CW01371440

The Gibraltar Crusade

THE MIDDLE AGES SERIES

Ruth Mazo Karras, Series Editor
Edward Peters, Founding Editor

A complete list of books in the series is available from the publisher.

The Gibraltar Crusade

Castile and the Battle for the Strait

Joseph F. O'Callaghan

PENN

UNIVERSITY OF PENNSYLVANIA PRESS

PHILADELPHIA

Copyright © 2011 University of Pennsylvania Press

All rights reserved. Except for brief quotations used for purposes of review or scholarly citation, none of this book may be reproduced in any form by any means without written permission from the publisher.

Published by
University of Pennsylvania Press
Philadelphia, Pennsylvania 19104-4112
www.upenn.edu/pennpress

Printed in the United States of America on acid-free paper
10 9 8 7 6 5 4 3 2 1

Library of Congress Cataloging-in-Publication Data
O'Callaghan, Joseph F.
  The Gibraltar crusade : Castile and the battle for the Strait / Joseph F. O'Callaghan.
    p. cm. — (The Middle Ages series)
  978-0-8122-4302-4 (hardcover : alk. paper)
  1. Crusades—13th–15th centuries. 2. Gibraltar, Strait of—Strategic aspects. 3. Gibraltar, Strait of—History, Military. 4. Castile (Spain)—History, Military. 5. Spain—History—711–1516. 6. Morocco—History, Military. 7. Granada (Kingdom)—History, Military. I. Title. II. Series
DP302.G39 O58   2011
946'.02—dc22   2010023080

In Honor of My Masters
Cyril E. Smith
James S. Donnelly, Sr.
Jeremiah F. O'Sullivan
Gerhart B. Ladner

Contents

List of Illustrations   ix

Genealogical Tables   xi

Chapter 1. Spain and the Strait of Gibraltar   1

Chapter 2. Alfonso X's African Crusade   11

Chapter 3. The Crusade Against the Mudéjars   34

Chapter 4. The Crusade Against the Marinids   60

Chapter 5. Sancho IV and the Conquest of Tarifa   88

Chapter 6. The Crusades of Gibraltar, Almería, and Algeciras   112

Chapter 7. The Early Crusades of Alfonso XI's Reign   137

Chapter 8. The Loss of Gibraltar and the Crusade of Salado   162

Chapter 9. The Crusade of Algeciras and Gibraltar   189

Chapter 10. Waging the Crusade of Gibraltar   218

Chapter 11. The Aftermath: The Strait of Gibraltar to 1492   256

List of Abbreviations   267

Notes   271

Bibliography   337

Index   365

Acknowledgments   375

Illustrations

FIGURES

1. King of Granada besieges Chincoya Castle   42–43

2. Christian knights defeat Marinid emir   64

3. Muslims besiege Christian town   106

4. Christians battle Muslims   230

MAPS

1. Castilian-Granadan frontier, ca. 1252–1350   2

2. Battle of Salado, 1340   181

3. Siege of Algeciras, 1342–44   194

Genealogical Tables

TABLE 1
KINGS OF CASTILE-LEÓN

Fernando III
1217-52

- Alfonso X, 1252-84
- Fadrique, d.1277
- Enrique, d.1303
- Felipe, d.1274
- Manuel, d.1283
- Leonor m. Edward I of England

Alfonso X 1252-84:
- Fernando de la Cerda, d. 1275
  - Alfonso
  - Fernando
- Sancho IV, 1284-95, m. María de Molina
  - Fernando IV, 1295-1312
    - Alfonso XI, 1312-50

Manuel d.1283:
- Pedro, d. 1283

Manuel d.1283 descendants:
- Pedro, d.1319
- Felipe, d.1327

Leonor line:
- Juan, d.1319
  - Juan el Tuerto, d.1326
- Jaime, d. 1284

TABLE 2
KINGS OF ARAGÓN

Jaime I
1213-76
┌─────────────┬──────────────────────┐
Pedro III   Violante m. Alfonso X of Castile
1276-85
┌─────────────┐
Alfonso III   Jaime II
1285-91   1291-1327
               ─────────
               Alfonso IV
               1327-36
               ─────────
               Pedro IV
               1336-87

TABLE 3
KINGS OF PORTUGAL

Afonso III
1248-79
─────────
Dinis
1279-1325
─────────
Afonso IV
1325-57

TABLE 4
THE NASRID KINGS OF GRANADA

```
Yūsuf
  |
  ├──────────────────────────────┐
Ibn al-Ahmar                   Ismāʿīl
(Muhammad I)                      |
  1237-73                       Faraj
  |                                |
  ├──────────┐                  Ismāʿīl I
Muhammad II  Nasr                1314-25
1273-1302   1309-14                |
  |                        ┌───────┴───────┐
Muhammad III          Muhammad IV        Yūsuf I
1302-1309               1325-33          1333-54
```

TABLE 5
THE MARINID SULTANS OF MOROCCO

```
                          Abū Yūsuf Yaʿqūb
                              1259-86
          ┌───────────────────────────────────┐
   Abū Yaʿqūb Yūsuf                      Abū Saʿīd ʿUthmān
      1286-1307                               1310-31
   ┌──────┴──────┐                              │
         Abū ʿĀmir ʿAbd Allāh              Abū l-Hasan ʿAlī
                                               1331-48
   Abū l-Rabīʿ Sulaymān    Abū Tābit             │
         1308-10             1307-8        Abū ʿInān Fāris
                                               1348-58
```

Chapter 1

Spain and the Strait of Gibraltar

The epic battle for control of the Strait of Gibraltar waged by Castile, Morocco, and Granada in the late thirteenth and early fourteenth centuries is a major, but often overlooked, chapter in the history of the Christian reconquest of Spain. It must also be seen in the broader context of the confrontation between Christianity and Islam during the crusading era.

The reconquest reached a climax with the fall of Seville in 1248 and the submission of the Moorish kingdom of Granada as a Castilian vassal state. The ensuing Castilian attempt to dominate the Strait is often regarded as a secondary episode in the reconquest. For some, the reconquest becomes important again only in the late fifteenth century when Ferdinand and Isabella conquered Granada, the last Muslim outpost in Spain. However, Castilian success in the fourteenth century in denying the Moroccans easy access to Spain made possible the ultimate conquest of Granada.

While Castile contested the battle for the Strait at the western end of the Mediterranean, the crusader states in the Holy Land ceased after 1291. Despite that overwhelming loss, the papacy, well into the fourteenth century, persistently attempted to convince western European rulers to liberate the Holy Land. Acknowledging the significance of that task, the Castilian kings contended that the Muslim presence in the Iberian Peninsula constituted a more immediate threat to Western Europe. Indeed, successive popes had recognized the importance of the reconquest by granting crusading privileges to those who participated in it.[1] As a continuation of that enterprise, the struggle to command the Strait also received the character of a crusade. The kings of Castile suggested that, once they had overthrown peninsular Islam and gained a base in Morocco, they could participate in a general European crusade to rescue the Holy Land.

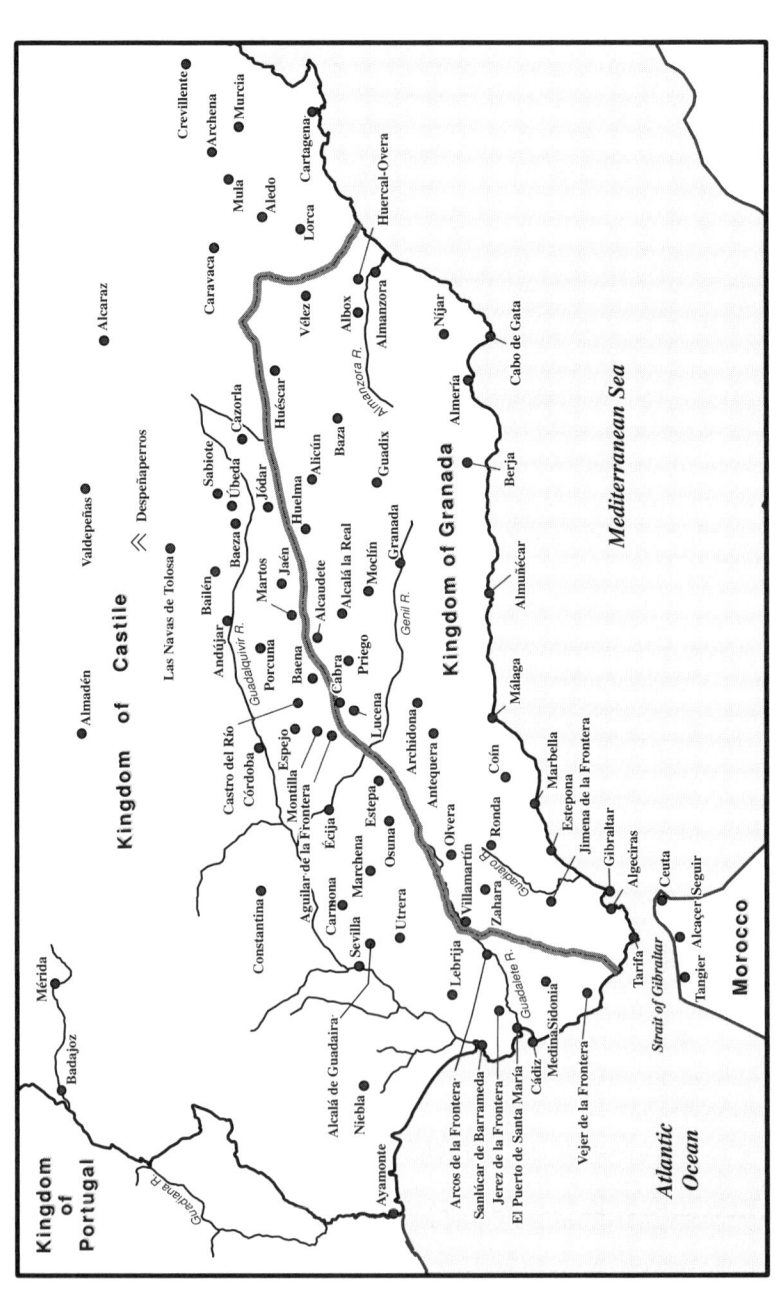

Map 1. The Castilian-Granadan frontier, 1252–1350.

The Strait, the Link Between Africa and Europe

For centuries the Strait of Gibraltar served, not as a barrier severing Europe from Africa, but as a bridge between the two continents. In Roman times the province of Mauritania Tingitana (now Morocco) formed part of a larger administrative unit known as the Diocese of Spain. When the Visigoths established their dominance over all of Spain in the sixth century they also asserted claims to Mauritania, but it is difficult to ascertain the extent of their authority there.[2]

Intent on spreading God's word, the Muslims raced across North Africa in the seventh century and traversed the Strait into Spain in 711. Within the century they were masters of the greater part of the Peninsula, or al-Andalus. Communication between al-Andalus and Morocco thereafter was continuous as a steady flow of warriors, farmers, herders, craftsmen, and merchants crossed and recrossed the Strait. Volunteers, determined to gain merit by engaging in the *jihād*, or holy war, also entered Spain. Scholars introduced the philosophical, medical, scientific, and religious ideas of the Hellenistic world. The great Muslim cities of Córdoba, Seville, Málaga, Granada, and Almería were now connected with the larger Islamic empire stretching across the Mediterranean. To the Arabs ancient Mauritania now became al-Magrib al-aksa, the far west. Medieval Christians called it Morocco in reference to the capital city of Marrakech.[3]

In the tenth century the caliph of Córdoba attempted to create a western Islamic empire straddling the Strait, but the collapse of the caliphate in the next century severed that connection. Nevertheless, Islamic Spain was destined to be part of a Moroccan empire ruled by the Almoravids in the late eleventh century and the Almohads in the twelfth.[4] The Muslim historian Ibn Khaldūn articulated the significance of Spain for the Islamic world:

> From the time that Spain was conquered by the Muslims, that land beyond the sea has always been a frontier of their empire, the setting for their holy wars, the field of martyrdom, and the gateway to eternal happiness for their soldiers. Muslim institutions in that country were constantly on a flaming brazier, so to speak, placed as they were between the claws and fangs of the lions of infidelity. Surrounded by a mass of hostile people, the true believers of Spain still find themselves separated from their coreligionists by the sea.[5]

Although the Christian kingdoms that survived the Muslim conquest were kept on the defensive, Alfonso VI (1065–1109), king of León-Castile, reached the southernmost extremity of the Peninsula at Tarifa. Riding out into the surf, he exclaimed in exultation: "This is the end of the land of al-Andalus and I have set foot on it."[6] Nevertheless, more than two centuries were to elapse before his successors could replicate that grand gesture.

The Ports of the Strait of Gibraltar

The Strait of Gibraltar, leading from the Mediterranean Sea into the Atlantic Ocean, is about thirty-six miles long and nine miles wide at its narrowest point. The depth of its waters varies between 980 and 3,000 feet. On the Spanish coast at the eastern end of the Strait, the Rock of Gibraltar, a limestone mountain, stands 1,396 feet high. Dominating Ceuta on the Moroccan shore, Mount Acho rises about 787 feet. Only fourteen miles apart, the Rock and Mount Acho, the ancient Pillars of Hercules, marked the farthest limits of the Mediterranean. Gibraltar (*Jabal Tārik*, the Rock of Tārik), about three miles long and a quarter mile wide, is connected to the Spanish mainland by a low-lying sandy isthmus.

The Bay of Algeciras, with a maximum depth of about 1,312 feet, forms a nearly full circle reaching from the Rock at the eastern end to Algeciras (al-Jazīrah al-Khadrā', the Green Island) on the west, a distance of six miles. The Miel and the Palmones Rivers flow into the bay while hills lead from the mountains down to the shore. About ten miles southwest of Algeciras is Tarifa, where hills rise gently from the beach to more than 500 feet. The strong winds from the Atlantic and from the Strait that make Tarifa a mecca for modern windsurfers wreaked havoc on Muslim and Christian fleets, especially in the fall and winter months. From Tarifa the shortest distance to Africa is nine miles. The struggle to rule the Strait focused on possession of these three sites, Gibraltar, Algeciras, and Tarifa.

Two ports served as points of embarkation for Moroccan armies invading Spain: Tangier on the Atlantic coast at the western end of the Strait and Ceuta about thirty miles to the east on the Mediterranean. Tangier, about thirty-six miles southwest of Gibraltar, was once the capital of Roman Mauritania. Ceuta is fourteen miles from Gibraltar. Ibn Khaldūn stated that "Ceuta and Tangier were always thought of as the most important governmental seats in the Almohad Empire, because they were both maritime fortresses, seaports, arsenals for shipbuilding, and points of embarkation for those wishing to participate in the holy war. On that account governance of those places was always entrusted to princes of the royal family."[7]

Islamic Spain in 1248

After the conquest of Seville in 1248 Islamic Spain was reduced to several kingdoms occupying a comparatively narrow belt of land generally south and east of the Guadalquivir River and reaching the shores of the Mediterranean. The Portuguese had occupied the Algarve, the southernmost section of modern Portugal, situated west of the Guadiana River. The region between the Guadiana and the Guadalquivir was subject to the Muslim king of Niebla. The largest of the Islamic kingdoms was Granada, whose boundaries roughly curved northward from Algeciras and Gibraltar through the mountains east and south of Seville, Córdoba, and Jaén and then southward to the Mediterranean coast below Murcia. Situated north and east of Granada was the kingdom of Murcia, extending along the coast from below Cartagena northward through Alicante almost to Denia.[8] Lying to the north were the dominions of the Crown of Aragón.

Numerous mountain ranges intersecting the kingdom of Granada served as an obstacle to easy conquest. Castles set on rocky mounts surveying the surrounding plain provided an initial line of defense and protection for the many small villages dotting the valleys and plateaus. Densely populated, the kingdom included many refugees from Christian Spain or their descendants. An abundance of wheat, fruits, olives, grapes, and other fruits and vegetables, as well as an active commerce with the Mediterranean world contributed to the general prosperity.

The Mediterranean clearly defined the southern boundary of the kingdom. Starting at Aguilas adjoining the kingdom of Murcia on the northeast, the coastline extends southward to Cabo de Gata and then west to Almería, a major seaport on the gulf of the same name. West of Almería are Almuñécar, Málaga, Marbella, Estepona, Gibraltar, and Algeciras.[9]

The inland frontier of the kingdom of Granada, a fluid zone rather than a fixed line, is less easily defined, as Christians and Muslims competed for control of certain regions. Frequent skirmishes, sieges, and even major battles occurred along the frontier with the Castilian kingdoms of Seville, Córdoba, and Jaén. The kingdom of Seville stretched southward from the city on the

Guadalquivir to the Gulf of Cádiz and beyond. After flowing about fifty miles the river empties into the Atlantic at Sanlúcar de Barrameda. Jerez de la Frontera is about twelve miles southeast of Sanlúcar. Eight miles south of Jerez is El Puerto de Santa María and about eight miles across the Gulf of Cádiz lies Cádiz itself. The coastline then turns to the southeast, passing by Vejer de la Frontera (about twenty-eight miles from Cádiz) and finally reaching Tarifa (about another twenty-eight miles from Vejer), directly opposite Morocco. Until 1292 the boundary between Christian and Muslim territory lay somewhere between Vejer and Tarifa.

Lying east and south of the Guadalquivir was a broad sector not entirely dominated by either side. Clashes of arms frequently occurred in this no-man's-land. A line of Castilian fortresses running westward from Estepa, through Osuna, La Puebla de Cazalla, and then turning southward to Morón de la Frontera, Arcos de la Frontera, and Vejer de la Frontera guarded the kingdom of Seville. Just east of that line were the Muslim strongholds of Pruna, Olvera, Zahara, Alcalá de los Gazules, and Jimena de la Frontera. Another series of Castilian outposts, namely, Cabra, Aguilar de la Frontera, Baena, Martos, La Guardia, Pegalajar, Jódar, Cazorla, and Castril defended the kingdoms of Córdoba and Jaén. Standing opposite them were the Granadan fortresses of Benamejí, Lucena, Luque, Rute, Zambra, Alcaudete, Bedmar, Quesada, Tíscar, and Huéscar. Beyond Huéscar, the frontier between Granada and Murcia underwent the least alteration during this period, although both sides frequently crossed the border with hostile intent.[10]

Fernando III, Granada, Morocco, and the Holy Land

By the middle of the thirteenth century, Castile, alone among the Christian states, had a frontier adjoining that of the kingdom of Granada. Thus, only Castile had a realistic possibility of peninsular expansion at Muslim expense. The Muslim kings of Granada, Niebla, and Murcia had all acknowledged the suzerainty of Fernando III (1217–52), the conqueror of Seville.[11] In 1246 Muhammad ibn Yūsuf ibn Nasr, known as Ibn al-Ahmar or Muhammad I (1237–73), king of Granada, pledged homage and fealty to him, promising court service, military service, and an annual tribute (*parias*). A truce of twenty years enabled him to consolidate his power in Granada. The Nasrid dynasty, which he founded, governed Granada until 1492. In like manner, Ibn Mahfūt, king of Niebla, and Ibn Hūd, king of Murcia, also accepted Castilian overlordship.[12]

Although the Moors no longer loomed as a threat to Christian Spain, Fernando III and his successors intended ultimately to expel them from the Peninsula. As early as the ninth century, if not before, the idea emerged that the Christian rulers of Asturias-León-Castile were the heirs of the Visigoths and as such had the obligation of recovering lands once subject to Visigothic rule, including the entire Iberian Peninsula and Mauritania. The Muslims were regarded as intruders who had usurped lands rightfully belonging to the Christians. The expulsion of the Moors and the reestablishment of Gothic rule over the whole of Spain was an ideal repeatedly expressed by Christian authors. The kings of Castile-León also aspired to conquer Morocco, believing that it had once been part of the Visigothic realm.[13] In more practical terms, the kings recognized the need to shut off the invasion route giving the Moroccans entry into the Peninsula by seizing Tarifa, Algeciras, and Gibraltar. If that could be accomplished, they hoped to isolate the kings of Granada and deprive them of receiving aid from their Moroccan coreligionists.

Secure in his ascendancy over the Moors of Spain, Fernando III proposed to establish a foothold in Morocco and also contemplated the possibility of leading a crusade to the Holy Land. With that in mind, he ordered the construction of galleys and other vessels. Many Moroccan lords, fearing his power, reportedly intended to surrender rather than oppose him. In the *Setenario* Alfonso X indicated that his father, by virtue of "his pacts with the Moors of Spain and with some of those in Africa," had great wealth, but as "the land beyond the sea was not wholly conquered and the Moors remained there," he was reluctant to assume the imperial crown of Spain.[14] Juan Gil de Zamora commented that "the Africans also offered him part of Africa."[15] These texts suggest that some Moroccan lords, like the kings of Granada, Niebla, and Murcia, paid tribute to Fernando III, but, as the greater part of Morocco was not subject to his rule, the Hispanic empire was incomplete.

By preparing a fleet at Seville, Fernando III likely intended to seize certain Moroccan seaports as a preliminary to a crusade to the Holy Land. In 1252 Pope Innocent IV approved a pact between the king and the Almohad caliph of Morocco. Although its provisions are unknown, Fernando III may have secured the caliph's pledge not to interfere with a possible eastern crusade.[16] The English historian Matthew Paris related that when Louis IX of France (1223–70) was captured in 1250 during his crusade to Egypt, Fernando III "took the cross, believing that to conquer the Holy Land was worthier than any other [deed]." Learning that King Henry III of England (1216–72) was planning a crusade to the Holy Land, he urged him to come first to Castile where he would provide him with supplies, arms, and a fleet and accompany him on his journey. Matthew Paris lamented that Fernando III's death in that year brought to naught his plans for a crusade. Louis IX, liberated from captivity but determined to recover the Holy Land, also had reason to deplore the death of Fernando III, "who, on account of his eminence, is called king of all Spain," and had gained great conquests over the infidels there. Louis IX's mother, Blanche of Castile, made frequent entreaties to her nephew Fernando III, who promised prompt and effective aid to the king of France. That was not to be.[17] The battle for control of the Strait of Gibraltar began in earnest with his son and successor, Alfonso X (1252–84).

Sources for Study

The principal Christian narratives for this period are the *Chronicles* of Alfonso X, Sancho IV, Fernando IV, and Alfonso XI, written in Castilian.[18] In the prologue to the *Tres Crónicas*, as the first three are known, the author emphasized the importance of recording the efforts of the Castilian kings to increase the Catholic faith by expelling the Moors from Spain. Alfonso XI, on discovering that the written history of the royal house ended with Fernando III,[19] commissioned an official account of the reigns of his three predecessors. As the prologue included Algeciras among his dominions, it was written after March 1344, but the date of initial composition of the full text is uncertain.

Alfonso XI apparently assigned the task of writing the *Tres Crónicas* to Fernán Sánchez de Valladolid (or de Tovar), the chancellor of the privy seal and chief notary of Castile. He is also the likely author of the *Chronicle of Alfonso XI*, a detailed account down to 1344. A few additional paragraphs summarize the king's last six years. The four chronicles follow an annalistic form, but the chronology does not always accord with documentary evidence. As a staunch royalist, the author's tone is laudatory and he is seldom critical of the monarchs he writes about. The original *Chronicle*, reedited between 1376 and 1379, is known today as the *Grand Chronicle of Alfonso XI*. Some chapters were expanded and others added, but the last section on the siege of Algeciras repeats the earlier text. Its picturesque and dramatic style distinguishes it from the more sober presentation of Fernán Sánchez.[20] Closely paralleling the prose *Chronicle* is Rodrigo Yáñez's *Poem of Alfonso XI*, a reasonably accurate presentation ending in 1344. The poet is clearly biased in favor of the king.[21]

Jofre de Loaysa, archdeacon of Toledo (d. 1307/10), composed a brief chronicle of the reigns of Alfonso X, Sancho IV, and Fernando IV down to 1305. As one intimately associated with the royal court, he is generally positive toward the kings. Though he wrote in Castilian, only a Latin version made at his request survives.[22] A translation of the Latin history of Archbishop Rodrigo Jiménez de Rada and a continuation down to 1327 has been attributed to Gonzalo de la Finojosa, bishop of Burgos (1313–27). The initial portion, described by Diego Catalán as the *Historia hasta 1288 dialogada* because of its use of dialogue, served as a source for the *Chronicle of Alfonso X*. The chronology of both works for the early years of Alfonso X is erratic.[23]

Also useful is the Catalan *Chronicle of Pedro IV of Aragón*, a purported autobiography that also recounts the reigns of his father and grandfather. As they were preoccupied chiefly with their Mediterranean empire, the *Chronicle*'s references to the struggle for the Strait are limited.[24] The *Chronicle of the First Seven Kings of Portugal*, attributed to Fernão Lopes (d. 1460), is useful for the reigns of Afonso III, Dinis, and Afonso IV, though it draws on the Castilian chronicles mentioned above. That is also true of the *Chronicle of Afonso IV* by Rui de Pina (d. 1521).[25]

The *Cantigas de Santa Maria*, a collection of miracle stories in praise of the Virgin Mary, includes a number of poems recounting events in the reign of Alfonso X.[26]

The Muslim narratives include Ibn Abī Zar''s *Rawd al-Qirtās*, a confused and often inaccurate history of Morocco and al-Andalus, reaching to 1326. The author tends toward hyperbole and is not always trustworthy. Ibn 'Idhārī's *Al-Bayān al-Mugrib*, a history of the rulers of Morocco, ends in 1306. Though little is known of him, his careful style, abundance of detail, and judicious assessments make his work particularly valuable.[27]

The two great historians of the fourteenth century, Ibn al-Khatīb (d. 1374) and Ibn Khaldūn (d. 1406), both served the kings of Granada and witnessed many of the events they recorded. The former composed *Al-Lamha al-badriyya fī l-dawla al-nasriyya*, a history of the kings of Granada to 1363, and *Al-Ihāta fī akhbār Garnāta*, a description of Granada with biographical sketches of notables. His writings have been translated only in part,[28] but Al-Makkarī (d. 1633) incorporated large sections of his work into his history.[29] Ibn Khaldūn's *Kitāb al-Ibar*, or *Book of Examples*, was a sort of universal history. The section dealing with the Berbers of North Africa, translated into French by the Baron de Slane, is especially helpful. One of the great historians of all time, his work is characterized by extensive detail, balanced presentation, and critical reflection.[30]

On the other side of the Strait, Ibn Marzūq (d. 1379) composed the *Musnad* in praise of the Marinid emir Abū l-Hasan, whom he served as a counselor and diplomat. He did not write a connected narrative and tended to pass over events that might tarnish his hero's reputation.[31]

The loss of the Castilian royal archives necessitates the reconstruction of their contents from originals in municipal, monastic, noble, and other repositories.[32] The Royal Academy of History published numerous documents of Alfonso X and a few of Sancho IV.[33] Mercedes Gaibrois and Antonio Benavides produced extensive diplomatic collections for Sancho IV and Fernando IV.[34] Manuel González Jiménez compiled royal documents of Alfonso X relating to Andalucía, and Esther González Crespo published a collection of Alfonso XI's charters.[35] The *Colección de documentos para la historia del reino de Murcia* includes a multitude of relevant texts.[36] Andrés Giménez Soler, Heinrich Finke, and Ángels Masià i de Ros transcribed many of the hundreds of letters of the kings of Castile, Aragón, Granada, and Morocco preserved in the archives of the Crown of Aragón.[37] Maximiliano Alarcón and Ramón García printed many Arabic documents from the same archive.[38] Some diplomatic correspondence between the kings of Granada and the emirs of Morocco during the fourteenth century has also been issued.[39] Numerous papal bulls of crusade published by the Écoles françaises d'Athènes et de Rome will be cited throughout this work.

Now let us turn our attention to the struggle between Muslims and Christians to hold sway over the Strait of Gibraltar from the accession of Alfonso X of Castile in 1252 to the death of his great-grandson Alfonso XI in 1350.

Chapter 2

Alfonso X's African Crusade

Alfonso X (1252–84), an exceptionally ambitious monarch, inherited his father's dream of establishing a foothold in Morocco and perhaps launching a crusade to liberate the Holy Land.[1] During the first decade of his reign, the new king, armed with papal bulls, proposed to carry out an African Crusade, but his pursuit of the throne of the Holy Roman Empire often distracted his attention from Morocco. Internal opposition from the Mudéjars, Muslims living under Castilian rule, and the hostility of Ibn al-Ahmar, king of Granada, ultimately thwarted his plans. The eventual intervention of a new dynasty emerging in Morocco, the Banū Marīn, or Marinids, known to the Castilians as the Benimerines, put him on the defensive.[2]

Alfonso X and His Moorish Vassals

Before intervening in Morocco Alfonso X had to assure the allegiance of the Muslim kings who had submitted to Fernando III and also to guarantee the security of Seville. He confirmed his father's pact of 1246 with Ibn al-Ahmar, who promised a yearly tribute of 300,000 *maravedíes* or half the revenue of his kingdom. The *Royal Chronicle* affirmed that the amount was 250,000 *maravedíes* but erroneously attributed that to Alfonso X's alteration of the coinage. The levy of such a weighty tribute was intended ultimately to demolish the kingdom of Granada. As a royal vassal, Ibn al-Ahmar's name was regularly recorded among the bishops and nobles confirming royal privileges.[3] Until 1264 he enjoyed peaceful relations with Alfonso X, meeting him every year near Seville to present his tribute and discharge his feudal obligation to attend his lord's court. In 1254, when summoned to the Cortes of Toledo to acknowledge Infanta Berenguela as heir to the throne, he was lodged in the

Huerta del Rey adjacent to the *alcázar*, or royal palace. Delighted to see him, Alfonso X showed him great honor. The Anonymous of Sahagún testified that Alfonso X was then much preoccupied with the Moorish kings, his vassals. More than likely, Ibn Mahfūt, king of Niebla, and Ibn Hūd, king of Murcia, also recorded as vassals confirming royal privileges, attended the Cortes. Their presence symbolized Alfonso X's supremacy over Spanish Islam.[4]

In order to retain Seville, the king set out to repopulate the city with Christian settlers and to strengthen Castilian control of the Guadalquivir River as it flowed southward to the Atlantic. Nevertheless, as the Muslim presence loomed large within a few miles of Seville, many colonists, wary of committing themselves to the hazards of life on the frontier, sold or abandoned their holdings.[5] Seville's uneasy situation became clear soon after Alfonso X's accession when the Moors of Tejada raided the municipal district. The king besieged Tejada, which promptly surrendered and was annexed to the municipality of Seville.[6]

Few Christians also dared to set down roots in the area south of the city where the Moors remained in possession of their lands. Although the Moors of Jerez, Medina Sidonia, Vejer, Arcos, Lebrija, and other towns had submitted to Fernando III, they opted to challenge the new king. Alfonso X quickly compelled Jerez to resume payment of tribute, while Arcos and Lebrija surrendered to his brother Enrique. Nevertheless, the security of the frontier would always be problematic so long as the Moors, despite their acceptance of Castilian suzerainty and the symbolic payment of tribute, preserved effective control of those towns.[7] The king's expansionist aspirations were complicated by his father's intention to create a lordship, including Jerez, Lebrija, Arcos, and Medina Sidonia, for his younger son Enrique. Recognizing that threat, Alfonso X destroyed the royal charters founding the lordship.[8] In retaliation, Enrique reportedly planned to seize the kingdom of Niebla, but was defeated near Lebrija in 1255 by Nuño González de Lara, the king's close friend. Abandoning Castile, Enrique found service with the emir of Tunis and later participated in the wars between the Guelfs and the Ghibellines in southern Italy. His withdrawal enabled the king to settle the disputed lands as he wished.[9]

Soon, however, Alfonso X began to restrict the Mudéjar presence. Thus, hoping to settle Christians in Morón de la Frontera on the Guadaira River, he ordered the Mudéjars to withdraw to Siliebar, a place of less strategic importance. He also urged Christians to purchase Mudéjar property in Arcos de la Frontera, and, as a defensive measure, ceded the nearby castle of Matrera to the Order of Calatrava.[10] While a significant Mudéjar population remained, especially in rural areas and in towns such as Jerez, the king was beginning to push the Christian frontier well beyond Seville into areas directly abutting the kingdom of Granada.

In the relative certainty that the kings of Granada, Niebla, and Murcia, now his vassals, would not take advantage of his preoccupation and attack him, Alfonso X initiated plans for a crusade in Africa. In line with traditional royal ideology, he believed that the kings of Castile, as heirs of the Visigoths, had the responsibility to recover the Visigothic realms.[11] In *Cantiga* 360 he pleaded with the Virgin Mary to help him to "expel the sect of Muhammad from Spain."[12] In his last will he emphasized that, in ancient times, God intended that all of Africa and all of Spain should belong to his Christian ancestors, but they lost it on account of their sins. His clear intention was to take possession once again.[13]

Readying a Fleet

Recognizing that an African expedition required a fleet, Fernando III granted specific privileges to mariners who would settle in Seville in the *barrio de la mar*, where their own *alcalde* would "judge every affair of the sea." They had to serve at sea for three months each year, at their own expenses.[14] The king also began reconstruction of the shipyards (*atarazanas*) at Seville. A dedicatory inscription tells us that Alfonso X, "king of the Spains," intent on conquering the southern regions, brought the work to completion in 1252.[15] The royal accounts of 1294 indicate that records were kept of income and expenditures.[16] The shipyards, situated along the Guadalquivir by the wall extending from the *alcázar* to the Torre del Oro, were about 200 yards long, with sixteen broad aisles, divided by strong pillars and ogival arches.[17] The preferred vessel for naval warfare was the lightly built galley, noted for its speed and maneuverability. Propelled by oarsmen, it also had a mast and sail to take advantage of the wind. Several galleys with a tier of twelve oarsmen on each side were depicted in Alfonso X's *Cantigas de Santa Maria*.[18]

The next task was to gather the requisite naval personnel. In 1253 the king gave a galley equipped with oars, sails, and supplies to Pelay Pérez Correa, master of the Order of Santiago, who promised to provide 200 armed men, at his own expense, for three months' service every year. While thirty would have iron weapons, ten archers (*ballesteros*) would be equipped with iron bolts and twenty crossbows (*ballestas*). Others had to have shields and iron caps "as is the custom of the galleymen." The Order pledged to appoint as captain (*cómitre*) a "good man, knowledgeable about the sea." The equal division of booty between the king and the Order was an innovation, inasmuch as his customary share was one-fifth. The galley had to be refitted every seven years. If it were lost, the Order would not have to replace it before that time. The knights would be bound by the same conditions if the king gave them another galley.[19]

Also in 1253 the king granted property in Seville and its neighborhood, as well as 100 *maravedíes*, to each of twenty-one ship captains (*cómitres*) from Cantabria, Catalonia, France, and Italy. Provided by the king with a properly equipped galley, each captain had to maintain 100 men outfitted with four *ballestas de estribera*, four *ballestas de dos pies*, 1,000 arrows, fifty lances, ten arm braces, ten shields, and ten iron caps. The two types of *ballestas*, or crossbows, mentioned were differentiated by the manner of arming them. The more primitive version (*ballesta de dos pies*) was held on the ground by both feet while a cord was drawn back and locked into place. A stirrup held down the *ballesta de estribera*. Each captain had to serve personally wherever the king required or else send someone certified as capable of command by the royal admiral. The galley would have to be refitted every seven years. Booty would be divided equally between the king and the captains. The galley had to be ready for service by 1 January 1255. In all, 21 galleys with 2,100 men were projected, but Julio González calculated only 18 and 1,900.[20] If the galleys were to accommodate 100–200 men, they probably were of considerable size. Perhaps some were comparable to a galley built in 1275 for Charles of Anjou, king of Naples and Sicily, that is 130 feet long and 12 feet wide, with two oarsmen on a bench on each side.[21]

Alfonso X also appointed an overall naval commander or admiral (Arabic, *amir al-bahr*, commander of the sea).[22] Although Ramón Bonifaz of Burgos organized a fleet in the Bay of Biscay for the siege of Seville, he was never officially designated as admiral. The first person known to hold the office of *almirante de la mar*, or admiral, was Roy López de Mendoza, who received Gelves on condition of maintaining two galleys for the king's service. As *almirante* he confirmed royal charters from December 1253 to January 1260.[23]

The Papacy, Henry III, and the African Crusade

In October 1252 as Alfonso X prepared his fleet, Pope Innocent IV (1243–54) ratified whatever accords he might make with the Saracens of Africa for the "glory of God, the honor of the Church and of the Christian people." The pope also acknowledged that Alfonso X, "for the increase of the Christian faith," planned to cross the Strait "with a great multitude of warriors against the Saracens of Africa, enemies of the Christian name." Therefore, Innocent IV authorized the absolution of all those who had incurred excommunication, provided that they participated in the enterprise, paid others to do so, or made a financial contribution. The king was permitted to use fines levied on usurers and property confiscated from thieves, if the legitimate owner did not claim it within a reasonable time. Early in the next year Innocent IV proclaimed a crusade, conferring the indulgence or remission of sins on all those who participated, just as if they made the pilgrimage to the Holy Land. The Franciscans and Dominicans were directed to preach the crusade throughout Castile, León, and Navarre. Money collected was to be deposited in a safe place and delivered to the king only when he began the campaign. The *tercias*, or third of the tithe, of the archdioceses of Seville and Compostela could be used to finance the crusade.[24]

Hoping to rouse general enthusiasm, Alfonso X may have announced his crusade and made the dramatic gesture of taking the cross in the spring of 1254 during the Cortes of Toledo. Innocent IV's remark in May that the king "had assumed the sign of the living cross against the Saracens of Africa" suggests a formal ceremony in which he publicly declared his intention to go crusading and took the customary crusader's vow.[25] Ibn al-Ahmar and the other Moorish kings present in the Cortes as vassals of Castile may have promised to collaborate with the expedition, at least to the extent of not interfering with it.

The king also enlisted the support of King Henry III of England. In return for Henry III's pledge to take part in the African Crusade, provided that the pope released him from his vow to go to the Holy Land, Alfonso X renounced his pretensions to Gascony.[26] When the English "army of crusaders—*crucesignatorum*—comes to the African regions in our company," Alfonso X promised, they would share equally in whatever lands were conquered.[27] Papal privileges customarily accorded to crusaders to the Holy Land were offered to participants in the African Crusade. Placed under the protection of the church, a crusader could not be compelled to pay interest on loans. If he had sworn to do so, his creditor had to relieve him of that obligation. If the creditor were a Jew, the secular arm could be summoned to enforce this order. Repayment of the crusader's debts was postponed until he returned home. If he responded to ordinary and diocesan judges, he could not be cited before extraordinary or papal judges. Moreover, clergy in the king's company were dispensed from the obligation of residence and could receive income from their benefices.[28]

Innocent IV's successor, Alexander IV (1254–61), seemed equally determined to advance the crusade. In 1255 he appointed Lope Fernández de Aín, bishop of Morocco, as his legate in Africa and authorized him to designate vicars to represent him. He was also instructed to establish bishops in newly reconquered dioceses if the ecclesiastical province to which they belonged was unknown. Acknowledging that the king was planning an expedition against the Saracens of Africa, the pope ordered Bishop Lope to preach the crusade in Spain and Gascony, offering the indulgence given for the Holy Land. This was more expansive than Innocent IV's bull which authorized preaching in Castile, León, and Navarre. Now, all of Spain was included, as well as Gascony because Henry III had expressed interest in the African Crusade.[29]

Nevertheless, when Henry III requested permission to substitute Africa for the Holy Land, Alexander IV refused, but he did allow him to lead a crusade against the papal archenemies, the Hohenstaufen of Sicily. Much to Alfonso X's dismay, the English king, in 1255, announced his intention to place his second son, Edmund, on the Sicilian throne and excused himself from participating in the African Crusade for at least six years. Still hoping to salvage something, Alfonso X appealed to him again, but in 1258 he refused. Thus, plans announced at Toledo in 1254 for a joint crusade in Africa were erased and, in the end, Henry III went neither to Africa nor to the Holy Land.[30]

Despite that disappointment, in 1255 the pope permitted Bishop Lope, "preacher of the cross in Spain," to absolve arsonists and those excommunicated for violence against clergy and to commute their penitential vows to visit the Holy Land, so they could go to Africa. Thus the African expedition had the character of a papal crusade endowed with a plenary indulgence and other privileges associated with crusading.[31]

Alliances with Pisa, Marseille, and Norway

Notwithstanding these preparations, several issues made it impossible for Alfonso X to carry out the African Crusade at this time. Aside from the revolt of his brother Enrique and a dispute with Aragón concerning claims to Navarre, the most important and prolonged distraction was the possibility of acquiring the title of Holy Roman Emperor, to which he had a claim through his mother, Beatrice of Swabia.[32]

His imperial ambitions were linked to the African Crusade when he entered agreements with Pisa and Marseille in 1256. The Pisan ambassador formally recognized him as king of the Romans. In return for his pledge to send at least 500 knights and a number of archers to Pisa, the city promised to provide, within forty days, ten armed galleys, at its expense, to serve for four months in Italy and Africa, and to share in his conquests. In 1257 Marseille also acknowledged his imperial rights and promised to make available, at its expense, ten galleys, together with their crews and armament, for three months' service between Easter and Michaelmas (29 September), anywhere from Sicily to Seville, against Christians and the Saracens of Africa. The city would receive a third of the booty. If the ships served beyond three months, the king would have to pay their expenses.[33]

In his quest for naval support, Alfonso X's diplomacy extended to the far north of Europe, to the kingdom of Norway. The initiative seems to have come from King Haakon IV (1217–63), who, on learning of Alfonso X's interest in the imperial crown, dispatched his envoys to Castile at the close of 1255. A Castilian alliance could assure Norway of a regular supply of grain, and, if Alfonso X succeeded in becoming emperor, he might give Norway control of Lübeck, a major North Sea port. The Icelandic chronicler Sturla Thordarson explained that "The king of Spain was then preparing his army against the infidels, and he much desired King Hákon to go with him and redeem his promise to take the cross; it was with the pope's consent that the cross could be redeemed there [i.e., Morocco], just as if one had traveled to Jerusalem."[34] A few years before, Haakon IV had promised Louis IX that he would accompany him to the Holy Land. Though assured that, with papal approbation, he could fulfill his crusading vow by participating in the projected African Crusade, Haakon IV likely did not intend to go crusading either in the Holy Land or Morocco. No treaty of alliance is extant, but a marital alliance between Haakon IV's daughter Kristin and Alfonso X's brother Felipe was arranged. Kristin married Felipe at Valladolid in 1258, but her death four years later effectively ended the alliance and Alfonso X's hope of securing Norwegian naval assistance.[35]

In April 1257 Alfonso X was elected as Holy Roman Emperor, but in the previous January, Henry III's younger brother, Richard of Cornwall, was also elected. In the long run, neither man was able to garner universal support or papal recognition. While satisfying dynastic ambitions, Alfonso X's election proved to be a serious financial drain on Castilian resources and a grave distraction from the African Crusade.[36]

African Contacts: Taount, Ténès, and Egypt

At the outset of his reign, as noted above, Alfonso X sought papal approval for his diplomatic outreach to the Muslim rulers in Africa, some of whom may have attended the Cortes of Toledo in 1254. When the king received Kristin of Norway in January 1258 during the Cortes of Valladolid, "Christian and infidel envoys," according to Sturla Thordarson, were among those present.[37] Representatives from Taount, Ténès, and perhaps Egypt may have been among them.

Sometime in 1256 or early in 1257 the ruler of Tagunt on the African coast sent an embassy to Castile, as two royal charters given to Alicante suggest. Intent on promoting military preparedness, Alfonso X granted the franchises enjoyed by the noble knights of Toledo to the citizens of Cartagena and Alicante who maintained horses and arms, and also to sea captains prepared for war. On 10 May 1257 he related that when he had previously visited Alicante, he had sent the men of that town "to receive the castle of Tagunt that they gave me beyond the sea." As he had visited Alicante in January, representatives of Tagunt probably notified him prior to that date of their ruler's willingness to cede the castle. Then on 10 April 1258, he declared that Alicante was one of the best seaports in Spain whereby he could "serve God in many ways and especially in the affair beyond the sea against the pagan people." He repeated that he had sent men "to receive the castle of Tagunt beyond the sea."[38]

These tantalizing references to Tagunt raise several perplexing questions. Where is Tagunt? From whom did the king receive this castle? Why was it given to him? The word "receive" suggests that it was offered, not taken by force. As to Tagunt's situation, Antonio Ballesteros proposed Tangier (Tanjar in the *Royal Chronicle*), but the spelling suggests otherwise. Charles Dufourcq put forward a more plausible explanation, Taount or Tāwunt, a fortress now in ruins, on the African coast west of Oran and adjacent to the port of Ghazaouet (al-Gazawat). Taount, controlled by the Banū Matghara, became an object of contention between Yagmurāsan b. Ziyyān (1235–83), a member of the 'Abd al-Wādid dynasty ruling Tlemcen, and Abū Yūsuf Ya'qūb, the Marinid emir. Perhaps on that account Harūn b. Mūsa, ruler of Taount, sought Alfonso X's protection and ceded the citadel to him. When the Marinids seized Taount in 1272, it seems likely the Castilian presence had disappeared long before.[39]

Two letters, one from the pope and another from the king of England, indicate that Alfonso X also reached out to another ruler. Alexander IV, on 26 September 1258, announced that Alfonso X had received the submission of "the illustrious king holding the *regnum Tenetu*." So that the Christian religion might flourish in that city, Alfonso X requested papal approval to build a church there. In December, Henry III congratulated Alfonso X for his efforts "not only to subjugate the barbarous natives to the cross, but also to bring them, especially the king of Thenecii and his nobles, to the light of truth and knowledge of God's name."[40] Both letters suggest that the king of Tenetu or Thenecii was favorable to Christianity and perhaps even offered to become a Christian.

I once thought that the *regnum Tenetu* or *Thenecii* should be identified with Tagunt or Taount, but Luis Villar García identified it with Tunis. *Tenecii*, the common Latin spelling of Tunis (in the genitive) in Aragonese documents, closely approximates the *Thenicii* of Henry III's letter. If one reads *Tenetu* as *Tenetii* the similarity is manifest. Nevertheless, it is extremely doubtful that Abū 'Abd Allāh Muḥammad al-Mustanṣir (1249–77), a member of the Hafsid dynasty then ruling Tunis, submitted to Alfonso X, as the papal letter suggests. A more likely possibility is Ténès, a port between Oran and Algiers. Alfonso X's proposal to build a church there suggests that it was a place of some consequence, and that there was a large enough Christian population, probably Castilian, Catalan, and Italian merchants, to justify such a structure. The king's envoys to the papal court may have expressed the situation in that exaggerated form in order to induce a favorable response from the pope. The ruler of Ténès may have sought Castilian backing against the 'Abd al-Wādids of Tlemcen and the Marinids of Morocco, but probably made no further commitment to Alfonso X. If he had become a Castilian vassal, he would surely have been recorded as such in royal privileges.[41]

Alfonso X also made diplomatic overtures to Egypt. Since the early thirteenth century, crusading strategists considered Egypt the key to control of the Holy Land. The Fifth Crusade and Louis IX's Sixth Crusade invaded Egypt, but failed miserably. In his *Petition* Alfonso X lamented that the Muslims ruled not only in Spain but also in Ultramar, that is, the Holy Land, and pleaded with the Virgin Mary to enable him to expel them all. His desire to deliver the Holy Land, according to Cristina González, caused him to order the composition of *La gran conquista de Ultramar*, an account of the crusades until the death of Louis IX at Tunis in 1270.[42]

An Egyptian diplomatic mission put in concrete form Alfonso X's aspirations concerning the Holy Land. It was his custom to celebrate the anniversary of Fernando III's death on 31 May in Seville. Expressing respect for the deceased monarch, Ibn al-Ahmar dispatched a retinue of notables accompanied by 100 footmen with great white candles to be placed about the royal tomb in the cathedral. On that same occasion, envoys from Alvandexaver, king of Egypt, brought rich cloths, jewelry, ivory, a giraffe, an ass with white and dark stripes (obviously a zebra), and other kinds of animals. Some of the animals were illustrated in *Cantiga* 29 (panel 5). When the animals died, the king had their hides displayed on the cathedral's exterior walls. A crocodile skeleton, hung from the ceiling in the cloister of the Patio de los Naranjos, gave its name to the Puerta del Lagarto adjacent to the Giralda.[43]

Distracted by the marvelous gifts from the east, the *Royal Chronicle* failed to mention the purpose or the date of the Egyptian embassy and only vaguely identified the Egyptian ruler as Alvandexaver. That seems to refer to Kutuz, the Mamlūk Sultan of Egypt (1259–60), whose honorific name was al-Muzaffar. His triumph at Ain Jalūd in September 1260 halted Mongol efforts to subjugate Syria and Palestine. In the next month, however, Baybars Bundukdārī (1260–77) assassinated Kutuz and succeeded as sultan of Egypt. Alfonso X was certainly familiar with him, as *Cantiga* 165 relates the attempt of Bondoudar (surely Baybars Bundukdārī), the sultan of Egypt, to take Tortosa on the Syrian coast in 1268.[44]

When Alfonso X summoned the Cortes of Toledo in 1259 "concerning the affair of the empire," he may have sent a legation to Egypt, not only to announce his new imperial status, but also to discuss the difficult situation of the Holy Land. While hoping to develop commercial relations with Egypt, he may also have wished to dissuade the Mamlūks from interfering in Morocco. If an embassy from Alvandexaver or Kutuz al-Muzaffar arrived in Seville at the time of Fernando III's anniversary, then that would have to have occurred in May 1260. Although there is no royal charter dated in the city at that time, the king was in Andalucía. If the envoys arrived in May 1261, when Alfonso X was certainly in Seville, they would have represented Baybars. As a usurper, he clearly wanted recognition from the principal Western rulers and, according to Arabic sources, sent his ambassadors to them. A few years later, in A.H. 664 (1265/66), when Alfonso X sent envoys to the ruler of the Assassins or Ismāʿīlis, a Syrian sect, the Mamlūks impeded their journey by levying customs duties on gifts for the Assassins. Although Muslim sources do not provide an itinerary, the envoys may have journeyed to Alexandria before continuing on to Syria. Despite that incident, Alfonso X and Baybars concluded a commercial treaty in A.H. 670 (1270/71).[45] Thus maritime contacts between the merchants of Seville and the Egyptians may have occurred more frequently than the documentation attests.

Aside from their commercial value, Alfonso X's relations with Taount, Ténès, and Egypt, ephemeral though they may have been, had a certain importance for his African Crusade, his quest for the throne of the Holy Roman Empire, and his interest in the plight of the Holy Land. All were now linked together. As Manuel González Jiménez emphasized: "From this perspective, leading a crusade could be the surest means of presenting oneself to the papacy and to Europe as a true emperor."[46]

Alexander IV, Jaime I, and the Crusade

Determined to press on with the African Crusade, Alfonso X continued to seek needed military and naval power. Meeting with representatives of the Castilian and Extremaduran towns at Segovia in 1256, he granted fiscal exemptions to urban knights who, as determined at an annual muster, maintained horses and arms suitable for war.[47] Then in 1257 he ordered San Esteban de Gormaz to be prepared to send 120 knights with horses and arms for a projected expedition against the Moors.[48] Early in 1258 during the Cortes of Valladolid he required the Galician and Asturian towns to meet his demand for a loan and to have their sailing ships (*naves*) and galleys ready at Cádiz on 1 May for the "affair of the crusade"—"fecho de la cruzada." Oviedo made a loan of 1,200 *maravedíes*. Perhaps the obligation of the Cantabrian towns to provide one or more galleys for the king's navy dates from this time.[49] Whether any naval action was undertaken after 1 May is unknown. The fleet may not have been ready and Henry III's failure to participate may have caused Alfonso X to postpone the expedition.

In April 1259, at the king's request, Alexander IV directed Bishop Remondo of Segovia to preach the crusade. José Goñi Gaztambide suggested, however, that the pope was beginning to question whether the African Crusade would ever occur. Thus in July, again in response to a royal petition, he declared that "if it should happen that you undertake war against the Saracens of Spain," the participants would gain the crusading indulgence. That made clear that the king's crusading plans extended not only to Africa but also to Islamic Spain.[50]

Plans for an African expedition moved ahead quickly in 1260. Alexander IV appointed Bishop Martín of Segovia to preach the crusade "against the

Saracens of Africa" throughout Spain. Recalling the help given by the mariner Roy García of Santander during his conquest of Murcia, the king rewarded him for the service he expected to receive "in this affair that we have begun beyond the sea for the service of God, the honor and benefit of ourselves and of all our kingdoms."[51]

Alfonso X also requested assistance from his father-in-law, Jaime I of Aragón (1213–76). Meeting at Agreda in March 1260, the two kings, aside from resolving smoldering resentments, discussed the African Crusade. Commenting that Alfonso X intended to move "against the Saracens for the exaltation of the Catholic faith," Jaime I declared that "this should be preached in our realm" and permitted his vassals to aid him against the Saracens. The only caveat was that no harm should be inflicted on the Hafsid sultan of Tunis, with whom Jaime I enjoyed friendly relations. Acknowledging the bad blood between Alfonso X and his brother Enrique, Jaime I refused to permit one of his nobles to accompany Enrique to Tunis.[52]

Knowing that the Tunisian sultans had intruded into Morocco in the past and probably would do so again, Alfonso X was annoyed by Jaime I's constraint and complained that he had excluded from the "fecho de la cruzada" magnates and knights who were not his vassals, but whose service could be of great value. Despite his grumbling, he pleaded with Jaime I to join the crusade. Jaime I, who was pondering a possible crusade to the Holy Land, affirmed that he had no objection to Aragonese knights taking part in "this crusade that you wish to have preached against the Moors." However, his truce with Tunis precluded any hostile Aragonese action there. A few months later Alfonso X expressed his disapproval of Jaime I's projected crusade to the Holy Land.[53]

Alcanatir, Cádiz, and El Puerto de Santa María

Hastening to the frontier in the early summer of 1260, Alfonso X appointed a new admiral to replace Roy López de Mendoza, who had died earlier in the year. Filled with "a great desire to carry forward the affair of the crusade beyond the sea, to the service of God and the exaltation of Christendom," the king designated Juan García de Villamayor as *adelantado de la mar*. Entrusted with all "the rights of the admiralty," he received authority over all the ports of the realm in matters relating to the sea. The use of the term *adelantado* rather than *almirante* seems to emphasize his jurisdictional responsibilities over those of a purely naval nature.[54]

With the goal of developing a naval base adjacent to the Atlantic Ocean, the king selected Alcanatir (al-Qanatir), a few miles south of Jerez. Endowed with a fine harbor sheltered from the open sea, Alcanatir, lying west of the Guadalete River, stood opposite Cádiz. The Moors of Cádiz apparently had acknowledged Fernando III's suzerainty, but Castilian settlement there did not begin in earnest until the summer of 1260. The appointment in 1261 of Pedro Lorenzo as archdeacon of Cádiz signaled its incorporation into the archbishopric of Seville.[55]

In the expectation that Alcanatir would "guard the Christians from the Moors and be a fortress whence to make war on the Moors of Spain and the Africans," the king began transforming it into a naval base in August and early September 1260.[56] In the *Cantigas de Santa Maria* he dedicated twenty-four *cantigas* to Alcanatir, now christened El Puerto de Santa María.[57] Reportedly inspired by Mary, Castilian settlers gave it its new name, but it is much more likely that the decision was the king's. When the *alguacil*, an official of Jerez, protested this alteration, the king ordered his officials to punish anyone using the new name. Even though many Christians were whipped, their ribs broken, and their ears cut off, the name could not be stamped out. At last, according to the king, the Virgin Mary intervened and persuaded the *alguacil*, for the good of his people, to accept the change. The *alguacil* also insisted that the king take possession not only of Alcanatir but also of all the adjacent villages. As a result, Alfonso X realized that Cádiz could be more quickly populated.[58] Although the focus of this story is a change of name, what likely disturbed the *alguacil* and the people of Jerez was the growing Castilian presence in the zone around El Puerto de Santa María and Cádiz. The new name manifested to all that the region now belonged entirely to the Christians. With good reason, the Moors could consider this constriction of their territory, albeit under Castilian suzerainty, as an arbitrary use of power by the king. Incapable of preventing it, they nevertheless harbored deep hostility that erupted in full-scale rebellion a few years later.[59]

Ceuta: Objective of the Crusade?

In the late summer of 1260, the African Crusade, so long in preparation, finally was launched, but there is some question as to its immediate objective. González Jiménez argued that the king, prompted by Ibn al-Ahmar, intended to attack Ceuta. Directly opposite Gibraltar, Ceuta was a rich emporium where merchants not only from the Muslim world, but also from Marseille, Pisa, Genoa, and Barcelona engaged in an active trade. Some years later, in *Cantiga* 169, Alfonso X declared his wish to "conquer Spain and Morocco as well as Ceuta and Arzila," an Atlantic port some miles north of Salé.[60]

For some time Fernando III and his son had Ceuta in their sights. Several letters from the chancery in Ceuta provide information about the relationship between Castile and the city.[61] After the fall of Seville, Ceuta, which had provided a fleet for its defense, accepted a truce and paid tribute to Castile. That agreement was probably reached in 1251, just before Fernando's death.[62]

Pressure from Castile, however, compelled Ceuta, about 1253 or 1254, to turn to the Almohad caliph Abū Hafs ʿUmar al-Murtadā (1248–66) for protection and financial aid. Emphasizing Ceuta's desperate situation, the citizens expressed their fear of a Christian attack, as the truce with Castile would expire within four months. The "wicked Alfonso," with the support of Jaime I, was mobilizing his forces and called upon the priests and friars, "who, raising crosses on high, impose them on the people to aid the king in a crusade." That language suggests the preaching of the crusade and the conferral of crosses, which crusaders sewed on their garments. To avert disaster the town council asked Alfonso X to renew the truce, but he refused. Determined to dominate the city, he demanded a tribute of 70,000 dinars in two years, an increase of 30,000 above the previous agreement. Those 30,000 dinars were the price of the Christian captives surrendered under the terms of the previous pact. Lamenting the drop in customs duties, as Christian merchants were no longer coming to Ceuta, the town fathers stressed that they could not meet Castilian demands. The public revenue, derived mainly from a tax on olive oil, was insufficient to pay the required tribute, especially because of a poor harvest. Strapped financially, the town council appealed to the Almohads, emphasizing that if the money were not paid promptly, the Castilians would besiege the city and take it. The payment of tribute seemed preferable to resistance.[63] Despite the silence of the sources, the tribute probably was paid and Ceuta was able to breathe freely for a time.

A few years later, probably in 1257, Abū-l-Qāsim al-ʿAzafī (1249–72) who transformed Ceuta into an autonomous lordship,[64] wrote to Ibn al-Ahmar, expressing his satisfaction that the Nasrids and the Marinids, who both aspired to dominate Ceuta, were at peace, at least for the time being, and were determined to defend the city against any enemies. Al-ʿAzafī also maintained a positive relationship with the Almohad caliph, with whom he exchanged correspondence.[65]

According to Alfonso X's own account in 1264, he summoned Ibn al-Ahmar to the Cortes of Toledo in 1259 "to advise us in this matter [the *fecho del imperio*] as a vassal and a friend in whom we trusted." If his imperial hopes came to naught, Ibn al-Ahmar promised to show him an even greater empire and help him to obtain it. That empire lay in Africa. Meeting at Jaén, probably in the summer of 1260, Alfonso X related that when he inquired as to Ibn al-Ahmar's meaning, he replied, "he would help us to take Ceuta, and we would win many Moors beyond the sea as friends who would help us and do what we wished to conquer the land."[66]

As a further indication that Ceuta was the target of the crusade, Fray Lorenzo of Portugal, a Franciscan friar who served as papal legate in Spain and "preacher of the cross throughout Spain" was named bishop of Ceuta around 1258. His appointment accorded with papal interest, seconded by the king, in developing the Christian mission in Morocco.[67] Nevertheless, he may never have set foot there and had no apparent successors until the Portuguese conquest in 1415.[68] Although it is likely that Alfonso X hoped to occupy Ceuta, one cannot say with certainty that he attempted to do so in 1260. Perhaps he and Ibn al-Ahmar planned a two-pronged attack by the Castilians on Salé and the Granadans on Ceuta.

The Crusade of Salé

As it happened, in 1260 a Castilian fleet sailing from El Puerto de Santa María sacked Salé (Salā), a port on the Atlantic coast of Morocco, separated from Rabat by the Bou Regreg River. Fifteen years previously Zeid Aazon, "the illustrious king of Salé," that is, the *sayyid* al-Hasan, a son of Abū Zayd, the last king of Valencia, who had converted to Christianity, made known his desire to become a Christian and offered his kingdom to the Order of Santiago. Although Innocent IV encouraged the knights, they were unable to act, preoccupied as they were with the peninsular reconquest. The Almohads, moreover, executed al-Hasan.[69]

Moroccan political uncertainties in 1260 invited Castilian intervention, as the Marinids dismembered the once-powerful Almohad Empire. While the Almohads still retained Marrakech, in July 1260 Rabat fell to the Marinid emir Abū Yūsuf Ya'qūb b. 'Abd al-Haqq (1259–86). A monarch of exceptional ability, he proved to be a grave threat to Castile during the next twenty-five years. His nephew Ya'qūb, then in control of Salé, perhaps hoping to set himself up as an independent ruler in alliance with Castile, appealed to Alfonso X, probably late in 1259 or early 1260, to send 200 cavalry. Expressing a common Muslim sentiment when speaking of the Castilian ruler, the historian Ibn 'Idhārī declared, "may God annihilate him." Despite that hostile remark, the king could not ignore this opportunity to secure a foothold in Morocco.[70]

During the late summer of 1260, while Alfonso X's fleet of 37 vessels of diverse sizes and capacities, namely, carracks, sailing ships, galleys, and barges, was being readied for action, he made his camp at El Puerto de Santa María.[71] Although the Moroccans were aware of this, they did not know the fleet's destination. Suspecting hostile intent, al-'Azafī, the governor of Ceuta, alerted all the coastal towns. A few residents of Salé withdrew to safety, but the majority, fearing nothing, stayed behind. Alfonso X entrusted command of the enterprise to Juan García de Villamayor, his *adelantado de la mar*, and Pedro Martínez de Fe, who bore the title of admiral. As an experienced seaman, his task was presumably to navigate to Salé, while Juan García was responsible for military operations. At the beginning of September the fleet took to the sea on a voyage usually of four days' duration. As Ibn 'Idhārī reported that the fleet was sighted off Salé on Wednesday, 8 September, it probably departed on 4 September.[72]

The fleet entered the Bou Regreg opposite Rabat on Friday, 10 September, as the fast of the month of Ramadan was ending. The citizens were in a joyous frame of mind. Initially, they thought that the ships were merchantmen, but they were quickly disabused of that idea when they watched armed soldiers disembark. Led by a company of archers, the troops marched toward the city and, as there was no protective wall by the riverbank, they gained entrance. Surprised, unarmed, and unprepared, the Muslims could not halt the enemy advance. A few threw javelins and twenty mounted horsemen offered combat, but they were easily overcome and, in the words of Ibn 'Idhārī, gained martyrdom. Watching from the citadel in Rabat across the river, Ya'qūb, the governor who had asked Alfonso X for 200 knights, was astounded and wrung his hands in sorrow and dismay. Killing the men, the Castilians drove women and children into the chief mosque, where they amused themselves with the women and virgins. Old women were killed. Homes were violated and mosques and houses were plundered and destroyed.[73]

For two weeks, while Pedro Martínez held the fleet conveniently offshore, Juan García and his troops pillaged Salé, seizing merchandise, gold, silver, valuable objects of all kinds, and numerous captives. Describing Salé, "a great and much honored town," as entirely destroyed, *Cantiga* 328 remarked that the booty taken was unimaginable. The surprise was such that the Marinid emir, Abū Yūsuf, accompanied by a small body of men, only laid siege to Salé on 13 September, five days after the initial assault. As other bodies of troops arrived during the next two weeks, he "roused them to the holy war." Rather than attempt to hold the town, Juan García decided to withdraw. Setting houses and markets on fire, the Castilians, in their hurry to leave, burned furniture, food, utensils, containers, beds, cotton, woolen, and linen goods, and whatever else they could not carry. In order to deceive the enemy they placed puppets in the embrasures of the walls and, laden with booty, vacated the town at nighttime, taking to their ships on Wednesday, 22 September. As "God had cleansed the land of their heresy," the Marinids took possession once more. Abū Yūsuf ordered the reconstruction of mosques and houses and built a wall along the riverbank to prevent similar incursions in the future.[74]

In their haste to escape, the Castilians failed to obtain sufficient water for their return voyage. Buffeted by strong winds as they made their way northward along the Moroccan coast, they tried to get water at various places, but the Moors repulsed them, even killing some. At Larrache, southwest of Tangier, the crew of one ship sold fifty-three Muslim captives in return for water. Exasperated with the leaders of the expedition for having abandoned Salé, one Castilian captain threatened to burn them alive. Twenty of his men offered to serve the Marinids and, after obtaining safe-conduct, made their way to the emir's court. Toward the beginning of October the crusaders reached El Puerto de Santa María. The Moors of Jerez and other towns ransomed about 380 of the 3,000 captives brought to Seville, mostly old men and women, and children. Around the middle of the month, Abū Yūsuf sent his lieutenant to ransom the remaining captives, including the chief judge of Salé. Rich families were able to ransom their own, while the poor were redeemed by the alms of their fellow Muslims. Some still remained in Christian hands, however, and the fate of other persons was entirely unknown.[75]

Meantime, the Almohad caliph al-Murtaḍā thanked al-ʿAzafī of Ceuta for his warning about the Castilian fleet and urged him to continue to monitor the enemy's plans, "so that with the help of God we may prepare and take steps to repel them."[76]

At the same time Abū Yūsuf's spies discovered that Alfonso X had organized a "very numerous and very well equipped contingent to support the infidels who had taken control of Salé." However, according to Ibn ʿIdhārī, when the king learned that the Marinids had recovered Salé, "he was about to explode and to die of grief." In his anger, he swore that he would punish the leaders of the expedition and would burn Juan García. On hearing this, Juan García, with three carracks, took refuge in Lisbon and did not return to Cádiz. Of the original thirty-seven ships only twenty-five returned home; the rest were probably dispersed or lost to storms. Contrary to Ibn ʿIdhārī, the *Royal Chronicle* affirmed that Alfonso X was quite happy with the outcome of the expedition. Winds may have driven Juan García to Lisbon, whence he returned to Castile, but it is also possible that Ibn ʿIdhārī, writing years later, has confused two events. Alfonso X may well have been angry with Juan García, but two years later he displayed his confidence in him by appointing him as one of his representatives to resolve a dispute with Portugal. That may be the reason for Ibn ʿIdhārī's statement that he went to Lisbon.[77]

When all is said and done, the question remains: why did Juan García attack Salé? Was Alfonso X angry that he did so, instead of attacking Ceuta? Ceuta was probably not the original objective and there is no reason to believe that Juan García would have changed that plan on his own authority. Rather, Alfonso X's intention was to take advantage of the proposal made by Yaʿqūb, the governor of Salé, and to establish a Castilian protectorate there and to place a garrison in the citadel. The time lapse between Yaʿqūb's proposal and the assault on Salé is unknown. In fact, Yaʿqūb may have changed his mind and seems to have been as surprised as anyone when the crusaders appeared. Ibn ʿIdhārī's statement that Alfonso X had ready a large and well-equipped force to support those who took Salé suggests that the occupation was intended to be permanent, but it would only be the first step. The king may have wished to use it as a base for expanding his control of the Moroccan coast northward to Tangier and Ceuta. Threatened by Abū Yūsuf's besieging army that increased every day, Juan García made the decision to withdraw. If the king were angry, surely it was because his grand design to use Salé as a Moroccan military outpost came to an abrupt end.

Meanwhile, Ibn al-Ahmar had his own ambitions for Morocco. Surely he knew that the Almoravids and the Almohads, after making themselves masters there, had invaded Spain where they vanquished the petty Muslim states. He had every reason to expect that the Marinids, once they consolidated their hold over the remnants of the disintegrating Almohad Empire, would invade the Peninsula and attempt to destroy his kingdom. As a precaution against that eventuality, he proposed the conquest of Ceuta to Alfonso X. Perhaps they agreed that while Castile would attack Salé, Granada would seize Ceuta. Probably in the fall of 1260 about the same time as the expedition to Salé or soon thereafter, Ibn al-Ahmar dispatched his fleet from Algeciras to Ceuta.[78]

Determined to defend his independence not only against the Almohads and the Marinids, al-'Azafī, the ruler of Ceuta, was also unwilling to accept Nasrid domination. When Granadan ships arrived before Ceuta and attempted to cut off food supplies, his fleet defeated them and only a few escaped. Their commander was killed and his body was hung from a rock overlooking the sea; his head, after being paraded through the city, was also hung. Stung by that reverse, Ibn al-Ahmar turned to Alfonso X for help.[79]

The Submission of Jerez de la Frontera

However disappointing the affair of Salé may have been, Alfonso X was resolved to continue his African Crusade. To that end, he convened the Cortes to Seville at the end of 1260 and early 1261, to seek counsel "concerning the affair of Africa that we have begun."[80] Mistakenly dating these events in 1255, the *Royal Chronicle* revealed the question put before the assembly. "As the king wished to serve God and to inflict damage and harm on the Moors, he proposed to conquer the land they held, especially what was near the city of Seville." When he asked whether he should attack Jerez or Niebla, the response was Jerez. Control of Jerez seemed necessary to assure the security of the recently developed naval base at El Puerto de Santa María and Cádiz, immediately to the south. His order, fifteen years later, that an accounting be undertaken of all taxes in arrears since the campaign of Niebla, suggests that he asked the Cortes for a tax levy to finance this campaign.[81]

Besieged for a month, and fearful that the Christians would destroy their orchards and olive groves, the Moors of Jerez decided to submit. Once the pressure of the siege was over, they thought that they might then free themselves of Castilian rule. Realizing that the siege would be prolonged and few Christians could be induced to settle there, Alfonso X accepted their proposal. The Moors, subject to an annual tribute, were allowed to reside in the town and retain their property. But the admission of a Christian garrison into the *alcázar* not only strengthened the king's hold over Jerez but also greatly enhanced the Castilian military position in the Guadalete River Valley. The king's good friend Nuño González de Lara was appointed *alcaide* or castellan. Ibn 'Idhārī dated the Castilian occupation in A.H. 659 (6 December 1260–25 November 1261). Jerez probably submitted sometime in the late spring or early summer of 1261.[82]

The Conquest of Niebla

Following the capitulation of Jerez, the king turned to the kingdom of Niebla just west of Seville. Ibn Maḥfūt, king of Niebla, had agreed to pay an annual tribute to Castile, but from time to time he waged the holy war, thereby provoking Castilian hostility. However, from February 1253 until late June 1261, he was recorded as a vassal confirming royal privileges.[83] The acquisition of Niebla would expand Castilian access to the Atlantic Ocean and reinforce Castilian claims to the Algarbe against the Portuguese. When Alfonso X began to call himself king of the Algarbe in 1261, he threw down a challenge, not only to the Portuguese, but also to Ibn Maḥfūt.

The *Royal Chronicle*, incorrectly dating this in 1257, stated that the king summoned magnates, knights, and town militias to participate in the siege of Niebla. A long siege seemed likely as Niebla was strongly fortified with a great store of provisions. Bombarded by siege engines, Niebla held out for nine and a half months, but, as the food supply dwindled, Ibn Maḥfūt surrendered toward the end of February 1262. The king provided him with an honorable retirement near Seville, but he eventually entered Almohad service and died in Morocco.[84]

González Jiménez suggested that Ibn Maḥfūt's resistance was merely a matter of form. By making a show of opposition and surrendering after an appropriate time, he saved his honor and that of his people as good Muslims. The fact that Alfonso X remained in Seville for most of the year and appeared at Niebla only on 12 February 1262 lends credence to this proposal. With the capture of Niebla, he also gained control of Gibraleón and the Atlantic port of Huelva, but the *Chronicle* errs in stating that he also acquired "the whole Algarbe." Afonso III of Portugal (1248–79) had already occupied the western Algarbe and had concluded a pact with Alfonso X concerning it in 1253.[85]

After the surrender of Niebla, the Moors were evacuated (though many remained in the surrounding area) and a Christian colony was begun. In 1263, announcing that "this is the first place that we conquered after we began to reign," the king provided for municipal government and defense and fixed the boundaries of Niebla, Huelva, Gibraleón, and Saltés.[86]

With Niebla firmly in his grasp, the king turned again to the development of the region around El Puerto de Santa María. Describing it as "one of the best places in the world to build a great town or a very great city," he erected a church there, welcomed new residents, and guaranteed the safety and security of merchants. As there had long been a Genoese colony in Seville, it was not surprising that Genoese merchants opted to settle in El Puerto, but there were others from as far away as Chartres in France and Catalan corsairs, regarded as a menace by everyone.[87]

In order to strengthen the Christian presence in Cádiz, the king, declaring that he had labored hard on the frontier and endured many illnesses in defense of his people, asked for financial aid from Oviedo and probably from other towns. While asserting great poverty, the people of Oviedo in 1264 agreed to lend him 1,000 *maravedíes*. Thanking them for their contribution to the "affair of Cádiz," he continued their exemption from *fonsadera*, a tax levied in lieu of personal military service.[88] The expansion of Christian settlement at Cádiz and El Puerto de Santa María eventually deprived the Moorish towns of Arcos, Jerez, Medina Sidonia, and others of easy access to the sea.[89]

Following the fall of Niebla, Alfonso X, looking back over his plans for the African Crusade, could count a measure of success. Two popes granted crusading bulls and allowed him to use ecclesiastical revenues. Nevertheless, he failed to persuade Jaime I or Henry III to participate; the latter refused to do so for the third time in 1262.[90] Perhaps in response to Castilian pleas, Haakon IV in the summer of 1262 sent two envoys to Tunis, but there is no indication of the outcome of their mission.[91] Despite the lack of enthusiasm from his royal colleagues, Alfonso X developed the shipyards in Seville, built a fleet, and established a naval base at El Puerto de Santa María and Cádiz. The immediate outcome of that effort was the expedition to Salé whose results were mixed. A great deal of booty was taken, but the king's expectation of establishing a base there, perhaps in preparation for further attempts to secure control of the Moroccan coast, was not met. While he may have been disappointed, he had greater success in taking control of the *alcázar* of Jerez and in occupying the shoreline around the mouth of the Guadalete and the Gulf of Cádiz. By annexing the kingdom of Niebla to the west of Seville, he strengthened his claims to the Algarbe and eradicated an independent Muslim state there.

The Demand for Tarifa and Algeciras

Despite the disappointing outcome of the Castilian assault on Salé and the abortive Granadan attack on Ceuta, Alfonso X and Ibn al-Ahmar still had ambitions in Morocco. When they met at Jaén, probably in May 1262, Ibn al-Ahmar suggested a joint venture against Ceuta. Arguing that an offensive could best be launched from Tarifa and Algeciras, Alfonso X asked the Nasrid king to yield those ports to him.[92] Ibn al-Ahmar promised to do so within thirty days, but after a lapse of two months, he still had not acted. Meeting Alfonso X at Seville, he said that, although his counselors advised him to the contrary, he would send his son to surrender the ports. If the meeting at Jaén took place in mid-May 1262, Algeciras and Tarifa should have been surrendered by mid-June, or at least around the middle of July. One would think, however, that just as the expedition to Salé set out from El Puerto de Santa María, an offensive against Ceuta could also be launched from there. Whether he realized it or not, Alfonso X was overreaching and expecting too much from his "friend and vassal to whom we have done much good and much honor and who is obligated to serve and love us loyally."[93]

Ibn al-Ahmar could only view the demand for Tarifa and Algeciras as a threat and apparently tried to put it off with honeyed words. An additional cause of alarm was the forced expulsion in 1263 of the Mudéjars of Écija and their replacement by Christian settlers. Alfonso X may have acted to provide greater security for a strategic area located about equidistant between Córdoba and Seville. His evident willingness to override agreements made with the Mudéjars, however, must have aroused resentment that eventually boiled over into rebellion. Surely Ibn al-Ahmar had to wonder whether there were any limits to Christian demands.[94]

Alfonso X, meanwhile, took measures to strengthen his military posture. The towns of Extremadura protested that, while serving on the frontier for three months, they had not received any share in the *fonsadera*. After consulting his counselors, the king enacted an ordinance on 29 April 1264 confirming tax exemptions given to municipal knights in 1256 and now extending them to their dependents. By rewarding them, he believed that they would be more disposed to serve him in the future.[95]

Intent on attacking Ceuta, Alfonso X solicited naval assistance from Genoa. On the same day that he enacted his ordinance on military service, Bonagiunta de Portovenere, a Genoese merchant, and his company agreed to build three galleys for the "admiral of Castile." Two weeks later, Raimundo Danza di Vintimiglia promised Hugo Vento, "admiral of the king of Castile," a loan for armament of the ships. As we hear no more of Admiral Hugo, Florentino Pérez Embid seems to be correct in noting that this was an isolated instance when the king attempted to secure Genoese collaboration in a naval enterprise.[96]

Alfonso X's ambitions to establish a base in Morocco and perhaps to conquer Ceuta were rudely interrupted in May 1264 by the revolt of the Mudéjars of Andalucía and Murcia who were roused to opposition by Ibn al-Ahmar. The African Crusade was ended once and for all. In the remaining twenty years of his reign, the king had to suppress this uprising, the most serious threat to his rule, and also to defend his realm against the Marinids of Morocco.

Chapter 3

The Crusade Against the Mudéjars

For more than ten years Alfonso X pursued his African Crusade and his quest for the imperial crown, confident that the kings of Granada and Murcia, as loyal vassals, would not impede him. In 1264, however, the revolt of the Mudéjars, aided and abetted by the Moorish kings, took him entirely by surprise and laid bare the vulnerability of his kingdom. Though guaranteed freedom of religion and the right to be governed by Islamic law, the Mudéjars repudiated their allegiance and maintained hostilities for several years. No longer could Islamic Spain be viewed as submissive and subjugated. In order to bring them to heel Alfonso X appealed to the pope to grant the usual crusading indulgences.

The Alienation of the King of Granada

Ibn al-Ahmar, king of Granada, provoked the Mudéjar revolt. Although he and Alfonso X seem to have developed a true friendship going beyond the strictly formal bond of lord and vassal, he came to realize that the Castilian's multiple actions imperiled his kingdom: the African Crusade; the naval bases at Cádiz and El Puerto de Santa María; the garrison in Jerez; the expedition to Salé; the conquest of Niebla; the expulsion of the Mudéjars of Écija; and the planned attack on Ceuta. If Tarifa and Algeciras fell into Castilian hands, his own ambition to dominate Ceuta would be thwarted. For his part, Alfonso X should have expected Ibn al-Ahmar's reaction to his demand for those ports.[1]

After the deposition of Ibn Maḥfūṭ of Niebla, the Nasrid king could suppose that Alfonso X would attempt to oust him as well. To avert that possibility, he turned to Abū Yūsuf Yaʿqūb, the Marinid sultan, who dispatched a contingent of light cavalry (*jinetes*) to Tarifa in 1263. Ibn ʿIdhārī, a most careful historian, not given to hyperbole, stated that 300 knights came to engage in the holy war. Ibn Abī Zarʿ, however, fixed their number at 3,000. Abū Yūsuf, according to Miguel Ángel Manzano Rodríguez, gained two advantages: (1) he got rid of a dissident Marinid faction; and (2) in preparation for a future invasion of the Peninsula, he secured an ally in the king of Granada.[2] The generous wages and other advantages provided to these newcomers by Ibn al-Ahmar stirred the resentment of the governors (*arraeces*) of Málaga and Guadix. Members of the Banū Ashqīlūlā, his relatives by marriage and close allies, they took even greater umbrage when he airily dismissed their complaints and, according to the *Royal Chronicle* (which counted 1,000 Marinid knights), actively sought to do him disservice. Jaime I reported that the arrival of the Marinids angered his son-in-law, who recognized them as a threat. Quartered at Málaga, they were transferred to Jerez when war broke out with Castile in 1264.[3]

The arrival of the Marinid troops may have prompted Alfonso X to demand an explanation when Ibn al-Ahmar came to Seville in 1264 to renew his twenty-year truce concluded in 1246. Accompanied by 500 knights, he encamped outside the city, but Alfonso X invited him to take up residence in the palace of Ibn ʿAbbad, the eleventh-century king of Seville, adjacent to the mosque. During the night the Christians erected a locked palisade on the street where the Moors were lodged, blockading their houses and impeding the passage of horses. Angered by this perceived treasonous stratagem, Ibn al-Ahmar ordered his men to break down the barricade and returned to Granada. Although Alfonso X swore that the palisade was intended to protect the Moors from Christian thieves, Ibn al-Ahmar was not convinced and vowed never to see the king of Castile again except in battle. After reaching Medina Sidonia, he ordered all the frontier outposts to prepare for war. He also declared his vassalage to ʿAbd Allāh Muhammad ibn Abū Zakariyāʾ, the emir of Tunis.[4] Alfonso X's brothers Enrique and Fadrique had taken refuge at the Hafsid court.

While Ibn al-Ahmar took the incident at Seville as an affront to his honor, Jaime I suggested that the Nasrid not only schemed with the Mudéjars to rise in rebellion on a fixed date, but also planned to seize Alfonso X, Queen Violante, and other members of the royal family in Seville. Informed of that plot, the king was able to escape the danger.[5]

The Beginning of the Revolt

The chronology of the Mudéjar revolt is uncertain in part because the *Royal Chronicle* placed the beginning in 1261 and gave a convoluted account of its progress. The rebellion started sometime between 29 April 1264, when Ibn al-Ahmar, as a royal vassal, was listed among those confirming Alfonso X's privileges, and 5 June, when his name was omitted.

In letters to the bishops of Cuenca, Segovia, and Sigüenza on 20 June 1264, Alfonso X recounted the origins of the uprising. After Ibn al-Ahmar promised to show him a great empire and proposed an assault on Ceuta, he delayed the surrender of Tarifa and Algeciras. Despite his dilatory tactics, Alfonso X willingly accepted his excuses. Meanwhile, Ibn al-Ahmar, betraying his suzerain's trust and revealing "the deceit and treason in his heart," became a vassal of the emir of Tunis and conspired with Alfonso X's other enemies. While simultaneously assuring the king that he was laboring in his service, he secretly plotted with the Mudéjars of Andalucía and Murcia to rise in revolt on a certain day. When Alfonso X was least suspicious and had only a small company with him in Seville, Ibn al-Ahmar sent his messengers to announce that he was no longer his vassal. Even before the messengers set out for home, he began to attack Castilian territory, waging war with his own forces and those from beyond the sea.[6]

Jerez was a principal center of the Mudéjar revolt. Chafing at the presence of the Castilian garrison stationed in the *alcázar* since 1261, the townspeople, after convincing the king that he had little to fear from them, built a wall separating the *alcázar* from the town. In late July or early August 1264, with the help of Marinid troops stationed at Málaga and contingents from Algeciras and Tarifa, they launched a fierce assault on the *alcázar*. Nuño González de Lara, the *alcaide*, who had only a few knights, appealed to Seville for help and demanded that the king come in person to take possession. Unwilling to take responsibility for the defense, Nuño yielded his post, leaving a token garrison behind.[7] *Cantiga* 345 pointedly remarked that that was something "which by law and custom ought not to be." By abandoning the *alcázar*, Nuño was acting contrary to the law set forth in the *Siete Partidas* (2,18) concerning an *alcaide*'s obligations. Although a troop of cavalry from Seville reached Jerez in two days, they were too late. By midday, the Moors had seized the *alcázar*, killing or capturing the forlorn defenders. *Cantiga* 345 then tells us that the king, while taking a siesta in Seville, dreamed that the Moors destroyed the chapel of Our Lady, but were unable to burn her statue. Waking, he discovered that Queen Violante had had the same dream. They both knew that the *alcázar* was lost.[8] The *alcázar* was taken on Friday, 8 August, according to the anonymous Muslim chronicle *Al-Dhakhīra al-Saniyya*. Although Alfonso X compensated Nuño González de Lara for his lost revenues, he later reproached him for his failure to hold Jerez.[9]

Following the lead of Jerez, the neighboring towns of Arcos, Lebrija, Medina Sidonia, and others repudiated Castilian suzerainty. A Castilian garrison holding the castle of Arcos was ousted. However, Alemán, a knight of Calatrava, ably defended the nearby fortress of Matrera, which Alfonso X had given to the Order in 1256.[10]

The Mudéjars of Murcia also rose in rebellion. Ever since 1243 the Banū Hūd had remained steadfast in their loyalty to Alfonso X, despite his efforts to strengthen the Christian population there. After the death of Abū Ja'far, king of Murcia, sometime late in 1263 or early 1264, his son Muhammad, succeeded him but was driven from the throne by his cousin Abū Bakr b. Hūd al-Wātiq, known to the Castilians as Alboaquez. However, when the Murcians expelled the Castilian garrison from the *alcázar* of Murcia, they accepted Ibn al-Ahmar as their suzerain. His appointment of Abū Muhammad b. Ashqīlūla as their governor indicated that al-Wātiq and the Banū Hūd were being pushed aside. The Moors of Lorca also threw off their allegiance to Castile. By Jaime I's reckoning, in a space of three weeks Alfonso X lost some 300 towns, castles, and other strongholds.[11]

The Castilian Response

Taken aback by the Mudéjar revolt and deceived by Ibn al-Ahmar's fine words, Alfonso X denounced the Moor's treachery. Proclaiming his "trust in God that this very great treason . . . will lead to [Ibn al-Ahmar's] harm and destruction," the king expressed the hope that the outcome would serve God, exalt Christendom, and render honor and benefit to himself and his people. As Ibn al-Ahmar duplicitously violated his pledges, Alfonso X demanded justice and determined to direct all his power against him. With that in mind, on 20 June he demanded that the bishops of Cuenca, Segovia, and Sigüenza preach a crusade throughout his realms and sent them copies of crusading bulls issued by Innocent IV and Alexander IV in 1246 and 1259. He also petitioned Clement IV (1265–68) to publish new crusading bulls. Moreover, he appealed for military assistance to Jaime I, and probably also to his son-in-law Afonso III of Portugal.[12] A few months later, when he came to terms with the latter concerning the Algarbe, he required the service of fifty knights for his lifetime and probably called on them in dealing with the Mudéjars.[13]

As Alfonso X, by his own admission, had only a small company with him at Seville when the rebellion broke out, he could not immediately mount a counteroffensive. A war on three fronts, namely, Lower Andalucía, Granada, and Murcia, lay before him. Neither the *Royal Chronicle* nor the documentary record provides a clear guide to events. While the king took necessary measures to defend frontier positions, such as Matrera, then besieged by the Moors, Ibn al-Ahmar responded with a vigorous attack wherever possible.[14]

The recovery of Jerez and other towns and fortresses leading to the Gulf of Cádiz was the king's most immediate concern. He began by besieging Jerez. At the end of five months the Moors, weary of bombardment by Castilian siege engines, proposed to surrender if the king permitted them to depart freely. Although he was exceedingly angry with them, he was anxious to regain possession, especially as there were reports that Abū Yūsuf, the Marinid emir, was preparing to invade the Peninsula. Rather than await the arrival of a new Marinid army, he allowed the Moors to evacuate the town. Moving southward, he received the submission of Vejer, Medina Sidonia, Rota, and Sanlúcar de Barrameda. On his return march, he expelled the Moors from Arcos and Lebrija. After garrisoning these fortresses, he returned to Seville, but, as winter was coming on, he released his troops, ordering them to be prepared to resume the campaign in the following April. According to *Cantiga* 345, he celebrated his triumph by restoring the statue of the Virgin Mary to the chapel in the citadel of Jerez.[15]

Local tradition dates the surrender of Jerez on the feast of St. Denis, 9 October 1264, five months after it began.[16] While in Jerez on 9 October 1264, he appointed an *alcaide* and issued several privileges.[17] In November, after returning to Seville, he extended privileges to Christian settlers in Arcos and in the following year affirmed that he had taken Jerez with the help of the Virgin Mary.[18]

Acknowledging the contribution of the military orders to the recent campaign, he attempted to convince the Order of Calatrava to transfer its headquarters from Calatrava la Nueva, a few miles below Villarreal, to Andalucía. Determined to effect the "destruction of the enemies of our faith," and in gratitude for the service rendered by the knights "when the king of Granada roused the country against us," in October 1264 he granted Calatrava the town and castle of Osuna, about twenty miles south of Écija, and also offered financial benefits. Osuna could better serve as a base from which to protect the frontier and to attack the kingdom of Granada, but the knights opted to maintain Calatrava la Nueva, at some distance from the frontier, as their principal seat. Thus Osuna never became more than a commandery.[19]

The Mudéjar revolt in Lower Andalucía was now crushed, but the departure of the Moors from Jerez and other towns necessitated their replacement with Christian settlers. Moreover, the task of subduing the king of Granada and the Mudéjars of Murcia remained to be accomplished.

Clement IV's Crusading Bulls

Attending at last to the king's pleas, in March 1265 Clement IV, invoking the traditional language used to describe crusades to the Holy Land (*negotium, peregrinatio*), published several crusading bulls. One ought not to be surprised, he remarked, that just as the slave girl Hagar fled from her mistress Sarah, her descendants, the Agarenes, like a menstruating woman, polluted Spain with their terrible filth. Nevertheless, the adherents of the Christian faith, though few in number, delivered themselves from the Agarenes, who had usurped their land, and restored it to the Christian religion.[20] Suddenly, however, the Saracens of Africa invaded Spain, slaughtering the faithful. The arrogance and pride of the Saracens compel us, said the pope, to relieve the Christian people in this time of danger. Therefore, he commissioned Archbishop Remondo of Seville to preach the crusade against the Saracens of Spain and Africa not only throughout Spain but also in the dioceses of Genoa and Pisa. All those who reverently took up the cross, affixing it to their shoulders and taking the vow to halt the wicked Saracens, would be granted remission of their sins. After confessing their sins and, with contrite hearts, serving personally at their own expense in the "Lord's battle," they would gain a plenary indulgence. Anyone unable to serve in person who paid the expenses of other suitable men could also win that reward. The indulgence was also accorded to those engaged in "the work of the pilgrimage" whose expenses were paid by others. Hoping to encourage others to share in "this pilgrimage," the pope offered the indulgence to persons who contributed financially or provided ships.

In accordance with Innocent IV's bull of 1254, Clement IV extended papal protection to all the crusaders, their families, and their property. Creditors, including Jews, were prohibited from demanding interest from debtors engaged in the crusade. The immunity from prosecution granted to crusaders going to the Holy Land was extended to crusaders in Spain. Preaching to the assembled clergy and people (even in places under interdict), Archbishop Remondo and his commissioners were to offer a remission of one hundred days to penitents confessing their sins. Persons excommunicated for trafficking with the enemy in prohibited goods or excommunicated for usury could be absolved, provided that they supported the crusade personally or financially. A fourth of the *decima* (a tenth of ecclesiastical revenues) could be directed to the crusade. If any crusaders (*crucesignati*) died in the affair they would gain the indulgence. The indulgence was also offered to the Templars, Hospitallers, knights of the Holy Sepulchre, Santiago, and other orders who participated in person or contributed financially. Preachers serving for one year were granted certain immunities. Appealing to all the faithful, the pope granted twenty days' indulgence to penitents who prayed for the king and queen and supported the crusade "against the enemies of the faith who recently invaded the bounds of his kingdoms." If insufficient support were given to the king of Castile in countering the Saracen invaders from Africa and the king of Granada, the pope directed Archbishop Remondo to halt until further notice preaching of the crusade to the Holy Land and collection of a subsidy for that purpose.[21]

While concession of the crusading indulgence was of paramount importance, the king was especially interested in obtaining financial support, and Clement IV did not disappoint him. Denouncing the treachery of the king of Granada who summoned the Saracens of Africa to his aid, the pope declared his intention to assist Alfonso X, "a warrior for the Lord" against this "common danger to the faithful people." As clergy and laity were equally affected, Archbishop Remondo was authorized to collect one one-hundredth over five years from the income of prelates and ecclesiastical institutions. That sum, originally intended for the Holy Land, would now be expended against the rebellious Moors.[22]

In June, Clement IV took further measures to promote the crusade. First, he designated Fray Juan Martínez, a Franciscan, recently elected bishop of Cádiz, to preach the crusade in conjunction with Archbishop Remondo. Learning that enemy forces had multiplied, the pope increased the amount of the levy on ecclesiastical income in Castile, León, and Portugal from one one-hundredth to a tenth (*decima*). Lest Alfonso X assume that this concession was unlimited, however, the pope restricted it to three years. Given the king's propensity to abuse papal financial concessions, the pope commanded Archbishop Remondo to admonish Alfonso X in secret that, by demanding the *tercias*, he was persisting in "notorious and mortal sin." If he ceased collecting the *tercias*, he would be permitted to take the *decima*. Should the archbishop's words fall on deaf ears, he was to halt publication of the bull granting that benefit. As Peter Linehan pointed out, however, Archbishop Remondo was unlikely to restrain the king. Despite these caveats, the contribution of the Spanish church to the crusade was substantially augmented.[23]

Although Alfonso X prohibited the collection of funds for any purpose other than the crusade, in July he made an exception in favor of the Order of the Hospital, permitting the knights to continue to collect money for the benefit of the Holy Land.[24]

The Crusade Against Granada

Meanwhile, Ibn al-Ahmar's forces threatened Castilian positions all along the frontier. The siege of Chincoya castle in the kingdom of Jaén recounted in *Cantiga* 185, though undated, may relate to this time. The Christian *alcaide* of Chincoya and the Muslim *alcaide* of nearby Bélmez appear to have been on good terms, but the latter treacherously seized the former and brought him to Ibn al-Ahmar's court. When the Nasrid king, depicted in the accompanying miniatures as a white-haired man, learned that only fifteen men defended Chincoya, he decided to besiege it. However, according to *Cantiga* 185, the defenders placed a statue of the Virgin Mary on the ramparts, prompting the king to abandon the siege, lest he incur her hostility. Despite Ibn al-Ahmar's lack of success, it is likely that many other poorly defended castles fell into his possession in the early stages of the uprising.[25]

The siege of Chincoya may have spurred the towns and nobles of Upper Andalucía to plan for a common defense. Córdoba, Jaén, Baeza, Úbeda, Andújar, San Esteban, Iznatoraf, Quesada, and Cazorla, and the nobles Diego Sánchez de Funes and Sancho Martínez de Jódar established a *hermandad*, or brotherhood, at Andújar on 26 April 1265. As loyal vassals of Alfonso X they swore to work together for their mutual benefit. Two knights representing each town would attend an annual assembly at Andújar after Easter to manage the affairs of the *hermandad*. A review of defenses, frontier weaknesses, and possible cavalcades into enemy territory were likely on the agenda.[26]

In the summer of 1265 Alfonso X advanced from Córdoba into the plain of Granada, pillaging as far as Alcalá de Benzaide (now Alcalá la Real) about forty miles north of the capital.[27] In the midst of the campaign, he rewarded

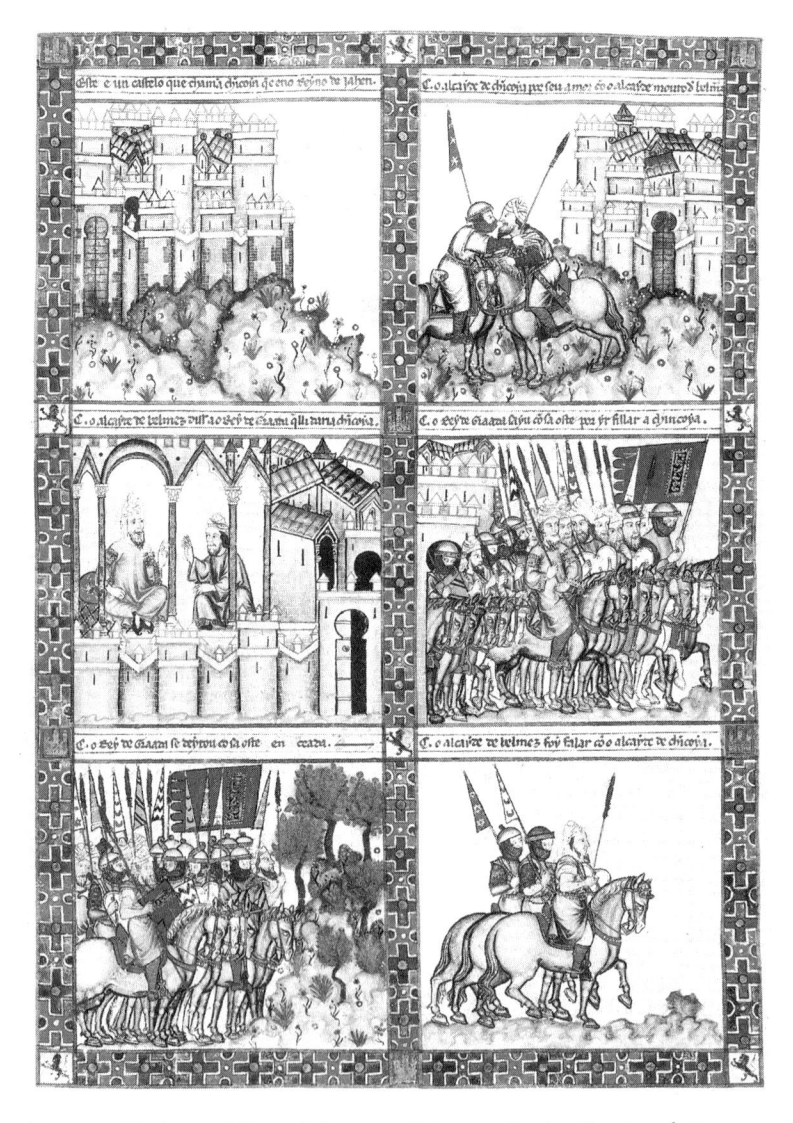

Figure 1. The king of Granada besieges Chincoya Castle. *Cantigas de Santa Maria*, 187. Escorial, MS T.I.1.

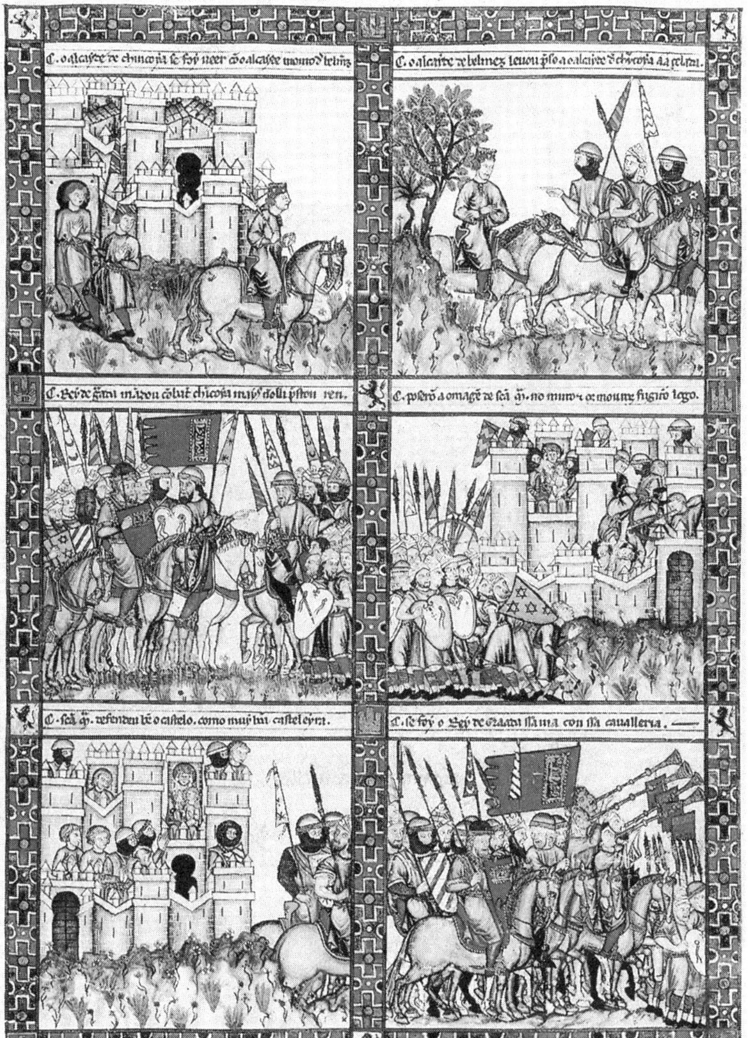

the municipal militias who accompanied him. On 22 June he conceded tax exemptions to the men of Ciudad Rodrigo, "who went to Jerez on my command in the host and came with me to Granada." Two weeks later, on 2 July, he rewarded the men of Salamanca for their service, and, after returning to Córdoba, he extended the *Fuero real*, his municipal law code, to Valladolid on 19 August.[28]

Although neither the *Royal Chronicle* nor the usual Muslim accounts mention a major battle between the Castilians and the Moors of Granada, two other sources do. The *Gran conquista de Ultramar*, a Castilian version of the crusades to the Holy Land begun during the reign of Alfonso X, reported that "in the year of the Incarnation 1264 [A.D. 1265] the king of Castile defeated the king of Granada between Córdoba and Seville; 4,000 Moorish knights were killed and many foot soldiers." If this, the only interpolation in the *Gran conquista* relating to Castilian history, is correct, then Alfonso X won a substantial victory over the Moors of Granada. The number of casualties, however, must be discounted. The Egyptian historian al-Nuwayrī (d. 1333) related that Granadan forces routed the Castilians on 10 July 1264, killing 45,000, and capturing 32 places, including Seville and Jerez. Alfonso X supposedly was so frightened that he moved the body of his father from Seville. Although that narrative is obviously distorted, it may contain an echo of a skirmish between Granadans and Castilians on 10 July.[29]

Perhaps as a consequence of such a conflict, Alfonso X and Ibn al-Ahmar concluded a truce, probably in late July or early August. González Jiménez suggested that the *Royal Chronicle*'s description of a meeting between them at Alcalá de Benzaide is a conflation of two encounters, one in 1265, when they arranged a truce, and the other in 1267, when they concluded a more permanent settlement. A suspension of hostilities was useful for both sides. Ibn al-Ahmar needed to suppress a growing restiveness among the Banū Ashqīlūlā, his longtime collaborators, and Alfonso X wanted to discuss the rebellion in Murcia with Jaime I.[30]

Jaime I's Murcian Crusade

While Andalucía and the kingdom of Granada remained the focus of Alfonso X's energy, his youngest brother, Manuel, and Pelay Pérez Correa, master of Santiago, attempted to halt the revolt in the kingdom of Murcia. In June 1264 Queen Violante, on her husband's urging, wrote movingly to her father, Jaime

I, avowing that without his assistance, she and her family might lose all that they possessed. Recognizing the danger of the situation, the king declared his intention to aid his son-in-law:

> I do not wish to betray my daughter nor my grandchildren, nor do I wish to disinherit them. . . . Although I need not aid him [Alfonso X] out of valor or duty, yet I should help him because he is one of the most powerful men in the world, and if I do not aid him now and he emerges safely from the conflict in which he now finds himself, he will always hold me as his mortal enemy. . . . If the king of Castile loses his kingdom we will be badly off in our kingdom. Therefore, it is better to hasten to defend his kingdom now than to have to defend ours later.

The Catalans, summoned to the Corts of Barcelona in July, consented to a tax called the *bovatge* for the projected campaign against the Moors. Meeting at Zaragoza in November, the Cortes of Aragón proved more obdurate and their opposition preoccupied him for many months thereafter.[31]

In May 1265 Clement IV commissioned Archbishop Benet of Tarragona and Bishop Andreu of Valencia to preach the crusade against the Moors throughout Jaime I's dominions. Protesting that the Mudéjars, driven by evil men and supported by a multitude from Africa, had thrown off the yoke of tribute, the pope declared that "warriors for the faith" would rise up to fight the "battles of the Lord" and triumph over the Saracens. Like a roaring lion, Jaime I, "a warrior from his adolescence," had already girded himself to punish the Saracens, the enemies of the faith. All those who reverently placed the sign of the cross on their shoulders, confessed their sins, and faithfully fulfilled their vow would gain full remission of their sins. Those who contributed financially in lieu of personal service would also earn the indulgence. Other crusading privileges including papal protection of the persons and property of crusaders and security against creditors were also granted. In addition, the pope permitted the king to collect the *decima* for three years; except in that part of the province of Tarragona subject to Castile. If the crusade ended before the expiration of three years, collection of the *decima* would cease.[32]

Infante Pedro, heir to the Aragonese throne, undertook the initial campaign against the rebellious Moors, devastating the countryside, probably in the late summer of 1265.[33] Setting out from Valencia at the end of October, Jaime I received the submission of the Moors of Villena and promised to intercede with their lord, Infante Manuel, to pardon them and allow them to keep their lands. Elda and Petrer also submitted. Advancing to Alicante on the coast, the king instructed his forces on the need to observe military discipline, acting only on his command and not separating themselves from the main army. In the same month the Moors of Elche, assured that they would be permitted to worship freely, to proclaim the call to prayer from the minaret, and to be governed according to Islamic law, also came to terms. They yielded the tower of Calahorra to the king, whose gift of 300 bezants to one of the Muslim negotiators helped to facilitate the agreement. At Orihuela Ibn Hūd, *arráez* of Crevillente, offered his submission. As the king prepared to attack Murcia, the principal rebel stronghold, Castilian forces commanded by Infante Manuel, joined him.[34]

Learning that 800 cavalry from Granada with 2,000 beasts of burden laden with food and 2,000 men-at-arms were en route to relieve Murcia, Jaime I moved rapidly to intercept them. Before giving battle, he confessed his sins, arguing with God that he ought to gain some merit by conquering Murcia and restoring it to Christian rule. After attacking the enemy, he put them to flight. In early December at Alcaraz, on the border between Castile and the kingdom of Valencia, he conferred for a week with Alfonso X about "the affair of the Saracens," but nothing is known of the decisions taken. Alfonso X presumably expressed his gratitude and authorized his father-in-law to reward his followers in Murcia once the war was concluded.[35]

At the beginning of the new year, Jaime I initiated the final stage of the campaign. Advancing southward from Orihuela, on 2 January 1266 he laid siege to Murcia on the Segura River. After a few armed clashes, the defenders, realizing the futility of resistance, offered to negotiate. If they submitted, Jaime I promised to ask Alfonso X to guarantee the legal situation they had enjoyed since 1244 when they first accepted Castilian suzerainty, including freedom of worship, the right of self-government in accordance with Islamic law, and retention of their property. If they refused, he threatened to take the town by force and to expel them all. Although they accepted his terms, they asked him to obtain Alfonso X's consent as well as his pardon. On the contrary, Jaime I declared that he would only do so after they surrendered. Having little choice but to agree, they inquired as to the extent of the area that would be reserved to them. He replied that the Christians would occupy the *alcázar* and the area from there to the gate opposite his encampment. The hapless Moors yielded the town to the victors on Sunday, 31 January 1266. Seeing his standard on the walls of the *alcázar*, Jaime I knelt down and kissed the ground in thanksgiving to God.

Four days later, on 3 February, he made his entrance into the town. When he demanded that the Moors hand over the mosque adjacent to the *alcázar*, they protested that the terms of the capitulation allowed them to retain all their mosques. Pointing out that they had ten other mosques, he queried: "Do you think it proper that you should retain the mosque at the gate of the *alcázar* and that I, when I am asleep, should have to hear in my head the cry, 'Allah lo Sabba O Allah?'" The latter was the king's garbled version of the Muslim call to prayer. Threatening to sack the town if they did not bow to his wishes, he had his way. As was his custom whenever he occupied a major town, he transformed the mosque into a Christian church dedicated to the Virgin Mary. After it was suitably decorated, in the company of the bishops of Barcelona and Cartagena and all the clergy bearing crosses on high and the statue of the Virgin Mary, he processed from his camp into the town and then to the church. Overcome with emotion, he wept copiously for more than a quarter of an hour. After intoning the chant *Veni Creator Spiritus*, the clergy celebrated the mass *Salve Sancta Parens*, usually said on feasts of the Virgin Mary. At the end of mass he took up residence in the *alcázar*. Many of his counselors complained that he should have expelled the Moors from the town, but he argued that if he wished he could confine them to the suburbs of Murcia and still be in conformity with the capitulation.[36]

Soon after, Clement IV, perhaps realizing that the king had completed his task, emphasized that he could continue to collect the *decima* granted for a three-year term provided that he engaged in the crusade for at least a year. A few months later the pope made the same point in a letter to the archbishop of Tarragona and the bishop of Valencia. Finally, in July the pope felicitated Jaime I for having reduced Murcia to obedience and for having restored it to Alfonso X. Yet at the same time he admonished him to overcome the weakness of the flesh and to abandon his mistress. Disinclined to support Jaime I's tolerant policy toward the Mudéjars, the pope exhorted him to expel them from his dominions.[37]

Entrusting the *alcázar* of Murcia to the Castilians, Jaime I notified Alfonso X that the Moors had surrendered the town along with twenty-eight castles between Murcia and Lorca. After rewarding his followers for their service during the campaign, he returned to his own realm in March. A few months later the rebels made their formal submission to Alfonso X. "Recognizing the error that the Moors of Murcia committed against the most high and noble lord, King Alfonso," representatives of the *aljama*, or municipal council, on 23 June 1266 renewed their allegiance and humbly begged his pardon, mercy, and favor. With that the Mudéjar uprising in the kingdom of Murcia was formally terminated.[38]

Continuation of the Crusade Against Granada

Gratified by Jaime I's subjugation of Murcia, Alfonso X was now able to give full attention to the kingdom of Granada. Despite the truce concluded in 1265, Ibn al-Ahmar, provoked by the opposition of the Banū Ashqīlūlā, resumed hostilities. The crusade against Granada took a surprising turn in 1266 when the Banū Ashqīlūlā offered their alliance to Alfonso X. Their resentment of Ibn al-Ahmar first manifested itself in 1257 when he designated his sons as his successors, effectively nullifying an earlier promise to cede half his kingdom to the head of the Banū Ashqīlūlā. Irritated by Ibn al-Ahmar's welcome to the Marinid troops in 1263–64, the Banū Ashqīlūlā feared that these newcomers would undercut their own preeminent position in control of the army. They soon concluded that he intended to deprive them of Málaga.[39]

The dissension between Ibn al-Ahmar and the Banū Ashqīlūlā found an echo in one of the *cantigas d'escarnho*, or songs of derision, popular in the Castilian royal court. In a satiric dialogue two poets debated whether María la Balteira, a female *juglar* or songstress who figures in several of these *cantigas*, had seduced the patriarch Fi d'Escalhola, that is, Ibn Ashqīlūlā (probably Abū Muhammad, who then held Málaga), as she had so many others.[40]

Defying their king, the Banū Ashqīlūlā asked Alfonso X for protection and offered their services to him. Delighted by this sign of dissension among the Moors, he declared that if Ibn al-Ahmar attacked them he would personally defend them. In addition to his written guarantee of their safety, he dispatched Nuño González de Lara with 1,000 knights to safeguard them. The *Royal Chronicle* says no more about Nuño's expedition, but it is possible that he advanced as far as Málaga.[41] As the price of their alliance, the Banū Ashqīlūlā may have pledged to surrender Antequera, Archidona, and the port of Marbella to Alfonso X. In return for many services received, he promised Antequera and Archidona to the Order of Santiago, whenever he acquired them, and he ceded Marbella to the bishopric of Cádiz. There is no indication, however, that the Castilians took possession of these places.[42]

Evidence of military operations in 1266 is quite slim and consists of only a few documentary references. The king, for example, ordered money collected as *fonsadera* to be returned to the men of Burgos who had responded to the summons to serve in the royal host. Granting houses in Baena to a vassal, he required him to "have a horse and arms of wood and iron . . . while this war that we have with the Moors lasts" and to serve should the war continue. The knights of Salamanca received various exemptions depending on the extent of their equipment. The term of service was limited to three months, but knights and foot soldiers could be excused if they paid *fonsadera*.[43] During most of the spring or summer of 1266, the king was in Seville, but there are a few intervals in the royal itinerary when a campaign could have been mounted.

There are other signs of military activity in the following year. In April 1267 Alfonso X obtained from Pontevedra and other towns of the archdiocese of Compostela "a *servicio* in aid of this war, from which we cannot excuse them."[44] Several papal bulls indicate that the *decima* was still being collected. In May Clement IV, for example, exempted the church of Santa Leocadia in Toledo and, on the king's request, directed Archbishop Remondo of Seville to hasten collection of the *decima* "unless the current storm should be settled in the meantime." However, in June the pope, while again stressing the need to collect the *decima*, required the king to notify all the bishops that he would not collect the *tercias* during the first year of the three-year period for which the *decima* was granted. If Afonso III halted his war against the Muslims, Archbishop Remondo was not to collect the *decima* in Portugal.[45]

As Archbishop Sancho II of Toledo, together with many others, had "assumed the sign of the living cross" and vowed to fight against "the perfidious Saracens," in 1267 Clement IV granted the crusading indulgence to him and all who confessed their sins and accompanied him to the frontier. As in the past, the same benefit was accorded to those who could not go personally but offered financial support. All the other privileges cited in previous crusading bulls were conceded to the archbishop and his companions.[46] Nothing further is known about Archbishop Sancho's crusade, but one possible consequence was the capture of the castle of Estepa near Écija, which the king granted to the Order of Santiago.[47]

The Treaty of Alcalá de Benzaide 1267

Despite the paucity of information, Alfonso X, in collaboration with the Banū Ashqīlūlā, seems to have maintained intense pressure on the kingdom of Granada. Realizing the peril arising from this coalition, Ibn al-Ahmar proposed a truce and offered to abandon the Mudéjars of Murcia if Alfonso X rejected the Banū Ashqīlūlā. Alfonso X met the king of Granada and his son, the future Muhammad II, at Alcalá de Benzaide and agreed to a truce, but no limitation of time was recorded. Ibn al-Ahmar, and his son after him, promised to pay an annual tribute of 250,000 *maravedíes* and to assist Alfonso X in recovering the kingdom of Murcia; he also requested that the life of al-Wātiq (Alboaquez) be spared. For his part Alfonso X asked Ibn al-Ahmar to grant a truce of one year to the Banū Ashqīlūlā. If he were unable to come to terms with them during that time, Alfonso X would no longer support them. The *Royal Chronicle*'s description of the treaty of Alcalá de Benzaide does not mention the renewal of vassalage by Ibn al-Ahmar, but only the payment of tribute. Indeed, he was no longer listed as a vassal confirming royal privileges.[48]

The *Royal Chronicle*, whose chronology in its early chapters is confused, placed the treaty of Alcalá de Benzaide in 1265. On the contrary, the Moroccan historian Ibn 'Idhārī, who was more nearly contemporary with this period, stated that the war lasted three years and that the truce was concluded in A.H. 665 (2 October 1266–21 September 1267), or 1267. The treaty may have been concluded in late May or early June.[49]

Alfonso X communicated his triumph to Clement IV who congratulated him in October because "that detestable traitor, that cunning enemy, the king of Granada, at last, submitted his iron neck to your authority." The pope also expressed the hope that the remnants of the barbarian rebellion would soon be crushed.[50]

As a further consequence of the treaty, Jaime I concluded a truce with Granada in January 1268 and another with al-'Azafi, lord of Ceuta, who seems to have supported the Mudéjar revolt. María del Carmen Mosquera Merino supposed that as Alfonso X asked his father-in-law to grant the truce, both Ibn al-Ahmar and al-'Azafi were tributary vassals of Castile.[51] Relations between the two Muslim rulers had improved since the Nasrid's naval assault on Ceuta some years before. Writing to Ibn al-Ahmar, probably in 1268 after the collapse of the Mudéjar uprising, al-'Azafi tried to lift his spirits. He mentioned Alfonso X and his two brothers, but without identifying them. More than likely he referred to Enrique who was captured at the battle of Tagliacozzo in 1268 and imprisoned. His brother Fadrique, expelled from Naples in 1269, took refuge in Tunis.[52]

The Resettlement of Andalucía

Victorious over his opponents, Alfonso X had now to undertake the work of reconstruction in Andalucía and Murcia. His chief goal seems to have been to expel the Mudéjars and persuade Christians to settle in the newly evacuated areas. In the lower Guadalquivir Valley he attempted to recreate Jerez as a

Christian town. Lands and houses were distributed among 1,500 foot soldiers, 200 urban knights (*caballeros villanos*), and 40 noble knights (*caballeros fijosdalgo*). With almost 2,000 inhabitants, mostly Christian, Jerez was by far the largest town in the region, surpassed only by Seville and Córdoba.[53] In 1269 and 1274 the boundaries between Jerez, Lebrija, Medina Sidonia, Arcos, Vejer, Alcalá de los Gazules, Tarifa, and Algeciras were laid down.[54]

Farther south, great energy was also expended in the development of Cádiz and El Puerto de Santa María. Permanent settlement of Cádiz was initiated in 1263 when Alfonso X granted property there to 100 colonists and took steps to encourage commerce. Once the Mudéjar revolt was crushed, in November 1264 lands were allotted to 200 lancers and 100 crossbowmen, many from ports on the Bay of Biscay.[55]

In 1263, when Cádiz was scarcely settled, Alfonso X petitioned Urban IV (1261–64) to establish a bishopric there, but the pope's death prevented his order from being carried out.[56] Three years later, however, Clement IV transferred the ancient see of Sidonia to Cádiz and commanded Archbishop Remondo of Seville to ordain the Franciscan Juan Martínez as bishop. Although he was displeased with the loss of territory for his see, the archbishop obeyed and in November 1267 agreed with Fray Juan Martínez on the delimitation of their respective dioceses.[57]

When the Dominican friar Maurice visited Cádiz around 1273, he found it to be "a strong and well-walled city" with a bishop. Although the future seemed bright for both Cádiz and El Puerto de Santa María, the continued threat of invasion from Morocco, which became a harsh reality in the 1270s, served as a deterrent to potential settlers. Despite the king's expectation that El Puerto de Santa María would become a great seaport, only a few brave souls were willing to commit themselves to full-time residence there. In the ensuing wars the Marinids so ravaged the area that the king, in the hope of attracting settlers, had to issue a new charter of population in 1281.[58]

As a means of encouraging settlement in the towns of the Guadalete Valley, the king offered many benefits. The noble knights of Arcos and Medina Sidonia, for example, were accorded the same privileges and tax exemptions as those of Toledo, and other settlers were guaranteed the franchises of Seville. Each town was permitted to have a weekly market and enjoyed rights of common pasturage with neighboring towns. However, some towns, such as Vejer de la Frontera (repopulated only in 1288, when it had 176 settlers), were not much more than advanced fortified positions.[59]

The revolt of the Mudéjars caused extensive economic distress, prompting widespread protests of the high cost of living. Summoning merchants and other good men from Castile, León, Extremadura, and Andalucía to an assembly at Jerez early in 1268, the king regulated prices and wages; stabilized the coinage; controlled exports and imports; and established customs stations on the Bay of Biscay, in Andalucía (Huelva, Cádiz, Vejer, Jerez, and Seville), and Murcia (Cartagena, Alicante, and Elche).[60]

The Repopulation of Murcia

Resettlement of the kingdom of Murcia also demanded Alfonso X's attention. Even while busy with the settlement of Lower Andalucía, he initiated the process of reconstruction in Murcia. In order to secure the city he compelled the Mudéjars to withdraw to the suburb of Arrixaca, where they could live according to Islamic law and worship freely. As a means of averting conflict with their Christian neighbors, a wall was constructed between the city and the suburb.[61] The leader of the Murcian rebels, al-Wātiq, or Alboaquez, according to the *Royal Chronicle*, threw himself on the mercy of the king, who spared his life and assigned him lands on which to live. Alfonso X likely designated ʿAbd Allāh ibn Hūd, identified as "rey de Murcia" in 1266 when the Mudéjars submitted to Jaime I and as "rey de los moros del arrixaca de Murcia" in 1279, to govern the large Muslim population still remaining.[62]

Symbolic of the tensions between Muslims and Christians was a Christian church dedicated to the Virgin Mary in the Arrixaca. *Cantiga* 169 related that, before the king's accession, the Moors begged permission to destroy the church, but he refused. After occupying Murcia in 1266, Jaime I authorized the *aljama*, or town council, to raze the church, but the Virgin Mary, according to the poet, thwarted their efforts. When Alfonso X visited Murcia in 1271–72 he agreed to allow demolition of the church, but the Moorish king refused, lest he incur Mary's wrath.[63]

After Alfonso X came to Murcia in February 1271, where he remained until the fall of 1272, the work of repopulation proceeded apace. As the apportionment of houses and lands was carried out, the area allotted to the Mudéjars was steadily reduced.[64] The king granted the *fuero* of Seville to Murcia, organized a municipal council, and made arrangements for the administration of justice, the collection of taxes, and economic development.[65] Similar measures were taken in other towns such as Lorca and Orihuela.[66] In the expectation that Alicante and Cartagena would become major seaports, Alfonso X attempted to stimulate maritime trade by regulating tariffs and offering concessions to foreign merchants. Anyone from his dominions who wished to go to the Holy Land was required to depart from Alicante or Cartagena. A bishopric was established at Cartagena. In like manner the king favored smaller settlements.[67]

After the Mudéjars of Elche, just south of Alicante, submitted to Jaime I, the king's brother Manuel, who held the lordship of Elche, agreed not to demand retribution on account of their rebellion. On the contrary, he guaranteed the security of their persons and property; their right to worship freely; to be governed by Islamic law; and to pay only taxes previously paid. Those who wished to leave were guaranteed safe conduct to another place. He also granted the Christian inhabitants the *fuero* of Seville and confirmed their privileges and the allotment of houses and lands.[68]

Despite the king's best efforts, the perils of frontier life deterred many from settling there permanently. Some, after a few years, gave up their holdings and retreated to the safety of other areas. As a result, a long time elapsed before the kingdom of Murcia was secure and well populated.

The Order of Santa María de España

In the twelfth century the kings of Castile-León had assigned defense of a broad zone south of Toledo and the Tagus River to the newly established military orders. As we have seen, Alfonso X attempted to involve them more immediately in the war along the frontier of Andalucía. Recognizing that control of the Strait of Gibraltar would necessitate naval power, however, he probably concluded that none of the existing orders, so accustomed to land warfare, would be able to engage effectively in maritime operations. Therefore, he founded the Confraternity, or Order, of Santa María de España, also known as the Order of the Star, in honor of his patron, the Virgin Mary, Star of the Sea, the seafarers' guide.[69]

In 1270 the king, seconded by Juan González, master of Calatrava, urged the Cistercian general chapter to approve constitutions for the new Order. The constitutions were based on those of the Order of Calatrava, an affiliate of the Order of Cîteaux and subject to annual visitation by the abbot of Morimond.[70] The king also appealed to Pope Gregory X (1272–76), who, in 1272, postponed his confirmation, commenting that the military orders, though humble in origin, had recently grown overmighty. He did suggest, however, that he would be open to reconsideration after the king had taken counsel with his court as to the wisdom of his action.[71] In the following year the chapter, which had delayed its response, acceded to the king's wishes. He explained that he had founded the Confraternity to battle for the faith "against the nefarious Saracens" and "for the fatherland against the barbarous nations in defense and expansion of the orthodox faith." The general chapter accepted Santa María as part of the Cistercian Order and assigned to the abbot of Grandselve the duty of visiting the Order annually and of appointing a prior to direct the conventual brethren.[72] Responding to a further royal petition, the general chapter in 1275 authorized the abbot of Grandselve to confirm the election of an abbot by the monastery of Cartagena.[73]

The Order's first headquarters was at Cartagena, but other houses were planned at San Sebastián on the Bay of Biscay, La Coruña on the northwest Atlantic coast, and El Puerto de Santa María. The king presumably expected the Order to develop its own fleet in those ports. In 1274 he assigned various fines levied by his court to the Order "for the affair of the sea."[74]

He entrusted direction of the new Order to his second son, Infante Sancho; then about fourteen years of age, he was recorded late in 1272 as *alférez* and admiral of the Confraternity of Santa María. Those titles implied both military and naval command.[75] When he was recognized as heir to the throne in 1276 after the death of his older brother, his responsibility for governing the Order probably ended and was transferred to Pedro Núñez de Guzmán, former grand commander of the Order of Santiago, with the military title of master of Santa María.

The king's creation of a new Order suggested his distrust of the more established military orders, now linked closely to the aristocracy. His appointment of Sancho to lead the new Order foreshadowed efforts of later monarchs to control the military orders by reserving the masterships to members of the royal family.[76] Foundation of a new Order without papal consent was among many abuses of power charged against Alfonso X in 1279 by Nicholas III (1277–80). According to the pope, churches were aggrieved many times over by the establishment of this new Order, but he did not specify the nature of those grievances.[77] Despite the pope's negative attitude, the Order survived for a few years.[78]

The King of Granada, the Banū Ashqīlūlā, and the Marinids

Although the treaty of Alcalá de Benzaide in 1267 terminated hostilities between Castile and Granada, the apparently cordial relationship previously existing between the two monarchs could not be restored. The enmity of the Banū Ashqīlūlā toward Ibn al-Ahmar remained a source of contention as he attempted to reduce them to obedience and Alfonso X continued to support them. During the one-year truce that the Nasrid king had given them, he failed to win them over. As the truce expired, he visited Alfonso X probably in Seville in June 1268, hoping to persuade him to abandon the Banū Ashqīlūlā. Knowing very well that as long as he encouraged them, Ibn al-Ahmar could never be at rest, Alfonso X reneged on his pledge. The Nasrid king was greatly displeased because he realized that he would now always be held in servitude to Castile.[79]

Sometime thereafter during an interview with Alfonso X, probably in Seville, Ibn al-Ahmar received an unexpected hint of support from disaffected Castilian nobles. Nuño, the son of Nuño González de Lara, visited his tent, grumbling about the many injuries and slights that his family had suffered at their king's hands. Cheerfully expressing his sympathy, Ibn al-Ahmar offered to assist them in obtaining justice, if they helped him topple the Banū Ashqīlūlā. Making a gift of jewels to Nuño, he told him to inform his father and his brother, Juan Núñez, of this proposal. However, the time was not yet ripe for joint action.[80]

In November 1269 another sign of discontent among the Castilian nobility appeared, which Ibn al-Ahmar eventually exploited to his advantage. During the Cortes of Burgos convened on the occasion of the marriage of Infante Fernando de la Cerda, the heir to the throne, the nobles acceded to the king's request for an extraordinary tax of six *servicios* so that he could "complete the business of the frontier."[81] Despite that acquiescence, tension between them and the king was revealed when Nuño González de Lara offered his services to Jaime I. Although Jaime I dissuaded him, an undercurrent of hostility remained. Alfonso X's request for six *servicios* may have been prompted by the need to complete the process of repopulation in Andalucía or Murcia, or by his desire to renew the war against Granada or the crusade in Africa.[82] An incidental reference to Castilian raids in 1269 on Larache and Shams (Tishams) on the North African coast southwest of Tangier suggests that the king may still have harbored hopes of establishing a foothold there.[83] However that may be, the Castilian nobility became increasingly distressed by the king's economic policies and the expense of his pursuit of the imperial crown.

Ibn al-Ahmar, meanwhile, abandoned peaceful attempts to resolve his dispute with the Banū Ashqīlūlā and besieged their stronghold of Málaga in June 1270, but without success.[84]

When Alfonso X and Jaime I met in February 1271 between Requena and Buñol and again at Alicante in February of the next year, they discussed the former's relationship with Granada and the Banū Ashqīlūla. Alfonso X informed his father-in-law that he knew that Castilian and Aragonese nobles had conspired with the Moors against them both. When he asked whether he should favor the king of Granada or the Banū Ashqīlūla, Jaime I counseled him to remain faithful to the one with whom he had first reached agreement. As that was Ibn al-Ahmar, he was obliged to observe the pact between them, provided that the Nasrid had not violated it. As Jaime I concluded that division among the Moors worked to the advantage of the Christians, it seemed best to Alfonso X to play them off against one another.[85]

As a further sign that Alfonso X was contemplating the eventual use of force against Granada, in January 1272 he pledged that when "God desires us to have it," he would give Alcalá de Benzaide (Alcalá la Real) to the Order of Calatrava, in recompense for many services received.[86]

The need to resolve his differences with the king of Granada became more urgent when he received news of the death in April 1272 of Richard of Cornwall, his rival for the imperial throne. Anxious to secure papal recognition as emperor and to undertake his "journey to the empire," he realized the need to pacify the restive Castilian nobility and to reach an accommodation with Ibn al-Ahmar. In September of the previous year, the Nasrid king, angered by Castilian support of the Banū Ashqīlūla, had appealed for help "against the enemies of Islam" to Abū Yūsuf Yaʿqūb, the Marinid emir. Although the prospect of waging the holy war in the Peninsula was attractive, Abū Yūsuf was then engaged in a struggle with the ʿAbd al-Wādids of Tlemcen and only after making peace with them in February 1272 was he prepared to respond to Ibn al-Ahmar's plea.[87]

Intent on coming to terms with the king of Granada, Alfonso X proposed a meeting at Jaén. In June 1272, however, he learned that a large number of Moroccan troops had landed in Spain. Ravaging the land, killing and capturing many, and plundering livestock, they attacked the castle of Vejer de la Frontera. On hearing that news, the king abandoned the projected meeting with Ibn al-Ahmar and ordered an all-out war against Granada.[88]

The Alliance of the Castilian Magnates and Ibn al-Ahmar

Much to Alfonso X's dismay, his magnates refused to respond to his summons to join Infantes Fernando and Manuel on the frontier. Instead, they appealed for help to Abū Yūsuf, the Marinid sultan. In its description of their rebellion and subsequent exile in Granada during 1272 and 1273, the *Royal Chronicle* (chapters 20–58) relied on a narrative probably composed during the rebellion of Infante Sancho ten years later and based on materials in the royal chancery. Included are fifty-seven documents copied either entirely or in part. González Jiménez characterized this account as "the best informed and coherent and also the oldest" section of the *Chronicle*. Although lacking a chronology, it reads like a contemporary newspaper report in orderly sequence and thus is "of incalculable value."[89]

The interception of eleven Arabic letters written by Abū Yūsuf and his son ʿAbd al-Wāḥid and addressed to the king's brother Infante Felipe, and the magnates Nuño González de Lara, Lope Díaz de Haro, lord of Vizcaya, Esteban Fernández de Castro, Gil Gómez de Roa, and Simón Ruiz de los Cameros, laid bare their treasonous behavior. Repeating their accusations that the king issued false coinage, violated their customary *fueros*, caused prices to rise, and gave free rein to merchants, Abū Yūsuf pledged military support against "Alfonso of the wrongs." He also invited Nuño to send his son to him, promising to make him king of the Christians in Morocco, that is, commander of the Christian militia in his service. He also offered to increase by twenty times the *soldadas*, or military stipend, of Gil Gómez de Roa if he would serve him "in Granada or Algeciras or beyond the sea."[90]

Also at some time during the year, Infante Felipe, Nuño González de Lara, Lope Díaz de Haro, Esteban Fernández de Castro, Fernán Ruiz de Castro, Juan Núñez de Lara (Nuño's son), Diego López de Haro (brother of Lope), Álvar Díaz de Asturias, Gil Gómez de Roa, Fernán Ruiz de Asturias, and Lope de Mendoza pledged homage and fealty to Ibn al-Ahmar. In particular they vowed to require Alfonso X to observe the treaty of Alcalá de Benzaide, "without any additions." That phrase probably meant that he would have to abandon the Banū Ashqīlūlā. The magnates also promised to aid Ibn al-Ahmar against his enemies, whether Christians or Moors. He agreed to come to their aid should Alfonso X deprive them of their lands. Neither side would make a separate peace with the king of Castile. Once peace was established, lands or fortresses taken in war would be restored to their original possessors.[91]

In spite of this evidence of treason, Alfonso X opted to negotiate with the dissidents. After they aired their grievances at the Cortes of Burgos in November 1272, he confirmed their *fueros* and made other concessions.[92] Unmoved by his conciliatory attitude, however, they repudiated the ties of vassalage and went into exile to Granada, plundering the countryside as they did so. As they journeyed toward the frontier, the king's messengers reminded them of the many favors he had conferred on them and charged them with violating the customs of the realm. Denouncing his brother Felipe, he declared that "the king of Granada is an enemy of God and of the faith and of the king and his kingdoms.... You, as the son of King Fernando and Queen Beatrice and brother of King Alfonso ought better to guard the lineage whence you come and the duty that you owe to it." In similar tones he upbraided the others: Nuño González de Lara, Lope Díaz de Haro, Fernán Ruiz de Castro, Esteban Fernández de Castro, Juan Núñez de Lara, and Álvar Díaz de Asturias. He also appealed to the knights and others accompanying them to return to his service. Also pleading with the magnates to abandon their course, Queen Violante and Archbishop Sancho of Toledo proposed that the king would grant a truce of one year from Christmas next to the king of Granada. Ibn al-Ahmar and the Banū Ashqīlūlā would observe a similar truce. In dealing with the Banū Ashqīlūlā, Alfonso X promised to follow the counsel of the queen, Infante Fernando, and the archbishop.[93]

Rejecting these efforts to recall them to their allegiance, the magnates continued on their way and received a warm welcome from Ibn al-Ahmar. Soon after their arrival, in response to his plea, they pillaged the area round Guadix belonging to the Banū Ashqīlūlā.[94] When the *arráez* complained to Alfonso X, he promised to compensate him from properties recovered from the magnates. The campaign was a short one, however, as Ibn al-Ahmar, now old and ill, summoned the magnates to Granada. He died soon after on 22 January 1273.[95] Although some of the Moorish lords wished to acknowledge one or another of the *arraeces* of Málaga or Guadix as the new king, so as to break the ties of the Banū Ashqīlūlā to Alfonso X, the Castilian nobles threw their support behind Ibn al-Ahmar's son, Abū 'Abd Allāh, who succeeded as Muhammad II (1273–1302).[96]

Alfonso X's Policy Toward Islamic Spain: A Balance Sheet

For nearly eight years following his abortive African Crusade, Alfonso X had to contend with the revolt of the Mudéjars and the ongoing conflict with the king of Granada. His adventuresome policy in Morocco and his expansionist efforts in Lower Andalucía produced negative consequences, which, perhaps, he did not foresee. The concession of papal crusading bulls offering the usual indulgence, but also many other privileges now commonly given to crusaders, facilitated Jaime I's subjugation of the Mudéjars of Murcia and Alfonso

X's suppression of the revolt in Andalucía. Perceiving the danger to his realm of a substantial disaffected Muslim population, the king initiated the process of repopulating the rebel areas with Christians, but that labor continued well beyond his time.

The treaty of Alcalá de Benzaide in 1267 may be said to have brought the crusade to an end, but a hostile undercurrent characterized relations between Alfonso X and Ibn al-Ahmar thereafter. Surely the king of Granada was unhappy to have to pay a hefty annual tribute of 250,000 *maravedíes*, knowing that his Castilian counterpart could use that money to finance military operations against Granada. Moreover, Alfonso X's persistent backing of the Banū Ashqīlūla was viewed as a deliberate and unforgivable violation of the treaty. Fearing Castilian power and the ruination of his dynasty, Ibn al-Ahmar exploited the enmity between the Castilian magnates and their king and also turned to the Marinids for military aid. The plundering of Vejer de la Frontera by a newly arrived Moroccan contingent foreshadowed the more serious Marinid intervention in the years to come.

When Ibn al-Ahmar established the kingdom of Granada at the midpoint of the thirteenth century, there was little reason to expect that the Nasrid dynasty that he founded would endure until 1492. He laid down the guidelines for survival followed by his successors during the next two and a half centuries. By skillful diplomacy and by counterbalancing the Castilian menace against the threat of conquest by the Marinids, the Nasrids were able to preserve their independence.

In January 1273 when Ibn al-Ahmar departed this life, Alfonso X's future seemed grim. The tranquility of his realm, a necessary condition for achieving his long-held aspiration to win the throne of the Holy Roman Empire, was imperiled by a defiant nobility in alliance with Granada. Soon the dreaded Marinid invasion would present an even greater danger. For the next seventy-five years the specter of an Islamic empire straddling the Strait of Gibraltar, absorbing the kingdom of Granada, and putting Christian Spain on the defensive, was raised once again.

Chapter 4

The Crusade Against the Marinids

In the last decade of his reign Alfonso X hoped to achieve his imperial ambitions, but his plans were disrupted by the Marinid invasion and the disputed succession to the throne. With papal support, he launched a crusade against the Marinids and, with the intent of preventing future Moroccan incursions into Spain, unsuccessfully laid siege to Algeciras. Concern about his health and mental stability, however, led his second son and designated heir, Sancho, to deprive him of royal authority in 1282. In the ensuing civil war, a desperate Alfonso X, feeling abandoned not only by his people but also by his royal contemporaries, turned for help to his nemesis, the Marinid emir.

Muhammad II, the Exiles, and the Journey to the Empire

In 1273, Alfonso X, anxious to obtain papal recognition of his imperial rights, strove to induce the exiled magnates to return to their allegiance. Although Muhammad II, the new king of Granada, was also eager to make peace, he refused to grant a truce to the *arraeces* of Málaga and Guadix, members of the Banū Ashqīlūlā. Knowing that they could always be used to threaten the Nasrids, however, Alfonso X would not forsake them. Rather, he required Muhammad II to cede Algeciras, Tarifa, and Málaga, to pay tribute, and to make a "great loan" to finance his imperial quest. Though displeased by these demands, Muhammad II offered to contribute 250,000 *maravedíes* for the journey to the empire, a sum that Alfonso X dismissed as hardly sufficient to pay for 400 knights. Infuriated by the continued obduracy of the magnates, the king ordered the destruction of their houses and threatened to resume the war against Granada. At the same time Juan González, master of Calatrava, acting on behalf of the king's eldest son, Fernando de la Cerda, proposed that the king accept Muhammad II as his vassal, uphold the treaty of Alcalá de Benzaide, and abandon the *arraeces*. He also settled outstanding issues with the nobility concerning their *fueros* and estates, but "not according to the king's wishes." Reluctant to confirm the master's decisions, Fernando sought his father's counsel.[1]

The outraged king decried the insolence of the rebels who aligned themselves with the Nasrid king. While he stressed Castile's military superiority over Granada, he also minimized the threat of invasion from Morocco, noting that the great Almohad caliph Miramamolín, with far greater power than the Marinids, was ultimately routed at the battle of Las Navas de Tolosa in 1212. Furthermore, he argued that Abū Yūsuf Ya'qūb, the Marinid emir, was unlikely to invade Spain, given his need to complete the subjugation of Morocco and to subdue Yagmurāsan, the emir of Tlemcen. He also questioned Abū Yūsuf's ability to secure enough ships and supplies to mount an invasion. Discounting the Marinid menace, he commented that the Moors had the habit of producing false letters to gain support from Morocco, just as Ibn al-Ahmar and Muhammad II had done. In underestimating the Marinids, he blundered seriously, as he would soon discover to his great regret.[2]

As another sign of future difficulties, the king mentioned that during his stay at Ávila, "I was sick with rheum and a little fever and I was greatly upset." Richard Kinkade, connecting this with the king's illness at Burgos in 1269, following a kick in the head by a horse, commented that "the fever and watery discharge of the eyes and nose . . . were most probably related to the worsening maxillary sinusitis and eventual squamous-cell carcinoma" that would afflict him and eventually lead to his deposition and death.[3]

In July his representatives, Queen Violante and Infante Fernando, negotiated a settlement with Muhammad II and the exiled magnates, obligating Alfonso X to observe the treaty of Alcalá de Benzaide. Muhammad II would pay 450,000 *maravedíes* as tribute for the past two years, the anticipated tribute for the next year, and 250,000 *maravedíes* for the imperial expedition. He would also grant the Banū Ashqīlūlā a truce for two years.[4]

Meanwhile, Alfonso X met Jaime I at Requena on the Valencian frontier, probably in August. They had already agreed to joint action against the Moors, but when Jaime I summoned the Catalan nobility to join the war "against the Saracens and perfidious Christians adhering to the king of Granada and other infidels, enemies of God and of the faith," they objected that they were not required to render military service outside of Catalonia.[5] Urging the need for immediate action to halt a Marinid invasion, Alfonso X asked Jaime I to send his forces into the area around Almería. This foreshadowed a later treaty allotting the conquest of Almería to Aragón. Although Jaime I promised to cooperate, he stressed the value of making peace. After his departure, as *Cantiga* 235 relates, Alfonso X fell ill and many feared for his life, but he was cured through the intercession of the Virgin Mary. Henceforth, however, his health continued to worsen and affected his behavior.[6]

Fearful that the agreement with the magnates and Muhammad II might fall apart and that troops who had served on the frontier for eight months might return home, Violante and Fernando urged the king to hasten to Andalucía. In an outburst of righteous anger, he deplored the magnates' demand that they receive stipends for their two years in exile and expenses for 1,000 knights for the imperial expedition, instead of 500, as originally proposed. Unwilling to endure any further offense to his honor, he upbraided them for pillaging the realm, collaborating with Muhammad II, and assaulting his vassals, the *arraeces*. Nevertheless, in December, after so many months of hostility, he journeyed to Seville where he received his opponents very well. As a sign of special honor, he knighted Muhammad II, who professed his vassalage and promised to pay an annual tribute of 300,000 *maravedíes*, an increase of 50,000. However, the Nasrid king would only agree to a truce of one year with the Banū Ashqīlūla. The magnates, received into favor once more, pledged to accompany Alfonso X on his imperial journey. Although it seemed reasonable to make peace with Abū Yūsuf, the king concluded that the Marinids would not invade Spain because of the pact between Castile and Granada. Furthermore, as all the ports were under Muhammad II's control, the Marinids, still contending with internal conflicts, would not have easy access to the Peninsula. This grave miscalculation would cost Alfonso X dearly.[7]

Preparing for his journey to the empire, the king designated Fernando de la Cerda as regent during his absence and, as a restraint on the king of Granada, admonished him to sustain the Banū Ashqīlūla. Although the *Royal Chronicle* asserted that Nuño González de Lara was appointed *adelantado mayor de la frontera*, his actual responsibility was as *tenente*, or castellan, of Écija. The apparent tranquility of the realm was such that Nuño even contemplated participating in the crusade to the Holy Land proclaimed by Gregory X.[8] The king's illegitimate son, Alfonso Fernández el Niño, stationed in Seville, had the primary task of protecting the frontier.[9]

As Alfonso X traversed Catalonia on his way to meet the pope, he became so ill that he seemed again at death's door. After recovering, he continued on to Beaucaire between Avignon and Arles where he met Gregory X in May

1275. By that time the German princes had elected Rudolf of Habsburg, and the pope had acknowledged him as emperor. Thus, Gregory X insisted that Alfonso X abandon his imperial pretensions once and for all.[10] Nevertheless, he persisted in using the imperial title "king of the Romans."

Notwithstanding his disappointment at Beaucaire, Alfonso X planned to join his supporters in Lombardy, but reports of an unexpected invasion of Spain by the Marinids compelled him to return home. At this time he fell sick again and was not immediately able to travel. Though his physicians gave him up for dead, *Cantiga* 235, a very personal account of these events, related that the Virgin Mary restored him to health.[11] When he regained Castile at the end of the year, his hope of empire was entirely dashed and he was confronted with the disastrous possibility of losing his kingdom as well.

The First Marinid Invasion

During his absence, Abū Yūsuf Yaʿqūb, who had recently occupied Tangier, set his sights on Ceuta and enlisted the aid of Jaime I, who hoped to further Catalan commerce in Morocco. In November 1274, Abū Yūsuf proposed that Jaime I provide him with 10 *naves* or sailing ships, 10 galleys, and 50 other ships (*leños* and *barcas*) as well as 500 knights. In return, he promised to pay 100,000 silver bezants for the armada and another 100,000 for a year's service. After the fall of Ceuta he would pay Jaime I another 50,000. The commander of the Christian cavalry would be paid 100 bezants daily and each knight would receive 2 each month. All would be provided with horses and camels and would have a church and oratory, as was the Christian custom. If the siege continued beyond a year, the Christians would be allowed to return home with their booty, but Jaime I would replace them. Perceiving this threat, al-ʿAzafī, lord of Ceuta, effectively undercut Jaime I's ambition by acknowledging Marinid rule and paying an annual tribute. As Dufourcq commented, however, the king of Aragón installed Abū Yūsuf in Ceuta to the detriment of the Christians of Spain. Although the emir did not use Ceuta as an embarkation point for his subsequent invasions of Spain, al-ʿAzafī provided ships for that purpose.[12]

While Alfonso X made his way to Beaucaire, Muhammad II reassessed the pact recently concluded at Seville. Judging that Alfonso X's absence offered a unique opportunity to crush the Banū Ashqīlūlā and secure the territorial integrity of the Nasrid kingdom, Muhammad II appealed for help to Abū Yūsuf. Although Christian and Muslim chroniclers affirmed that the

Figure 2. Christian knights defeat Abū Yūsuf, the Marinid emir. *Cantigas de Santa Maria*, 181. Escorial, MS T.I.1.

sultan demanded the surrender of Algeciras and Tarifa and the inland town of Ronda, that is questionable.[13]

Abū Yūsuf was said to have expressed a desire to participate in the *jihād* in Spain as early as 1245, but he lacked the means to do so at that time. However, in 1269, after the death of the last Almohad caliph, he occupied his capital, Marrakech, and the greater part of Morocco, save the eastern region of Tlemcen, was soon in his hands.[14] The Marinid chronicler Ibn Abī Zar' declared that Ibn al-Ahmar, at the time of his death, had advised his son to seek the help of the Marinids and to grant them whatever lands they wanted. The first part of that statement is probably true, but the second part is doubtful. Nevertheless, by inviting the Marinids into Spain Muhammad II was playing a dangerous game. Surely he knew that in the past the Almoravids and the Almohads had swallowed up the petty Muslim kingdoms that they ostensibly came to save. Did he expect that, once Alfonso X was punished, the Marinids would withdraw and that they would willingly restore Algeciras and Tarifa to him?[15]

The first Marinid contingent landed in Spain on 13 May 1275.[16] With a fleet of 20 ships organized by al-'Azafī at Ceuta, 5,000 knights were transported from Alcácer Seguir to Tarifa. Asserting his independence of the kingdom of Granada, the governor of Algeciras yielded the port to the Marinids on 28 May and acknowledged Abū Yūsuf as his lord. Without meeting any significant Christian opposition, the Marinids raided as far as Vejer de la Frontera and Jerez.[17] As soon as he learned of the invasion, Fernando de la Cerda, not yet twenty years old, hastened to the frontier but died suddenly at Villarreal on 25 July 1275. His death at such a crucial moment left the defense of the realm in disarray and threw open the question of succession to the throne.[18]

Soon after Abū Yūsuf sailed from Tangier and landed at Peña del Ciervo near Tarifa on 16 August. At Algeciras he met Muhammad II and Abū Muhammad b. Ashqīlūla, the *arráez* of Málaga, and his brother Abū Ishāq of Guadix, who had acknowledged Marinid suzerainty. Despite the intense enmity between the king of Granada and the Banū Ashqīlūla, the emir persuaded them, at least for the moment, to put aside their differences and to join in war against "the polytheists." According to Ibn Khaldūn, however, the emir gave a cold reception to Muhammad II who was so offended that he returned to Granada.[19]

The Marinids then set out to ravage the Guadalquivir valley. The vanguard of 5,000 men commanded by the emir's son Abū Ya'qūb devastated the countryside around Almodóvar del Río, west of Córdoba, and Baeza and Úbeda, east of Jaén. The castle of Palma del Río was taken by assault. *Cantiga*

323 recorded the looting of Coria del Río, a village near Seville: "when Abū Yūsuf crossed the Strait / from Algeciras and ravaged the land of Seville / and the Moors burned many villages" (10–13). As the fields were set ablaze, Ibn Abī Zarʻ remarked that "it seemed that the countryside was illuminated by the rising sun." The marauding soldiers swept up people, livestock, and goods of all sorts. At the same time Muhammad II pillaged the kingdom of Jaén.[20] News of the Marinid invasion also roused the Mudéjars of Murcia and Valencia who attempted to throw off the Christian yoke. The Virgin Mary, according to *Cantiga* 169, foiled their attempt to seize control of the city of Murcia. In the neighboring kingdom of Valencia, the old rebel al-Azraq also mounted an offensive against Jaime I.[21]

Gregory X and the Crusade Against the Marinids

When Pope Gregory X proclaimed a crusade to the Holy Land during the Second Council of Lyon in 1274, several Spaniards indicated their desire to participate but the Marinid invasion made that impossible. Jaime I's advanced age deterred him and the Moroccan onslaught required the presence in Spain of Nuño González de Lara and his son Juan Núñez. The pope reminded Infante Manuel that "it is not appropriate for you to desert your brother" when his kingdoms were under attack by the Saracens.[22]

The Spanish church, by contributing the *decima*, or tenth, of ecclesiastical income for six years, was expected to assist in financing the crusade. Papal instructions concerning preaching of the crusade and collection of the *decima* were sent to the bishops of Navarre and Aragón and the heads of the Franciscan and Dominican Orders in Spain. The Orders of Santiago and Calatrava were exempt from payment because they fought "in defense of the Christian faith against the Saracens of Africa" and because of the hazards to which they were continually exposed in "the defense of Christendom in the regions of Africa." Anxious to persuade Alfonso X to renounce his imperial claims, in June 1274 the pope suggested the possible diversion of the *decima* to the war in Spain. A year later, at Beaucaire, Gregory X, considering that the "Saracens, the enemies of the cross, coming from Africa . . . dared to invade your kingdoms," conceded the *decima* to the king for six years. The knights of Calatrava and Santiago who were engaged "in the defense of the Christian faith against the Saracens of Africa" were exempted. Ironically, on the very same day, he threatened to excommunicate him if he did not repay a loan from the curia.[23]

Gregory X's most important concession was the bull of crusade given to Archbishop Sancho II of Toledo in September 1275. As "the perfidious Saracens, after gathering a multitude from the regions of Africa, with insolent treachery" invaded Spain, the archbishop, "taking the sign of the living cross," assembled a host to oppose them. The pope granted the crusading indulgence to all those who, truly repentant and having confessed their sins, took the sign of the cross. The text of this bull, embodying the many privileges granted to crusaders, was nearly identical to that of Clement IV, issued in July 1267.[24]

By then Castile had suffered grave disasters and any thought that Castilian knights might participate in the crusade to the Holy Land was erased for good.

The Battles of Écija and Martos

After his initial campaign of devastation, Abū Yūsuf advanced on Écija on the Genil River, about midway between Seville and Córdoba. There, Nuño González de Lara, the castellan of Écija, no longer dreaming of a crusade to the Holy Land, prepared to halt the Muslim assault. While some advised him to avoid a pitched battle, others averred that retreat would forever be a blot on his honor. With great hyperbole Ibn Abī Zarʿ pictured Nuño, "the cursed one," riding in the midst of thousands of soldiers covered with breastplates and coats of mail, their banners flying and trumpets blaring. Prior to his encounter with the enemy, Abū Yūsuf, performing ritual ablutions, raised his hands and recited the Prophet's prayer: "O God, help this host; save it and strengthen it in the war against your enemies. Favor it and protect it." Then mounting his horse and appointing his son Abū Yaʿqūb to command the vanguard, he exhorted his men:

> O band of Muslims, warriors for the faith! This is a great day and a great setting for martyrdom! Behold, Paradise opens its gates for you and adorns its pavements. Strive to gain it, because God has purchased the lives and goods of believers to guide them to Paradise. O legion of Muslims, fight with all your strength against the polytheists. Whoever among you dies will die a martyr; whoever lives will be rich, rewarded, and renowned. Be patient, emulating one another in battle; stand firm and fear God so you may be successful!

Roused by his words, and desiring martyrdom, the troops embraced one another, said their good-byes, and recited in a loud voice the *shahada* or profession of faith, "there is no God but God, and Muhammad is God's Prophet."[25]

Soon the battle was joined. Arrows flew, swords clashed, and blood spilled. Overwhelmed, the Christians were routed and Nuño was killed together with many knights. The emir lamented his death, as he would have preferred to have taken him alive. In a needless act of barbarity, he ordered the heads of dead Christians to be cut off and thrown into a heap. Mounting the pile, the muezzins proclaimed morning and afternoon prayers on the field of battle. With grotesque exaggeration, Ibn Abī Zarʿ asserted that more than 18,000 Christian knights were slain, while only a handful of Muslims (32 in all) won the crown of martyrdom. The battle "in which God exalted Islam and humiliated the idolaters" occurred, according to him, on 8 September. The date given by the *Anales Toledanos III*, namely, Saturday, 7 September 1275, may be correct. Although Abū Yūsuf planned to seize Écija, during the night 300 Christian knights gained entrance and, holding firm against the Marinids, compelled him to withdraw. As he announced his victory, the people rejoiced and in thanksgiving gave alms and freed slaves. Captives bound with ropes, chains, and irons preceded him when he made his triumphal return to Algeciras on 18 September. Nuño's head was brandished on a stake so that everyone could see it. Reportedly included in the booty were 124,000 head of cattle; 7,830 captives, men, women and children; 14,700 horses, mules, and asses; and an innumerable quantity of shields, swords, and other materials.[26] The Marinid triumph found its way to the later pages of the Egyptian historian, al-Maqrīzī (d. 1442), who reported the death of the Christian commander and 10,000 of his men. The booty was so immense that 14,600 camels were needed to carry it from the battlefield.[27] In a praise poem the *arráez* of Málaga, Abū Muhammad b. Ashqīlūlā, saluted the emir as "defender of the people" and exalted him as "a good caliph," a title implying he was heir to Muhammad.[28]

In a gesture no doubt calculated to offend, Abū Yūsuf sent a unique symbol of his victory to Muhammad II, namely, the severed head of Nuño González de Lara. Known as *al-faqīh*, the jurist, the king of Granada was a man of some refinement and was likely repelled by this act of cruelty. As a leader of the exiled Castilian magnates, Nuño was well known to him and they may have forged a bond of friendship or at least of respect. The Nasrid king had the dead warrior's head embalmed in musk and camphor and secretly sent it to Córdoba to be interred together with his body. In doing so, according to

Ibn Khaldūn, he yielded to sentiments of friendship, the desire to retain the good opinion of the Christians, and the hatred he bore for the Marinid emir.[29]

Hearing of the disaster at Écija, Archbishop Sancho II of Toledo, a son of Jaime I, accompanied by knights and town militias, hastened toward the frontier. By then he may have received Gregory X's crusading bull. At Jaén he learned that the Nasrids were plundering around Martos, a fortress pertaining to the Order of Calatrava. Rather than await the arrival of Lope Díaz de Haro, lord of Vizcaya, and perhaps share the glory of victory with him, the archbishop advanced toward Martos. Moving rapidly ahead, he suddenly found himself surrounded and was captured. Stripping him of his arms and clothing, the Moors decided to take him to the king of Granada, but two Moroccans insisted that he should be handed over to Abū Yūsuf. However, one man, crying out, "May Allah not allow so many good men as are here to be killed by a dog," killed the archbishop. After cutting off his head and his hand with his episcopal ring, the Moors departed. The battle of Martos took place on 20 October. On the next day, Lope Díaz de Haro caught up with the enemy and recovered the archbishop's cross and killed the Moorish *alférez* carrying it. On the following day he was able to retrieve the archbishop's headless body. The Moors sent his head and hand to Toledo for burial.[30]

On receiving news of the tragic deaths of Nuño González de Lara and Archbishop Sancho, Infante Sancho, Alfonso X's second son, now just seventeen years old, hastened to Córdoba. Reorganizing frontier defenses, he ordered a fleet to be readied at Seville to blockade Algeciras. Although the sultan appeared before the gates of the city with banners displayed and drums sounding, he did not attempt a siege. Instead, turning southward, he threatened Jerez and regained Algeciras on 16 November. There he spent the winter, building a new town called al-Binya to serve as a convenient base for future landings in Spain.[31]

Meanwhile, the Castilian fleet engaged the Moors off Tarifa, destroying eleven ships.[32] That loss and the possibility that his communications with Morocco might be severed encouraged Abū Yūsuf to hasten his return to Morocco. In late December or early January 1276, he and Muhammad II agreed to a truce with Castile for two years. After six months in Spain, he landed at Alcácer Seguir on 19 January 1276. The first Marinid invasion was at an end.[33]

Prior to his departure, Muhammad II's secretary addressed a poem to Abū Yūsuf, expressing his continuing fear of Castile and his desire to retain Marinid support. He exhorted him to cleanse himself of sin by taking up arms in "the holy war, the first of the pious works." Lamenting the dominance of the infidels, he asked: "how can you endure the insults of the Trinitarians, the oppressors of those who believe in the one God?" Mosques were converted into churches and defiled as wine and pork were served. Priests mounted the minarets and rang bells. Instead of pious people at prayer, a mob of arrogant reprobates was in the ascendant. Many men and women had been taken captive, and young girls, separated from their families, lived in chains wishing only to die. Parents regretted having brought children into the world to suffer death or imprisonment at the hands of unbelievers. So many martyrs had been sent to death at the point of a lance on the field of battle. The poet pleaded for help: "The holy war is a duty required of you. Hasten to fulfill this most essential and rigorous obligation." Some might live to enjoy the glory of victory, but others, falling as martyrs, would be received into Paradise to be served by beautiful virgins.[34] Painting a dire picture of the evils inflicted by the Christians, the poet appealed to the traditional notion that good Muslims ought to wage the holy war against the infidels. Those who died in doing so would receive the reward of martyrdom, life eternal in Paradise. As we shall see, Muhammad II had reason later to regret his appeal to the Marinids.

At the conclusion of his first campaign in Spain Abū Yūsuf could take a certain satisfaction. The Marinids had wreaked destruction far and wide and had defeated and killed one of Castile's principal nobles, Nuño González de Lara, in a pitched battle. Castile's woes were further compounded by the defeat and death of Archbishop Sancho of Toledo. The emir had not acquired any significant Castilian territory, but the ports of Algeciras and Tarifa, ceded by the king of Granada, gave him a permanent foothold in Spain. He also enjoyed the alliance of the Banu Ashqīlūla. Though he had retreated to Morocco, both Muslims and Christians knew that he would soon return to Spain.

Delayed by a recurrence of illness at Montpellier, Alfonso X, who was "very angry and ill," reentered his kingdom late in 1275.[35] Given the likelihood of a resumption of hostilities, the towns of Castile and Extremadura summoned to Alcalá de Henares promised him an annual levy of *moneda* for three years.[36] Aside from seeing to the defense of his realm, his most immediate concern was the succession to the throne. The question was whether Alfonso, the older of the two sons of Fernando de la Cerda, who was only five years old, or the king's second son, Infante Sancho, should be designated as the royal heir. Taking what seemed to be the wiser course, the king recognized Sancho, the hero of the recent war, during the Cortes of Burgos in May 1276. Philip III of France, as uncle to the Infantes de la Cerda, however, became increasingly hostile.[37]

Preparation for Renewal of the Crusade

After the death of Archbishop Sancho II, Gregory X designated Archbishop Remondo of Seville as "executor of the business of the cross." In February 1276 he directed Fray Juan Arias, the Dominican provincial in Spain, to appoint the most capable friars to preach the crusade, offering the indulgence to all who "took the cross to wage war against the Saracens of Africa and Spain" or subsidized others. Crusaders would enjoy all the benefits granted by the papacy. Preachers were authorized to condemn anyone giving aid and counsel to the enemy or providing him with arms and supplies. As guidance for the preachers, Archbishop Remondo appended the crusading bulls issued by Clement IV on 26 June and 2 July 1265. Nevertheless, Fray Juan Arias raised many questions, prompting the archbishop to issue a sharply worded reply on 21 March. He emphasized that Jerez and other towns were especially vulnerable to enemy attack and pointed to the need to bring in the harvest before the Moors could destroy it.[38] The lack of an up-to-date crusading bull was overcome on 9 April when Innocent V (January–June 1276) repeated the substance of Clement IV's earlier bulls and confirmed Archbishop Remondo's responsibility to preach the crusade.[39]

Alfonso X also appealed to Jaime I and to Edward I of England. The former agreed to send his son Pedro with 1,000 knights and 5,000 infantry for three months "in the service of God and the aid of the king of Castile in the region of Spain [i.e., Muslim territory] against the Saracens." Jaime I died on 27 June, however, and was succeeded by his son, now Pedro III (1276–85), whose immediate concern was to suppress the revolt of the Valencian Mudéjars.[40] In January 1276 Edward I ordered the people of Bayonne in Gascony to provide Castile with warships "to resist the Saracens by sea," but he excused himself from personal participation because of his wars in Wales and his plan to lead a crusade to the Holy Land.[41]

Alfonso X also reached out to Baybars, the sultan of Egypt. Toward the end of 1275, a Castilian emissary visited Baybars, who sent his own ambassadors to Spain. Sailing from Alexandria in May 1276, they seem to have landed at Valencia, and, after meeting Jaime I, continued on to Vitoria where Alfonso X received them warmly. They returned to Alexandria in August or September. A year later, in July, Alfonso X's envoys, on arrival at Cairo, discovered that Baybars was dead, but they met his son al-Malik al-Saʿīd. Another embassy arrived in Cairo in February 1280. The sources say nothing of the purpose or

72 Chapter 4

outcome of these diplomatic exchanges, but one may surmise that Alfonso X sought to induce the Mamlūks to lend their support against the Marinids, restore Jerusalem to Christian rule, and encourage trade relations.[42]

Hostilities with France and the Moors placed a heavy drain on the royal treasury, which was relieved somewhat when Burgos and other cities as well as the prelates consented to an aid during the Cortes of Burgos in 1276. After protesting the king's incessant demands for money and attempt to collect arrears of taxes dating back to 1261, the towns in the Cortes of Burgos in 1277, in exchange for exemption from all other tributes, granted him an annual *servicio* for life.[43]

Afflicted by a deadly cancer, Alfonso X fell gravely ill at Vitoria in the fall of 1276 and seemed at death's door. Thereafter his behavior became more extreme, causing great consternation. In March 1277, "on account of certain things that he knew about them," he ordered the sudden arrest and execution of his brother Infante Fadrique and the magnate Simón Ruiz de los Cameros. Fadrique, after long years in exile, may have conspired to take advantage of the king's illness and Sancho's youth to seize power. The brutal execution of the two men, without due process of law, would later be cited in justification of rebellion against the king.[44]

The Second Coming of the Marinids

In 1277 the Marinids invaded Spain for the second time, apparently before the expiration of the truce. As the *Royal Chronicle* makes no reference to this invasion, the chief sources are Ibn Abī Zarʿ and three letters from the chancery of Ceuta, which provide additional details, but without a chronological framework.[45] Pope John XXI (1276–77) was informed on 9 May 1277 that "a great body of Moors had crossed the Strait and were ravaging the land." This was likely an advance contingent of a larger force.[46]

The main army crossed the Strait from Alcácer Seguir to Tarifa at the end of June. From Algeciras, Abū Yūsuf proceeded to Ronda, where the Banū Ashqīlūlā joined him. Notably absent was Muhammad II, who perhaps feared that the Marinids might overthrow him. Abū Yūsuf determined to attack Seville, whose citizens, he believed, had been lulled into a false sense of security because the city had not been assaulted since 1248. In July he marched northward to Alcalá del Río and Gerena and then to Italica, the ruined Roman municipality just north of the city. After 200 Marinids drove 300 Castilian knights and 2,000 infantry across the Guadalquivir, he turned against Seville.[47] On the Prophet's birthday, 2 August, Abū Yūsuf decided to give battle. Praying for divine assistance, he addressed his men:

> Oh, band of the Banū Marīn! Fight for God in his holy war. . . . May God grant that no one who fights against the enemies of God, the infidels, will suffer the torment of fire. . . . May God grant that the prize of the holy war be great and its merit eminent before God. May the one who dies in it live and gain such a high dignity that is inaccessible!

Fired up by his words, the Marinids shouted "God is great!" and the profession of faith. As they advanced with drums loudly beating and flags flying, the Christians turned in flight like frightened prey before a lion. Many were killed and the Guadalquivir ran red with their blood; dead bodies floated on the water. After spending the night before Seville, drums beating incessantly and fires lighting up the sky so that night was turned into day, the emir withdrew on the next morning. Moving northward along the Guadalquivir, he took the castles of Guillena, Cantillana, and Alcolea del Río. Turning southward toward Morón de la Frontera, he returned to Algeciras on 29 August. Setting out again on 15 September, he destroyed vineyards and olive groves, burned the harvest, and demolished villages. A troop of 3,000 Marinids attacked the castles on the lower Guadalquivir, namely, Rota, Sanlúcar de Barrameda, Galiana, and Alcanatir. Although Abū Yūsuf briefly laid siege to Jerez, he soon withdrew to Algeciras.[48]

Urging Muhammad II of Granada to join him, Abū Yūsuf set out from Algeciras on 30 October. After meeting near Archidona and taking the castle of Benamejí, the two kings marched northward, carrying off livestock, olive oil, wheat, and barley in great quantities. While they encircled Córdoba for three days, marauding parties pillaged the neighborhood of Baeza, Úbeda, Jaén, Cañete de las Torres, Porcuna, Martos, Arjona, and Andújar.[49] *Cantiga* 215 described the desolation as churches were plundered, bells carried off, altars robbed, crucifixes and statues destroyed. Unable to destroy a statue of the Virgin Mary, a band of Moors sold it to Muhammad II, who handed it over to the Christians with orders to return it to Alfonso X. The moral of the story, according to *Cantiga* 215, was that "that band of Moors was defeated and [Mary's] image was avenged."[50]

Now, according to Ibn Abī Zarʿ, Alfonso X, considering the destruction caused by the Moors, sent representatives to ask "for pardon and peace."

74 Chapter 4

Manzano Rodríguez suggested, however, that the frontier towns, suffering the terrible ravages of war, rather than the king, sued for peace. While the Marinids were wreaking havoc in Andalucía, Alfonso X remained at Burgos, wishing to journey to the frontier, but constrained by poor health from doing so. Muhammad II agreed to a settlement, and Abū Yūsuf, after returning to Algeciras on 28 November, concluded a truce of uncertain duration on 24 February 1278.[51]

When the emir departed for Morocco at the end of May, the second Marinid invasion was over. Extensive plundering enriched the Marinids, inflicted great damage on the economy, and put fear into the hearts of Christians living on the frontier. Although he routed the Castilians on the outskirts of Seville, the significance of that encounter was probably much less than Ibn Abī Zarʿ made it out to be. The emir made no serious attempt to besiege any large town, nor did he permanently annex Christian territory. However, in September 1277, the Banū Ashqīlūlā, concluding that they could not hold Málaga against the king of Granada, offered it to the Marinids, who occupied it in mid-February 1278. As a consequence, the emir's relationship with Muhammad II grew ever colder.[52]

Preparing for the Crusade of Algeciras

In the ensuing months Alfonso X had much to suffer as his marriage broke down and his illness recurred. Much to his distress, in January 1278, Queen Violante, accompanied by her daughter-in-law Blanche and the Infantes de la Cerda, took refuge in Aragón, where Violante's brother, Pedro III, gave them a warm welcome. When Alfonso X fell ill in April and seemed on the point of death, he entrusted even greater responsibility to Infante Sancho, but mounting antagonism toward the king provoked an attempt at assassination.[53]

Once recovered, he determined to thwart further Marinid invasions by laying siege to Algeciras. The situation was complicated, however, by the continued enmity of France and papal insistence on launching a crusade to the Holy Land. So long as the Marinid threat persisted, Castile could have no part in such a crusade. Rather, Alfonso X endeavored to gather financial support for a crusade against Algeciras. Pope Nicholas III (1277–80) apparently did not issue a new bull of crusade, but Archbishop Remondo of Seville, the promoter of the crusade, probably used one published by Innocent V. Both Gregory X and Innocent V had allowed the tenth (*decima*) of ecclesiastical revenue authorized by the Council of Lyon in 1274 for the relief of the Holy Land to be diverted to the war against the Moors. When the Castilian bishops complained that the money was being sent to the East, Nicholas III postponed collection for a year and exempted the Orders of the Hospital, Santiago, and Calatrava, as they were directly involved in war against the Moors.[54]

As the Council of Lyon required kings to fine those who lent money at interest or usury, Alfonso X, seeing this as a useful source of income, demanded substantial sums from several towns for "the affair of the frontier." Alba de Tormes, for example, pledged 10,000 *maravedíes*; Burgos promised 60,000; and Alcalá de Henares agreed to pay usury fines "for the crusade." When Archbishop Remondo wrote concerning financial aid for "the affair of the crusade," Burgos was reluctant to contribute, but in February 1279 in response to the king's plea to act so that the "affair of the crusade might go forward," the city promised to pay six *servicios* in five years, in lieu of outstanding taxes and fines.[55]

Two matters complicated royal fund-raising. First, Nicholas III denounced him for continuing to collect the *tercias* beyond the term previously authorized and for extorting subsidies from the clergy. Secondly, Infante Sancho diverted tax moneys intended for the siege of Algeciras so that his mother, Violante, could return to Castile. An outraged king would have his vengeance a year later.[56]

Recognizing the need for a fleet to interdict all communication between Algeciras and Morocco, the king assembled at Seville eighty galleys, twenty-four *naves* or sailing ships, and a large number of other vessels (*galeotas*, *leños*). The ships were provided with crews, arms, crossbows, biscuit, and other necessities and siege engines were constructed. Pedro Martínez de Fe, who had served previously in the expedition to Salé, was appointed as admiral.[57]

The Crusade of Algeciras

When Alfonso X dispatched his fleet to blockade Algeciras in the late summer of 1278, Ibn Abī Zarʿ accused "the cursed one" of violating the truce. Taking advantage of the appearance of the fleet, Muhammad II persuaded the Marinid governor of Málaga to surrender the port on 31 January 1279. When Abū Yūsuf learned of this treachery, he planned to set out for Spain, but heavy rains, floods, winds, and reports of rebellion in Morocco deterred him. Meantime, Muhammad II, intent on expelling the Marinids from the Peninsula, formed an alliance with Alfonso X. Both men also turned to Yagmurāsan, emir of Tlemcen, with the expectation that he would be able to distract Abū Yūsuf.

Although Alfonso X appointed his third son, Infante Pedro, then nineteen, to command the host, effective leadership probably rested with the king's illegitimate son, Alfonso Fernández el Niño, a man well experienced in frontier warfare. With great exaggeration, Ibn Abī Zarʿ reported that 30,000 Christian knights and 300,000 infantry surrounded Algeciras in the spring of 1279. While siege machines and cannons battered the walls, skirmishes took place every day and night. As food supplies dwindled, hunger decimated the population. Parents feared that if their children were captured they would be compelled to apostasize. As the term of service for many of the besiegers came to an end, some returned home while others, hoping to share in the plunder, remained. Lacking changes of clothing and suffering from a shortage of food, many mariners succumbed to sickness, probably scurvy, and lost their teeth. Some left their ships to take shelter in huts on shore. Hard-pressed for funds, Alfonso X found it difficult to pay them. Though he obtained loans from the merchants in Seville, he was still able to send little help.

Busy suppressing rebellions in Morocco, Abū Yūsuf instructed his son Abū Yaʿqūb to relieve Algeciras, thereby initiating the third Marinid invasion. Aware of the deteriorating situation, Abū Yaʿqūb sent representatives to discuss a possible settlement, but also to assess the Castilian situation. The Marinids offered to pay Alfonso X 200,000 *doblas* and to cede Algeciras to Muhammad II. Thus, if the Castilians seized it, the Marinids could disclaim any responsibility. On the face of it, Abū Yaʿqūb was prepared to betray the king of Granada who unwittingly would be left at the mercy of the Castilians and would be blamed for the loss of Algeciras. Castilian magnates experienced in dealing with the Marinids surely viewed this proposal with extreme skepticism. Infante Pedro rightly responded that he would have to consult his father. As the Marinid emissaries observed that the Castilian galleys were unprotected and many mariners were ill, they urged Abū Yaʿqūb to send galleys to attack them so that much needed supplies could be brought to Algeciras.[58]

Fifteen ships were readied in Tangier and other ports while Abū Hātim al-ʿAzafi of Ceuta armed another forty-five. Men seeking to gain merit in the holy war were recruited for the army. Perceiving a shift in the balance of power, Muhammad II repudiated his alliance with Castile and gathered twelve ships, thus bringing the total of Muslim vessels to seventy-two. As his fleet passed in review at Tangier, Abū Yaʿqūb proclaimed: "Go with God's blessing and favor." After reciting the profession of faith and asking God's help, on 19 July the mariners sailed from Tangier to Gibraltar. There, preachers reminded them of the rewards promised by God to those fighting for the faith. Now zealous for martyrdom, they embraced one another, asking pardon, and lifted their sails to assault the "polytheists."

The Christians, according to Ibn Abī Zarʿ, were frightened by the enormous number of enemy ships; yet he declared that the Muslims had 70 ships and the Christians 400, an unbelievable numerical discrepancy. While four Marinid galleys burned Castilian galleys near Isla Verde just off Algeciras, another ten galleys assaulted the main body of the Castilian fleet near Algeciras Nueva. In the midst of a heavy rain, battle was joined; arrows were shot into the air; swords were drawn; and many fell dead or wounded. As their losses mounted, the Christians turned in flight; some threw themselves into the sea where the Muslims killed them and burned their deserted ships. Others scuttled their ships and fled to land in small boats. The Moors also disembarked and killed the Castilians, many of whom were ill and incapable of mounting a defense. Six Moorish galleys then brought in food to Algeciras. The destruction of the Castilian fleet occurred on the Prophet's birthday, Monday, 24 July 1279.[59]

Three Castilian vessels, hoping to make their escape, were driven toward Tangier. The three commanders, including Admiral Pedro Martínez de Fe, landed but, while speaking to Abū Yaʿqūb, their ships sailed away, eventually reaching Cartagena. Whether, as the *Royal Chronicle* put it, a storm came up and they feared to be driven aground, or whether, fearing capture, they deserted their commanders and made for the open sea is uncertain. The admiral and his two subordinates were held captive for two years, when they escaped.

As they witnessed the ruination of the Castilian fleet, the Muslims in Algeciras, who had given themselves up for lost, rejoiced and welcomed the victors, while Infante Pedro decided to abandon the siege. As the Christians began their withdrawal, leaving behind siege machinery, weapons, jewels, and clothing, the Muslims killed and wounded some and captured others. Supplies of fruit, barley, and wheat dumped by the enemy were brought into Algeciras to relieve the hungry defenders. Abū Yaʿqūb crossed from Tangier to Algeciras on 11 August. As the place where the Christians had encamped was considered difficult to defend should another siege occur, he ordered the settlement of the Villa Nueva of Algeciras. The Miel River divided the Villa Vieja, or Old Town, from the Villa Nueva.[60]

Learning of the obliteration of his fleet and seeing his bedraggled army returning in humiliation to Seville, Alfonso X realized that his grand plan for the conquest of Algeciras had come to an ignominious end. Nevertheless, Castile, though badly wounded in body and spirit, did not suffer any loss of territory. While the Marinids successfully retained possession of Algeciras, the king of Granada had deprived them of Málaga and probably also of Ronda. By his double-dealing, however, Muhammad II made enemies of both Abū Yūsuf and Alfonso X.

In the ensuing months, Alfonso X strengthened frontier defenses by resuming his earlier policy of entrusting key fortresses to the military orders. In 1264 he had given Osuna to the Order of Calatrava and Estepa to the Order of Santiago in 1267. Now in 1279, he granted Medina Sidonia and Alcalá de los Gazules to the Order of Santa María de España. He anticipated that the knights would establish their principal house at Medina Sidonia, the most important Castilian advanced position. He also donated Morón to the Order of Alcántara and made additional grants to Calatrava and to Infante Pedro.[61]

The War Against Granada

In November, after the relief of Algeciras, the emir, Abū Yūsuf, summoned his troops to the holy war against Muhammad II, but raids by Yagmurasān of Tlemcen made an invasion impossible at that time. Alfonso X also wished to punish the king of Granada, who had played him falsely, and agreed to a truce with the Marinids. While Muhammad II emerged as the common enemy and the emir's son, Abū Ya'qūb, invited Alfonso X to join him in besieging Granada, it is not certain that a coordinated assault was planned.[62]

Announcing that he had made peace with Abū Yūsuf and intended to go to war against Granada, Alfonso X summoned the host to Córdoba in the spring. His efforts to enlist the support of his grandson Dinis (1279–1325), king of Portugal, were unavailing. However, Pedro III permitted him to secure ten to fifteen galleys in the Crown of Aragón and, as before, Edward I authorized him to construct ships at Bayonne. With military uses in mind, Alfonso X reserved the skins of horses, mules, and asses for making saddles, shields, and scabbards; shoemakers and others who used those materials for other purposes would be fined.[63] The king apparently did not ask Nicholas III, who regarded him with hostility, for crusading privileges. If a crusade was preached, earlier papal bulls were probably used. More than likely, the *decima* and the *tercias* were still being collected.

Meanwhile, an initial Marinid offensive against the port of Marbella and Ronda was unsuccessful. In June 1280 Alfonso X planned to march from Córdoba to Alcalá de Benzaide (Alcalá la Real) where Infante Sancho, advancing from Jaén, would join him. The king, felled again by a cancer that forced his eye out of its socket, so that he nearly lost it, had to abandon any thought of campaigning. Nevertheless, Sancho, supported by the Banū Ashqīlūlā, longtime enemies of the Nasrids, besieged Granada for two weeks.

A military disaster brought the campaign to an abrupt end. On Saturday, the eve of St. John (23 June), Gonzalo Ruiz Girón, master of the Order of Santiago, advanced as far as the castle of Moclín perched on a high hill overlooking the plain of Granada, about equidistant from Alcalá de Benzaide and the Nasrid capital.[64] When a band of 100 Moorish knights appeared, the master, a man of great courage, rashly attacked them. Executing a classic maneuver, the Moors turned in flight and led him into an ambush where 2,000 knights waited. The Moors chased the wounded master and his company, capturing many and, according to the *Royal Chronicle*, killing 2,800 men. Among the dead were most of the knights of the Order of Santiago. Ibn Khaldūn reported that 700 knights were killed or wounded, a number that seems more reasonable. Nevertheless, the Christians suffered a grievous blow.

Hearing of the rout at Moclín, Sancho promptly mounted his horse and, with lance in hand, commanded his men to remain calm, thereby saving them from an even worse catastrophe. So horrific was the destruction wrought at Moclín, however, that many soldiers deserted and headed for home. Still hoping to achieve some success, Sancho on 25 June advanced toward Moclín, burning the wheat fields and pillaging the outskirts of Granada; but within a few days he brought his campaign to a halt.[65]

Thus, the first stage of the war, intended to chastise the king of Granada, ended badly. The death of the master of Santiago shortly after and the loss of so many of his knights left the future of the Order in doubt. Alfonso X resolved that issue by uniting the Orders of Santiago and Santa María de España under Pedro Núñez, the first master of the latter Order. As the combined force was known as the Order of Santiago, the independent history of the Order of Santa María came to an end.[66]

Although the *Royal Chronicle* emphasized that Alfonso X was very pleased with Sancho's conduct of the campaign, signs of tension suggest otherwise. While still in Córdoba, for example, Sancho, in a blatant attempt to secure the backing of the Order of Calatrava in any future dispute over the succession, promised that, once he became king, he would grant Villarreal (Ciudad Real) to the knights. The king, who had established Villarreal in 1255 as a symbol of royal power in the heart of the Order's lordship, had every reason to be affronted and could denounce his son for an apparent usurpation of authority.[67]

Moreover, Sancho, as the overall commander, could be blamed for the disaster at Moclín. The failure of the siege of Algeciras could also be laid at his door because he sent Queen Violante tax moneys earmarked for the siege. In September 1280, as a lesson for Sancho, the king ordered the arrest of Zag de la Maleha, the royal *almojarife mayor* responsible for tax collection. Seized in front of the infante's residence in Seville, he was dragged through the streets as far as the riverbank, until dead. Although Sancho thought to intervene, his advisers warned against it. The king replenished his treasury, at least temporarily, on 19 January 1281 by ordering the arrest of the leaders of all the Jewish communities and demanding that they pay a huge ransom of 12,000 *maravedíes* a day, or 4,380,000 a year, about double the annual amount paid by the Jews to the crown.[68]

The plundering of the Jews found an echo in *Cantiga* 348, which tells the story of a king who raised a great army "to destroy the Moors." Although his tax collectors failed to provide him with sufficient funds, the Virgin Mary, in a dream, revealed a vast treasure hidden by those "who are much worse than the Moors." She showed him great quantities of silver, gold, precious stones, silk cloths, rich tapestries, and jewels belonging to "the Jews, his enemies, who are worse than the Moors." *Cantiga* 348 emphatically expressed the intensity of Alfonso X's anger at his perceived betrayal by Zag de la Maleha.[69]

The relationship between the king and his son was strained further when the former endeavored to accommodate the claims to the throne of Alfonso de la Cerda. Anxious to placate Philip III, the prince's uncle, Alfonso X also wanted to respond to Nicholas III's desire for a crusade to liberate the Holy Land. If he could convince the kings of France and England to participate in an invasion of Morocco, he thought that they could "conquer the Holy Land from there."[70] However, when he offered to give Alfonso de la Cerda the kingdom of Jaén to hold in vassalage of Sancho, who would inherit all the other Castilian dominions, the infante expressed strong displeasure. In turn, Alfonso X reacted angrily. The bad blood stirred up eventually brought the king of Castile to his knees.

The king and his son were also at odds when Alfonso X, who had never given up his imperial ambitions, sent 2,000,000 *dineros* or 133,333 *maravedíes*, as well as 300 knights and 100 archers, to serve the marquess of Montferrat, his ally in Lombardy, for one year. An irritated Sancho believed that both the money and the troops could be put to better use, especially, for example, against the Marinids.[71]

In June 1281, Alfonso X, intent on waging unremitting war against Muhammad II, invaded the lowlands of Granada. As Infantes Sancho and Pedro advanced, Muhammad II sent 50,000 Moors and as many archers and other mounted men to repel them. These figures, of course, are exaggerated. The Castilians were on the point of fleeing in disorder when Sancho rallied them and the king sent Infante Juan to his aid. With renewed vigor, they inflicted a grave defeat on the enemy before the walls of Granada on 25 June. Offering to negotiate, Muhammad II promised to pay a third of his revenues in tribute, but Alfonso X demanded the surrender of all his castles and fortresses. Rejecting that ultimatum as outrageous, Muhammad II broke off negotiations. Soon thereafter Alfonso X and Sancho returned to Córdoba, ending hostilities for the time being.[72]

Cantiga 366, after describing the campaign of pillage, reported that when the king returned to Seville his illness recurred and his legs swelled up so much that they could not fit in his pants. After a brief respite, according to *Cantiga* 367, he made a pilgrimage to El Puerto de Santa María, but his legs, turning red, swelled again so that he could not put on his boots, and a yellow fluid oozed from his veins. Through the intercession of the Virgin Mary, however, he recovered. Recalling his earlier ambition to establish a naval base at El Puerto de Santa María, he not only recounted the wonders worked there by the Virgin Mary, but also granted a settlement charter in December 1281.[73] Nevertheless, his affliction could not be concealed from his family and courtiers who must have questioned his ability to fulfill his royal duties.

As the financial burden of the assault on Granada became insupportable, the towns pleaded with Sancho to inform his father "that the men were very poor and the tributes great." During the Cortes of Seville in November 1281, Alfonso X emphasized the need for additional funds to prosecute the war against Granada, but rather than levy a new tax, he proposed to issue new coinage, much to the dismay of the townsmen. When the king announced his intention to grant the kingdom of Jaén to his grandson Alfonso de la Cerda, Sancho vigorously protested. He also suspected that a mission sent to Pope Martin IV (1281–85) to obtain "graces for the war against the Moors" was intended to win papal support for the plan to partition the realm. In a bitter exchange of words, the king threatened to disinherit Sancho.[74]

The Revolt of Infante Sancho

Following the Cortes, Sancho, with his father's consent, journeyed to Córdoba to negotiate a truce with Granada. Muhammad II renewed his vassalage, agreed to pay tribute, and promised to aid Castile against its enemies. In Alfonso X's view, however, Sancho concluded a treaty with the Nasrid ruler "contrary to us and our dominions." He charged Sancho with acting treacherously, entering an alliance with Muhammad II, and appropriating the tribute for himself. Ignoring his father's summons to Seville, Sancho journeyed northward to Valladolid where he convoked the estates of the realm in April 1282. Among those present were Queen Violante, the king's brother Manuel, and his sons Pedro, Juan, and Jaime. Acknowledging the king's impairment, the assembly, while leaving him with the royal title, transferred his powers to Sancho. In scathing language Alfonso X denounced his son's treason on 9 November and disinherited him and his descendants.[75]

Deserted by his family and many of his people, the king reached out in vain to his royal colleagues. However, his grandson Dinis of Portugal sided with Sancho, and Pedro III was planning an adventure in Sicily. Edward I, though emphasizing the great distance between his realms and Spain, promised to send 100 Gascon knights. Philip III failed to respond. Pope Martin IV expressed the hope that the quarrel might be resolved, but could do little else.[76]

Meantime, Córdoba and six frontier towns (Jaén, Baeza, Úbeda, Andújar, Arjona, and San Esteban), and three nobles (Gonzalo Ibáñez de Aguilar, Sancho Sánchez de Jódar, and Sancho Pérez de Jódar) organized a *hermandad*, or brotherhood, for mutual defense. They had established a similar association in 1265 during the Mudéjar revolt.[77]

The Fourth Marinid Invasion

In an extraordinary diplomatic twist, Alfonso X, feeling alone in the world, appealed to his erstwhile enemy Abū Yūsuf, the Marinid sultan. Speaking in his king's name, the Castilian envoy spoke these words: "O victorious king, the Christians have violated their oath of fidelity and, together with my son, have rebelled against me. They say: 'he is an old man who has lost his judgment and whose reason is disturbed.' Aid me against them and I will go with you to meet them." Commenting on the alacrity of Abū Yūsuf's pledge to aid "his old enemy," and his hope to turn the quarrel among the Christians to his own advantage, Ibn Khaldūn remarked that "he was happy to be able to intervene . . . and to gratify . . . his love of the holy war."[78]

In his frantic search for allies Alfonso X may also have turned to the Egyptian sultan Qalāwūn (1279–90). In June 1282 Castilian ambassadors reached Cairo and in the following year Qalāwūn sent his envoys to Castile. They soon realized the futility of their mission and wished to return home, but the king insisted that they stay. Abū Yūsuf interceded for them, even offering to pay their expenses, but they were still in Seville when Alfonso X died. Only reluctantly did his son give them permission to depart.[79]

However that may be, Abū Yūsuf crossed the Strait from Alcácer Seguir to Algeciras in July 1282 and established his camp at Zahara, northwest of Ronda. There, exhibiting the honor due to a sovereign, he received Alfonso X, "humble and beaten," who declared that he had no one to defend him, save the emir. Lacking funds, he offered the crown of his father and grandfathers as a pledge of repayment of a loan. Out of pity, Abū Yūsuf gave the feeble king 100,000 gold dinars. The Castilian royal crown was still in the palace in Marrakech in Ibn Khaldūn's time and was considered one of the glories of the dynasty. Its whereabouts today are unknown.[80]

The two monarchs then set out to expel Sancho's partisans from Córdoba. When Alfonso X demanded the keys of the city, Diego López de Haro, speaking on behalf of the magnates, accused him of executing his brother Fadrique and Simón Ruiz de los Cameros without a trial. As he was in the company of Abū Yūsuf, the enemy of the faith, who had killed Nuño González de Lara in the battle of Écija as well as Archbishop Sancho II, the magnates refused to meet him. Unable to take Córdoba, Abū Yūsuf withdrew after three weeks and, after pillaging the countryside, returned to Algeciras. With typical hyperbole, Ibn Abī Zar' declared: "this was an expedition unlike any other in past ages."[81] Alfonso X related that, having recovered his health and being able to ride and walk, he had "remained almost four months in his [Abū Yūsuf's] power with the few forces that we had." On returning to Seville he expected to receive some sign of support from the pope, the king of France, and other kings, but found "only fine words."[82]

Meeting again at Zahara, on 24 October 1282, Alfonso X and Abū Yūsuf pledged to collaborate against their common enemies. The emir ratified in advance whatever agreement Alfonso X might reach with Philip III, probably with respect to the succession. On the same day Abū Yūsuf urged the

84   Chapter 4

French king to help Alfonso X, who had suffered the malice of fortune. As all religions would find Sancho's revolt abominable, he felt obliged to defend the king, even though "we differ from him in matters of dogma and belief. For, in fact, we are his enemies. Our hostile disposition has always been very pronounced and we have always manifested a great aversion to one another." Given Sancho's detestable actions, however, the emir asserted that he would assist Alfonso X "with our person, our wealth, our relatives, our children, and our armies." He emphasized that he did so out of the purest of motives, with no concern for his own interest and no desire to obtain any part of Alfonso X's dominions. Acknowledging the familial ties binding the royal houses of Castile and France, he exhorted Philip III to succor Alfonso X.[83]

Despite that appeal, Philip III was unlikely to intervene. He could perceive the conflict as an opportunity for his nephew Alfonso de la Cerda that should be allowed to play itself out. Soon to be of greater interest was the possibility of establishing one of his sons on the Aragonese throne. When Pedro III invaded Sicily in the summer of 1282, Martin IV deposed him and in 1284 offered the Aragonese crown to Philip III's younger son, Charles of Valois. Thus, rather than heed Abū Yūsuf's plea, the French king expended his energy on his son's behalf.

In the light of Ibn Khaldūn's remark that Abū Yūsuf hoped to profit from the Castilian war, the emir's assertion that his motives were purely altruistic seems disingenuous or even hypocritical. Contemporary observers surely knew he intended to benefit from his intervention.

A month after meeting the emir, Alfonso X disinherited Sancho and in his will, drawn up on 8 November 1283, he explained the reasons for his alliance with Abū Yūsuf:

> Seeing ourselves bereft of everything in the world, except only the mercy of God, we thought of Abū Yūsuf, king of Morocco. . . . He put himself forward before the Christian and Moorish kings to uphold right and truth and made known that he was troubled and sorry for the evil and the harm that we had received. He said that, although we follow different religions [*leyes*] and that his dynasty in Morocco was always opposed to Spain, he did not wish to be concerned about that. Rather, knowing the long and honorable descent of our dynasty, he believed that none could be held in such great esteem in the world; nor could there be any greater honor for his religion than to protect our dynasty so that it would not be destroyed and we would not be killed or injured

by such great treason as that which the traitors have committed against us. Concerning this he sent to us, promising to aid us with his body and his lineage, his vassals, and his power and wealth until we should recover everything of ours. . . . And he did so, sending us first his sons and relatives, and then crossing over in his own person with his noble cavalry and great wealth, so that many good things derived from his coming.[84]

The king's language is reminiscent of Abū Yūsuf's letter to Philip III. His alliance can only be regarded as the act of a desperate man. It is a terrible irony that the king who expressed the hope "that I can expel the sect of Muhammad from Spain" was reduced to begging for help from Abū Yūsuf, who only a few years before had burned and pillaged his realm.[85]

The End of the Marinid Invasion

As the year 1282 drew to a close, Sancho recognized his need for allies and turned to Muhammad II, who also required help to prevent the Marinids from seizing Málaga and Ronda. The two men met at Priego, about thirty miles northeast of Granada. As the price of his alliance Muhammad II demanded restoration of Campillo de Arenas, about twenty-five miles north of Granada, which he had previously lost to Alfonso X. In the next year Pedro III acknowledged that both he and Sancho were obliged to aid Granada in case of a Marinid attack. Thus, a bizarre state of affairs played out before the Christian and Muslim worlds: the Christian king Alfonso X was in alliance with the Muslim emir Abū Yūsuf against the Christian infante Sancho and his ally, the Muslim king Muhammad II. Political realities obviously trumped religious considerations and the spirit of the crusade vanished.[86]

Meantime, Alfonso X, perhaps reflecting on the harm that he had done by inviting the Marinids into his realm, proposed a truce with Sancho. After consulting his mother, his uncle Manuel, his brothers, and various magnates and prelates at Burgos in April 1283, Sancho responded positively, but wished first to take counsel with representatives of the towns and summoned them to Córdoba.[87] That tentative agreement was soon overridden, however, by a renewal of hostilities by Abū Yūsuf, who had spent the intervening months in Algeciras.

In preparation for an attack on Granada, Abū Yūsuf asked Alfonso X to supply him with 1,000 knights. However, he could only muster 600 and they preferred to keep their distance from the Marinids, thereby arousing the emir's suspicions. At the end of March 1283, Abū Yūsuf struck at Málaga and "the whole of al-Andalus was in flames." Hard-pressed, Muhammad II appealed to the emir's son Abū Yaʿqūb to mediate the situation. Realizing that it was perhaps easier and more profitable to plunder Christian territory, both sides were reconciled and agreed to ravage the land of the "idolaters." At that point the alliance between Muhammad II and Sancho was at an end.[88]

Abū Yūsuf set out from Algeciras on 29 June on another punitive expedition. The account given by Ibn Abī Zarʿ has usually been accepted, but Abū Hātim al-ʿAzafī, lord of Ceuta, in a letter to Abū Yūsuf, and the *Historia dialogada hasta 1288* provide more precise information. According to Ibn Abī Zarʿ, the emir, after plundering about Córdoba, encamped near Baeza; then in two days of forced marches through deserted regions he came to a place called *al-burt*. The word, meaning "el puerto," could refer to any of the many ports or passages through the mountains. Ambrosio Huici thought it was Talavera, a town west of Toledo, but an advance over more than one hundred and fifty miles from Baeza to Talavera seems extraordinary. *Al-burt* was surely not Talavera. Rather, the *Historia dialogada* stated clearly that the emir passed through El Puerto del Muradal (Despeñaperros) on his way to Montiel. Abū Hātim al-ʿAzafī traced the march from Córdoba to Jaén and Úbeda and then northward through difficult terrain. On the third day after crossing *al-burt* (probably following the modern highway N-IV), the Marinids attacked Montiel (a fortress belonging to the Order of Santiago) and Almedina. Returning by a different route, they assaulted Vilches and Santiesteban del Puerto before reaching their encampment near Baeza. The emir then returned to Algeciras and departed for Morocco early in November. This was Abū Yūsuf Yaʿqūb's last campaign during the reign of Alfonso X. He did not reappear in Spain until two years later.[89]

Although the Marinids failed to permanently occupy any important fortress they enriched themselves with captives, livestock, and goods of all sorts, and gained spiritual merit by participating in the holy war. As Ibn Khaldūn identified those as Abū Yūsuf's goals, one would have to say that he achieved them and undoubtedly gained fame and honor among his people as a great warrior.

The End of the Reign of Alfonso X

The Marinid invasion did not serve Alfonso X well, as it did not result in Sancho's downfall. Yet the infante's position deteriorated as his younger brothers, in the hope of gaining greater rewards, returned to their father's side. Adding to Sancho's woes, Martin IV charged him with treason, excommunicated him, and imposed an interdict on the kingdom.[90] In a codicil to his will, dated 22 January 1284, Alfonso X reiterated his condemnation of Sancho's treason and rewarded Infantes Juan and Jaime by assigning the kingdoms of Seville and Badajoz to the former and the kingdom of Murcia to the latter.[91] Meanwhile, attempts to reconcile the king and his son failed. Nevertheless, in a letter addressed to Martin IV on 23 March, Alfonso X declared that he pardoned his son and asked the pope to lift the censures against him. Soon after, on 4 April 1284, Alfonso X el Sabio died in Seville and was buried in the cathedral.[92]

The last decade of Alfonso X's reign was tumultuous. His magnates revolted and went into exile in Granada; his imperial ambitions collapsed; his oldest son and heir died, creating a succession crisis; the Marinids took advantage of his absence and invaded his realm; Nuño González de Lara and Archbishop Sancho II died attempting to halt the Marinid advance; the siege of Algeciras failed; his health steadily declined; his son Sancho rebelled against him; and the king of Granada played him false. He suffered the ultimate humiliation of having to beg for help from Abū Yūsuf, the Marinid ruler, who had invaded his kingdom three times and wrought terrible devastation. The crusading king, who had pleaded in the past for papal bulls of crusade with their attendant spiritual and financial privileges, found himself in the end allied with and dependent on a Muslim prince. Whatever hopes he had of ejecting the Moors from Spain and liberating the Holy Land were entirely shattered. Nevertheless, his son Sancho, who succeeded him, took up his plan to take possession of the ports on the Strait and to halt Marinid intrusions.

Chapter 5

Sancho IV and the Conquest of Tarifa

Sancho IV (1284–95), aged twenty-six at his accession and known to subsequent generations as "el Bravo," the Bold or the Brave, was a courageous ruler confronted by seemingly insurmountable obstacles.[1] His nephew Alfonso de la Cerda, challenged his right to rule and Pope Martin IV had excommunicated the king, placing an interdict on his kingdom and refusing to sanction his marriage to his cousin María de Molina. Thus, as their children could be regarded as illegitimate, their rights to the throne would be disputed.[2] Compounding these problems was the likelihood of a new Moroccan invasion. The Marinid threat bracketed the opening and closing years of his reign. After an initial incursion there ensued several years of peace followed by the resumption of hostilities. Given papal opposition, Sancho IV apparently did not request crusading indulgences for his wars against the Muslims. However, his success in defending his realm against the Marinids is testimony to his tenacity and his conquest of Tarifa his enduring legacy.

The Marinids and the Nasrids

When Sancho IV ascended the throne, Abū Yūsuf, the Marinid sultan, had withdrawn to Morocco. Nevertheless, as Moroccan soldiers remaining in the Peninsula committed depredations along the frontier, armies and fleets had to be readied to oppose them. Thus, it is likely that, in addition to *moneda forera* usually granted to a new king, he requested other taxes during the Cortes of Toledo in May 1284. Appealing to many places for financial aid "for this journey to the frontier," he also admonished Burgos to fulfill its obligation to send its militia to the frontier and to pay a promised 33,000 *maravedíes*.[3]

After confirming his alliance with his uncle Pedro III, the king journeyed to Córdoba where he received the submission of many of his father's adherents. Although his brother Juan was tempted to challenge him for the kingdom of Seville, which Alfonso X had awarded to him in his last will, the people acknowledged Sancho IV. In return for the city's loyalty he exempted it from all tolls and guaranteed freedom of travel to anyone transporting much needed wheat and other grains to Seville and other frontier locations. In order to better defend the frontier, he appointed an *adelantado mayor* for Andalucía and another for Murcia, as well as castellans to hold critical fortresses.[4]

Muḥammad II of Granada, worried about a long-term Moroccan presence in Spain, had entered an alliance with Infante Sancho against his father and Abū Yūsuf. However, before the death of Alfonso X, he abandoned the infante and made peace with the Marinids. Now, in the absence of Abū Yūsuf, he changed course again, declaring his vassalage to Sancho IV and promising to pay tribute. From August 1284 onward he was recorded as a vassal confirming royal privileges. As an ally of Sancho IV, Pedro III counseled Muhammad II not to align himself with Morocco.[5]

In the summer of 1284, Abū Yūsuf, the Marinid emir, who had only recently laid waste Andalucía as an ally of Alfonso X, sent to Seville to inquire about the young king's intentions. Sancho IV replied that "he had bread in one hand and a stick in the other, and if anyone should attempt to take the bread, he would strike him with the stick." Realizing that that was a signal for war, both monarchs began to make the necessary preparations. Pedro III informed his nephew that he was pleased "with what you have done with the king of Granada and the affair of Abū Yūsuf." One may presume that he was satisfied that Sancho IV had accepted the former as his vassal and had defied the latter.[6]

Sancho IV probably discussed the Marinid threat during the Cortes of Valladolid in early December. Orders were given to collect *fonsadera* and *acémilas*, a payment made instead of providing pack animals for the royal host. All the seaports were required to ready ships for war. The royal *camarero mayor*, or chamberlain, Juan Mathe de Luna, was given the task of collecting 20,000 *maravedíes* for the fleet.[7] Although the *Royal Chronicle* affirmed that the king enlisted the services of the famous Genoese admiral Benedetto Zaccaria, the *Annales Ianuenses* say nothing about this at this time. The *Chronicle* seems to have retrojected Zaccaria's employment in 1291 to 1284 when in fact he appears to have been occupied elsewhere. Thus, there is no evidence that he participated in the defense of the Strait in the early years of the reign.[8] Payo Gómez Charino held the post of *almirante de la mar* from 1284 to 1286, but his responsibility was probably more jurisdictional than naval. Effective command of the fleet may have been entrusted to Pedro Martínez de Fe, known as the *almirante de Sevilla*, even though he had failed Alfonso X in the unsuccessful siege of Algeciras.[9]

Recognizing that these military operations would necessitate substantial funds, in 1285 Sancho IV authorized Abraham el Barchilón to collect all royal revenues, including past debts owing since 1273, but excepting *fonsadera* and *moneda forera* then being collected. The nobles assembled at Burgos received their usual stipends and pledged to participate in defense of the frontier, and the towns consented to *servicios* and agreed to send their contingents to the host.[10]

The prospect of a French crusade against Aragón, however, had the potential to distract Sancho IV from the Marinid threat. In February he promised that if the Moroccans did not invade Castile, he would aid Pedro III, but if they did so, he would oppose them. In the spring when Philip III asked him not to intervene he demurred, but he also turned aside Pedro III's plea for assistance because he had to confront the Marinids. If he had sided with either of his Christian neighbors, it would probably not have been to his ultimate advantage, so neutrality may have seemed the wisest course.[11]

The Fifth Marinid Invasion

Beginning his fifth expedition into Spain, Abū Yūsuf crossed the Strait from Alcácer Seguir to Tarifa on 12 April 1285. From there he advanced to Jerez, initiating a siege that lasted until late summer. His raiding parties laid waste to Vejer de la Frontera, Medina Sidonia, Alcalá de los Gazules, Sanlúcar de Barrameda, Alcanatir, and Rota, cutting down trees, orchards, and vineyards, destroying villages, and killing or capturing many inhabitants. While he assaulted Jerez on 5–6 May, a Marinid detachment of 1,000 cavalry moved against Seville, routing the enemy sent out to oppose them. Turning eastward against Carmona and Alcalá de Guadaira, the Marinids burned the harvest and ruined trees. As additional troops arrived from Morocco, further attacks were directed against Sanlúcar, Écija, Alcalá de Guadaira, Marchena, Carmona, Rota, Arcos de la Frontera, Seville, Medina Sidonia, and Alcalá de los Gazules.

The emir attacked Jerez again on 22 May before turning against Alcanatir (El Puerto de Santa María) on 28 May, burning the suburbs, killing or capturing men, women, and children, and seizing livestock. On the last day of the month he assailed Jerez again, while dispatching his son, Abū Ya'qūb, with 5,000 regulars, 2,000 volunteer horse, 13,000 foot, and 2,000 archers (these numbers are highly inflated) to raid Seville and its environs on 1 June. During June and early July Jerez was assaulted daily while raiding parties pillaged the countryside about Carmona, Seville, Niebla, Écija, Jaén, and Sanlúcar de Barrameda. Despite this wide-ranging campaign of devastation, Jofre de Loaysa pointed out that no significant fortress or town was captured. If Jerez were to be taken, a lengthy siege, uninterrupted by Castilian assaults on the besieging army, would be required. Ibn Abī Zar', who provided an extremely detailed account of these military operations, commented that the Marinid "encampment became like a city where all sorts of craftsmen and merchants gathered.... All kinds of artisans worked their trades, except the textile workers, although there was a market for wool and cotton.... If you lost your companion in the markets, you would not find him for two or three days because there were so many people." Speaking of the Christians defending their homes, the poet Abū Fāris remarked that "they fought only to be devoured by the birds and the wolves."[12]

Although Sancho IV determined to relieve Jerez, he did not arrive at Seville until the beginning of July. Abū Yūsuf sent his son Abū Ya'qūb with 12,000 *jinetes* or light cavalry, to pillage about Seville, but the king opted not to engage them until his entire force had gathered. Fifteen days later Infante Juan, other nobles, and the military orders, in all 4,000 knights, joined him; but the town militias had not yet arrived. During a vigil of arms in the cathedral of Seville Sancho IV promised to make a pilgrimage to Santiago de Compostela. Then, informing the emir that he intended to give battle within five days, he marched toward Jerez. Abū Yūsuf reportedly had 18,000 knights, but, faced with dwindling supplies, he chose not to await the king and lifted the siege on 2 August, a little less than four months after its inception. Ibn Khaldūn dated the withdrawal at the end of September. Jofre de Loaysa, who stated that he "withdrew or rather fled" from Jerez, said that the siege lasted six months, or until October. However that may be, the hazard of a pitched battle was grave, and no doubt weighed heavily in the emir's decision. Victory, despite greater numbers, was never guaranteed.[13]

The emir also took into account the arrival at El Puerto de Santa María of a fleet of about 100 galleys and sailing ships from the Cantabrian ports. Realizing that the fleet might sever his communications with Morocco, he hastened to Tarifa. When he sent his envoy 'Abd al-Haqq to the fleet, Sancho

IV's counselor Fernán Pérez Maimón, who had organized it, showed him bread in his right hand and a stick in his left and said: "'Abd al-Haqq, tell your lord, King Abū Yūsuf, that I, Fernán Pérez Maimón, servant of my lord, King Don Sancho, say to you that the words that he said to you last year in Seville when you came to him with his [Abū Yūsuf's] mandate, are now fulfilled: I have here bread and I have here a stick." According to Ibn Abī Zar', a Marinid fleet of thirty-six warships from Ceuta, Tangier, Algeciras, Tarifa, and other ports came out to oppose the Christians, who, out of fear, sailed away. More than likely the two armadas did not join battle because peace negotiations commenced. When Sancho IV reached Jerez he wanted to give battle, but Infante Juan and Lope Díaz de Haro argued that the Marinids in effect were defeated and he should not expose his body to the risk of combat. Both sides were having difficulty in securing provisions. The king was insistent but when the magnates declared that they intended to return to Seville, he had to give in. Returning to Seville, he decided to negotiate with Abū Yūsuf, who, according to Jofre de Loaysa, sent a peace legation to him. Muhammad II did so as well.[14]

An Interval of Peace

Ibn Abī Zar' asserted that Sancho IV, seeing his kingdom ruined, his soldiers killed, his women captives, and knowing that the ships had been defeated, submitted humbly and sued for peace. Abū Yūsuf reportedly dictated the following terms:

> that you not attack any Muslim territory, nor any of their ships, nor do injury to my subjects or others whether on land or sea. In your country you will be my servant in whatever I may command you or forbid you. If Muslims journey through your land for trade or to earn their living, they will not be impeded by day or night, nor will any tribute be demanded of them; you will not interfere between Muslim kings, not even by one word, and you will not ally yourself with any of them in war.

Sancho IV probably did not bow to the emir's arrogance as Ibn Abī Zar' affirmed and certainly did not assume the servile role attributed to him. His council now debated whether to make peace with the Marinids or the Nasrids. Most argued that he should come to terms with Abū Yūsuf so that he could aid his uncle Pedro III against the French invaders. Infante Juan and Lope Díaz de Haro, on the contrary, favored a settlement with Granada. Sancho IV sensibly concluded that it was more important to alleviate the Marinid threat. Stressing that Abū Yūsuf was a man who kept his word, the Moroccan envoy 'Abd al-Haqq told the king: "You have risen unjustly against your father; you have been a perjurer, and the people have turned away from you because they have little faith in you." Sancho IV supposedly replied that he would be glad to be the emir's servant. 'Abd al-Haqq stated that "you must not intrude yourself in the affairs of the Muslims for any reason . . . and abandon any pact that you have with Ibn al-Ahmar [Muhammad II], leaving to one side his affairs, and send his ambassadors back to him."

When the Granadan emissaries asked what response they should bring home, Sancho IV affirmed that he did not intend to ally with Muhammad II, who was not his equal nor his relative, but rather one who customarily served the kings of Castile as their vassal. On the contrary, he noted that Abū Yūsuf, who ruled on both sides of the Strait, was "the only king on earth whom I fear." Ibn Abī Zar' put a lengthy speech in Sancho IV's mouth in which he purportedly admitted that both he and his father had been defeated by Abū Yūsuf and that he lacked the power to oppose him. Inasmuch as he could not defend himself against the Marinids, he asked rhetorically, "how can I defend him [Muhammad II] against others," and concluded that he would never make a treaty with Granada. Disgruntled, the Granadan envoys withdrew while preparations were begun for a meeting between Sancho IV and Abū Yūsuf.[15]

The two monarchs met on 21 October at the castle of Fuente de la Peña on the Guadalete River near Jerez. As Abū Yūsuf evidently journeyed the greater distance, that would seem to give the lie to Ibn Abī Zar''s rhetoric implying Sancho IV's abject submission. After exchanging gifts and observing the usual ceremonies, they ratified a treaty previously drafted. As Abū Yūsuf was in his seventies, Sancho IV asked that his son and heir, Abū Ya'qūb Yūsuf, should be present to ensure that the pact would be binding in the future. According to the *Royal Chronicle*, Abū Yūsuf agreed to pay 2,500,000 *maravedíes* in compensation for the damage inflicted during the campaign. That was the equivalent of the tribute of 250,000 *maravedíes* owed by the king of Granada for the ten years from 1275 when the Marinids invaded Spain. If the conditions stipulated by 'Abd al-Haqq and quoted by Ibn Abī Zar' are accurate, it would seem that the Marinid ruler was concerned lest Sancho IV enter a hostile alliance with Muhammad II and perhaps with the ruler of Tlemcen, a longtime enemy of the Marinids. The two monarchs agreed to a truce, probably for three years, and the free passage of Muslim merchants through Castilian lands, a commonplace in treaties of this era. In response to the emir's request, thirteen loads of Muslim books that had fallen into the hands of Christians and Jews were returned. Included were copies of the Koran, commentaries on the Koran, collections of traditions, books of law, grammar, and literature. The emir sent them to a school in Fez.[16] Ibn Abī Zarʿ presented this campaign as a glorious triumph for the Marinids that resulted in the humiliating submission of Sancho IV. However, they failed to take Jerez and were forced to withdraw before his advance and to pay a substantial indemnity for damages caused to his kingdom.

Although Abū Yūsuf was intent on wresting Málaga from Nasrid control, he fell ill toward the end of January 1286 and died at Algeciras on 20 March. His great achievement was the establishment of the Marinid empire in Morocco. In addition to his many wars with the emir of Tlemcen, he persuaded the king of Granada to surrender Algeciras and Tarifa so that over a period of nearly eleven years he was able to invade Spain on five occasions. His armies caused terrible destruction of property and the capture of innumerable men, women, and children who were condemned to a life of slavery. Nevertheless, his attempts to besiege Seville, Córdoba, Jaén, and Jerez were unsuccessful as circumstances compelled him to withdraw in each instance. While some small castles and villages were taken, he made no permanent conquests in the kingdom of Castile, but he did retard the development of El Puerto de Santa María and Cádiz. Although he occupied Málaga and Ronda, the Nasrids, uncertain allies determined to preserve their independence both of Castile and Morocco, were able to regain possession. Moreover, unlike the Almoravids and Almohads of an earlier time, Abū Yūsuf was unable to oust the Nasrid dynasty and to seize their kingdom.[17]

Following the suspension of hostilities, Sancho IV took steps to protect the frontier and rewarded his followers for their recent services. For example, he granted privileges to Rota "for the great harm that you received from the Moors in this war," and he thanked the Cantabrian seaport of Castrourdiales for providing "a *nave* and a galley . . . when Abū Yūsuf besieged the town of Jerez." Acknowledging the service of the knights of Alcántara, he confirmed his father's grant of Morón and Cote; he also entrusted the defense of Vejer, Medina Sidonia, and Alcalá de los Gazules to the reconstituted Order of Santiago. As the Galician towns of Santa Marta, Ferrol, Puentedeume, Vivero, La Coruña, Pontevedra, Bayona, Guarda, Lobera, and Cedeira had supplied one or more ships to the royal fleet, they were exempted from two *servicios* promised at Seville.[18]

Meantime, Abū Yūsuf's son, Abū Ya'qūb Yūsuf (1286–1307), on learning of his father's death, hastened from Morocco to Algeciras. Preoccupied by the need to establish himself firmly at home, he made peace with Muhammad II and yielded all the towns previously occupied, except Algeciras and Tarifa. After confirming the peace with Castile on 28 May and leaving 3,000 men in the Peninsula, he withdrew to Morocco.[19] Two years later, the Banū Ashqīlūlā, abandoned by both Castile and Aragón, ceded Guadix to Abū Ya'qūb in exchange for lands in Morocco. He, in turn, surrendered Guadix to Muhammad II, who had taken possession of Comares, one of the strongholds of the Banū Ashqīlūlā in 1284. They had already lost Málaga to a younger branch of the Nasrid royal family. When the Banū Ashqīlūlā crossed the Strait to Morocco a persistent thorn in the side of the kings of Granada was finally removed.[20]

In 1288 when Sancho IV renewed the truce with Morocco he agreed to provide Abū Ya'qūb with 300 knights.[21] In order to meet this expense he levied a *moneda* and thanked Seville for consenting to it.[22] As Christian knights had long served the Almohads and the Marinids, there was nothing unusual about this request. Abū Ya'qūb probably needed the knights to confront domestic challenges to his rule and to oppose the emirs of Tlemcen. As it was apparent that he did not intend to continue his father's aggressive policy in Spain and greatly reduced his involvement in peninsular affairs, the frontier remained at peace for several years.

Intent on concentrating his power against Tlemcen, Abū Ya'qūb also reached out to Alfonso III, the new king of Aragón (1285–91), offering to provide him with 2,000 men on condition that he remain at peace with the king of Granada and the lord of Ceuta. The emir, who regarded them as his vassals, was wary of possible Aragonese designs on Ceuta. Suggesting an alliance, Alfonso III advocated a policy of free trade and security for merchants and their property, and proposed to supply the emir with five to ten galleys in exchange for 500 knights. However, as he was not prepared to make peace with Muhammad II and the emir was unwilling to upset peaceful relations prevailing among Morocco, Granada, and Castile, no treaty was signed.[23] When negotiations with Morocco collapsed, Alfonso III, in 1287, concluded an alliance against the Marinids with 'Uthmān, the emir of Tlemcen.[24]

Alfonso III, seeing a rapprochement between France and Castile as a threat to his own throne, and annoyed by Sancho IV's failure to aid his father during the French Crusade, turned against him.[25] In 1288 he proclaimed Alfonso de la Cerda as king of Castile and persuaded him to cede titular possession of the kingdom of Murcia.[26] If he could occupy it, he would have direct access to Granada and the possibility of further conquest of Muslim lands. For the moment, however, he convinced Muhammad II to participate in a coalition against Castile.[27] As a countermeasure, Sancho IV induced Philip IV of France (1285–1314) to withdraw his support of Alfonso de la Cerda and to collaborate against Aragón, now viewed as the common enemy.[28] Thwarted on every side, Alfonso III made peace with France in 1291. However, his death soon after and the accession of his brother, Jaime II (1291–1327), fundamentally altered Castilian-Aragonese relations. When ambassadors from Granada and Morocco inquired of his intentions, Jaime II put them off with a request for further information. Indeed, from the outset he determined that the future of his kingdom lay in peninsular expansion at Nasrid expense. Thus, he decided to join Castile in an assault on Granada.[29]

A New Offensive Against the Marinids

As his truce with Morocco expired in 1291, Sancho IV, no longer fearful of France or Aragón, decided to take Algeciras from the Marinids. In preparation, he ordered collection of *fonsadera* and *acémilas*.[30] In May, Muhammad II, who had as much reason to be afraid of the Marinids as anyone, renewed his vassalage and the payment of tribute to Castile, but he was also prepared to change sides if that seemed beneficial. As Sancho IV made a pilgrimage to Santiago de Compostela to request the saint's blessing on his projected offensive, Marinid troops were beginning to cross the Strait.[31]

Anticipating that eventuality, the king organized a fleet and contracted with the Genoese mariner Benedetto Zaccaria at a monthly salary of 6,000 *maravedíes*. Sailing from Genoa on 19 March with seven galleys, he joined five others at Seville. Then, on 6 August, he won a major victory over twenty-seven Marinid galleys at Marzamosa or Qasr Masmuda off Alcácer Seguir; twelve galleys were taken and the rest put to flight. On the following day he dragged the captured vessels along the coast in view of the emir, who, "defeated and dishonored," withdrew to Fez. Ibn Abī Zarʿ briefly mentioned the defeat and Ibn Khaldūn declared that "God wished to test the Muslims."[32]

Although Zaccaria's victory halted the transfer of troops from Morocco for the time being, the second stage in the campaign began in late September. Abū Yaʿqūb, after readying new ships and armaments, crossed the Strait from

Alcácer Seguir to Tarifa, apparently without hindrance. As none of the sources refers to any attempt to intercept him, it seems reasonable to suppose that Zaccaria had returned to Genoa. If he had been employed for six months beginning in March, that term would have ended in August. However that may be, during the next three months the Marinids besieged Vejer de la Frontera and carried out daily raids around Jerez and as far north as Alcalá del Río near Seville.[33]

Sancho IV took a number of steps to counteract the Marinid offensive. In a pact with King Dinis of Portugal, on 15 September, he arranged the marriage of his son and heir, Fernando, with Dinis's daughter, Constanza. Nothing was said of military collaboration against the Muslims, but the statement that the treaty would lead "to the great confusion and destruction of the enemies of the faith" seems to imply as much.[34]

Sancho IV also benefited from the renewal of amicable relations with Aragón. Resolved that he had little to gain from continuing enmity toward Castile, in September Jaime II offered peace and friendship and ordered the cessation of hostilities on behalf of Alfonso de la Cerda.[35] He also renewed the alliance of his predecessors with Muhammad II, who pledged 100 *jinetes* for three months' service against his Christian enemies. On the other hand, complaining of Moroccan acts of piracy against Catalan ships, Jaime II refused any Marinid alliance.[36]

The kings of Castile and Aragón met at Monteagudo on 28 November 1291 and on the following day concluded a treaty of friendship.[37] Meeting again at nearby Soria on 1 December, they acknowledged that by reason of dissension among Christians, "Spain was divided and the Moors, the enemies of the faith, were emboldened and strengthened in their desire to conquer it and to expel and uproot the holy faith of Our Lord Jesus Christ and to spread and plant the barbaric sect." Pledging mutual aid, they agreed to delimit their respective spheres of influence and potential conquest in North Africa. The river Mulawiya, near the modern boundary between Morocco and Algeria, marked off the zones set aside for each one; thus expansion into Morocco was reserved for Castile, while Algeria and Tunisia fell to Aragón. The pact was sealed by the betrothal of Jaime II and Sancho IV's daughter Isabel, then only eight years of age. Although they were related within the prohibited degrees of kindred and no papal dispensation had been obtained, their marriage was justified because "Christendom was never in greater peril than it is now."[38] In addition to the loss of Tripoli and Acre in the Holy Land, marking the effective end of the crusader states there, the two monarchs noted that "the Moors of Africa had transferred into Spain as many as 15,000 men on horseback or more with the king of Morocco and they were conquering the land with great power." "Fired," therefore, "by a love for the Christian faith," they determined to defend themselves against the infidels. Should they be needed, Jaime II promised to provide Castile with twenty galleys at his own expense for four months.[39]

While Jaime II gave Sancho IV full power to negotiate the resolution of outstanding issues among Aragón, France, and the papacy, Sancho IV similarly authorized him to arrange an accord with Morocco. Jaime II had already notified his subjects living there to leave because he expected to support Castile against the Marinids. He also informed Muhammad II on 1 December that he would observe all the Nasrid's agreements with Castile.[40] While the kings of Aragón and Castile were feasting at Calatayud, ambassadors of the emir of Tlemcen arrived and pledged to make war against the Marinids.[41] At that time Sancho IV received word that Abū Ya'qūb, faced with difficulties of supply, had abandoned the siege of Vejer after three months and had withdrawn to Algeciras and then to Morocco on 24 December.[42]

Preparations for the Siege of Tarifa

Early in 1292, Sancho IV, at peace with France and Aragón and allied with Portugal, Granada, and Tlemcen, determined to take decisive action to undercut the continuing Marinid threat to Andalucía. The fall of Acre to the Muslims in 1291, however, presented a potential distraction as Pope Nicholas IV (1288–92) summoned the Christian world to a crusade. In accordance with his directive ordering the convocation of councils for the liberation of the Holy Land, Archbishop Gonzalo of Toledo summoned a provincial council at Valladolid to meet in April 1292, but there is no surviving documentation relating to it.[43] If the bishops did assemble, they likely agreed that the war in Spain was of more immediate concern than the crusade to the Holy Land; whether they declared that one could gain the crusading indulgence by participating in the upcoming campaign against the Marinids is unknown, but it is possible. Neither they nor the king had any intention of diverting Castilian funds to the Holy Land, however; indeed in February the pope complained that he had received nothing from Spain. Lest there be any doubt about the relative importance of the wars against Islam in the east and in the west, Sancho IV, on 21 April, asked the Leonese bishops in a provincial council at Santiago de Compostela to pray for his army soon to besiege to Algeciras. He was convinced that his journey to the frontier would redound to "the service of God and the benefit and honor of all of Christendom."[44]

In order to finance the campaign the king, as Francisco García Fitz pointed out, drew on three principal sources: (1) a *servicio* granted by the prelates in November 1291; (2) the *fonsadera*, and (3) three *servicios* contributed by the towns in 1292.[45] Meeting at Medina del Campo in November 1291, the bishops authorized 1,400,000 *maravedíes* for the siege of Algeciras, thereby enabling him to equip a large fleet in the ports of Castile, Asturias, and Galicia. He also used the annual *servicio* granted at the Cortes of Haro in 1288 for a term of ten years to pay the stipends of the nobility.[46] The sum of 274,535 *maravedíes* was collected as *fonsadera* in the four dioceses of Palencia, Burgos, Calahorra, and Segovia. Data concerning about two dozen other bishoprics in León, Extremadura, and parts of Castile are lacking.[47] The levy of *fonsadera* evoked considerable protest because royal officials ignored exemptions.[48]

After visiting the Marian shrine of Villa Sirga near Burgos, celebrated in several of his father's *Cantigas*, Sancho IV in April asked the towns for three *servicios* to maintain the siege of Algeciras. Although the *Royal Chronicle* reported that they did so easily, that seems astonishing because the three *servicios* seem to have been in addition to the annual tax granted at Haro in 1288. On the other hand, the Moroccan threat was a very real one and it would have been difficult to raise strenuous objections to his plea.[49] The amount collected was 1,455,588 *maravedíes*. Of that 1,117,851 was derived from six bishoprics and 337,737 from thirteen towns. As that figure reflects only the sums recorded from a limited number of bishoprics and towns, the total amount was likely a good deal higher. García Fitz has provided tables illustrating these resources and some of the expenses involved. Loans by various individuals also have to be included. Given the incomplete status of royal accounts, all of these sums are approximations.[50]

The money collected was used for a variety of expenses, principally for the maintenance of an army and a fleet, though the documentation does not assign specific quantities for these purposes.[51] On the other hand, by the end of 1292 the king received 35,400 *maravedíes* of the 54,000 due from the bishoprics of Palencia, Calahorra, and Burgos for siege engines and weapons that he had ordered made in Castile. Two separate payments of 11,244 and 24,000 *maravedíes* were received to transport siege engines from the northern ports to Seville.[52] Moreover, at a cost of 2,056 *maravedíes*, the king commissioned the construction of a galley with 130 oars, and thus of considerable size.[53]

The Conquest of Tarifa

As Abū Ya'qūb's forces renewed their depredations along the frontier in the spring of 1292, Sancho IV appealed in vain to Dinis of Portugal for financial assistance. Jaime II, however, dispatched ten galleys to Seville and instructed their commander to aid Castile or to reach an accord with Abū Ya'qūb. After discussion with Sancho IV, the possibility of negotiating with Morocco was shelved.[54] The king, who hastened to Seville at the end of May, initially planned to besiege Algeciras,[55] as Archbishop Rodrigo of Santiago affirmed when he announced that he had been summoned "to the army which [the king] was organizing against Algeciras." The king changed his mind, however, and opted to go against Tarifa at the tip of the Peninsula just opposite Morocco. He commented that "his cavalry would be able to make a better sally there when the Moors came over."[56] Ibn Khaldūn declared that Muhammad II, fearful of Marinid ambitions, made a secret agreement with Sancho IV:

> In that conference they recognized at once that the sultan had great facilities to invade Spain: the Strait was not wide; the fortresses that defended both sides belonged to him; and even without a fleet at his disposition he could maintain communications between the two countries by means of galleys and other vessels. They agreed, therefore, that of all those strongholds Tarifa was the most important and if they could take it, it would serve as a vantage point to dominate the Strait and a harbor for a fleet capable of battling against all the ships that the ports of the Maghrib might put to sea.[57]

Meantime, María de Molina gathered necessary supplies at Seville and asked the Franciscans and Dominicans "to pray to God for the king while he is before Tarifa."[58] Military contingents summoned by bishops, nobles, military orders, and towns, as well as armed galleys from the ports on the Bay of Biscay, began to appear before Tarifa after the feast of St. John (24 June). Esteban Bernáldez, "capitán mayor en la mar por nuestro sennor el rey," was probably one of several Castilian mariners participating in the siege. According to the *Annales Ianuenses*, Benedetto Zaccaria was "general and supreme admiral," commanding not only the ten Catalan ships but also an unspecified number of Genoese galleys.[59] Utilizing eleven newly built engines of war, the Christians bombarded Tarifa constantly by land and by sea. At the same time, while the emir of Tlemcen ravaged eastern Morocco, Muhammad II provided the army besieging Tarifa with men, arms, and victuals, and aided the blockade of the Strait. Attacking Marinid outposts, his forces seized Estepona on the coast to the west of Málaga.[60]

Tarifa fell to the Christians after a siege of four months. The besieging forces broke into the suburb on 20 August 1292 and took the town by force on the feast of St. Matthew, 21 September. Following the usual custom, the defenders, after capitulating, were given safe conduct and allowed to depart carrying their movable goods. The *Annales Ianuenses* stated that more than 3,000 men at arms defended the place and nearly 8,000 men, women and children were found there. By contrast, the number of Christian knights was 664.[61] The victors made their entrance on 13 October.[62]

Neither the *Royal Chronicle* nor the other sources explicitly stated whether Sancho IV participated in the siege, but there are ample gaps in the royal itinerary during which he could have been there. The *Royal Chronicle* emphasized that he labored with "such great toil and hardship that was the start of the illness that he had later and of which he died."[63] Surely he made a triumphal entrance into Tarifa once it was taken. Obviously elated by his success, he dated his *Libro de los castigos*, dedicated to his son Infante Fernando, "in the year when, with the help of God, I won Tarifa from the Moors who had held it for six hundred years since King Rodrigo, the last king of the Goths, lost it on account of the wickedness and abominable treason of the evil Count Don Julian." Spanish historiography had long attributed Rodrigo's defeat at Muslim hands in 711 to the treachery of Count Julian, who supposedly facilitated the Muslim invasion. The king's statement that "a Moor is nothing more than a dog" perhaps reflects his assessment of his great rivals Muhammad II and Abū Ya'qūb.[64]

Archbishop García of Seville consecrated the mosque of Tarifa as a Christian church. Rodrigo Pérez Ponce, the master of Calatrava, one of the king's close confidants, was assigned 2,000,000 *maravedíes* annually to defend Tarifa. Recognizing the necessity of protecting the Strait against a new attack from Morocco, the king covered the expense of maintaining a fleet there for two months. Tarifa, "a sentinel on the Strait guarding against African invasions," was, in the words of Mercedes Gaibrois, Sancho IV's most important contribution to the centuries-old work of reconquest.[65]

Soon afterward, while expressing his pleasure at the news that Tarifa had fallen, Jaime II announced that he would pay the expenses of ten Catalan galleys for two months and that he had instructed his commanders not to withdraw from the Strait until Sancho IV authorized them to do so. Even so, the king of Aragón was financially strapped, as he asked María de Molina for a loan of 500,000 *maravedíes*; he promised to repay her from booty seized in the Aegean. Given Castile's own financial situation, it seems unlikely the queen could make such a loan.[66]

Sancho IV's elation following his victory was dampened in December when Muhammad II's ambassadors asked him to surrender Tarifa. The Nasrid king apparently believed that Tarifa, once part of his realm but occupied by the Marinids, should now be restored to him. Ibn Khaldūn related that when the two kings met prior to the campaign Sancho IV pledged to cede Tarifa as remuneration for Nasrid collaboration. Reporting the same promise, Ibn Abī Zarʿ stated that Muhammad II offered to trade six castles for Tarifa.[67] In the following March, Sancho IV, addressing the prelates of his realm, emphasized that the fall of Tarifa distressed both Abū Yaʿqūb and Muhammad II because "it was the best and the most secure passage that they had to our land." On that account they offered many castles and money in exchange for it. As he had conquered it "for [God's] service, our great honor, and for all the people of our realm," he declared that he would not yield Tarifa to "the power of the enemies of the faith," no matter what they offered.[68] The king of Granada may have misunderstood the terms of his agreement with Sancho IV, or the latter may have deceived him or may have reneged on his pledge once Tarifa was in his hands. Muhammad II's intense reaction when his demand was rejected would seem to confirm his understanding that Tarifa had been promised to him and that Sancho IV, by refusing to hand it over, had betrayed him.[69]

Diplomatic Alterations

Given the hostile reaction in both Granada and Morocco, the defense of Tarifa became Sancho IV's primary concern. Meeting Jaime II at Guadalajara in January 1293, he enlisted his aid in dealing with the Moors.[70] Hoping to ease the situation, Jaime II urged Muhammad II not to turn against Castile, but rather to maintain the love that "ought to exist between a lord and a very good and most honored vassal." He also attempted to mediate a settlement with Abū Yaʿqūb which would have secured the Castilian grip on Tarifa.[71]

Celebrating his recent triumph, Sancho IV summoned the Cortes to Valladolid in May 1293. He lauded the "great services" that he received from the knights and good men of the municipalities of Andalucía, León, Castile, and Murcia especially when "Abū Yūsuf and Abū Ya'qūb, his son, besieged Jerez two times and we went in our person and lifted the siege, and also . . . the service that they rendered to us in the siege of Tarifa." He also thanked them for protecting "our sovereignty against the wicked and false moves that Infante Don Juan made against us." The king's brother, who had always been a thorn in his side and had recently rebelled, took refuge in Portugal before the year was out. The bad blood between them would manifest itself again in a more brutal way. Aside from attending to the petitions of the assembly, the king stressed that he had had great need of the sixth *servicio* for the "journey to Tarifa."[72]

Meanwhile, Muhammad II, angered by Sancho IV's refusal to surrender Tarifa, resolved to repair his frayed relationship with Morocco. Assured that Abū Ya'qūb would welcome him, he crossed the Strait to Ceuta and met Abū Ya'qūb at Tangier on 24 October.[73] Muhammad II, bearing many gifts, including an exemplar of the Koran from the era of the Umayyad caliphs of Córdoba, asked forgiveness for his earlier hostility. Pledging friendship, the two monarchs agreed to collaborate in a future siege of Tarifa. A month later, Muhammad II, accompanied by a troop of Marinid soldiers, returned home. While Ibn Abī Zar' reported that the Marinid emir surrendered to Muhammad II Algeciras, Ronda, and some twenty-one castles between Ronda and the valley of the Guadiaro River, Ibn Khaldūn affirmed just the opposite, namely, that Muhammad II restored these fortified positions (of which he had gained control) to the Marinids. Indeed, there is little reason to believe that the Marinids, following the loss of Tarifa, would give up control of Algeciras, the only port giving them access to the Peninsula. Sancho IV himself reported that Muhammad II yielded "Algeciras and Ronda and their castles" to the Marinids so that they could come to his aid.[74]

Troubled by news of the coalition between Granada and Morocco, Sancho IV and Jaime II took military and diplomatic steps to defend the Strait. While the former asked the ports on the Bay of Biscay to arm eleven galleys, the latter promised to provide another fifteen.[75] Sancho IV hoped to impede any accommodation between the Muslim powers, and Jaime II, anxious to restore everything to good estate, again offered to mediate between Granada and Castile. Although Gaibrois suggested that his words were insincere, one need not draw that conclusion.[76] Nevertheless, Castilian relations with Aragón and Portugal seemed to become lukewarm, chiefly because Sancho IV was thought to be aligning himself too closely with France. The withdrawal of Catalan ships from the Strait at the end of 1293 after three months' service appeared to suggest that Jaime II was distancing himself from Castile. If the ships were still needed, he argued, Castile would have to pay the cost. After receiving payment, he ordered the preparation of the galleys and encouraged traitors, counterfeiters, and highwaymen, in return for a royal pardon, to volunteer for service. He also prohibited the export of weapons and food to the Moors and prepared to send fifteen ships to "combat the perfidious Saracens." And yet he also limited the number of ships to be armed for Castilian service.[77]

Preparations for the Defense of Tarifa

In preparation for the expected Muslim offensive, Sancho IV took several measures, spiritual, military, and financial. As the papacy refused to legitimate his marriage and his children, he had little expectation of obtaining a new bull of crusade. Moreover, the death of Pope Nicholas IV in April 1292 was followed by an interregnum lasting until the election of Celestine V in July 1294. As the papal throne was vacant, the king trotted out an old bull issued by Innocent IV in 1246 authorizing the archbishop of Seville to preach a crusade against the Muslims.[78]

The king's most important act was to entrust the defense of Tarifa to Alfonso Pérez de Guzmán. Since 1279 he had commanded Christian militias in the service of the Marinid emirs. They were soldiers of fortune, mostly from Castile.[79] Having returned home in July 1291, Alfonso Pérez offered to hold Tarifa as its *alcaide* for 600,000 *maravedíes*. The royal accounts record only that he received 120,000 *maravedíes* as his *soldadas*, or wage. At the end of August 1293, envoys from 'Uthmān, the emir of Tlemcen, arrived at court and likely renewed the alliance against the Marinids.[80]

The task of financing the defense of Tarifa was enormous but the king was fortunate to have the services of a capable moneyman, Juan Mathe de Luna, the *camarero mayor*. His accounts for the period December 1293 to June 1294 reveal that he collected 515,792 *maravedíes* chiefly from bishops, clergy, Moors, and Jews in frontier communities. He also reported expenses totaling 27,624 *maravedíes* for salaries for tax collectors, messengers, pack animals, sacks, ropes, and straw. The main expense, 687,440 *maravedíes*, was for the maintenance of the fleet (oars, arms, wheat, wood, bacon, cheese, beans, chickpeas, and so on). The fleet included three Genoese galleys commanded by Micer Rufin, a subordinate of Benedetto Zaccaria. Men and provisions for twelve frontier castles (food, lookouts, guards, sentries, porters, spies, footmen, cavalry, and *almogávares* (skilled raiders, lightly armed) amounted to 261,843 *maravedíes*. Salaries for various commanders, crossbowmen, and squires came to 19,831 *maravedíes*. An additional 21,050 *maravedíes* (not all related to defense) was expended on various matters (naval armaments, mules, horses, messengers, and so on) and still another 1,366 *maravedíes* on messengers. The sum of all these expenses during this critical period was 1,534,946 *maravedíes*, a million more than the revenue he collected. As royal accounts are haphazard and incomplete, one cannot provide an accurate balance sheet.[81] The queen also ordered two ships, laden respectively with 2,500 and 1,700 *quintales* of iron (a *quintal* was about 100 pounds) and 90 *quintales* of hemp fiber to be sent to Seville, probably for outfitting the fleet.[82]

In order to raise necessary revenue, late in 1293 the king levied the *sisa*, a tax on commercial transactions that proved to be immensely unpopular.[83] In addition to the annual *servicio* promised for ten years by the Cortes of Haro, he also collected *fonsadera* and *acémilas*.[84]

In March 1294 at Valladolid he requested financial aid from the prelates, reminding them that Muhammad II and Abū Ya'qūb were determined to wage "the most forceful and vigorous war" by sea and by land to recover Tarifa. To oppose them, he planned to set out for the frontier with a great host and had sent to Aragón to secure twenty-five galleys; another twenty were being readied at Seville. Trusting that his actions would serve God, Christendom, and his realm, he pleaded with the prelates to provide him with large quantities of money by the following May and requested a specific amount from each one.[85]

The total was 734,000 *maravedíes*. The varying sums are indicative of the comparative wealth of each see. The contributions of several other bishoprics do not appear in these accounts, for example, Túy, Astorga, Cádiz, and Cartagena. In February, the king demanded 140,600 *maravedíes* from forty-two religious houses and an additional 10,000 from the Order of the Holy Sepulchre.[86] If all the bishoprics and monasteries paid the amount requested, he could expect 984,600 *maravedíes*. However, some, including the archbishop of Santiago, evidently failed to do so; thus, the king ordered the sale of archiepiscopal property in order to make up the necessary sum.[87]

The Defense of Tarifa

Early in 1294 Abū Ya'qūb sent a Marinid army to Spain to lay siege to Tarifa. Manzano Rodríguez emphasized that this hardly represented a major

Figure 3. Muslims besiege a Christian town. *Cantigas de Santa Maria*, 99. Escorial, MS T.I.l.

commitment on the part of the emir, who remained in Fez and made no attempt personally to intervene in the Peninsula. Ibn Abī Zarʿ made the excuse that Morocco was ravaged by famine and plague.[88]

However that may be, the Moroccan forces probably did not initiate the siege until an unexpected collaborator arrived. While preparing to defend the frontier, Sancho IV determined that he could not risk the continued presence of his rebellious brother Juan in Portugal and asked King Dinis to compel him to leave. The *Royal Chronicle* reported that Juan boarded a ship in Lisbon bound for France but contrary winds drove the vessel to Tangier. That seems unlikely. Gaibrois suggested that in the spring of 1293 Dinis sent his envoys to Morocco to prepare the way for Infante Juan. Informed of his arrival, Abū Yaʿqūb decided to enlist him in the siege of Tarifa. Lest he be detained in Morocco, Juan, who was anxious to avenge himself on his brother, accepted the emir's proposal. Supplied with horses and provisions for himself and his vassals and a troop of 5,000 *jinetes* or light cavalry, he crossed to Spain in late April or early May 1294 to collaborate with the Marinids in the siege of Tarifa.[89]

Alfonso Pérez de Guzmán, the *alcaide* of Tarifa, was in charge of the defense. His young son, Pedro Alfonso, had fallen into the hands of Infante Juan, who threatened to execute him if his father failed to surrender the town. Alfonso Pérez refused, saying that he had pledged homage to the king to hold Tarifa and would not surrender it even if his other five sons were in the infante's power. Indeed, he said he would give him a knife to kill his son and then, in an act of hard-hearted bravado, threw a knife down from the wall. Angered by this show of defiance, Juan ordered the boy to be murdered in cold blood before his father's eyes. Yet, as the *Royal Chronicle* commented, "with all that, he could not take the town."[90]

By putting the chivalric principle of fidelity to one's lord before his paternal duty to love his son, Alfonso Pérez gained the sobriquet "El Bueno" and was rewarded by the crown for his heroism. The *alcázar* of Tarifa today is called the Castillo de Guzmán el Bueno and his statue stands at the entrance.[91] While one may admire his steadfast loyalty to the king, it must be said that the language employed by Gaibrois to describe his action is excessive. She wrote of "the most glorious deed of this loyal knight"; "the supreme heroism achieved by this immortal noble"; "his stoicism of classic moral beauty"; "this glorious episode"; and the "heroic sacrifice" of the "sublime defender of Tarifa." Most astounding is her reference to this "martyr father." Perhaps Alfonso Pérez de Guzmán thought that Infante Juan would not dare to murder his son. Surely he was shocked when he witnessed the crime, but if anyone should be called a martyr it is his son.[92]

While the siege was in progress, Jaime II continued his diplomacy with Granada and Morocco. Articulating his concern about the discord between Granada and Castile, in April he urged Muhammad II to resolve his differences with Sancho IV. A little more than two months later when Abū Ya'qūb offered to come to terms, Jaime II promised to send an envoy to suggest ways of making peace beneficial to all. A settlement became urgent in August when Castilian and Catalan ships arrived and threatened to cut off the Moroccans from their lines of retreat.[93]

Ibn Abī Zar' emphasized that shortages of food, the high price of wheat, and the spread of disease also contributed to the decision to abandon the siege after four months. According to the *Royal Chronicle*, Abū Ya'qūb, fearing that Sancho IV would then move against Algeciras, yielded it to the king of Granada to defend as best he could. The emir, as Manzano Rodríguez put it, effectively abandoned any political aspirations in the Peninsula. It is notable that neither Abū Ya'qūb, nor Muhammad II, nor Sancho IV personally took part in the siege of Tarifa.[94]

Preparations for the Siege of Algeciras

Although Alfonso Pérez de Guzmán traditionally has been hailed as the hero of the defense of Tarifa, Gaibrois rightly pointed out that without the labors of Juan Mathe de Luna, *camarero mayor*, and Fernán Pérez Maimón, *canciller del seello de la poridad* (chancellor of the privy seal), the outcome might have been quite different. While the former raised the necessary funds, Fernán Pérez was largely responsible for securing galleys from Catalonia and from the Vizcayan seaports to blockade the Strait. Within a few weeks after the siege of Tarifa was lifted, on 17 September, the two men presented the king with a plan to secure control of the Strait. The objective was to seize Algeciras, now in the hands of Muhammad II. If the siege were begun by land and by sea by the first of May of the following year, they argued, Algeciras could be taken within three or four months, that is, by the end of the summer. Once Algeciras was in Christian hands, the coast would be safeguarded against its enemies on both sides of the Strait. Moreover, the maintenance of a permanent fleet in the Strait at enormous expense would not be necessary; only a few ships would be needed for defense. In order to accomplish this task, Jaime II would have to allow his galleys to remain in the Strait at least until March and indeed through the summer, if that were possible.[95]

In practical terms the siege would require a fleet of thirty well-armed galleys, twenty from Aragón and ten from Seville. An army recruited from the magnates and their vassals, as well as the municipal militias of Extremadura and León would also be needed. The two royal counselors urged the king to make a personal plea for the assistance of the towns, rejecting any excuses. The army should be organized in two *quadrillas*, or troops, the first to blockade Algeciras by land, the other to attempt the capture of two or three other places. All should be in readiness by 1 April so that the siege could begin by land and by sea on 1 May. If the blockade were effective and all supply lines were cut off, hunger and want would compel the defenders to capitulate.

After outlining the plan of attack, Juan Mathe and Fernán Pérez summarized the cost of the entire operation. The expense of the thirty galleys for six months from April to September would be 1,440,000 *maravedíes*. Each galley would cost 8,000 per month, or 240,000 per month for all thirty. Siege engines would cost an additional 250,000 for six months. Thus the total for ships and war machines would amount to 1,690,000 *maravedíes*; the text incorrectly states this as 1,790,000.

Next, they estimated the expense of maintaining the fleet for six months from October 1294 through the winter to 1 April. Included were fifteen Catalan galleys together with wages, bread, oil, and meats costing 120,000 *maravedíes* each month, or a total of 720,000 for six months; three Genoese galleys at a monthly cost of 30,000 for eight months (August through March) amounted to 240,000; and nine galleys from Seville, costing 63,000 each month, for seven months (September through March) would require 441,000. The sum total was 1,401,000 *maravedíes*, but the document gave it as 1,463,000.[96]

Finally, the king's counselors detailed other essential needs. Personnel included 100 seamen, two masters to emblazon shields and helmets, and four Jews to make *perpuntes* or military jackets. Provisions included: 200 clubs for throwing (*porras que luego sean lanzadas*); as many *fojas* as are available (these were probably sheets of iron used as armament); 100 pairs of coats-of-mail (*lameras*); 240 swords and knives; javelins (*gorgueces*); 360 lances; 260 darts or bolts; 100 crossbows; twine for 100 cords, probably for crossbows; 20 *arcos de saetas de estribera*, and 20 *arcos de saetas de dos pies* (the former was held down by a stirrup while a cord was drawn back and locked into place; the latter was held on the ground with both feet); tillers (*pendones*); 10 *quintales* or 1,000 pounds of nails; 36 *arrobas* or 900 pounds of pitch (*pes*) or tar (an *arroba* was about 25 pounds); 12 *arrobas* or 300 pounds of burlap (*estopa*); 50 *arrobas* or 1,250 pounds of tallow for caulking (*sevo para despalmar*); tackle or rigging (*jarcia*); 8 yards (*entenas*) to which lateen sails were affixed;[97] and 10,000 *arrobas* or 250,000 pounds of biscuit (*bizcocho*), costing 20,000 *maravedíes* each month.[98]

The king, apparently agreeing to act on these recommendations, ordered preparations to begin in the following year and rewarded Juan Mathe de Luna and Fernán Pérez Maimón for their endeavors by giving each man the title *almirante de la mar*.[99] At the end of the year he ordered a bull of Clement IV (issued on 26 June 1265) authorizing the archbishop of Seville to preach the crusade to be copied with the evident intention of utilizing it for the siege of Algeciras. The king probably had little expectation of obtaining a new crusading bull from Pope Celestine V, who was elected on 7 July but resigned on 12 December.[100] In order to attract settlers the king granted numerous financial exemptions to Tarifa.[101] He also rewarded Admiral Benedetto Zaccaria with lordship of half of El Puerto de Santa María on condition that he always maintain an armed galley to defend the maritime approaches to Seville. Alfonso Pérez de Guzmán purchased the other half and later gave it as a dowry to his daughter Leonor when she married Don Luis de la Cerda. Micer Bonavena (or Bonavía), another Genoese, was *alcaide* of El Puerto de Santa María for Guzmán el Bueno.[102]

While Castile readied for war, letters of credentials given by Jaime II to his emissaries suggest an active correspondence between the two kings. Although these documents tell us nothing of the subjects under discussion, one may suppose that the continuance of Catalan ships in the Strait in preparation for the siege of Algeciras was high on the list.[103] Writing to Muhammad II, Abū Yaʿqūb, and Abū Hātim, the ʿAzafid lord of Ceuta, Jaime II reminded them of the friendship that had long existed between their houses.[104] As the new year approached, Sancho IV's health deteriorated steadily, so that Jaime II proposed a meeting with María de Molina, probably to resolve issues concerning his marriage to her daughter Isabel, the projected siege of Algeciras, and so forth. In Dufourcq's judgment Jaime II had been reluctant to send his ships in support of the Castilian defense of Tarifa, but if he failed to collaborate in the attack on Algeciras he risked losing the friendship of his father-in-law. After the withdrawal of the Marinids, he was anxious to assure both Muslim rulers that he wished to maintain friendly relations with them. This was important not only to foster Catalan trade in North Africa but also to discourage any support that Granada or Morocco might give to the Mudéjars of Valencia. His attempt to juggle these disparate interests was viewed negatively in Castile and contributed to a growing estrangement that María de Molina may have hoped to resolve by meeting with him.[105]

The Death of Sancho IV

Sancho IV fell ill early in 1295 and died in Toledo on 25 April at thirty-six, leaving the throne to his nine-year-old son, Fernando IV. In his will he entrusted the boy and the defense of the realm to the care of his mother, María de Molina. He also extracted a promise from Juan Núñez de Lara, the younger, to loyally defend his son's rights to the throne. A few weeks before his death he spoke to his first cousin Juan Manuel, urging him to support Queen María and to conduct himself as a loyal vassal toward the new king. Perhaps he expected trouble from the brother who had so often opposed him, "that sinner Infante Juan who is lost wandering in the land of the Moors."[106] While the king had extended a warm welcome to his uncle Infante Enrique, who had spent many years abroad in North Africa and Italy and had just been released by the Angevins of Naples after twenty-six years in prison, his return to Spain boded ill for the future.[107]

    Sancho IV had ascended the throne under difficult circumstances but succeeded in retaining his position in the face of strong opposition. With that bravado that gained him his sobriquet, El Bravo, he met the challenge of a Marinid invasion and compelled the emir Abū Yūsuf to abandon his campaign. Several years later he took the initiative and seized the important seaport of Tarifa after a siege of several months. Then he organized the defense of Tarifa against an attempt by Marinid forces and Infante Juan to recover possession. As a consequence, Abū Ya'qūb withdrew from the Peninsula, leaving Muhammad II of Granada to fend for himself, and did not reappear until the following reign. Sancho IV could be pleased that he had expelled the power of the Marinids beyond the sea. His conquest and defense of Tarifa was the first step toward closing the gates of the Peninsula to future Moroccan invasions. Secure in his grasp of Tarifa, the king planned an assault on Algeciras, but death cut short his plans and the minority of his son prevented any further action for more than seven years.

Chapter 6

The Crusades of Gibraltar, Almería, and Algeciras

As the thirteenth century waned, the struggle to command the Strait took second place to the effort to secure the throne for the boy king, Fernando IV (1295–1312).[1] After he reached adulthood, he joined Jaime II of Aragón in a crusade against the kingdom of Granada. Although Fernando IV captured Gibraltar in 1309, he had to abandon the siege of Algeciras and Jaime II similarly failed to take Almería. Fernando IV resumed his crusade against Algeciras, but his untimely death and the minority of his son once again interrupted Castilian efforts to seize control of the Strait. Gibraltar, his principal conquest, remained in Christian hands for not quite a quarter of a century.[2]

The Frontier and the Anti-Castilian Coalition

The accession of Fernando IV, nine years of age, threw Castile into turmoil that lasted until he achieved his majority in 1301. While keeping custody of his person, his mother, María de Molina, a woman of great prudence and common sense, had to yield guardianship of the realm to Infante Enrique, a younger brother of Alfonso X, now returned home after many years of exile and imprisonment.

Meantime, a sense of unease prevailed along the frontier as the towns realized that a royal minority left them vulnerable to Muslim attack. As a means of mutual protection, they revived their *hermandades*, or brotherhoods. Seville, Córdoba, Écija, and Jerez formed a *hermandad* in 1295 and pledged to aid the king in case of attack by either Muslims or Christians (art. 15).[3] Farther east, Jaén, Baeza, Úbeda, Andújar, Arjona, San Esteban, and Juan Sánchez de

Bedmar and his brother Simón Pérez renewed their *hermandad* dating from 1282 and promised to turn back any invasion by the Moors (art. 2).[4] Still farther east, the towns of the kingdom of Murcia, namely, Murcia, Cartagena, Lorca, Alicante, Mula, Guardamar, Molinaseca, and Alhama also organized a *hermandad*.[5]

Castile's Christian neighbors, however, posed a greater threat than the kingdom of Granada. Jaime II of Aragón, having abandoned any aspiration to intervene in Sicily, hoped to expand his peninsular dominions and organized a coalition with the aim of dismembering the Crown of Castile. In the early months of 1296, Jaime II, Alfonso de la Cerda, whom he recognized as king of Castile, Dinis of Portugal, and Infante Juan, Sancho IV's younger brother, assaulted Castile from different directions.[6]

Jaime II also cultivated good relations with the rulers of Morocco and Granada. Preoccupied with internal problems and the hostility of the emirs of Tlemcen, however, the Marinid sultan Abū Yaʿqūb was not ready to engage in peninsular affairs. Muhammad II of Granada, on the other hand, recognized the opportunity to undo some of the damage inflicted by Sancho IV. The two Muslim monarchs met at Tangier in 1295 to confirm the Marinid cession of Algeciras and Ronda to Granada, thereby restoring the territorial integrity of the kingdom of Granada. Muhammad II was now poised to broaden his frontiers. Though he acknowledged the importance of recovering Tarifa, he determined first to buttress his northern frontier. In the waning months of 1295 he seized the hilltop fortress of Quesada, southeast of Úbeda, and routed Rodrigo Pérez Ponce, master of Calatrava, at Iznalloz, a few miles north of Granada.[7]

Recognizing the value of maintaining good relations with Granada, Jaime II proposed a treaty of friendship and commerce. Granada would be permitted to arm galleys each year in his dominions, provided they were not used against Christians. Should he have need, Muhammad II would send him 10 to 500 knights who would not be deployed against the Moors; Jaime II would pay their expenses and would be entitled to a fifth of the booty, excepting towns, castles, and persons. As a sign of "his love and pleasure," Muhammad II would pay an annual tribute of 3,000 gold *doblas* and he would also make peace with Alfonso de la Cerda. In May 1296 negotiations ultimately resulted in a pact of friendship and commercial interchange that became a model for subsequent accords between Aragón and Granada.[8]

Early in 1297 when Jaime II seized Alhama in the kingdom of Murcia, Muhammad II, worried that an offensive might be directed against him, expressed his misgivings; but Jaime II assured him that he had invaded Murcia "against our enemies of Castile" and that he intended to maintain his alliance with Granada. Some months later he urged Muhammad II as well as Abū Yaʿqūb, the Marinid emir, to support Alfonso de la Cerda's claims to the Castilian throne.[9]

Infante Enrique's Proposal to Surrender Tarifa

Earlier, in June 1296, Infante Enrique offered to surrender Tarifa to Muhammad II as an inducement to withdraw from the anti-Castilian coalition. Jerónimo Zurita reported that the Nasrid king made an astounding counteroffer. In exchange for Tarifa, he proposed to renew his vassalage to Fernando IV; give him 8,000,000 *maravedíes* (probably as the purchase price), as well as an advance payment of the tribute for the next four years; surrender Quesada and twenty-two other castles; summon the Marinids to Spain to drive Infante Juan and Alfonso de la Cerda out of the kingdom; join in ousting Jaime II from Murcia; and pay 400,000 *maravedíes* annually to support the Castilian fleet until the recovery of Murcia was complete. The invitation to the Marinids to assist Fernando IV in expelling his enemies seems extraordinary, as one would think that Muhammad II would not wish to bring them back to Spain.

Alfonso Pérez de Guzmán, who held Tarifa in the king's name, undercut Enrique's plan. Turning to Aragón, he stated that he would not yield Tarifa on the command of anyone. Should the Moors besiege Tarifa, he asked Jaime II to send a fleet to oppose them. If Castile cut off his salary as tenant of Tarifa, he requested Jaime II to lend him the money. On receipt, he would do homage to the Aragonese king and would not cede Tarifa to Fernando IV until his salary was restored. Finally, he asked that the merchants of Seville and Córdoba should be guaranteed safe and secure passage throughout the Crown of Aragón. Jaime II, however, emphasized that he would only send his ships to disrupt a Nasrid siege of Tarifa if Alfonso Pérez joined him in opposing Fernando IV. He would assure the safety of merchants provided that they did no harm to Alfonso de la Cerda, Infante Juan, or Dinis of Portugal.[10] In this instance, Alfonso Pérez, acknowledging the debility of the Castilian monarchy, was prepared to accept Aragonese suzerainty in order to save Tarifa.

As his plan to yield Tarifa came to naught, Enrique was returning to Castile at the end of the year when he attacked a troop of Nasrid cavalry near Arjona, northwest of Jaén. Defeated and nearly captured, he was rescued by

Alfonso Pérez. Among the spoils was his horse, which Muhammad II, in a gesture of chivalry, returned to him.[11]

Still persisting, Enrique informed the Cortes of Cuéllar in 1297 that the sale of Tarifa would bring the war with Aragón, Portugal, and Granada to an end. María de Molina, however, staunchly opposed him, arguing that the money obtained from the sale would scarcely resolve the crown's financial problems. Even more strenuously she contended that to yield the fortress that Sancho IV had captured after the expenditure of so much energy would be a grave blow to Christendom and might lead to a new Moroccan conquest of Spain as in the time of the last Visigothic king, Rodrigo. As she carried the day, Enrique was discomfited once more.[12] Aware of the precariousness of their situation, Córdoba, Seville, Úbeda, and Juan Sánchez de Bedmar concluded a pact broadening their *hermandad*.[13]

Soon after, Fernando IV, prompted by his mother, demonstrated his gratitude to Alfonso Pérez de Guzmán, who had successfully held the frontier for him. In fulfillment of his father's oral promise, the king ceded Sanlúcar de Barrameda at the mouth of the Guadalquivir to Alfonso. The charter recalled his service to Sancho IV in the conquest and subsequent defense of Tarifa, the sacrifice of his son during the siege by Infante Juan, and his more recent defense of Tarifa against the kings of Granada and Portugal. Until 1640 Alfonso Pérez's descendants held Tarifa in lordship; from the fifteenth century they had the ducal title of Medina Sidonia. Ten years later Fernando IV granted Vejer de la Frontera to him, especially for the 56,000 gold *doblas* that he had lent to Sancho IV for the maintenance of his castles and vassals; for the fleet that he armed during the war; and also for money provided to secure from the papacy the legitimation of the marriage of Sancho IV and María de Molina and their children.[14]

Despite his previous failure, Enrique again urged the wisdom of selling Tarifa during the Cortes of Valladolid in 1298, but the queen successfully opposed him as before. In the spring of the following year he set out for the frontier to assume the office of *adelantado mayor de la frontera*. Reiterating her opposition to his proposed sale of Tarifa, María de Molina urged the towns not to accept him as *adelantado* unless he swore never to surrender it to the Moors. Apparently he did so.[15] Meantime, Alfonso Pérez de Guzmán, backed by the municipal council of Seville, again appealed to Jaime II for military support. As this matter concerned the good estate of Christendom, the king promised to bring it to the attention of the pope.[16]

The Muslim Offensive Against Castile

Although the Marinid sultan Abū Ya'qūb had refrained from intervening in the Peninsula, the weakened condition of the Castilian monarchy prompted him to send troops to collaborate with the Nasrids. Neither the Muslim nor the Christian chronicles mentioned this, but Bernat de Sarrià, in August 1299, informed Jaime II that the Marinids, probably in May or June, inflicted a humiliating defeat on the Castilians near Seville, killing 600 knights and 3,000 infantry. Among the dead were the archbishop of Seville, the bishop of Córdoba, and many other prelates. The Marinids then laid siege to Tarifa while Muhammad II, with 5,000 knights, besieged Jaén for two and a half months. Infante Enrique and the master of Santiago, apparently representing María de Molina, proposed to surrender Tarifa provided that Granada and Morocco joined forces with Castile against Aragón. Such an alliance would bode ill for the kingdoms of Valencia and Murcia, especially as the king of Granada had already sent thirty *morabites*, or itinerant preachers, to rouse the Moors of Valencia to rebellion.[17]

The peace plan described by Bernat de Sarrià sounds much like the offer made by Muhammad II in 1296. The surrender of Tarifa was put forward as the incentive for a triple alliance of Castile, Morocco, and Granada against Aragón that would also undermine Alfonso de la Cerda's royal aspirations. Although Bernat implied that María de Molina favored the cession of Tarifa, that seems unlikely, given her previous steadfast resistance. Nevertheless, Alfonso Pérez's refusal to step aside thwarted any plan to hand Tarifa over to the Moors. Thus, the triple alliance never became a reality.

Muhammad II soon resumed his offensive along his northern frontier. Anticipating that threat, the municipality of Úbeda received the Order of Calatrava into its *hermandad* in 1300 and adhered to agreements made by Calatrava and Alfonso Pérez de Guzmán, probably for joint action against the Moors.[18] In June Muhammad II seized Alcaudete, about twenty miles southwest of Jaén. After repairing the walls, he ravaged about Martos and as far north as Andújar, then toward the outskirts of Jaén. After three days of further pillaging, he returned to Granada, leaving on the frontier 3,000 *jinetes* "who had come on pilgrimage from the land of Abū Ya'qūb." They were Moroccan volunteers who had come to Spain to gain merit by taking part in the holy war. Meantime, emissaries from María de Molina, Fernando IV, and Infante Juan, who had recently returned to his allegiance and in whom the king of

Granada had the most confidence, visited his court and discussed the possibility of an accord concerning Tarifa. Muhammad II and his counselors were now in something of a quandary. Should they make peace with Castile, which lacked the funds necessary to prosecute the war effectively, or break friendly relations with Aragón?[19]

Jaime II and Muhammad II Renew Their Alliance

Early in 1300 Jaime II proposed a renewal of the 1296 pact, guaranteeing free trade, exchange of prisoners, construction of Catalan galleys for Nasrid use against Muslims, reservation of a fifth of the booty to Jaime II, and provision of Moorish knights to serve him against Christians. Muhammad II would pay an annual tribute of 1,500 gold *doblas*, half the amount specified in 1296. As Jaime II planned to send a fleet to Sardinia and Corsica in the following summer, he also asked for a loan of 20,000 gold *doblas*, offering as security two crowns, one of his own and the other his father's. He also urged Muhammad II to take military action against Castile.[20]

Promising not to make a separate peace and assuring the safety of merchants, the two kings renewed their alliance on 29 April 1301. Jaime II agreed to provide Granada with five to ten galleys when needed, at a cost to Granada of 1,250 *libras reales de Valencia* for four months. In turn, Muhammad II, when asked, pledged to send 200 to 1,000 *jinetes* to Jaime II who would pay their daily wage of three *sols de reales de Valencia*. Each monarch would retain whatever towns or places he acquired from Castile, provided they did not belong to the kingdoms of Murcia or Granada.[21] At the instance of Muhammad II the treaty was revised on 23 June to include the explicit Nasrid claim to Alcalá de los Gazules, Vejer de la Frontera, and Medina Sidonia. A new treaty drawn up at Zaragoza in September 1301 and ratified at Granada on 1 January 1302 acknowledged his right to those places and also to Tarifa, as well as Jaime II's claims to Murcia. Muhammad II and the Infantes de la Cerda, who accepted his rights to Tarifa and other frontier places, also agreed to an alliance against Fernando IV.[22]

Although Jaime II admitted Nasrid rights to Tarifa and other towns, it is unlikely that he would have facilitated their conquest. Indeed, Bernat de Sarrià advised him to appeal to the pope to prohibit María de Molina from surrendering Tarifa. Moreover, Jaime II arranged to supply wheat to Tarifa. As Dufourcq noted, he thus helped his Castilian enemies to resist his Muslim friends. Nevertheless, in his desire to thwart any accommodation between Granada and Castile, he exhorted Muhammad II to maintain his alliance with Aragón and with Alfonso de la Cerda. He also hoped that Abū Yaʻqūb, the Marinid emir, would join the alliance against Castile.[23]

Jaime II's effort to place Alfonso de la Cerda on the Castilian throne and to annex the kingdom of Murcia unraveled in the next few years. By 1300 Dinis of Portugal recognized the need for a settlement and Infante Juan acknowledged Fernando IV in June. When Pope Boniface VIII legitimated Fernando IV on 6 September 1301, his title to the throne was no longer open to question.[24] In the previous year the pope had given the boy king access to a major source of revenue that would enable him to withstand his opponents. Acknowledging that Fernando III had been allowed to collect the *tercias* to defend his realms against the Saracens, the pope authorized Fernando IV to do so for three years but no longer.[25] In December 1301 the king, now sixteen years of age, reached his majority and assumed personal responsibility for governing the realm.

Muhammad III and His Christian Neighbors

The death of Muhammad II in April 1302 (possibly poisoned by his heir) brought his long reign of nearly thirty years to a close. Building on his father's achievement, he helped to consolidate the Nasrid dynasty and also made some territorial gains in the kingdom of Jaén, especially Quesada and Alcaudete. Nevertheless, his efforts to recover Tarifa and the adjacent fortresses were unsuccessful.[26]

His son Abū ʻAbd Allāh Muhammad, known as Muhammad III (1302–9), maintained hostilities with Castile, friendly relations with Jaime II, and support for Alfonso de la Cerda.[27] Within two weeks of becoming king, he seized Bedmar just south of Úbeda and other neighboring strongholds. Among the prisoners was María Jiménez, widow of the *alcaide*. Nasrid forces also attacked Jódar, northeast of Bedmar, and recovered Quesada, which had fallen to the Christians in 1300. After parading María Jiménez through the streets of Granada, he sent her to the Marinid emir Abū Yaʻqūb, who was quite enamored of her. In addition to Granada, Almería, and Málaga, Muhammad III's inclusion of Algeciras, Ronda, and Guadix in the royal intitulation in 1302 indicates that he, rather than the Marinids, was in effective possession of those places.[28]

Depicting the fall of Bedmar as a great blow to Christendom, Fernando IV persuaded the Leonese and Extremaduran and Castilian towns meeting separately in the Cortes of Medina del Campo and the Cortes of Burgos to grant him five *servicios* to protect the frontier.[29] Although Boniface VIII urged him to seek peace with Alfonso de la Cerda, he declared that he could not do so because the infante had joined the Moors in an invasion of his kingdom.[30] Nevertheless, as a preliminary to a final settlement, he agreed to a truce with Dinis of Portugal and Aragonese envoys in April 1303.[31] He also negotiated a truce with Granada, to which Abū Yaʿqūb adhered.[32]

Muhammad III, meantime, realized that Granada had gained little by collaborating with Jaime II. Thus, in February 1303 he was only willing to accept a truce of one year rather than a treaty of alliance. Wary of a possible rapprochement between Granada and Castile, and anxious to secure free trade in the Strait, Jaime II proposed an alliance with Abū Yaʾqūb, who hoped to obtain Aragonese help against Tlemcen.[33] About the same time, Enrique, breaking with Fernando IV, entered an alliance with Jaime II and Alfonso de la Cerda. Nevertheless, his death on 12 August 1303 eliminated a threat to the young king of Castile.[34]

The Proposed Crusade of the Order of Santiago

While Nasrid forces threatened the frontier, Juan Osórez, master of Santiago, asked Fernando IV's authorization to preach the crusade in the archbishopric of Toledo and the bishoprics of Cuenca, Córdoba, and Jaén. As there is no evidence that Boniface VIII issued any new crusading bulls, the master probably intended to use papal bulls issued in the thirteenth century. The king agreed that the *fecho de la cruzada* was to "the great service of God and myself and the protection of my kingdom" and the release of captives taken in defense of the faith. Therefore, on 1 July 1303, he ordered the civil and religious authorities to assemble the people to listen to crusade preachers. Officials were authorized to collect bequests for the crusade made by deceased persons. If anyone stipulated that the remainder of his estate should be given to God, the king commanded that it be assigned to the crusade. Money bequeathed to the anonymous poor for food and clothing would also be used for the crusade, particularly for the maintenance of castles and the release of captives. As was the custom in the time of Alfonso X and Sancho IV, a fifth of the property of those dying intestate would also be directed to the crusade. Two years later, at the master's request, Fernando IV commanded local officials to allow the friars of Santiago to go about the country preaching the crusade. In accordance with papal bulls, all those who joined the Order in the defense of the frontier or supported it financially could gain the same indulgence given to those who went to the Holy Land.[35]

Peace with Granada and Aragón

Fernando IV, however, was not prepared to embark on a general crusade against Granada at this time. In August 1303 he concluded a treaty at Córdoba with Granada for three years. Whereas Tarifa would remain in Castilian hands, Granada would retain Alcaudete, Bedmar, Quesada, and other places taken since the death of Sancho IV. In return, Muhammad III would renew his vassalage and pay the same tribute given to Sancho IV. Jofre de Loaysa, commenting that the amount of tribute was much less than that paid to Alfonso X and Sancho IV, also complained that Muhammad III was not required to surrender places previously taken, which "seemed to many to redound not to the honor of the king of Castile, but indeed to his ignominy."[36] Muhammad III probably concluded that a pledge of vassalage and tribute was a small price to pay for Castilian acceptance of his conquests.

Even though Muhammad III assured Jaime II that their truce remained in effect, the latter was sorely angered by the treaty of Córdoba and decided to hasten negotiations for an alliance with Abū Ya'qūb. Assured of Jaime II's continued friendship, the emir offered to act as mediator with the king of Granada and to supply 1,000 or 2,000 men for war against Castile.[37]

Nevertheless, as his coalition against Castile collapsed, Jaime II made peace with Fernando IV at Campillo on 9 August 1304. Jaime II restored the kingdom of Murcia to Castile, except for Alicante, Orihuela, Elche, and lands north of the Segura River. In return for an extensive patrimony, Alfonso de la Cerda renounced his claims to the Castilian throne, thus ending a conflict that had disturbed the tranquility of the realm for nearly thirty years. Two days later the Aragonese and Portuguese kings agreed to make peace with Muhammad III as a vassal and friend of Fernando IV.[38]

Muhammad III and the Conquest of Ceuta

The accord with Castile allowed Muhammad III to attempt to extend his power to the Moroccan coast by seizing Ceuta. Taking advantage of Abū Yaʿqūb's preoccupation with Tlemcen, he encouraged the ʿAzafid lords of Ceuta to rebel in 1304.[39] Appealing to Jaime II, Abū Yaʿqūb promised him a share of 30,000 gold *dinars* in the booty, if the rebels surrendered upon the arrival of Catalan ships, or 50,000 if force were needed to compel surrender.[40] Jaime II replied that, as he had made peace with Castile, he would not require Marinid military assistance, but, as a gesture of friendship, he was willing to lease galleys to the emir. Thus Abū Yaʿqūb was left to his own devices.[41]

Seizing the opportunity, Muhammad III, in May 1306, dispatched a fleet to capture Ceuta and to dispossess the ʿAzafids. Possession of Ceuta and Algeciras now enabled him to straddle both sides of the Strait. Thanking Jaime II for not providing galleys to the Marinids, he also advised him to warn Catalan merchants of the dangers to be encountered there.[42] The Marinids attempted to blockade Ceuta but were driven off in June 1307. In addition to making an alliance with the emir of Tlemcen, Muhammad III sent troops to occupy the Moroccan ports of Alcácer Seguir, Alarche, and Arcila on the Atlantic coast.[43]

The murder on 10 May 1307 of Abū Yaʿqūb Yūsuf, the Marinid emir, who had been besieging Tlemcen, turned everything upside down.[44] Learning of his death, ʿUthmān ibn Abī l-ʿUlā, another member of the ruling dynasty, declared himself sultan, but eventually had to take refuge in Granada. There, as *shaykh al-guzāt*, he commanded the volunteers of the faith (*mujāhidīn*), Moroccan soldiers enlisted in the service of the Nasrids.[45] A rival candidate for the Marinid throne, Abū Tābit (1307–8), a grandson of Abū Yaʿqūb Yūsuf, lifted the siege of Tlemcen and recovered possession of Alcácer Seguir and Arcila. However, while awaiting Muhammad III's response to his demand for the surrender of Ceuta, Abū Tābit died at Tangier. His brother Abū l-Rabīʿ Sulaymān (1308–10) arranged a truce, leaving Ceuta in Nasrid hands.[46] However, he was unable to induce Jaime II to lend him military and naval assistance; the king argued that the treaty of Campillo prohibited him from taking hostile action against the king of Granada as a Castilian vassal.[47]

The Treaty of Alcalá de Henares 1308

Muhammad III's occupation of Ceuta, Algeciras, Gibraltar, Málaga, and Almería gave him a strong position in the Strait of Gibraltar that was not viewed with equanimity by his neighbors in Morocco, Castile, and Aragón. Observing his aggressive attitude, Fernando IV prepared to jettison the pact concluded at Córdoba in 1303 and to join Aragón and Morocco in a coalition against Granada. Organizing an armada for that purpose, he discussed a joint campaign against the Nasrids with Jaime II, who also made a pact with Abū l-Rabīʿ Sulaymān.[48]

The kings of Castile and Aragón signed a treaty of alliance at Alcalá de Henares on 19 December 1308. The treaty was reminiscent of twelfth-century pacts whereby their predecessors had divided Islamic Spain between them. Declaring his desire to exalt "the faith of our Lord Jesus Christ" and to "expel from Spain those who do not believe in the Catholic faith who are here to the dishonor of God and the great damage and danger of all Christendom, and because we have never found any security or affirmation in what they promised us," Fernando IV pledged to join Jaime II "in making war by sea and by land against the king of Granada and his realm." The campaign would begin on the feast of St. John (24 June) of the following year. Jaime II, who had no direct access by land to Granada, was allotted a sixth of that kingdom, including the port of Almería on the southeastern coast. Should Almería and its territory not constitute a sixth, the archbishop of Toledo and the bishop of Valencia would assign additional lands to him; should it be greater than a sixth they would make the appropriate adjustment. The recent Nasrid conquests of Quesada, Bedmar, Alcaudete, Locubín, and Arenas were reserved to Castile. "For as long as the war lasts until the conquest of Granada is completed," Jaime II promised to aid Castile with ten galleys and five sailing ships (*leños*). Once the war began Fernando IV guaranteed to provide ten galleys and three *leños*. The two kings vowed not to make peace separately or without the consent of Infante Juan and Infante Pedro, Fernando IV's younger brother. Although Juan objected to the cession of a portion of the kingdom of Granada to Aragón, Pedro supported his brother's decision. The king also authorized Jaime II to act on his behalf to persuade the emir of Morocco to join forces against Granada.[49] Several marriages between the Castilian and Aragonese royal families were intended to strengthen the alliance.[50] The Catalan chronicler Ramon Muntaner, commenting on the wisdom of the proposed joint expedition, noted that it would require the king of Granada to fight on two fronts.[51]

In order to obtain the necessary funds Fernando IV convened the Cortes of Madrid in February 1309. Acknowledging his good intentions, the Cortes granted him five *servicios* for the current year and three for each year thereafter. While the *Royal Chronicle* presented this as fairly routine, a Catalan observer reported that the Cortes was unwilling to grant any tax until the king justified the need. Moreover, objections were raised to the cession of a part of the kingdom of Granada to Aragón. The Cortes eventually acquiesced, but limited the grant of three *servicios* to a term of three years beyond the present year. Fernando IV reportedly intended to begin his advance to the frontier at the end of May with 8,000 knights, but it seemed likely that he would have only 4,000. Infante Juan argued that, rather than besiege Algeciras, he should plunder the plain of Granada. His misgivings about the projected campaign foreshadowed more serious trouble once hostilities got under way.[52]

Clement V's Concession of the Crusade

Jaime II and Fernando IV now appealed to the pope to grant the crusading indulgence and the right to collect the *decima*, or tenth, on ecclesiastical property.[53] In 1300 Boniface VIII had authorized Fernando IV to take the *tercias* for three years, and the king probably requested renewal in 1303 and in 1306. He informed Clement V (1305–14) that the kings of Castile customarily took two-thirds of the third of the tithe reserved for the *fabrica*, or upkeep, of churches, but he noted that he had not received any of that money in the previous three years. The pope authorized him on 1 January 1308 to take half of that amount, reserving the other half for the *fabrica*.[54]

In February 1309 Jaime II protested that the papal announcement of a crusade to the Holy Land gave comfort to the Moors of Spain and Morocco who still posed a grave threat. Muhammad III possessed a large army and Abū l-Rabīʿ was as powerful as the sultan of Babylon and their troops could cross the Strait several times a day. It was common opinion that only 10 percent of the Granadan population was Saracen in origin; the rest were descended from Christian women who had the misfortune of being captured and made concubines. Thus, the kings of Aragón and Castile requested papal support for their plan to blockade the Strait with forty galleys; to expel the Saracens from Spain; and to maintain a constant vigil against future invasions. Jaime II also asked that the *decima* granted to him in 1305 for the conquest of Corsica and Sardinia could be diverted to the war against Granada. As it only amounted to 18,000 *libras barcelonesas,* he petioned the pope to pay the wages of 1,000 knights and the maintenance of five galleys for three years. Acknowledging that the conquest of Granada would serve God and the church, the pope agreed to transfer the *decima* for the conquest of Sardinia to the war against Granada, but he refused any other financial support.[55]

In the papal consistory the cardinals also expressed reservations. As the conquest of Granada was believed to pertain to Castile, they noted that no evidence that Fernando IV consented to Aragonese participation was presented and they questioned whether the goal was to conquer Granada or merely to compel the payment of tribute.[56] If the pope knew that Jaime II planned to collaborate with the Marinids against Granada—a point his envoy did not mention—that might have raised another objection.[57] Despite these misgivings, the pope eventually acceded to the request for the *decima* and the bull of crusade.

Applauding Jaime II's determination to "extirpate from the kingdom of Granada the fetid nation, the enemies of the Christian faith," Clement V, on 21 March 1309, conceded two-thirds of the *decima* for the war against Granada and one-third for his proposed conquest of Sardinia. A month later, on 24 April, he promulgated the bull of crusade in the Crown of Aragón, granting a plenary indulgence to those who confessed their sins and served in the war against Granada continuously for a year, or intermittently for three years, or who paid the expenses of others or gave financial support. Clergy who participated were dispensed from the obligation of residence and could sell or rent the income from their benefices.[58]

Clement V addressed six similar bulls to Fernando IV: the concession of the crusade indulgence; the appointment of the archbishop of Toledo as papal legate; the concession of the *decima*; the appointment of collectors; and the application to the crusade of fines for usury and rapine. On 29 April, he conceded the *decima* of all ecclesiastical revenues (except in the lands of the Orders of the Hospital, the Temple, Calatrava, and Santiago) for three years from the feast of St. John onward. This was the first time since the middle of the thirteenth century that the pope gave crusading privileges for the war in Spain. Both Alfonso X and Sancho IV had used earlier papal bulls for their crusading efforts. When Fernando IV complained in June that the pope had not yet acceded to his request for the *decima*, Jaime II assured him that bulls similar to those he had received would soon reach the Castilian court.[59]

Writing to Cardinal Jacopo Colonna, Jaime II proclaimed his intention to bring about "the exaltation of the Catholic faith and the suppression of the sect of Muhammad." Both he and Fernando IV were united by their vows to cause "the suppression and eradication of the fetid nation of the Saracens in Hispania Citerior." His use of the word *votis* indicates that both kings had taken the crusader's vow.[60]

In July Jaime II requested additional favors. The bishop of Valencia, as promoter of the crusade in the Crown of Aragón, would be authorized to absolve crusaders and their supporters of any sentence of excommunication incurred for striking a cleric; to commute vows, except that of chastity, so that those who had taken a vow to do something else could participate in the crusade; to absolve all sins, except those reserved to the Holy See; and to allot a third of the plenary indulgence to crusaders serving for four months at their own or another's expense. A similar benefit would be accorded to anyone who paid a crusader's expenses; if the crusader served for six months, his sponsor would gain half the indulgence, or two-thirds if he served for eight months. Anyone who gave alms for the crusade would also receive a partial indulgence. As many Gascons, Toulousains, Provençals, and Navarrese wanted to take part in the crusade, the king asked that the bishop be allowed to grant them the indulgence, even though they were not Aragonese subjects. Finally, he begged that, once he had taken Almería, a bishopric should be established there, directly subject to the Roman church, rather than to any metropolitan bishop.[61]

Describing Jaime II as an "athlete of Christ," in September Clement V directed the bishop of Valencia to establish a chapter of canons at Almería to elect a bishop. The pope also acceded in part to the king's petitions concerning excommunication and the absolution of sins reserved to the papacy, not including the murder of a cleric or arrest of a bishop. He also agreed to the commutation of vows, except those of chastity, monastic life, and pilgrimage to the Holy Land. Further, he permitted the absolution of excommunicated clerics who celebrated the liturgy.[62]

Jaime II also pressed for financial support, even asking for a direct subsidy from the papal treasury. Besides the *decima* already granted, he requested a double *decima* for three years. He also urged that an indulgence comparable to that conceded to the Hospitallers for the crusade to the Holy Land should be given for the war against Granada. Furthermore, he wanted the right to recruit men in the service of the churches of his realm. Finally, he pleaded that individuals be permitted to redeem their crusading vows by making a monetary payment. In other words, he preferred to have the money that would enable him to hire competent mercenaries, rather than depend upon the goodwill of men otherwise unfit for war.[63]

The cardinals were not disposed to agree, but, at length, in mid-November, the pope asked the Aragonese prelates to make a voluntary aid to the king from their own property, the property of their churches, and of the people subject to them.[64] Given the emptiness of the papal treasury, the pope could not make any direct contribution, but he did agree that the indulgences of the Hospitallers could be diverted to the crusade in Spain. No pope had ever granted a double *decima*, but once the original concession of the *decima* reached its term, he was willing to extend it, provided the war against Granada continued. The king was also permitted to collect fines incurred by his subjects engaged in illicit trade with the Saracens. Anyone who had taken a crusading vow could fulfill it by making a financial contribution. Clement V exhorted the king to bring the crusade to a happy end by extirpating the barbarous nations and avenging the injury done to the Savior.[65]

As a further means of support, the pope asked pastors of parishes to grant the fruits of their benefices for one year to the crusade and urged them to exhort their people, both in confession and in their homilies, to contribute financially to the crusade. Moreover, a prayer against the perfidy of the pagans was to be said at every mass. Priests and faithful who fulfilled the papal commands would gain an indulgence. Papal tax collectors were instructed to deliver the Castilian *decima* for the next three years to Jaspert, viscount of Castellnou, whom Fernando IV had appointed as his admiral, so that the money could be used for the crusade.[66]

While the pope provided spiritual and financial assistance, the Catalan theorist Ramon Llull actively linked the war against the Muslims in Spain and Morocco with the recovery of the Holy Land. In addition to urging a missionary effort to convert the Moors, he also argued that the unification of the military orders would provide a more effective counterweight to Islam. While Jaime II and Fernando IV were planning their assault on Granada, Llull presented a copy of his book *Liber de acquisitione Terrae Sanctae* to the pope. In it he proposed that while a great crusade moved from Constantinople into Syria and Egypt, in the West the Christians would undertake the conquest of Granada and the Moroccan port of Ceuta. By means of this pincers movement he hoped that Islam could be crushed. At that very time Jaime II was engaged in diplomatic efforts concerning the recovery of Ceuta.[67]

The Marinid Recovery of Ceuta

As the treaty of Alcalá envisaged the tripartite alliance of Aragón, Castile, and Morocco, Jaime II endeavored to secure the adherence of Abū l-Rabīʿ, the Marinid emir. Offering to send Catalan galleys to deliver Ceuta from Granadan control, he asked Abū l-Rabīʿ to pay 2,000 gold *dinars* for each galley for four months' service and 1,000 *doblas* per galley for every four months thereafter; to pay the wages of 1,000 Aragonese knights; and not to make a separate peace with Granada. Once Ceuta was captured all its movable goods would be reserved to the king of Aragón.[68]

When Muhammad III complained that Catalan naval preparations were directed against him, Jaime II assured him that that was not the case. Though he asserted that he was preparing for the conquest of Sardinia, Muhammad III was not convinced.[69] Meantime, the master of Calatrava was beginning incursions into Granadan territory and the bishop of Cartagena seized the castle of Lubrín on 13 March. To guard against an Aragonese attack on Almería, the governor there arrested all Catalan merchants and confiscated their goods.[70] Complicating Muhammad III's situation, internal discontent gave way to open rebellion. His brother Abū l-Juyūsh Nasr (1309–14) seized the throne on 14 March 1309, forcing him to withdraw to Almuñécar. Intent on thwarting the projected alliance of Aragón, Castile, and Morocco, Nasr sent his envoys to the Marinid court at Fez in April.[71]

In that very month, Jaspert de Castellnou asked Jaime II to send five Catalan galleys and two sailing ships to join five Castilian galleys in the Strait by mid-May. About the appointed time, a Catalan fleet of sixteen galleys arrived in the Strait.[72] Without waiting for them, however, Abū l-Rabīʿ launched an attack on Ceuta on 12 May.[73] Early in July he concluded an alliance that gave Jaime II much less than he had proposed earlier. Reserving Ceuta for himself, the emir allotted its movable property to Jaime II and conceded certain commercial benefits to Catalan merchants.[74] He also sent 1,000 measures of wheat and 2,000 of barley to Aragón and opened Moroccan ports to Catalans wishing to purchase grain. However, he said nothing about payment for Catalan galleys or troops.[75]

A few weeks later, on 20 July, the Marinids, without Catalan assistance, seized Ceuta. Although Abū l-Rabīʿ promised to deliver the movable goods to Jaime II, he did not do so. Moreover, having eliminated the Nasrids from Morocco, he made peace with them in late September.[76] Thus, Jaime II's expectations of enlisting Morocco in the Aragonese-Castilian alliance collapsed entirely.[77] As he informed Fernando IV, "it seems to us, King, that from now on we can regard that king as an enemy."[78]

The Conquest of Gibraltar

Although the joint Castilian-Aragonese Crusade was projected for the feast of St. John, the allies did not meet that deadline. Resolved to besiege Algeciras, Fernando IV's army appeared before that port at the end of July.[79] Meantime, by virtue of an agreement reached at Valladolid on 3 July 1309 Dinis of Portugal sent a contingent of 700 knights to participate in the siege and provided a loan of 16,600 silver marks.[80]

A few days after the siege of Algeciras was initiated, Alfonso Pérez de Guzman and Jaspert de Castellnou reconnoitered by sea the fortress of Gibraltar, about five miles directly across the Bay of Algeciras; the overland journey covered about fifteen miles. With the king's consent, Alfonso Pérez besieged Gibraltar by land while Jaspert and the Catalan ships blockaded it by sea. As two siege engines battered the walls, the Moors, unable to withstand the attack, surrendered on 12 September 1309. In accordance with the terms of capitulation, about 1,125 Muslims emigrated to Morocco rather than submit to Christian rule.[81] Fernando IV came to Gibraltar probably on 14 September. An old man evacuating the fortress poignantly expressed the plight of the Spanish Muslims when he addressed him:

> My lord, why do you drive me hence? When your great-grandfather King Fernando took Seville he drove me out and I went to live at Jerez, but when your grandfather Alfonso took Jerez he drove me out and I went to live at Tarifa, thinking that I was in a safe place. Your father King Sancho came and took Tarifa and drove me out and I went to live here at Gibraltar, thinking that I would not be in any safer place in the whole land of the Moors . . . but now I see that I cannot remain in any of these places, so I will go beyond the sea and settle in a place where I can live in safety and end my days.[82]

After entering the town the king gave thanks to God and ordered the repair of damaged walls and the construction of a shipyard where galleys could be safely docked. He also granted a *fuero* to Gibraltar on 31 January

1310. Archbishop Fernando of Seville consecrated the mosque as a Christian church.[83] While Gibraltar was not as important as Algeciras, its conquest was a notable achievement, giving the Castilians a firm base on the Strait. However, it proved not to be permanent, as the Muslims recovered possession in 1333.

The joy that the Christians felt was soon tempered when Alfonso Pérez de Guzmán was killed in a skirmish on 19 September. While the Castilians were besieging Jimena de la Frontera, he invested Estepona, a port lying northeast of Gibraltar. ʿUthmān ibn Abī l-ʿUlā, the Marinid prince commanding the Nasrid army, after routing an Aragonese detachment at Marchena near Almería, hastened to deliver Estepona. Although Ibn Khaldūn reported that he killed 3,000 men, including Alfonso Pérez, Christian sources recorded a loss of 30 knights and 1,000 foot soldiers. Another Muslim force drove off Castilian soldiers besieging Gaucín, northwest of Estepona.[84] Fernando IV, in acknowledgement of Alfonso Pérez's many services, "especially in defending the frontier," granted the dead warrior's estates to his wife and children.[85] The most effective Castilian military leader of his day, Alfonso Pérez de Guzmán must be credited with preserving Sancho IV's conquest of Tarifa.

The Siege of Algeciras

With the fall of Gibraltar King Nasr of Granada realized the importance of coming to terms with the Marinids, lest the Castilians continue their assault with impunity. In mid-September he made peace with Abū l-Rabīʿ, to whom he surrendered Algeciras, Ronda, and their dependencies. Thus, for the first time since the Marinids had withdrawn their forces in 1294, they now had a strong position in the Peninsula. Abū l-Rabīʿ promptly sent troops, money, and horses to relieve Algeciras.[86] Ironically, Castile and Aragón, whose forces were besieging Algeciras, were at peace with Morocco. By the terms of the treaty of Fez the emir had not committed himself to the Aragonese-Castilian alliance and complained of Catalan attacks on Moroccan ships and asked Jaime II to terminate naval assistance to the Castilians besieging Algeciras. As his fleet was short of food and money to pay the crew, Jaspert de Castellnou asked the king whether he ought to seek a loan from Abū l-Rabīʿ.[87]

As Nasr was no longer responsible for the defense of Algeciras, he could now direct his attention to the siege of Almería. When reports indicated that 1,000 horsemen and twenty galleys and sailing ships from Ceuta, Tangier, and Granada were preparing to relieve Almería, Jaspert proposed a retaliatory attack on the Moroccan coast. Although Jaime II decided to focus on the conquest of Almería, his ships, by blockading Ceuta, thwarted a Marinid attempt to transport 1,000 knights to Spain.[88]

Meantime, long-festering dissension within the Castilian camp before Algeciras broke open. From the outset Juan, the king's uncle, and Juan Manuel, the king's cousin, objected to the cession of a sixth of the kingdom of Granada to Aragón. As to strategy, rather than a protracted siege of Algeciras, they preferred to enrich themselves by plundering Granadan territory. Complaining that the king ignored their advice, Juan informed Jaime II that he and Juan Manuel were thinking of withdrawing. To avert that catastrophe, Jaime II appealed to all parties to resolve this issue. Suffering from a shortage of funds, Fernando IV owed Juan 26,000 *maravedíes* for five days' service and Juan Manuel 100,000 for twenty days. Although Jaspert declared that it would be shameful if they left the host, they did so in late October, taking 500 knights with them. Nevertheless, Fernando IV seemed determined to continue the siege, even though he had only 600 knights and insufficient funds to sustain his army. When Jaime II learned that Juan and Juan Manuel had deserted their king, he exhorted them to remain, but it was too late.[89]

Several important contributions helped to relieve the financial shortage. The bishop of Astorga, for example, contributed 3,100 gold *doblas* for the maintenance of ten galleys and three sailing ships, while the master of Alcántara loaned 3,000 *doblas*. The Genoese of Seville also lent 8,911.5 *doblas*. Acknowledging that "I was much helped and assisted by you in time of war," the king, in June 1310, promised to repay them in two installments. Even Queen Constanza did her bit by pawning her crowns and jewels.[90]

Some of the king's counselors feared that if the Moors discovered his weakened condition, they would surely attack. The arrival of his brother Felipe and the archbishop of Santiago with 400 knights provided some reinforcement, but when Diego López de Haro, one of the leading Castilian nobles, fell ill, many believed that if he died the king would have to abandon the enterprise. Heavy rains lasting three months also heightened a sense of misery. The Moors were also anxious to be done with the affair and often offered to negotiate, promising to surrender other fortresses if the crusaders would withdraw. Yet Fernando IV insisted that he would rather die before Algeciras than be dishonored by withdrawing. María de Molina, to whom he had entrusted the government of Castile and León during his absence on the frontier, asked all the religious communities to lead solemn processions, pleading with God to stop the rains. The chronicler, however, made the point that the rains worked to Castile's advantage because they prevented the Moors from attacking.[91] Nevertheless, pressure to end the siege steadily intensified.

The Crusade of Almería

When the Castilians initiated the siege of Algeciras, Jaime II prepared to besiege Almería, a seaport located about ninety miles southeast of Granada.[92] In anticipation, he provided for the defense of the Valencian frontier and authorized his treasurer to raise the necessary funds to prosecute the war.[93] He planned to raise an army of 1,000 knights, each accompanied by eight foot soldiers, two archers, and two squires, or a total of 12,000 men. Zurita commented that he also asked the abbot of San Juan de la Peña to send him the arm or some other relic of St. Indalecio, in ancient times the reputed bishop of Urci and a disciple of the Apostle St. James. As Almería was built on the ruins of Urci, Jaime II wanted to name St. Indalecio as patron of his crusade. While he sailed from Valencia on 18 July, his army marched overland through enemy territory. Blockading Almería by land and sea, around the middle of August, he built a palisade and a ditch to protect his host from counterattack. His army was powerfully equipped with mangonels, trebuchets, and other siege machinery off-loaded from ships. The *Royal Chronicle* made the curious remark that, whereas the Moors did not object to Fernando IV's siege of towns that were his by right, they believed that Jaime II's action against Almería was dishonorable.[94]

A Muslim eyewitness account emphasized that the defenders had taken pains to fortify the walls and to secure substantial food supplies, which were rationed during the course of the siege. When the crusaders first appeared they were richly appareled and accompanied by the sound of trumpets and drums. Seeing their great numbers, the people of Almería were discouraged, but after a few skirmishes, they took heart and realized that all was not lost.[95]

A week after arriving at Almería, on 23 August, Jaime II achieved an openfield victory over the enemy, who reportedly lost 6,000 men.[96] Clearly that figure was intended to convey the significance of the victory rather than the exact number of those killed. Informed that thousands of Saracens died, Clement V congratulated the king on achieving an admirable victory. Cardinal Nicola de Prato also sent his congratulations. The king himself announced the victory that "we achieved by God's power over the perfidious Saracens," and asked the physician Arnald de Vilanova, for "the utility of all of Christendom," to intercede with the pope for additional aid.[97]

In early September the crusaders, bringing up siege engines and scaling ladders, attempted an assault on Almería, but the defenders poured boiling oil on them and forced them to withdraw. Despite that setback, using catapults and trebuchets, they launched rocks weighing twenty-five to thirty pounds into the city; as many as 22,000 were said to have fallen. There were numerous casualties and the sole Muslim catapult was knocked out; but the defenders later built three others. ʿUthmān ibn Abī l-ʿUlā, commander of the Nasrid army, on 17 September routed an Aragonese detachment at Marchena near Almería. When some of the crusaders dressed in Muslim clothing seemingly came to relieve the city, other crusaders pretended to pursue them, prompting the Muslim defenders to come out; as soon as they did so they were attacked and were fortunate to escape to safety within. During another assault by the crusaders the Muslims emptied the cesspits and poured human excrement on them, soiling their fine clothes and humiliating them.[98]

Despite their inability to gain entrance into the city, the crusaders, on 15 October, repulsed a major attack by 60,000 men. That figure, given by Jaime II, surely is an exaggeration. He also reported that 2,000 of the enemy were killed and many prisoners were taken. Fearing the possibility of reprisals, he warned the cities of Murcia and Lorca to guard against a Muslim attack. When a breach was opened in the walls on 5 January 1310, the Christians attempted to take advantage, but the defenders held them off. The discomfort of the crusading army was intensified by the lack of food and other supplies, as winds blowing from the west prevented Christian vessels from bringing needed relief. Meanwhile, ʿUthmān ibn Abī l-ʿUlā so vigorously harassed the crusaders that they were compelled to lift the siege.[99] At the end of December Jaime II agreed to a truce.[100]

The End of the Crusade

As the futility of continuing the crusade became increasingly apparent, toward the end of January 1310 Fernando IV abandoned the siege of Algeciras and Jaime II departed from Almería.[101] Lacking sufficient ships to transport his army, however, Jaime II left many men behind. Many were captured or killed as they pillaged Granadan territory on their way homeward.[102] Once they were gone, the people of Almería destroyed the siege works left behind lest they be used again.[103] Meantime, as negotiations to end the war were begun, it was proposed that Nasr renew his vassalage to Castile and pay an annual tribute;

Jaime II would receive a sixth of that.[104] Tensions continued, however, as Infante Pedro captured Tempul east of Jerez.[105] Moreover, Fernando IV asked Jaime II to send five to ten galleys and five *leños* by 1 May to join ten Castilian galleys and three *leños* in patrolling the Strait.[106]

A peace treaty between Castile and Granada was completed on 26 May 1310. For the next seven years both monarchs pledged to aid one another against all enemies and not to support anyone rebelling against the other. Committing himself to both court service and military service, Nasr continued to be recorded as a vassal in Castilian royal privileges. When summoned, he would send a representative to the Castilian royal court once a year for a period of twenty days and would provide troops for three months' service at his own expense. Further, he promised to pay an annual tribute of 11,000 gold *doblas* in three installments. All merchants were guaranteed security and freedom of access to markets, subject to the usual customs duties. Fernando IV consented to appoint an official to resolve disputes between Muslims and Christians along the frontier; thus, the office of *juez de la frontera* came into existence. The *Royal Chronicle* also stipulated that Quesada and Bedmar were restored to Castile and that Nasr paid an indemnity of 150,000 *doblas*. According to the king's own statement, a *dobla* was worth 26 *maravedíes* of the *moneda blanca*; thus 150,000 *doblas* was the equivalent of 3,900,000 *maravedíes*.[107] No text of a pact between Aragón and Granada appears to be extant, but Nasr promised to pay Jaime II an indemnity of 65,000 *doblas*; of that amount Fernando IV agreed to provide 30,000.[108]

Aside from the capture of Gibraltar, the crusade did not achieve its objectives. The projected alliance of Castile, Aragón, and Morocco failed to materialize as Abū l-Rabīʿ, after recovering Ceuta, made peace with Nasr, who ceded Algeciras to him. Thus the Marinids, without much effort, again had a foothold in the Peninsula. The lateness of the year also contributed to the failure of the crusade. Neither the Castilians nor the Aragonese commenced the crusade on St. John's Day as planned. The Castilians began the siege of Algeciras at the end of July and the Aragonese appeared before Almería a month later. As fall turned toward winter, incessant wind, rain, and snow made life miserable for the crusaders, who also suffered from shortages of food and other supplies. Worst of all, the desertion of Infante Juan and Juan Manuel, whom Catalan sources accused of accepting Nasrid money, demoralized both Castilians and Aragonese. Dismissing the Castilians, Ramon Muntaner boasted that, "if the kingdom of Granada had been [Jaime II's] conquest, it would have belonged to the Christians a long time ago."[109]

Instability in Morocco and Granada

Fernando IV, angered by the desertion of Infante Juan and Juan Manuel, was resolved to resume his crusade, but first he had to face the demands of the prelates and the fractious nobility.[110] In May 1311, declaring his intention "to make war against the Moors for the service of God," he extended numerous privileges to the clergy. Though he planned to commence his campaign on St. John's Day, conflict with the nobility made that impossible. After a failed attempt to assassinate Infante Juan, he came to terms with the magnates in October.[111]

Internal challenges to Abū l-Rabīʿ of Morocco and Nasr of Granada encouraged Fernando IV to revive his crusade. In the fall of 1310 the Christian militia in Marinid service rebelled and appealed to the king to send ten galleys and forty transports to Hunayn, west of Tlemcen. As recompense for deposing Abū l-Rabīʿ, the king would receive Algeciras and 200,000 *doblas*. Offering Jaime II 40,000 *doblas*, Fernando IV asked him to supply half the ships, but the king of Aragón, recalling the duplicitous conduct of the Moroccans in the past, refused. Although the rebellion collapsed, the reign of Abū l-Rabīʿ ended abruptly when he died in November.[112]

In the spring of 1311 Abū Saʿīd ʿUthmān b. Abū Yūsuf (1310–31), the new Marinid emir, dreaming of conquest in al-Andalus, prepared a fleet to invade Spain. However, on the feast of Santiago, 25 July, off Algeciras, nine Castilian galleys and four *leños* dispersed a much larger Muslim fleet of thirteen galleys and five *leños*. Seven hundred Moors were killed or captured and two galleys were taken and burned. Stung by that defeat, Abū Saʿīd ʿUthmān abandoned his intervention in Spain and restored Algeciras, Ronda, and their dependencies to Nasr of Granada.[113]

During this time conspiracies directed against Nasr upset the stability of the kingdom of Granada. When he fell ill in November 1310 and seemed on the verge of death, his brother, Muhammad III, whom he had deposed, hoped to regain his throne. Early in the next year when Nasr recovered, Muhammad III retreated to his refuge at Almuñécar, where he died in 1314. A more serious uprising occurred in February 1312 when Abū Saʿīd Faraj, the *arráez* of Málaga, revolted and proclaimed his son Abū l-Walīd Ismāʿīl as king. Although Ismāʿīl routed his uncle Nasr at Atosa near Granada, Infante Pedro drove him back to Málaga on 28 May.[114]

Hoping to take advantage of the volatility of the situation, Fernando IV and Jaime II, meeting at Calatayud in November 1311, pledged to make war on the Moors. Nevertheless, as Jaime II was preoccupied with his invasion of Sardinia, he could not resume hostilities against Granada. Although Edward II of England, citing his war with the Scots, refused financial aid, Dinis of Portugal made a contribution. The Cortes of Valladolid in March 1312 also granted Fernando IV five *servicios* and a *moneda forera* for the war. In July, besides the five *servicios*, he asked the towns of the archbishopric of Toledo for another *servicio* to maintain his fleet. He also urged his lieutenants in Murcia to ravage the kingdom of Granada every day "as cruelly as you possibly can."[115]

The Crusade of Algeciras Resumed

After withdrawing from Algeciras and Almería, Fernando IV and Jaime II attempted to explain to Clement V why they terminated their crusade. Rebuking Infante Juan and Juan Manuel for desertion and reproaching Jaime II for giving credence to the Marinid emir, the pope emphasized that, among the unfortunate consequences of the crusade, Christian military strength was discredited and the Moors were better prepared for future attacks. Despite Fernando IV's insistence that a papal refusal to grant a subsidy would jeopardize Spain and Christendom, the pope noted that previous Spanish kings had defeated the Muslims without any aid from the church.[116] Nevertheless, he ordered the imposition of ecclesiastical censures on those who failed to contribute financially to the struggle.[117]

In his need for funds to prosecute the war, the king stepped up collection of the *decima*.[118] In 1309 Clement V had granted the *decima* for three years, but after the fall of Gibraltar, he ordered the Castilian bishops, gathered in provincial councils, to advise him whether to sanction collection for the entire term. In July 1311 he announced that the *decima* for the third year would not be collected.[119] The king apparently ignored that restriction and also collected the *tercias* without papal authorization.[120] Although the pope was reluctant to allow the king to tap ecclesiastical revenues, he did issue four crusading bulls on 1 August 1312 repeating the terms of similar bulls published in 1309. He also permitted the diversion to the crusade of all fines levied for usury and other offenses.[121]

Meanwhile, Fernando IV joined his brother Pedro who had been besieging Alcaudete since June 1312.[122] Infante Juan was expected to bring reinforcements, but, fearful that the king would kill him, he failed to do so. The surrender of Alcaudete on 4 September may have been the price that Nasr had to pay to enlist Castilian support against the revolt of Ismāʿīl of Málaga. Three days later, Fernando IV, who had returned to Jaén, died at the age of twenty-seven.[123] Pedro, after proclaiming his deceased brother's infant son, Alfonso XI, made peace with Nasr and arranged for the defense of the frontier.[124]

Shortly before the king died, Clement V, exasperated by the continued collection of the *tercias* without papal consent, imposed an interdict on Castile.[125] When he learned of the king's death, he halted the dispatch of the crusading bulls, which thus remained without effect. Concluding that Jaime II could not effectively prosecute the war alone, he denied his request for the *decima*.[126]

The Achievement of Fernando IV

The reign of Fernando IV began badly, as his neighbors challenged his right to rule and attempted to dismember his realms. Muhammad II seized Quesada and Alcaudete and his son Muhammad III secured a foothold in Morocco by capturing Ceuta, only to lose it to Abū l-Rabīʿ, the Marinid emir. Once Fernando IV reached adult age, he collaborated with Jaime II in a crusade directed at the capture of Algeciras and Almería. Although neither objective was achieved, the Castilians did occupy Gibraltar. As Fernando IV resumed his crusade, his brother Pedro recovered Alcaudete, but the king's sudden death brought the crusade to a halt. One can only speculate whether Fernando IV, had he lived longer, would have achieved greater success in the reconquest. Giménez Soler described him as more loyal than his father, less immoral than his son, and, like both of them, an enthusiast for the reconquest.[127] The ensuing struggle over the regency for his son, Alfonso XI, proved disastrous for Castile.

Chapter 7

The Early Crusades of Alfonso XI's Reign

In spite of the disorder of the early years of Alfonso XI (1312–50), his uncle Infante Pedro carried out several crusades against the kingdom of Granada.[1] Nevertheless, his sudden death and that of his uncle Infante Juan, during their crusade in 1319, plunged the kingdom into turmoil. During those years, however, the Marinids remained apart from the Peninsula, and discord among the Nasrids minimized their opportunities to seize Castilian territory. After attaining his majority in 1325, Alfonso XI, supported by papal crusading bulls, began a frontal assault on the kingdom of Granada, frightening Muhammad IV, who summoned the Marinids to his aid.

Castile and the Civil War in Granada

As the new king, whose mother died in 1313, was little more than one year old, his grandmother, María de Molina, his uncle Pedro, and his great-uncle Juan contended for control of the regency.[2] While María de Molina took charge of his person, the infantes, especially Pedro, assumed the duty of defending the realm.[3] In May, the towns of Andalucía, forming the Hermandad General at Palma del Río, between Córdoba and Seville, acknowledged Pedro and his mother as regents. In order to raise funds necessary to secure the coast against possible Marinid attack, they enacted a complex series of financial articles.[4] Nevertheless, the perennial conflict with Tlemcen precluded Abū Saʿīd, the Marinid emir, from intervening in the Peninsula. Having ceded Algeciras to Nasr in 1312, he no longer had a foothold in Spain.[5] En route to the frontier, in November 1313, Pedro met urban representatives of the *hermandad*, as well as the archbishop of Seville and the bishop of Córdoba, at Villarreal.[6]

By then the kingdom of Granada was in disarray. In August 1312, shortly before the death of Fernando IV, King Nasr renewed his vassalage and the payment of tribute, and Pedro confirmed that agreement.[7] However, Nasr's circumstances changed quickly when Ismāʿīl ibn Faraj challenged his right to rule and marched on Granada. Besieged in the Alhambra, Nasr appealed to Pedro, who was not able to respond immediately. Thus, Ismāʿīl seized the Alhambra in February 1314 and compelled Nasr, the last representative of the direct line of the Nasrid dynasty, to withdraw to Guadix, northeast of Granada. Although Ismāʿīl seems to have guaranteed his security for life, Nasr was unwilling to accept his reduced status. When Pedro seized the castle of Rute, northwest of the city, he informed Nasr that, in exchange for his help, he expected to receive either Guadix or a more valuable kingdom; presumably he had Granada in mind.[8]

Ismāʿīl ibn Faraj ibn Nasr, or Ismāʿīl I (1314–25), a member of a collateral branch of the Nasrid royal family, brought renewed stability to the kingdom. So long as Nasr attempted to break out of his exile in Guadix, Ismāʿīl I seemed prepared to maintain peaceful relations with Castile and Aragón. He assured Jaime II of his friendship and guaranteed the security of Catalan merchants in the Nasrid kingdom. However, when Moorish troops plundering the Castilian realm of Murcia advanced into the neighboring kingdom of Valencia, Jaime II protested. Ismāʿīl I likely was also responsible for stirring up hostility against Castile along the frontier of the kingdom of Jaén. In December 1314 "wicked Christians" reportedly joined the Moors in attacking Quesada and Bedmar and even the *alcázar* of Jaén.[9]

Nasr, meanwhile, made insistent appeals for help to Pedro, but ongoing concerns about the regency made it impossible for him to act in force. Turning to Jaime II, Nasr denounced the treason of his "wicked vassal," Ismāʿīl I, and accused him of violating his pledge to leave him undisturbed in Guadix. While responding in a friendly manner, Jaime II offered no assistance. On the contrary, writing to Pedro and Juan, he expressed his expectation that the Moors would be destroyed and invited them to outline a plan for cooperative action against them. Given the dissension among the Nasrids, Pedro, though he intended to meet Nasr at Úbeda, argued that the time was ripe to seize the kingdom of Granada and offered Jaime II a sixth part, if he renewed the treaty of Alcalá of 1308. In January 1316, Nasr reminded the king that Pedro, Juan, and María de Molina planned to aid him in recovering his kingdom.[10]

In the spring of 1316 the prelates of the realm, assembled at Medina del Campo and Olmedo, pledged a *servicio* and an *ayuda* or aid in support of

Pedro's projected campaign.[11] When he dispatched a convoy to supply Guadix, however, 'Uthmān ibn Abī l-'Ulā, now commanding Ismā'īl I's forces, intercepted it on 8 May. In the ensuing battle near the castle of Alicún, Pedro, aided by Nasr, achieved a complete victory, killing 1,500 Muslims and 40 magnates. Forced to lift the siege of Guadix, Ismā'īl I retired to Granada. In June Pedro captured the castles of Cambil, Alhamar, and Benaxixar southeast of Jaén and then arranged a truce until 31 March of the following year; it was later extended for six months. On his return to Córdoba, the frontier towns gave him a *servicio* of 1,000,000 *maravedíes*. Representatives of the towns also visited the royal court of Granada, probably to arrange the exchange of captives. Although Aragón was included in the truce, Nasrid forces, passing through Murcia, raided Jaime II's kingdom of Valencia. Although he demanded a halt to these expeditions, he was planning "a good invasion" of the kingdom of Granada in the coming year.[12]

Planning the Crusade

For the campaign against Granada to be most effective, Pedro and Jaime II realized the importance of securing papal support. Castilian relationships with the papacy were frayed, however, as Clement V had imposed an interdict because of Fernando IV's continued use of the *tercias* without authorization. Protesting that they could not live without the spiritual benefits of the church, the *hermandad* of Andalucía in January 1313 invited the archbishop of Seville and the bishops of Córdoba and Jaén to join an appeal to the pope. Late in the year the pope relented and lifted the interdict.[13] After Clement V's death in April 1314, the papacy remained vacant for twenty-seven months, so there was no possibility of obtaining crusading benefits. The election of John XXII (1316–34), however, brought that unhappy period to an end.

In the interim, Jaime II organized a confraternity in 1315 in Barcelona to wage war against the Saracens. Charitable contributions would be used to ready a fleet for that purpose.[14] John XXII granted an indulgence of five years to the people of Mallorca who were preparing a fleet to defend themselves against Muslim raids. He also allowed them to use for four years the *decima* for the crusade to the Holy Land authorized by Clement V in the Council of Vienne.[15] In 1316 some 500 Norman and French knights, who had taken the crusading vow, indicated their desire to accompany Jaime II on his crusade against "the enemies of the faith" in the following summer. Though he accepted their offer, he had to wait until the expiration of the truce with Granada at the end of March.[16]

John XXII seemed favorably disposed to the pleas of Pedro and Jaime II. Though he promised Pedro an aid large enough to bring the proposed attack on Granada to a successful conclusion, he was not prepared to accord similar benefits to Jaime II, who seemed aloof from the struggle. Nevertheless, Cardinal Napoleone Orsini, the king's agent in the papal court, expressing the hope that Jaime II's "most glorious affair" would achieve many good things, counseled him to explain his plans more specifically. Beginning abruptly at this point, the *Poema de Alfonso XI* related that the pope, conceding the bull of crusade and the *decima*, urged Pedro to ignore his truce with Ismāʿīl I and to conquer Granada.[17]

In February 1317 John XXII authorized the archbishops of Toledo and Seville and the bishop of Córdoba to preach a crusade against Granada under Pedro's leadership. During the next three years everyone who served continuously and without interruption for a full year, whether on land or at sea, could gain the indulgence granted for the crusade to the Holy Land. All would enjoy papal protection for the duration of the campaign.[18] Moreover, for three years 150,000 gold florins, taken from the *tercias* and the *decima* levied by Clement V for the Holy Land, would be diverted to the war against Granada.[19] Of that amount 12,000 to 14,000 florins should be used to arm six galleys for four months.[20] Anyone supplying arms and other strategic war materials to Granada was condemned, but could be absolved after making monetary compensation.[21]

A comment by Al-Makkarī suggests how the Muslims perceived Pedro's crusading plans. He tells us that "the king, Don Betroh [Pedro] repaired to Toledo, where he had a conference with the head of the church, whom the Christians call Bábá (Pope); that he worshipped him, went on his knees before him, and communicated to him his design of conquering whatever provinces still remained in the hands of the Moslems; that the Bábá, in short, strengthened him in his purpose." Perhaps these words are an echo of a ceremony in Toledo when Pedro, kneeling before the archbishop, took the crusader's vow and then listened to his exhortation.[22]

Also in February John XXII authorized Jaime II to divert to the war against Granada 35,000 to 40,000 pounds (*libras*) from the *decima* intended for the Holy Land and to use the remainder for the siege of Almería. Crusade collectors were ordered to deliver the money to the king so long as hostilities were in progress.[23] While these concessions were welcome, they fell short of what the pope had granted to Pedro. Emphasizing the need "to eradicate the cursed and fetid sect of the abominable Muhammad residing in these parts of Spain," Jaime II noted that the king of Granada, realizing that the pope wished to bring about his ruin, was prepared to surrender his kingdom to the Marinids, rather than have it fall to the Christians. To guard against a likely Moroccan invasion, Jaime II asked for help, especially for a fleet to close the Strait. He also postponed a response to Nasr's latest pleas for assistance.[24] The *Royal Chronicle*'s statement that Ismāʿīl I ceded Algeciras, Ronda, Castellar, Jimena, Estepona, and Marbella to Abū Saʿīd confirmed Jaime II's words.[25] In April, John XXII, admonished Jaime II to clarify his plans for the war against Granada.[26]

The Crusade of 1317–18

In March 1317, after the assembly of Carrión authorized a tax levy of five *servicios*, Pedro prepared for his crusade. Nevertheless, Infante Juan, apparently distressed by Pedro's reluctance to share the *tercias* and *decima*, refused to join him. Other magnates, including Pedro's younger brother, Felipe, also refused to do so. In spite of this disloyalty, Pedro ravaged the vineyards and fields in the plain of Granada in late July. About the same time Yahyā b. Abī Tālib al-ʿAzafī, lord of Ceuta, besieged Gibraltar for several days and defeated a Christian fleet in the Strait, presumably one organized by Pedro.[27] Continuing his campaign, Pedro captured the castle of Bélmez de la Moraleda after a siege of three weeks. In December he urged the archbishop of Toledo and the bishop of Córdoba to collect the funds authorized by John XXII for the crusade. Unable to check the Castilian advance, Ismāʿīl I agreed to a truce and pledged to resume the payment of tribute.[28]

Preparing to resume the crusade in the spring, Pedro, Juan, and Juan Manuel agreed to share the crusade revenues. In support of the crusade, the Castilians gathered in the Cortes of Valladolid in June 1318 granted five *servicios* and a *moneda forera*, as did representatives of the towns of Extremadura and the kingdoms of Léon and Toledo in the Cortes of Medina del Campo in early September.[29] Pope John XXII, on 13 August 1318, issued a bull of crusade to Infante Juan and allowed him a share in the 150,000 gold florins cited above, provided that he remained at peace with Pedro and continually waged war against the Moors with 500 knights and six galleys for six months and with three galleys for an additional six months.[30]

Perhaps encouraged by these concessions, Jaime II tried again to persuade the pope to grant him the *decima* for six years. Though pleased to hear that Pedro was amenable to Jaime II's participation in the crusade, the pope remarked that the *decima* was intended for the expedition to the Holy Land and asked the king to make a special request for the Granada crusade. Three cardinals appointed to study the matter proposed a grant for three years, but they demanded to know when the king planned to set out, how many knights and how many galleys he would have, and the length of the projected campaign. As an indication of their expectations, they affirmed that Pedro had agreed to serve personally for three years with a certain number of knights and to deploy a certain number of galleys in the Strait for the whole year and to double the number in the summer. Saracens, other than captives, would not be permitted to remain in conquered territory. Those who wished to be baptized would be set free. Mosques would be turned into churches. One out of every ten cities, towns, or castles taken would be reserved for the Roman See. The church would have the *decima* and first fruits in every place that was captured. Pedro also pledged not to make war or peace with the Saracens without papal approval.

The papal documents conceding the *decima* to Pedro do not refer to these conditions, and it seems unlikely that he accepted all of them. The conversion of mosques into churches was traditional policy as was the guarantee of safe conduct given to Muslims who wished to withdraw to Muslim territory; but it was also traditional to allow Muslims to remain under Christian rule subject to the payment of tribute. Pedro apparently pledged not to make peace without papal authorization, as he justified his rupture of the truce in 1319 on that account. Yet it seems highly unlikely that he agreed to cede one out of every ten cities, towns, or castles to the papacy. No king of Castile had ever agreed to that proposition.

No doubt astonished by these representations, Jaime II responded that, accompanied by 2,000 knights and 30,000 foot soldiers, he planned to plunder Granada once a year for two years, to seize towns and castles, and to give battle to the king of Granada, should he present himself. Galleys would also be put to sea in support of this effort. As he was motivated only by the desire to serve God and the Roman See and to exalt the Catholic faith, he would not enter a truce with Granada. Although he required the *decima* for six years, the pope restricted it to three years, in the amount of 400,000 *sueldos* (which Jaime II considered inadequate), provided that the king invaded Granada each year and agreed to the conditions cited above. A report that the papal treasurers ordered that the money collected should be brought to the curia raised the suspicion that it would be used for the Holy Land rather than the war against Granada.[31]

In September 1318 Pedro informed Jaime II that, as his troops were exhausted by a campaign of four or five months and he needed to replenish his treasury, he made a truce with Ismāʿīl I until the following March. He invited Jaime II to join the effort to serve God and to gain honor for himself and his kingdom in the spring. Minimizing the value of minor incursions, however, Jaime II stressed that to be most effective an invasion of Granada had to be carried out with the greatest force to inflict the greatest damage.[32]

The Final Crusade of Infante Pedro and Infante Juan

Fully aware of the imminent crusade, Ismāʿīl I appealed in 1318 to the Marinid emir Abū Saʿīd for help. Prior to taking any action, however, the emir demanded the surrender of ʿUthmān ibn Abī l-ʿUlā, the Marinid prince and former pretender to the Moroccan throne, who commanded Marinid troops in Nasrid service. He probably knew that that was unlikely, and, given his concern to regain possession of Ceuta, he likely had no intention of intervening in the Peninsula. Thus, Ismāʿīl I was left without allies.[33]

In preparation for the crusade, Infantes Pedro and Juan summoned their vassals to Córdoba in June 1319. The *Grand Chronicle of Alfonso XI* related that one could find little to blame in Pedro's conduct, save this one instance of breaking the truce with Granada. Some suspected that that was why he met his death during the campaign. He justified himself by remarking that when Clement V granted the *tercias* and *decima* and the bull of crusade, he required Pedro, "on pain of obedience and love for the Holy See," not to make peace with "the enemies of the cross." Thus, Pedro informed Ismāʿīl I that he could not maintain the peace because of the papal command and the threat of excommunication. For that reason he also refused to accept the Nasrid tribute money. Determined to "observe the truth established by God," Ismāʿīl I charged Pedro with breaking faith and called on God to judge between them. In turn, Pedro remarked: "I would not be a son of King Don Sancho, if, within a few years, if God gives me life, I did not cause the house of Granada to be restored to the Crown of Spain."[34] Infante Juan informed Jaime II that, in order to cause the greatest damage, he planned to move southward from Córdoba while Pedro advanced from Úbeda. Jaime II was unable to participate because of illness, but his son Alfonso, "who had a great desire to serve God," appealed to the pope to support his planned invasion of Granada. The papal response is unknown, and there is no evidence that Alfonso took part in the crusade.[35]

Pedro's first objective was Tíscar, a castle perched on a peak known as the Peña Negra, just south of Quesada. Fernando III had captured it in 1224, but the Moors recovered possession probably about the time they seized Quesada. For thirteen days Pedro's siege engines battered its formidable walls, but to little avail. At last, on the night before Pentecost (26 May), a small band scaled the Peña Negra and killed the Moorish guards, thus enabling Pedro to break into the fortress. Once the Moors surrendered, he allowed them to depart with their movable goods. Infante Juan, reportedly displeased by Pedro's victory, joined him at Alcaudete. Setting out in mid-June, they approached the city of Granada on the vigil of St. John (23 June).[36]

Dismayed by the Castilian attack, Ismāʿīl I entrusted the defense of Granada to ʿUthmān ibn Abī l-ʿUlā. With about 5,000 knights he confronted the Christian army of 9,000 knights and many foot soldiers. On Monday, 25 June, ʿUthmān harassed the rear guard commanded by Infante Juan who summoned Pedro to his aid. When Pedro ordered his standard-bearer to lead his men into battle, they hesitated to do so, but a knight with sword and shield in hand pushed forward, crying out: "There are the Moors. Let us attack them, because it is better to die for God and to be honored for doing good, than to live a dishonored life forever!" At that a Moorish knight, warning Pedro that he could not escape death or imprisonment, threw down his spear as a challenge to battle. Angered, Pedro dashed forward, shouting "Santiago and Castile," though some of his men, fearing that he would be killed, tried to stop him. As he broke loose and rode ahead, he became entangled in the reins and was thrown from his horse. Speechless and bleeding from his nose and mouth, he lay motionless: "El infante fue tornado/ Syn ferida e syn batalla"—"The infante was toppled / Without a wound, without a battle." His men removed his armor and, as he expired, covered him with a scarlet cloth and placed his lifeless body on a mule. When the masters of Santiago, Calatrava, and Alcántara, the archbishop of Seville, and the bishop of Córdoba, who were in the vanguard about a mile and a half away, learned of his death, they fled.[37]

When Juan heard of Pedro's death, he exhorted his troops, telling them that with God's help they could overcome the Moors. Suddenly, however, he lost both understanding and speech and seemed neither dead nor alive. Later that night he died. Placing his body on a horse, leaving their standards and abandoning their camp, the crusaders began their retreat. Not knowing what had happened, but seeing the Castilians in disorder, the Moors plundered their encampment and killed or captured as many as they could.[38]

Pedro's vassals carried his body home for interment in the royal monastery of Las Huelgas de Burgos. Juan's vassals, however, betrayed their lord in a most grievous manner. Instead of guarding his body and bringing it safely back to Castile, they lost it under the cover of night, or, rather, one should say that they abandoned it in the land of the Moors. Distressed by this unpardonable breach of feudal etiquette, the infante's son Juan ordered a search, but without success. The Moors, however, found the body, unmarked by any wounds, and brought it to Granada. There, Ismāʿīl I placed it in a coffin covered with cloth of gold and surrounded by blazing candles and all the Christian captives. "As he had never received injury or harm" from Infante Juan, Ismāʿīl I appointed a Moorish honor guard to accompany a contingent of Christian knights sent to fetch the body, which was also buried at Las Huelgas. Both Pedro and Juan seem to have died from natural causes, perhaps cardiac arrest. Pedro was not quite twenty-nine years of age, but Juan was fifty-seven. The strenuous nature of the campaign, Juan's age, the heat of the day, and lack of water may have contributed to their demise. Seeing this tragedy as a divine judgment, the *Grand Chronicle* remarked that the wheel of fortune turned in a bad way, so that without a clash of arms, without any wounds inflicted, the infantes were dead. Whether that was because of their wicked intentions or the sins of the Christians, it was the will of God.[39]

Proclaiming that "God willed the triumph of his religion and the disgrace of infidelity," Ibn Khaldūn declared that Pedro's head was placed on the walls of Granada where it remained in his lifetime. Al-Makkarī recounted an even more elaborate fable. Pedro's wife and son were reportedly among the prisoners and, as ransom, the Castilians offered to surrender Tarifa and Gibraltar. Pedro's body, wrapped in cotton in a wooden coffin, supposedly was placed on the wall at the entrance to the Alhambra. None of this is true. The head or the body may have belonged to some other unfortunate Christian. Pedro's own people retrieved his body on the battlefield. His wife was at Córdoba, awaiting the birth of her child. If she had been taken prisoner, the ample correspondence of her father, Jaime II, would surely have recorded that fact. The notion that Tarifa and Gibraltar were offered as ransom seems to reflect the Muslim chronicler's nostalgia for their loss. Whereas the death of the infantes put an end to Nasr's aspirations to regain the Nasrid throne, his archenemy Ismāʿīl I could rejoice that the end of his kingdom had been postponed indefinitely.[40]

Compounding the sense of shock following the loss of the infantes were reports of extortion by men employed by the archbishops of Toledo and Seville and the bishop of Córdoba to collect money for the crusade. Although John XXII appointed a commission to investigate and to determine the whereabouts of the money, we hear nothing further of this.[41]

The End of the Crusade: The Truce of Baena

Meantime, the Hermandad General de Andalucía made a truce with Granada until Alfonso XI should come of age. Ismāʿīl I accepted it provided that the new regent confirmed it. Several meetings of the Hermandad reflected the uncertainty of the situation. Gathered at Palma del Río in July, the Hermandad declared, in accordance with the wishes of María de Molina, that it would not accept anyone as regent without the consent of the realm. Ratifying that decision a month later at Peñaflor (or Santa María de Villadiego near Palma del Río), the Hermandad decided to calculate revenues and expenditures for the defense of the frontier. In September the master of Calatrava and representatives of Jaén, Baeza, and Arjona, adhered to the *hermandad*, as did Úbeda and Baeza in November. The realm was thrown into disorder once more as Infante Juan's son Juan, known as *el tuerto*, the one-eyed, Juan Manuel, and Infante Felipe, the queen's youngest son, all claimed a share in the regency and attempted to win recognition from the regional *hermandades*. In April 1320 Baeza and Santiesteban recognized María de Molina as regent and pledged to guard against disorder.[42]

    Both the pope and the king of Aragón expressed their concern for the safety of the frontier. Urging the master of Calatrava to guard against Muslim incursions, John XXII expected that the prelates and nobles would convene shortly "so that the business of the war of the kingdom of Granada might be powerfully and forcefully resumed." Jaime II, who was wary of a Muslim attack on the kingdom of Valencia, exhorted his son-in-law, Juan Manuel, who had already hastened to Andalucía, to avert the grave danger threatening Castile by taking in hand the affairs of Alfonso XI.[43]

    Given the danger threatening the realm, the Hermandad, meeting at at Peñaflor on 23 April 1320, intended to negotiate a treaty with Ismāʿīl I and to ask John XXII to grant the *tercias* and *decima* as well as a bull of crusade for the defense of the realm. In addition to funds already derived from the *decima*, María de Molina was asked to utilize the royal revenues of Andalucía especially for the defense of Tarifa and Gibraltar. Town militias pledged to guard against Moorish attacks during the harvest season. The Hermandad would only accept the person chosen as regent by the Cortes when he or she gave written consent to the treaty to be concluded with Granada. By negotiating with Ismāʿīl I the Hermandad was acting independently of the crown. This also seems to be the first instance that a body, other than the king, requested a crusading bull.[44]

The Hermandad concluded a treaty of peace with Ismāʿīl I at Baena in June 1320. Agreeing to a truce of eight years, both parties promised to aid one another against their respective enemies. In a clause evidently directed against Nasr of Guadix, the Christians promised not to establish an alliance with another Moorish king. The export of wheat and livestock, except horses, would be permitted without an increase in customs duties. If a Moor fled to Christian territory, he would be repatriated, unless he became a Christian. Escaping Christian captives would be free, but whatever goods they brought with them would be returned to their owners. The same rule would apply to Moorish captives who fled. Castles ruined in the recent wars, including Alcaudete taken by Fernando IV in 1312, could not be rebuilt. All claimants to the regency would be obliged to observe these terms. As each town was asked to send representatives to Baena to confirm the treaty, Úbeda did so on 18 June.[45]

Meantime, the regency remained unsettled. When Córdoba recognized Juan Manuel, the towns of the kingdoms of Seville and Jaén protested that that was contrary to their sworn agreement not to act unilaterally. In December 1320 when those towns recognized Felipe as regent, he pledged to confirm the treaty arranged by the Hermandad.[46] In April 1321 the Cortes of Valladolid accepted Felipe, Juan Manuel, and Juan el Tuerto as regents. However, the death of María de Molina in June was a great misfortune as there was now no one with sufficient prestige to mediate among the contending regents.[47]

Perhaps in response to the Hermandad's pleas, John XXII in June 1321 granted the crusading indulgence and directed his legate Cardinal Guillaume Peyre de Godin and the Castilian prelates to enlist the faithful. The archbishop of Toledo and the bishops of Cartagena and Cuenca were delegated to preach the crusade.[48] Given the turbulence over the regency it seems likely that this crusading effort was ineffectual, except perhaps on a very local level. The pope also lauded King Dinis of Portugal for his desire to protect the Peninsula against the Moors and granted him the *decima* for three years. Perhaps contemplating some action in Morocco, Dinis had appointed the Genoese Manuel Pessagno (Peçanho) as his admiral, but nothing came of it.[49]

Jaime II declared that the Hermandad's treaty with Granada was a disservice to God and a diminishment of the sovereignty of Castile. Perhaps his principal objection was that the Hermandad acted without any apparent authorization by the crown. In the circumstances it is difficult to fault the Hermandad because Alfonso XI was only nine years of age and no one as yet had been recognized as regent. Jaime II still hoped to obtain papal consent to convert the *decima* granted for the crusade to the Holy Land to the war against Granada for six years. His motivation was "not any desire to acquire territory, but to avenge the injuries inflicted by the perfidy of the Saracens on the Christians of Spain." However, the papal consistory rejected this proposal.[50]

Thus, in mid-May 1321 Jaime II concluded a peace treaty for five years with Ismāʿīl I. Neither monarch would aid the enemies of the other. Merchants would be guaranteed secure passage for themselves and their goods through both realms. Ships from Tlemcen coming to Aragonese ports would be treated as neutral. Saracens could freely emigrate from the Crown of Aragón to Muslim lands. Certain restrictions were imposed on the export of horses and arms. The treaty marked the end of Jaime II's hopes of expanding his peninsular dominions. Henceforth he directed his attention to the conquest of Sardinia and Corsica. The treaty had advantages for the adjacent kingdom of Murcia, as it guaranteed an interval of tranquillity for five years. Nevertheless, there were complications. Negotiating a truce with Juan Manuel, *adelantado mayor de Murcia*, Ismāʿīl I wanted to insert a clause allowing Moorish forces to pass through Murcia in case of war against Aragón and to oblige the Murcians not to warn their fellow Christians. Jaime II, of course, strongly objected. As he readied a fleet for the conquest of Sardinia and Corsica, the kings of Granada and Tlemcen and the lord of Ceuta reportedly feared that he intended to attack them. In order to avert that, it was rumored that they planned a landing on the Valencian coast north of Alicante and that Ismāʿīl I would invade Valencia through Murcia. The Valencian Mudéjars were expected to rise in rebellion. The rumors proved to be unfounded and in 1326 he renewed his pact with Granada.[51]

Muhammad IV and Alfonso XI

Several factors, meanwhile, emboldened Ismāʿīl I, despite the treaty of Baena, to launch an offensive against Castile. Nasr's death in 1322 removed that thorn in Ismāʿīl I's side and the contention among the Castilian regents allowed him to act as he wished. In mid-July 1324 he captured the fortress of Baza near

Guadix. Moving northeastward he seized Orce, Galera, and Huéscar, belonging to the Order of Santiago on the border of the kingdom of Murcia. Cannons and gunpowder were used in the attack on Galera, apparently the earliest instance of this in Spain. After a bloody battle on 10 June 1325 he took Martos, a bastion of the Order of Calatrava south of Jaén. The master of Calatrava was accused of failing to provide for a proper defense of Martos.

Returning to Granada, Ismāʿīl I quarreled with his cousin, Muhammad b. Ismāʿīl, governor of Algeciras, and ʿUthmān ibn Abī l-ʿUlā, commander of the Nasrid army, who conspired to kill him. As Muhammad and his son accompanied Ismāʿīl I through a narrow passageway in the Alhambra, they turned on him and stabbed him. The royal *alguacil* attempted to defend him and, though wounded himself, was able to carry his body into the palace where surgeons attempted to revive him. Meantime, the attackers were seized and beheaded. In order to deflect suspicion from himself, ʿUthmān helped to arrest them. When Ismāʿīl I, one of the most effective kings of Granada, died of his wounds on 6 July, his eldest son, then only twelve years of age, was proclaimed as the new king, Muhammad IV (1325–33).[52]

Not long afterward, the tumultuous minority of Alfonso XI was terminated. Celebrating his fourteenth birthday on 13 August 1325, he dismissed his three regents and soon executed Juan el Tuerto for treason. After the death of Felipe in 1327, Juan Manuel remained as the only surviving regent and mistakenly assumed that he would now dominate the young king.[53] The king also prohibited the *hermandad*, thus effectively dissolving the Hermandad General de Andalucía. Formed to defend the frontier during his minority, he now perceived it as a potential challenge to his authority.[54]

Juan Manuel and the Battle of the River Guadalhorce

In the spring of 1326, ʿUthmān ibn Abī l-ʿUlā, now commanding the Nasrid army on behalf of Muhammad IV, resumed hostilities and recovered the castle of Rute taken by Infante Pedro twelve years before. As *adelantado mayor de Murcia* and *adelantado mayor de la frontera*, Juan Manuel was immediately responsible for defending the frontier.[55] Informed of his plan to take up arms against Granada, John XXII, in August 1326, promised future assistance.[56] Accompanied by the bishop of Jaén, the magnates, military orders, and urban militias, Juan Manuel marched southward from Córdoba in late July to Teba and Ardales on the Guadalhorce River near Antequera. When the Nasrid cavalry attacked, he prayed: "Lord, remember me and the Christians gathered here in praise and reverence of the Holy True Cross on which Jesus Christ suffered on Mount Calvary." Then, leaping on his horse, he cried out "God and Saint Mary," and called on Santiago, "the shield of Christendom," to help repel the enemy. In the melee the staff flying the standard, or *pendón*, of Baeza was broken. Depicting St. Isidore of Seville on horseback and bearing a sword in one hand and a cross in the other, the *pendón* probably originated in the thirteenth century. This is the first mention of its use in battle in the fourteenth century.[57]

Shouting "Santiago and Castile," Juan Manuel rallied his troops, forcing the Moors to flee toward Antequera. Unable to stem the rout, 'Uthmān, "like a rabid wolf," threw his lance at the enemy and tore his long, white beard, swearing not to take up his sword again for a year. Meantime, the victors promised to fast and to give alms in gratitude for divine favor. Although many Moors lay dead on the battlefield (3,000 according to the *Poema de Alfonso XI*), no more than 80 Christians had fallen. A banner of the king of Granada was among the prizes taken. Juan Manuel related that "the Lord defeated all the power of the king of Granada" on a Friday, the feast of the beheading of St. John, 29 August. On the next day, he advanced toward Teba and Ardales while the Moors withdrew to Antequera. Returning to Córdoba, he was received with great honor. Alfonso XI was overjoyed, but he was also annoyed that his counselors had insisted that he remain apart from the frontier.[58] Both Jaime II and John XXII congratulated the victor.[59]

The Muslim defeat intensified rivalry among the lords seeking to dominate Muhammad IV. In 1328 at the age of fifteen he executed his vizier and assumed direct control of his affairs, much as Alfonso XI had done in 1325. 'Uthmān, the military commander who rebelled against him, appealed in vain to Jaime II to facilitate his escape to North Africa. Forcing 'Uthmān to submit, Muhammad IV nevertheless restored him to his command.[60]

Alfonso XI's Early Crusade Proposals

Juan Manuel's triumph spurred Alfonso XI to undertake his first incursion into Muslim territory. The poet Rodrigo Yáñez stated that, for inspiration, the king read books describing the deeds of "the noble Cid Ruy Dias" and the cavalcades of noble kings against the Moors.[61] As early as October 1325 he dispatched envoys to the papal court, perhaps to seek crusading benefits, though the specific mission was not identified.[62] John XXII's entreaty in 1326 that the archbishop of Compostela, who had already incurred great expense in attending the Cortes, should not be required to participate in the war against Granada revealed the king's intentions.[63]

The king also requested that the pope grant the crusading indulgence to members of the confraternity of Santa María del Pilar, recently established in Seville "for the exaltation of the Catholic faith against the perfidious Agarenes [another name for Muslims] attacking the Christians in those parts." More than 2,000 knights belonging to the society were prepared "to oppose the said enemies of the Catholic faith." The indulgence was requested for those who, having repented and confessed their sins, served in person in the confraternity's ships or on land for a whole year, or for three months each year over four years, or provided financial support. Anyone who died in the enterprise should gain a plenary indulgence. As the pope was unfamiliar with the confraternity, he appointed several officials to inquire about its membership and purpose.[64] Aragonese settling in Seville after 1248 founded the confraternity. In 1317 Infante Pedro granted a site for a hospital to lodge pilgrims and care for the sick, and the king extended his protection in 1322. A document of 1327 referred to the confraternity's military and naval purposes, citing knights on cavalcade as well as ships of various types and "all our other ships on the sea." In 1333 its members included the king and queen, the royal princes, prelates, and nobles.[65]

In addition to the bull of crusade, the king also asked for the *decima* as well as the *tercias*, which, in fact, he was already taking. Jaime II learned that the king's envoys, "with Castilian arrogance," had made "many inconvenient and unworthy petitions," and would obtain little.[66] When John XXII rejected their pleas in 1327, Alfonso XI expressed his consternation, prompting the pope to reply that, although his predecessors had granted the *decima* and the *tercias* for the crusades to the Holy Land and in Spain, the kings had often diverted the money to other purposes. Unless the king was prepared to offer guarantees, the pope would not accede to his request. At the same time he required the Spanish bishops to pay the *decima* authorized by Clement V for the crusade to the Holy Land fourteen years before.[67]

Despite the pope's negative response, Alfonso XI for the first time set out for the frontier in the summer of 1327.[68] Welcoming him to Seville was 'Uthmān's son Ibrāhīm, who had participated in the recent rebellion against Muhammad IV, and now entered Castilian service.[69] His presence was discounted, however, by the defection of Juan Manuel, who refused to join the king or surrender frontier revenues in his possession. The campaign's first objective was Olvera, a stronghold near Antequera. The defenders, worn down by siege engines bombarding the walls, surrendered toward the end of July and were permitted to depart with their movable goods.[70] Alfonso XI captured the neighboring castles of Pruna, Torre Alháquime, and Ayamonte, but these conquests proved ephemeral, as the Moors recovered them within a few years.[71] On returning to Seville, the king offered prayers of thanksgiving in the confraternity's church of Santa María del Pilar.[72]

During the campaign of Olvera, Alfonso Jofre Tenorio, *almirante mayor de la mar*, with a fleet of six galleys, eight *naos*, and six *leños* (*naos* and *leños* were types of sailing ships), gave battle to Muhammad IV's twenty-two galleys in the waters off Almería and Málaga. The Castilians seized three enemy galleys, sank four others, and killed 1,200 Moors. Tenorio brought the three captured galleys to Seville and, preceded by 200 captives, made a triumphal entry into the city. As a mark of honor, the elated king met him outside the walls.[73]

Realizing that Alfonso XI would likely soon resume his campaign, Muhammad IV turned for help to the Marinids, ceding Ronda and Marbella to them in 1327, and, in the following year, Algeciras.[74] To counter that move, the king, in the expectation of securing Portuguese military and naval support, contracted to marry María, daughter of Afonso IV of Portugal (1325–57).[75] The marriage was solemnized in 1328.[76] By doing so, he repudiated his earlier pledge to marry Juan Manuel's daughter.[77] Anticipating that, Juan Manuel had refused to participate in the king's recent campaign and now sought an alliance with Muhammad IV. Intercepted documents revealed that he suggested that they wage war against Castile. If that were not possible, he offered to become a vassal of the Nasrid king, and to serve him with 1,000 knights. Should that idea be declined, Juan Manuel, who possessed extensive dominions throughout Castile, proposed to sell certain fortresses that would give Muhammad IV greater power than any of his predecessors and enable him to levy war from the frontier as far north as Toledo and Castile. When Alfonso XI learned of Juan Manuel's treason, he ordered his messengers to be hung, after their hands and feet were cut off and their eyes were gouged out. While Juan Manuel, from his strongholds of Escalona and Peñafiel, ravaged Castile, Muhammad IV accepted the proffered alliance and began an attack on the frontier.[78]

Planning a New Crusade

Meanwhile, in March 1328 when Alfonso XI appealed for crusading indulgences and the attendant financial benefits, John XXII concluded that the king could do nothing without the aid of Juan Manuel, a powerful, but rebellious, magnate.[79] Thus, he sent his legate to reconcile the two opponents. Emphasizing the many honors he had given to Juan Manuel, Alfonso XI accused him of forsaking his post, leaving Andalucía unprotected, and refusing the royal summons to join the attack on Olvera. Worst of all, in alliance with the king of Granada, "an enemy of the law of God and of Christendom," he plundered and burned Castile.[80] The king, who requested the concession of the *decima* for ten years to be paid in five, also explained that, as his predecessors had taken the *tercias*, he did not believe it necessary to ask the papacy for permission. The cardinals found that to be disingenuous.[81]

Nevertheless, in June the pope granted the bull of crusade and the right to collect the *decima* and the *tercias* for four years. Those who died on the crusade or elsewhere as a result of wounds received were guaranteed a plenary indulgence. The archbishop of Seville and the bishops of Córdoba and Jaén were designated to confer the crusader's cross on both Castilians and foreigners. Charged with collection of the *decima* and the *tercias*, the three prelates were required to secure the money in the churches and to render accounts to the pope.[82]

Several conditions were attached to these concessions. Should the king be unable to lead the crusade in person, he would appoint a capable commander with at least 500 knights. The king would be expected to command many more knights than that. Waged for four years, the war would be not merely defensive, but would aim to seize the enemy's towns and fortresses. Casualties would be replaced immediately by fresh troops. In newly conquered towns churches would be restored or built and endowed with sufficient personnel and financial support. Moors living in conquered places to the scandal of Christians would be forbidden to proclaim the name of Muhammad and to go on pilgrimage to Mecca. Christians would be obliged to pay tithes. Sentences of excommunication and interdict would be strictly enforced, and ecclesiastical immunities and privileges would be observed. The sacred vessels could not be pawned, sold, or alienated in any way. In December 1328 Alfonso XI thanked the pope.[83]

Meantime, Alfonso XI was busily seeking an alliance with his Christian neighbors. After the death of Jaime II of Aragón, his son Alfonso IV (1327–36) urged Alfonso XI to make peace with Juan Manuel, whom he denounced for aligning himself with the Moors. Although Alfonso IV, in 1328, renewed for five years his father's pact with Granada, he was increasingly disturbed by Muhammad IV's alliance with Abū Saʿīd, the Marinid emir, who was reported to be preparing an invasion of Spain.[84] Therefore, at Tarazona on 6 February 1329, Alfonso IV pledged to collaborate with Alfonso XI against the Moors. Neither would make peace without the other. Aragonese troops would be permitted to traverse the Castilian kingdom of Murcia into Moorish territory and to purchase necessary supplies.[85] Alfonso XI urged his royal colleague to accompany him to the frontier on 1 May, but he preferred to act independently. Intent on acquiring Almería, he planned to march through Murcia, while ten Catalan galleys proceeded along the coast. The Corts of Valencia contributed 100,000 *libras* for the campaign.[86] In March, protesting persistent Muslim attacks he nullified his pact with Muhammad IV and declared war against Granada.[87]

Turning to the papacy, Alfonso IV requested the bull of crusade and other benefits, including the *decima* for ten years; the revenue of all vacant benefices in the first year of a five-year period, and a third of that revenue in the other four years; and permission for crusading clerics to retain their benefices. Although he did not wish to be obliged to begin the crusade on a fixed date or to participate in person, John XXII insisted that he serve personally each year and would only grant the *decima* for three years. According to the king's estimate, an annual income of 20,000 *libras* from the *decima* would only sustain his army for three months. In all, he expected to have 2,500 knights, 30,000 foot soldiers, and twenty galleys. Despite his plea for some modification, the papal response was negative.[88]

Northern European Crusaders

Meanwhile, northern Europeans, whose ancestors had taken part in earlier crusades to Jerusalem, now looked to Spain. After the end of the crusader kingdom of Jerusalem in 1291, various plans were advanced for the recovery of the Holy Land but with little success. Aware of the Muslim presence in Spain, northerners realized that, by participating in the defense of Christendom there, they could gain honor as well as the crusading indulgence. Some, such as the Pastoureaux, were clearly undesirable. French peasants, stirred by popular preachers to liberate the Holy Land, they entered the Crown of Aragón in

1320 on the pretext of carrying out a crusade against Granada. Recognizing their potential for destruction, Jaime II ordered their expulsion.[89]

In February 1328, however, Alfonso IV endeavored to enlist potential crusaders among the nobility of France and Germany.[90] Count Philip of Valois had obtained a bull of crusade from John XXII in March 1326, but failed to act on it. In August of the following year the pope reissued the bull, provided that Philip served continuously for a full year or gave twelve months' service over two years.[91] Though he succeeded to the French throne as Philip VI in 1328, he still aspired to undertake a crusade against Granada with the king of Navarre, the dukes of Brittany, Burgundy, and Bourbon, the counts of Hainaut, Flanders, Alençon, and Beaumont, and a force of 2,000–2,500 knights. Nevertheless, his rivalry with Edward III of England eventually compelled him to abandon those plans.[92]

Another prospective crusader was John, count of Luxembourg and king of Bohemia. At first Alfonso IV told him to postpone his arrival until the conflict between Alfonso XI and Juan Manuel could be resolved. Then, in February 1329, he encouraged him to hasten to Aragón with 200 knights and 400 crossbowmen. Fearful of the "disorder and scandal" that a large army passing through his dominions might cause, however, Alfonso IV instructed his envoy to the French court not to discuss the crusade with any other nobles. In the end, John delayed his departure indefinitely and seems never to have come to the Peninsula.[93] Addressing the kings of Aragón, Castile, and Portugal, Philip of Évreux, king of Navarre, expressed his desire to participate in the crusade, solely out of love of God, reserving only the right to booty and prisoners taken by his men. John XXII, on 24 February 1330, rewarded him for his zeal by granting him the bull of crusade and the *decima* of Navarre for two years.[94]

Many nobles of lesser rank were also attracted by the possibility of a crusade in Spain. Theobald of Blazón, whose ancestor had taken part in the Crusade of Las Navas de Tolosa in 1212, announced in August 1329 that he and other French lords were prepared to join Alfonso IV's crusade in the following year. Count William of Hainaut also indicated his desire to take part.[95] Henry, lord of Seuilly, asked John XXII for the bull of crusade.[96] The pope asked Alfonso IV to welcome Count William of Jülich in Prussia, who proclaimed his desire to avenge the "atrocious injuries inflicted on the faithful of the orthodox faith by the blasphemers of the Christian name in the kingdom of Granada."[97] Aside from Walter of Enghien, who, accompanied by an Aragonese messenger, made the journey to the Granadan frontier, it is uncertain whether any of these men actually participated in the crusade.[98] Some perhaps did so, but others, distracted by their own concerns and by the uncertainty of Alfonso IV, likely remained at home.

The Portuguese chronicler Rui de Pina related that ambassadors from the king of France and various German magnates visited the kings of Aragón, Castile, and Portugal to propose a collaborative crusade to deliver the Holy Land. After listening to their plea at Seville, Alfonso XI sought the counsel of Afonso IV. Replying to the French argument that "we would surely save our souls, if we go against the Moors and wage war against them," the Portuguese monarch pointed out that "we can do this in our own land." Not only would the Spanish kings "win land from the infidels that our children will later inherit," but "we would be delivered from the disdain and vituperation of other Christians who blame our ancestors for allowing the Moors to live among us." It was foolish to undertake a long journey to make war when the enemy was at the gates. To lose people and treasure in an attempt to conquer strange lands to be inherited by the children of others was unreasonable, especially when there were lands closer to hand that "our children will directly inherit." That would be tantamount to trying to put out the fire in someone else's house while one's own was burning. If we did that, said the king, people would think we were fools and would "inscribe us in the *Book of Fools*." The kings of Spain, in his judgment, ought rather to wage war against the "family of dogs inhabiting the mountains of the kingdom of Granada" as well as their neighbors, the Marinids. Once they were destroyed, then the conquest of the Holy Land could be undertaken. "It would seem unreasonable to seek war with the Moors in foreign lands, while those in your own were left in peace."[99] Although this letter is undated and the king of France is not named, he may have been Charles IV or, more likely, Philip VI, who succeeded to the French throne in 1328 and whose interest has been cited above. However that may be, to my knowledge, the French effort to enlist the peninsular monarchs in the fate of the Holy Land is unknown.

The Crusade of 1330

Focusing rather on the Peninsula, Afonso IV and Alfonso XI prepared for war against Granada. After obtaining the bull of crusade from John XXII in February 1330 and the right to the *decima* and the *tercias* for ten years, Afonso IV sent to the frontier 500 knights, commanded by the master of the Portuguese Order of Christ.[100] The Cortes of Madrid in June 1329, responding to Alfonso

XI's plea for financial assistance so that he could "conquer the land that the Moors, the enemies of the faith, kept from him by force," authorized four *ayudas*. After many false starts, he also reached an accord with Juan Manuel. Setting out from Córdoba in July 1330, Alfonso XI intended to expand the area around Olvera, which he had taken in 1327, by attacking the nearby fortress of Teba, situated in the foothills of the mountains of Ronda. The formidable Castillo de la Estrella, or Castle of the Star, overlooked the village. As siege engines were brought up and siege towers were constructed, the siege began on 7 August. With 6,000 knights, ʿUthmān ibn Abī l-ʿUlā, the commander of the Nasrid forces, faced the Christians across the Guadateba River. During one skirmish, a "foreign count who had left his land to serve God and to test his body against the enemies of the Cross," left the main body of the army, "as he ought not to have done," and advanced against the Moors. "Through his own fault," he was attacked and killed.[101] The count in question may have been one or another of the French and German nobles mentioned above. One such person was Sir James Douglas, a loyal vassal of King Robert Bruce of Scotland. Unable to fulfill his vow to go crusading in the Holy Land, Bruce asked that after his death Douglas should bury his heart near the Holy Sepulchre. After Bruce died in June 1329, Douglas, carrying the deceased monarch's heart in a silver casket, sailed from Scotland to the Bay of Biscay and then to "Sebell the Graunt," or Seville the Grand. His intention surely was to continue to the Holy Land.[102]

Hearing of his arrival, Alfonso XI, the "kyng of Spayne," offered him gold and silver, horses and arms in return for his service. Although Douglas refused those gifts, he declared his willingness to fight against the Saracens. According to the Scottish historian John Barbour (d. 1395), Alfonso XI set out to oppose the "kyng of Balmeryñe" that is, the emir of the Benimerines or Marinids, who had entered Spain. In fact, the ensuing battle did not involve the Marinids, but rather the forces of the king of Granada. After reminding his men that by their service to God they would enjoy heaven's bliss, Douglas, who was assigned to the vanguard, advanced against the enemy. In a symbolic gesture, he hurled the silver casket enclosing Bruce's heart into the midst of the Saracens, shouting out: "Pass thou forward and I shall follow or else die." When battle was joined, many were slain and the Saracens turned in flight. Pursuing them, Douglas, with only about ten men, got ahead of the main army that resisted the impulse to chase the enemy. Suddenly surrounded by Moors, he and his company were killed. As the Saracens withdrew, his men recovered his body and also found the casket with Bruce's heart. The grieving

Scots eventually made their way home, where Douglas was given honorable burial and Bruce's heart was interred in Melrose Abbey.[103] The people of Teba have renamed their Plaza de España in honor of Douglas and erected a stone monument testifying to his heroism. Angus MacKay commented that Bruce participated posthumously in a crusade and that in this instance "Andalucía was another Holy Land and a kind of Jerusalem."[104]

The action of the anonymous count or Sir James Douglas seems typical of crusaders with little experience of warfare against the Muslims either in the Holy Land or in Spain. So many of them thought that through mere bravado they could overcome the enemy. Jean Froissart commented that, as Douglas always wished to be the first to attack, he and his men rushed forward, leaving the main army behind, only to be slaughtered by the Moors. As they did so often, the Moors likely feigned retreat in order to disconcert the Christians. While the Castilians recognized this tactic and held back, Douglas did not and paid with his life. The Moors, who were as well attuned to the code of chivalry as the Christians, probably discovered Douglas's body and the silver casket containing Bruce's heart and returned them to the Scots.

After a month in the siege, the master of the Order of Christ, informed Alfonso XI that he and the Portuguese knights had fulfilled their three months' service (counting the journey to and from Teba) and intended to depart. The king attempted to dissuade them in vain.[105]

Meanwhile, 'Uthmān ibn Abī l-'Ulā, "a powerful warrior . . . and a good knight," and "very wise in the ways of war," planned to entrap the Castilians. Sending 3,000 of his knights to the Guadateba River in the hope of luring the crusaders into combat, he concealed another 3,000 in a nearby valley. However, Alfonso XI learned of the plan and drove the Moors back across the river, killing or capturing many. The Christians might have inflicted greater damage, but they halted their pursuit to plunder the enemy's camp of tents, animals, clothing, and whatever else was left behind. On the following morning, 'Uthmān enticed about 500 crusader foot soldiers to cross the river and then, turning about, killed about fifty and chased the others. Rescuing the survivors, Alfonso XI forbade anyone to cross the river without authorization. Soon after, his siege engines breached the wall of Teba, enabling his men to enter and to put the Moors to the sword. They surrendered on 30 August 1330 and were permitted to withdraw safely with only the clothes on their backs. After taking Teba, the king seized the nearby castles of Pego and Cañete la Real, and the abandoned towers of Las Cuevas del Becerro and Ortegícar.[106] Alfonso XI rewarded the knights of Santiago for their service and granted a charter to Teba and offered tax exemptions to those who would settle there and in other captured positions. Although he had succeeded in expanding his frontier south of Olvera, west of Antequera, and north of Ronda, the Moors recovered many of these places not long afterward.[107]

While Alfonso XI was busy with the siege of Teba, he hoped that Alfonso IV and Juan Manuel would also enter the fray. However, the king of Aragón, concerned about an uprising on Sardinia, had to counter Muslim naval actions off the Valencian coast and overcome difficulties in obtaining secure passage through Murcia to Granada and the reluctance of the knights of the Hospital to participate. In mid-August 1330 the host, including Juan Manuel, the papal legate, Cardinal Pedro Gómez Barroso, bishop of Cartagena, and about 700 to 800 knights and 2,000 foot soldiers, began the crusade. Hearing mass on Sunday morning, 26 August, they "took the cross," that is, they took the crusader's vow and placed the sign of the cross on their garments. Lacking siege machinery, they opted to ravage Huércal and other villages in the valley of the Almanzora River, but by Saturday, 1 September, they returned to Lorca. For all practical purposes, their crusade was finished. However, Juan Manuel, proposing to carry on the war by sea from the port of Cartagena, asked Alfonso IV for assistance in arming and provisioning his galleys. Still unwilling to collaborate with the king of Castile, he expected to accompany Alfonso IV in the expedition projected for the following year. Although Alfonso XI would have preferred to have his services, he agreed that that arrangement was best for everyone. The *Royal Chronicle*, however, accused Juan Manuel of failing to make war against the Moors and, indeed, of informing the king of Granada that he preferred to observe the peace rather than disrupt it.[108]

Peace Between Castile and Granada

The Castilians, having pressed the war everyday from the end of July to the beginning of September, at considerable cost, were exhausted, and Alfonso XI doubted that he would soon be able to resume his crusade. Muhammad IV, whose kingdom had been severely ravaged, indicated his desire for peace. Although Alfonso XI initially rebuffed his overtures, concern about the uncertain allegiance of Juan Manuel, the expense of the recent crusade, and the lengthy service required of his vassals convinced him to come to terms.[109]

Peace was concluded in Seville on 19 February 1331 for a period of four years, beginning on 1 March. In Muhammad IV's name his emissaries kissed

Alfonso XI's hand as a sign of vassalage and promised to pay an annual tribute of 12,000 gold *doblas*, the equivalent of 246,000 *maravedíes*. Payable in three equal installments, that amount approached the 250,000 *maravedíes* paid as tribute in the reign of Alfonso X. He also promised to send one of his relatives to Alfonso XI's Cortes once a year and to remain there for twenty days. Given the shortage of food resulting from the devastation of the countryside, Muhammad IV asked that his people be able to purchase Castilian wheat and livestock subject to a duty of one-twentieth, 5 percent.[110]

Alfonso IV had previously expressed concern that Alfonso XI, contrary to the treaty of Tarazona, might make peace with Granada without him. Although he was included in the treaty of Seville, he objected strenuously, especially as he expected northern crusaders to arrive in the spring. That possibility was eliminated, however, when Philip VI asked that the crusade be postponed. Several Muslim attacks on the Valencian frontier and rumors that Muhammad IV was assembling a large army for an invasion give evidence of uncertainty about the inclusion of Aragón in the treaty.[111]

The Order of La Banda and the Ideal of Chivalry

The truce enabled Alfonso XI to address economic and financial difficulties but with mixed results. By minting new coins, he remedied the shortage of money, but manipulations by his physician, Samuel ibn Wakar, caused a general rise in prices. When Yūsuf of Écija, the royal *almojarife mayor*, leased collection of frontier revenues (*almojarifazgo*), Samuel persuaded the king to halt exports to Granada, contrary to the truce. That led to a decline in revenue and in Yūsuf's profit, but, more seriously, it also provoked Muhammad IV, who now turned to Morocco for help. The king also enacted measures to maintain readiness for war. In order to prevent knights from selling their horses abroad, he enacted an ordinance in May 1331 requiring them to have horses and imposed a penalty on those riding on mules. However, because of the ban on mules, many were exported, resulting in a shortage; it was also discovered that horses could not do many of the hard tasks of mules, and so he repealed the ordinance after two years.[112]

In 1331 the king proposed to establish a new military order, to be endowed with the properties once held by the Order of the Temple, prior to its suppression by Clement V in 1312. Pointing out that Templar holdings in Castile had already been assigned to the Order of the Hospital, John XXII rejected the king's proposal. The new Military Orders of Montesa and Christ had been allotted Templar estates in Aragón and Portugal respectively, but, in the pope's judgment, they were of little avail in the war against the Moors because of internal disputes. Consequently he did not expect much from a new Castilian order.[113]

Nevertheless, in 1332 Alfonso XI created the Order of La Banda, the Band, or the Scarf, by having the knights and squires of his household wear a dark sash across white garments. "Men, wanting to have that sash," he hoped, "would have reason to do chivalric deeds." Members had to be royal vassals sworn never to abandon his service. This was, however, an Order of Chivalry, quite distinct from the older Military Religious Orders that were organized as monastic communities. The king did not entrust the Order with the defense of fortresses nor did its members fight as a unit.[114]

Chivalric motives also prompted the king's journey to Santiago de Compostela, where, after the vigil of arms, he received knighthood from the image of St. James. After his anointing and coronation at Las Huelgas de Burgos in June 1332, he knighted many young men, including Richard de Labret, or d'Albret, viscount of Tartas, one of the French lords who had expressed interest in the crusade.[115] By establishing the Order of La Banda and conferring knighthood, the king intended to highlight the importance of chivalric ideals to the development of an effective military force.

Awaiting the Marinids

His need for such a body would become apparent soon after when the Marinids returned to the Peninsula. During the king's minority, the Marinids were absent from the peninsular wars, so Infante Pedro was able to divert the focus of military action from Algeciras to the city of Granada, the heart of the Nasrid kingdom. If Granada could be taken, the rest of the kingdom might follow. The unexpected death of Pedro and Juan in 1319 brought their crusade to an abrupt halt. When Alfonso XI attained his majority, he continued Pedro's strategy of attacking the heartland of Granada. Juan Manuel gained a notable victory at the Guadalhorce River and Alfonso XI captured Olvera and other fortresses in 1327. Three years later the fall of Teba pushed the frontier closer to Granada, but the gains achieved ultimately proved ephemeral. Realizing the peril to his kingdom, Muhammad IV, as his predecessors had done, appealed for help to the new Marinid ruler, Abū l-Hasan. Thus, for nearly a decade thereafter the conflict shifted again to the Strait.

Chapter 8

The Loss of Gibraltar and the Crusade of Salado

Preoccupied by their ambition to conquer Tlemcen, the Marinid emirs had not been directly involved in peninsular affairs for nearly two decades. Responding, however, to Nasrid appeals, the Marinids reappeared, delivering a grave blow to Castile by seizing Gibraltar. Alfonso XI's resolve to reclaim that stronghold led to a decisive confrontation with the Marinid sultan Abū l-Hasan (1331–48), at the Salado River. There, the kings of Castile, Portugal, Granada, and Morocco risked life, honor, and kingdoms in a pitched battle with profound consequences for all.

The Loss of Gibraltar

Arriving in Fez in September 1332, Muhammad IV was warmly received by Abū l-Hasan, who had just ascended the Marinid throne.[1] Though unable to intervene personally at that time, he promised military assistance and sent Muhammad IV home, laden with gifts. The Nasrid king immediately encouraged Juan Manuel to join him in opposing Alfonso XI.[2]

At the beginning of 1333, Abū l-Hasan, "a king wise in the ways of war," dispatched his son, Abū Mālik ʿAbd al-Wāhid, with 5,000 soldiers to Algeciras. After taking the Rock of Gibraltar and occupying the shipyard, the Marinids encircled the town. As Juan Manuel was ravaging the Castilian countryside, the king could not personally rescue the beleaguered fortress. Thus, he commanded his admiral Alfonso Jofre Tenorio, who had fifteen galleys and six *naves*, to supply Gibraltar with food, while the masters of the military orders, several magnates, and frontier militias attempted to break the siege.

Nevertheless, the Marinid blockade was complete, so no relieving force could enter. Siege engines battered the walls, knocking down two towers. About the same time, Muhammad IV, after vainly assaulting Castro del Río, southeast of Córdoba, captured the castle of Cabra.[3]

Realizing the need for prompt action, Alfonso XI, after obtaining loans from Valladolid, Burgos, and Toledo, arrived in Seville on 8 June. After some initial resistance, he also persuaded Juan Manuel to collaborate with him. João, the son of Afonso IV of Portugal, also joined him. The relieving army probably set out from Seville on 16 June, moving slowly toward Gibraltar, about 110 miles away. When the king reached Jerez on 18–19 June, still four days' march from Gibraltar, he received word that the defenders had surrendered after a siege of five months and were allowed to leave. The Moroccan chronicler Ibn Marzūq related that, when he was a student in Tlemcen, his teacher announced: "Rejoice, community of the faithful, because God has had the goodness to restore Gibraltar to us!" The students erupted in cries of praise and thanksgiving and shed tears of joy.[4]

Gibraltar was unprepared for a long siege because Vasco Pérez de Meira, the *alcaide*, had used money intended for its defense for his own benefit. In the last month the starving defenders were reduced to boiling and eating the leather of their shields and shoes as well as stray rats, cats, and dogs. Admiral Tenorio attempted to relieve their distress by launching bags of flour from two trebuchets mounted on his ships, but only a few bags fell within the castle. Firing missiles from their siege engines, the Moors forced Tenorio to withdraw. The *Royal Chronicle* fixed the blame for this disaster on Vasco Pérez. Four years later, "the unlucky knight who lost Gibraltar" was among the defenders of Tlemcen against Abū l-Hasan.[5]

Alfonso XI and the Siege of Gibraltar

Determined to recover Gibraltar, Alfonso XI hastened from Jerez to the Guadarranque River where, on 26 June, he encountered about 6,000 Moorish knights. Pursuing them across the river, his men were trapped between the Guadarranque and the Palmones River, not far from Algeciras. As the Moors turned about and gave battle, about 1,500 Castilian infantry drove the enemy back to Algeciras.[6] Alfonso XI established his main encampment on the sandy isthmus connecting Gibraltar to the mainland.[7] Another detachment, loaded on Tenorio's ships, made their way to the red sands or Tierra Bermeja along the western side of the peninsula. As they disembarked in a disorderly way, the Moors drove them back to their ships and many drowned in the sea. Meantime, a band of about 1,500 Castilians scaled to the top of the Rock where they were isolated with insufficient food. The problem of supply was acute, as transports from Seville were delayed by a lack of wind. Alfonso IV promised to send Catalan ships, but they were late in arriving.[8] Afonso IV also sent a fleet, but as soon as their funds ran out, they returned home, while the siege was still in progress.[9]

Judging that he could not continue the siege, Alfonso XI ordered a retreat, but the arrival of eight ships loaded with food changed his mind. When the Moors attacked, the Castilians, crying out "Santiago and Castile for King Alfonso the Fortunate," drove them back to the castle. Observing this, the soldiers on the Rock hastened down to join their fellows. Siege machines bombarded the castle and the Moorish galleys in the harbor. The Moors, however, covering their ships with wooden beams so that little damage was done, built a heavy wooden stockade to prevent Tenorio from entering the harbor. The Castilians moved wooden towers mounted on wheels up against the castle and showered stones and arrows down on the defenders while sappers worked to undermine the walls. However, the Moors shot arrows and threw down stones and *alquitrán*, a combustible mixture of tar, grease, and oil. As the towers were set on fire, the Castilians had to abandon them.[10]

As the siege wore on and the food shortage became acute, despite the king's efforts, increasing numbers deserted. Among them was Juan Manuel, who, once again began to plunder Castile. Meantime, Abū Mālik called on Muhammad IV for help. As a diversionary tactic, he seized the castle of Benamejí and pillaged the lands around Córdoba before marching toward Gibraltar. Abū Mālik and Muhammad IV then advanced to within three miles of Alfonso XI's headquarters. His initial reaction was to give battle, but his counselors, noting that combat in an open field was too risky, dissuaded him. Instead, he ordered his men to dig a ditch across the isthmus to impede enemy encroachment. Sentries were posted and a bell was set up to warn of approaching attack. For several days, with some minor skirmishing, the two armies faced each other.[11]

Both sides realized that they had reached a stalemate. Abū Mālik and Muhammad IV were unable to relieve Gibraltar, but Alfonso XI knew that if he captured it he would be besieged in turn and would not be able to return home without engaging in battle. Moreover, Juan Manuel's continued depredations compelled him to seek a solution. A truce was arranged, and the pact between Castile and Granada concluded in February 1331 was confirmed. Muhammad IV then visited Alfonso XI and, after sharing a leisurely meal with him, presented him with lavish gifts: a sword with a scabbard covered with cloth of gold, emeralds, rubies, sapphires, and a large pearl; a basinet, or helmet, covered with gold and jewels, especially two rubies about the size of chestnuts, mounted in front, one above the other; and cloth of gold and silk made in Granada. After two and a half months, the siege ended, probably on 24 August 1333. Ibn Khaldūn, who related that Alfonso XI, on foot and bareheaded as a sign of respect, received Muhammad IV at his tent, declared that, "Abū l-Hasan thus had the good fortune to achieve a conquest that crowned his reign with an imperishable glory."[12] In recompense for their services Alfonso XI granted lands to Admiral Alfonso Jofre Tenorio and the masters of Alcántara and Santiago.[13]

If the king had been able to move more quickly, he might have saved Gibraltar, but that was not to be. Gibraltar was now definitively in Muslim hands and would remain so until 1462. Resolved to regain possession, however, Alfonso XI realized the need to institute important military, financial, and legal reforms.

An Interval of Peace

As he departed from Gibraltar, Muhammad IV was assassinated on 25 August by the sons of 'Uthmān ibn Abī l-'Ulā, the exiled Marinid prince, who had died in 1330. Fearing that the king's alliance with Abū Mālik and his settlement with Alfonso XI might embolden him to act against them, they charged that Muhammad IV, by dining with the king of Castile and wearing clothes that he gave him, had become a Christian and sold his kingdom to the Castilians.[14] The dead king's brother, Abū l-Hajjaj Yūsuf I (1333–54), one of the most able Nasrid monarchs, was proclaimed in his stead. He promptly deported 'Uthmān's family and confirmed the truce with Alfonso XI and agreed to include Aragón.[15]

Although it was feared that Abū l-Hasan was contemplating an invasion of the Peninsula, he was not prepared to do so while still at war with Tlemcen. Thus, representatives of Castile, Granada, and Morocco signed a treaty of peace on 26 February 1334 at Fez that would extend for four years from 1 March 1334 to 28 February 1338. Knowing that his kingdom required a long period of tranquility, Alfonso XI had little choice but to release Granada from payment of tribute. Otherwise the treaty followed the usual pattern of allowing free trade, payment for damages, and freedom for escaped captives; ruined castles would not be rebuilt. Though the emir promised not to send additional troops to Spain, he insisted on his right to freely rotate his garrisons there. Moreover, Alfonso XI agreed to allow Marinid ships to be outfitted in Castilian ports.[16]

Though Alfonso IV had taken a secondary role in the recent conflict, he adhered to the treaty of Fez in May and made a separate peace for four years with Yūsuf I on 3 June 1335. When he died on 24 January 1336, his son Pedro IV (1336–87) succeeded him and prolonged the truce with Granada for five years, thus initiating a long period of peace between the two realms.[17]

Peace was also essential for Alfonso XI who needed to subdue Juan Manuel and other dissident nobles.[18] As an example to others, he executed Juan Alfonso de Haro for failing to fulfill his duty to participate in the siege of Gibraltar. Although the chronicler remarked that "he died justly and without blame to the king," later generations recalled that the king, to the consternation of his nobles, acted without giving Juan Alfonso a hearing. By early summer 1338 he finally resolved his differences with Juan Manuel, who now promised to serve him loyally.[19]

In order to provide adequately for the defense of the frontier, Alfonso XI appealed to Seville and other frontier towns to grant an *alcabala*, a sales tax on bread, wine, fish, and clothing for three years. He also demanded a loan from Seville to maintain 3,000 knights garrisoned on the frontier. Anxious that his knights not lose their military capability, he encouraged them to participate in tournaments. Besides detailing the military obligations of the urban militias, at Burgos in 1338 he enacted an ordinance regulating the military service of the nobility.[20]

Preliminaries to War

Abū l-Hasan, meanwhile, seeking to complete the subjugation of Tlemcen, sought an extension of the truce. Showered with gifts of jewelry, swords covered with gold and silver and precious stones, cloth of gold and silk, horses, falcons, camels, and storks, Alfonso XI accepted his proposal.[21] Nevertheless, both men, expecting to resume their struggle, prepared for war. After seizing Tlemcen in April 1337, Abū l-Hasan, according to Ibn Khaldūn, wished to undertake the *jihād* against the infidels of Spain. In explanation of his motivation, the *Grand Chronicle* related that Muslim holy men accused him of causing the death of at least 300,000 Moors. Swearing on the Koran to atone for his sins, he declared that, "if he did not fix his tents at the gates of Seville . . . the whole world could say that he was no king." His son, Abū Mālik crossed the Strait with 4,000 to 8,000 knights, probably as replacements for peninsular garrisons, but everyone knew that they would soon be used against Castile. Boasting that "my lance is feared from the gates of Algeciras as far as Toledo," Abū Mālik promised to conquer Tarifa, the key to the Peninsula. Alfonso XI commanded Admiral Tenorio to guard the Strait and to prevent the arrival of additional Moroccan forces.[22]

The king also strove to establish friendly relations with Portugal and Aragón. By taking Leonor de Guzmán as his mistress and marginalizing Queen María, he had alienated his father-in-law, Afonso IV of Portugal, who even appealed to Abū l-Hasan for help. Nevertheless, a truce concluded in December 1337 brought hostilities to a halt, and papal legates facilitated the reconciliation of the two kings in September of the following year.[23]

Pedro IV, fearing that a Marinid invasion would encourage Yūsuf I of Granada to attack the kingdom of Valencia, armed thirty galleys to impede hostile movement in the Strait. Although he sought agreement with Abū l-Hasan in April 1338, he concluded a treaty with Castile at Madrid on 1 May 1339. Alfonso XI promised to intercept Muslim forces crossing through Murcia into Valencia and to permit Aragonese troops to pass through Murcia to Granada. Neither king would make a separate peace with the Moors. To defend the Strait from May to September, Castile would provide twenty galleys and Aragón ten; in the winter the numbers would be reduced to eight and four respectively.[24] In June Pedro IV dispatched Jofre Gilabert de Cruilles, whom he had appointed as his admiral, to the Strait with ten galleys.[25]

Alfonso XI soon realized that thirty Castilian and Catalan galleys would be insufficient to hold back the Moroccans. Thus he added thirty galleys, fifteen *naos*, and ten *leños* and pleaded for a Catalan increase from ten to fifteen galleys. At the end of September when Jofre Gilabert announced that his term of service was finished, the king provided the necessary funds to retain the ten Catalan galleys until the middle of February. He also planned to station fourteen galleys, six *naos*, and four *leños* in the Strait from mid-February to June and asked Pedro IV to send five additional galleys. The Aragonese king was skeptical, however, and ordered Jofre Gilabert to determine whether it was necessary to maintain twenty-four galleys from October through April. Meanwhile, it was rumored that Abū Mālik had gathered 8,000 knights for the invasion and would be joined by 18,000 or 19,000 from Granada. Abū l-Hasan was said to be assembling forty ships and that forty Genoese vessels, then serving France in its war with England, would join him. Preparing for a Muslim attack, Pedro IV, in March 1339, summoned his vassals, requested a subsidy from his bishops, informed the pope of the imminent danger, and appealed to Philip VI of France to prevent the Genoese from going over to the Moroccans.[26]

Anticipating a Marinid invasion, the kings of Castile and Aragón turned to Pope Benedict XII (1334–42) for assistance. In 1336 the pope had admonished Alfonso XI to resolve his quarrel over Navarre lest "the perfidious Saracens" should attack. The king explained that financial aid from the church was all the more necessary because the kingdom was impoverished by the many wars against the Moors.[27] In August 1339 Benedict XII protested hat the king had seized the revenues of ecclesiastical benefices, including the *tercias*, held by foreigners. In May of the following year, however, he lifted the sentence of excommunication incurred by the king for taking the *tercias* during the previous three years without papal authorization. Despite papal objections, the king probably continued to collect the *tercias* and other ecclesiastical revenues whenever he could.[28]

In August 1337 Pedro IV asked Benedict XII to grant him the *decima* for six years payable in three. Earlier in the year, in March, the pope commented that the king displayed too much interest in Islamic customs and admonished him not to forget the struggles of his ancestors against Islam. He upbraided him for taking pleasure in the company of Saracen young men, and, most shameful of all, wearing Muslim dress on occasion. Rejecting the king's excuse that these young men were instructing him in the art of war, the pope told him that he could surely find suitable Christian tutors. Lest excessive familiarity with the Saracens threaten the salvation of his soul, the pope exhorted him to seek the company of prudent persons and, like his devout predecessors, to hear daily mass and the canonical hours. Heeding that warning, Pedro IV became somewhat more circumspect, but retained an avid interest in Islam and patronized three different Catalan translations of the Koran.[29]

While awaiting a response from the pope, Alfonso XI's attention was directed to another potential source of revenue. Declaring that "my lord the king goes out to make war against his foes while they sit at home eating and drinking," Gonzalo Martínez, master of Alcántara, proposed that he plunder the Jews. By doing so, he could bring into his treasury 4,000,000 *maravedíes*, an amount double their annual taxes. However, Gil de Albornoz, archbishop of Toledo, opposed that plan and there is no sign that it was implemented.[30]

The Beginning of Hostilities

Despite the truce, the opening salvo in the next stage of the conflict started in the late spring of 1339, when the Marinids, from their base at Ronda, began to devastate the countryside. Setting out from Seville, Alfonso XI, after ravaging about Antequera, Archidona, and Ronda, gave battle to the enemy on 21 July. Shouting "Santiago and Castile for Good King Alfonso," the Castilians put the Moors to flight. As it was apparent that the war would be a lengthy one and that his resources were strained to the utmost, the king obtained consent to an extraordinary tax from various towns summoned to Madrid in November. During his absence, numerous hostile encounters between Christians and Muslims took place. Gonzalo Martínez, master of Alcántara, led a pillaging expedition to Locubín, Alcalá de Benzaide, and Priego, just north of Granada. Yūsuf I countered by besieging Siles, a fortress in the Sierra de Segura. Alfonso Méndez de Guzmán, master of Santiago, with 1,000 horse and 2,000 foot soldiers relieved Siles, driving off the opposing army of about 2,000 horse and 6,000 foot soldiers.[31]

The Marinid prince, Abū Mālik, with 6,000 knights and many infantry, set out from Algeciras to plunder Medina Sidonia, Jerez, and Lebrija, and sent a detachment to despoil the outskirts of Seville. Joined by the master of Alcántara, the militia of Seville engaged the Moors in a brutal clash and drove them from the field. A few days later Abū Mālik withdrew toward Alcalá de los Gazules and fixed his camp near the Alberite River, where the pursuing Christians surprised him at dawn. As they cried out "Santiago and Castile for King Don Alfonso," the Moors responded "Benamarin!" However, the advantage lay with the Castilians who routed their opponents. Vainly attempting to halt the flight of his men, Abū Mālik was killed. Ibn Khaldūn attributed his death to his youthful lack of experience, though one may question that judgment. Ibn Marzūq hailed the dead prince as a "martyr to the faith." Writing later in the century, Pedro López de Ayala stated that the battle took place on 20 October 1339.[32] In his *Libro de la Montería*, a book on hunting, Alfonso XI mentioned the *arroyo*, or brook, in which Abū Mālik's body was found.[33]

One of the sad consequences of the Christian victory was the rupture between Alfonso XI and Gonzalo Martínez, master of Alcántara. The immediate cause seems to have been Gonzalo's rivalry with Alfonso Méndez de Guzmán, master of Santiago, and brother of the king's mistress. Refusing to obey the royal summons to Madrid, Gonzalo took refuge in Valencia de Alcántara and appealed, in vain, to Afonso IV of Portugal for support. Then, in a betrayal of the ideal on which the Military Order of Alcántara was founded, he proposed an alliance with Yūsuf I and ordered the *alcaides* of Morón and other frontier outposts to aid the Moors. Compelled to surrender, Alfonso XI upbraided him for his treasonous conduct and, despite the pleas of Benedict XII, ordered him to be hung and his body burned. Thus a man, who had long enjoyed the king's confidence, met a tragic end, a victim of his own treachery.[34]

During Alfonso XI's absence from the frontier, the Marinids despoiled the land about Arcos, Jerez, and Medina Sidonia until the people of Jerez defeated them. The chronicler commented that royal cavalry conducted themselves in an upright manner, frequently confessing their sins and receiving communion every Sunday. "And thus, as they lived such a life, one ought not wonder that so few of them should overcome the Moors."[35]

The Letter of the Sultan of Babylon

Meantime, on learning of his son's death, Abū l-Hasan took "consolation in the thought that the young man died fighting for the faith and would obtain an ample reward from God." No one who saw his body, covered with blood and abandoned by his men, "would not be filled with sorrow, even though he was a Moor." In lines recalling the eleventh-century king Alfonso VI, entitled *imperator toletanus*, the poet Rodrigo Yáñez attributed this vow to Abū l-Hasan:

> I will conquer Castile
> and destroy Christendom
> and crown myself
> in the city of Toledo
> and there make my seat
> and be called emperor.[36]

Both the *Grand Chronicle* and Rodrigo Yáñez declared that Abū l-Hasan received a letter from the sultan of Babylon exhorting him to conquer all the kingdoms of Spain and to capture Alfonso XI.[37] Whereas both sources paraphrased the letter, an anonymous Englishman, who participated in the battle of Salado, recorded a French translation of an original Arabic text, found in the enemy camp. The sultan identified himself as "Goldifa, un ley exarif," probably meaning the caliph, Mawlay al-Sharif, that is, noble prince, or alternatively, "un rey exarif," or noble king (al-mālik al-Sharif). Describing himself as lord of Asia, Africa, and Europe, he lamented the death of Abū l-Hasan's son, now enjoying the bliss of Paradise, and commanded the emir to destroy all of Christendom. The caliph empowered his wise men to grant pardon to those going to war against the Christians. Those who died would be raised up to Paradise within three days with their wives; there, each man, attended by seven virgins, would feast on cakes, honey, butter, milk, and cheese. Anyone who contributed financially to the war would enjoy the same pardon. Admonishing Abū l-Hasan to show no mercy to the Christians, the caliph ordered him to destroy their churches, converting them into stables, their altars into mangers, and their crosses into hitching posts. "Smash their children against the wall; slit open the wombs of pregnant women; cut off the breasts, arms, noses, and feet of other women. Do all this to dishonor Christendom. Do not leave until you have destroyed Christendom from sea to sea."[38]

Is this an authentic letter found in the Marinid camp at Salado or Christian propaganda intended to arouse the faithful? Some unusual characteristics suggest that it is not genuine, at least as we have it now. The caliph does not identify himself nor the "king of Belmaryn," the addressee. The letter, which may be incomplete, is also undated. The anonymous introduction to the letter states that the author was the sultan of Babylon, a title given in the fourteenth century to the Mamlūk rulers of Egypt. The Egyptian sultan at this time, al-Nāsir Muhammad (1309–40), may have written the letter, because Abū l-Hasan had informed him that his son had crossed the Strait to Algeciras in 1333.[39] The promise of Paradise to those fighting the Christians conformed to Islamic tradition, but the offer of pardon to the participants in the war or financial contributors seems very similar to papal bulls of crusade. Did the Muslims borrow this idea, or did a Christian propagandist attribute this Christian practice to the Muslims? On balance, I believe that the letter was Christian propaganda, but it is reasonable to suppose that the sultan of Egypt encouraged Abū l-Hasan to conquer Spain.

The Naval Battle of Algeciras 1340

In the fall of 1339 and the spring of 1340, the Castilian and Catalan armada guarding the Strait suffered two severe blows. Jofre Gilabert, the Catalan admiral, with eight galleys defeated thirteen Moorish galleys and seven *leños* on 6

September, but, soon after, while attempting a landing near Algeciras, he was killed by an enemy arrow and his ships sailed for home. As the winter wore on, the Castilian admiral Alfonso Jofre Tenorio found himself in an increasingly weakened position. Some of his ships were undermanned due to illness and death. In March 1340 the king attempted to remedy the situation and to construct new galleys. Though he appealed to Pedro IV to send ships, he failed to do so; nor did he break his truce with Granada, as Alfonso XI asked.[40]

Across the Strait Abū l-Hasan assembled sixty galleys and as many as 250 other ships, which evaded Tenorio and made their way to Gibraltar. Though he blockaded the harbor, he was driven off by a powerful storm, enabling the Marinids to cross the bay to Algeciras. While he returned to blockade Algeciras, malicious rumors were spread abroad that the Marinids had bribed him to allow them to cross the Strait. Assured of his absolute loyalty, the king sent six new galleys to Tenorio, bringing his total to thirty-three. When the Marinid ships came out to give battle on Saturday, 8 April 1340, Tenorio's ships failed to act in unison, leaving his galley exposed to a fierce enemy attack. Three times the Moors attempting to board his galley were repelled, but there were too many. Despite his tenacious resistance, standing with the royal standard in one hand and a sword in the other, he was killed. The Marinids cut off his head and threw it into the sea and sent his body as a trophy to Abū l-Hasan. Many of his mariners suffered a similar fate. Captives were paraded in chains through the streets of Ceuta. Proclaiming himself "lord of the sea," Abū l-Hasan cited a prophecy of Muhammad that the Moors would penetrate Spain as far as Compostela and declared that the victory was a sign from God that he would conquer Castile. Rodrigo Yáñez attributed to him the desire to bring to Morocco the heads of the kings of Spain fixed on his standards.[41]

Tenorio's failure to hold his fleet together and poor morale resulting from inadequate supplies and a lack of pay contributed to the Christian defeat. The Moors had forty-four galleys and thirty-five *leños*, with 300 to 400 men-at-arms and 200 archers and crossbowmen on each ship. Tenorio, according to one count, had about forty-four galleys and an indeterminate number of *naos*. Twenty-eight galleys and seven *naos* were captured. Ten Castilian galleys and one Catalan, which had not been fully engaged, fled to Cartagena. No more than five escaped to Tarifa.[42] Benedict XII, seeing this disaster as a divine punishment on Alfonso XI for his harsh treatment of the master of Alcántara, pressed him to change his life and turn to God in order to achieve victory over his enemies.[43]

Alfonso XI Seeks Naval Help

The complete destruction of the Castilian fleet removed the last obstacle to Abū l-Hasan's invasion. To counter that, Alfonso XI repaired old ships and built new ones, so that besides the five galleys that had escaped from the battle, he had fifteen others and twelve *naos*. Afonso IV of Portugal, responding to a plea from his daughter Queen María, sent twenty galleys, commanded by the Genoese merchant Manuel Pessagno, to Seville. Although Alfonso XI wanted him to go to Algeciras, he sailed instead to the relative safety of Cádiz. Meantime, the kings of Portugal and Castile concluded an alliance on 1 July 1340 and pledged not to make a separate peace with the Marinids.[44] Alfonso XI, on 24 May, pointedly commented that Pedro IV had yet to provide galleys for the defense of the Strait as he was obliged to do under the treaty of 1339. Four months later, on 23 September, Pedro IV announced that he was sending galleys, but financial difficulties resulted in delays. Lending him the money to arm twelve galleys for three months' service, Alfonso XI also counseled him to prepare for a land war.[45]

With some trepidation, Alfonso XI also turned to Simon Boccanegra, the doge of Genoa. He feared that the Genoese might aid the enemy, because, as the chronicler put it, "the Genoese always had the habit of helping whoever paid them money; in this regard they cared nothing for Christendom nor for anything else that was good." At the king's request, in June Benedict XII appealed to Boccanegra, who sent fifteen galleys commanded by his brother Egidio. Castile provided food and paid 800 gold florins for each galley, or a total of 12,000 every month (about 1,600 *maravedíes* per galley). Additional galleys would be hired at the same amount.[46]

Benedict XII and the Bull of Crusade

Responding to the king's request, Benedict XII on 7 March 1340 proclaimed the crusade throughout Castile, León, Aragón, Navarre, and Mallorca, and granted the *tercias* and the *decima* for three years. While collecting those levies, the king was forbidden to demand any other subsidy from the clergy.[47] The bishops of Cuenca and Ávila were appointed to preach the crusade and to bestow the crusader's cross. Crusaders were expected to serve for a year; one could also gain the indulgence by making a financial contribution sufficient to support a soldier for one year. Although the *Royal Chronicle* asserted that Archbishop Gil de Albornoz of Toledo was designated to preach the crusade, no papal bull mentions him. Contributions would be gathered according to conditions established by John XXII.[48] Thanking Benedict XII for his beneficence, on 10 May Alfonso XI accepted the stipulations concerning the *tercias* and the *decima*.[49] As a further sign of his support, Benedict XII sent a crusading banner to Alfonso XI.[50] In August, the pope exhorted all the peninsular prelates to summon their people to repentance and to participate in processions and public prayers so that the Christian kings might triumph over the enemies of the faith, especially the emir of Morocco.[51]

Alerting the pope to the Marinid invasion, Pedro IV painted a terrible picture of the fate awaiting the people at the hands of the Moors, "rabid wolves, thirsting for Christian blood." Forcible conversion to Islam, the burning of churches, destruction of relics, and rape were among the many crimes to be expected unless Benedict XII came to the aid of the impoverished king, who requested the following: concession of the crusading indulgence to all participants and financial contributors; the *decima* for six years, payable in the first three, though that would only yield 20,000 *libras*; the first year's revenue of vacant ecclesiastical benefices; pious legacies whose purpose was unspecified; bequests intended for the Holy Land; and diversion to the defense of Valencia of the feudal tribute owed for Sardinia. As José Goñi Gaztambide put it, "undoubtedly Pedro IV argued well, but he argued late because the battle of Salado was already an historical event." When the royal ambassador tendered his memorial to the pope on 7 December Salado had already been fought and won.[52]

Two Italian sources refer to the participation of northern crusaders. One referred to many pilgrims from France, Germany, and Italy. Another mentioned unbelievable numbers of knights from Germany, France, Navarre, and Provence, the participation of the kings of Navarre and Aragón, and of King Dinis of Portugal. Neither Philip of Navarre nor Pedro IV was present and Dinis was dead; but his son, Afonso IV, did take part in the conflict.[53]

The Siege of Tarifa

The long-awaited invasion began on 4 August 1340 when Abū l-Hasan landed at Algeciras. The size of his army given by the *Royal Chronicle*, 40,000 knights and 400,000 infantry, is grossly inflated; Rodrigo Yáñez's statement that

60,000 men crossed the Strait in four months must also be discounted. The sultan planned to besiege Tarifa, and then Jerez, before moving against Seville. Once Alfonso XI was overcome, no king or emperor would dare challenge him. The Christian religion would be cast down, Islam would be exalted, and he would be the "best king who ever reigned in Africa, a saint and a peer of the great Prophet Muhammad."[54]

Initiating the siege of Tarifa on 23 September, Abū l-Hasan summoned the defenders to surrender. They reminded him, however, that their swords were still red with his son's blood and vowed not to clean them until they washed them again in the blood of his soldiers. Infuriated, he swore to slaughter them all. His twenty siege engines, bombarding the fortress by day and night, broke up a great part of the wall and one of the towers, but the Christians held their ground. Meantime, Alfonso Ortíz Calderón, prior of the Hospital, with fifteen galleys, twelve *naos*, and four *leños*, summoned Manuel Pessagno, the Portuguese admiral, to join him at Tarifa; but he refused to move from Cádiz, apparently to guard against a possible Marinid attack on the coast of the Algarve. Overly confident that Tarifa would soon be his, Abū l-Hasan had retained only twelve galleys in Algeciras, but he soon realized that if the Christians gained control of the Strait, his retreat to Morocco would be cut off. Here the *Grand Chronicle* related a fabulous story about a disturbing nightmare that occurred to the emir's wife Fātima that portended disaster. Although she warned him, he dismissed her words as womanly fears. Nevertheless, he consulted a seer who interpreted her dream as a warning from God and urged him to abandon the campaign.[55]

In Seville, meanwhile, Alfonso XI consulted the leaders of the crusade as to the best course of action. Though one advised him to abandon Tarifa, he declared that he would rather lose his head with the crown of Spain than do something so shameful. Given the numerical superiority of the Moors, however, he sent his wife, Queen María, to secure the assistance of her father, Afonso IV. Convinced that if things went badly for Castile, Portugal would be unable to defend itself against the Moors, he summoned his vassals to prepare for war "against the enemies of the Holy Cross."[56]

About 10 October the Castilian fleet suffered an unexpected calamity when nine galleys, and a number of other ships were destroyed by a heavy storm. Some ships were driven as far eastward as Cartagena and Valencia. Many mariners were lost, but others were taken captive and some embraced Islam in order to save their lives. An elated Abū l-Hasan took this news as a sign of God's favor that he would conquer all of Spain. He vowed that he would not abandon the siege of Tarifa and that one day he would become lord of Toledo. At the same time he asked the defenders of Tarifa to send two representatives to a parley. On their arrival, a translator told them to kiss the ground before the emir, as was the Muslim custom, but they adamantly refused. When the emir urged them to submit, they emphasized that the town was well fortified and that the defenders were not country bumpkins but proven knights of long service to their king, who would rather die than surrender. Irritated by their response, Abū l-Hasan declared that he would seek out Alfonso XI wherever he was to be found and give battle. When he offered the emissaries meat to eat on a Friday, they refused; they also rejected his attempt to bribe them with gold coins. After their departure, in a gesture of intimidation, he paraded captive mariners before the walls of Tarifa and then executed them.[57]

The Christian Advance to the Salado River

Afonso IV, accompanied by prelates, nobles, and the masters of the Military Orders of Avis and Christ, reached Seville in early October. The prior of the Hospital in Portugal bore a relic of the Holy Cross (Santo Lenho, now preserved in the cathedral of Évora).[58] As Alfonso XI had expended great sums on the defense of the frontier, paying the troops a monthly wage, and providing financial aid to his father-in-law, he had to pawn his jewels and to seek a loan from the people of Seville. At best he would have supplies for fifteen days but would not be able to provide for Tarifa, unless he broke the siege. After their soldiers took the crusader's cross and confessed their sins, the two kings set out from Seville on 16 October and urged Abū l-Hasan to await their coming.[59]

The royal envoys informed Abū l-Hasan that the Christians, having undertaken this pilgrimage (*rromería*) to save their souls, and having received absolution for their sins, were determined to die rather than to flee. Sneering disdainfully, he asserted his intention to take Tarifa, Jerez, and Seville, and to conquer the whole of Spain. Encouraged by Yūsuf I of Granada, who exhorted him to trust that God would give him victory, he announced that he was ready for battle. When one of his advisers suggested sending the women and children to the safety of Algeciras, he refused, arguing that men, fighting in the presence of women, are moved to great deeds in the hope of winning their love and admiration. "If we are defeated or killed," he concluded, "we will have no need of women, and those who die will be saved and we will find them in the Holy House of the Great Prophet Muhammad." On the other side, Juan

Manuel, now again loyally serving his king, confidently declared that, with the help of God and Santiago, he would provide a banquet for the two kings in Abū l-Hasan's tent.[60]

When the crusaders reached the Guadalete River just beyond Jerez on 22 October, Pere de Moncada, the Catalan admiral, arrived with galleys dispatched by Pedro IV. The Portuguese admiral Pessagno was given permission to return to Lisbon, presumably because his term of service was up. Continuing on their way, on Sunday, 29 October, the two kings arrived at La Peña del Ciervo (The Hill of the Deer), rising to a height of about 1,437 feet and about five miles northwest of Tarifa. There they established their camp. About midway between Tarifa and La Peña was the Arroyo del Salado, a small stream, tributary to the Río de la Jara emptying into the Atlantic Ocean. When Abū l-Hasan and Yūsuf I saw the Christian army, they drew back from Tarifa, burning their siege engines, and stationed their forces on the surrounding hills. The Moors supposedly had 53,000 knights and 600,000 infantry, but these numbers are unreliable. Given the scarcity of supplies, Alfonso XI decided to give battle on the following day.[61]

Alfonso XI, who had about 8,000 knights and 12,000 infantry, planned to attack Abū l-Hasan's army. Afonso IV, who had no more than 1,000 knights, would take the offensive against Yūsuf I and his 7,000 knights on the left. In order to counterbalance the Nasrid forces, Alfonso XI sent 3,000 knights to join the Portuguese king. In the vanguard, led by Juan Manuel, a French knight living in Úbeda, named Yugo, was appointed to carry the crusade banner. The main body of the army consisted of knights in the service of the king's illegitimate sons, Enrique (b. 1334) and Fadrique (b. 1335), who were both under age; archbishops and bishops; magnates; knights of the royal household; the master of Santiago; and municipal militias. The king brought up the rear. Foot soldiers from the Basque provinces and Asturias, armed with shields, helmets, lances, and crossbows, were stationed on the left flank next to the forces of Afonso IV. Álvar Pérez de Guzmán held the right flank. On the advice of Juan Manuel, the king dispatched 1,000 knights and 4,000 foot soldiers at night to join the defenders of Tarifa and the mariners who were ordered to land. Pushing past 3,000 Muslim knights, they forded the Salado River and made their way safely to Tarifa.[62]

Prayer Before Battle

After a restless night, Alfonso XI rose at dawn. Kneeling by his bed, he prayed that God would remember him and the Christians gathered there on account of the "holy Catholic faith." Acknowledging his sins and pleading for God's pardon, he placed "the crown of Spain" in God's hands. If God should be angry with him so that he did not survive the battle, he asked God to remember Spain, lest it should be lost. After confessing his sins, he asked Gil de Albornoz, archbishop of Toledo, then just thirty years of age, to say mass in honor of the Holy Cross. Placing the king's arms upon the altar, the archbishop pleaded with God to exalt the holy Catholic faith and to honor the crown of Castile. As he did so, the king prostrated himself, asking God's pardon. When the archbishop elevated the host, the king wept, confessing his sins and saying:

> Lord, almighty, king of all that is, there is no other: I ask your grace to remember these faithful Christians and the kingdoms of Spain and me, your earthly king whom you have placed in your stead. Lord, I acknowledge that I am a very sinful king. Know, Lord, that in the beginning of my reign, when some of my subjects made a great disturbance I attacked them in order to become master of my realms. I admit my guilt. Also, Father of mercy, if I did you any service, I consider myself fortunate and I believe that for that little service that I did you will pardon the great sin of which I am guilty. And, Lord, forgetting kingdoms, wife and children, and the world's luxuries, I am come to this place very willingly to suffer death for you. And, Lord, if you are angry with me and have rendered judgment that I should not escape with my life, remember Castile, that you have ennobled over all the lands of the world, and grant it honor and victory, and advance the Holy Cross on which you suffered death. If it has to be otherwise, I ask your favor that I may be the first to die, so that I may not see the devastation of my people over whom you made me king and lord. I well believe and I am certain, Lord, that there is more mercy in you than the sins of any man and, for the small service that a man does to you, you reward him more than a hundred times over. And remember the words of your Prophet Isaiah, that you will receive every sinner who turns to you with a good heart and pardon his sins many though they be. And for this, Lord, I, king and sinner, turn

to you with a good heart and a good will and ask your favor for me and the Christians assembled here with me, that you will not abandon us. I place in your hands the kingdoms of which you made me lord, and the crown of Spain.[63]

Then the king and all those in the host, "as true and faithful Christians," received the Eucharist.[64] After exhorting them, the archbishop absolved them from their sins. Writing to the pope after the battle, he testified that the king had triumphed over all that had kept him in chains as he confessed his sins and that "there could be no doubt that he would conquer the Saracens."[65] Then he consecrated the king's arms, asking God to grant grace and strength so that they might be honored in the battle to come:

Today you will save your soul.
You will honor the holy religion
And gain such fame
As no king ever had.

After donning his armor and mounting his horse called Valencia ("Valor," "Bravery"), Alfonso XI declared that with God's help the siege of Tarifa would be lifted and the Christian religion would be exalted. Castile would gain honor and fame that would be spoken of for many years to come.[66]

In like manner, Afonso IV and his men confessed their sins, attended mass, and received the Eucharist. Attempting to raise their spirits, the king's confessor reminded them that God would be with them and advised those who were afraid of dying to remain behind. Recalling the loss of Spain by King Rodrigo, the last of the Visigoths, the subsequent ravages of Almanzor, and the creation of the kingdom of Portugal by Afonso I Henriques, Afonso IV begged God's pardon for his sins and exhorted his troops, saying that whether they lived or died that day they would be remembered forever. He ordered his standard-bearer to bring forward the Santo Lenho, the relic of the True Cross kept in the monastery of the Hospitallers in Marmelar, so that all would know that God favored them. During the ensuing battle, a priest dressed in white and mounted on a white mule, held aloft the relic, fixed on a spear, so that all might see it.[67]

The Battle of Salado

On a bright, sunny morning, Monday, 30 October 1340, with the royal and crusading banners leading their way, the crusaders moved off from La Peña del Ciervo and advanced toward the enemy.[68] About the same time the defenders in Tarifa and the contingents sent to their aid marched out to the north. The Moors had taken up positions near the fords over the Salado River so as to prevent the Christians from crossing. The bishops prayed, granting absolution and the Eucharist to everyone, as they chanted "Salve Regina." In Abū l-Hasan's tent holy men prayed, while he read "the false Koran recounting the commandments of his false religion," and placed about his neck a reliquary containing a piece of cloth belonging to the Prophet Muhammad. Informed that Alfonso XI was preparing to cross the Salado, he called for his great standard named Almançora, the Victorious, and commanded one of his vassals to guard it that day. As he mounted his horse, he observed that the sea and the shore below seemed entirely covered by Christian knights. Reminding his men that they were fighting for Islam, he proclaimed that if they were victorious they would be "the most honored and blessed men who ever were or will be." Renowned forever, they would conquer Spain and the Christians would lose it just as King Rodrigo had lost it centuries before.[69]

As they prepared to engage in this "holy and blessed battle," the Christian vanguard, led by Juan Manuel, advanced to the riverbank where they met stiff resistance. Advised of this, Alfonso XI sent to inquire why, but Juan Manuel made no move to hasten the crossing. When his standard-bearer, in obedience to the king's command, began to cross the river, Juan Manuel struck him with his mace, knocking him off his horse. Many were disturbed by his action, thinking that he did not wish to serve the king. Nevertheless, about 800 knights began to cross over a small bridge defended by 2,500 Muslim knights. When the king sent a detachment of 1,500 knights to their aid, they were able to beat back the Moors. Meantime, Juan Núñez de Lara and the master of Santiago crossed the river and engaged Abū 'Umar, the emir's son, with 3,000 knights. Driven back, the Moors fled up a hill toward the emir's encampment with the Christians in hot pursuit. As the forces from Tarifa joined the attack, the defenders fled, leaving the emir's wives and children unprotected.[70]

When Alfonso XI forded the river, his standard-bearer led many of his troops up the hill toward Abū l-Hasan's camp, leaving the king in the valley with only a small number of men. Seeing his difficulty, the Moors attacked

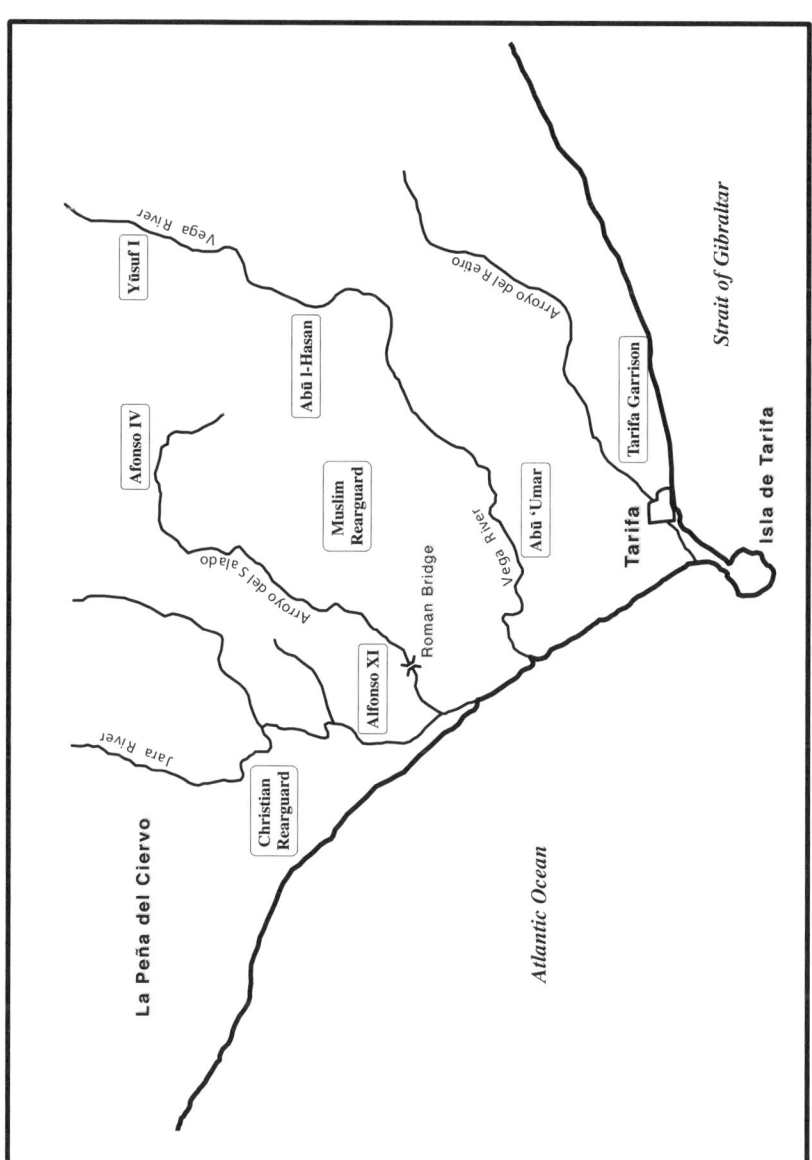

Map 2. The Battle of Salado, 1340.

and an enemy arrow lodged in his saddle. At this moment, said the chronicler, "Castile and all the chivalry of Spain was at the point of being conquered." But the king rallied his men, shouting "Santiago and Castile." Rising up in his saddle so his men might see him, he proclaimed: "Today I will see who my vassals are and they will see who I am." As he was about to charge, Archbishop Gil seized his rein and cautioned him: "My Lord, take care and command your men; don't put Castile in danger, for the Moors are beaten and I trust in God that you will emerge as victor this day."[71]

Although the number of those remaining with the king was small, they took courage and followed him as he plunged ahead into the Marinid army. As the troops who had occupied the emir's camp hastened down the hill to rescue their king, yelling "*Real, real*, for Good King Don Alfonso," the Moors found themselves engulfed on all sides. Shouting "Benamarin," Abū l-Hasan tried in vain to rally them, but they fled in panic. In fear of death, "he put his honor under his feet" and joined the flight, leaving his wives and children in enemy hands. According to Mūsā II, emir of Tlemcen, writing many years later, when Abū l-Hasan (who had more than 60,000 men) shifted the position of the main body of his army, those on his flanks assumed that he was defeated and began to flee. Mūsā concluded: "The disgrace of this rout fell on Abū l-Hasan, who humiliated the head of Islam and filled the idolaters with joy."[72]

Meanwhile, Afonso IV, joined by the Basque infantry, crossed the river and assaulted the forces of the king of Granada, who wore a golden helmet. When the relic of the True Cross was brought forward the Portuguese turned the tide and compelled the Moors to flee. While the Castilians and the Moroccans were still engaged, Yūsuf I abandoned the battlefield. Seeing that, the emir shouted: "Look at that madman, that cowardly king of Granada routed by the king of Portugal." Ibn al-Khatīb, the vizier of Yūsuf I, who took part in the battle and whose father fell that day, commented that the Granadan forces were about to overcome Afonso IV, when reinforcements came up to repel the attack. Both Alfonso XI and Afonso IV pursued the enemy as far as the Guadamecí River about five miles from the battlefield.[73]

The battle lasted about three hours, from about 9 a.m. until noon, but the pursuit of the enemy continued until late afternoon. As soon as the Moors turned in flight, many crusaders halted in order to plunder the royal encampment. Sadly, "vile men" massacred the women and children there, including the emir's wife Fātima, daughter of the king of Tunis. Aside from lamenting the tragedy of killing defenseless women and children, the leaders of the crusade knew that a great ransom had been lost. Ibn Khaldūn remarked that the women put up a stiff resistance, but that seems highly improbable. All over the battlefield countless numbers of Moors were killed, wounded, or captured. Among the captives were the emir's son Abū 'Umar Tāshufīn, other members of the royal family, and many distinguished nobles. Recording the recollection of an earlier author, the seventeenth-century historian, Al-Makkarī, commented that Almighty God allowed the emir's army of 60,000 men to be scattered like dust before the wind. Defeated and a fugitive, Abū l-Hasan had to return to his own realms, while thousands of Muslims won the crown of martyrdom that day.[74]

Thinking that Abū l-Hasan would attempt to cross the Strait that night, Alfonso XI ordered Pere de Moncada, the Catalan admiral, to guard against this, but he would not do so, even though his galleys were paid for by the king of Castile. Throughout the battle the admiral had remained on his galley and would not allow any of his mariners to land and to aid their fellow Christians. From Algeciras Abū l-Hasan made his way to Gibraltar while Yūsuf I fled to Marbella and then to Granada. Trying to console his men, the emir declared that God had ordained the Christian victory, but in the privacy of his chamber, he deeply lamented the outcome. Lest word of that catastrophe reach Morocco and encourage his son 'Abd al-Rahmān to rise in rebellion, he sent a ship immediately to Ceuta to proclaim his victory. Before the night was over, he sailed to Ceuta where he was received with honor. In the words of Giménez Soler, "For the last time Africa was expelled from Spain."[75]

The poet Rodrigo Yáñez, interpreting a prophecy of Merlin, compared the battle of Salado to a great struggle involving a crowned lion (Alfonso XI), a sleeping lion (Afonso IV), a porcupine (Abū l-Hasan), and a dragon (Yūsuf I). The porcupine escaped death but lost his sword and his honor on that day.[76]

Although 200,000 Moors were said to have died in the battle, a Genoese sent by Abū l-Hasan to discover the fate of his wives and children reported that 400,000 (an unlikely number) persons were missing from the list of those who had crossed the Strait in sixty galleys in the previous five months. In the two weeks after the battle only twelve galleys were needed to carry the survivors to Morocco. As Alfonso XI had food supplies for no more than two to four days, he decided not to attempt to capture Algeciras. Archbishop Gil de Albornoz lamented: "If we had provisions for a month, we would surely have conquered the castle of Algeciras." After repairing the walls of Tarifa, the king began the homeward journey on Wednesday, 1 November. Prior to his departure, he asked Admiral Pere de Moncada, whose expenses he was paying, to continue to guard the Strait.[77]

The Aftermath of the Crusade

On their return the kings of Castile and Portugal made a pilgrimage to El Puerto de Santa María, a shrine celebrated by Alfonso X in his *Cantigas de Santa Maria*.[78] When they neared Seville, the archbishop and chapter came out to meet them in a great procession. The banners seized in that "holy battle" were carried into the city on the necks of captured Moors. The booty was immense. There were great quantities of gold and silver, both in coins and in bars; gold and silver rings; jewelry and precious stones; cloth of gold and silk; swords garnished with gold and silver; spurs and belts of gold and silver; saddles and bridles; and tents of exquisite workmanship. Many men, however, had hidden booty and refused to hand it over for general distribution.[79] Among the most precious items was a copy of the Koran written by Caliph ʿUthmān b. ʿAffān (644–56) and once preserved in Umayyad Córdoba. Abū l-Hasan had acquired it when he took Tlemcen in 1337, but he lost it at Salado. After many inquiries he discovered that it was in Portugal and sent a merchant to recover it. It cost him thousands of dinars, even though the cover and its decoration had been ripped off.[80]

Bound with ropes and penned in a corral near the *alcázar* of Seville were many captives from the Marinid royal house, including the emir's son, and the sons of other distinguished families. Alfonso XI invited Afonso IV to take whatever he wanted, but he took only some swords, saddles, bridles, and spurs, leaving all the money. Alfonso XI handed over to him the emir's son and some of the other captives who could be ransomed. Five of the captured banners, probably those taken from Yūsuf I, were taken back to Lisbon. The armor worn by Afonso IV in the battle is preserved in the National Museum in Lisbon.[81] Alfonso XI rewarded those who had contributed to the victory at Salado in various ways.[82]

Many captured banners were placed in the cathedral of Seville where they remained for many years. A portion of the booty was used to finance decoration of the cathedral's Puerta del Perdón. Two banners are now conserved in the sacristy of the cathedral of Toledo. One made of silk of a rich yellow-orange color, measures about 12.25 feet long and about 3.75 feet wide. Across the top is a sleeve through which a pole was run so that it could be suspended horizontally. In a rectangular space just below the sleeve is an Arabic epigraph: "May the aid and protection of Allah and manifest victory be with our Lord Abū l-Hasan, *amīr al-muslimīn*," that is, lord of the Muslims. In the center of the banner is a large square with a border. Inside the square are sixteen circles shaped like half moons. A narrow strip at the bottom records that this was made for the emir in December 1339. Hanging from the bottom are nine *farpas*, or scallop points. More than likely, this banner was placed in the royal encampment.

A second banner, of a bright yellow color, but now deteriorated and lacking the upper sleeve as well as the bottom section and the scalloped points, displays a similar central field with nine circles. A text reads: "May victory be with our Lord Abū l-Hasan, *amīr al-muslimīn*." Still a third banner of green silk and exhibiting similar motifs, measures about 12.8 feet by 8.8 feet. An Arabic inscription indicates that it belonged to the emir's father, Abū Saʿīd, in the year 1312. Inscriptions such as "There is no God but God!" and "Muhammad is God's Messenger!" and verses from the Koran are woven into the fabric at various places. Although Huici suggested that the Marinid emirs followed the Almohad tradition of using a white banner, Abū l-Hasan's tent was red. The banners of the king of Granada were red.[83]

News of the victory had already been sent to the pope. On the very day of the battle, 30 October, Archbishop Gil de Albornoz wrote to Benedict XII and to Bishop Annibale de Ceccano of Frascati. Proclaiming the extraordinary character of the victory and the untold number of Moors who were killed, he emphasized the valor of the nobles battling out of zeal for the faith. The triumphant king prayed that God would expel from Christian territory the "awful stench of the sons of darkness, whose victory would have brought ruin to Christendom."[84] Later the archbishop established a liturgical commemoration of the victory, *Victoriae Benamarin super flumen Salsum*, to be celebrated on 30 October; this was included in the liturgical books of the archiepiscopal see as late as 1819.[85]

Prior to the battle, on 20 October, the bishop and municipal council of Valencia went in procession through the streets, asking God to grant victory to the crusaders. Then, on 11 November, another procession celebrated the Christian triumph. The citizens gave thanks to "Our Lord God, who in his mercy, gave victory to the high kings of Castile and Portugal in their pitched battle with the infidel kings of Benamarin and Granada and their troops."[86] In years thereafter, many Portuguese dioceses introduced a feast entitled *Victoria Christianorum* that was celebrated even in the twentieth century.[87]

As a sign of gratitude, the king dispatched Juan Martínez de Leyva, with a most magnificent caravan, to Avignon to present to Benedict XII his royal banner and other banners seized in that "holy battle." He also made a gift of the horse he had ridden that day as well as a number of Moorish captives and their horses, and various objects of booty. In order to continue the war against the Muslims, he instructed his emissary to ask the pope for additional financial aid. Many cardinals and ordinary citizens came out of the city to greet the Castilian ambassador. The captured horses, each with a sword and shield affixed to the saddle horn, preceded him. Castles and lions signifying Castile and León covered the king's steed. Following it were twenty-four Moors, each carrying a captured banner. Receiving Juan Martínez with honor, Benedict XII descended from his throne, took the royal banner in his hand, and intoned the triumphant hymn: "Vexilla Regis prodeunt; fulget Crucis misterium"—"Abroad the regal banners fly, now shines the Cross's mystery." The cardinals, archbishops, and clergy present all joined in singing the hymn. The pope ordered the royal banner and the trophies of war to be hung from the ceiling of his chapel.[88]

When he first heard of the royal triumph, the pope ordered processions and granted pardon of their sins to those who gave thanks to God. In his homily during mass, he compared Alfonso XI's victory to King David's defeat of two kings of the Philistines (2 Samuel 8:3–7). Like King Antiochus, who sent offerings to Simon, the high priest of Jerusalem, in recognition of his high priesthood, so Alfonso XI sent gifts to the pope, holding the place of the sovereign high priest (1 Maccabees 15:1–9). With other laudatory words, he praised the king who risked his body for the increase of the holy Catholic faith.[89]

In December the pope wrote a warm letter of felicitation to Alfonso XI. Commending the kings of Castile and Portugal for putting their quarrels aside and turning away from sin to act jointly against the Moors, he stressed that God gave them victory. At the same time he admonished Alfonso XI to guard against succumbing again to the concupiscence of the flesh. Urging him to combat both visible and invisible enemies, he assured him that if he conquered the interior enemy, God would enable him to emerge triumphant with even greater glory over his enemies and the enemies of he faith. Thus, the glory of his name and his fame would be spread about the world and at the last he would be "crowned with the diadem of eternal life."[90] In May of the following year Benedict XII thanked Alfonso XI for the splendid gifts and exhorted him to press on in defense of the faith. A similar congratulatory letter was sent to Afonso IV.[91]

Pedro IV, on 8 December, also congratulated Alfonso XI on his victory over "the evil enemy of our Catholic faith and the cross of our Lord Jesus Christ and over his perfidious and wicked people." Two days before the king briefly alluded to "the victory now gained against the Agarene ruler in Spain" and enunciated his hope that it would lead to the extermination of both him and his people. A few days later he assured the king of Castile that he was ordering Pere de Moncada to remain in the Strait through the coming month of March. In addition, he was sending money to pay the crew and hoped to send two other galleys to the Strait by that time.[92]

The Meaning of the Crusade of Salado

The Crusade of Salado, one of the decisive battles of the Middle Ages, marked a significant turning point in the relationship between the Christian and Muslim worlds. Comparing Salado with the Crusade of Las Navas de Tolosa in 1212, the *Royal Chronicle* emphasized that the victory in "the holy battle" fought near Tarifa was greater and more worthy of praise. Unlike Alfonso VIII, the victor at Las Navas, Alfonso XI had little time to prepare and lacked any significant support from beyond the Pyrenees. Whereas the kings of Aragón and Navarre contributed in a decisive way to the triumph at Las Navas, the only peninsular king to aid Alfonso XI was Afonso IV of Portugal. Aside from the Portuguese, only one knight from the kingdom of Aragón and two squires from Mallorca were present. The victory at Salado was attributable to *soli hispani*, to the Spaniards alone. Archbishop Rodrigo Jiménez de Rada had said as much of Las Navas de Tolosa.[93]

Whether one accepts the chronicler's argument or not, both battles had profound consequences. Las Navas de Tolosa marked the beginning of the end of Almohad power and opened Andalucía to the great Christian conquest of the second quarter of the thirteenth century. The battle of Salado, on the other hand, signaled the beginning of the decline of the Marinids, who never again invaded the peninsula in force. Manuel García Fernández emphasized that control of maritime traffic in the Strait was now in the hands of the Christians, in particular, the Genoese as allies of Alfonso XI.[94]

The number of combatants is difficult to determine, given the obviously inflated figures provided by the sources. There were about 8,000 Castilian knights and 12,000 infantry and 1,000 Portuguese knights. Another 1,000 in Tarifa would bring the total to about 22,000 men. The Marinids supposedly had 70,000 knights and 400,000 foot soldiers, and the king of Granada had 7,000 knights and 700,000 infantry. Archbishop Albornoz estimated Muslim strength at 40,000 knights and 400,000 foot soldiers, but one cannot accept these numbers. For many years a Christian militia served in the emir's army and likely took part in the battle. Fighting on the side of Alfonso XI was Sulaymān, one of the sons of ʿUthmān b. ʿAbī-l-ʿUlā, the Marinid prince who had once commanded the Granadan army. The number of dead Muslims, according to the *Chronicle of Alfonso XI* was 200,000, a number raised to 450,000 by the *Chronicle of Afonso IV*. By contrast, only fifteen to twenty Christians were said to have died. These figures are simply unbelievable. Huici's judgment, that the Christians had about 22,000 men and the Muslims about 60,000, attempts to make sense out of a seemingly irrational subject. Whatever the actual numbers may have been, it seems certain that both armies were the largest to engage in a pitched battle in the Iberian Peninsula in the medieval era.[95]

In addition to superior numbers, Abū l-Hasan ruled over an empire in Morocco that was much more extensive, more heavily populated, and wealthier than Castile. In 1317 Alfonso XI's annual income was calculated at 1,000,000 *maravedíes*, leaving him with a shortfall of 9,600,000 *maravedíes*. Later, in order to relieve Tarifa he was compelled to pawn the crown jewels. In contrast to his perennial poverty, the emir, according to Huici's estimate, had revenues twenty times greater. Without the grant of extraordinary taxes by the Cortes, loans, and the papal concession of the *decima* and the *tercias*, Alfonso XI would have been unable to defend his realm.[96]

Four monarchs, two representing the Christian faith and two representing Islam, participated in the battle. Two emerged victorious and two went down in defeat. Two were relatively young men but the other two were in middle age. At the time of the battle Alfonso XI was just twenty-eight years of age, while his father-in-law, Afonso IV, was forty-nine. The Marinid emir, Abū l-Hasan, was forty-three; but Yūsuf I of Granada was only twenty-two. Afonso IV, a warrior king known as "El Bravo," survived his son-in-law by seven years, but his later years were torn by family strife. Although Abū l-Hasan, one of the great conquerors of the Marinid dynasty, was able to achieve one more great military victory at Tunis, internal discord and rebellion by his sons eventually brought his reign to an end. Deprived of the possibility of Moroccan support thereafter, Yūsuf I had to bear the brunt of a renewed Christian attack, but he also opened a new and brilliant era in the cultural life of the kingdom of Granada. Elated by his triumph at Salado, Alfonso XI now took up the task of conquering Algeciras and Gibraltar.

Chapter 9

The Crusade of Algeciras and Gibraltar

In the decade following his victory at Salado, Alfonso XI directed his efforts and his treasure to the conquest of Algeciras and Gibraltar. Possession of those ports, he recognized, was essential to protect against a renewed invasion from Morocco. After a siege of nearly two years Algeciras was forced to surrender in 1344, though it exhausted his treasury and his troops. Nevertheless, after allowing time for his people to catch their breath, he returned to the attack, this time against Gibraltar. His campaign and his life ended abruptly, however, when he was struck down by the plague in 1350.

Financing the War

Despite the euphoria after the battle of Salado, Alfonso XI knew that the war would likely be resumed in the following spring and he would have to replenish his treasury. Urban representatives summoned to Llerena, north of Seville, in early December 1340, though feeling the weight of many taxes previously levied, acknowledged their responsibility for "the protection and defense of the realm" and granted an unspecified amount of new taxes.[1] He also demanded a substantial sum from the Jewish communities.[2] Journeying to the shrine of the Virgin Mary at Guadalupe in the province of Cáceres, he offered thanks for "the marvelous victory" achieved through her intercession.[3]

Afonso IV of Portugal, who had shared in the glory of Salado, seemed prepared to continue his military alliance with Castile. Benedict XII on 30 April 1341 granted him the bull of crusade as well as the right to take the *decima* for two years for the war against the Moors of Granada and Murcia. The archbishop of Braga was appointed executor of the bull.[4] A month later, Philip VI of France expressed his concern to the pope about enemies threatening

Christendom.⁵ Neither king, however, participated further in military operations against the Moors.

The Conquest of Alcalá de Benzaide

By late April 1341 Alfonso XI initiated a frontal assault on the kingdom of Granada. Although some suggested that he could easily take Algeciras, he believed that first he had to strengthen his fleet and obtain renewed crusading benefits from the pope. Instead, he opted to strike at Alcalá de Benzaide about thirty miles north of Granada, first ravaging its wheat fields and then planning a siege. Lest the Moors strengthen its defenses, he let it be known that he intended to attack Málaga and sent ships loaded with wheat and barley to await him off the adjacent coast. Deceived by his actions, Yūsuf I transferred many of his soldiers from frontier outposts, including Alcalá de Benzaide, to Málaga. The king, however, reversed direction and marched on Alcalá de Benzaide, whose formidable fortress, known as La Mota, dominated the surrounding area. A contingent sent to besiege the nearby castle of Locubín forced its surrender. As eight siege engines bombarded the walls of Alcalá de Benzaide, sappers set to work undermining them. Yūsuf I advanced to Moclín, a few miles north of Granada, but, no doubt remembering the unfortunate outcome of the encounter at Salado, he refused to accept the Castilian challenge to battle. Bereft of any help, the defenders surrendered on 20 August and, leaving their arms and supplies behind, were allowed to depart. Alcalá la Real, the name by which this fortress is known today, commemorates Alfonso XI's conquest. Hoping to end the Castilian offensive, Yūsuf I proposed a truce. However, when Alfonso XI refused to include Abū l-Hasan, the Nasrid king, knowing that he might have future need of Marinid support, terminated negotiations. In the ensuing weeks, Alfonso XI seized Priego, Carcabuey, and the castle of Matrera, near Villamartín, while the master of Santiago recaptured the castle of Benamejí. As it was now September and the rains were heavy, he concluded his campaign. He had good reason to be satisfied because of the recovery of several places previously occupied by the Christians and he had advanced his frontier ever closer to the seat of Nasrid power.⁶ Benedict XII on 26 September congratulated him on the conquest of Alcalá de Benzaide and Locubín.⁷

During the siege of Alcalá de Benzaide, Egidio Boccanegra, brother of the doge of Genoa, arrived at Seville with fifteen galleys. Pedro IV instructed his admiral, Pere de Moncada, not to withdraw from the Strait until the following

January when he expected to send ten new galleys. In order to maintain his fleet, he appealed to Benedict XII to authorize the use of revenues pertaining to the Order of the Hospital for that purpose.[8]

The *Alcabala*

As the year drew to a close, Alfonso XI decided to concentrate his energy on the capture of Algeciras, the chief port giving the Marinids entry into the Peninsula. As none of the other European kings, save Afonso IV, had come to his aid at Salado, Alfonso XI knew that he could not depend upon them to oppose the Marinids and their allies, the Nasrids of Granada. Recalling the loss of Christian lands to the Moors who invaded Spain centuries before, Alfonso XI concluded that if he did not conquer Algeciras, his people and all of Christendom would be in great danger.[9]

Abū l-Hasan reportedly was preparing a great fleet to avenge his earlier defeat. Interpreting the emir's mind, the poet Rodrigo Yáñez affirmed that if Algeciras were conquered, the ports would be unprotected, Granada would be lost, and "Don Alfonso, king of Spain, will then be emperor." Worst of all, he would cross the Strait to invade the emir's lands. In these lines the poet expressed the traditional aspirations of the kings of Castile, as heirs of the Visigoths, to repossess all of Spain, including Morocco, once believed to be part of the Visigothic realm. The titles "king of Spain" and "emperor" articulated their pretensions to ascendancy over the entire Peninsula.[10]

Realizing that the realm was impoverished by the many levies already imposed, Alfonso XI decided to demand an *alcabala*, or sales tax, on all commercial transactions for one year. At an assembly at Burgos in January 1342 he argued that the conquest of Algeciras was essential to the well-being both of Christendom and his kingdom. With 3,000 knights he intended to lay siege to Algeciras and not to withdraw until he could take it. However, the *servicios* hitherto collected were insufficient to cover half the cost of the stipends given to his vassals, payments to town militias, and the maintenance of Genoese galleys. After the citizens of Burgos gave consent, the prelates, magnates, and knights followed suit. Similar assemblies held at León, Zamora, and Ávila also consented.[11]

Naval Battles in the Strait

Early in May 1342 Abū l-Hasan assembled a large fleet of about eighty galleys and other warships at Ceuta with the aim of attacking the Castilian fleet guarding the Strait at Getares just south of Algeciras. In order to prevent twelve other galleys from joining the main body of the fleet, Admiral Egidio Boccanegra sent ten galleys to attack them. Four enemy ships were burned, two were destroyed, and six were captured. Although Alfonso XI was pleased by this news, he took steps to arm additional galleys at Seville. In addition, Afonso IV sent ten Portuguese galleys under the command of Admiral Carlo Pessagno, the son of Manuel Pessagno.[12] As Nicolas Agrait pointed out, the monthly cost of equipping a galley and paying the crew was about 9,000 *maravedíes*; thus the expense of maintaining a fleet of about forty-four ships for one month was about 396,000 *maravedíes*.[13]

The conduct of the Catalan admiral Pere de Moncada, who left the Strait in pursuit of Moorish ships laden with arms, oil, cloth, and other merchandise, displeased Alfonso XI. After seizing two enemy ships along the Barbary Coast, Moncada, instead of returning to the Strait, made for Barcelona. Excusing his admiral, whose action was injurious to "the enemies of the faith who were in great need," Pedro IV nevertheless ordered him to Valencia, where other galleys were being readied. By 1 June Moncada and twenty galleys were expected to set sail for the Strait.[14]

Although the king had not planned an offensive in 1342, news of Marinid naval preparations persuaded him to hasten to Seville in mid-May. Summoning the military orders and the municipal militias of Andalucía, he moved to Jerez. There he requisitioned quantities of wheat and barley from the archdiocese of Seville and also collected the *tercias*.[15] Meanwhile, the Muslim fleet had crossed the Strait to the mouth of the Guadamecí River near Tarifa, where Boccanegra and Pessagno blockaded it. When thirteen galleys put out from Algeciras to aid their fellow Muslims, ten Christian galleys engaged them in a fierce battle, seizing two, sinking four, and forcing seven to run aground. A quantity of gold and silver intended to pay the Marinid troops in Algeciras fell into Christian hands, much to the joy of Alfonso XI, who could divert it to his own army. In another engagement the Christians defeated the Moors, who lost twenty-six galleys; some were sunk, others burned, and still others captured. The Christians lost only three *naos*. Following this, as the two months for which his fleet was paid had elapsed, Carlo Pessagno wished to return to Portugal, but Alfonso XI, offering to pay him for two additional months, persuaded him to remain. Four days after the Marinids were defeated in the Strait, Pere de Moncada, the Catalan admiral, en route to the Strait with twenty galleys, prevailed over thirteen Muslim galleys near Estepona. Four galleys loaded with wheat were captured; two were driven aground, and the other seven returned to Morocco. These naval battles occurred during late May and June.[16]

In his concern to thwart any Marinid invasion, Alfonso XI hastened to Getares with 2,300 knights and 3,000 foot soldiers. Reconnoitering Algeciras, its harbor, fortifications, vineyards, orchards, and wheat fields, he decided to initiate the siege with the men at hand and summoned all his vassals to join him. While urging his admirals to maintain a strict watch over the Strait, lest the Marinids attempt to dispatch another fleet from Morocco, he also gathered forage and shipped wheat and barley down the Guadalquivir. In order to facilitate the transfer of troops and supplies he built several bridges and improved the roads from Jerez to Algeciras.[17]

Beginning the Siege of Algeciras

"If I conquer Algeciras, I will be lord of Spain." With that thought in mind, Alfonso XI set out from Jerez on 25 July 1342, making his way to Getares near Algeciras on 1 August. Accompanying him were Gil de Albornoz, archbishop of Toledo, the bishop of Cádiz, the masters of the military orders, the militias of Seville, Córdoba, Jerez, Écija, Carmona, Niebla, and Jaén, and various nobles from Andalucía. He had 2,600 knights and 4,000 crossbowmen and lancers. On 3 August he established his base northwest of the town on a hill near the Palmones River. His fleet, commanded by Egidio Boccanegra, stood offshore. As a reward for services already rendered, he granted Palma del Río to Boccanegra.[18]

During the ensuing twenty months Christians and Muslims engaged in a duel to determine who should have Algeciras.[19] Defended by formidable stone walls intersected by strong towers, Algeciras, since the late thirteenth century, was divided by the Miel River into the Villa Vieja and the Villa Nueva. An exterior wall and a moat provided further protection. Behind its ramparts were 30,000 people, including 800 knights, 2,000 archers, and 14,000 infantry. The Castilians blockaded the town by land and by sea, though they were not able to seal it off completely until January 1344. The defenders, well supplied

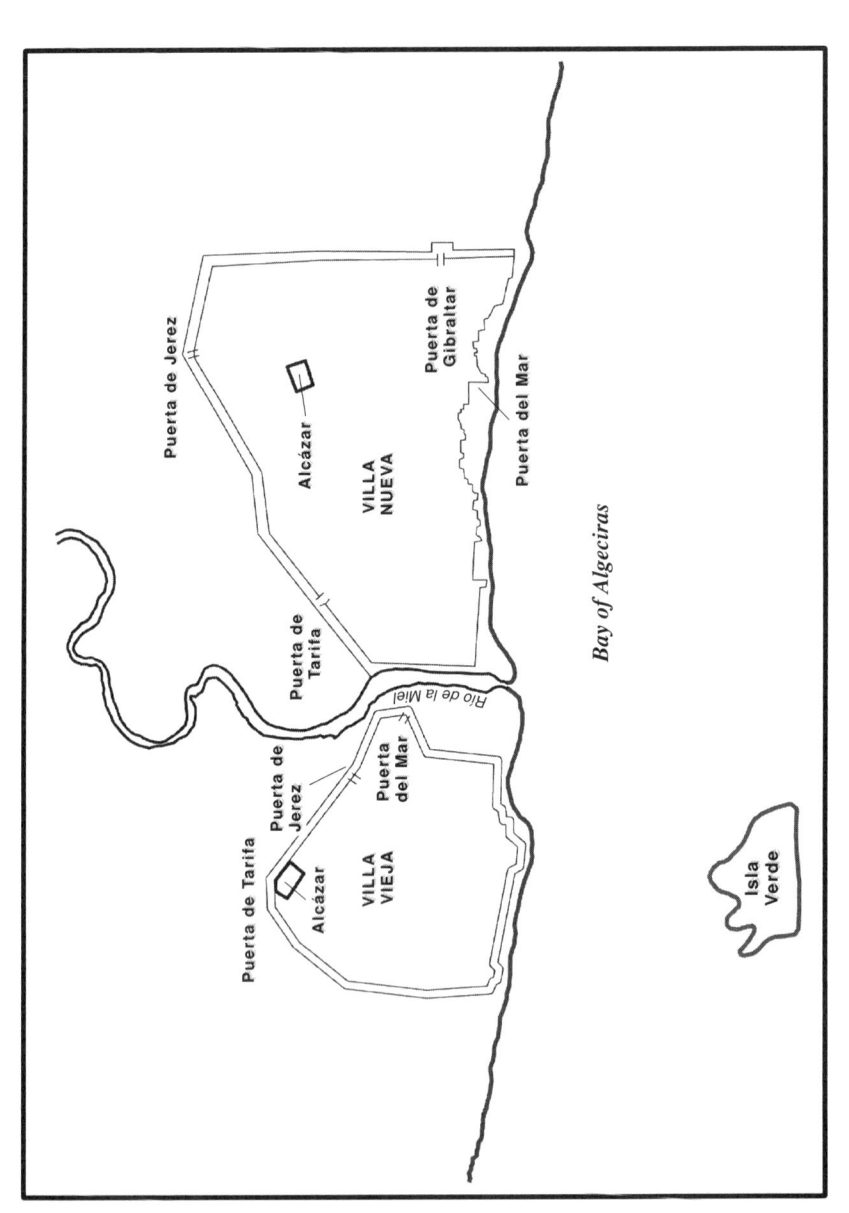

Map 3. The siege of Algeciras, 1342–1344.

with food and arms, were able to hold out with only minimal support from Granada or Morocco. Small boats breaking through the blockade, usually at night, brought in additional food, and this was a principal reason for the prolongation of the siege. As the siege went on, a steady stream of prelates, magnates, knights, knights of the military orders, and town militias, especially those of the frontier towns, arrived and were given responsibility for certain areas.[20]

Nearly every day the defenders launched projectiles against the Castilian lines. In January 1343 the king ordered Iñigo López de Orozco, his *capitan mayor de los trabucos y engeños*, to bring to Algeciras trebuchets and siege engines made in Seville by Genoese craftsmen.[21] Most terrifying were iron balls, burning like fire, shot from cannons (*truenos*). Anyone struck by a cannonball was beyond the help of any surgeon. Burning gunpowder caused ulcerations that led inevitably to death.[22] The Muslims had the advantage here as the Castilians do not seem to have had cannons.[23] When the Christians mounted one of their twenty-six engines on its carriage, the Moors fired and knocked it out, but two rapid-fire, double-arch trebuchets countered the enemy barrage. The besiegers also built wooden towers that could be moved on wheels close to the walls. From these heights archers and crossbowmen could fire arrows into the town. From time to time the Moors made sorties outside the walls to engage the enemy. While the Christians cried out "Santiago," the Moors shouted "Benamarin!" In these innumerable skirmishes both sides suffered casualties. During the winter of 1342–43 heavy rains caused great distress among the besiegers. As tents riddled with holes offered little protection against the elements, the king ordered the construction of wooden huts. He also moved his base camp closer to Algeciras, southwest of the Villa Nueva, and seized the tower of Cartagena between Algeciras and Gibraltar.[24]

Throughout the long months the task of feeding the besieging army was a major concern. The shortage was such that in the summer of 1343 a *fanega* (about 1.6 bushels) of wheat cost 2.5 maravedíes and a *fanega* of barley 12 *dineros*, at the rate of 10 *dineros* to the *maravedí*. Large quantities of these grains were sent from Old Castile to the ports on the Bay of Biscay and then shipped to Algeciras. Nevertheless, the price of a *fanega* of wheat rose to 15 *maravedíes* and of barley to 6. The cost of transporting a *cahiz* (about 12 *fanegas*) of wheat in Andalucía rose from 18 *maravedíes* in September 1342 to 24 *maravedíes* three months later. Responding to an appeal for help, Pedro IV authorized the shipment of 1,000 *cahices* (about 1,600 bushels) of wheat. The king of Portugal also sent provisions. Much of the supply was reserved for a later day when the need would be greater. In July 1343, however, fire swept through the camp, destroying a goodly portion of the food supply as well as merchandise offered for sale. Enterprising merchants had set up shop on a street in the midst of the camp where they sold cloth of gold, silk, wool, and jewels.[25]

Faced with disaster, the king, according to the poet Rodrigo Yáñez, turned to prayer. Reminding God of his service and his wars against the Moors undertaken to increase the faith, he admitted his sinfulness, but asked God not to abandon him or his people:

> If you are angry with me,
> Here take my life away,
> But, Lord, let not Castile,
> The flower of Spain, be lost.

Soon food supplies shipped from many different areas arrived to relieve the distress.[26]

Both sides employed spies to observe their opponents. Alfonso XI ordered the seizure of stray Moors who might provide information. If they were reluctant to speak, torture was applied. In the hope of disrupting the besieging army, the defenders attempted to assassinate the king. One potential assassin was stopped, tortured, and executed. Two others were apprehended, tortured, and beheaded. Their heads were then catapulted into the town. In retaliation, the defenders executed two Christian captives and threw their heads into the royal camp.[27]

The Naval Blockade

The success of the siege depended heavily on maintaining the naval blockade. Thus Alfonso XI was greatly distressed in September 1342 when Pedro IV, citing his conflict with the king of Mallorca, withdrew his fleet commanded by Pere de Moncada, "a young man of little wisdom." Acknowledging his treaty obligation to provide ships, in November the Aragonese king dispatched ten galleys under his vice admiral Mateu Mercer. Afonso IV also sent ten galleys commanded by Admiral Carlo Pessagno. They were paid for two months' service, but that time was effectively reduced to three weeks because of the round-trip journey from Lisbon. The chronicler complained that "it would have been better if they had not come because the Moors took heart when they withdrew." He also lamented that only one Portuguese knight and not a single squire participated in the siege. This was all the more surprising because everyone knew that if the Moors overcame Castile Portugal would soon suffer.[28]

In the spring of 1343 Egidio Boccanegra commanded a fleet of fifty Genoese and Castilian galleys, as well as forty Castilian warships (*naves*). A storm drove two of the ten Catalan galleys aground, but the Christians were able to save them from being burned by the Moors. A Castilian galley and two large *naos* and some smaller vessels transporting food were broken up. In response to Alfonso XI's plea that the Catalans extend their tour of duty for another four months, Mateu Mercer appealed to Pedro IV to pay his crew and send fresh sailors. He promised to do so as soon as he had resolved affairs in Mallorca, but Alfonso XI had to remind him that the Catalan galleys needed basic sustenance and armament. In response, Pedro IV sent mixed messages, telling Alfonso XI that he commanded Mateu Mercer not to leave the Strait, while summoning him to Mallorca. On his own authority, Alfonso XI ordered Mateu not to depart. At last, in July Pedro IV announced that he was sending ten galleys to the Strait.[29]

Diversions by the King of Granada

Aside from the fear that Abū l-Hasan would come to the relief of Algeciras, Alfonso XI also had to guard against a possible attack on his rear by Yūsuf I of Granada. Still smarting from his defeat at Salado, he was slow to make any hostile move. Then in January 1343, joined by Marinid knights from Ronda, he pillaged the land around Écija and massacred Christians at Palma del Río. Alerted to this incursion, the militias of Córdoba, Seville, and other towns forced the Moors to withdraw. A month later Yūsuf I seized the castle of Benamejí and the town of Estepa, both belonging to the Order of Santiago.[30]

In February 1343, considering that the siege had already been in progress since August, some among Alfonso XI's counselors thought that it was time to make peace. Afonso IV of Portugal had indicated that he could provide no support other than the galleys he had already sent, and neither the pope nor the king of France had responded to the king's pleas for help. Inasmuch as Abū l-Hasan had not yet dispatched his army to Spain, Yūsuf I also thought it wise to come to terms. Negotiations collapsed, however, when Alfonso XI demanded that he break with the Marinids and allow him to proceed with the siege of Algeciras without interference. Realizing that his alliance with Morocco still afforded some protection, Yūsuf I refused. Soon after a Marinid force of 1,000 knights and 2,000 foot soldiers from Málaga and Ronda again plundered the area around Écija, but a contingent of 200 knights and 1,500 foot soldiers, surprised them at midnight. Shouting "Santiago," they captured 300 of the enemy and killed 650. As it was time for the spring harvest, the king arranged to defend various frontier outposts and prevent burning crops.[31]

Meantime, Abū l-Hasan was diverted from executing an invasion of Spain by the rebellion of his son ʿAbd al-Rahmān. Ostensibly attempting to placate him, the emir offered him half the realm, but when the opportunity arose, he ordered him to be beheaded. These internal troubles perhaps ultimately contributed to the loss of Algeciras. Nevertheless, Abū l-Hasan did send a detachment of troops to Estepona on the coast east of Gibraltar. Emboldened by their presence, on 1 May 1343 Yūsuf I advanced to the Guadiaro River about fifteen miles from the Castilian encampment. While preparing for battle, Alfonso XI sent his envoy to inquire as to his intentions.[32]

Northern European Crusaders

About this time several distinguished northern European crusaders joined the besieging army. In a skirmish in August 1342 Godefroy, count of Los, who had come from Germany with six knights, was killed when he led his men ahead of the main army. The Moors burned his corpse. Alfonso XI advised the other Germans to show greater caution, as they were not used to fighting the Moors. Early in 1343 the Catalan Bernat Rocaberti, viscount of Cabrera, also came to Algeciras, as did the king's nephew, Fernando of Aragón, marquess of Tortosa.[33]

Prior to the siege of Algeciras, Edward III of England and Philip VI of France, bitter rivals in the Hundred Years' War, sought an alliance with Alfonso XI. A Franco-Castilian treaty signed in 1337 provided for military and naval support against mutual enemies, but did not mention the Marinids. With the hope of securing their collaboration against the Moors, the king offered to mediate between France and England. Writing to Benedict XII on 26 May 1341, Philip VI expressed regret at not being able to provide immediate aid to Castile. When French and English crusaders came to take part in the siege, they also hoped to gain Castilian support, especially naval assistance, in the ongoing war between their respective sovereigns.[34]

After the arrival of some French and German knights in April 1343, the royal camp eagerly awaited the appearance of the earls of Derby and Salisbury, who came "for the salvation of their souls" and to "gain the pardon that was granted." After lodging in Seville in the house of the Bardi, Genoese merchant bankers, they reached Algeciras in May. Although Edward III commissioned Henry, earl of Derby, and William Montague, earl of Salisbury, to seek Castilian naval assistance against France, Alfonso XI, in the present circumstances, was unable to promise anything. If it were not for the lull in the Hundred Years War, it seems unlikely that the earls would have come to Algeciras. Once there, however, they vigorously participated in many skirmishes and the earl of Derby even sustained a facial wound. Both men also accompanied Admiral Boccanegra when he engaged the Moors in a naval battle off Ceuta in August 1343. Soon afterward, however, Edward III summoned them home and ordered the earl of Derby to proceed to Avignon as his representative. Alfonso XI thanked them for their service and they parted as good friends. On the return journey, the earl of Salisbury fell ill in Seville, but when he heard that a Moorish force had come to Gibraltar, he wanted to return to the siege, but his doctors dissuaded him. The English earls served about five months in the siege of Algeciras and, on the whole, acquitted themselves well. Edward III expressed his gratitude to Boccanegra for his hospitable reception of the English crusaders.[35]

English participation in the siege found an echo in Geoffrey Chaucer's *Canterbury Tales*. Among the pilgrims described in the prologue was "a true, a perfect gentle-knight," who had taken part in the conquest of Algeciras and had fought against the Marinids: "In Gernade at the seege eek hadde he be/ of Algezir and riden in Belmarye"—"In Granada he had also been at the siege of Algeciras and rode in Benamarin" (ll. 56–57). Whether a fictitious person or not, he exemplified real knights who had been there.[36]

Also anxious to obtain Castilian naval support, Philip VI sent his emissaries to Algeciras. In June 1343 Gaston de Béarn, count of Foix, and his brother Roger Bernard, viscount of Castelbon, with a few Gascon companies, arrived. A month later Philip of Évreux, king of Navarre, and his men appeared. Using the language of crusading, the poet Rodrigo Yáñez described them as "romeros en romeria"—"pilgrims on pilgrimage." Although Philip had only 100 knights and 300 foot soldiers, he shipped a substantial quantity of meat, barley, wine, and bacon from the Bay of Biscay to the siege. In order to avoid unnecessary clashes between erstwhile enemies, Alfonso XI assigned the Navarrese, Gascons, and French areas of operation apart from the English and Germans.

As they were unfamiliar with the style of warfare employed by the Moors, he warned them all not to advance against the enemy unless they followed the royal standard.[37]

Failing to heed his command, the count of Foix, crying "France! France!" rushed into the midst of the Moors, but as the poet noted, "it would have gone badly for the French, if it were not for the Castilians." The author of the *Royal Chronicle* seems to have held the Gascons in low regard, complaining that the count of Foix and the viscount of Castelbon avoided combat. The former seemed more intent on gaining the king's confidence, no doubt in an attempt to persuade him to accept an alliance with France, while his brother told jokes and made everyone laugh. Just two months after his arrival, Gaston de Foix asked Alfonso XI to pay his expenses; otherwise he would not be able to remain. Although he was hard-pressed financially, the king realized that the departure of the Gascons would hearten the Moors and so he asked the Genoese and other merchants for a loan. With that he was able to pay the count and his brother and their men for a month. Gaston received 200 *maravedíes*, Roger Bernard, 50, each knight, 8, and each foot soldier, 2. The king soon had reason to be annoyed with the Gascons, for when he asked Gaston to guard a wooden tower, he refused, alleging that he did not feel well. The chronicler made the point that "just as it is right to relate the good deeds accomplished by those who serve well, so one ought not to forget what is done by those who do not wish to do well. Otherwise both would be treated equally."[38]

In late August 1343, twenty days after accepting the king's money for his service, Gaston de Foix informed Alfonso XI that he had to return home. Expecting the Moors to mount an offensive in September, the king tried to persuade him to remain through that month, but lacked the wherewithal. When Roger Bernard, viscount of Castelbon, offered to stay if Alfonso XI paid his expenses, the count denounced him. Gaston also tried to persuade Philip of Navarre to leave as well. Although Bernat of Cabrera urged him to remain, Gaston made his way to Seville where he fell ill and died. In effect, Count Gaston de Foix, after arriving at the royal camp before Algeciras toward the end of June, left about the end of the third week in August. At most he served at the siege for about two months, but if we are to believe the chronicler, his contribution was negligible if not lacking altogether. Perhaps he was not in good health and thus wished to return to the comfort of home.[39]

Late in the summer Philip of Évreux, king of Navarre, also fell seriously ill. Alfonso XI sent his physicians to treat him. While they proposed that the king follow a diet, his own physician opposed them, insisting that he eat meat and drink wine every day and withdraw from the siege. One might suspect that Alfonso XI's doctors, among whom was R. Shemarya of Negroponte, a distinguished astronomer and physician, had access to greater medical knowledge derived from the Muslim world. Be that as it may, in September Philip left Algeciras only to die at Jerez at the age of thirty-seven.[40] In November Clement VI (1342–52) consoled his widow, Queen Jeanne of Navarre. He had arrived at the siege in July and, unlike the count of Foix, acquitted himself well.[41]

Another northern crusader, Jean de Rye, lord of Balançon, had the misfortune of being captured. Although Clement VI, on 12 June 1344, suggested that an exchange of prisoners might give Jean de Rye his freedom, Alfonso XI seems to have done little if anything to bring that about. When the pope wrote to him again on 29 April 1347, he noted that Jean had been taken to Morocco as a prisoner in the service of Balec Agorg, a familiar of the Marinid emir. As Alfonso XI held Balec's son captive, the pope proposed an exchange. By 1352 Jean had returned to his native home, but the date and manner of his liberation is unknown. In any case, his experience in the Peninsula seems to have facilitated his later career as a diplomat in the French service, often as an ambassador in Spain.[42]

The contribution of northern crusaders to the siege of Algeciras, while not negligible, was not substantial. Their number was comparatively small. Most displayed their bravery as good knights, but their actions were not decisive one way or the other. The poet Rodrigo Yáñez summed up this episode:

> The foreigners have returned
> Each to his own land.
> The Castilians, Who know how to endure wars remained.[43]

Crusade Finance

As the siege wore on, the expense of maintaining a large army and a fleet for so many months threatened to exhaust the king's resources. Collecting as much silver as possible, he sent it to Seville to be minted, but he also debased the coinage. In February 1343 the magnates, knights, and townsmen in his company urged him not to do so and promised that the whole realm would grant him a *moneda forera* to purchase the coinage already minted. Minting of the debased coinage was halted and in May he asked for a *moneda*. His counselors urged him, however, to seek loans of money and livestock from his vassals and from the towns. His tax collectors were simultaneously collecting *fonsadera* and other customary revenues. He also pawned his golden crowns set with precious jewels as well as gold cups of great value.[44]

Realizing that these domestic resources were inadequate, late in 1342 the king dispatched Archbishop Gil de Albornoz to Philip VI of France and Alfonso Ortíz Calderón, prior of the Hospital, to Clement VI to request financial aid. In his plea to the pope, he argued that his finances were stretched to the limit and, though his people willingly responded to his frequent demands for money, they were impoverished and their contributions were insufficient to maintain his army and his fleet. The *tercias*, the *decima*, and other ecclesiastical revenues amounted to very little and could scarcely cover the cost of the war. Thus he asked Clement VI to lend him 100,000 gold florins. In June the pope arranged a loan of 20,000 gold florins from the Italian banker Guido, son of Francesco Malaballa, to be repaid by Christmas 1344. The *tercias* and *decimas* previously granted by the papacy as well as the king's revenues were pledged as security for repayment. Should Alfonso XI default on the loan, he would be subject to excommunication. The amount of the loan was a far cry from 100,000 florins. At the rate of 1 florin to 20 *maravedíes* the sum requested and the sum received approximated 2,000,000 and 400,000 *maravedíes* respectively. While acknowledging "the scant generosity" of the pope, Luciano Serrano commented that Clement VI expected to devote most of the available papal funds to the liberation of the Holy Land.[45]

When Clement VI, on 22 October 1343, accepted the king's ratification of the terms of the loan, he also affirmed that he had granted the crusade indulgence to all those in the Iberian Peninsula and in Europe generally who personally participated in the siege of Algeciras. In addition the king was authorized to collect the *decima* and the *tercias* for five years, but he had to use them solely on the prosecution of the war.[46]

Alfonso XI had to use the proceeds of the loan to pay his debts to the Genoese and thus was still in great need. Shortly, however, Archbishop Albornoz sent word that the king of France had made a gift of 50,000 florins (about 100,000 *maravedíes*), but half of it went to Alfonso XI's Genoese creditors. The remainder paid the expenses of the fleet, but that left nothing for his troops. In October Philip VI's contribution of 15,257 gold *escudos*, 23,651 gold florins, and 80,000 *dineros* was deposited in the royal treasury. In response to the king's indigent circumstances, the prelates, magnates, masters of the military orders, knights, and townsmen who were with him granted him two *monedas* and urged him to obtain loans. Some of his counselors and members of his household lent him what they could. He also acquired 5,000 cows and 20,000 sheep from the northern regions of his realm.[47]

Proposals for a Truce

As mentioned above, in May 1343 when Yūsuf I advanced to the Guadiaro River, Alfonso XI inquired as to his intentions. The Nasrid king, preferring a diplomatic settlement rather than the hazard of another battle, offered to renew his vassalage and the payment of tribute and some portion of Alfonso XI's expenses; now he also proposed a long-term truce that would include the Marinids. Although some of Alfonso XI's counselors argued that he should accept those terms, others insisted that the Moors would not observe the truce and he would have great difficulty in assembling an army to challenge them again. Aware that northern European crusaders were on their way, the king decided to prolong the negotiations.[48]

Although Abū l-Hasan wished to give battle once more, Yūsuf I contended that a reprise of the encounter at the Salado River was unwise. When his emissaries returned from Morocco in July, they visited the Castilian encampment where they saw an ample supply of food; a street where merchants sold cloth and jewels; and more than 600 helmets elaborately worked with horns and wings, and images of lions, wolves, and other animals, belonging to the northern crusaders. Impressed by the apparent good order, the Moors concluded that Alfonso XI would not easily come to terms. Realizing all the more the necessity of Marinid support, Yūsuf I pleaded with Abū l-Hasan to come to Spain or at least to send one of his sons so that the siege of Algeciras could be broken.[49]

As the summer wore on skirmishes outside the walls of Algeciras continued, as did encounters on the frontier between the kingdoms of Jaén and Granada, as well as around Lorca in the kingdom of Murcia. In August and September, however, the northern European crusaders began their journey home. The situation soon became worse. In October after storms dispersed the Christian fleet, sixty Moroccan galleys and many smaller ships, each carrying 160 horses, crossed the Strait to Estepona and then to Gibraltar. Accompanying them were 2,000 knights.[50]

Their arrival greatly increased the threat to the besiegers, who were suffering severe hardship from the chronic shortage of food and lack of pay. When

Boccanegra threatened to leave if he did not receive payment for four months' service, the king confessed that he did not have the money. He feared that Boccanegra would go over to the enemy if they paid him. Indeed, Abū l-Hasan had offered money to Simon Boccanegra, the doge of Genoa, to entice him to abandon Alfonso XI and enter his service. Suspicious of the Genoese, the king recalled that his great-grandfather Alfonso X had been compelled to lift the siege of Algeciras when the Genoese aided the Marinids. In order to avert a repetition of that treachery, the king gathered all the silver he could and borrowed money wherever he could to pay the Genoese. Despite his suspicions of their loyalty, they did not play him false and participated in the siege until the end.[51]

After the departure of the northern European crusaders, Yūsuf I thought that Alfonso XI would be more open to negotiation. Setting the figure of 300,000 gold *doblas* as compensation for his expenses, the king of Castile hoped to use that money and the Nasrid tribute to pay his troops, his fleet, and his loans. He also hoped to win Yūsuf I over to his side or at least to sow division between Granada and Morocco. With a safe-conduct from Alfonso XI, Yūsuf I crossed the Strait to consult Abū l-Hasan, who gave him the money for the indemnity. Suspecting that Boccanegra intended to seize the galley carrying the Nasrid king and the Marinid *doblas*, Alfonso XI summoned the admiral to his side. Although a Genoese ship commanded by Boccanegra's nephew latched on to Yūsuf I's galley, the Moors of Gibraltar drove off the Genoese and rescued the king and his treasure. The captain of the Genoese galley wisely escaped Alfonso XI's wrath by sailing to Genoa. Apologizing to the king of Granada for this violation of his safe-conduct, Alfonso XI also protested to Boccanegra but took no action against him because he still needed his services.[52]

Although the *Royal Chronicle* reported that Yūsuf I received an unspecified number of Marinid *doblas*, Ibn Marzūq, an eyewitness, related an entirely different story. Arguing that Algeciras had abundant provisions and the enemy was demoralized, Abū l-Hasan refused the Nasrid's request for 70,000 to 100,000 gold dinars to pay off the Christians. Ibn Marzūq noted that, aside from food and other supplies regularly sent to al-Andalus, the sultan expended 50,000 dinars every month to sustain the defenders there and in Gibraltar. Yūsuf I asked for twice that amount. At best, the sultan seems to have agreed to sell grain to the defenders in Algeciras at the price prevailing before the siege, so that they would not suffer want. Thus, it would seem that Yūsuf I returned home almost empty-handed. If the Genoese had captured him, they likely would have been disappointed to discover that he had scant treasure. As a further consequence, plans for a peace settlement were deferred once again because of Abū l-Hasan's refusal to cooperate.[53]

Thus, the siege dragged on. As summer turned to fall the condition of the besiegers deteriorated even more. Contrary winds prevented the delivery of food supplies and resulted in a rise in the cost of wheat and barley. The troops were also reduced to penury, as the king had no money to pay them. Their living conditions grew steadily worse, as their tents were destroyed by harsh weather and even the wooden huts that they had built were falling down. Through all this the king tried to keep up morale by frequent exhortations and promises of victory.[54]

The Battle of the Palmones River

Seeking to take advantage of the enemy's distress, in November Yūsuf I and the Marinids advanced from Gibraltar to the Palmones River east of Algeciras, but after a few skirmishes they withdrew. Alfonso XI then attempted to burn the Moorish fleet by sending into its midst two large *naos* and six barges laden with dry wood that was set ablaze; but the Moors, by covering their ships with large blankets soaked in the ocean, averted disaster. To add to the king's misery, the Catalans commanding twenty galleys announced that, as they had not been paid, they intended to leave. Borrowing money from Catalan and Genoese merchants and giving pledges of repayment, he was able to retain them for two more months.[55]

At the beginning of December 1343 the king of Granada and the Marinids crossed the Guadarranque River and came up to the Palmones River while thirty of their galleys maintained close contact along the coast. As two Muslim detachments crossed the Palmones, leaving three others behind, the Christians rang bells and made other signals in preparation for an attack. At the ninth hour or about 3 p.m., however, the Moors and their thirty galleys withdrew without giving battle. Nevertheless, on Friday, 12 December, the Moors of the Villa Vieja attacked the Christian ships just offshore, firing arrows and launching cannonballs. Smoke signals sent up from the tower of the mosque summoned the Moorish army at Gibraltar. Once again Yūsuf I and the Marinids attempted to cross the Palmones River against Castilian opposition. Alfonso XI could not match the enemy's 10,000 men, because he had to leave 2,000 knights and 5,000 foot soldiers to maintain the siege. Nevertheless, he rallied his men and pushed the enemy back, pursuing them as they fled to Gibraltar and Castellar. By nightfall, the field belonged to Castile.[56] Informed of Alfonso XI's victory, Pedro IV extended his congratulations on 31 December, commenting that it was a "great service to God and the exaltation of the Catholic faith and to your honor which we take as our own." A month later Alfonso XI appealed to his Aragonese colleague to allow Catalan merchants to bring needed food supplies to the besieging army.[57]

As 1344 dawned, Alfonso XI attempted to isolate Algeciras entirely, so that no food could be brought in, especially at nighttime. Tree trunks driven into the Bay of Algeciras and linked by chains stretching across the harbor prevented any boat from breaking out into the Strait. Two weeks of heavy rains in February caused great hardship to both sides and strong winds wrecked five galleys. The Moors had only enough food to last until March and as more and more men died of starvation, the defense became all the more problematical. Yūsuf I again proposed a truce and Abū l-Hasan, seeing all his efforts to succor the town thwarted by the Christian fleet, concluded that Algeciras was lost. Alfonso XI's forces were also depleted and so he appealed to the towns of Andalucía and Extremadura, the Order of Santiago, and Murcia and Lorca for additional help.[58]

The Surrender of Algeciras

Acknowledging that Alfonso XI seemed determined to persist to the end, on 21 March 1344, Yūsuf I outlined possible terms of surrender. The defenders would be permitted to depart with their movable goods, and Granada, Morocco, and Castile would accept a truce for fifteen years. He promised to renew his vassalage to Castile and to pay an annual tribute of 12,000 *doblas* or 246,000 *maravedíes*, the approximate amount Muhammad IV had agreed to pay in 1331. Some of Alfonso XI's counselors urged him to reject these proposals and, once additional reinforcements arrived, to take Algeciras by force and kill everyone except those who could be held for ransom. Others argued that an assault might not succeed, especially as the Nasrid and Marinid armies were close by and would come to the rescue. The possibility of Genoese treachery was also considered. Observing the impecunious state of his realms and the death of so many of his men from wounds or illness, Alfonso XI decided to accept the surrender, but he limited the term of the truce to ten years. As Manuel García Fernández noted, whereas in 1334 the emir dictated the terms of the truce, now it was Alfonso XI's turn to do so. The truce signified "the definitive triumph of Castile" in controlling traffic in the Strait.[59]

The kings of Castile and Granada concluded a peace treaty on Thursday, 25 March 1344 in the royal encampment before Algeciras. The treaty included Abū l-Hasan, identified only as "el rey de allen mar"—"the king beyond the sea," Pedro IV, and the doge of Genoa. After extending his friendship to Yūsuf I, Alfonso XI promised that during the ensuing ten years he would not support anyone rebelling against him and would forward to him, unopened, any correspondence he might receive from them. Granadan and Moroccan merchants would be permitted to travel freely and securely in Castile, but they could not export horses, arms, or wheat. Ordering Murcia to observe the truce, the king expanded the list of *cosas vedadas*, or goods whose export was prohibited, to include wheat, rye, barley, hemp, spelt, armor, fodder, and other things that could be used to support a fleet. To discourage robbers from seeking refuge in his realms, he promised to execute anyone who failed to return stolen property within two months. He also pledged to appoint good men to resolve disputes along the Murcian border. Yūsuf I, identifying himself as king of Granada, the servant of God, and "Almiramomelim," swore to uphold the terms of this pact. Ordinarily he was entitled *amīr al-muslimīn*, or prince of the Muslims. His usage of "amīr al-mu'minīn," prince of believers or commander of the faithful, the traditional title of the caliphs, suggests that Yūsuf I considered himself the successor of Muhammad. In another document he called himself "rey de los creyentes," equivalent to the caliphal title "prince of believers." Although the tribute was not mentioned, it may have been discussed in the first section of the treaty, now missing, or in another document, no longer extant.[60]

On the following day, 26 March, about 9 a.m., the Moors delivered the Villa Nueva of Algeciras to Juan Manuel, acting in the king's name, and withdrew to Gibraltar. The standards of Castile and Aragón were mounted on the walls.[61] On 27 March, the eve of Palm Sunday, the Villa Vieja surrendered, and its inhabitants, under a royal safe-conduct, departed to Gibraltar with all their goods. The royal banner and those of the princes, prelates, magnates, knights, and municipalities that had participated in the siege were displayed on the walls. On Palm Sunday, 28 March, Alfonso XI, accompanied by the bishops, magnates, and other warriors, all bearing palms, processed into the town. Mass was celebrated in the great mosque, now rededicated as a church under the title Santa María de la Palma. Taking up residence in the *alcázar*, the king received the Muslim *alcaide* of Algeciras and other knights and honored them with gifts. Christian and Muslim soldiers, enjoying the security of the truce, passed from one camp to the other, perhaps to exchange war stories or to engage in trade.[62]

Meantime, many Marinids withdrew to Morocco where the emir received them warmly, bestowing on them robes of honor, horses, and other gifts. In all he expended 35,000 gold dinars and distributed 5,000 garments. On the other hand, he imprisoned the commander of the Marinid force defeated at the Palmones River.[63] A late fourteenth-century chronicler recorded that in 1346 Alfonso XI also released Abū l-Hasan's daughters who had been captured in the battle of Salado. In gratitude the emir sent him gifts of jewelry, cloth of gold and silk, swords, spurs of gold and silver, and horses and lions. If this be true, then it would seem that not all the females in the royal encampment at Salado were slaughtered.[64]

News of the king's victory spread quickly, prompting general rejoicing. The *Martyrology of Solsona*, recording the capture of Algeciras on 26 March 1344 after a siege of nearly two years, reported that this feast was celebrated through the entire province of Tarragona.[65] When informed of Alfonso XI's triumph, Pedro IV expressed his pleasure, but also commented that, as the twenty galleys he had promised would no longer be needed, they could be diverted to his war against Mallorca.[66] Clement VI extended his congratulations in July.[67] Regretting his own inability to join in the struggle against the infidels, Edward III congratulated Alfonso XI in August and also broached the possibility of an alliance.[68]

Pedro IV evidently was not pleased that Alfonso XI, seemingly as a matter of course, included him in the pact. Stressing his independence, he authorized his galleys to attack Nasrid shipping in the waters off Murcia; when the Castilian ruler questioned him, he refused responsibility for any damages because he had not made peace with Granada. Despite that, when Yūsuf I in August proposed a truce for ten years among Aragón, Granada, and Morocco, Pedro IV willingly consented. After receiving a copy of the treaty, Abū l-Hasan in October authorized Yūsuf I to make peace with Aragón in his name. The treaty was concluded 25 February 1345.[69]

Prior to leaving Algeciras on 8 April, Alfonso XI provided for its defense and administration.[70] Initiating the customary process of repopulation, he distributed property to the participants in the siege in the hope that they would settle there permanently. Among the beneficiaries was Admiral Egidio Boccanegra. The *Libro de Repartimiento*, however, is no longer extant.[71] The *Ordenamiento de Algeciras* enacted on 4 February 1345 outlined the responsibilities of municipal officials.[72] Although Clement VI established a bishopric at Algeciras as the king requested, he united it to the see of Cádiz. Thus, Bartolomé, bishop of Cádiz became bishop of Cádiz and Algeciras.[73]

Over time Alfonso XI's efforts to maintain a firm hold on Algeciras languished. Many potential settlers were probably deterred by the close proximity of the Muslims in Gibraltar and across the Strait. Whatever the reason, the city did not flourish, and the population steadily dwindled, especially during the civil wars following his reign. In 1369 Muhammad V (1354–59, 1362–91) of Granada seized Algeciras and burned it to the ground, rendering it uninhabitable. Antonio Torremocha remarked that the surrender of Algeciras brought to an end "the most distinguished period in the history of Algeciras, the six centuries during which it was one of the principal ports of al-Andalus, a political, economic and religious center situated north of the Strait of Gibraltar."[74]

An Interlude of Peace

The conclusion of a ten-year truce allowed Castile to recover from the hardships of war and to experience again the more orderly processes of government. Though Alfonso XI's kingdoms "were in very great poverty because of the many tributes they had paid," the time had come to pay the bills.[75] As he had borrowed 333,700 *maravedíes* from the archbishop and chapter of Seville, he allowed them to retain the *decima* for two of the three years authorized by Clement VI; he reserved the *decima* for the third year.[76] As a reward for faithful service he exempted the knights of Córdoba and Seville from *moneda forera*.[77] In three successive assemblies held at Alcalá de Henares, Burgos, and León in the spring of 1345, he dealt with other issues arising from the siege. Knights and squires who had failed to participate, though paid to do so, would be identified and punished. Although the towns asked him to restore the fees of scribes and notaries that he had taken to build a shipyard, he refused, as his financial need was still great. Each assembly authorized the *alcabala* for six years to sustain Algeciras and other frontier outposts. Sales of horses and arms, essential to military defense, were exempted from this tax.[78]

Three years later, during the Cortes of Alcalá de Henares, the king repeated regulations concerning the military obligations of royal vassals enacted at Burgos in 1338 (art. 29–32). Acknowledging that his previous ordinances concerning the export of horses had made it difficult for the nobles to maintain horses and arms, he encouraged horse-raising and required each man to keep one or more horses and mules for military service, depending on his assessed wealth (art. 17, 56–85). Despite the complaints of the townsmen, he retained control of the money-changing business because he had to accumulate quantities of gold and silver for the war against the Moors (art. 44). Although the towns protested that, because of a poor harvest, they were unable to pay the *alcabala* and the *tercias* (art. 35), the Cortes apparently consented to the continued levy of the *alcabala* for the defense of Algeciras and the maintenance of the fleet.[79]

During this time, the kings of France and England continued their efforts to secure an alliance with Alfonso XI. In July 1345 he renewed his pact with Philip VI, who, prompted by his desire to serve God and to increase Christendom and in consideration of the sums that Alfonso XI had already expended in the war against the Moors, pledged to pay Castilian expenses in case of a new Marinid invasion. He also permitted his subjects to join Alfonso XI in the war against the Marinids.[80] Remaining true to his alliance with France, Alfonso XI in 1347 pledged to send Boccanegra with a fleet to defend Calais against English attack.[81] During the siege of Algeciras, Boccanegra had indicated to the earl of Derby that he was willing to enter English service, but three years later alliances had shifted.[82] In preparation for Boccanegra's service in France, in 1348 the king elaborated the rights and responsibilities of the admiral as recorded in the "charter of admiralty that he has from us and according to the usage of our fleet." The crews on all the ships (that were to aid France against England) were instructed to obey the admiral as though he were the king himself. The admiral dispensed justice to his mariners whether on land or sea.[83]

The Projected Crusade to the Canary Islands

While Alfonso XI attended to these matters, he was reminded of traditional Castilian claims to North Africa and their practical application to the Canary Islands. No one was more effusive in praising the king for his great victory at Salado than Álvaro Pelayo, a distinguished canonist and bishop of Silves (d. 1353). In 1341, when the battle was still fresh in the collective memory, he dedicated his *Speculum regum*, or *Mirror of Princes*, to "the most generous and most victorious Lord, Prince, and King of the Visigoths and earthly vicar of Christ in the province of Baetica [the ancient civil and ecclesiastical province whose capital was Seville] and the surrounding kingdoms of Spain."[84] In speaking of the king in those words Álvaro recalled a long-standing tradition that the kings of Castile-León, as heirs of the Visigoths, were obliged to recover all the territory once belonging to their realm. His description of the king as Christ's vicar in Baetica or Andalucía and in the other kingdoms of Spain is reminiscent of claims to ascendancy over the entire Peninsula put forward by Alfonso XI's predecessors.

The bishop then commended Alfonso XI for overcoming "the Ishmaelites, the Moors and Arabs, the bastard sons of Muhammad, the false Prophet, a magician and a camel driver," and for defeating the "barbarians," the "proud Vandals." The Vandals were a Germanic tribe, who, after overrunning Roman Spain, had subjugated North Africa. Álvaro also dismissed the Moors as "the greatest blasphemers" and as "Agarenes descended from Hagar, the slave." References to Ishmaelites and Agarenes were a commonplace of Christian polemical literature against Islam. In the Hebrew Scriptures, Abraham sired Ishmael by Hagar the slave.[85]

Álvaro warned Alfonso XI not to rest on his laurels or to trust in Muslim promises of peace because "God's enemies cannot be your friends." Exhorting the king not to loosen the belt of his knighthood, nor to pay off his troops, he advised him to take possession of the land from the "enemies of the faith."[86] He presented the king with a clear objective:

> Africa, where once the name of Christ was sincerely revered, but where Muhammad is exalted today, belongs to you by right. The kings . . . of the Goths from whom you descend subjected Africa to the faith. Because of our sins, the enemies of the faith, and yours, have now occupied it. Take it, as the other western lands, for it is yours by hereditary right. Because it is yours, subject it to the faith and possess it in the name of Christ.[87]

The conquest of Africa was justified because the Visigoths were believed to have ruled the Roman province of Mauritania, now coinciding with the Marinid kingdom of Morocco.[88]

Whereas Álvaro's work might be dismissed as mere rhetoric, the potential exploitation of the Canary Islands, a chain of seven islands lying nearly 700 miles southwest of Gibraltar and 70 miles due west of Africa, anticipated Castilian and Portuguese overseas expansion and required Alfonso XI's attention. Clement VI broached the question of sovereignty when, on 15 November 1344, he granted the Canary, or Fortunate, Islands as a papal fief to Luis de la Cerda, a grandson of Fernando de la Cerda, the French ambassador to the papal court.[89] As no other Christian had any special right to the Islands the pope ceded them to Luis, who proposed to acquire them "for the exaltation of the faith and the honor of the Christian name" and "to eradicate the filthiness of pagan error."[90] The pope also encouraged the kings of Aragón, Castile, Portugal, France, and Naples, the prince of Dauphiné, and Genoa to assist Luis in establishing his lordship there.[91] As an inducement, in January 1345 Clement VI proclaimed a crusade, offering the usual indulgence to those who participated in the conquest of the Islands.[92] At the same time he granted Afonso IV the *decima* for two years for the war against the Marinids. No doubt the Portuguese king understood the papal concession to include the conquest of the Canary Islands.[93]

Despite Clement VI's assertion that no other ruler had a right to the Islands, Afonso IV and Alfonso XI promptly protested. Pointing out that he had supplied several Genoese ships sailing from Lisbon to the Canaries in 1341, Afonso IV put forward Portuguese claims on 12 February 1345. He argued that the Islands were nearer to Portugal than to any other Christian realm and that the Portuguese had initially discovered and explored them. Moreover, he had dispatched an expedition that brought men, animals, and goods back to Portugal. His plan to send a fleet to the Canaries had been thwarted by war with Castile in 1336–38 and then by his participation in the battle of Salado. A report attributed to Giovanni Boccaccio stated that an expedition sailed from Lisbon on 1 July 1341 and returned in November.[94] Afonso IV was precluded by his war with the Moors from assisting Luis de la Cerda, but he argued that the pope should have asked the Portuguese, who had begun this enterprise, to bring it to conclusion.[95]

As Alfonso XI had commenced the siege of Gibraltar, he could not intervene and contented himself with a theoretical argument in favor of Castilian dominion over the Canary Islands. In language evocative of Álvaro Pelayo, he pointed out that his ancestors had seized lands from the African kings and defended them at great cost in men and money. The "conquest of the kingdom of Africa," he announced, "is known to pertain to us and to our royal right, and to no one else." His claim extended to the Canary Islands, adjacent to Africa. Nevertheless, out of devotion to the Holy See and his ties of blood with Luis de la Cerda, he promised to obey the pope in this regard.[96] Pedro IV, without alleging any claims of his own, also seems to have indicated his willingness to assist Luis de la Cerda.[97] The projected crusade came to naught, however, when Luis died in the battle of Crécy in 1346.

Although neither Castile nor Portugal attempted to translate its claims into reality until the end of the fourteenth century, Clement VI's bull pointed not only to the future exploitation of the Canary Islands, but also to exploration of the African coast and the eventual discovery of America. As a consequence of those developments, the locus of energy shifted from the Strait of Gibraltar to the Atlantic Ocean.

The Siege of Gibraltar

When the issue of the Canary Islands arose, Alfonso XI was already engaged in the siege of Gibraltar. Captured by Fernando IV in 1309 and lost to the Marinids in 1333, Gibraltar, "or Gebel Tarif, as the Moors call it," took its name from Tarik ibn Ziyad, who landed there in the time of Rodrigo, the last Visigothic king. The *Chronicle of Alfonso XI* added that Algeciras belonged to Count Julian, "the wicked man on whose counsel the Moors came to Spain." Tradition had it that Count Julian, feeling betrayed by King Rodrigo, facilitated the invasion led by the Berber commander Tarik. Even Ibn Marzūq related that story.[98] The noted traveler Ibn Battūta visited Gibraltar just after the death of the "tyrant of the Christians, Alfonso." After observing the fortifications erected by Abū l-Hasan, he declared that he would like to spend the remainder of his days defending the "Rock of Victory." He quoted a Muslim author who said: "the Rock of Conquest or Victory is the stronghold of Islam placed there to choke the throats of the worshippers of idols." The conquest of Spain had its beginning in Gibraltar, a place of holy war.[99]

Alfonso XI felt the loss of Gibraltar very deeply. Now in firm control of his kingdom, his self-confidence renewed by his triumph at Algeciras, he was determined to recover possession. The ten-year truce concluded in March 1344, however, would seem to have postponed any attempt to do so for many years, but events in Morocco provided the opportunity to resume the war. Pedro IV notified Alfonso XI in January 1346 that Abū l-Hasan was readying a fleet of eighty galleys for an assault on Cartagena and the neighboring kingdom of Valencia. Juan Manuel also reported his suspicion that Abū l-Hasan had assembled ninety galleys ostensibly for an attack on Tunis, but he suggested that his real objective was Alicante on the Valencian coast.[100] Both men were mistaken. In the spring of 1347 Abū l-Hasan marched on Tunis, taking it in September. Thus, for a brief time, he controlled North Africa from Morocco through Algeria to Tunisia. No sooner had he achieved this remarkable feat than it fell apart. After his defeat in April 1348 at Qayrawān in Tunisia, his son Abū 'Inān Fāris rebelled and seized Fez, the Marinid capital. As the

Marinid empire began to disintegrate, the Black Death also decimated the population. While Abu l-Hasan was blockaded in Tunis, Alfonso XI decided to undertake the siege of Gibraltar.[101]

Abū 'Inān's rebellion provided the casus belli justifying the king's actions. The governor of Gibraltar, responsible for its defense, abandoned Abū l-Hasan and recognized Abū 'Inān as the Marinid emir. Ronda, Zahara, Jimena de la Frontera, Marbella, and Estepona followed suit.[102] Alfonso XI concluded that an assault on Gibraltar would not violate his truce with Abū l-Hasan, who no longer controlled the Marinid peninsular outposts. Anticipating that eventuality, Yūsuf I, in April 1349, informed Abū 'Inān that he had dispatched archers to assist in the defense of Gibraltar and planned to provide additional infantry.[103] As Yūsuf I threw his support to Abū 'Inān, the Castilian king took that as a violation of the peace of Algeciras. In April of the previous year, before the siege began, Yūsuf I's forces had seized 30,000 sheep and their shepherds in the vicinity of Lorca; whether this portended a major offensive by the king of Granada or not, Alfonso XI ordered the people of Murcia to prepare for war. In July 1349, once he began the siege, he ordered the Murcians to make war against Granada and to send twenty archers to Algeciras.[104]

Neither the *Royal Chronicle* nor any other source offers a detailed account of the siege of Gibraltar, but documentary evidence indicates the king's presence there in July 1349. He may have begun the siege in late June.[105] It is likely that he summoned his fleet to blockade Gibraltar by sea. In need of naval assistance, he asked Pedro IV to honor his treaty obligation and to supply ten galleys. To ease whatever scruples Pedro IV might have, he noted that just as his truce with Abū l-Hasan would remain in effect, so would that with Granada. For that reason Catalan naval commanders were instructed not to injure any person or place subject to the king of Granada. When Yūsuf I heard of Alfonso XI's request for galleys, he reminded Pedro IV of the ten-year truce concluded at Algeciras and urged him to observe it. Despite that, after long negotiations the two kings reached agreement on 29 August 1349. Pedro IV dispatched four galleys with 400 archers and Bernat, viscount of Cabrera, later arrived with four additional galleys. Some time later the commander of the four Catalan galleys abandoned the siege without Alfonso XI's consent and as a consequence Pedro IV threw him into prison.[106] Afonso IV also provided galleys.[107]

Whether Alfonso XI appealed to the pope to issue a new crusading bull is unknown, but it is possible that he utilized Clement VI's bull of 1343. The pope had already offered financial support in 1346 when he authorized the king to use the *decima* for two years to defend against an expected Moroccan invasion, and the *tercias* for six years.[108]

The difficulties of food supply and finance encountered during the siege of Algeciras arose once more. In August, for example, Alfonso XI dispatched his *despensero* to Aragón to purchase wheat.[109] Given the inadequacy of his ordinary resources, he appealed to the prelates and cathedral chapters to contribute financially. When the bishop and chapter of Ávila failed to do so, he ordered the municipal council to demand payment. If the clergy refused, he empowered the municipal officials to seize their property and to offer it for sale to the ten richest men in each locality. If need be, clerics could be seized until they agreed to purchase the property in question.[110] The effect of this high-handed tactic is unknown, but obviously church leaders were greatly offended by it. At some time during 1349, the king also obtained consent to a levy of three *monedas*.[111] In August he notified Murcia that a *moneda* and two *servicios* for the war against Granada would be levied. The second *moneda* was collected in December. In addition to these sums, he also collected the *tercias* granted by Clement VI as well as the *alcabala*, *almojarifazgo*, and *yantar*.[112] As many urban knights sought to evade military duty, he ordered a list to be drawn up of all Murcian citizens, who, by reason of their income, were obliged to maintain horse and arms. By selling properties belonging to the royal domain, the king found an additional means of raising money.[113] In order to encourage participation in the siege he exempted from *fonsadera* vassals of the Order of Santiago "for their contribution to the campaign."[114]

As the siege wore on, Alfonso XI apparently reached out to Abū l-Hasan, perhaps hoping that he would surrender Gibraltar in return for Castilian aid in recovering his throne. Writing to Pedro IV, Abū l-Hasan indicated that the king of Castile had supported him at Qayrawān (presumably referring to his defeat in April 1348) and had often sent his ships to him; two of them reached him in Algiers where he had taken refuge. Although the text is at times illegible, it seems likely that Alfonso XI sent ships to aid the emir in making his escape from Algiers. The king also confirmed his decision to faithfully observe the pact between them, a reference no doubt to the ten-year truce concluded after the fall of Algeciras. In another fragmentary sentence, the emir stated that when Alfonso XI "received our response he wished to withdraw from Gibraltar" but soon after death intervened.[115]

The End of Alfonso XI

Like thousands of others throughout Europe, Alfonso XI fell victim to the bubonic plague, the Black Death, the *mortandad grande*, as it was called, the scourge of all of Europe. Originating in Central Asia, the plague spread westward, striking Barcelona, Valencia, and Almería on the Mediterranean coast in 1348. From there it made its way inland to Granada, Málaga, Antequera, and other towns of the kingdom of Granada.[116] Apparently as a safeguard against contamination, in February 1349 Alfonso XI ordered the municipal council of Murcia not to send any messenger to the royal court until the following May.[117] The plague did not spare the Castilian encampment at Gibraltar and the king himself was found to have a small tumor. His counselors urged him to abandon the siege because of the pestilence, but he refused, commenting that the Moors had seized Gibraltar during his reign and that it would be a great shame for him to lift the siege out of fear of death. According to the *Royal Chronicle*, he died on Friday of Holy Week, 26 March 1350; his son Pedro I testified, however, that death came on the night of Thursday, 25 March. He was just thirty-eight years of age. With his death the siege of Gibraltar came to an end.[118]

When the Moors of Gibraltar learned of his death, they prohibited anyone to attack the Christians. "A noble king and prince of the world had died, by whom not only were the Christians honored, but also the Moorish knights who had received great honors from him." When the Christians withdrew from Gibraltar with his body, the Moors all came out of the town to watch. The body was taken to Seville and interred in the royal chapel in the cathedral. Although he had ordered his interment in the cathedral of Córdoba next to his father, Fernando IV, only in 1371 was the transfer carried out by his son Enrique I. Immediately after his death, the nobles proclaimed as king his only legitimate son, Pedro I (1350–69), a boy of fifteen, then in Seville. Fearing the vengeance of Pedro I and his mother, the long-suffering Queen María of Portugal, the deceased king's illegitimate sons and other relatives did not go to Seville.[119]

Alfonso XI's great rival Abū l-Hasan, without being able to recover his throne, died on 23 May 1351. The greatest of the Marinid emirs, he had substantially expanded their empire, but ultimately was dispossessed by his own son, Abū 'Inān Fāris. Although the Marinids retained Gibraltar and a few other peninsular positions, dynastic disputes prevented them from invading

Spain ever again. The life of Yūsuf I of Granada, one of the most notable of the Nasrid kings, was also cut short on 19 October 1354 when he was stabbed to death while at prayer in the great mosque of Granada by an apparently deranged person. His funerary inscription hailed him as a martyr.[120]

Alfonso XI was one of ablest of the Castilian kings, an energetic warrior who prosecuted the war against the Muslims with great persistence. In the words of the chronicler, "he was a great warrior knight against the Moors and their evil sect."[121] His conquest of Alcalá de Benzaide and other fortresses advanced the frontier closer to the seat of the kingdom of Granada. His triumph over the combined forces of Granada and Morocco at the battle of Salado in 1340 was his greatest military achievement, ranking with Alfonso VIII's triumph at Las Navas de Tolosa in 1212, as one of the most decisive battles of the reconquest. His victory brought an end to the Marinid threat to the Peninsula and made it possible for him to conquer Algeciras after a siege of twenty months. That endeavor demonstrated his determination. If he had lived, he likely would have continued the siege of Gibraltar until it, too, fell into his hands. Beyond that, it seems reasonable to believe that, if he had been able to gather the necessary financial resources, he would have carried on a war of attrition against Granada, steadily taking one fortress after another. His contemporary Ibn al-Khatīb remarked that, "if God had not looked with eyes of mercy on the Muslims and put an end to his life," he would have finished off the kingdom of Granada.[122] None of that was to be, however. Gibraltar remained in Marinid hands and the Nasrids recovered Algeciras twenty-five years after his conquest. Following his death, the siege of Gibraltar was abandoned and the reconquest that he had pushed so vigorously was left in abeyance for nearly a century and a half.

Chapter 10

Waging the Crusade of Gibraltar

For nearly a century the kings of Castile, intent on controlling the principal seaports on the Strait and reducing Muslim territory in the Peninsula, waged bitter war against the Marinids and the Nasrids. That enormous task required the organization and maintenance of armies and navies as well as immense sums of money. Arguing that the threat of Islam to Western Christendom was especially grave, kings simultaneously sought the blessing of the church for their war against the Muslims. The popes, though torn by their desire to liberate the Holy Land, despite growing odds against any possibility of success, conferred on the battle for the Strait all the trappings of a crusade. Crusaders could gain remission of sins and kings could divert a portion of ecclesiastical revenues to the crusade.

The Nature of War and the Defense of the Realm

The business of making war and the obligation to defend the realm especially against the Moors received extended treatment in Alfonso X's law codes, the *Espéculo* (cited as *E*) and the more comprehensive *Siete Partidas* (*SP*).[1] Drawing on the wisdom of the ancients, but also on contemporary military experience, royal jurists explained the fundamentals of military organization and campaigning.[2] Surely each of the Castilian monarchs of this period studied these texts. Among them was Sancho IV, for whose benefit Juan Gil de Zamora provided a summary of the treatise on war by the Roman Vegetius.[3] Sancho IV also remarked on the hazards of warfare in his *Libro de los castigos* (*LC*), a mirror for princes intended for the guidance of his son, the future Fernando IV.[4] Juan Manuel, who had an active role in the crusade, also commented on his own knowledge of warfare in his *Libro de los estados* (*LE*), written around 1330. The anonymous *Libro de los doze sabios* (*LDS*), usually dated in the reign of Fernando III, though it may be later, also offered general observations on warfare.[5]

At a time when the menace of Islam loomed large, the king scarcely needed to be reminded that his primary responsibility was to preserve the peace and to defend his people and his realm against external enemies (*SP* 2,1,5; 2,10,1–3; *E* 2,1,5). The statement that one could justly undertake a war to recover lands and rights wrongfully taken away was surely written with the Moors in mind (*SP* 2,23,1). Though not explicitly described as such, wars "against heretics and Moors and all the enemies of holy church or those who are not of our faith" (*E* 3,5, prologue), were certainly considered as just. For centuries Spanish Christians believed that the reconquest was justified because the Moors had occupied lands that did not belong to them.[6] Alfonso X expressed that view when he declared that he hoped to "expel the sect of Muhammad from Spain." His stated intention "to carry forward the affair of the crusade beyond the sea, to the service of God, and the exaltation of Christendom" signaled his belief that the overthrow of Islam in Spain and Morocco was preparatory to a crusade to the Holy Land.[7]

The root of the conflict between Christians and Muslims, according to Juan Manuel, was not a difference of religious belief, nor were Christians called upon to impose their religion by force. Muhammad, he argued, was a "false man" who convinced simple people that he was a prophet sent by God. As his followers conquered many lands that had been Christian, Christians were justified in attempting to recover them. Thus, the war of reconquest was a just war:

> On this account there is war between Christians and Moors and there will be until the Christians have recovered the lands that the Moors took from them by force. There would not be war between them on account of religion or sect because Jesus Christ never commanded that anyone should be killed or compelled to accept his religion; for he does not want forced service, but only that which is done willingly and with a good heart. Good Christians hold that the reason why God consented that they should receive such harm from the Moors is so that they would be able to wage war justly against them and so that those who died in [the war], having fulfilled the commandments of the Church, would be martyrs and, by their martyrdom, their souls would be cleansed of whatever sin they had committed. (*LE* 1:30)

The natural bond created between a person and the land of his birth inspired a love of country and the consequent obligation to defend it (*SP* 2,11,1–3; 2,12; 2,20,1–8; *E* 3,4; 3,5.2; *LC*, ch. 10).[8] As the danger touched everyone, all men were bound to respond to the summons to repel an enemy attack, or to join the king in an invasion of enemy territory. In numerous charters, the king, exercising an inalienable attribute of sovereignty, required his vassals "to make war and peace" at his command.[9] Men responding willingly could gain both spiritual and temporal rewards. A share in the booty might make one rich and, should one die in battle, there was the promise of eternal life in Paradise and everlasting glory for oneself and one's family. Those who failed to answer the summons could be denounced as traitors and, depending on the circumstances, could suffer exile, confiscation of property, everlasting infamy, or execution. (*E* 3,5,1–5; *SP* 2,28,1–11).[10] Alfonso XI threatened with death citizens of Córdoba who excused themselves without cause.[11]

Royal messengers delivered the summons personally to prominent individuals or proclaimed it to the towns. When no formal summons was issued men had to hasten to whatever place was threatened. The term of service ordinarily was three months. Only those with a rightful excuse, such as illness or an impediment encountered on the journey, were exempt. Everyone had to appear with horses, arms, and equipment appropriate to his station (*SP* 2,19,3–9; 2,21; *E* 3,5,1–6, 10–11). In 1277 the Asturian *hermandad* echoed these ideas when its members pledged "to defend and to protect the land of our lord the king." In the same year the bishops notified the pope that the king planned to go to the frontier "to guard his kingdoms from the dangers that are there and that may increase."[12]

Prior to initiating a conflict, kings were advised to reflect carefully on their reasons for doing so. If their cause were just, they would be better able to secure allies as well as divine aid (*SP* 2,23,2). Jaime I acted on that principle, when, in response to his son-in-law's pleas, he announced his intention to suppress the Mudéjars of Murcia, lest they threaten his realm. Similarly Afonso IV took part in the crusade of Salado in order to deflect the Marinids from a possible attack on Portugal.[13]

As a warrior of many years experience, Sancho IV counseled his son to be wary of the errors that could occur during warfare. Whereas mistakes made in other circumstances might be corrected, blunders committed in battle, a siege, or a raid often had permanent and unwanted consequences. A company might be taken in an ambush; a great army might be destroyed; and a fleet lost. Death and eternal infamy were often the fate of men engaged in warfare, as the king reminded his son: "Although a man might die, the evil that he did never dies and men will always remember it and speak of it and wonder at it." Before undertaking war, one ought to accurately assess one's own strength and that of the enemy as well as the potential damage inflicted on or by the enemy. Careful preparation was essential and once a war began it should be carried out forcefully and quickly, lest one's troops be exhausted and wish to withdraw (*LC*, ch. 40).

Reflecting on his own struggles with Alfonso XI, Juan Manuel cited the many evils resulting from warfare: "poverty, hardship, grief, dishonor, death, division, sorrow, disservice to God, depopulation of the world, and lack of law and justice." For all these reasons one might wish to avoid war, but, in Juan Manuel's judgment, when a man suffered dishonor he had no alternative but to go to war. Death was preferable to dishonor (*LE* 1:70). The *Libro de los doze sabios* urged the prospective conqueror first to set his own house in order, ruling with justice and subjecting the powerful so that his name might be feared. Both loved and feared by his vassals, he ought to consider carefully the circumstances of the conquest he wished to undertake, choosing the optimum time and season. Placing his affairs in the hands of God and the Virgin Mary, he should commend himself to God, the "Lord of Battles." His purpose should be to "increase the law of God" and not to seek worldly glory. If his enemies learned to fear him, half the conquest would be accomplished (ch. 26–27).

Organization of the Army

In order to dominate the Strait the king's first task was to organize a capable military force (*hueste*). As commanding general, he was accompanied by his *mesnada*, an elite body of knights constituting his household guard, and the adult male members of the royal family. The core of the army was composed of knights of the military orders; royal vassals, including magnates and prelates, each with his retinue of knights; and municipal militias.[14]

Archbishops and bishops regularly participated in military campaigns, but warrior bishops typical of an earlier time were no longer quite so prominent. Although their principal task was to provide spiritual sustenance to the king and his troops, they usually brought a contingent of knights to battle. Archbishop Sancho II of Toledo was defeated, captured, and beheaded when he attempted to halt the Marinid invasion of 1275.[15] Ten years later when

Sancho IV confronted the Marinids, Bishop Alfonso of Coria had no qualms about assuming military accoutrements.[16] The archbishops of Seville and the bishops of Córdoba and Jaén together with their vassals frequently participated in military operations, but whether they actively engaged in combat is uncertain. Archbishop Gil de Albornoz of Toledo was constantly by Alfonso XI's side at Salado. Numbers of priests and friars also ministered to the spiritual needs of the troops.

The Military Orders of Calatrava, Santiago, and Alcántara (and to a lesser extent, the Hospitallers and the Templars, until their suppression in 1312), by reason of their profession, were a major military element. Founded in the twelfth century to defend the realm against Islam, and entrusted with custody of frontier castles, they were a first line of defense. Their knights, equipped and ready for war, could be summoned at almost any moment. In the king's war councils, the masters of the Orders drew on their personal military expertise, but also that gained by their communities over many years of conflict with the Muslims. The Order of Santiago nearly became extinct following the loss of many of its knights at Moclín in 1280, but the king rescued it from oblivion by merging the surviving remnant with the Order of Santa María.[17] The master of Santiago reported in 1301 that the Order had 1,000 knights, brothers, and *hidalgos*, but it is not clear how many were prepared for battle.[18] Agrait suggested that the three Orders could provide as many as 2,000 knights.[19]

Magnates (*ricos hombres*) and noble knights (*caballeros fijosdalgo*) formed a privileged military caste, whose primary duty as royal vassals was to defend the realm and, if necessary, to give up their lives. Men of distinguished lineage, the magnates were expected to possess the virtues of wisdom, understanding, loyalty, courage, moderation, justice, and prowess, and to be able to judge the quality of horses and arms. From early youth they were trained in the use of weapons and at an appropriate age were admitted to the Order of Chivalry.[20] In order to maintain their readiness for war, they were advised to be temperate in eating, drinking, and sleeping, and to read histories of great feats of arms. If a warrior sold, maltreated, or lost his horse or weapons, gambled them away, engaged in trade, fled in battle, or abandoned his lord, he would lose his status as a knight. A royal squire would strip him of his spurs and sword (*SP* 2,21,1–25). At any given time there were about two to four dozen magnates. In order to carry out their responsibilities the king gave them monetary stipends (*soldadas*). These were either outright cash grants or shares in royal rents. Nobles who failed to respond when summoned to war or to bring the required number of knights would lose whatever they received from the king (*SP* 4,25,7–9).[21]

Alfonso XI attempted to reform the military structure by increasing the number of royal vassals and by stipulating conditions for military service. The foundation of the Order of the Band, while exalting the chivalric virtues, was also intended to augment the number of his vassals. At his coronation in 1332 he knighted 21 magnates and 86 other nobles; some knighted their own vassals, bringing the total of new knights to 135. So that his knights not lose their military capability, he encouraged them to participate in tournaments. At Easter 1335, for example, he summoned the members of the Order of the Band and other knights to Valladolid to take part in a great tournament.[22]

Intent on strengthening his army, the king, in an assembly at Burgos in 1338, enacted an Ordinance concerning the military obligations of royal vassals (art. 14–32). A vassal had to expend one-third of his stipend on arms and equipment for himself and his horse. For every 1,100 *maravedíes* of the remaining two-thirds of his stipend, he had to recruit one horseman, accompanied by a lancer and a crossbowman (*ballestero*). At a cost of 1,300 *maravedíes* a magnate entitled to have his own standard had to be accompanied by ten lightly armed knights for each heavily armed knight (*ome a cauallo el cuerpo e el cauallo armado*). Warhorses had to be worth 800 *maravedíes* or more; if not, the king would seize them. The armor required of a heavily armed knight included a coat of mail (*loriga*), scaled jacket (*foja*), thigh guards (*quijotes*), shin guards (*canilleras*), padded jacket (*gámbax*), iron cap (*capelina*), and neck guard (*gorguera*). In the mind of the chronicler, these were "laws holy and advantageous to all the men of the realm."[23]

Municipal militia forces, including both mounted men (*caballeros villanos*) and foot soldiers (*peones*), formed a significant part of the royal army.[24] Municipal *fueros* set forth the military obligations of the townsmen, but as the frontier in Andalucía seemed ever more remote from the northerly regions of Castile, Extremadura, and León, many towns were reluctant to respond to the summons to war. Thinking that the town militias were indispensable for the defense of Andalucía and the projected African Crusade, Alfonso X took several measures to remind the towns of their duty. In the Cortes of Seville in 1252 (art. 44) he required every man with a horse and arms to be prepared for war in accordance with his *fuero*.[25]

As an incentive to perform their duty, the king also granted tax exemptions to the urban cavalry. In 1255 citizens of Burgos provided with horses and arms were exempted from all tributes. This exemption was extended in the next year to knights owning arms and horses worth more than 30 *maravedíes*, and also to their wives and children. A knight's son, who, at age sixteen, maintained the status of a knight, would enjoy this exemption; as would a knight's widow who remained unmarried. Similar charters given to other towns ordered the municipal militia to muster (*alarde*) twice yearly on 1 March and 29 September (Michaelmas) in the presence of royal officials who would determine whether the knights had the required horses and arms.[26] In April 1264 the king enacted the Ordinance of Extremadura refining those provisions (art. 4–5, 7–9, 12–15).[27] Faced with the revolt of the Mudéjars and the Marinid invasion, the king, over the next decade, confirmed and amplified these tributary exemptions.[28]

Thus, members of the urban cavalry constituted an elite dominating the political and social life of the towns.[29] Nevertheless, townsmen living at a considerable remove from the frontier grew lax in maintaining the necessary equipment or attempted to avoid their obligation to serve. In several *cantigas d'escarnho*, or songs of derision, Alfonso X denounced in scathing language men who came to battle without proper equipment, or made the flimsiest excuse for not serving, or simply deserted.[30] The *Libro de los doze sabios* counseled the king only to bring militiamen chosen by trustworthy persons. Soldiers who did not know how to wield a lance were of no use. The weak undermine the strong, and cowards cause good men to flee. The strongest and most forceful men should always be put in the vanguard. Greedy men whose only desire was for riches and who would sell their honor for money should be excluded (*LDS*, ch. 29, 33).

The need to be prepared for war was an everyday reality for people living on the frontier. Not only did they have to maintain town walls and other fortifications, but their militias also had to be constantly at the ready. During the settlement of Andalucía after the conquest of Seville, many men owning horses shared in the distribution of houses and lands and voluntarily served in the municipal militias. In time, however, fewer men opted to do so. Requiring an ever-larger number of knights from the towns, Alfonso XI in the Ordinance of Burgos in 1338 undertook a major reform, replacing the popular cavalry (*caballería popular*) with a cavalry based on income or personal wealth (*caballería de cuantía*). Whereas the former was voluntary, the latter was compulsory. Regulations set down in the *Siete Partidas* concerning the term of service and failure to respond to the summons were repeated.[31] In addition to confirming their traditional tax exemptions, in the Cortes of Alcalá in 1348 (art. 77–79) he required anyone having a certain level of wealth (not counting his house) to have one or more horses, each worth at least 600 *maravedíes*, ready for war, and to respond to his summons.[32] These regulations remained in effect for the remainder of the medieval era.[33]

From time to time other peninsular rulers, namely, Jaime I, Jaime II, and Alfonso IV of Aragón, and Afonso III and Afonso IV of Portugal collaborated with the kings of Castile in the war against the Moors. Alfonso X's efforts to enlist the English kings, however, were unavailing. Nevertheless, several northern European nobles participated in the Spanish crusade. Representing King Robert Bruce of Scotland, Sir James Douglas fought and died in the crusade of Teba. Gaston de Béarn, count of Foix, Henry, earl of Derby, William, earl of Salisbury, and Philip of Évreux, king of Navarre, took part in Alfonso XI's siege of Algeciras, though for limited periods of time. The *Libro de los doze sabios* admonished the king to honor foreigners who came to serve and to pay them their due, for "largess is a beautiful thing" and brings renown (*LDS*, ch. 38).

Kings also came to rely ever more on mercenaries, professional soldiers who fought for pay. These included *almogávares*, who fought both on foot and on horseback; living on the frontier, they made lightning attacks on the enemy in the hope of profiting from whatever booty they could seize (*CSM* 277, 374).

Military forces included both cavalry and infantry. Among the former were heavily armored knights, riding *a la brida*, that is, with their legs stretched straight out in the stirrups so that they could use maximum force in attacking the enemy. More common and probably more useful in frontier warfare were lightly armed horsemen, carrying a lance and a sword and wearing only a thin coat of mail and an iron cap. Striving for speed and mobility, they rode *a la jineta*, in the manner of the Moors, with their legs bent in short stirrups. Their horses, unlike those of heavily armed knights, were unprotected by any armor. Knights with elongated shields, lances, cylindrical or bowl helmets, chain mail and armor, horses with protective leather or mail are depicted in *Cantiga* 63.[34] Foot soldiers, usually wearing leather jackets and iron caps, were armed with lances, javelins, and a variety of swords, knives, and axes. As they could make their way into areas inaccessible to cavalry, they had to be physically prepared to endure long marches and the heat of the frontier. Crossbowmen (*ballesteros*), similarly dressed, used their weapons to good effect to cut down the enemy, especially armored knights (*SP* 2,22,7). The bolt of a crossbow had a range of about 328 feet. Also essential, especially when a siege was undertaken, were artillery experts who constructed and manned siege engines, including trebuchets and catapults, as well as wooden siege towers (*SP* 2.23.24). Both Christians and Muslims customarily employed the ambush (*SP* 2,23,30).[35]

The number of soldiers varied depending on the nature of the military action being undertaken. As a general rule the numbers given in both Christian and Muslim chronicles are highly exaggerated and must be used with extreme caution. More trustworthy are numbers cited in documents. A small raiding party might consist of several hundred knights while a major expedition might involve as many as 1,500–2,000 knights. If the ratio of infantry to cavalry were between 4:1 and 5:1, then 1,500 knights would likely be accompanied by 6,000–7,000 foot soldiers.[36] The Marinids threatening Seville in 1285 supposedly had 5,000 regulars, 2,000 volunteers, 13,000 foot soldiers, and 2,000 archers, but those figures are questionable. When Sancho IV mustered his army there, 4,000 knights were said to be present, but the number may have been smaller.[37] Alfonso IV estimated that he would need at least 2,500 knights and 30,000 foot soldiers for his crusade against Granada.[38] Prior to the battle of Salado, the Christians, according to Huici's estimate, had about 22,000 men. Included were 8,000 Castilian knights and 12,000 infantry, 1,000 Portuguese knights, and another 1,000 from Tarifa. Muslim sources affirmed that the Marinids had 70,000 knights and 400,000 infantry and that Yusuf I had 7,000 knights and 700,000 infantry. Such numbers are fantastic.[39] Reviewing his troops in 1342 before the siege of Algeciras, Alfonso XI determined that he had 2,600 knights and 4,000 infantry. That seems reasonable, but the size of a besieging army was always changing as troops came and went over many months.[40]

Early in the reign of Alfonso XI, Pedro López de Ayala calculated that the Nasrids could count on the service of 4,000 knights, including 3,000 *jinetes* from Morocco. The rest were *andalusos*, or natives of Andalucía. He suggested that 2,000 Aragonese knights could easily lay waste the kingdom of Granada. Derived from the Berber tribe of Zanata, *jinete* described a skilled rider capable of rapid maneuvers and lightly armed with a javelin, sword, and shield. According to his estimate, there were 1,600 knights stationed in Granada, 400 in Guadix, 250 in Baza, 200 in Algeciras and Vera, 150 in Ronda, 100 in Vélez Rubio and Alcalá de Benzaide, and less than 100 in several other fortresses. Each garrison was responsible for the defense of an adjoining segment of the frontier.[41]

Military Commanders and Their Standards

Under the overall command of the king were officers with distinctive responsibilities. Sancho IV advised his son to entrust command to men with military skills or maritime experience and always to have at his side a knight practiced in battle, with whom he could take counsel (*LC*, ch. 40). Chief among the military commanders was the *alférez*, or royal standard-bearer, usually a member of the royal family, who functioned as the king's lieutenant and dispensed military justice (*SP* 2,9,16). At other times a magnate, such as Juan Manuel, might be in command. Some commanders were appointed because of noble birth or official position, but their most important quality was the wisdom to seek out those with military expertise. Aside from being courageous, skillful, and prudent, commanders ought to be masters of the military art (*sabidores e maestros de fecho de guerra*). They should know how to lead and to inspire their men by words and deeds. Prior to undertaking any operation, they should study the situation and attempt to gain advantage either in greater numbers or by choosing the most favorable position. Their troops should be required to be thoroughly familiar with their arms and horses through regular practice (*SP* 2,23,4–10; *LE* 1:70).

Especially important for an army marching through enemy territory was the *adalid* (Arabic *al-dalīl*). As one familiar with the area, he could guide the army safely and securely, avoiding dangerous passes, identifying places suitable for an ambush, for the placement of sentries, or for encampments. On the recommendation of twelve *adalides*, who reviewed his qualifications, a man could be appointed to this post. Raised on a shield by the twelve and turned successively to the four directions, he raised his sword on high, making the sign of the cross, and declared: "In the name of God I defy all the enemies of the faith, of the king, and of the kingdom." The king then gave him a banner signifying his new office. Henceforth he ranked among the knights. As a commander, he always proceeded in the vanguard. He had authority to settle disputes, oversee the distribution of booty, and promote officers of lesser rank (*SP* 2,22,1–4; 2,23,19; 2,26,11; 2,28,2). The *almocadén* (Arabic *al-muqaddam*), or infantry commander, served under the *adalid*, and like him was promoted on the recommendation of a committee of twelve *almocadenes* who determined that he was knowledgeable in war, agile, courageous, and loyal. Given a lance with a small pennant so that he could be recognized, he was raised up on two lances and, facing each of the four quarters, swore the same oath as the *adalid* (*SP* 2,22,5–6; *LC*, ch. 40).

The use of military standards or banners was essential so that commanders might be recognized and located during the heat of battle. Knights often identified themselves by distinctive markings on their armor, helmets, and even their horses (*CSM* 63). During Alfonso XI's siege of Algeciras horns and figures of animals adorned the helmets of northern European crusaders. Only the king was entitled to have a square standard, probably quartered in castles and lions, much like the royal seal. A magnate commanding at least 100 knights could have a square, scalloped standard. The military orders ordinarily displayed a distinctive form of the cross on their banners, garments, and tents (*CSM* 205). Municipalities also had their standards. Most banners were triangular pennants, but others were rectangular and divided into two parts (*SP* 2,23,12–15). Both Muslim and Christian banners were illustrated in the *Cantigas de Santa Maria*. The Virgin Mary and Child were depicted on the banner of Christian knights in Morocco, who also carried a cross. The Marinid standard was white with red, vertical zigzag lines (*CSM* 181). A rectangular panel on Ibn al-Ahmar's red standard exhibited Arabic letters, probably a verse from the Koran. Christians and Muslims carried triangular pennants with various designs (stripes, chevrons, etc.) and used trumpets to summon the troops, to sound a charge or a retreat (*CSM* 187).[42] Two of the Marinid standards captured in the battle of Salado are yellow in color and contain lines calling on Allah to protect and grant victory to Abū l-Hasan.[43]

Military Operations

Adequate preparation was essential for a successful campaign. That involved recruiting suitably equipped armies, requisitioning necessary supplies, fortifying, garrisoning, and supplying frontier castles and towns, and securing intelligence concerning the enemy's intentions and movements. Juan Manuel emphasized the need to keep one's plans secret (*SP* 2,23,2; *LE* 1:70–71). The *Libro de los doze sabios* affirmed that the king should treat traitors with cruelty, especially those who communicated with the enemy and revealed his plans (*LDS*, ch. 17, 28).[44] Discipline and unity had to be maintained. For security, soldiers on the march had to keep their ranks. The vanguard, the rear, and the flanks had to be protected, as well as the baggage train. Scouts sent on ahead reported on the nature of the terrain and the presence of the enemy, while foraging parties searched for food. Difficult passages where troops could not easily aid one another ought to be avoided. Warning that companies marching at night might be separated from one another, Juan Manuel counseled that the best way to maintain unity was to place a trumpeter in the van, in the middle, and in the rear. He had high praise for an iron lamp (*farahon*) that neither water nor wind could extinguish. The campsite had to be chosen with care so that the troops would not be at a disadvantage, should the enemy attack. Water, wood, straw, and grass had to be easily accessible. Sentinels (*atalayas, escuchas*) were posted to guard against surprise attacks; others were designated to protect pack animals, flocks, and siege engines. No one was allowed to leave his post, to break out of an ambush, or to attack the enemy without authorization. If anyone killed, wounded, or dishonored his commander, he would be executed as a traitor (*SP* 2,23,28–29; *LE* 1:70–71; *LDS*, ch. 31–32).[45]

During several centuries of combat Christians and Muslims learned much from one another and so it is not surprising that they often employed similar strategy and tactics. Military operations were essentially of three types: plundering expeditions, sieges, or pitched battles.[46] Forays into enemy territory (whether by Christians or Muslims) were usually carried out in the spring or early fall and were intended to punish, mainly by the destruction of crops. However, such booty as sheep, cattle, and other livestock, household goods, jewelry, weapons, and, above all, people could enrich the raiders. From time to time the magnates, rather than commit themselves to a lengthy siege, counseled a strategy of pillage. Pillaging expeditions were relatively inexpensive to mount, could be conducted quickly, usually did not involve armed encounters with large bodies of the enemy, and brought the most immediate profit. However, they seldom resulted in the conquest of additional territory. Juan Manuel commented that Moorish knights having no arms other than a shield, javelin, and sword, and a minimum of food, such as bread, figs, raisins, or fruit, and not encumbered by foot soldiers or pack animals, were accustomed to strike rapidly and stealthily. They did it so well that 200 knights could accomplish more than 600 Christians. Plunder was held in common for later distribution; a soldier reserving anything for himself would be punished. If the raiders had to take shelter overnight, they did so in small companies and sent a few men on with their booty. When Christians pursued the Moors they ought first to seize their plunder and then send on men to scout possible ambushes (*LE* 1:70–71, 75–78).

Sieges of towns and castles were more prolonged and more expensive. If a fortress was well provisioned and well defended, it could hold out for months or years at a time. Smaller places with fewer defenders and limited provisions were much more vulnerable. Exterior walls protected every town, but once they were breached, the citadel, usually on a height within, provided a further refuge for the defenders. Juan Manuel recommended that a moat and a stout wall with openings for archers and lancers could serve as a first line of defense. Piles of stones should be at hand to hurl down on men attempting to

Figure 4. Christians battle Muslims. *Cantigas de Santa Maria*, 63. Escorial, MS T.I.1.

scale the walls or to bring up wooden siege towers. Sufficient food and water was also necessary (*LE* 1:77–78). Trebuchets and other artillery were used to break down walls while sappers attempted to undermine them. Using ladders to scale the walls or crossing to the walls from wooden siege towers, soldiers could gain entrance and engage the enemy in hand-to-hand combat. The defenders responded in kind, by pouring hot oil or throwing stones down upon them. All the elements involved in a siege are illustrated in *Cantigas* 15, 28, and 99. In the fourteenth century the use of cannons and gunpowder came into play, at first among the Nasrids and later among the Christians. Even though cannons made much noise and frightened people, they do not seem to have played a decisive role in the capture of any town. According to Ibn al-Khaṭīb, the Nasrids first used Greek fire, an incendiary chemical mixture, during the siege of Huéscar in 1324.[47] Both besiegers and defenders required a regular supply of food and water, missiles, and other necessities for men and beasts.

The *alcaide*, or castellan, was obligated to vigorously defend a fortress and never to surrender it, even if his wife or children or friends were tortured, maimed, or killed (*SP* 2,18,1–32; *LE* 1:71).[48] Sancho IV remarked that to appoint as *alcaide* someone who could not be trusted to hold a fortress against all odds was like giving a knife to one's enemy so that one could be killed (*LC*, ch. 40). The contrast between the conduct of two famous *alcaides* is remarkable. Whereas Nuño González de Lara abandoned the citadel of Jerez (*CSM* 345), Alfonso Pérez de Guzmán refused to surrender Tarifa despite the murder of his son.[49]

Although the Marinid siege of Jerez in 1285 and Alfonso XI's siege of Teba in 1330 were notable, the most significant sieges were those of Tarifa (by Castile in 1291; by the Marinids in 1294); Algeciras (1278–79, 1310, 1312, 1342–44), and Gibraltar (1309, 1333, 1349–50), as well as Almería (1309). In each instance naval forces were necessary. Although Gibraltar was taken in 1309, the Marinids recovered it in 1333, and Alfonso XI died while besieging it in 1349–50. His siege of Algeciras lasting nearly two years demonstrated the difficulty of capturing a well-fortified and provisioned port with access to the sea. Foul weather, illness, and disease ruined more than one siege. At times troops having served for three months wanted to go home and the king often was unable to raise the money to pay them. The Portuguese withdrew from Alfonso XI's siege of Algeciras when they counted the time of their departure from home to the site of the siege and their return journey. Particularly important were sufficient funds to pay the troops for as long as necessary. In most instances the defenders were starved into submission; only rarely was a fortress taken by assault.

Pitched battles, in which the combatants risked kingdoms, life, fame, and fortune, were comparatively rare. So much depended on the number, experience, and quality of the troops and military leadership and the terrain. Capable leadership at every level, good order and discipline, access to water, and protection of the supply train were essential, according to Juan Manuel. A day or two of rest after a long march would best prepare the troops for battle. Before engaging in combat, a general ought to know the strength of the enemy and the abilities of his commanders. Then, exhorting his own men, he should remind them of their duty, promise good rewards, describe the reason for the conflict, the offense committed by the enemy, and the necessity of avenging dishonor. He should also speak of the great deeds of previous kings who, with limited numbers, had defeated larger hosts. As to the battlefield, he should seek as many advantages as possible, for example, having the sun and the wind at his back and in the face of his opponents. His army should occupy the best possible ground, such as a height near a river or stream. Battle should be joined quickly and forcefully. Every effort should be made to disperse the enemy and to prevent him from regrouping. When advancing against the enemy, troops could form a point, headed by three knights followed by successive ranks of five, eight, twelve, and twenty. Cavalry so closely packed that the heads of horses in one line nearly touched the haunches of those in front could execute a massive assault. The general and the *alférez* bearing his standard should be in the middle of the host. If the enemy broke into the main body of the army, troops stationed on the two flanks should be ready to encircle him. Two things above all were essential for victory: understanding and courage. The general had to comprehend every aspect of the combat and had to possess the courage, determination, and decisiveness to emerge victorious. Faintness of heart often brought defeat. During the heat of battle, a general could not turn the pages of a book to find out what to do (*LE* 1:72–79).

Failure of leadership may have caused the defeat and death of Nuño González de Lara and Archbishop Sancho II of Toledo respectively at Écija and Martos (1275), the master of Santiago at Moclín (1280), and Infantes Pedro and Juan in the plain of Granada (1319). In the battle of Teba (1330), Sir John Douglas was the victim of a favorite tactic of the Moors.[50] In the hope of inducing the Christians to break ranks and to pursue them, the Moors feigned flight (*torna fuye*). Once they took the bait, the Moors turned about, encircled them, and slaughtered them. Juan Manuel emphasized that Christians had to guard against this ploy, as 100 Moorish knights could easily wipe out 300 Christians. He also related that he had heard that Infantes Pedro and

Juan were overcome when their men chased the fleeing Moors who then came about and destroyed them. Although the Moors belonged to a false sect rejected by God, in Juan Manuel's judgment, "in this world there are no better men-at-arms or [men more] knowledgeable about war" (*LE* 1:76–79).

The most important of all these military engagements was the battle of Salado in 1340, an extraordinary victory for Christian arms. Thousands of men commanded by the kings of Castile, Portugal, Granada, and Morocco participated and the booty was immense. Salado was a decisive event in that it effectively terminated the Marinid threat to Spain.

Naval Warfare

Attempts to take seaports on the Strait required fleets. In the *Siete Partidas* (2,24,1–10), Alfonso X, "the true creator of the Castilian naval force," after emphasizing that the sea was an exceedingly perilous place, gave a detailed exposition of naval warfare.[51]

As a fleet of galleys filled with armed men was comparable to an army (*hueste mayor*) commanded by the king, so the admiral, "the leader of all those who go in ships to make war at sea," had the same power as if the king himself were present. Given that great authority, the admiral should be a person of good lineage, endowed with a sense of honor, knowledge of maritime and landed affairs, and the courage necessary to attack the enemy and to provide strong leadership. As disobedience could lead to disaster, his crew, on penalty of death, should immediately execute his orders. By generously sharing booty with his men, the admiral would win their respect and loyalty. He should know how to delegate responsibilities and should be loyal both to his lord and to his men. Prior to assuming office, the admiral, as though he were preparing for knighthood, ought to keep a vigil in church. On the next day, dressed in rich silks, he would receive from the king a ring on his right hand signifying the honor bestowed on him, and a naked sword symbolizing his power. As a sign of his command, the king would place in his left hand a standard bearing the royal arms. Then the admiral should promise to defend the faith and to uphold the king's sovereignty and the common good of the realm, even to the point of death. After promising to loyally fulfill all his responsibilities, he was vested with all the authority of the admiral (*SP*, 2,9,24; 2,24,3).[52]

Aside from Roy López de Mendoza, Juan García de Villamayor, Pedro Martínez de Fe, Alfonso Jofre Tenorio and other Castilians, the kings occasionally hired Genoese mariners such as Benedetto Zaccaria and Egidio Boccanegra to serve as admirals of their fleet. In 1291 Zaccaria agreed to provide twelve galleys at a monthly cost of 6,000 *maravedíes*, and in 1339 Boccanegra contracted for fifteen galleys at the rate of 12,000.[53]

Under the admiral's command were captains (*cómitres*), who had similar authority in their own ships. If any man thought he was competent to command a ship, he should inform the king or the admiral, who would summon twelve men knowledgeable in matters of the sea to assess his qualifications. If he was suitable, he would be clothed in red, given a standard with the royal arms, and take possession of his galley to the sound of trumpets and pipes. Although the king appointed these "commanders of the sea," in his absence the admiral could invest them. He could not inflict corporal punishment on them nor seize their landed property, but he could require them to make amends for their offenses from their movable goods (*SP* 2,24,4).

Navigators or pilots (*naucheres*), familiar with currents, winds, weather, islands, and harbors had a major function involving the safety of the ship. As such they were expected not only to be loyal and courageous, but also intelligent and capable of giving sound advice to the commander. The navigator was vested with his office by being brought to the ship and given a tiller (*espadilla*) and a rudder. His responsibility was a grave one and if the ship was lost through his treachery or negligence, he would be executed. Also essential were marines or men-at-arms (*sobresalientes*) armed with crossbows and other weapons, ready to engage the enemy in combat. Mariners handling the everyday business of propelling the ship either with oars or sails and guarding arms and provisions were, of course, indispensable (*SP* 2,24,5–6).

Among the variety of ships plying the waters of the Strait of Gibraltar were sailing ships (*naos, naves*) with one or two masts; carracks, *leños*, barks, and above all, galleys. Oarsmen could swiftly and easily maneuver war galleys (*galeotas, tardantes, saetas*). Many were built in the shipyards of Seville or in the Cantabrian ports, but Castile was never able to produce enough and had to appeal to Aragón, Portugal, and Genoa for others. The number of oarsmen and the number of marines serving on them varied depending on the size of the galley. Sailing ships of various types are illustrated in the *Cantigas de Santa Maria* (5, 9, 33, 35, 36, 95, 193, 264, 328, 379).[54]

As noted, a fleet of galleys was like an army, but smaller squadrons were often used for rapid pursuit of enemy ships. The wood used to build them should be duly seasoned and they should be properly equipped with banks of oars, a rudder, sails, masts, anchors, ropes, and cables for towing. Arms included coats of mail, cuirasses, quilted jackets, shields, helmets, knives, daggers, spades, axes, clubs, lances, iron hooks to repel boarders or to latch onto enemy ships to prevent them from escaping, crossbows, darts, stones, and as many arrows as possible. Jars of lime were useful for blinding the enemy just as jars of soap could make them slip and fall. Liquid pitch was needed to set fire to enemy ships. Food supplies included biscuit that would not spoil, salt meat, vegetables, cheese, garlic, onions, water, vinegar, cider, and wine. The crew were admonished to be moderate in both eating and drinking and to guard against too much wine as it could dull the brain. Supplies had to be guarded and not wasted. Noting the hazards of warfare at sea, including the possibility of drowning, and the close quarters that made it difficult to rest or to sleep quietly, the king emphasized that the crew should be paid promptly and receive their share of booty (SP 2,24,7–10).

Fleets were employed not only to guard the Strait, but also to intercept enemy invaders and interdict supplies to ports under siege. Several naval battles occurred during this time. Tenorio suffered a grave defeat and was killed by the Marinids in the Bay of Algeciras in 1340. Boccanegra's victory over the Marinid fleet during the siege of Algeciras helped to compel the surrender of that port.[55] When a naval battle was imminent, oarsmen maneuvered their galleys close to one another, attempting to ram the enemy ship, perhaps disabling it, running it aground, or seizing it with grappling hooks. Once the galley was caught, marines leaped into it from their galley and proceeded to kill, wound, or disarm the enemy. Sometimes Greek fire (*alquitrán*) was used to burn enemy ships. Naval warfare suffered from the same problems as land warfare, namely, the inadequacy of supplies, food, water, armament, and the hazards of the weather. The winds of the Atlantic and the Strait could be particularly treacherous and heavy rain especially in the fall and winter made life miserable for seamen.

The Aftermath of Battle

A military encounter often produced heroes and cowards as well as those who, in lesser ways, were derelict in their duty. A variety of punishments, including warnings, flogging, branding, or execution were meted out to those who disobeyed orders, provoked fights, stole, wounded or killed their fellows, gave information or deserted to the enemy. Those who fled in battle or failed to defend the royal standard were held in particular contempt and condemned as traitors. In the words of the thirteenth-century *Poema de Fernán González* (v. 444) such a one "should lie in hell with Judas." Knights were also deprived of their rank, suffering the ignominy of having their spurs, swords, and belts stripped from their bodies (*SP* 2,21,25).[56] While the negligence of some soldiers led to their disgrace, others distinguished themselves and received appropriate rewards. The first man to gain entrance to a town or castle would receive 1,000 *maravedíes*, the next one, 500, and the third one, 250. They would also be given good houses in the town, though the *alcázar* would always be reserved for the king (*SP* 2,27,1–10; *E* 3,5,7–8).

The conclusion of a campaign was marked by the distribution of booty, which could be plentiful, though impossible to quantify. The chronicles refer generally to riches, tapestries, jewels, carpets, rugs, pillows, furniture, horses and other animals, and people who were probably enslaved. All the spoils were placed in a common store under the guard of royal officials who would arrange an auction. A soldier who held anything back could be severely punished, even to the point of death. When the Christians plundered the Marinid camp at Salado, many tried to conceal the riches they found.[57] A fifth (*quinto*) of the proceeds from the auction was reserved for the king and the rest was distributed among the troops, each sharing in accord with the extent of his service. Compensation was also provided to the families of the dead and wounded as well as to those who lost horses or arms (*E* 3,7,1–17; *SP* 2,26,1–8).[58] The riches that might accrue from booty encouraged soldiers to pillage or besiege a fortress or to expose their bodies to the dangers of a pitched battle. As a further inducement the king granted shares in the royal fifth to the frontier towns or directed that the funds be used to fortify frontier outposts.[59]

Inevitably a campaign resulted in casualties. The numbers reported by the chronicles are fantastic (the Christians lost only twenty men at Salado!), but they do suggest the extent of suffering caused by raids, sieges, and battles. Nevertheless, those who were wounded as well as the widows and children of warriors who were killed received compensation depending on their injuries (*E* 3,6,1–9; 3,7,11; *SP* 2,25, 1–5). Physicians or others with some medical knowledge patched up the wounded, who at times were transferred to field hospitals. The military orders maintained hospitals for their men and each large town usually had a hospital of sorts.[60]

Warfare was brutal, involving as it did the devastation of crops, buildings, and other forms of property. The burning of fields and the killing or seizure of livestock must have had disastrous consequences for those dependent on them for their livelihood. Whereas combatants could expect to be wounded or killed, noncombatants finding themselves in a war zone ran similar risks. Those ill-fated souls who had the misfortune of being caught unawares out in the open rather than behind the walls of towns or castles might be thankful that they escaped with their lives, but an extremely harsh existence awaited them. They could be bound in chains, beaten and thrust into dank prisons, or sold into slavery. Women were often put in the harem, and it appears that several of the Nasrid kings were the children of Christian mothers taken as slaves. Ridwān, who rose to the position of *ḥājib* in the Nasrid court, had been captured as a child.[61] The *Cantigas de Santa Maria* described the cruel fate of prisoners, who were said to suffer a "double martyrdom" (*CSM* 83.18). Pedro Marín related the stories of some who escaped through the intercession of Santo Domingo de Silos.[62] The law endeavored to protect the property rights of captives during their confinement (*SP* 2,29,1–12). Ransomers, usually merchants engaged in cross-border commerce, played a significant role in the liberation of captives. The *alfaqueque* designated by the king or a municipality received a commission of 10 percent or a gold *maravedí* for each person ransomed (*SP* 2,30,1–3).[63] Ransom, especially of important figures, could be a significant source of income. The ransom paid for the 3,000 Moors carried off from Salé is unknown, but it must have been quite substantial. Occasionally, peace treaties stipulated that captives should be given their freedom.

Truces and Treaties

Eventually, opposing sides turned to negotiations for peace. At times a truce for a limited term of years was agreed upon, but that was intended merely as a respite so the contending parties could heal their wounds and prepare to resume hostilities at a later date. At other times treaties intended to establish peace for many years were drawn up. Juan Manuel argued that, until one had gained an advantage, one ought not to negotiate with the enemy and then, rather than put forward one's own proposals, one ought to listen to one's opponent. If the terms offered seemed good, they ought to be accepted and negotiations should not be prolonged in the hope of securing better terms. If the negotiations dragged on, the ultimate agreement might not be as beneficial as the earlier one (*LF* 1:71).

Many military operations ended with a truce for a determined term of years or a more elaborate treaty. The treaty of Jaén concluded by Fernando III and Ibn al-Ahmar in 1246 provided for a truce of twenty years. In subsequent years the kings of Castile and Granada signed other treaties usually involving a pledge of vassalage and the payment of tribute. Treaties often provided for freedom of commerce between the opposing kingdoms and for the release of captives. Examples of treaties include: Alcalá de Benzaide in 1267 between Alfonso X and Ibn al-Ahmar; 1291 between Sancho IV and Muhammad II; Córdoba in 1303 between Fernando IV and Muhammad III; 1310 between Fernando IV and Nasr.[64] Alfonso XI also concluded several treaties with Muhammad IV (1331) and Yūsuf I (1333, 1334, 1344).[65] Jaime II also made his own treaty arrangements with Granada and Morocco. The alliance between Alfonso XI and Alfonso IV stipulated that neither would make a separate peace, but the king of Castile did just that in 1331.[66]

Funding the Crusade

Before undertaking any military operation sufficient financial support was necessary. The cost of sustaining the century-long struggle to dominate the Strait must have been staggering, but unfortunately only partial financial records are extant. The royal accounts for 1293–94 provide a narrow glimpse of financial activity during the reign of Sancho IV.[67] A proposal for military action against Algeciras presented in 1294 suggests something of the budgetary process.[68] For the most part, however, one is left with incidental information derived from chronicles and documents.

Traditionally kings were expected to live off their ordinary revenues such as estate rents, fines, fees, and tributes from the Mudéjar and Jewish communities. Taxes on migratory sheep and customs duties, of more recent origin, were also important.[69] That income was insufficient, however, to support the continuing war against the Moors. In order to obtain extraordinary aid, the king had to ask consent of the Cortes, an assembly of prelates, magnates, and municipal representatives of towns, or a partial assembly of one or more of the estates of the realm. Kings justified their need by citing "the affair of Africa" (Seville, 1261); "the affair of the frontier" (Burgos, 1269); the war against Granada and Morocco (Burgos, 1277; Seville, 1281); the siege and defense of Tarifa (Haro, 1288; Medina del Campo, 1291); the siege of Algeciras (Madrid, 1309; Valladolid, 1312); the defense of the frontier (Valladolid and Medina del Campo, 1318); the war against the Moors (Madrid, 1329). Despite strong resistance, the patriotic duty of defending the realm usually resulted in a positive response to the king's request.[70]

Directly associated with military operations was *fonsadera*, or scutage, a payment in lieu of personal military service, that enabled the king to hire mercenaries to serve as long as they were paid. Sancho IV in 1291 collected 274,535 *maravedíes* as *fonsadera* in the four dioceses of Palencia, Burgos, Calahorra, and Segovia. Alfonso XI levied *fonsadera* in support of his campaigns in 1330 and 1332, the battle of Salado in 1340, the siege of Algeciras in 1343–44, and the siege of Gibraltar in 1349.[71] The collection of *fonsadera* evoked considerable protest when royal officials ignored the many exemptions already granted.[72] Somewhat comparable was *galera*, the obligation of the Cantabrian coastal towns to provide one or more galleys for the royal fleet. Laredo, for example, was required to provide a galley with sixty oars and sixty men for three months.[73] Towns generally were subject to *acémilas*, that is, a certain number of beasts of burden to transport supplies, or a fixed sum. From at least the late twelfth century the export of horses was prohibited because they were needed for warfare.[74]

An important source of extraordinary income was the tribute (*parias*) paid by Muslim rulers. Since the eleventh and early twelfth centuries, the petty kings of the *taifas* had done so to guarantee their survival. The consolidation of power by the Almoravids and later by the Almohads interrupted payment, but as the Almohad Empire dissolved Fernando III was able to impose tribute on the Muslim successor states. In 1246 Ibn al-Ahmar, the founder of the Nasrid dynasty, became a Castilian vassal and agreed to pay an annual tribute of 150,000 *maravedíes*. In addition, the kings of Murcia and Niebla and dependent towns such as Jerez and even the Moroccan lord of Ceuta paid tribute. The king of Granada agreed to pay Alfonso X as tribute half his annual revenues, which were estimated at 600,000 *maravedís*.[75] In the late thirteenth and early fourteenth centuries the amount seems to have been about 250,000 *maravedíes*. When war broke out, payment was withheld but was usually resumed once peace was restored. Thus, Ibn al-Ahmar ceased to pay tribute during the Mudéjar revolt of 1264–66, but apparently did so following the treaty of Alcalá de Benzaide in 1267. After the Marinid invasion of 1275, payment stopped until Muhammad II renewed his vassalage in 1291. During the reigns of Fernando IV and Alfonso XI the tribute was expressed in gold *doblas*. The 18,000 *doblas* promised in 1310 and the 12,000 in 1331 were probably the equivalent of 250,000 *maravedíes*. Jaime II of Aragón also benefited from tribute.[76] Despite intermittent collection, the tribute money ironically contributed to the undoing of the Muslims as it enabled the Castilians to conquer many small towns and fortresses as well as Tarifa, Gibraltar, and Algeciras.

Extraordinary Taxes: *Moneda and Servicio*

Among the principal extraordinary taxes approved by the Cortes or other assemblies for the war against the Moors were *moneda forera* and the *servicio*.[77] *Moneda forera* was a contribution owed to the king at the time of his accession, but the Cortes often made additional grants. Originally a tax of one *maravedí* due from each nonnoble freeman, it was payable every seven years in return for the royal promise not to alter the coinage.[78] The Cortes of Valladolid in 1258 approved a double *moneda* for Alfonso X's journey to the empire. The nobles' demand in 1273 that it should be collected only every seven years suggests that he may have taken it more frequently. The assembly of Valladolid in 1282 granted it to Infante Sancho and he took it again at his accession in 1284. Fernando IV obtained *moneda* in 1295 and in 1312 to support the siege of Algeciras. On several occasions the Cortes conceded it to Alfonso XI (Valladolid 1318, 1325; Madrid 1329), as did the assemblies of Burgos, Zamora, and León in 1336, and the towns gathered at the siege of Algeciras in 1343 and 1344. The Cortes of Palencia in 1286 fixed the amount at 10 percent of movable goods (art. 17). The royal accounts of 1293–94 indicate that it was usually 6 *maravedíes* in León and 8 in Castile. As a symbol of sovereignty, *moneda forera* was inalienable, but Alfonso X exempted cathedral canons as well as knights of Seville, Toledo, Córdoba, and Madrid.[79]

The towns usually authorized *servicios*, but the prelates occasionally also did so. When a *servicio* was stated as equal to *moneda forera* it was a poll tax, but ordinarily it was a levy on movable property. Several *servicios* or *monedas* were often identified as an aid (*ayuda*). The word *servicio* was used for the first time when the prelates made a grant to Alfonso X at Valladolid in 1255. Although the nobles in the Cortes of Burgos in 1269 agreed to allow the king to collect six *servicios*, each equivalent to a *moneda*, from their vassals, three years later, during the Cortes of Burgos, they insisted that he cease doing so. However, at Almagro in the following year he promised to cancel only two of the six. In return for confirming their *fueros*, the towns and monasteries in the Cortes of Burgos in 1272 consented to an annual *servicio*, equal to a *moneda*, for as long as he thought necessary. Two years after that the Cortes of Burgos asked him to renounce his right to an annual *servicio*, in exchange for two *servicios* collectible in that year. When the Marinids invaded in 1275 the towns of Castile and Extremadura consented to an aid amounting to a *moneda* each year for three years for the defense of the frontier. After he pledged not to demand a *servicio* without their consent, the prelates in the Cortes of Burgos in 1276 approved a levy of three aids on their vassals. Nevertheless, as the struggle against the Moors drained the royal treasury, he contracted in 1276 with Jewish tax farmers to recover taxes owed since 1261. In response to the popular outcry, he exempted the townsmen in the Cortes of Burgos in 1277 from the payment of arrears provided that they give him an annual *servicio* equal to a *moneda* for the rest of his life. When he initiated the siege of Algeciras in 1278, he asked the Cortes of Segovia for an additional *servicio*, but it was insufficient to meet his needs. As extraordinary taxation became increasingly burdensome, the Cortes of Seville in 1281 complained that the townspeople were "very poor and the tributes great."[80]

Although Sancho IV promised to alleviate the financial load, he could not escape the need for extraordinary taxes. Prior to his accession the *hermandad* of León and Galicia and the assembly of Palencia in 1283 granted him a *servicio*. Preparing for his journey to the frontier, he asked the towns and monasteries for an aid in 1284, and in 1285, following his father's example, he arranged for the collection of taxes due since 1273. In 1285 he was promised *servicios* at Burgos and two *servicios* at Seville for the relief of Jerez. During the Cortes of Haro in 1288 he canceled all arrears of taxes in exchange for an annual *servicio* payable for the next ten years. Despite that financial cushion, the war against the Moors continued to strain the royal treasury, and in 1291 he had to ask the prelates at Medina del Campo for a *servicio* of 1,400,000 *maravedíes* for the siege of Tarifa. In the following spring, apparently without convoking the Cortes, he asked the towns for three *servicios* for the siege of Algeciras. Responding to the protests of the Cortes of Valladolid in 1293, he declared that in the future he would ask consent before imposing an extraordinary tax. However, he also established the *sisa*, a sales tax of 1 percent in lieu of *servicios*, *moneda forera*, or *fonsadera*. As the *sisa* soon became an irritant, María de Molina, after her husband's death, announced its abolition. When the Moroccans besieged Tarifa in 1294 the king demanded aid from the clergy, apparently without convening the prelates to ask consent.[81]

During the reign of Fernando IV, the Cortes regularly authorized *servicios* and in increasing amounts (Cuéllar 1297, one; Valladolid 1298, two; Valladolid 1299, three; Valladolid 1300, Burgos and Zamora 1301, Medina del Campo and Burgos 1302, the Extremaduran towns in 1303, Medina del Campo 1305, five). After he levied five *servicios* in 1306, evidently without consent, the Cortes of Valladolid in 1307 demanded that he always ask consent but also approved a levy of three *servicios*. Despite his promises, in the fall of 1307 he collected five *servicios* without consent. In support of the projected crusade against Granada, the Cortes of Madrid in 1309, while alleging the poverty of the realm, authorized five *servicios* for that year and three for each of the next three years. The fall of Gibraltar and the initiation of the siege of Algeciras prompted the Cortes of Valladolid in 1312 to approve five *servicios* and a *moneda*. As that was not enough, he had to ask the towns of the archbishopric of Toledo for another *servicio* for the fleet to defend Tarifa and Gibraltar.[82]

In the minority of Alfonso XI, there were the usual complaints of excessive tributes and insistence on the principle of consent, and occasional accounting of revenues and expenditures revealed huge deficits. In order to meet the needs of government, the Cortes approved levies of varying amounts (Valladolid 1314, five *servicios*; Burgos 1315, two *servicios* and three aids each amounting to a *moneda* for the defense of the frontier; Valladolid and Medina del Campo 1318, four *servicios* and a *moneda*). In addition, the prelates at Medina del Campo in 1316 granted one *servicio* and an aid, and the frontier towns in that year authorized one *servicio* of 1,000,000 *maravedíes* for the war against Granada. The *hermandad* of Carrión in 1317 approved five *servicios*, and the *hermandad* of Burgos in 1320, seven, but at other times the regents seem to have imposed these taxes without consent. In 1320, for example, María de Molina collected six *servicios*, and Juan Manuel took seven and a half in 1321. Juan el Tuerto received five *servicios* in 1323 and Juan Manuel asked the same amount in 1324.

When Alfonso XI came of age, he altered the system of extraordinary taxation. Initially, the Cortes of Valladolid in 1325 approved five *servicios* and a *moneda* and the Cortes of Madrid in 1329, pleased that he was about to take the offensive against the Moors, authorized four *ayudas* and a *moneda*. The prelates at Medina del Campo in 1326 also gave him a *servicio*. Thereafter he no longer summoned the Cortes regularly, choosing rather to meet with smaller gatherings that were less likely to oppose his plans. In 1336 at Valladolid the nobles agreed to a levy of five *servicios* and a *moneda*, and the towns assembled at Burgos and León also gave consent. The prelates at Madrid in 1337 and the towns in 1339 authorized unspecified amounts. After his triumph at Salado the towns meeting at Llerena in 1340, in expectation of a renewed enemy assault, agreed to a small quantity of *servicios* and *monedas*.[83]

In the absence of detailed financial records, the amount of each *servicio* is difficult to determine. However, on the basis of the royal accounts for 1288, 1292, and 1294, Ladero Quesada calculated that Sancho IV obtained more than 1,500,000 *maravedíes* from each *servicio*, but in 1316 Infante Pedro received considerably less, only 1,000,000 *maravedíes*. The ordinary amount may have been between 1,000,000 and 1,500,000.[84]

Acknowledging the inadequacy of income taxes, Alfonso XI decided to levy the *alcabala*, an indirect sales tax on bread, wine, fish, and clothing, payable by nobles, clergy, and the people generally. As the Moors had just recovered Gibraltar in 1333 he appealed to Seville, Córdoba, and Murcia, hoping that once they consented smaller towns would also do so. In preparation for the siege of Algeciras, he decided to extend the *alcabala* to all commercial transactions. Emphasizing that the siege was essential for the welfare of the kingdom and of Christendom, he summoned four separate assemblies of varied composition at Burgos, León, Zamora, and Ávila in 1342 to obtain consent. In 1345 after the fall of Algeciras the assemblies of Alcalá, Burgos, and León sanctioned the *alcabala* for six years, in lieu of other taxes. The rate was 3⅓ percent. Although the Cortes of Alcalá in 1348 protested the burden imposed on the people who suffered from poor harvests, it agreed to the continuance of the *alcabala* for the defense of Algeciras. Thus, the king relied most heavily on this tax to bring the siege of Algeciras to a successful conclusion and to finance the siege of Gibraltar.[85]

The *Tercias* and the *Decima*

Of particular value were revenues derived from the church. The most common levy on ecclesiastical income was the *tercias*, a third of the tithe intended for the upkeep of the churches, but in actuality two-ninths of the tithe. Though authorized by the pope for a limited term, kings tended to collect it regularly, much to papal annoyance. Although kings recognized the spiritual value of bulls granting the crusading indulgence, they were especially concerned that the pope also concede the *decima*, a tenth of ecclesiastical income. In addition to the *tercias* and the *decima*, from time to time kings also requested special aids (*ayudas*) from the clergy. Like everyone else, the bishops and clergy were not happy to have to pay these taxes, but they could hardly refuse to support measures intended to defend the realm against the Moors.[86]

In 1247 Pope Innocent IV authorized Fernando III to take the *tercias* for three years for the conquest of Seville.[87] Collection beyond that term seems to have taken place so much so that in the Cortes of Seville in 1252, Alfonso X, in response to episcopal complaints, promised to consider the issue at a later date.[88] In the *Fuero real* (1,5,4), however, while requiring everyone to pay tithes, he also justified the royal right to the *tercias* and reiterated that principle at a meeting with the bishops at Valladolid in 1255. Thereafter, despite their grumbling, royal officials continued to collect the *tercias*. In 1265 in the midst of the Mudéjar revolt, Pope Clement IV permitted the king to take the *decima* for three years but insisted that he give up the *tercias*. At the time of the Marinid invasion in 1275 Gregory X also refused to allow collection of the *tercias*, but he did approve the *decima* for six years. Four years later Nicholas III protested that the king was still taking the *tercias*, but Alfonso X and Sancho IV continued to do so.[89] In 1296 Boniface VIII, in his bull *Clericis laicos*, condemned the seizure of ecclesiastical revenues by the secular power. Although he threatened Fernando IV for doing so, in 1300 he authorized the king to take the *tercias* for three years. Clement V made a limited grant of the *tercias* in 1308 but in 1312, apparently because the king had failed to secure renewal, he put an interdict on the kingdom.[90] The pope also allowed Fernando IV and Jaime II to take the *decima* for three years for their proposed crusade in 1309, but the king of Aragón complained that it only yielded 18,000 *libras*.[91]

In support of Infante Pedro's crusade, John XXII in 1317 permitted him to take the *tercias* and the *decima* for three years. The amount to be collected, however, was limited to 150,000 florins or 3,000,000 *maravedíes*.[92] Jaime II was allowed to use a portion of the *decima* intended for the Holy Land.[93] Although the pope objected that Alfonso XI had been taking both the *tercias* and the *decima* without authorization, he gave his approval in 1328 for four years.[94] Two years later he permitted Afonso IV to take the *tercias* and the *decima* for ten years.[95] As Alfonso XI continued to collect these revenues beyond the term allowed, he incurred the sentence of excommunication, but Benedict XII lifted it in 1340. In preparation for the crusade of Salado, the pope also authorized the king to take the *tercias* and the *decima* for the next three years.[96] In 1343 during the siege of Algeciras Clement VI conceded the *tercias* and the *decima* for five years. Six years later while the king was engaged in the siege of Gibraltar, the pope made a further grant for one year.[97]

The persistent collection of the *tercias* and the *decima* over so many years, in spite of the protests of the clergy and the resistance of the popes, is evidence that the kings believed the yield was worth the trouble.

Loans

From time to time the kings of Castile asked for loans from the Jews or the people of Seville, the Genoese, Philip VI of France, the papacy, and others.

An *empréstito* was usually a forced loan required from a town, which had little prospect of being repaid.[98] During the siege of Seville in 1248 Fernando III requested an exceptional aid or *empréstito* from the Galician towns, and perhaps from others as well, to support his labors for the exaltation of Christendom. He promised to repay it when he next levied *moneda*, perhaps in 1251. Anyone whose income was over 300 *maravedíes* was assessed at the rate of 5 percent.[99] Although Alfonso X pledged in 1255 not to exact an *empréstito* without consent he apparently continued to do so.[100] In 1262 he demanded 1,000 *maravedíes* from Oviedo for the maintenance of his fleet. Intent on his journey to the empire, in 1273 he demanded an *empréstito* from the king of Granada. During the siege of Algeciras in 1278 he asked the merchants in Seville for loans.[101] Sancho IV may also have resorted to borrowing, though the evidence is unclear. In return for the loan of 56,000 *doblas*, Fernando IV in 1307 gave the town of Véjer to Alfonso Pérez de Guzmán. When the king embarked on the crusade of 1309 he obtained loans of 3,000 *doblas* from the master of Alcántara and 8,911.5 *doblas* from the Genoese of Seville. Queen Constanza pawned her crowns and jewels and Dinis of Portugal also made a loan of 16,600 silver marks.[102]

Alfonso XI actively borrowed money or imposed *empréstitos*. When the Marinids laid siege to Gibraltar in 1333 he demanded loans from Valladolid, Burgos, Toledo, and Seville. He promised the merchants of Valladolid that he would not do so without their consent, but it is uncertain whether he abided by that pledge. In preparation for the crusade of Salado, he pawned his jewels and required a loan from Seville. During the siege of Algeciras he again pawned his golden crowns and jewels and borrowed money from the Genoese and other merchants as well as his own vassals.[103] Pope Clement VI arranged a loan of 20,000 gold florins from an Italian banking house, although the king had asked for 100,000. Philip VI of France came through with a gift of 50,000 florins.[104]

In addition to all the revenue sources mentioned, one can add several listed by Fernando IV in 1303. These included bequests intended for the crusade, property willed to God, and funds bequeathed to the poor. From the reigns of Alfonso X and Sancho IV it was customary to dedicate to the crusade a fifth of property belonging to persons dying intestate.[105]

Much of this evidence is anecdotal and derives from the chroniclers. If extensive royal accounts were available, it would seem that, in order to meet the extraordinary needs of a nearly constant battle with the Moors, borrowing was a consistent element of royal policy.

The Expenses of War

Whatever the source of royal revenues, a substantial portion was expended on the defense of the frontier. The principal expenditures were *soldadas*, the stipends paid to the great men in return for their military service; wages for knights and foot soldiers; the custody of royal castles; and the maintenance of a fleet in the Strait.

Perhaps the most important expense was *soldadas*. Although the Cortes of Valladolid in 1258 inferred that the standard stipend for a magnate was 10,000 *maravedíes*, that amount seems to have risen over the years. Out of a spirit of generosity, but also intent on binding the magnates more closely to him, Alfonso X substantially increased their stipends.[106] Objecting that Fernando IV neglected to pay them for their service, Infante Juan and Juan Manuel withdrew from the siege of Algeciras with 500 knights. The former was owed 26,000 *maravedíes* for five days service and the latter, 100,000 for twenty days, or approximately 5,000 per day. During the Marinid siege of Gibraltar, Juan Manuel, who boasted that he had 1,000 knights at his disposal, demanded that the king increase his annual stipend from 400,000 *maravedíes* to 600,000. He also insisted that his annual income from royal lands should be increased from 180,000 *maravedíes* to 300,000. Juan Núñez de Lara made a similar demand. Agrait pointed to other magnates who received stipends of 100,000 and 80,000.[107]

According to figures given in the Ordinance of Burgos in 1338, a knight's wage for three months would be 900 *maravedíes*, or 3,600 for a year; a heavily armed knight would receive 1,100 *maravedíes*, or 4,400 annually. A lancer paid 1 *maravedí* per day would earn 90 over three months and 365 for a year. The daily wage of a crossbowman was 1.3 *maravedíes* per day, or 117 for three months and 474.5 for a year. The lack of financial records makes it impossible to determine the cost of assembling an army, but the anecdotal evidence indicates that it was highly expensive and strained the royal treasury.[108]

Additional sums were expended for the custody and maintenance of castles. Pedro Martínez de Fe, for example, was allotted 12,000 *maravedíes* to maintain Serpa and Moura near the Portuguese frontier. After the fall of Tarifa, Sancho IV allotted 2,000,000 *maravedíes* annually to Rodrigo Pérez Ponce, master of Calatrava, for its defense. In 1293, however, Alfonso Pérez de Guzmán, who received 120,000 *maravedíes* as *soldadas*, was appointed *alcaide* of Tarifa with an annual stipend of 600,000 *maravedíes*.[109]

The hiring, construction, and maintenance of a fleet, including the purchase of supplies and wages for sailors to defend the Strait, was an especially expensive proposition. The cost of the eighty galleys and twenty-four *naves* and other ships employed by Alfonso X in the siege of Algeciras in 1278 and Sancho IV's fleet of 100 *naves* and galleys in 1285 must have been enormous. For the defense of Tarifa Sancho IV contracted with the Genoese mariner Benedetto Zaccaria to maintain twelve galleys in the Strait for 6,000 *maravedíes* per month.[110] When Juan Mathe de Luna and Fernán Pérez Maimón presented a plan in 1294 for an attack on Algeciras, they indicated the potential expense. A new galley was built for 10,000 *maravedíes* and four were purchased from the Genoese for 33,000. Assuming the service of thirty galleys for six months, they calculated that the monthly cost for each galley would be 8,000 *maravedíes*, or 240,000 for all. The total for six months would be 1,440,000 *maravedíes*. During the same term, the expense for siege engines would be 250,000 *maravedíes*. Maintenance of the fleet would require an additional 1,401,000 *maravedíes*. In all, they estimated an expenditure of 3,091,000 for six months.[111] In 1339 after the destruction of his fleet Alfonso XI contracted for fifteen Genoese galleys at 800 florins (or 16,000 *maravedíes*) each month; the admiral would be paid 1,500 (30,000 *maravedíes*) per month. Agrait estimated that the cost of a galley fell between 7,000 and 13,000 *maravedíes*. In 1343 during the siege of Algeciras the monthly expense of maintaining a fleet of forty-five Castilian and Aragonese galleys at 9,000 *maravedíes* each and fifteen Genoese at 16,000 each would be 645,000 *maravedíes*. Over a year the total would be 7,740,000. Thus vast sums of money were required for the maintenance of the fleet.[112]

Asunción López Dapena estimated that in 1294 Sancho IV expended 1,515,423 *maravedíes* for the defense of the frontier. For the period 1293–94 she determined that his income was 6,457,998 *maravedíes* and outgo 6,704,583, leaving a deficit of 246,585 *maravedíes* of 3.8 percent.[113] Deficit spending seems to have been characteristic of this period. As a consequence of the steadily mounting stipends paid to the magnates, a deficit of 4,500,000 *maravedíes* was reported in the Cortes of Burgos in 1308.[114] An accounting presented in the assembly of Carrión in 1317 revealed that Alfonso XI's income was 1,600,000 *maravedíes*, not including revenues from the frontier, but his expenditures were 9,600,000, leaving a deficit of 8,000,000.[115] By contrast, Pedro López de Ayala calculated that Muhammad IV's daily revenue was 1,000 *doblas de mihareses*, or approximately 20,500 *maravedíes*. Annually that would amount to 365,000 *doblas*, or 7,482,500 *maravedíes*. In the course of a month he expended

24,000 *doblas*, or 492,000 *maravedíes*, for military purposes. That would be 288,000 *doblas*, or 5,904,000 *maravedíes*, for the year.[116]

In the absence of detailed financial records, the miscellany of figures presented above cannot tell us the sum total of royal revenue at any moment or how much the king expended on any military operation. The incidental references to specific expenses suggest that the cost of maintaining war against the Moors of Granada and Morocco over nearly a century was extraordinary and strained the financial resources of the crown in ways one can only imagine.

The Religious Dimension of the Crusade

From the early twelfth century the papacy consistently acknowledged that the Christian war against Spanish Islam served Christendom and therefore those who participated in it would gain the same indulgence given to crusaders to the Holy Land. Nevertheless, the Spanish Crusade always had to compete with the Holy Land Crusade. Although Spain could not challenge Jerusalem, the burial place of the Lord, kings and bishops still emphasized that the war against the Moors was as important as the war in the Holy Land.[117] Christian sources often described that war as a *cruzada* or *crusada*. From the time of Urban II the crusade was thought of as a pilgrimage. Adopting that concept, the poet Rodrigo Yáñez spoke of the Christians assembled on the battlefield of Salado as "romeros en rromeria"—"pilgrims on pilgrimage."[118]

Each of the Castilian kings ruling during this period, save Sancho IV, benefited from crusading bulls published by successive popes. Both Innocent IV in 1253 and Alexander IV in 1259–60 supported Alfonso X's African Crusade.[119] When the Mudéjar revolt erupted he urged the bishops to preach the crusade using bulls issued by those popes in 1246 and 1259, but Clement IV in 1265 authorized the crusade both in Castile and in Aragón. Two years later he extended the crusade to Archbishop Sancho II of Toledo.[120] Following the Marinid invasion in 1275 Gregory X directed another crusading bull to the archbishop. After the archbishop's tragic death at Martos, Innocent V proclaimed the crusade in 1276.[121] Given Sancho IV's excommunication and the generally hostile reaction of the papacy, no pope offered him the crusading indulgence. For the defense of Tarifa, during the papal interregnum of 1292–94, he resurrected papal bulls of 1246 and 1265.[122] In 1303 Fernando IV threw his support behind the crusading plans of the master of Santiago who also seems to have used papal bulls of an earlier date.[123] Clement V authorized the crusade proposed by Fernando IV and Jaime II in 1309 and did so again three years later when the former resumed the siege of Algeciras.[124] Pope John XXII issued crusading bulls in favor of Infantes Pedro and Juan in 1317–18,[125] and in support of Alfonso XI's first crusade of 1329.[126] In 1340 Benedict XII proclaimed the crusade of Salado and in the following year granted the bull of crusade to Afonso IV of Portugal.[127] Clement VI promulgated the crusade for the siege of Algeciras in 1343.[128] Thus, at least fourteen papal bulls conferring the crusading indulgence were directed to Spain during this period. Not counted were the numerous bulls conceding financial aid and those issued to northern European knights who wished to participate in the crusade in Spain.

The crusading indulgence granted remission of sins to all those, who, having confessed their sins, participated personally or contributed financially to the crusade. Crusaders also enjoyed the entire panoply of ancillary privileges accorded to participants in the crusade to the Holy Land, including papal protection for crusaders and their families, immunity from prosecution, and exemption from the payment of interest while on crusade.[129] Whereas kings recognized the spiritual benefit of the crusade, as it indicated that the pope was on their side, and it seemed to mean that God sanctioned their efforts, they also realized the financial benefits, especially the right to take the *tercias* and the *decima*. The impact of those concessions has been discussed above.

Once the crusade was proclaimed the pope usually designated one or more bishops to preach it. Preaching was sometimes limited to Castile, but at other times it was extended to the entire Peninsula and even to France. Under the supervision of the bishop(s) appointed by the pope, there were innumerable other preachers, often Franciscan and Dominican friars, who proclaimed the crusade in churches and other public places, even in those under interdict. Thus far no texts of crusading sermons have come to light, but Archbishop Remondo of Seville, appointed in 1265 to promote the crusade, indicated that preachers ought to discuss the indulgence and the privileges accorded to crusaders and warn their listeners against aiding the Moors in any way. Perhaps repeating the ideas and even the language of crusading bulls, preachers emphasized the threat of Islam and probably used traditional condemnatory language when speaking of the Moors. No doubt they asked for donations (including bequests by deceased persons) from those who could not personally participate and commuted the vows of persons intending to go to the Holy Land who now opted for the crusade in Spain. Preachers similarly could grant absolution to usurers and others engaged in illicit commerce with the Moors, on condition that they take part in the crusade.[130]

At the time of Alfonso X's African Crusade, a Muslim source from Ceuta remarked that friars preaching the crusade elevated the cross and distributed crosses to their listeners.[131] The taking of the cross, which was sewn on one's garments, usually on the shoulder, was an outward sign of one's vow to serve in the crusade. Papal documents referred to such persons as *crucesignati*, while vernacular texts used the word *cruzados*. After conquering Seville, Fernando III declared his intention to lead a crusade to the Holy Land and took the cross around 1250–51. With his African Crusade in mind, Alfonso X did so in 1254, probably during the Cortes of Toledo. Both Fernando IV and Jaime II took the crusader's vow in anticipation of their crusade in 1309.[132] An incidental remark by Al-Makkarī suggests that in 1317 Infante Pedro, kneeling before the archbishop of Toledo, took the crusader's vow and listened to the archbishop's exhortation. Prior to the campaign of 1330 Juan Manuel, Juan Núñez de Lara, and the bishop of Murcia, heard mass and "took the cross." During the crusade of Salado, German and French contingents, wearing the cross, received absolution for their sins. The ceremony for taking the cross was likely quite solemn and was attended by the celebration of mass.[133]

The concession of the bull of crusade implied that God was on the side of the Christians. To make doubly sure of divine aid, kings sometimes made a pilgrimage to a notable shrine. In an attempt to develop El Puerto de Santa María by encouraging pilgrims to visit, Alfonso X dedicated twenty-four *cantigas* to the shrine of the Virgin Mary there. Suffering from severe illness in the midst of his campaign against Granada, he made a pilgrimage there in 1281 to beseech the Virgin's help.[134] In 1291 Sancho IV, preparing to take the offensive against the Marinids, went on pilgrimage to Santiago de Compostela, and in the following year, prior to defending Tarifa against the Moroccans, he visited the shrine of the Virgin Mary at Villa Sirga, whose cult his father had encouraged.[135] Alfonso XI's pilgrimage in 1332 to Santiago de Compostela was motivated in part by his desire for the saint's protection in his wars against the Moors.[136]

Prayer by individuals or by communities was also a means of invoking God's assistance. *Cantiga* 374 related that a band of raiders (*almogáveres*) from Jerez, disappointed by their lack of success, turned to prayer and observed a vigil in honor of the Virgin Mary before their raids, and from then on they took much booty.[137] Sancho IV requested prayers for the success of his assault on Tarifa from the Leonese bishops meeting in council at Compostela and from the cathedral chapter of Compostela.[138] María de Molina made a similar plea for prayers to the Franciscans and Dominicans.[139] As heavy rains impeded

Fernando IV's siege of Algeciras, she pleaded with religious communities to lead solemn processions in the hope that God would send better weather.[140] When Clement V authorized the crusade of 1309 he asked pastors to say a prayer condemning Muslim perfidy.[141] Prior to the battle of Salado Benedict XII urged the bishops to call for public penance, processions, and prayers for peace among the Christian rulers, so that God might give them victory over the enemies of the faith.[142]

As outward signs of God's presence, the Christians customarily carried religious banners, often depicting the Virgin Mary. During Juan Manuel's crusade of Guadalhorce in 1326 the Castilians carried the *pendón* of Baeza. Dating from the early thirteenth century, this banner depicted a mitered St. Isidore of Seville on horseback with a sword in one hand and a cross in the other. Benedict XII sent a special banner to Alfonso XI for the crusade of Salado. Religious themes also characterized Moorish banners, which usually had verses of the Koran, praising God or invoking God's name. Aside from banners, other holy objects might be carried into battle. When Jaime II undertook his crusade in 1309, for example, he had a relic of St. Indalecio, reportedly a disciple of the Apostle St. James and bishop of Urci, the foundation on which Almería was built.[143] During the crusade of Salado, the prior of the Hospital in Portugal carried a relic of the True Cross (Santo Lenho). In the midst of battle a priest raised it on high to encourage the crusaders.[144] In that very same battle Abū l-Hasan, who wore a bit of cloth belonging to the Prophet Muhammad, also carried a special copy of the Koran, which he lost. After the expenditure of large sums of money, he later recovered it from Portugal.[145] More than likely each soldier, trusting in God's protection, carried some religious object as well as personal mementos.

Prior to engaging in combat, Christian soldiers were prepared both temporally and spiritually. Not only were the commanders expected to encourage them to act with energy and resolve, but preachers would also remind them of the spiritual aspect of the task. Alfonso X's jurists recommended that this should be done when the men were assembled before breakfast (*SP* 2,23,5).[146] Emphasizing that the outcome of battle was in God's hands, Juan Manuel urged his men to be confident in God and to pray that their actions would serve God. Before going to war against the Moors they should confess their sins and make amendment and be prepared "to receive martyrdom and death to defend and exalt the holy Catholic faith" (*LE* 1:76).

The *Grand Chronicle of Alfonso XI* portrayed the battle of Salado as a *santa batalla*, or "holy battle," an expression not much different from "holy war," which also seemed to imply that it was just. The sacred character of the conflict was enhanced by the liturgical ceremonies preceding combat. The troops customarily confessed their sins, heard mass, listened to a sermon exhorting them to trust in God, and received the Eucharist. Before the great encounter at Salado, Alfonso XI confessed his sins to Gil de Albornoz, archbishop of Toledo, who celebrated the mass of the Holy Cross. Following the usual practice in such circumstances, the archbishop gave general absolution of sins to all those present. After all had received the Eucharist, he blessed the king's arms and called on God to grant victory. Afonso IV and the Portuguese crusaders similarly confessed their sins, heard mass, and received the Eucharist. While the royal preacher stressed that God was on their side, the king reminded them of the loss of Spain by Rodrigo, the last Visigothic king, and the foundation of the kingdom of Portugal.[147]

The liturgy preceding battle had a long history, as kings pleaded with God to grant them victory. The celebration of mass, the confession of sins, the reception of the Eucharist, and the blessing of arms were all part of the process. The prayer of Alfonso XI before the battle of Salado, while it may reflect the memory of eyewitnesses such as Archbishop Gil de Albornoz or Fernán Sánchez de Valladolid, the royal chancellor and presumed author of the *Royal Chronicle*, nevertheless rings true. The sentiments expressed were typical and there is no reason to doubt that the king prayed in such a manner and even asked God's pardon for his illicit relationship with Leonor de Guzmán. It also made sense for the Portuguese preacher to recall Rodrigo, Almanzor, and Afonso Henriques.[148]

The Muslim warriors participated in similar rituals. Before the battle of Écija in 1275, the Marinid emir Abū Yūsuf prayed to God for assistance against his enemies. Rousing his troops, he summoned them to fight boldly knowing that God was with them and that, if they fell in battle, they would gain entrance into Paradise as martyrs to the faith. Bravely rising, his men loudly proclaimed the profession of faith, "there is no God but God, and Muhammad is God's Prophet." Two years later he made a similar plea for divine aid and reminded his soldiers of the rewards to be gained by fighting against the enemies of the faith. The Marinids responded with the cry "God is great!" and the profession of faith.[149] On the morrow of Salado, Muslim holy men offered prayers as the emir Abū l-Hasan read the Koran and then exhorted his men to fight courageously for Islam and to conquer Spain.[150]

In the midst of combat Christians customarily cried out "Santiago" or "St. Mary and Santiago" or "Castile" or "Castile and King Alfonso." During the battle that cost him his life in 1317, Infante Pedro rushed against the enemy, crying out, "Santiago and Castile." Attacked by Moorish cavalry from Antequera in 1326, Juan Manuel offered a prayer to God, and then, barking, "God and Saint Mary," he appealed to Santiago to halt the enemy. The Muslims usually invoked Allāh and Muhammad, often shouting "Allāh Akhbar" ("God is great") or "Benamarin." Although Santiago, St. Isidore of Seville, San Millán de la Cogolla, or St. George reportedly intervened in battles of an earlier epoch, no accounts of their miraculous intervention are extant from this period.[151]

Both Christians and Muslims believed that those who fell in battle would be accounted as martyrs to the faith and would enjoy the bliss of Paradise. This was a theme used by both Christian and Muslim preachers before battle began. Appeals were also made to the obligation to serve one's king and country and to defend the faith. A man who truly loved his country might also have to give up his life for it, if that should be necessary (*SP* 4,24,4). A man who died "for the faith, or defending his country, or for the honor of his king" should be lauded for his loyalty. Passing "from this life to Paradise," he earned "a firm renown for himself and for his lineage forever" (*E* 3,7,11; *SP* 2,25,3).[152] In the thirteenth-century *Poema de Fernán González*, the count of Castile similarly assured his vassals who died in battle of eternal life in Paradise. Alfonso X's *Estoria de Espanna* also recorded the count's prayer that if he and his men were killed in battle against Almanzor, they would be gathered into Paradise. In like manner, Muslim sources affirmed that 'Uthmān b. Muhammad b. 'Abd al-Haqq, a Marinid prince in exile in Granada, won the "crown of martyrdom."[153]

Juan Manuel's extended discussion of martyrdom in the war against the Moors probably reflects ideas presented by friars appointed to preach the crusade. Just as Jesus suffered death on the cross for the redemption of sinners, so Christian warriors should prepare to die and receive the crown of martyrdom. However, not everyone who died in battle would be accounted as a martyr; excluded were robbers and rapists and others who committed grave sins. On the other hand, those who were truly repentant and went to war with the right intention and died in defense and exaltation of the holy Catholic faith "are without doubt holy and proper martyrs and suffer no other penalty than death." Citing the example of Fernando III, Juan Manuel argued that even those who did not fall in battle but, with good intentions, endured the hardship and travail of war against the Moors were martyrs (*LE* 1:76).

Both Christians and Muslims firmly believed that God was on their side and that the outcome of war was a sign of divine favor or punishment. If the Christians were triumphant, said Juan Manuel, they ought to thank God who gave them victory. God also allowed them to suffer defeat on account of their sins. If that should happen, they ought to ask God's pardon and amend their lives (*LE* 1:77). At the conclusion of a campaign the victors customarily gave thanks to God. After Juan Manuel's triumph at the Guadalhorce River, his men praised God and in thanksgiving pledged to fast and give alms.[154] Alfonso XI and Afonso IV made a pilgrimage to El Puerto de Santa María following the battle of Salado, and the former also gave thanks to the Virgin Mary at her shrine at Guadalupe.[155]

When a city or town was captured, the royal standards were placed on the walls and the clergy, performing a ritual purification, consecrated the principal mosque as a Christian church. Making a ceremonial entrance, the king usually proceeded to the newly converted church to offer thanks to God. Alfonso X, for example, dedicated a chapel to the Virgin Mary in the citadel of Jerez. When the Mudéjars of Murcia surrendered, Jaime I demanded that they give up the mosque next to the *alcázar* because he did not wish to be disturbed by the call to prayer. Once Tarifa fell to Sancho IV in 1292, Archbishop García of Seville dedicated the mosque to Christian worship. His successor, Archbishop Fernando, performed the same ritual in the mosque of Gibraltar in 1310. When Alfonso XI, as a conquering hero, returned to Seville in 1327 from his campaign against Olvera, he was met by a procession of prelates and citizens and went to the church of Santa María del Pilar to offer prayers of thanksgiving, as his predecessors had done on other occasions.[156] After taking Algeciras, the banners of the victors were displayed on the towers and walls, and on Palm Sunday Alfonso XI, in the midst of a procession of prelates and knights, all carrying palms, made his triumphal entrance. Mass was celebrated in the church of Santa María de la Palma, the former mosque, now ritually sanctified. Although Clement VI agreed to erect a bishopric there, as the king requested, he united Algeciras to the diocese of Cádiz, established in the time of Alfonso X.[157]

War, Money, and Prayer

Three elements made for a successful crusade: competent military leadership and organization; sufficient financial resources; and God's beneficent response to prayer. The battle for control of the Strait of Gibraltar involved thousands of soldiers and mariners, horses and armaments of all kinds, cannons, siege machines, and ships. Raids, sieges, and battles, great and small, marked the seasons and ravaged the landscape. The consequences were manifold: crops and buildings destroyed; goods and livestock carried off as plunder; men, women, and children captured and enslaved; soldiers and civilians maimed, wounded, or killed; and the impoverishment of the realm by the outlay of millions of *maravedíes*. Enveloping the entire enterprise was a spiritual aura, brought to life by indulgences, preaching and blessing, processions, the invocation of divine aid, and promises of eternal life in Paradise. Both Christians and Muslims, whether disheartened by the ignominy of defeat or delighting in the ecstasy of victory, accepted the outcome as the judgment of God.

Chapter 11

The Aftermath:
The Strait of Gibraltar to 1492

The Gibraltar Crusade, the preoccupation of the kings of Castile for almost one hundred years, from the accession of Alfonso X in 1252 until the death of Alfonso XI in 1350, achieved mixed results. Reflecting on that venture, several questions may be asked. Why did the Castilian monarchs feel impelled to engage in the battle for control of the Strait of Gibraltar? What did they accomplish and what did they fail to do? What remained to be done in the nearly 150 years from the demise of Alfonso XI to the fall of Granada in 1492?

The Rationale of the Battle for the Strait

Several factors explain the importance of the battle for the Strait in Castilian royal policy. From the late eleventh century onward the kings of Castile had to confront successive invasions by the Almoravids and then by the Almohads of Morocco. After Alfonso VIII's triumph over the Almohads at Las Navas de Tolosa in 1212, Andalucía was opened to Castilian conquest. Taking advantage of that, Fernando III, after the fall of Córdoba in 1236 and the submission of Jaén in 1246, capped his military career by seizing Seville in 1248. In doing so, he gained access, via the Guadalquivir, to the Atlantic Ocean and made possible a future opening to the Mediterranean Sea. The expansionist drive manifested by these achievements was built into the psyche of the kings of Castile, as Fernando III made clear in his final counsel to his son Alfonso X:

> My Lord, I leave you the whole realm from the sea hither that the Moors won from Rodrigo, king of Spain. All of it is in your dominion,

part of it conquered, the other part tributary. If you know how to preserve in this state what I leave you, you will be as good a king as I; and if you win more for yourself, you will be better than I; but if you diminish it, you will not be as good as I.[1]

In speaking in that manner, Fernando III was recalling the long tradition linking the kings of Castile with their Visigothic predecessors and evoking an ideological rationale for territorial expansion. Throughout Castilian history, the kings of Castile were reminded that they were the heirs of the Visigoths and, hence, obliged to reconstitute the Visigothic kingdom. Visigothic rule, it was believed, had extended not only to the entire Iberian Peninsula, but also to ancient Mauritania, or Morocco.[2]

Castilian ambitions in Morocco were expressed in 1291 when Sancho IV and Jaime II of Aragón concluded the treaty of Monteagudo. Forming an alliance to halt the expansion of the "madness" of the "Moors, enemies of the faith," they pledged to aid one another in defending their respective kingdoms and in "conquering others beyond the sea." The river Mulawiya between Morocco and Algeria delimited the zones reserved to each for commercial exploitation and possible conquest. Castile would have a free hand in Morocco, and Aragón in Algeria and Tunis. A generation later, when the issue of the Canary Islands came into view, Álvaro Pelayo reminded Alfonso XI that, as heir of the Visigoths, Africa belonged to him and he should take it.[3]

As we have seen, from time to time the idea was put forward that Christian ascendancy in the western Mediterranean would eventually make possible a grand crusade for the liberation of the Holy Land in which the kings of Castile would have a part together with the other European powers.

As it happened, Castilian aspirations to expand within the Iberian Peninsula at Muslim expense ultimately goaded the king of Granada into appealing for help to the Marinids of Morocco. As a consequence, from the last quarter of the thirteenth century to the middle of the fourteenth, Castilian expansionism drew a belligerent response. Mindful that the Muslims had once ruled nearly all of Spain, the Marinid sultans dreamed of incorporating it into their empire. Thus Christian imperialism confronted its Islamic counterpart. From that time onward the kings of Castile, by taking possession of the ports on the Strait, hoped to halt the Marinids, who were only the latest in a series of Moroccan invaders going back as far as 711. For seventy-five years following Abū Yūsuf Yaʿqūb's incursion in 1275 the specter of an Islamic empire straddling the

Strait of Gibraltar, absorbing the kingdom of Granada, and putting Christian Spain on the defensive, was very real.

Aside from political and economic considerations, the battle for the Strait took on a religious dimension as it set Christians against Muslims. The chronicles and other documents of this time are replete with statements condemning opponents in religious terms. To the Christians, Muslims were infidels and Muhammad was a false prophet. Muslims, while acknowledging Jesus as one of the prophets antecedent to Muhammad, regarded Christians as polytheists because of their belief in the Trinity. Religion thus set them at odds with one another. As Christianity was, in effect, the official religion of Castile and Islam the official religion of Granada and Morocco, there was little room for the type of secular tolerance characteristic of modern Western states. Religious minorities were permitted to exist but did not enjoy the fullness of rights and privileges accorded to members of the dominant religious group.[4]

The co-existence of Christians and Muslims in the Iberian Peninsula over so many centuries often resulted in accommodations that Europeans without any direct experience of Islam found disturbing. Whereas Christians in northern Europe might strenuously object to any compromise with the Muslims, the Mozarabs, or Christians living under Muslim rule, and Christians living independently in Castile realized that one could not overthrow the Muslims by mere words. Thus, from time to time truces and peace treaties were necessary to provide breathing space and time for recuperation. In peacetime a certain amount of cross-border trade took place, and both Christians and Muslims profited from it. The notion that the king of Granada should be accepted as a vassal of the kings of Castile would have horrified some of the purists of an earlier age, who denounced any arrangement with Islam as unacceptable.

One of the anomalies of the struggle for the Strait was the presence of Christian soldiers in the service of Muslim rulers. Rodrigo Díaz de Vivar, el Cid Campeador, is an example of a Christian knight, exiled from his native Castile, who rendered military service first to the Muslim kings of Zaragoza and later to the Muslim king of Valencia.[5] Other Christian knights, while retaining their religious belief and practice, enlisted in the Almohad armies and fought against their Muslim enemies in Morocco.[6] Whether they also participated in the wars against the Christians in Spain is uncertain. Among the most distinguished of these warriors was Alfonso Pérez de Guzmán, the hero of Tarifa, who in his earlier years had served the Marinid emir. The interchange between Christians and Muslims also produced another disconcerting event when Alfonso X's disaffected nobles, led by his brother Infante Felipe, found employment with the king of Granada. At a later date the king's son Infante Juan, in the service of the Marinids, demanded that Alfonso Pérez de Guzmán surrender Tarifa.[7] Such conduct is explicable in light of the political circumstances of the time and ultimately did not detract from the religious character of the confrontation between Christians and Muslims.

A Century of Success and Failure

The Gibraltar Crusade pitted four Castilian kings against seven kings of Granada and six sultans of Morocco. All of the Castilian monarchs had to contend with dynastic conflicts and rebellions that often diverted them from the struggle to control the Strait. Each of them achieved notable successes, offset, however, by grievous losses. Throughout their history the Nasrid kings of Granada preserved their autonomy by accepting a feudal dependence on Castile, but when threatened by Castilian aggression, they welcomed their fellow Muslims into the Peninsula. Yet, they were always wary of the possibility that the Moroccans might swallow up their kingdom. In the long run, the Nasrids successfully negotiated the hazards of life between their more powerful Christian neighbor to the north and their Muslim neighbor to the south. Although the Marinids secured control of Algeciras and Gibraltar, internal rebellions and the desire to extend their rule in North Africa eastward to the kingdom of Tlemcen frequently distracted them from the pursuit of conquest in the Iberian Peninsula. In reviewing Marinid interventions in Spain, one must conclude that, while they wreaked havoc far and wide, ultimately they failed to achieve any enduring territorial gains.

Alfonso X, a man of maturity and long military experience against the Moors at the time of his accession, initiated the drive toward the Strait of Gibraltar, but his actions provoked the first Marinid invasion of Spain. From his father, Fernando III, he inherited the idea of implanting a Castilian presence in Morocco. The possibility of success seemed good, inasmuch as the Almohad dynasty was in decline and the Marinids had yet to establish themselves. However, his assault on the Moroccan port of Salé in 1260, the first stage in his projected African Crusade, proved abortive. Despite that, he pressed on, imposing a Castilian garrison in Jerez in 1261, subjugating the kingdom of Niebla in 1262, and taking the first tentative steps to develop El Puerto de Santa María and Cádiz on the Gulf of Cádiz. Those advances helped to provide greater security for the kingdom of Seville and to further Castilian expansion along the length of the Guadalquivir River. However, when he demanded that Ibn al-Ahmar, the founder of the Nasrid dynasty, surrender Tarifa and Algeciras, the king of Granada, perceiving that as a grave threat to his realm, provoked the revolt of the Mudéjars. That put an end to the African Crusade. While the king suppressed the revolt in Andalucía, his father-in-law, Jaime I of Aragón, subdued the rebels in Murcia. Although Ibn al-Ahmar was compelled to renew his vassalage and the payment of tribute in 1267, his relations with Alfonso X thereafter remained uneasy. Countering Alfonso X's support of the Banū Ashqīlūlā, he welcomed dissident Castilian magnates to his court. Nevertheless, continued Castilian pressure prompted Muhammad II, like his father, one of the ablest of the Nasrid kings, to summon the Marinids to his aid.

In 1275 during Alfonso X's journey to the empire, Abū Yūsuf Yaʿqūb, the emir largely responsible for establishing Marinid rule in Morocco, made his first incursion into the Peninsula. The sudden death of the king's oldest son, Fernando de la Cerda, followed by the defeat and death of Nuño González de Lara and Archbishop Sancho II of Toledo in the battles of Écija and Martos left the kingdom, in the king's absence, without a leader. Nevertheless, Infante Sancho, then seventeen, organized the defense, blockaded the Strait, and brought this first invasion to a halt. After confronting a second Marinid offensive in 1277, Alfonso X, in the hope of impeding access to the Peninsula, mounted an unsuccessful siege of Algeciras in 1278–79. Still another disaster occurred when the knights of Santiago were wiped out at Moclín by the forces of the king of Granada in 1280. These troubles were multiplied when Infante Sancho, taking advantage of a general malaise brought on by his father's illness and erratic behavior, rebelled in 1282. In desperation, the old king turned to his nemesis Abū Yūsuf, who launched another invasion, this time as Alfonso X's ally. When the king died in 1284 so many of his grandiose plans had ended in failure. However, even though he was unable to establish a permanent base in Morocco and failed to capture Algeciras, his consolidation of the kingdom of Seville, absorption of the kingdom of Niebla, imposition of a Christian presence in Jerez, El Puerto de Santa María, and Cádiz, and control of the Guadalquivir River prepared the way for permanent domination of Lower Andalucía.

The rebel Sancho IV came to power at the age of twenty-six and displayed great courage in challenging the Marinids, but his life and reign were cut short. His right to rule disputed by many, he soon had to face a new Marinid incursion. In the spring and summer of 1285 Abū Yūsuf besieged Jerez and ravaged the countryside. Facing the enemy boldly, the king sent a fleet to blockade the Strait, mustered his army, and offered to give battle. The emir wisely withdrew, abandoned the siege of Jerez, and agreed to a truce. Although his death in 1286 removed a formidable adversary, his son Abū Yaʿqūb Yūsuf eventually proved equally aggressive. Nevertheless, the interval of peace enabled Sancho IV to repair relations with his Christian neighbors and to prepare to defend the frontier against a future Marinid attack. In 1292, aided by Catalan ships, he besieged and captured Tarifa. An attempt by the Marinids and the king's uncle Infante Juan to recover Tarifa in 1294 was turned aside by the determined defense organized by Alfonso Pérez de Guzmán. At this point, Abū Yaʿqūb Yūsuf, attracted by the possibility of expansion in Morocco, withdrew from the Peninsula, ceding Algeciras to Muhammad II. Sancho IV intended to attack that bastion, but his death and the succession of a minor son postponed any further action. The conquest of Tarifa, Sancho IV's great achievement, gave Castile a valuable port at the southernmost tip of the Peninsula directly opposite Morocco. It remained the only Castilian conquest not undone by the Muslims.

During the difficult minority of Fernando IV opposition to his claim to the throne, fostered especially by Jaime II of Aragón, once a Castilian ally, continued. The withdrawal of Abū Yaʿqūb from peninsular affairs greatly benefited the kingdom during those troubled years. However, Infante Enrique, the king's great-uncle, returned from long years of exile and demanded a share in the regency. More than once, over the objections of the king's mother, María de Molina, Enrique attempted to placate Muhammad II of Granada by proposing to sell Tarifa to him. The resistance of Alfonso Pérez de Guzmán to the surrender of Tarifa effectively brought that idea to naught. This turbulent period came to an end when Fernando IV reached his majority in 1301 and all foreign opposition to his right to rule ended two years later. In 1308 he joined Jaime II in an alliance against Granada. Allotted a sixth of the Nasrid kingdom, the Aragonese king's crusade against Almería failed. At the same time, Fernando IV's crusaders seized Gibraltar in 1309, but he had to abandon the siege of Algeciras, largely because of the desertion of Infante Juan and Juan Manuel. Taking advantage of the civil war in Granada between the brothers Muhammad III and Nasr, the king invested Algeciras once more in 1312, but his death brought the siege to an end. Although Fernando IV could count the conquest of Gibraltar among his notable accomplishments, the Marinids regained possession twenty-four years later.

In other circumstances, the accession of the infant king Alfonso XI could have resulted in the grave loss of territory to the Moors, but neither the Marinids nor the Nasrids were prepared to profit from it. The Marinid emir Abū

Sa'īd yielded Algeciras to Nasr of Granada and effectively ceased to participate in peninsular affairs. Civil war between the Nasrids Nasr and Ismā'īl I prompted the regents Infante Pedro and Infante Juan to advance boldly to the capital, but each man died suddenly in the midst of battle in 1319. As pretenders to the regency again plunged Castile into confusion, Ismā'īl I, who had driven Nasr from the throne, made some territorial gains, but an assassin's knife brought his reign to a halt.

After Alfonso XI attained his majority and made himself master of his realm, he directed an offensive against Granada. Alarmed by this onslaught, Muhammad IV appealed for help to Abū l-Hasan, the Marinid sultan, who invaded Spain, seized Gibraltar in 1333, and turned aside Alfonso XI's belated attempt to recover it. After making peace with Castile, Muhammad IV, like his father before him, had the misfortune of being assassinated by his fellow Muslims, who charged him with adopting Christian ways. With the intention of repossessing Tarifa, Abū l-Hasan invaded again in 1340 and his vessels inflicted a terrible defeat on the Castilian fleet. Accompanied by his ally Afonso IV of Portugal, Alfonso XI met the combined armies of Abū l-Hasan and Yūsuf I of Granada at the Salado River in October 1340. The ensuing clash of arms, one of the great pitched battles of the medieval era, ended in an overwhelming triumph for the Christians. Henceforth, Abū l-Hasan and his successors abandoned any serious attempt to extend their authority in the Peninsula. Heartened by his victory, Alfonso XI laid siege to Algeciras in 1342, taking it two years later. Turning then to Gibraltar, he commenced the siege in 1349, but when he fell victim to the plague in the following year the siege was abandoned. His attempt to control the Strait had both positive and negative consequences. During his reign, the Marinids reclaimed Gibraltar and the Nasrids repossessed Algeciras in 1369. On the other hand, his victory at Salado hastened the decline of the Marinids, who never again mounted a major offensive against Castile.[8]

The End of the Marinid Presence in Spain

During the quarter century following the death of Abū l-Hasan in 1351, the Marinids yielded control of their last strongholds in the Peninsula, namely, Gibraltar, Ronda, and Marbella. Aside from strengthening the fortifications of Gibraltar, his son Abū 'Inān (1348–58) indicated little interest in peninsular adventures, directing his attention rather to eastward expansion in North

Africa. After he was strangled in 1358, the Marinid kingdom was thrown into chaos. Several weak emirs dominated by their viziers succeeded to the throne. That circumstance and a dynastic war in Castile eventually made it possible for the Nasrids to recover possession of Gibraltar, Ronda, and Marbella.[9]

About 1361, Muhammad V, one of the great kings of Granada, occupied Ronda and Marbella with Marinid acquiescence. After Enrique of Trastámara murdered his half brother Pedro I of Castile (1350–69) in 1369, the Nasrid ruler occupied Algeciras. He calculated that Enrique II (1369–79), needing to establish himself on the throne in the face of opposition from his peninsular neighbors, would be unable to counteract his move. However, rather than attempt to strengthen the defenses of Algeciras as previous occupiers had done, Muhammad V dismantled them about three years later. As a consequence, Algeciras lost much of its importance as a gateway to the Strait. Around that time he also disbanded the Marinid volunteers of the faith (*al-guzāt al-mujāhidīn*), who had long constituted an important element in the Granadan army.[10] In 1374 Abū l'Abbās Ahmad, in return for Nasrid support in gaining the Marinid throne, ceded Gibraltar, the last Marinid outpost in Spain, to Muhammad V.[11] Ironically, the Nasrid kings, who had long been dependent on the Marinids to save them from destruction at Castilian hands, now dominated Moroccan politics and treated the Marinids as clients. The Marinid dynasty lasted until 1465, but they never again attempted to invade the Peninsula.

The End of the Reconquest

Whereas Muhammad V secured control of Algeciras and Gibraltar, the kings of Castile in the late fourteenth and fifteenth centuries took only a transitory interest in the affairs of the Strait. For nearly a century and a half after the death of Alfonso XI the reconquest and Castilian efforts to dominate the Strait were interrupted. The kingdom of Granada seemed not to constitute any real danger to Castile and the Marinid dynasty was in decline. Thus, the Castilian monarchs, no longer anxious about the imminent danger of Islam, turned to other affairs and failed to press the reconquest with any vigor.

The first Trastámara rulers were preoccupied with the task of securing their hold on the throne, but during the lengthy minority (1406–19) of Juan II (1406–54), his uncle and regent Fernando conquered Antequera in 1410. This was the most important achievement of the reconquest since Algeciras fell to

Alfonso XI in 1344. Fernando de Antequera, as he came to be known, probably would have pressed on with the war, but his election as king of Aragón two years later removed him from the Granadan frontier.[12] Aside from Juan II's victory over Granadan forces at La Higueruela in 1431, the most notable event prior to the coming of Ferdinand and Isabella was the seizure of Gibraltar in 1462 by Juan Alfonso de Guzmán, first duke of Medina Sidonia, a descendant of Alfonso Pérez de Guzmán, the hero of Tarifa. For many years Gibraltar was regarded as the property of the Guzmán family, but in 1501 Isabella the Catholic annexed it to the crown.[13]

With the marriage of Ferdinand of Aragón (1479–1516) and Isabella of Castile (1474–1504) the task of reconquest was resumed. When they asked Pope Innocent VIII for crusading indulgences in 1485, they reminded him that if "these infidels . . . are not ejected and expelled from Spain," Christendom would always be threatened by the danger at the gates.[14] By steadily forging ahead, the Catholic monarchs took possession of Granada in January 1492. Writing to Pope Alexander VI on 2 January 1492, they said: "It pleased our Lord to give us a complete victory over the king and the Moors of Granada, enemies of our holy Catholic faith. . . . After so much labor, expense, death and shedding of blood . . . this kingdom of Granada, which was occupied for over seven hundred and eighty years by the infidels," has been conquered.[15] The conquest of Granada brought an end to independent Muslim rule in Spain and the medieval crusades against Islam.[16]

A Foothold in Morocco

Although the kings of Castile had long aspired to establish a foothold in Morocco, the Portuguese anticipated them by seizing Ceuta in 1415 and Tangier in 1471.[17] The capture of Ceuta marked the beginning of the Portuguese overseas empire, but also reminded Spanish theorists of Castile's ancient claim to North Africa. Repeating arguments put forward by Álvaro Pelayo in the fourteenth century, Alfonso de Cartagena declared that "the conquest of that region of Africa beyond the sea, formerly called Tingitana and today Benamarin [a reference to the Benimerines, or Marinids] and of the adjacent islands . . . usually called the Canary Islands," pertained to the king of Castile.[18] Similarly Rodrigo Sánchez de Arévalo expressed the hope that Castilian royal power would be established in "the barbarous regions of Africa," and that those lands, once held by the Visigothic kings, would be recovered.[19] Diego de Valera asserted that God had chosen King Ferdinand not only to rule the Spains but also "to subjugate the lands beyond the sea to the glory and exaltation of our Redeemer, the increase of the Christian religion, and to the great honor and excellence of your royal crown."[20]

In response to such exhortations, the Catholic monarchs Ferdinand and Isabella seized Melilla directly opposite Málaga in 1497. Cardinal Francisco Jiménez de Cisneros, who was most enthusiastic about intervention in North Africa, persuaded Ferdinand to send a fleet to take the port of Mazalquivir on the Gulf of Oran in 1505. Taking up ideas developed in the late thirteenth and fourteenth centuries by crusade propagandists such as Ramon Llull for a combined Christian offensive against the Islamic world in both East and West, Cisneros dreamed not only of the conquest of North Africa but also of rescuing the Holy Land. When he discovered that European monarchs were disinterested in that grand scheme, he turned to a more easily attainable objective, planning and carrying out the successful occupation of Oran in 1507.[21] Subsequent efforts to extend the Spanish hold on the North African coast met with only partial success but the attraction of the New World and other considerations distracted the Spanish monarchs.

Spanish aspirations in North Africa found some satisfaction in 1906 when, through an international agreement, Spain was given a protectorate over the northern provinces of Morocco, while the French assumed a protectorate over the rest. When Spain annexed Portugal in 1580, Ceuta came under Spanish rule. In 1956 Morocco gained its independence of both Spain and France, but Spain retained possession of certain *plazas de soberanía* including Ceuta (ceded by Portugal in 1668), Tetuán (acquired in 1860, but ceded to Morocco in 1956), and Melilla. Morocco, however, regards those ports as part of its territory now occupied by a foreign power.

Looking back on the century covered by this book, the kings of Castile, while unsuccessful in their efforts to gain a foothold in Morocco, ultimately blocked the Marinids from extending their empire into Spain. In the Peninsula itself, of all the ports on the Strait of Gibraltar, only Tarifa, taken by Sancho IV in 1292, remained permanently in Castilian hands. Gibraltar, occupied by Fernando IV in 1309, and Algeciras, taken by Alfonso XI in 1344, reverted to Muslim rule before the end of the century. Although the Castilians regained Gibraltar in 1462, an Anglo-Dutch fleet seized it in 1704 during the War of the Spanish Succession. Spanish refugees from Gibraltar, settling in the ruins of Algeciras, gradually brought that ancient town to life once again. To this day, however, Gibraltar remains under British rule.

Abbreviations

ACA	Arxiu de la Corona d'Aragó, Barcelona.
AEM	*Anuario de Estudios Medievales.*
BAE	*Biblioteca de Autores Españoles.*
BRAH	*Boletín de la Real Academia de la Historia.*
CAX	*Crónica de Alfonso X.* Ed. Cayetano Rosell. *BAE* 66:1–66.
CAX (GJ)	*Crónica de Alfonso X, según el Ms. II/2777 de la Biblioteca del Palacio Real (Madrid).* Ed. Manuel González Jiménez. Murcia: Real Academia Alfonso X el Sabio, 1998.
CAXI	*Crónica de Alfonso XI. BAE* 66:173–392.
CCPIV	*Chronique catalane de Pierre IV d'Aragon et III de Catalogne.* Ed. Amédée Pagès. Toulouse: E. Privat, 1941.
CDACA	*Colección de Documentos inéditos del Archivo de la Corona de Aragón.* Ed. Prosper Bofarull et al. 41 vols. Barcelona: Imprenta del Archivo, 1847–1910.
CDAXI	González Crespo, Esther. *Colección documental de Alfonso XI: Diplomas reales conservados en el Archivo Histórico Nacional, Sección de Clero, Pergaminos.* Madrid: Universidad Complutense, 1985.
CDIE	Juan Manuel, *Chronicon Domini Ioannis Emmanuelis.* In *MFIV*, 1:675–80.
CFIV	*Crónica de Fernando IV. BAE* 66:93–170.
CGPIII	*Crònica general de Pere III el Cerimoniós dita comunament Crònica de Sant Joan de la Penya.* Ed. Amadeu-J. Soberanas Lleó. Barcelona: Alpha, 1961.
CJI	*Crònica de Jaume I.* Ed. J. M. Casacuberta and E. Bagüe. 9 vols. Barcelona: Barcino, 1926–62.
CLC	*Cortes de los antiguos reinos de León y Castilla.* 5 vols. Madrid: Real Academia de la Historia, 1861–1903.

CODOIN	*Colección de documentos inéditos para la historia de España*. Ed. Martín Fernández Navarrete et al. 112 vols. Madrid: Calera and others, 1841–95.
CODOM	*Colección de documentos para la historia del reino de Murcia* 22 vols. thus far (Murcia: Academia Alfonso X el Sabio, 1963–). Consejo superior de investigaciones científicas.
CSIV	*Crónica de Sancho IV. BAE* 66:69–90.
CSJP	*The Chronicle of San Juan de la Peña: A Fourteenth-Century Official History of the Crown of Aragón*. Tr. Lynn H. Nelson. Philadelphia: University of Pennsylvania Press, 1991.
CSM	*Cantigas de Santa Maria*, ed. Walter Mettmann. 4 vols. Coimbra: Universidad de Coimbra, 1959–74. Reprint, 2 vols. Vigo: Edicions Xerais de Galicia, 1981.
CSPRP	*Crónica dos sete primeiros reis de Portugal.* Ed. Carlos da Silva Tarouca. 2 vols. Lisbon: Academia Portuguesa da Historia, 1952.
DAAX	Manuel González Jiménez, *Diplomatario andaluz de Alfonso X.* Seville: El Monte, Caja de Huelva y Sevilla, 1991.
E	Alfonso X, *Espéculo: Texto jurídico atribuído al Rey de Castilla Don Alfonso el Sabio*. Ed. Robert A. MacDonald. Madison, Wis.: Hispanic Seminary, 1990.
EEMCA	*Estudios de Edad Media de la Corona de Aragón.*
ELEM	*En la España Medieval.*
ES	*España Sagrada*. Ed. Enrique Flórez et al. 52 vols. Madrid: Antonio Marín and others, 1754–1918.
ETF	*Espacio, Tiempo y Forma, Serie III.*
GCAXI	*Gran crónica de Alfonso XI.* Ed. Diego Catalán. 2 vols. Madrid: Gredos, 1977.
HID	*Historia, Instituciones, Documentos.*
LC	Sancho IV, *Libro de los castigos. Castigos e documentos para bien vivir ordenados por el rey don Sancho IV.* Ed. Agapito Rey. Bloomington: Indiana University Press, 1952.

LDS	*Libro de los doze sabios o tractado de la nobleza y lealtad.* Ed. John K. Walsh. Madrid: Anejos de la Boletin de la Real Academia Española, 1975.
LE	Juan Manuel, *Libro de los estados.* Ed. Ian R. Macpherson and Robert Brian Tate. Madrid: Clásicos Castalia, 1991.
MFIV	Benavides, Antonio. *Memorias de Fernando IV de Castilla.* 2 vols. Madrid: José Rodríguez, 1869.
MH	*Monumenta Henricina.* 15 vols. Coimbra: Comissação executivo das comemorações do V centenário da morte do Infante D. Henrique, 1960–74.
MHE	*Memorial Histórico Español.* 50 vols. Madrid: Real Academia de la Historia, 1851–1963.
PAXI (1864)	Rodrigo Yáñez, *Poema de Alfonso XI.* Ed. Tomás Antonio Sánchez. In *Poetas castellanos anteriores al siglo XV.* Madrid: M. Rivadeneyra, 1864. 477–551.
PCG	*Primera crónica general de España.* Ed. Ramón Menéndez Pidal. 2 vols. Madrid: Gredos, 1955.
RABM	*Revista de Archivos, Bibliotecas y Museos.*
RFLH	*Revista da Faculdade de Letras. História.*
Rui de Pina, *CAIV*	Rui de Pina, *Chronica de el rey Dom Afonso IV.* Lisbon: Paulo Craesbeeck, 1653. Reprint Lisbon: Biblion, 1936.
SP	*Las Siete Partidas del Rey Don Alfonso el Sabio.* Ed. Real Academia de la Historia. 3 vols. Madrid: Imprenta Real, 1801.

Notes

CHAPTER I. SPAIN AND THE STRAIT OF GIBRALTAR

1. Joseph F. O'Callaghan, *Reconquest and Crusade in Medieval Spain* (Philadelphia: University of Pennsylvania Press, 2003).
2. Joseph F. O'Callaghan, *A History of Medieval Spain* (Ithaca, N.Y.: Cornell University Press, 1975); Roger Collins, *Visigothic Spain, 491–711* (Oxford: Blackwell, 2004).
3. Roger Collins, *The Arab Conquest of Spain, 710–797* (Oxford: Blackwell, 1989); Richard Fletcher, *Moorish Spain* (Berkeley: University of California Press, 1992).
4. Bernard F. Reilly, *The Contest of Christian and Muslim Spain, 1031–1157* (London: Blackwell, 1992).
5. Ibn Khaldūn, *Histoire des Berbères et des dynasties musulmanes de l'Afrique septentrionale*, trans. Baron de Slane, 4 vols. (Paris: Imprimerie du Gouvernment, 1852–56), 4:71.
6. Ibn Abī Zar', *Rawd al-Qirtās*, tr. Ambrosio Huici, 2 vols. (Valencia: Anubar, 1964), 1:277; Bernard F. Reilly, *The Kingdom of León-Castilla Under King Alfonso VI, 1065–1109* (Princeton, N.J.: Princeton University Press, 1988), 166.
7. Ibn Khaldūn, *Histoire*, 4:63.
8. Rachel Arié, *L'Espagne musulmane au temps des Nasrides (1232–1492)* (Paris: Boccard, 1973), 29–60; Cristóbal Torres Delgado, *El antiguo reino nazarí de Granada (1232–1340)* (Granada: Anel, 1974), 60–140; Miguel Angel Ladero Quesada, *Granada: Historia de un país islámico (1232–1571)* (Madrid: Gredos, 1969), 9–35, 73–76; L. P. Harvey, *Islamic Spain, 1250 to 1500* (Chicago: University of Chicago Press, 1990), 1–40; Francisco Vidal Castro, "Historia política," in María Jesús Vigueira Molins, ed., *El reino nazarí de Granada (1232–1492)*, in *Historia de España fundada por Ramón Menéndez Pidal* (Madrid: Espasa-Calpe, 2000), 3:47–208.
9. Torres Delgado, *Granada*, 25–60; Raúl González Arévalo, "La costa del reino de Granada en la documentación náutica italiana (siglos XIV–XVI)," *ELEM* 31 (2008): 7–36.
10. Mercedes Borrero Fernández, "La frontera de Sevilla con el reino de Granada en tiempos de Alfonso X," and Francisco García Fitz, "La frontera castellano-granadina a fines del siglo XIII," in Cristina Segura Graiño, ed., *Relaciones exteriores del reino de Granada: IV Coloquio de Historia Medieval Andaluza* (Almería: Instituto de Estudios Almerienses, 1988), 13–21, 23–35; Manuel García Fernández, *El reino de Sevilla en tiempos de Alfonso XI (1312–1350)* (Seville: Diputación Provincial, 1989), 41–76, "La frontera de Granada a

mediados del siglo XIV," *Revista de Estudios Andaluces* 9 (1987): 69–86, and "Fortificaciones fronterizas andaluzas en tiempos de Alfonso XI de Castilla (1312–1350)," *Castillos de España* 95 (1988): 51–58; Cristóbal Torres Delgado, "El ejército y las fortificaciones del reino nazarí de Granada," *Gladius*, special vol. (1988): 197–217; Arié, *L'Espagne*, 230–38.

11. Julio González, *Reinado y diplomas de Fernando III*, 3 vols. (Córdoba: Monte de Piedad y Caja de Ahorros, 1986); Manuel González Jiménez, *Fernando III el Santo: El rey que marcó el destino de España* (Seville: Fundación José Manuel Lara, 2006); idem, ed., *Sevilla 1248: Congreso Internacional Conmemorativo del 750 Aniversario de la Conquista de la Ciudad de Sevilla por Fernando III, Rey de Castilla y León* (Madrid: Fundación Ramón Areces, 2000).

12. *PCG*, 2:722, 745–46, ch. 1037, 1069–70; Arié, *L'Espagne*, 61–68; Torres Delgado, *Granada*, 101–44; Ladero Quesada, *Granada*, 75; Harvey, *Islamic Spain*, 20–29; Hugh Kennedy, *Muslim Spain and Portugal: A Political History of Al-Andalus* (London: Longman, 1996), 273–77.

13. O'Callaghan, *Reconquest*, 1–22.

14. *PCG*, 2:770–71, ch. 1131; *Setenario*, ed. Kenneth Vanderford (Buenos Aires, 1945; reprint Barcelona: Crítica, 1984), 15, ley 9; 23, ley 10.

15. Fidel Fita, "Biografías de San Fernando y de Alfonso el Sabio por Gil de Zamora," *BRAH* 5 (1885): 321, ch. 21.

16. Augusto Quintana Prieto, *La documentación pontificia de Inocencio IV (1243–1254)*, 2 vols. (Rome: Instituto Español de Historia Eclesiástica, 1987), 2:709, no. 803.

17. Matthew Paris, *Chronica majora*, ed. H. R. Luard, 7 vols., Rolls Series (London: Longman, 1872–83), 5:170, 231–32, 311; José Manuel Rodríguez García, "Fernando III y sus campañas en el contexto Cruzado Europeo, 1217–1252," *Archivo Hispalense* 234–36 (1994): 205–17; Élie Berger, *Saint Louis et Innocent IV: Étude sur les rapports de la France et du Saint-Siège* (Paris: Thorin & Fils, 1893), 345 n. 1.

18. Cayetano Rosell edited all four in *Crónicas de los reyes de Castilla desde don Alfonso el Sabio hasta los católicos don Fernando y doña Isabel*, 3 vols., Biblioteca de Autores Españoles (*BAE*) 66, 68, 70 (1875; reprint, Madrid: Real Academia Española, 1953), 66:1–392.

19. Alfonso X's *Estoria de Espanna* extended to the death of Fernando III. Ramón Menéndez Pidal edited it with the title *Primera crónica general de España*, 2 vols. (Madrid: Gredos, 1955). Cited as *PCG*.

20. *Gran crónica de Alfonso XI*, ed. Diego Catalán, 2 vols. (Madrid: Gredos, 1977), 1:1–267. Cited as *GCAXI*.

21. Rodrigo Yáñez, *Poema de Alfonso XI*, ed. Tomás Antonio Sánchez in *Poetas castellanos anteriores al siglo XV* (Madrid: M. Rivadeneyra, 1864), 477–551, cited as *PAXI (1864)*; *Poema de Alfonso XI*, ed. Yo Ten Cate (Madrid: CSIC, 1956); Diego Catalán Menéndez Pidal, *Poema de Alfonso XI: Fuentes, dialecto, estilo* (Madrid: Gredos, 1956).

22. Jofre de Loaysa, *Crónica de los reyes de Castilla Fernando III, Alfonso X, Sancho IV, y Fernando IV (1248–1305)*, ed. Antonio García Martínez (Murcia: Diputación de Murcia, 1961).

23. Gonzalo de la Finojosa, "Continuación de la Crónica del Arzobispo Don Rodrigo

Jiménez de Rada," ed. Marqués de Fuensanta in *Colección de documentos inéditos para la historia de España*, ed. Martín Fernández de Navarrete et al., 112 vols. (Madrid: Calera and others, 1841–95), vols. 105–6, cited as *CODOIN*; Diego Catalán, *La Estoria de España de Alfonso X: Creación y evolución* (Madrid: Universidad Autónoma de Madrid, 1992), 248–53.

24. *Chronique catalane de Pierre IV d'Aragon III de Catalogne*, ed. Amédée Pagès (Toulouse: E. Privat, 1941), cited as *CCPIV*; *Chronicle of Pere III of Catalonia (Pedro IV of Aragon)*, tr. Mary Hillgarth, 2 vols. (Toronto: Pontifical Institute of Mediaeval Studies, 1980).

25. *Crónica dos sete primeiros reis de Portugal*, ed. Carlos da Silva Tarouca, 2 vols. (Lisbon: Academia Portuguesa da Historia, 1952), cited as *CSPRP*; Rui de Pina, *Chronica de el rey Dom Afonso o Quarto* (Lisbon: Paulo Craesbeeck, 1653; reprint, Lisbon: Biblion, 1936), cited as Rui de Pina, *CAIV*.

26. *Cantigas de Santa Maria*, ed. Walter Mettmann, 4 vols. (Coimbra: Universidad de Coimbra, 1959–74; reprint, 2 vols., Vigo: Edicions Xerais de Galicia, 1981), cited as *CSM*; Joseph F. O'Callaghan, *Alfonso X and the Cantigas de Santa Maria: A Poetic Biography* (Leiden: Brill, 1998).

27. Ibn Abī Zarʿ, *Rawd al-Qirtās*, tr. Ambrosio Huici, 2 vols. (Valencia: Anubar, 1964); Ibn ʿIdhārī, *Al-Bayān al-Mugrib fi Ijtisār ajbār Muluk al-Andalus wa al-Magrib*, tr. Ambrosio Huici, 2 vols. (Tetuán: Editora Marroquí, 1954).

28. Ibn al-Khatīb, *Historia de los reyes de la Alhambra: El resplandor de la luna llena (Al-Lamha al-badriyya)*, ed Emilio Molina López, tr. José María Casciaro Ramírez (Granada: Universidad de Granada, 1988); *Al-Lamha al-badriyya fī l-dawla al-nasriyya*, ed. Ahmad ʿĀsī and Muhibb al-dīn al-Khatīb (Beirut: Dār al-Afāq al-Jadīdah, 1978); *Al-Ihāta fī akhbār Garnāta*, ed. Muhammad ʿAbd Allāh ʿInān, 4 vols. (Cairo: Maktabat al-Khānjī, 1973–77).

29. Ahmad ibn Mohammed al-Makkarī, *History of the Mohammedan Dynasties in Spain, Extracted from the Nafhu t-tib min ghosni-l-Andalusi-r-rattab wa tarikh Lisanu-d-Din ibni-l-Khattib*, ed. and tr. Pascual de Gayangos, 2 vols. (London: Oriental Translation Fund, 1840–43; reprint, New York: Johnson, 1964).

30. Ibn Khaldūn, *Histoire*.

31. Ibn Marzūq, *El Musnad: Hechos memorables de Abū l-Hasan, sultán de los Benimerines*, ed. and tr. María Jesús Viguera (Madrid: Instituto Hispano-Arabe de Cultura, 1977).

32. Joseph F. O'Callaghan, "Origin and Development of Archival Record-Keeping in the Crown of Castile-León," in Lawrence J. McCrank, ed., *Discovery in the Archives of Spain and Portugal: Quincentenary Essays, 1492–1992* (New York: Haworth, 1993), 3–18.

33. "Documentos de la época de D. Alfonso el Sabio," *MHE* 1:1–344, 2:1–135; "Documentos de la época de D. Sancho el Bravo," *MHE* 3: 421–68.

34. Mercedes Gaibrois de Ballesteros, *Historia del reinado de Sancho IV*, 3 vols. (Madrid: Revista de Archivos, Bibliotecas y Museos, 1922–28); Antonio Benavides, *Memorias de Fernando IV de Castilla*, 2 vols. (Madrid: José Rodríguez, 1869). Cited as *MFIV*.

35. Manuel González Jiménez, *Diplomatario andaluz de Alfonso X* (Seville: El Monte, Caja de Huelva y Sevilla, 1991), cited as *DAAX*; Esther González Crespo, *Colección documental de Alfonso XI: Diplomas reales conservados en el Archivo Histórico Nacional, Sección de*

Clero, Pergaminos (Madrid: Universidad Complutense, 1985), cited as *CDAXI*, and "Inventario de documentos de Alfonso XI relativos al reino de Murcia," *ELEM* 17 (1994): 235–59.

36. Juan Torres Fontes, ed., *Colección de documentos para la historia del reino de Murcia* (*CODOM*), 22 vols. thus far (Murcia: Academia Alfonso X el Sabio, 1963–).

37. Andrés Giménez Soler, *La Corona de Aragón y Granada: Historia de las relaciones entre ambos reinos* (Barcelona: Casa Provincial de Caridad, 1908); Heinrich Finke, *Acta Aragonensia: Quellen zur deutschen, italienischen, französischen, spanischen, zur Kirchen- und Kulturgeschichte aus der diplomatischen Korrespondenz Jaymes II (1291–1327)*, 3 vols. (Berlin, 1908–22; reprint, Aalen: Scientia Verlag, 1966–1966); Àngels Masià i de Ros, *Jaume II: Aragó, Granada i Marroc* (Barcelona: CSIC, 1989) and Ángeles Masiá de Ros, *Relación castellano-aragonesa desde Jaime II a Pedro el Ceremonioso*, 2 vols. (Barcelona: CSIC, 1994), are the same person.

38. Maximiliano Alarcón y Santón and Ramón García de Linares, *Los documentos árabes diplomáticos del Archivo de la Corona de Aragón* (Madrid: E. Maestre, 1940).

39. Mariano Gaspar Remiro, ed., *Correspondencia diplomática entre Granada y Fez (siglo XIV): Extractos del "Raihana Alcuttab" de Lisaneddin Abenal-jatif el andalosí* (Granada: El Defensor, 1916).

CHAPTER 2. ALFONSO X'S AFRICAN CRUSADE

1. See *Crónica de Alfonso X según el Ms. II/2777 de la Biblioteca del Palacio Real (Madrid)*, ed. Manuel González Jiménez (Murcia: Real Academia Alfonso X el Sabio, 1998). Cited *CAX (GJ)*, this supersedes *Crónica de Alfonso X*, ed. Cayetano Rosell, *BAE* 66:3–66, cited *CAX*. See also *Chronicle of Alfonso X*, tr. Shelby Thacker and José Escobar, intro. Joseph F. O'Callaghan (Lexington: University Press of Kentucky, 2002); "Documentos de la época de Alfonso el Sabio."

2. Joseph F. O'Callaghan, *The Learned King: The Reign of Alfonso X of Castile* (Philadelphia: University of Pennsylvania Press, 1993) and the Spanish edition, *El rey sabio: El reinado de Alfonso X de Castilla*, tr. Manuel González Jiménez (Seville: Universidad de Sevilla, 1996); O'Callaghan, *Alfonso X and the Cantigas de Santa Maria*; Manuel González Jiménez, *Alfonso X el Sabio* (Barcelona: Ariel, 2004) and *Alfonso X el Sabio, 1252–1284* (Palencia: Diputación Provincial, 1993). I will cite González Jiménez's biography of 2004. See also Antonio Ballesteros y Beretta, *Alfonso X el Sabio* (1963; reprint Barcelona: El Albir, 1984); H. Salvador Martínez, *Alfonso X, el Sabio: Una biografía* (Madrid: Polifemo, 2003).

3. *CAX (GJ)*, 5–7, ch. 1; *CAX*, 4, ch. 1; Ibn 'Idhārī, *Al-Bayān*, 3:162; Ibn Khaldūn, *Histoire*, 4:74; Al-Makkarī, *History*, 2:339–45, bk. 8, ch. 5; Ballesteros, *Alfonso X*, 61–66; Miguel Ángel Ladero Quesada, *Fiscalidad y poder real en Castilla (1252–1369)* (Madrid: Editorial Complutense, 1993), 47–52; Francisco García Fitz, "¿Una España musulmana, sometida y tributaria? La España que no fue," *HID* 31 (2004): 227–48.

4. *CAX (GJ)*, 10–11, ch. 3; *CAX*, 5, ch. 3; Ibn 'Idhārī, *Al-Bayān*, 3:235; *Crónicas anónimas de Sahagún*, ed. Antonio Ubieto Arteta (Zaragoza: Anubar, 1987), 153, ch. 87.

5. Julio González, *Repartimiento de Sevilla*, 2 vols. (Madrid: CSIC, 1951; reprint, Seville: Ayuntamiento de Sevilla, 1998); *CAX (GJ)*, 9, ch. 2; *CAX*, 4, ch. 2; Manuel González Jiménez, Mercedes Borrero Fernández, and Isabel Montes Romero-Camacho, *Sevilla en tiempos de Alfonso X el Sabio* (Seville: Ayuntamiento de Sevilla, 1987), 16–41; Manuel González Jiménez, *Alfonso X*, 60–67, and *La repoblación de la zona de Sevilla durante el siglo XIV: Estudio y documentación* (Seville: Universidad de Sevilla, 1975); Antonio Ballesteros y Beretta, *Sevilla en el siglo XIII* (Madrid: Juan Pérez Torres, 1913).

6. *CAX (GJ)*, ii, 8–9, ch. 2; *CAX*, 4, ch. 2; Gonzalo de la Finojosa, "Continuación," 106:13, ch. 238; González, *Repartimiento de Sevilla*, 2:152–53; *DAAX*, 89, no. 85.

7. *PCG*, 2:770, ch. 1130; *CAX (GJ)*, 12–14, ch. 4; *CAX*, 4–6, ch. 2; Ibn 'Idhārī, *Al-Bayān*, 3:275; Jofre de Loaysa, *Crónica*, 60, ch. 218.1; González, *Fernando III*, 1:241.

8. *DAAX*, 5–6, 14, nos. 3, 15; González, *Fernando III*, 1:105–6, 115–16; Ballesteros, *Sevilla*, xii–xiii, no 10; González Jiménez, *Fernando III*, 238–40, and *Alfonso X*, 58–60.

9. *CAX (GJ)*, 22–25, 99–102, ch. 8, 30; *CAX*, 7–8, 25–26, ch. 8, 30; O'Callaghan, *Learned King*, 73–75.

10. *DAAX*, 158–60, 188, 198–202, nos. 147, 169, 179–80.

11. Juan Gil de Zamora, *De preconiis civitatis Numantine*, in Fidel Fita, "Dos libros (inéditos) de Gil de Zamora," *BRAH* 5 (1884): 147, and *Liber de preconiis Hispaniae*, ed. Manuel de Castro y Castro (Madrid: Universidad de Madrid, 1955), 21, 23, 75, Tr. 2, Tr. 5, ch. 11.

12. *CSM*, 2:280–81, 370–72, nos. 360, 406; O'Callaghan, *Cantigas*, 93–95.

13. *DAAX*, 561, no. 521; Georges Daumet, "Les testaments d'Alphonse X le Savant, roi de Castille," *Bibliothèque de l'École des Chartes* 67 (1906): 93; González Jiménez, *Alfonso X*, 107–11.

14. González, *Fernando III*, 3:408–12, no. 825; Marcos Fernández Gómez, Pilar Ostos Salcedo, and María Luisa Pardo Rodríguez, eds., *El libro de privilegios de la ciudad de Sevilla* (Seville: Ayuntamiento de Sevilla, 1993), 137–41, no. 1.

15. Ballesteros, *Alfonso X*, 676. John Clark kindly assisted me in translating the inscription, now in the Hospital de la Caridad.

16. Asunción López Dapena, *Cuentas y Gastos (1292–1294) del rey D. Sancho IV el Bravo (1284–1295)* (Córdoba: Monte de Piedad y Caja de Ahorros, 1984), 641.

17. González, *Repartimiento de Sevilla*, 1:294, 516–20; Florentino Pérez Embid, "La marina real castellana en el siglo XIII," *AEM* 6 (1969): 158–65; Leopoldo Torres Balbás, "Atarazanas hispano-musulmanas," *Al-Andalus* 11 (1946): 179–209; Rafael Cómez Ramos, "Notas sobre las atarazanas de Sevilla," *Archivo Hispalense* 254 (2000): 165–77.

18. Amparo García Cuadrado, *Las Cantigas: El Códice de Florencia* (Murcia: Universidad de Murcia, 1993), 339–59; O'Callaghan, *Reconquest*, 150.

19. *DAAX*, 33–34, no. 37; González, *Repartimiento de Sevilla*, 1:293–98, and 2:172–74; José Manuel Rodríguez García, "La Marina alfonsí al asalto de Africa, 1240–1280: Consideraciones estratégicas e historia," *Revista de Historia Naval* 85 (2004): 27–55.

20. *DAAX*, 50–52, no. 53; Julio González, "Origen de la marina real de Castilla," *RABM* 54 (1948): 229–53, and *Repartimiento de Sevilla*, 1:297–98, 2:155, 157–58, 162–72; Ballesteros, *Sevilla*, lxxi–lxxii, no. 69, and *Alfonso X*, 78.

21. John H. Pryor, *Geography, Technology and War: Studies in the Maritime History of the Mediterranean, 649–1571* (Cambridge: Cambridge University Press, 1988), 64–66.

22. Florentino Pérez Embid, *El Almirantazgo de Castilla hasta las capitulaciones de Santa Fe* (Seville: Universidad de Sevilla, 1944); Rafael Gibert, "Almirante en la historia del derecho," *Revista de la Facultad de Derecho de la Universidad Complutense de Madrid* 18 (1976): 137–51.

23. González, *Repartimiento de Sevilla*, 2:155; *DAAX*, 80–85, no. 80; Juan Torres Fontes, *Fueros y privilegios de Alfonso X el Sabio al reino de Murcia*, *CODOM* 3 (Murcia: Academia Alfonso X el Sabio, 1973), 69–71, no. 52; José Manuel Calderón Ortega and Francisco Javier Díaz González, "Los almirantes y la política naval de los reyes de Castilla en el siglo XIII," *Anuario de la Facultad de Derecho de Alcalá de Henares* 8 (1998–99): 103–25, esp. 109–13.

24. Quintana Prieto, *Inocencio IV*, 2:709, 711–12, 741–42, nos. 803, 807–8, 833, 839–40; Élie Berger, *Les Registres d'Innocent IV*, 4 vols., Bibliothèque des Écoles Françaises d'Athènes et de Rome ser. 2, no. 1 (Paris: A. Thorin, 1884–1921), 3:117, 119, 155, 173, nos. 6014, 6029–30 reg., 6212–14, 6316; José Goñi Gaztambide, *Historia de la bula de la cruzada en España* (Vitoria: Editorial del Seminario, 1955), 187–88 n. 3; Ladero Quesada, *Fiscalidad*, 191–203, 207–9; Carlos de Ayala Martínez, *Directrices fundamentales de la política península de Alfonso X: Relaciones castellano-aragonesas de 1252 a 1263* (Madrid: Universidad Autónoma de Madrid, 1986), 80–84.

25. Quintana Prieto, *Inocencio IV*, 2: 837–38, no. 955; Berger, *Registres d'Innocent IV*, 3: 410, no. 7496; O'Callaghan, *Learned King*, 7–8, 24, 31–37, 46.

26. Cayetano J. Socarras, *Alfonso X of Castile: A Study on Imperialistic Frustration* (Barcelona: Ediciones Hispam, 1976), 251–52, app. 8.

27. Thomas Rymer, *Foedera, conventiones, litterae et cuiuscunque acta publica inter reges Angliae et alios quovis imperatores, reges, pontifices, principes*, 3rd ed., 10 vols. (The Hague: Joannes Neaulme, 1739–45), 1.1:179–81, 185; *DAAX*, 135–36, no. 131; José Manuel Rodríguez García, "Henry III, Alfonso X of Castile and the Crusading Plans of the Thirteenth Century (1245–1274)," in Björn Weiler and Ifor Rowlands, eds., *England and Europe in the Reign of Henry III (1216–1272)* (Aldershot: Ashgate, 2002), 99–120; Anthony Goodman, "Alfonso X and the English Crown," in Juan Carlos de Miguel Rodríguez, Angela Múñoz Fernández, and Cristina Segura Graiño, eds., *Alfonso X el Sabio: Vida, obra y época: Actas del Congreso internacional de estudios medievales conmemorativos del VII Centenario de la muerte de Alfonso el Sabio* (Madrid: Sociedad Española de Estudios Medievales, 1989), 39–54, esp. 40–45, and "England and Iberia in the Middle Ages," in Michael Jones and Malcolm Vale, eds., *England and Her Neighbours, 1066–1453: Essays in Honour of Pierre Chaplais* (London: Hambledon, 1988), 73–96, esp. 74–82; Francisco J. Hernández, "Relaciones de Alfonso X con Inglaterra y Francia," *Alcanate* 4 (2004–5): 167–242; Ayala Martínez, *Directrices*, 61–70; Maureen Purcell, *Papal Crusading Policy, 1244–1291* (Leiden: Brill, 1975), 111–12.

28. Quintana Prieto, *Inocencio IV*, 2: 837–38, 876–77, nos. 955, 1000; Berger, *Registres d'Innocent IV*, 3:496, no. 7496 reg.; Ballesteros, *Alfonso X*, 103; James A. Brundage, *Medieval Canon Law and the Crusader* (Madison: University of Wisconsin Press, 1969), 159–90.

29. Ildefonso Rodríguez de Lama, *La documentación pontificia de Alejandro IV*

(1254–1261) (Rome: Instituto Español de Historia Ecclesiástica, 1981), 61–62, 67, 74–77, 83–84, 130, 133–34, nos. 36–37, 43, 53, 62, 125, 129; Charles Bourel de la Roncière, *Les registres d'Alexandre IV (1254–1261)*, 3 vols., Bibliothèque des Écoles Françaises d'Athènes et de Rome ser. 2, no. 15 (Paris: Fontemoing, 1902–59), 1:75, 126–27, 145, nos. 274–75 reg., 298, 416 reg., 483, 862, 873, 902; Odoricus Raynaldus, *Annales ecclesiastici ab ano MCXCVIII ubi desinit Cardinalis Baronius*, ed. J. D. Mansi, 15 vols. (Lucca: Leonardo Venturini, 1738–47), 2:534, a. 1255, no. 49; Ballesteros, *Alfonso X*, 135–36; Demetrio Mansilla, *Iglesia castellano-leonesa y curia romana en los tiempos del rey San Fernando* (Madrid: CSIC, 1945), 86 n. 123; O'Callaghan, *Reconquest*, 117–23.

30. Rymer, *Foedera*, 1.1:194, 1,2:6–7, 27, 39; *Crónicas anónimas de Sahagún*, 153, ch. 87; Ballesteros, *Alfonso X*, 135; Goñi Gaztambide, *Historia*, 189; Goodman, "Alfonso X," 45–48.

31. Rodríguez de Lama, *Alejandro IV*, 124–25, no. 117; Bourel, *Alexandre IV*, 1:259, no. 862; Goñi Gaztambide, *Historia*, 187–88; Peter Linehan, *The Spanish Church and the Papacy in the Thirteenth Century* (Cambridge: Cambridge University Press, 1971), 202–3; O'Callaghan, *Learned King*, 162–71.

32. O'Callaghan, *Learned King*, 73–75, 152–56, 198–99.

33. Socarras, *Alfonso X*, 259–64, app. 9–10; Paul Scheffer-Boichorst, "Kleinere Forschungen zur Geschichte Alfons X von Castilien," *Mitteilungen des Instituts für Österreichische Geschichtsforschung* 9 (1888): 226–48, esp. 241–48, nos. 1–3; Ballesteros, *Alfonso X*, 155–56, 159–60, 169–70.

34. Bruce Gelsinger, "A Thirteenth-Century Norwegian-Castilian Alliance," *Medievalia et Humanistica* n.s. 10 (1981): 55–80, esp. 65. Sturla Thordarson, *Hákonar saga Hákonarsonar*, in C. R. Unger, ed., *Codex Frisianus: En Samling af norske Konge-Sagaer* (Christiania: P. T. Mallings, 1871), 548–59, ch. 289, 292–93, 295, 299, 301; P. A. Munch, Tomás Antonio Sánchez, Pascual de Gayangos, Antonio Ballesteros Beretta, and Juan Pérez de Guzmán y Gallo, "La Princesa Cristina de Noruega y el Infante don Felipe, hermano de don Alfonso el Sabio," *BRAH* 74 (1919): 45–61; Vicente Almazán, "El viaje de la Princesa Cristina a Valladolid (1257–1258) según la saga islandesa del rey Hákon," *Archivos Leoneses* 73 (1983): 101–10; Ballesteros, *Alfonso X*, 189–93; Purcell, *Papal Crusading Policy*, 110–11.

35. The information in *CAX (GJ)*, 8–12, ch. 2–3, *CAX*, 5, ch. 3, and Gonzalo de la Finojosa, "Continuación," 106:12, ch. 238, is largely erroneous. O'Callaghan, *Learned King*, 202–3; González Jiménez, *Alfonso X*, 125–28; Ayala Martínez, *Directrices*, 187–89.

36. O'Callaghan, *Learned King*, 200–202, and "Paths to Ruin: The Economic and Financial Policies of Alfonso the Learned," in Robert I. Burns, S.J., ed., *The Worlds of Alfonso the Learned and James the Conqueror: Intellect and Force in the Middle Ages* (Princeton, N.J.: Princeton University Press, 1985), 41–67; González Jiménez, *Alfonso X*, 111–20.

37. Quintana Prieto, *Inocencio IV*, 711, no. 807; *Crónicas anónimas de Sahagún*, 153, ch. 87; Gelsinger, "Norwegian-Castilian Alliance," 61.

38. Torres Fontes, *Fueros*, 40, 53–57, 63–64, nos. 28, 38, 40, 46.

39. Ballesteros, *Alfonso X*, 259; Charles-Emmanuel Dufourcq, *L'Espagne catalane et le Maghrib aux XIIIe et XIVe siècles* (Paris: Presses Universitaires de France, 1966), 24, 134 n. 10; Ibn Khaldūn, *Histoire*, 4:61–62.

40. Luis Miguel Villar García, *Documentación medieval de la catedral de Segovia (1115–1300)* (Salamanca: Universidad de Salamanca, 1990), 274–75, no. 166; Rymer, *Foedera*, 1.2:367, 372.

41. Ballesteros, *Alfonso X*, 262–68; O'Callaghan, *Learned King*, 73–75; González Jiménez, *Alfonso X*, 86–87, 140–41.

42. *CSM*, 2:358, no. 401, ll. 22–31; O'Callaghan, *Cantigas*, 94–96; Cristina González, *La tercera crónica de Alfonso X: La gran conquista de Ultramar* (London: Tamesis, 1992) and "El último sueño de Alfonso X: La Gran conquista de Ultramar," *Exemplaria Hispánica* 1 (1991–92): 97–117; Manuel Alejandro Rodríguez de la Peña, "La cruzada como discurso político en la cronística alfonsí," *Alcanate* 2 (2000–2001): 23–41.

43. *CAX (GJ)*, 28, ch. 10; *CAX*, 8, ch. 9.

44. *CSM*, 1:552–554, no. 165; O'Callaghan, *Cantigas*, 96–97.

45. Pedro Martínez Montávez, "Relaciones de Alfonso X de Castilla con el sultán mameluco Baybars y sus sucesores," *Al-Andalus* 27 (1962): 343–76, esp. 346–55, 355–60, citing al-Maqrīzī, *Sulūk*, 1.3:543; Ballesteros, *Alfonso X*, 305–6; O'Callaghan, *Learned King*, 206–7; Ayala Martínez, *Directrices*, 291–93.

46. González Jiménez, *Alfonso X*, 110.

47. *MHE*, 1:89–100, nos. 43–45; O'Callaghan, *Learned King*, 92–93.

48. Juan Loperráez, *Descripción histórica del Obispado de Osma*, 3 vols. (Madrid: Imprenta Real, 1788), 2:163; Antonio Ballesteros y Beretta, *El Itinerario de Alfonso el Sabio* (Madrid: Tipografía de Archivos, 1935), 182–83.

49. Ciriaco Miguel Vigil, *Colección histórico-diplomática del ayuntamiento de Oviedo* (Oviedo: Pardo-Gusano, 1889), 46, no. 22; Ladero Quesada, *Fiscalidad*, 45–46; Joseph F. O'Callaghan, *The Cortes of Castile-León, 1188–1350* (Philadelphia: University of Pennsylvania Press, 1989), 102.

50. Villar García, *Segovia*, 280–81, no. 169; Toribio Mingüella, *Historia de la diócesis de Sigüenza*, 3 vols. (Madrid: RABM, 1900–1913), 1:599–601, no. 225; *DAAX*, 313–16, no. 286; Goñi Gaztambide, *Historia*, 189–90.

51. Villar García, *Segovia*, 284, no. 171; Carlos de Ayala Martínez, *Libro de privilegios de la Orden de San Juan de Jerusalén en Castilla y León (siglos XII–XV)* (Madrid: Editorial Complutense, 1995), 554–56, no. 338; Torres Fontes, *Fueros*, 69–71, no. 52.

52. Ambrosio Huici Miranda and María Desamparados Cabanes Pecourt, *Documentos de Jaime I de Aragón*, 5 vols. thus far (Valencia: Anubar, 1976–88), 4:255, 363, nos. 1170, 1181; *MHE*, 1: 155–56, 158, nos. 72, 74; Jerónimo Zurita, *Anales de la Corona de Aragón*, ed. Ángel Canellas López, 9 vols. (Zaragoza: CSIC, 1970–85), 1:598–99.

53. *MHE*, 1:156–59, 165–66, nos. 73, 75, 80; Huici and Cabanes Pecourt, *Jaime I*, 4:264–65, no. 1183; *CDACA*, 6:149–50, 153–54, nos. 34–36; Ayala Martínez, *Directrices*, 273–77.

54. *DAAX*, 253–54, no. 231; *MHE*, 1:164–65, no. 79; Francisco Veas Arteseros and María del Carmen Veas Arteseros, "Alférez y Mayordomo Real en el siglo XIII," *Miscelánea Medieval Murciana* 13 (1986): 39–40.

55. Ibn 'Idhārī, *Al-Bayān*, 3:29–30; Al-Himyarī, *Kitāb ar-Rawd al-mi'tar*, tr. María

Pilar Maestro González (Valencia: Gráficas Bautista, 1963), 16–17, 290–98; Jofre de Loaysa, *Crónica*, 60, ch. 218.1; *DAAX*, 275, no. 247.

56. *CSM*, 2:337–38, no. 385.

57. *CSM*, 2:199–201, 272–79, 288–89, 292–99, 306–9, 312–13, 317–24, 326–30, 337–38, 342–43, 345–52, nos. 328, 356–59, 364, 366–68, 371–72, 375, 377–79, 381–82, 385, 387, 389, 391–93; Jesús Montoya Martínez, *Cancionero de Santa María de El Puerto* (El Puerto de Santa María: Ayuntamiento, 2006) and "Las Cantigas de Santa Maria, fuente para la historia gaditana," in *Cádiz en el siglo XIII: Actas de las "Jornadas Conmemorativas del VII Centenario de la muerte de Alfonso X el Sabio"* (Cádiz: Universidad de Cádiz, 1983), 173–91; O'Callaghan, *Cantigas*, 172–91.

58. *CSM*, 2:199–201, no. 328; *CAX (GJ)*, 23, ch. 8; *CAX*, 7, ch. 8; O'Callaghan, *Cantigas*, 100–101; Rafael Sánchez Saus, "Cádiz en la época medieval," in Francisco Javier Lomas Salmonte et al., *Historia de Cádiz* (Cádiz: Sílex, 2005), 175–201.

59. Manuel González Jiménez, "El Puerto de Santa María en tiempos de Alfonso X el Sabio," in Manuel González et al., eds., *Nuestros orígenes históricos como el Puerto de Santa María* (El Puerto de Santa María: Ayuntamiento de El Puerto de Santa María, 1989), 11–31, and "De al-Qanatir al Gran Puerto de Santa María," in *El Puerto de Santa María entre los siglos XIII y XVI: Estudios en homenaje a Hipólito Sancho de Sopranis en el centenario de su nacimiento* (El Puerto de Santa María: Ayuntamiento de El Puerto de Santa María, 1995), 37–52; Leopoldo Torres Balbás, "La mezquita de al-Qanatir y el santuario de Alfonso el Sabio en el Puerto de Santa María," *Al-Andalus* 7 (1942): 417–37.

60. *CSM*, 1: 562, no. 169; O'Callaghan, *Cantigas*, 138–39; González Jiménez, *Alfonso X*, 138–39.

61. Jalaf al-Gāfiqī al-Qabtawrī, *Rasā'il dīwāniyya min Sabta*, ed. M. al-Habīb al-Hīla (Rabat, 1979), cited by María del Carmen Mosquera Marino, *La señoría de Ceuta en el siglo XIII: Historia política y económica* (Ceuta: Instituto de Estudios Ceutíes, 1994), ch. 7.

62. Al-Qabtawrī, *Rasā'il*, 109–12, cited by Mosquera Marino, *Señoría de Ceuta*, 185–89, 197, 202.

63. Al-Qabtawrī, *Rasā'il*, 113–21 (eighth of eleven letters in the collection), cited by Mosquera Merino, *Señoría de Ceuta*, 189–202, esp. 191–93.

64. Ibn 'Idhārī, *Al-Bayān*, 3:215–17; Ibn Khaldūn, *Histoire*, 4:63–64; Mosquera Merino, *Señoría de Ceuta*, 139–45; Francisco García Fitz, "Alfonso X y sus relaciones con el Emirato granadino: Política y guerra," *Alcanate* 4 (2004–5): 35–77, esp. 37–38.

65. Al-Qabtawrī, *Rasā'il*, 123–27 (the ninth letter), cited by Mosquera Merino, *Señoría de Ceuta*, 202–6; Ibn 'Idhārī, *Al-Bayān*, 245–46.

66. *DAAX*, 313–16, no. 286; Mingüella, *Sigüenza*, 1:599–601, no. 225; Antonio Ballesteros y Beretta, "Itinerario de Alfonso X, rey de Castilla," *BRAH* 107 (1935): 30, and *Alfonso X*, 363; O'Callaghan, *Learned King*, 206–7; González Jiménez, *Alfonso X*, 137–38; Mosquera Merino, *Señoría de Ceuta*, 145–46.

67. Scheffer-Boichorst, "Kleinere Forschungen," 246, no. 1; *DAAX*, 254, no. 231; Ballesteros, *Alfonso X*, 155, 159–60, 272–73; González Jiménez, *Alfonso X*, 138; Linehan, *Spanish Church*, 202–3.

68. Atanasio López, *Memoria histórica de los obispos de Marruecos desde el siglo XIII* (Madrid, n.p., 1920), 12–31; Juan de Samargo, "Obispado de Ceuta," *Transfretana: Revista del Instituto de Estudios Ceutíes* 6 (1994): 129–35.

69. Quintana Prieto, *Inocencio IV*, 1:251–52, no. 216; Ibn 'Idhārī, *Al-Bayān*, 2:153.

70. Ibn Abī Zarʻ, *Rawd al-Qirtās*, 2:571; Ibn 'Idhārī, *Al-Bayān*, 3:260; Ibn Khaldūn, *Histoire*, 4:46–47.

71. *CSM*, 2:200, no. 328, l. 32.

72. Ibn 'Idhārī, *Al-Bayān*, 3:261–62. *CAX (GJ)*, 53–55, ch. 19, and *CAX*, 13–14, ch. 19, erroneously dated this in 1269; Ballesteros, *Alfonso X*, 279–84; Montoya Martínez, "Las Cantigas," 173–81.

73. Ibn 'Idhārī, *Al-Bayān*, 3:262–66.

74. *CSM*, 2:200, no. 328, ll. 30–35; Ibn 'Idhārī, *Al-Bayān*, 3:267–69, 272; Ibn Abī Zarʻ, *Rawd al-Qirtās*, 2:571–72; Ibn Khaldūn, *Histoire*, 4:46–47; Ibn Marzūq, *El Musnad*, 102.

75. Ibn 'Idhārī, *Al-Bayān*, 3:269–71.

76. Ibn 'Idhārī, *Al-Bayān*, 3:265–66, extracted the caliph's letter dated 10 October 1260.

77. Ibn 'Idhārī, *Al-Bayān*, 3:268–70; *CAX (GJ)*, 54, ch. 19; *CAX*, 13–14, ch. 19; Ballesteros, *Alfonso X*, 274–84, and, "La toma de Salé en tiempos de Alfonso X el Sabio," *Al-Andalus* 8 (1943): 89–128; Ambrosio Huici, "La toma de Salé por la esquadra de Alfonso X," *Hespéris* 39 (1952): 41–52; Charles Emmanuel Dufourcq, "Un projet castillane du XIIIe siècle: La croisade d'Afrique," *Revue d'histoire et du civilisation du Magreb* 1 (1966): 26–51; Pérez Embid, "La marina real," 167–70; Ayala Martínez, *Directrices*, 279; Concepción Cereijo Martínez, "La política marina de Alfonso X: La toma de Salé en la Crónica de Alfonso X y en las Fuentes musulmanas," *Revista de Historia Naval* 25 (2007): 37–57; María Inmaculada Marín Buenadicha, "Una contradicción historiográfica: El suceso de Salé," in Miguel Rodríguez, Múñoz Fernández, and Segura Graiño, eds., *Alfonso X el Sabio*, 225–36; O'Callaghan, *Learned King*, 172–74; González Jiménez, *Alfonso X*, 136–41.

78. Ibn 'Idhārī, *Al-Bayān*, 3:275–76, reported the attack on Ceuta in A.H. 659 (6 December 1260–25 November 1261).

79. Ibn 'Idhārī, *Al-Bayān*, 3:275–76; Mosquera Merino, *Señoría de Ceuta*, 145–46, 206–7; Arié, *L'Espagne*, 62–63; Ayala Martinez, *Directrices*, 269; Francisco García Fitz, "La conquista de Tarifa en la estrategía de expansión castellano-leonesa del siglo XIII," in Manuel González Jiménez, ed., *Tarifa en la Edad Media* (Tarifa: Ayuntamiento de Tarifa, 2005), 103–25, esp. 108–9.

80. Matías Rodríguez Díez, *Historia de la ciudad de Astorga*, 2nd ed. (Astorga: Porfirio López, 1909), 715–20; Manuel González Jiménez, "Cortes de Sevilla de 1261," *HID* 25 (1998): 295–311; O'Callaghan, *Cortes*, 21–22, 189.

81. *CAX (GJ)*, 12, ch. 4; *CAX*, 5–6, ch. 4; *MHE*, 1:308–24, esp. 311–12, no. 140.

82. *CAX (GJ)*, 12–13, ch. 4; *CAX*, 5–6, ch. 4; Ibn 'Idhārī, *Al-Bayān*, 3:275; Gonzalo de la Finojosa, "Continuación," 106:13, ch. 238; Al-Himyarī, *Kitāb*, 211–12; O'Callaghan, *Learned King*, 174–75; González Jiménez, *Alfonso X*, 142–44; Francisco García Fitz, *Castilla y León frente al Islam: Estrategias de expansión y tácticas militares (siglos XI–XIII)* (Seville: Universidad de Sevilla, 1998), 61–62.

83. Ibn ʿIdhārī, *Al-Bayān*, 3:285; *DAAX*, 11–12, no. 12; *CSM*, 1:593–94, no. 183; Alejandro García Sanjuán, "La conquista de Niebla por Alfonso X," *HID* 27 (2000): 89–112; Fátima Roldán Castro, "Ibn Mahfuz en Niebla (siglo VII/XIII)," *Anaquel de Estudios Árabes* 4 (1993): 161–78.

84. *CAX (GJ)*, 16–19, ch. 6; *CAX*, 6, ch. 6; Gonzalo de la Finojosa, "Continuación," 106:13–14, ch. 238; Ibn ʿIdhārī, *Al-Bayān*, 3:285; *DAAX*, 280–81, no. 253; O'Callaghan, *Cantigas*, 106–7.

85. González Jiménez, *Alfonso X*, 52–58, 146–49, and "Las relaciones entre Portugal y Castilla durante el Siglo XIII," *RFLH* ser. 2, 15 (1998): 1–24; Ballesteros, *Alfonso X*, 315–18; O'Callaghan, *Learned King*, 156–59, 175–78; García Fitz, "Alfonso X y sus relaciones," 50–53; Florentino Pérez Embid, *La frontera entre los reinos de Sevilla y Portugal* (Seville: Ayuntamiento de Sevilla, 1975).

86. *DAAX*, 292–93, 295–98, 305–6, 326, 353–57, 538–39, nos. 262, 266, 269, 275, 279, 284, 301–2, 311–12, 323–25, 508.

87. *CSM*, 2:322–23, no. 379, and 2:199–202, no. 328; O'Callaghan, *Cantigas*, 177–78.

88. Vigil, *Oviedo*, 56–57, 59, nos. 30, 32; Ballesteros, *Alfonso X*, 283, 367; Ladero Quesada, *Fiscalidad*, 41–45.

89. Miguel Ángel Ladero Quesada and Manuel González Jiménez, "La población en la frontera de Gibraltar y el repartimiento de Vejer (siglos XIII y XIV)," *HID* 4 (1977): 199–204.

90. Rymer, *Foedera*, 1.1:420–21.

91. Sturla Thordarson, *Hákonar saga*, 568, ch. 320; Gelsinger, "Norwegian-Castilian Alliance," 67.

92. In *Learned King*, 178–80, in a *lapsus mentis* I inadvertently wrote of the demand for Tarifa and Gibraltar.

93. *DAAX*, 313–16, no. 286; Mingüella, *Sigüenza*, 1:599–601, no. 225; O'Callaghan, *Cantigas*, 138–39.

94. María Josefa Sanz Fuentes, "Repartimiento de Écija: Estudio y edición," *HID* 3 (1976): 535–41; Manuel González Jiménez, "Población y repartimiento de Écija," in *Homenaje al Profesor Juan Torres Fontes*, 2 vols. (Murcia: Universidad de Murcia, 1987), 1:691–711; *Alfonso X*, 171.

95. *CAX (GJ)*, 34–36, ch. 12; *CAX*, 10, ch. 12; Aquilino Iglesia Ferreirós, "El privilegio general concedido a las Extremaduras en 1264 por Alfonso X: Edición del ejemplar enviado a Peñafiel el 15 de abril de 1264," *AHDE* 53 (1983): 456–521; González Jiménez, *Alfonso X*, 158–61.

96. Pérez Embid, "La marina real," 175–77.

CHAPTER 3. CRUSADE AGAINST THE MUDÉJARS

1. See Alfonso X's letters detailing the treachery of Ibn al-Ahmar; *DAAX*, 313–16, no. 286; Diego Colmenares, *Historia de la insigne Ciudad de Segovia*, new ed., 3 vols. (Segovia:

Academia de Historia y Arte de San Quirce, 1969–75), 1:264; Mingüella, *Sigüenza*, 1:599–601, no. 225; González Jiménez, *Alfonso X*, 166–73.

2. Ibn 'Idhārī, *Al-Bayān*, 3:285, 288; Ibn Abī Zar', *Rawd al-Qirtās*, 2:575; Ibn Khaldūn, *Histoire*, 4:48–49; Al-Makkarī, *History*, 2:341, 343, bk. 8, ch. 5; Miguel Ángel Manzano Rodríguez, *La intervención de los Benimerines en la Península Ibérica* (Madrid: CSIC, 1992), 4–6, 324.

3. *CAX (GJ)*, 37, ch. 13; *CAX*, 10, ch. 13; *CJI*, 7:34–36, ch. 378; María Jesús Rubiera de Epalza, "Los Banū Escallola, la dinastía granadina que no fue," *Andalucía Islámica* 2–3 (1981–82): 85–94; Arié, *L'Espagne*, 49–60; Torres Delgado, *Granada*, 61–100.

4. Ibn 'Idhārī, *Al-Bayān*, 3:285–86.

5. *CJI*, 7:34–36, ch. 378; *Annales Ianuenses (1249–1264), Monumenta Germaniae Historica, Scriptores*, 18:248; *Chronicon Marchiae Tarvisinae et Lombardiae (aa. 1207–1270)*, ed. L. A. Botteghi (Città di Castello: S. Lapi, 1916), 54.

6. *DAAX*, 313–16, no. 286; Colmenares, *Segovia*, 1:264; Mingüella, *Sigüenza*, 1:599–601, no. 225.

7. *CAX (GJ)*, 12–13, 29–32, 100, ch. 4, 10, 30; *CAX*, 5–6, 8–9, 25–26, ch. 4, 10, 30; Gonzalo de la Finojosa, "Continuación," 106:13, ch. 238; González Jiménez, *Alfonso X*, 175; Antonio Sánchez de Mora, "Nuño González de Lara: 'El más poderoso omne que sennor ouiese et más honrado de Espanna,'" *HID* 31 (2004): 631–44.

8. *CSM*, 2:242–45, no. 345; O'Callaghan, *Cantigas*, 114–21; Rafael Cómez Ramos, *Las empresas artísticas de Alfonso X* (Seville: Diputación Provincial de Sevilla, 1979), 143–51, and fig. 22.

9. *Al-Dhakhīra al-Saniyya fī ta'rikh al-dawla al-marīniyya*, ed. Mohammed Ben Cheneb (Algiers: 1920), 111–12, cited by Arié, *L'Espagne*, 63–64, who mistakenly dated the assault on 13 Shawwāl 622/31 May 1264; A.H. 622 corresponds to A.D. 1225. Huici, in n. 1 of his edition of Ibn 'Idhārī, *Al-Bayān*, 3:275, cited *Al-Dhakīra*, 111–12, stating that the Marinids seized the *alcázar* on Friday, 13 Shawwāl, 8 August 1264. I wish to thank Miguel Ángel Manzano Rodríguez for correctly interpreting this information for me.

10. *CAX (GJ)*, 29–32, ch. 10; *CAX*, 9, ch. 10.

11. *CAX (GJ)*, 29–32, ch. 10; *CAX*, 9, ch. 10; Ibn 'Idhārī, *Al-Bayān*, 3:287; *CJI*, 7:34–36, ch. 378; Ballesteros, *Alfonso X*, 396; García Fitz, "Alfonso X y sus relaciones," 53–57.

12. *DAAX*, 313–16, no. 286; Colmenares, *Segovia*, 1:264; Mingüella, *Sigüenza*, 1:599–601, no. 225; González Jiménez, *Alfonso X*, 176.

13. *DAAX*, 318, no. 290; O'Callaghan, *Learned King*, 157–60.

14. *CAX (GJ)*, 34–35, ch. 12; *CAX*, 9–10, ch. 11–12.

15. *CAX (GJ)*, 38–40, ch. 14; *CAX*, 10–11, ch. 14; *CSM*, 2:245, no. 345, ll. 106–14; González, *Repartimiento de Sevilla*, 1:79–82; González Jiménez, *Alfonso X*, 178–79.

16. *CAX (GJ)*, 38, ch. 14; *CAX*, 10, ch. 14; Hipólyto Sancho de Sopranis, *Historia de Jerez de la Frontera*, 3 vols. (Jerez: Jerez Industrial, 1964–65), 1:22.

17. *DAAX*, 319, nos. 292–94; Gonzalo de la Finojosa, "Continuación," 106:14, ch. 238; Manuel González Jiménez and Antonio González Gómez, *El libro del repartimiento de Jerez de la Frontera: Estudio y edición* (Cádiz: Instituto de Estudios Gaditanos, Diputación

Provincial, 1980), 7. In *Learned King*, 187–88, on the basis of these two sources, I argued that the surrender ought to be dated on 9 October 1266. I am now convinced that 1264 is correct.

18. *DAAX*, 321–22, 330–31, nos. 296, 306; González Jiménez, *Alfonso X*, 179.

19. *DAAX*, 319–21, 323–25, nos. 295, 297–99; Manuel González Jiménez, "Osuna en el siglo XIII," in Manuel García Fernández and Juan José Iglesias Rodríguez, eds., *Osuna entre los tiempos medievales y modernos (siglos XIII–XVIII)* (Seville: Universidad de Sevilla, 1995), 27–38.

20. On the Saracens as Agarenes, descendants of the slave girl Hagar, see O'Callaghan, *Reconquest*, 15.

21. Santiago Domínguez Sánchez, *Documentos de Clemente IV (1265–1268) referentes a España* (León: Universidad de León, 1996), 111–15, 118–19, nos. 4–5, 10; Edouard Jordan, *Les registres de Clément IV (1265–1268): Recueil des bulles de ce pape*, 2 vols., Bibliothèque des Écoles Françaises d'Athènes et de Rome ser. 2, no. 11 (Paris: Thorin, 1893–1945), 1:4–7, nos. 15, 17 reg.; F. Javier Pereda Llarena, *Documentación de la Catedral de Burgos (1254–1293)* (Burgos: Garrido Garrido, 1984), 102–8, no. 73; Goñi Gaztambide, *Historia*, 192–94; Brundage, *Canon Law and the Crusader*, 159–90.

22. Domínguez Sánchez, *Clemente IV*, 109–10, no. 3; Jordan, *Clément IV*, 1:6–7, no. 16.

23. Domínguez Sánchez, *Clemente IV*, 134–36, 140–42, nos. 25, 31–32; Jordan, *Clément IV*, 1:23, 29–30, 350–52, nos. 89 reg., 126, 890, 896; Pereda Llarena, *Burgos (1254–1293)*, 98–101, nos. 71–72; Linehan, *Spanish Church*, 207–8; Goñi Gaztambide, *Historia*, 194–96.

24. Ayala Martínez, *San Juan*, 561–62, no. 342.

25. *CSM*, 1:597–600, no. 185; O'Callaghan, *Cantigas*, 110–13; Jesús Montoya Martínez, "El Castillo de Chincoya," *Boletín de Estudios Gienenses* 101 (1980): 17–25.

26. Manuel Nieto Cumplido, *Orígenes del regionalismo andaluz, 1235–1325* (Córdoba: Monte de Piedad y Caja de Ahorros de Córdoba, 1979), 122–25, no. 5; *MHE*, 1:221–23, no. 101.

27. *CAX (GJ)*, 34–35, ch. 12, and *CAX*, 9–10, ch. 11–12, erroneously dated these events in 1263.

28. Ballesteros, "Itinerario de Alfonso X," *BRAH* 109 (1936): 381, n. 1, 382, n. 1; *MHE*, 1:224–27, no. 102; Mateo Hernández Vegas, *Ciudad Rodrigo: La catedral y la ciudad*, 2 vols. (Salamanca: Imprenta comercial salmantina, 1935), 1:169; Ángel Barrios García, José María Monsalvo Antón, and Gregorio del Ser Quijano, *Documentación medieval del Archivo municipal de Ciudad Rodrigo* (Salamanca: Diputación Provincial de Salamanca, 1988), nos. 3–4; Julián Sánchez Ruano, *Fuero de Salamanca* (Salamanca: Sebastián Cerezo, 1870), xxi.

29. *La gran conquista de Ultramar: Biblioteca Nacional MS 1187*, ed. Louis Cooper (Madison, Wis.: Hispanic Seminary, 1989), 257, ch. 556; Martínez Montávez, "Relaciones," 360, citing al-Nuwayrī, *Nibāya*, 31–32.

30. *CAX (GJ)*, 40–43, ch. 15; *CAX*, 11, ch. 15; González Jiménez, *Alfonso X*, 181–83.

31. *CJI*, 7:36–78, ch. 379–405, esp. 382; Ballesteros, *Alfonso X*, 388–90; Zurita, *Anales*, 1:614–25.

32. Domínguez Sánchez, *Clemente IV*, 127–31, 145, 147–48, 165–66, nos. 20, 35, 37, 57; Jordan, *Clément IV*, 1:26, 30, 32, 79, nos. 112 reg., 128, 134, 300; Goñi Gaztambide, *Historia*, 196–98.

33. Bernat Desclot, *Cronica*, ed. M. Coll i Alentorn, 5 vols. (Barcelona: Barcino, 1949–51), 3:5–7, ch. 65; Ramon Muntaner, *Cronica*, ed. Enric Bagüe, 2d ed., 9 vols. (Barcelona: Barcino, 1927–52), 1: 36–40, ch. 12–13.

34. *CJI*, 7:80–98, ch. 407–22; Zurita, *Anales*, 1:630–32; Pierre Guichard, *Un señor musulman en la España cristiana: El ra'is de Crevillente (1243–1318)* (Alicante: Instituto de Estudios Alicantinos, 1976).

35. *CJI*, 8:1–23, ch. 423–33; Desclot, *Cronica*, 1:7–9, ch. 65; Muntaner, *Cronica*, 1: 42–46, ch. 16–17; Zurita, *Anales*, 1:632–34; Ballesteros, *Alfonso X*, 394–96; Juan Torres Fontes, *La reconquista de Murcia en 1266 por Jaime I de Aragón* (Murcia: CSIC, 1967).

36. *CJI*, 8:23–40, ch. 439–51; Zurita, *Anales*, 1:656–59; Ballesteros, *Alfonso X*, 395–401; González Jiménez, *Alfonso X*, 183–85.

37. Domínguez Sánchez, *Clemente IV*, 165–66, 169–70, 181–82, 224–27, nos. 57, 61, 74, 114; Jordan, *Clément IV*, 1:79, 334, 385, nos. 300, 848 reg., 1086; Goñi Gaztambide, *Historia*, 198–200.

38. Juan Torres Fontes, *Documentos del siglo XIII*, CODOM 2 (Murcia: Academia Alfonso X el Sabio, 1969), 22–28, nos. 23–31; *MHE*, 1:231–32, no. 105; *CJI*, 8:42–48, ch. 453–56.

39. *Dhakhīra*, 108, cited by Arié, *L'Espagne*, 65–66; Ibn Khaldūn, *Histoire*, 4:88–89; Harvey, *Islamic Spain*, 30–33; Francisco García Fitz, "Alfonso X, el reino de Granada y los Banū Ašqīlūla: Estrategías políticas de disolución durante la segunda mitad del siglo XIII" *AEM* 27 (1997): 216–37.

40. Manuel Rodrigues Lapa, *Cantigas d'escarnho e de maldezir dos cancioneiros medievais galego-portugueses*, 2nd ed. (Vigo: Galaixa, 1970), 620–21; Rubiera, "Los Banū Escallola," 90–91.

41. *CAX (GJ)*, 40–41, ch. 15; *CAX*, 11, ch. 15.

42. *DAAX*, 341–44, nos. 314–15; González Jiménez, *Alfonso X*, 186–87.

43. Emiliano González Díez, *Colección diplomática del Concejo de Burgos (884–1369)* (Burgos: Ayuntamiento de Burgos, 1984), 119, no. 37; *DAAX*, 331–32, no. 309; Sánchez Ruano, *Fuero de Salamanca*, xxi–xxii.

44. Antonio López Ferreiro, *Fueros municipales de Santiago y de su tierra* (Santiago de Compostela, 1895; reprint, Madrid: Castilla, 1975), 286; Ladero Quesada, *Fiscalidad*, 57–75.

45. Domínguez Sánchez, *Clemente IV*, 247–51, nos. 129–31; Jordan, *Clément IV*, 140–41, 405, nos. 458 reg., 459, 1205; Ballesteros, "Itinerario," *BRAH* 109 (1936): 452 n. 1; Sánchez Ruano, *Fuero de Salamanca*, xxii.

46. Domínguez Sánchez, *Clemente IV*, 260–63, no. 140; Jordan, *Clément IV*, 157–59, no. 500; Ballesteros, *Sevilla*, clxii, no. 155.

47. *DAAX*, 362, no. 332; González Jiménez, *Alfonso X*, 187.

48. *CAX (GJ)*, 40–43, ch. 15; *CAX*, 11, ch. 15; González Jiménez, *Alfonso X*, 181–82; Arié, *L'Espagne*, 67; García Fitz, "Alfonso X y sus relaciones," 56–60.

49. Ibn 'Idhārī, *Al-Bayān*, 3:337; Ballesteros, "Itinerario," *BRAH* 109 (1936): 447–48.

50. Domínguez Sánchez, *Clemente IV*, 273–74, no. 151; Jordan, *Clément IV*, 414, no. 1264.

51. Dufourcq, *L'Espagne*, 163, citing ACA Reg. 15, fol. 130v; Mosquera Merino, *Señoría de Ceuta*, 216–18.

52. Ibn al-Qabtawrī, *Rasā'il*, 129–34, cited by Mosquera Merino, *Señoría de Ceuta*, 208–10; Máximo Diago Hernando, "La monarquía castellana y los Staufer: Contactos políticos y diplomáticos en los siglos XII y XIII," *ETF* 8 (1995): 51–83, esp. 17–29.

53. González Jiménez and González Gómez, *Jerez de la Frontera*.

54. *DAAX*, 364, 379–81, 393–94, 396, 440–43, nos. 335, 355, 371, 374, 416; Ladero Quesada and González Jiménez, "Gibraltar," 226–28, no. 3; González Jiménez, *Alfonso X*, 191–98.

55. *DAAX*, 293–94, 332–33, nos. 263–64, 310; Hipólyto Sancho de Sopranis, "La incorporación de Cádiz a la Corona de Castilla bajo Alfonso X," *Hispania* 9 (1949): 355–86, and "La repoblación y repartimiento de Cádiz por Alfonso X," *Hispania* 15 (1955): 490–503; González, *Repartimiento de Sevilla*, 1:82–85; Manuel González Jiménez, "La obra repobladora de Alfonso X en las tierras de Cádiz," in *Cádiz en el siglo XIII*, 7–20.

56. Jean Guiraud, *Les registres d'Urbain IV (1261–1264): Recueil des bulles de ce pape*, 4 vols., Bibliothèque des Écoles Françaises d'Athènes et de Rome ser. 2, no. 13 (Paris: Fontemoing, 1892–1958), 164, no. 348; Demetrio Mansilla, "Creación de los obispados de Cádiz y Algeciras," *Hispania Sacra* 10 (1957): 243–71, esp. 263, no. 1; Ballesteros, *Alfonso X*, 329.

57. Domínguez Sánchez, *Clemente IV*, 161–62, 245–47, nos. 53, 128; Jordan, *Clément IV*, 55, 140, nos. 204, 457; *DAAX*, 365–67, nos. 336, 338; Pablo Antón Solé, "La iglesia gaditana en el siglo XIII," in *Cádiz en el siglo XIII*, 37–48; José Sánchez Herrero, "El episcopología medieval gaditano, siglos XIII al XV," *ELEM* 1 (1980): 443–65, esp. 446–48.

58. "Fragmento del itinerario del Hermano Mauricio y del señor Andrés Nicolas, año 1273," in José García Mercadal, *Viajes de extranjeros por España desde los tiempos más remotos hasta fines del siglo XVI* (Madrid: Sociedad General Española de Librería, 1952), 223–24; *DAAX*, 516–19, no. 487.

59. *DAAX*, 369–70, 372–76, 388–90, nos. 325, 342–43, 345–46, 348, 356–57, 362–67; Ladero Quesada and González Jiménez, "Gibraltar," 204, 209.

60. *CLC*, 1:64–85; *DAAX*, 376–78, no. 349; O'Callaghan, *Cortes*, 22, 187–90; González Jiménez, *Alfonso X*, 210–13.

61. Juan Torres Fontes, "El estatuto concejil murciano en la época de Alfonso X el Sabio," *Documentos del siglo XIII*, CODOM, 2:xxi–lxxvi; González Jiménez, *Alfonso X*, 199–205.

62. Torres Fontes, *Fueros*, 27–28, 64–65, nos. 30, 69, and "Los mudéjares murcianos en la Edad Media," *Actas del III Simposio Internacional de Mudejarismo* (Teruel: Instituto de Estudios Turolenses, 1986), 55–66, and "Jaime I y Alfonso X: Dos criterios de repoblación," *Actas del VII Congreso de Historia de la Corona de Aragón* (Barcelona: Fidel Rodríguez Ferrán, 1962), 342–40; *CAX (GJ)*, 41–44, ch. 15–16; *CAX*, 11, ch. 15–16.

63. *CSM*, 1:560–62, no. 169; O'Callaghan, *Cantigas*, 121–25.

64. Juan Torres Fontes, *Repartimiento de Murcia* (Murcia: Academia Alfonso X el Sabio, 1960), v–xi, 1–251.

65. Juan Torres Fontes, *Documentos de Alfonso X el Sabio*, *CODOM* 1 (Murcia: Academia Alfonso X el Sabio, 1963), 17–21, 35–36, 39, 43, 47, 54, 56, nos. 11, 24, 26, and *Fueros*, 113–14, no. 104, and "El estatuto concejil," xxi–lxxvi; Ángel Luis Molina Molina, *Documentos de Pedro I*, *CODOM* 7 (Murcia: Academia Alfonso X el Sabio, 1978), 53, 139–40, nos. 29, 77; *MHE*, 1:230–31, 278–87, nos. 104, 128.

66. Juan Torres Fontes, *Repartimiento de Lorca* (Murcia: Academia Alfonso X el Sabio, 1977), 1–51; and *Repartimiento de Orihuela* (Murcia: Academia Alfonso X el Sabio, 1988), 1–87; and *Fueros*, 86–93, 97–101, 103–7, 113–14, 117–31, 134–35, 137, 143–47, 153, nos. 67–69, 71, 73–76, 82–86, 89, 92–93, 95–96, 104–16, 120–22, 125, 128, 131, 134, 142; Juan Manuel del Estal, *Documentos inéditos de Alfonso X el Sabio y del Infante, su hijo, Don Sancho* (Alicante: Juan Manuel del Estal, 1984), 101, no. 1, and "Problemática en torno a la conquista y repoblación de las ciudades musulmanes de Orihuela y Alicante por Alfonso X el Sabio," *La ciudad hispánica durante los siglos XIII al XVI*, 2 vols. (Madrid: Universidad Complutense, 1985), 2: 798–810.

67. Torres Fontes, *Fueros*, 82–87, 93–96, 100–102, 107–13, 132–33, 136–42, 150–52, nos. 64–66, 77–79, 87 88, 91, 97–101, 103, 116–19, 123, 126–27, 137, 139–40; and "El obispado de Cartagena en el siglo XIII," *Hispania* 13 (1953): 340–401, 515–80; *MHE*, 1:233, no. 106; Juan Manuel del Estal, *Alicante, de villa a ciudad (1252–1490)* (Alicante: Juan Manuel del Estal, 1990).

68. Torres Fontes, *Documentos del siglo XIII*, 21–22, 31–33, 36–38, 44, 60–63, 66–70, nos. 22, 35–36, 39, 42–43, 49, 63–67, 71–72, 74–75, and *Fueros*, 3:104, 112, 152–53, nos. 94, 102, 141.

69. O'Callaghan, *Cantigas*, 159–62.

70. J. M. Canivez, *Statuta capitulorum generalium Ordinis Cisterciensis*, 8 vols. (Louvain: Revue d'Histoire ecclésiastique, 1933–41), 3:91, ad annum 1270, no. 74; Joseph F. O'Callaghan, "The Affiliation of the Order of Calatrava with the Order of Cîteaux," in *The Spanish Military Order of Calatrava and Its Affiliates* (London: Variorum, 1975), no. 1.

71. Santiago Domínguez Sánchez, *Documentos de Gregorio X (1272–1276) referentes a España* (León: Universidad de León, 1997), 150–51, no. 43; Jean Guiraud, *Les registres de Grégoire X (1271–1276): Recueil des bulles de ce pape*. Bibliothèque des Écoles Françaises d'Athènes et de Rome ser. 2, no. 12. (Paris: Thorin, Fontemoing, 1892–1906), 75–76, no. 200.

72. Canivez, *Statuta*, 3:122, ad annum 1273, nos. 37–38; Juan Torres Fontes, "La Orden de Santa María de España," *AEM* 11 (1981): 810–14, nos. 1–4, and "La Orden de Santa María de España," *Miscelánea Medieval Murciana* 3 (1977): 75–118.

73. Juan Menéndez Pidal, *Noticias acerca de la Orden militar de Santa María de España instituída por Alfonso X* (Madrid: RABM, 1907) 20, no. 2.

74. Ordinance of Zamora, art. 31, *CLC*, 1:91–92.

75. Torres Fontes, "La Orden de Santa María de España," *AEM* 11 (1981): 810–11, nos. 1–2; Juan Pérez Villamil, "Orígen e instituto de la Orden militar de Santa María de España," *BRAH* 74 (1919): 243–71.

76. Manuel González Jiménez, "Relaciones de las órdenes militares castellanas con la

Corona (siglos XIII–XIV)," *HID* 18 (1991): 209–22; Carlos de Ayala Martínez, "La monarquía y las órdenes militares durante el reinado de Alfonso X," *Hispania* 178 (1991): 409–65.

77. Santiago Domínguez Sánchez, *Documentos de Nicolás III (1277–1280) referentes a España* (León: Universidad de León, 1999), 340–45, esp. 342, no. 118; Jules Gay, *Les registres de Nicolas III (1277–1280): Recueil des bulles de ce pape*, Bibliothèque des Écoles Françaises d'Athènes et de Rome ser. 2, no. 14 (Paris: A. Fontemoing, 1898–1938), 342, no. 743; O'Callaghan, *Learned King*, 58–63.

78. Juan Torres Fontes, "La Orden de Santa María de España y el Maestre de Cartagena," *Murcia Murgetana* 10 (1952): 95–102, and "La Orden de Santa María de España y el Monasterio de Santa María la Real de Murcia," *Alcanate* 2 (2000–2001): 83–96.

79. *CAX (GJ)*, 44–45, ch. 16; *CAX*, 11–12, ch. 16; González Jiménez, *Alfonso X*, 216.

80. *CAX (GJ)*, 45, ch. 16; *CAX*, 11, ch. 16; Arié, *L'Espagne*, 67; Ballesteros, *Alfonso X*, 403–7.

81. *CLC*, 1:85–86, no. 15; *CAX (GJ)*, 49–53, ch. 18; *CAX*, 13, ch. 18; O'Callaghan, *Cortes*, 23, 131.

82. *CJI*, 9:12–14, ch. 497–99; Zurita, *Anales*, 1:674–80; O'Callaghan, *Learned King*, 76–77; González Jiménez, *Alfonso X*, 219.

83. Manzano Rodríguez, *Intervención*, 12, citing *Al-Dhakhīra al-saniyaa fi ta'rikh al-dawla al-marīniyya*, ed. A. Benmansour (Rabat: Dar al-Mankhur, 1972), 121.

84. Arié, *L'Espagne*, 67, citing *Al-Dhakhīra*, 137.

85. *CJI*, 9:16–18, 22–24, ch. 501, 505–7; Zurita, *Anales*, 1:681–82; Robert I. Burns, S.J., "Warrior Neighbors: Alfonso el Sabio and Crusader Valencia, an Archival Case Study in His International Relations," *Viator* 21 (1990): 147–202, esp. 165–67.

86. *DAAX*, 411–12, no. 391.

87. Ibn 'Abī Zar', *Rawd al-Qirtās*, 2:585, dated the appeal in A.H. 669 (1271); Ibn Khaldūn, *Histoire*, 4:60, put it in 670 (1271–72). *Al-Dhakhīra*, 126, 130, cited by Manzano Rodríguez, *Intervención*, 8 n. 20, mentioned appeals in both years.

88. *CAX (GJ)*, 70–76, ch. 22; *CAX*, 17–18, ch. 22; *CAXI*, 204–5, ch. 51; Ibn Khaldūn, *Histoire*, 4:89; Arié, *L'Espagne*, 67.

89. *CAX (GJ)*, xxxi–xxxvi.

90. *CAX (GJ)*, 70–76, ch. 22; *CAX*, 18–19, ch. 22, includes letters to Felipe, Nuño, and Lope, and summarizes the others. Gonzalo de la Finojosa, "Continuación," 106:20–21, ch. 240, related that Abū Yūsuf sent the magnates' incriminating letters to Alfonso X.

91. See the text, which is undated, in *CAX (GJ)*, 123–26, ch. 43, and *CAX*, 32–33, ch. 43. Arabic and Latin copies were made but do not seem to be extant.

92. *CAX (GJ)*, 76–92, ch. 23–26; *CAX*, 19–23, ch. 23–26; O'Callaghan, *Learned King*, 214–23, and *Cantigas*, 127–30, and *Cortes*, 23–25.

93. *CAX (GJ)*, 92–116, ch. 27–40; *CAX*, 23–31, ch. 27–40.

94. Rubiera, "Los Banū Escallola," 92.

95. Emilio Lafuente y Alcántara, *Inscripciones árabes de Granada* (Madrid: Imprenta Nacional, 1859), 207–8; Al-Makkarī, *History*, 2:344–45.

96. *CAX (GJ)*, 37–40, 70–76, ch. 13–14, 22; *CAX*, 17–19, ch. 13–14, 22; *CAXI*, 204–5,

ch. 51; Gonzalo de la Finojosa, "Continuación," 106:19–20, ch. 240; Ibn Khaldūn, *Histoire*, 4:89; Arié, *L'Espagne*, 67; O'Callaghan, *Learned King*, 223–24; García Fitz, "Alfonso X y sus relaciones," 60–65.

CHAPTER 4. CRUSADE AGAINST THE MARINIDS

1. *CAX (GJ)*, 127–42, ch. 44–51; *CAX*, 33–38, ch. 45–51; Harvey, *Islamic Spain*, 151–64; García Fitz, "Conquista de Tarifa," 109–11; González Jiménez, *Alfonso X*, 262–67; O'Callaghan, *Learned King*, 223–28.

2. *CAX (GJ)*, 144–51, ch. 52 and *CAX*, 38–41, ch. 52; Paula K. Rodgers, "Alfonso X Writes to His Son: Reflections on the *Crónica de Alfonso X*," *Exemplaria Hispanica* 1 (1991–92): 60–79.

3. *CAX (GJ)*, 144, ch. 52; *CAX*, 38, ch. 52; Richard P. Kinkade, "Alfonso X, *Cantiga* 235, and the Events of 1269–1278," *Speculum* 67 (1992): 296; O'Callaghan, *Cantigas*, 131.

4. *CAX (GJ)*, 152–57, ch. 53–54; *CAX*, 41–43, ch. 53–54; González Jiménez, *Alfonso X*, 268.

5. *MHE*, 1:271–73, no. 125; Zurita, *Anales*, 1:703–4, 706.

6. *CAX (GJ)*, 164–65, ch. 57; *CAX*, 45, ch. 57; *CSM*, 1:721–24, no. 235; Kinkade, "Alfonso X, *Cantiga* 235," 297–98; O'Callaghan, *Cantigas*, 131–32; Burns, "Warrior Neighbors," 167 n. 35; Ballesteros, *Alfonso X*, 670–71.

7. *CAX (GJ)*, 157–70, ch. 55–56, 58; *CAX*, 43–48, ch. 55–56, 58; O'Callaghan, *Learned King*, 228–29; González Jiménez, *Alfonso X*, 268–71; Ballesteros, *Alfonso X*, 680.

8. Domínguez Sánchez, *Gregorio X*, 314–16, nos. 166–67.

9. *CAX (GJ)*, 170–72, ch. 59; *CAX*, 47–48, ch. 59; O'Callaghan, *Learned King*, 229–30; González Jiménez, *Alfonso X*, 273–75; Ballesteros, *Alfonso X*, 680.

10. O'Callaghan, *Learned King*, 231–33; González Jiménez, *Alfonso X*, 278–86; Ballesteros, *Alfonso X*, 680; Carlos de Ayala Martínez, "Alfonso X, Beaucaire y el fin de la pretensión imperial," *Hispania* 47 (1987): 5–31; Zurita, *Anales*, 1:736–46.

11. *CSM*, 1:722, no. 235; Kinkade, "Alfonso X, *Cantiga* 235," 302–6; O'Callaghan, *Cantigas*, 133–35; González Jiménez, *Alfonso X*, 290–92.

12. Ibn Khaldūn, Histoire, 4:66; Louis de Mas Latrie, *Traités de paix et de commerce et documents divers concernant les relations des chrétiens avec les arabes de l'Afrique septentrionale a moyen âge*, 2 vols. (Paris, 1866; reprint, Philadelphia: Burt Franklin, 1963), 2: 285–86, no. 3; Antonio Capmany y de Montpalau, *Antiguos tratados de paces y alianzas entre algunos reyes de Aragón y diferentes principes infieles de Asia y Africa desde el siglo XIII hasta el XV* (Madrid: Imprenta Real, 1786), 1–4; Zurita, *Anales*, 1:758; Dufourcq, *L'Espagne*, 168; Mosquera Merino, *Señoría de Ceuta*, 152–60.

13. *CAX (GJ)*, 175–77, ch. 61; *CAX*, 48–49, ch. 61; Ballesteros, *Alfonso X*, 633–37; Mariano Arribas Palau, "Los Benimerines en los pactos concordados entre Aragón y Granada," in *Actas del Primer Congreso de Estudios Árabes e Islámicos, Córdoba 1962* (Madrid: Comité Permanente del Congreso de Estudios Árabes e Islámicos, 1964), 179–88; García Fitz, "Conquista de Tarifa," 109–14.

14. *Al-Hulal al-Mawsiyya: Crónica árabe de las dinastías almorávide, almohade y benimerín*, tr. Ambrosio Huici Miranda, *Colección de crónicas árabes de la Reconquista* 1 (Tetuán: Editora Marroquí, 1952), 196–99; Ibn Khaldūn, *Histoire*, 4:76; Ibn Marzūq, *El Musnad*, 101, ch. 1; *CSM*, 1:588–89, no. 181; O'Callaghan, *Cantigas*, 135–37.

15. Manzano Rodríguez, *Intervención*, xxvi, 3–4; María Jesús Viguera, "La intervención de los Benimerines en al-Andalus," *Actas del Congreso Relaciones de la Península Ibérica con el Magreb, siglos XIII–XIV* (Madrid: CSIC, 1988), 237–48, and "Religión y política de los Benimerines," *Ilu* (1995): 285–88.

16. Francisco García Fitz, "Los acontecimientos político-militares de la frontera en el último cuarto del siglo XIII," *Revista de Historia Militar* 32 (1988): 9–71, esp. 15 (diagram of the campaign).

17. Ibn Abī Zarʿ, *Rawd al-Qirtās*, 2:591–94; Ibn Khaldūn, *Histoire*, 4:76–77; Harvey, *Islamic Spain*, 154–55, quoting *Al-Dhakhīra al-Saniyya*; Al-Makkarī, *History*, 2:345; Arié, *L'Espagne*, 69–70; Manzano Rodríguez, *Intervención*, 18–19; Ballesteros, *Alfonso X*, 633–37; García Fitz, "Acontecimientos, 10–18, and "¿Hubo estrategía en la edad media? A propósito de las relaciones castellano-musulmanas durante la segunda mitad del siglo XIII," *RFLH* ser. 2, 15 (1998): 837–54.

18. *Anales Toledanos III*, *ES* 23:420; Jofre de Loaysa, *Crónica*, 78–80, ch. 12–13; *CAX (GJ)*, 183–84, ch. 64, and *CAX*, 51, ch. 64; Manuel González Jiménez, "Unos anales del reinado de Alfonso X," *BRAH* 192 (1995): 477, ch. 6; Gonzalo de la Finojosa, "Continuación," 106:16–17, 22, ch. 238–39; O'Callaghan, *Learned King*, 235–36.

19. Ibn Abī Zarʿ, *Rawd al-Qirtās*, 2:594–96; Ibn Khaldūn, *Histoire*, 4:77–79, 89–90; Harvey, *Islamic Spain*, 155–56, quoting *Al-Dhakhīra al-Saniyya*; *Al-Hulal*, 201; Manzano Rodríguez, *Intervención*, 19–20; Rubiera, "Los Banū Escallola," 92–93.

20. Ibn Abī Zarʿ, *Rawd al-Qirtās*, 2:596–97; Ibn Khaldūn, *Histoire*, 4:77–79; *CSM*, 2:188–89, no. 323, O'Callaghan, *Cantigas*, 137–38.

21. *CSM*, 1:561–62, no. 169; O'Callaghan, *Cantigas*, 138–39; Burns, "Warrior Neighbors," 171.

22. *CJI*, 9:42–58, ch. 523–35; Domínguez Sánchez, *Gregorio X*, 314–316, 339–40, 348, nos. 166–67, 192, 198; Guiraud, *Grégoire X*, 280, 345, nos. 646 reg., 840 reg.; Zurita, *Anales*, 1:707–16; Ballesteros, *Alfonso X*, 773–76; Goñi Gaztambide, *Historia*, 225, n. 139.

23. Domínguez Sánchez, *Gregorio X*, 240–43, 257–58, 267–87, 341–42, 368–70, 378–79, nos. 110–11, 128–29, 136–40, 193–94, 214–15, 222; Guiraud, *Grégoire X*, 281, 359–60, nos. 649 reg., 910, 912.

24. Domínguez Sánchez, *Gregorio X*, 343–45, no. 195; Guiraud, *Grégoire X*, 269, no 629 reg.; Goñi Gaztambide, *Historia*, 201–2.

25. Ibn Abī Zarʿ, *Rawd al-Qirtās*, 2:598–600.

26. Ibn Abī Zarʿ, *Rawd al-Qirtās*, 2:600–602; Harvey, *Islamic Spain*, 157, quoting *Al-Dhakhīra al-Saniyya*; *Anales Toledanos III*, *ES* 23:420; Al-Makkarī, *History*, 2:345–46; *CAX (GJ)*, 178–80, ch. 62; *CAX*, 49–50, ch. 62; Jofre de Loaysa, *Crónica*, 82, ch. 14–15; Gonzalo de la Finojosa, "Continuación," 106:21–22, ch. 240; Manzano Rodríguez, *Intervención*, 23–24.

27. Martínez Montávez, "Relaciones," 360, n. 51, citing al-Maqrīzī, *Histoire des sultans mamlouks de l'Égypte*, tr. Étienne Quatremère, 4 pts. in 2 vols. (Paris: Oriental Translation Fund, 1837–45), 1.2: 125–26.

28. Ibn Khaldūn, *Histoire*, 4: 79–80; Ibn Marzūq, *El Musnad*, 101, ch. 1.

29. Ibn Abī Zarʿ, *Rawd al-Qirtās*, 2:602; Ibn Khaldūn, *Histoire*, 4:80.

30. *CAX (GJ)*, 180–81, ch. 63 and *CAX*, 50–51, ch. 63; Gonzalo de la Finojosa, "Continuación," 106:22, ch. 240; Al-Makkarī, *History*, 2:346; González Jiménez, *Alfonso X*, 299–303; Torres Delgado, *Granada*, 191–94; Zurita, *Anales*, 1:758–61.

31. Ibn Abī Zarʿ, *Rawd al-Qirtās*, 2:605–6; Ibn Khaldūn, *Histoire*, 4:81; Ibn Marzūq, *El Musnad*, 102, ch. 1; CAX *(GJ)*, 185–87, ch. 65 and *CAX*, 51–52, ch. 65; Manzano Rodríguez, *Intervención*, 26–30.

32. Pedro Marín, *Los miraculos romanzados de como sacó Santo Domingo de Silos los cautivos de la catividad*, ed. Sebastián de Vergara (Madrid: Francisco del Hierro, 1736); José María Cossío "Cautivos de moros en el siglo XIII: El texto de Pero Marín," *Al-Andalus* 7 (1942): 49–112, esp. 57; Juan Torres Fontes, "La cautividad en la frontera gaditana (1275–1285)," *Cádiz en el siglo XIII*, 75–92, esp. 84; Mosquera Merino, *Señoria de Ceuta*, 165.

33. *CAX (GJ)*, 189–90, ch. 67; *CAX*, 52–53, ch. 67; Manzano Rodríguez, *Intervención*, 28–29.

34. Ibn Khaldūn, *Histoire*, 4:930–96.

35. Bernat Desclot, *Crònica*, 3:10–13, ch. 66; *CSM* 1:722–23, no. 235; Ramon Muntaner, *Crònica*, 1:61, ch. 24; Ballesteros, *Alfonso X*, 769–78; Kinkade, "Alfonso X, Cantiga 235," 311–12.

36. González Díez, *Burgos*, 129–30, no. 44; *CAX (GJ)*, 189–90, ch. 66–67; *CAX*, 52–53, ch. 66–67.

37. *CAX (GJ)*, 193, ch. 68, and *CAX*, 53, ch. 68; Gonzalo de la Finojosa, "Continuación," 106:17, ch. 238; O'Callaghan, *Learned King*, 236–41; González Jiménez, *Alfonso X*, 305–14; Ballesteros, *Alfonso X*, 785–87, 841–48.

38. Peter Linehan, "*Quaedam de quibus dubitans*: On Preaching the Crusades in Alfonso X's Castile," *HID* 27 (2000): 129–54; González Jiménez, *Alfonso X*, 297.

39. Atanasio López, "Cruzada contra los saracenos en el reino de Castilla predicada por los franciscanos de la Provincia de Santiago," *Archivo Ibero-Americano* 9 (1918): 322–27; Raynaldus, *Annales*, a. 1276, no. 20 fragment; Goñi Gaztambide, *Historia*, 202.

40. *CJI*, 9:82–91, ch. 554–60; Bernat Desclot, *Crònica*, 3:13–17, ch. 67; Ramon Muntaner, *Crònica*, 1:635, ch. 26; Zurita, *Anales*, 1:762–70; Ballesteros, *Alfonso X*, 775–77.

41. Rymer, *Foedera*, 1.2:151–52, 157–58, 160, 177.

42. Martínez Montávez, "Relaciones," 360–71, citing al-Nuwayrī, *Nibāya*, 48, Ibn al-Furāt, *Ta'rīj*, 1:157, 7:44, al-Maqrīzī, *Sulūk*, 1.3:621, 666–67, and al-Yūnīnī, *Dayl*, fol. 95r.

43. O'Callaghan, *Cortes*, 135–36, and *Learned King*, 243–44, and 340 n. 35; González Jiménez, *Alfonso X*, 314–16.

44. *CSM*, 1:660–61, 721–24, nos. 209, 235; Jofre de Loaysa, *Crónica*, 96, ch. 23; *CAX (GJ)*, 194, ch. 68; *CAX*, 53, ch. 68; Kinkade, "Alfonso, Cantiga 235," 313–18; O'Callaghan, *Cantigas*, 141–51, and *Learned King*, 241–43; Ballesteros, *Alfonso X*, 818–27.

45. Manzano Rodríguez, *Intervención*, 36–37; García Fitz, "Acontecimientos," 18–23, esp. 20 (diagram), and "Alfonso X y sus relaciones," 66–77.

46. J. M. Escudero, "Súplica hecha al Papa Juan XXI para que absolviese al rey de Castilla, D. Alfonso X, del juramento de no acuñar otra moneda que los dineros prietos," *RABM* 2 (1872): 58–59; Ballesteros, *Alfonso X*, 836–37.

47. Manzano Rodríguez, *Intervención*, 37–40, citing al-Qabtawrī, *Rasā'il, Risāla I*, the first of the Ceutan letters; Mosquera Merino, *Señoría de Ceuta*, 180–82.

48. Ibn Abī Zarʿ, *Rawd al-Qirtās*, 2:608–13; Ibn Khaldūn, *Histoire*, 4:85–87, 90; Manzano Rodríguez, *Intervención*, 41–42, 46–47, citing al-Qabtawrī, *Rasā'il, Risāla I*; *Al-Hulal*, 201.

49. Ibn Abī Zarʿ, *Rawd al-Qirtās*, 2:614–16; Ibn Khaldūn, *Histoire*, 4:88; Manzano Rodríguez, *Intervención*, 48–55, citing al-Qabtawrī, *Rasā'il, Risāla III*; Mosquera Merino, *Señoría de Ceuta*, 183–85.

50. *CSM*, 1:674–76, no. 215; O'Callaghan, *Cantigas*, 152–53; Jesús Montoya Martínez, "Historia de Andalucía en las Cantigas de Santa María," in *Andalucía medieval: Actas del I Congreso de Historia de Andalucía, diciembre de 1976*, 2 vols. (Córdoba: Monte de Piedad y Caja de Ahorros, 1978), 1:266–68.

51. Ibn Abī Zarʿ, *Rawd al-Qirtās*, 2:616–18; Ibn Khaldūn, *Histoire*, 4:88; *Al-Hulal*, 201; *CSM*, 1:721–24, no. 235; Manzano Rodríguez, *Intervención*, 34–44; Torres Delgado, *Granada* 194–95; Arié, *L'Espagne*, 71.

52. Ibn Abī Zarʿ, *Rawd al-Qirtās*, 2:618–19; Ibn Khaldūn, *Histoire*, 4:90–91, 97–98; Arié, *L'Espagne*, 71–72.

53. Juan Gil de Zamora, *Liber de preconiis civitatis Numantine*, 146; O'Callaghan, *Learned King*, 240–47, and *Cantigas*, 156–59; González Jiménez, *Alfonso X*, 324–28.

54. Domínguez Sánchez, *Nicolás III*, 191–206, 226, 263–65, 267–69, 286–87, nos. 15–28, 46, 73, 75, 81; Gay, *Nicolas III*, 9–11, 56–58, nos. 27–32, 34, 36–37, 39–41, 186–88; Ballesteros, *Alfonso X*, 847.

55. Ángel Barrios García, Alberto Martín Expósito, and Gregorio del Ser Quijano, *Documentación medieval del Archivo municipal de Alba de Tormes* (Salamanca: Universidad de Salamanca, 1982), 52–53, no. 14; González Díez, *Burgos*, 141–42, 143–46, 147–49, 152–55, 157–62, nos. 57, 59–62, 64–66, 70–72, 75–77, 79; Ballesteros, *Alfonso X*, 853–56, 875, 880, 885.

56. Domínguez Sánchez, *Nicolás III*, 334–45, nos. 114–18; Linehan, *Spanish Church*, 218–20; O'Callaghan, *Learned King*, 58–63, 248; González Jiménez, *Alfonso X*, 329–32.

57. *CAX (GJ)*, 195–96, ch. 69; *CAX*, 53–54, ch. 69.

58. *CAX (GJ)*, 195–96, 200–202, ch. 69, 72; *CAX*, 54–56, ch. 69, 72; Ibn Abī Zarʿ, *Rawd al-Qirtās*, 2:621–22; García Fitz, "Acontecimientos," 27 (diagram).

59. Ibn Abī Zarʿ, *Rawd al-Qirtās*, 2:622–23, 625–27; Ibn Khaldūn, *Histoire*, 4:101; Manzano Rodríguez, *Intervención*, 60–63; Ballesteros, *Alfonso X*, 885–904; Pérez Embid, "Marina real," 179–83; Mosquera Merino, *Señoría de Ceuta*, 252–59

60. *CAX (GJ)*, 202–4, ch. 72; *CAX*, 56–57, ch. 72; Gonzalo de la Finojosa, "Continuación," 106:18–19, ch. 239; Antonio Torremocha Silva, *Algeciras entre la Cristiandad e el Islam:*

Estudio sobre el cerco y la conquista de Algeciras por el rey Alfonso XI de Castilla (Algeciras: Instituto de Estudios Campogibraltareños, 1994), 67–112.

61. *DAAX*, 475–82, 484–87, 493–94, 495, 500, nos. 451–58, 466, 468; González Jiménez, *Alfonso X*, 332–35.

62. Ibn Abī Zarʻ, *Rawd al-Qirṭās*, 2:628–32; Ibn Khaldūn, *Histoire*, 4:102; *CAX (GJ)*, 204, ch. 72; *CAX*, 57, ch. 72; Manzano Rodríguez, *Intervención*, 64–65.

63. *CAX (GJ)*, 205–6, ch. 73; *CAX*, 57, ch. 73; *MHE*, 2:7, 18, nos. 152, 170; Rymer, *Foedera*, 1.2:184.

64. For a plan of the castle of Moclín, see Torres Delgado, *Granada*, plate 2.

65. *CAX (GJ)*, 207–9, ch. 74; *CAX*, 57–58, ch. 74; Ibn Khaldūn, *Histoire*, 4:102–3; *Anales Toledanos III*, *ES* 23: 413–14; Manzano Rodríguez, *Intervención*, 65–66; González Jiménez, *Alfonso X*, 336–37.

66. Torres Fontes, "La Orden de Santa María de España," *Miscelánea Medieval Murciana* 3 (1977): 95–102; O'Callaghan, *Cantigas*, 159–62.

67. Ignacio José Ortega y Cotes et al., *Bullarium ordinis militiae de Calatrava* (Madrid: A. Marín, 1761), 144.

68. *CAX (GJ)*, 209–10, ch. 74; *CAX*, 58, ch. 74; Yitzhak Baer, *A History of the Jews in Christian Spain*, 2 vols. (Philadelphia: Jewish Publication Society, 1966), 1:124–30; González Jiménez, *Alfonso X*, 338–39.

69. *CSM*, 2:250–51, no. 348; O'Callaghan, *Cantigas*, 162–65.

70. Domínguez Sánchez, *Nicolás III*, 394–402, nos. 147–48, 150; O'Callaghan, *Learned King*, 250–51; González Jiménez, *Alfonso X*, 339–41.

71. *CAX (GJ)*, 210–11, ch 74–75; *CAX*, 58–59, ch. 75; Carlos de Ayala Martínez, "Paces castellano-aragonesas de Campillo-Agreda (1281)," *ELEM* 5, 2 (1986): 155–56; Ballesteros, *Alfonso X*, 931–34.

72. *Anales Toledanos III*, *ES*, 23:421; *CAX (GJ)*, 214–15, ch. 75; *CAX*, 59, ch. 75; Jofre de Loaysa, *Crónica*, 98–100, ch. 25–26; Ballesteros, *Alfonso X*, 941–45.

73. *CSM*, 2:292–94, 295–307, nos. 366–67; *DAAX*, 516–20, 540–41, 555, 564–65, 568, nos. 487–88, 510, 519, 522, 527; O'Callaghan, *Cantigas*, ch. 9; González Jiménez, "El Puerto de Santa María," 11–31.

74. *CAX (GJ)*, 214–19, ch. 75; *CAX*, 59–60, ch. 75; *CSM*, 2:339–41, no. 386; O'Callaghan, *Cantigas*, 168–71, and *Learned King*, 255–56; González Jiménez, *Alfonso X*, 342–45.

75. *CAX (GJ)*, 219–25, ch. 76; *CAX*, 59–61, ch. 75–76; *DAAX*, 532–34, no. 503 bis; Peter Linehan, "El cuatro de mayo de 1282," *Alcanate* 4 (2004–5): 147–66; González Jiménez, *Alfonso X*, 345–52; Ballesteros, *Alfonso X*, 992–94.

76. *DAAX*, 548–54, no. 518; Daumet, "Testaments d'Alphonse le Savant," 70–99; Rymer, *Foedera*, 1.2:202.

77. Nieto Cumplido, *Regionalismo*, 131–36, nos. 9–11; *MHE*, 2:72–75, nos. 205–6; O'Callaghan, *Learned King*, 258–64.

78. Ibn Abī Zarʻ, *Rawd al-Qirṭās*, 2:635; Ibn Khaldūn, *Histoire*, 4:105–6.

79. Martínez Montávez, "Relaciones," 372–73, citing Tāqī al-Dīn Ahmad ibn ʻAlī al-Maqrīzī, *Kitāb al-sulūk fī maʻrifat duwal al-mulūk*, ed. Muhammad Mustafā Ziyāda, 2 vols.

(El Cairo, 1939–42), 1.3:706, and Rukn al-Dīn Baybars al-Mansūrī, *Zubdat al-fikra fī ta'rīj al-hiŷra*, University of Cairo, Ms 24.028, vol. 9, fol. 129v; Émile Fricaud, "1283 (682 H): Des émissaires du Sultan Qalāwūn dans la Castille d'Alphonse X et de son fils Sanche IV," *TextArab* 40 (juillet–aout 1996): 8–9. Ahmed Salama of Marlboro College kindly translated this text for me.

80. Ibn Abī Zar', *Rawd al-Qirṭās*, 2:636; Ibn Khaldūn, *Histoire*, 4:105–7; *Al-Hulal*, 202; Gonzalo de la Finojosa, "Continuación," 106:24, ch. 242–43; *CAX (GJ)*, 250–62, ch. 97–98; García Fitz, "Acontecimientos," 36 (diagram).

81. Ibn Abī Zar', *Rawd al-Qirṭās*, 2:635–36; Ibn Khaldūn, *Histoire*, 4:107; Manzano Rodríguez, *Intervención*, 67–71; Ballesteros, *Alfonso X*, 986–92.

82. *CAX (GJ)*, 226–29, ch. 76; *CAX*, 62, ch. 76; Gonzalo de la Finojosa, "Continuación," 106:27–30, ch. 240; *DAAX*, 552, no. 518.

83. Silvestre de Sacy, "Mémoire sur une correspondance de l'empereur de Maroc Yakoub, fils d'Abd-alhakk, avec Philippe-le-Hardi, conservée dans les Archives du Royaume," *Histoire et Mémoires de l'Institut Royal de France, Académie des Inscriptions et Belles Lettres* 9 (1831): 478–506; Mas Latrie, *Traités*, 2:96–97; Manzano Rodríguez, *Intervención*, 68.

84. *DAAX*, 532–35, 548–54, nos. 503 bis, 518; González Jiménez, *Alfonso X*, 353–63.

85. *CSM*, 2:280–81, 370–72, nos. 360, ll. 24–27, 406, ll. 38–41.

86. *CAX (GJ)*, 229, ch. 76; *CAX*, 62, ch. 76. Ibn Abī Zar', *Rawd al-Qirṭās*, 2:637; Giménez Soler, *Corona*, 21 n. 1; Ballesteros, *Alfonso X*, 1008–9.

87. González Díez, *Burgos*, 214–15, no. 128.

88. *CAX (GJ)*, 232, ch. 77; *CAX*, 63, ch. 77; Gonzalo de la Finojosa, "Continuación," 106:31–34, ch. 244; Ibn Abī Zar', *Rawd al-Qirṭās*, 2:637; Ibn Khaldūn, *Histoire*, 4:108.

89. Ibn Abī Zar', *Rawd al-Qirṭās*, 2:638–39; Ibn Khaldūn, *Histoire*, 4:108–9; Gonzalo de la Finojosa, "Continuación," 106:30, ch. 243; Manzano Rodríguez, *Intervención*, 72–80, citing al-Qabtawrī, *Rasā'il, Risāla II*; Mosquera Merino, *Señoría de Ceuta*, 182–83.

90. F. Olivier-Martin, *Les registres de Martin IV (1281–1285): Recueil des bulles de ce pape*, Bibliothèque des Écoles Françaises d'Athènes et de Rome ser. 2, no. 16 (Paris: Fontemoing, 1901–35), 219–20, nos. 479–80.

91. *DAAX*, 557–64, no. 521; Jofre de Loaysa, *Crónica*, 108, ch. 220.32; *CAX (GJ)*, 233–42; ch. 77; *CAX*, 65–66, ch. 77; Gonzalo de la Finojosa, "Continuación," 106:35–36, ch. 244–45.

92. Rymer, *Foedera*, 1.2:230; O'Callaghan, *Learned King*, 266–69; González Jiménez, *Alfonso X*, 364–71; García Fitz, "Acontecimientos," 29–40.

CHAPTER 5. SANCHO IV AND THE CONQUEST OF TARIFA

1. The chief narrative is the *Crónica de Sancho IV*, *BAE* 66: 69–90 (*CSIV*).

2. Mercedes Gaibrois de Ballesteros, *Historia del reinado de Sancho IV*, 3 vols. (Madrid: Revista de Archivos, Bibliotecas y Museos, 1922–28). In 1:1–cxlviii, she published a "Libro

de diferentes cuentas de entrada y distribución de las Rentas reales y gastos de la Casa real (1293–1294)," and in 1:cxlix–clxxxiv, a "Registro de Cancillería de los años 1283 a 1286." Vol. 3 contains 601 royal charters. See also her *María de Molina, tres veces reina* (1936; reprint, Madrid: Espasa-Calpe, 1967), and "Tarifa y la política de Sancho IV de Castilla," *BRAH* 74 (1919): 418–36, 521–29; 75 (1919): 349–55; 76 (1920): 53–77, 123–60, 420–48; 77 (1920): 192–215; reprint, *Tarifa y la política de Sancho IV* (Madrid: Real Academia de la Historia, 1920); José Manuel Nieto Soria, *Sancho IV, 1284–1295* (Palencia: Diputación Provincial, Editorial La Olmeda, 1994).

3. *CSIV*, 69, ch. 1; Gaibrois, *Sancho IV*, 3:i–iii, xi, nos. 1, 5, 15; González Díez, *Burgos*, 219–20, nos. 134–35.

4. *CSIV*, 69, ch. 1; Jofre de Loaysa, *Crónica*, 110–14, ch. 221.33–35; Gaibrois, *Sancho IV*, 1:1–11, and 3:xviii, no. 27; Rogelio Pérez Bustamante, *El gobierno y la administración de los reinos de la Corona de Castilla (1230–1474)*, 2 vols. (Madrid: Universidad Autónoma, 1976), 1:358–59, 399–400.

5. Gaibrois, *Sancho IV*, 1:60–64 and 3:viii–x, no. 12; Giménez Soler, *Corona*, 22 n. 2; Arié, *L'Espagne*, 75–76; Torres Delgado, *Granada*, 200–202.

6. *CSIV*, 69–70, ch. 1; Gonzalo de la Finojosa, "Continuación," 106:37, ch. 246; Giménez Soler, *Corona*, 23 n. 2.

7. Luis Fernández, "Colección diplomática del monasterio de San Pelayo de Cerrato," *Hispania Sacra* 26 (1973): 299–301, no. 11; Gaibrois, *Sancho IV*, 1:61–62, and 2:213, n.1.

8. *CSIV*, 70, ch. 1; Jofre de Loaysa, *Crónica*, 112, ch. 221.34; Gaibrois, *Sancho IV*, 3: vi, no. 9; Pérez Embid, *Almirantazgo*, 9–18, 92–100.

9. Gaibrois, *Sancho IV*, 1:61, and cliv, "Registro de Cancillería de los años 1283 a 1286" (10 September 1284).

10. *CSIV*, 70–71, ch. 2; Antonio Ubieto Arteta, *Colección diplomática de Cuéllar* (Segovia: Diputación Provincial, 1961), 82–87, no. 38; Gaibrois, *Sancho IV*, 1:55–60, and 1:clviii, clxxviii, clxi–clxiii, clxvii, clxx, clxxviii, and 3:l–li, no. 79; Baer, *Jews*, 1:131–32.

11. *CSIV*, 71, ch. 1–2; Zurita, *Anales*, 2:187, 211–13; Georges Daumet, *Mémoire sur les relations de la France et de la Castille de 1255 à 1320* (Paris: Fontemoing, 1913), 88; Gaibrois, *Sancho IV*, 1:55–58; Nieto Soria, *Sancho IV*, 68–71.

12. Ibn Abī Zar', *Rawd al-Qirtās*, 2:640–43, 655–60, 669; Ibn Khaldūn, *Histoire*, 4:110–15; *Al-Hulal*, 202; *CSIV*, 70, ch. 1; Jofre de Loaysa, *Crónica*, 114, ch. 221.36–37; Manzano Rodríguez, *Intervención*, 81–100; García Fitz, "Acontecimientos," 41–54, esp. 45 (diagram); Gaibrois, *Sancho IV*, 1:64–67; Nieto Soria, *Sancho IV*, 71–74.

13. Ibn Abī Zar', *Rawd al-Qirtās*, 2:668–69; Ibn Khaldūn, *Histoire*, 4:114; *CSIV*, 70–71, 73, ch. 2, 3; Gonzalo de la Finojosa, "Continuación," 106:37–38, ch. 246; Gaibrois, *Sancho IV*, 1:67–68; Nieto Soria, *Sancho IV*, 71–72; García Fitz, *Castilla y León*, 273–75.

14. Ibn Abī Zar' *Rawd al-Qirtās*, 2:640–71; *CSIV*, 71–72, ch. 2; Jofre de Loaysa, *Crónica*, 116, ch. 221.37; Gaibrois, *Sancho IV*, 1:69–71, and 1:clxv–clxvii; Mosquera Merino, *Señoría de Ceuta*, 259–72; Manzano Rodríguez, *Intervención*, 100–101.

15. Ibn Abī Zar', *Rawd al-Qirtās*, 2:672–77; *CSIV*, 72, ch. 2; Arié, *L'Espagne*, 76; Torres Delgado, *Granada*, 202–3.

16. *CSIV*, 72, ch. 2; Ibn Abī Zarʿ, *Rawd al-Qirṭās*, 2:679–84; Ibn Khaldūn, *Histoire*, 4:117–18; *Al-Hulal*, 202; Manzano Rodríguez, *Intervención*, 101–2.

17. Ibn Abī Zarʿ, *Rawd al-Qirṭās*, 2:681–84; Ibn Khaldūn, *Histoire*, 4:118–20; Manzano Rodríguez, *Intervención*, 110–17; García Fitz, "Conquista de Tarifa," 116–18.

18. *CSIV*, 72, ch. 2; Ladero Quesada and González Jiménez, "Gibraltar," 230–32, nos. 6–8; Gaibrois, *Sancho IV*, 1:79, and 1:clxv–clxviii, and 3:lv–lvii, lx, lxix, nos. 85, 88, 92, 108; Nieto Soria, *Sancho IV*, 72–73.

19. Ibn Abī Zarʿ *Rawd al-Qirṭās*, 2:685–89; Ibn Khaldūn, *Histoire*, 4:120–21; *CSIV*, 72, ch. 2; Gaibrois, *Sancho IV*, 1:98, 103–4; Arié *L'Espagne*, 76; Torres Delgado, *Granada*, 204–5; Harvey, *Islamic Spain*, 159–60.

20. Ibn Abī Zarʿ *Rawd al-Qirṭās*, 2:692; Ibn Khaldūn, *Histoire*, 4:125; Manzano Rodríguez, *Intervención*, 125–29; Rubiera, "Los Banū Escallola," 93–94.

21. *CSIV*, 80, ch. 5; Gonzalo de la Finojosa, "Continuación," 106:43–47, ch. 247; Manzano Rodríguez, *Intervención*, 130–32.

22. Fernández Gómez, Ostos Salcedo, and Pardo Rodríguez, *Sevilla*, 228–29, no. 29; Gaibrois, *Sancho IV*, 1:179–80.

23. Dufourcq, *L'Espagne*, 206–7, 210–15; Gaibrois, *Sancho IV*, 1:104; Zurita, *Anales*, 2:281.

24. Alarcón y Santón and García de Linares, *Documentos árabes*, 394–97, no. 155.

25. *CSIV*, 72–74, 79–82, ch. 2–3, 5–6; Jofre de Loaysa, *Crónica*, 118, 126–36, ch. 221.38, ch. 222.43–45; Gaibrois, *Sancho IV*, 1:88–104; Daumet, *Mémoire*, 91–94; Zurita, *Anales*, 2:280–81, 346–50, 356–59, 365–67.

26. Gaibrois, *Sancho IV*, 3:cxxiv–cxxvi, nos. 205, 223–24, 226–27; Andrés Giménez Soler, *Don Juan Manuel: Biografía y estudio crítico* (Zaragoza: F. Martínez, 1932), 221–23, no. 2.

27. Giménez Soler, *Corona*, 24 nn. 1–2; Gaibrois, *Sancho IV*, 3: cxxxviii–cxxxix, no 230; Zurita, *Anales*, 2:375–78; Arié, *L'Espagne*, 76; Torres Delgado, *Granada*, 206.

28. Zurita, *Anales*, 2:280–81, 346–50, 356–59, 365–67, 411–12, 415; Dufourcq, *L'Espagne*, 217–18; Gaibrois, *Sancho IV*, 1:236; Nieto Soria, *Sancho IV*, 96–113.

29. Giménez Soler, *Corona*, 26 nn. 1–2; Ángeles Masiá de Ros, *Relación castellano-aragonesa desde Jaime II a Pedro el Ceremonioso*, 2 vols. (Barcelona: CSIC, 1994), 1:37–39.

30. Colmenares, *Segovia*, 2:84; Gaibrois, *Sancho IV*, 2:123–24 n. 4.

31. *CSIV*, 84–85, ch. 7–8; Ibn Abī Zarʿ, *Rawd al-Qirṭās*, 2:695; Ibn Khaldūn, *Histoire*, 4:130–31; Arié, *L'Espagne*, 77; Gaibrois, *Sancho IV*, 2:94–101, and "Tarifa," *BRAH* 74 (1919): 431.

32. *CSIV*, 86, ch. 8–9; Ibn Abī Zarʿ, *Rawd al-Qirṭās*, 2:695; Ibn Khaldūn, *Histoire*, 4:130–31; Jacopo d'Oria, *Annales Ianuenses*, ed. Cesare Imperiale, *Fonti per la Storia d' Italia* 5 (1929): 127–29, 136–37; Pérez Embid, *Almirantazgo*, 9–18, 92–100; Gaibrois, *Sancho IV*, 2:121–24; Zurita, *Anales*, 2:439–40; Roberto Lopez, *Genova marinara nel duecento: Benedetto Zaccaria, ammiraglio e mercante* (Milan: Giuseppe Principato, 1933).

33. Ibn Abī Zarʿ, *Rawd al-Qirṭās*, 2:695–96; Ibn Khaldūn, *Histoire*, 4:130–31; *Al-Hulal*, 202; *CSIV*, 86, ch. 9; Gaibrois, *Sancho IV*, 2:138, and "Tarifa," *BRAH* 74 (1919): 434–36;

Manzano Rodríguez, *Intervención*, 132–35; Torres Delgado, *Granada*, 206; Mosquera Merino, *Señoría de Ceuta*, 271–98.

34. *CSIV*, 85, ch. 8; Gaibrois, *Sancho IV*, 3:ccxxxiv–ccxxxviii, no. 369; Manuel García Fernández, "La política internacional de Portugal y Castilla en el umbral de la Baja Edad Media: Nuevas reflexiones sobre los viejos sistemas de alianzas dinásticas peninsulares (1279–1357)," *Revista de Ciencias Históricas* 14 (1999): 61–80, esp. 65–67.

35. "Documentos de la época de D. Sancho el Bravo," *MHE*, 3:460–61, nos. 3–4; Gaibrois, *Sancho IV*, 3:ccxli, no. 372, and "Tarifa,"*BRAH* 76 (120): 420, no. 1.

36. *MHE*, 3:451–52; Dufourcq, *L'Espagne*, 218–20, citing ACA Reg. 90, fol. 17–18v, 22v–3, 25v; Torres Delgado, *Granada*, 206; Nieto Soria, *Sancho IV*, 111–13.

37. *MHE*, 3:453, and 462–63, no. 5; Masiá de Ros, *Relación*, 1:39–42.

38. *MHE*, 3:453, 456–57, and 463–68, nos. 6–7; Gaibrois, *Sancho IV*, 2:135–49, and 3:ccl–cclvii, nos. 384–86, and cclviii–cclxi, nos. 388–91; Dufourcq, *L'Espagne*, 220–21, citing ACA Reg. 55, fol. 52v.

39. Gaibrois, *Sancho IV*, 3:ccl–cclvii, no. 384; *CSIV*, 86, ch. 8; Jofre de Loaysa, *Crónica*, 136, ch. 51; Ramon Muntaner, *Cronìca*, 5:52–56, ch. 176–77; *CDIE*, 1:676; Zurita, *Anales*, 2:422–29; Torres Delgado, *Granada*, 206; Manzano Rodríguez, *Intervención*, 137–38.

40. Giménez Soler, *Corona*, 31; *MHE* 3:467–68, no. 7; Gaibrois, *Sancho IV*, 2:170, 194 n. 1, 3:cclx, no. 390; Dufourcq, *L'Espagne*, 221–22, citing ACA, Pergaminos de Jaime II, nos. 68, 70; Manzano Rodríguez, *Intervención*, 138.

41. *MHE*, 3:451–52; Ibn Khaldūn, *Histoire*, 4:138; Giménez Soler, *Corona*, 26; Gaibrois, *Sancho IV*, 2:148–49, and 1:lviii, and "Tarifa,"*BRAH* 75 (1919): 432–33; López Dapena, *Cuentas*, 463; Zurita, *Anales*, 2:429.

42. Ibn Abī Zarʿ, *Rawd al-Qirtās*, 2:695–96; Ibn Khaldūn, *Histoire*, 4:131; *CSIV*, 86, ch. 9; Arié, *L'Espagne*, 78.

43. Fidel Fita, *Actas inéditas de Siete Concilios españoles celebrados desde el año 1282 hasta el de 1314* (Madrid: F. Maroto, 1882), 183–88; Gaibrois, *Sancho IV*, 2:171–72; Linehan, *Spanish Church*, 241–43; Torres Fontes, "Obispado de Cartagena," 524–25.

44. Ernest Langlois, *Les registres de Nicolas IV (1288–1292): Recueil des bulles de ce pape*, Bibliothèque des Écoles Françaises d'Athènes et de Rome ser. 2, no. 5 (Paris: E. Thorin, 1886–93), no. 6857; Gaibrois, *Sancho IV*, 3:cclxxxii, no. 420.

45. Francisco García Fitz, "La defensa de la frontera del bajo Guadalquivir ante las invasiones benimerines del siglo XIII," in Mercedes García Arenal and María J. Viguera, eds., *Relaciones de la Península Ibérica con el Magreb (siglos XIII–XVI)* (Madrid: CSIC, 1988), 275–323, esp. 276–77.

46. *CSIV*, 86, ch. 8; Gaibrois, *Sancho IV*, 2:138, and "Tarifa," *BRAH* 74 (1919): 349–52, 522; Pérez Embid, *Almirantazgo*, 9–18, 92–100.

47. Gaibrois, *Sancho IV*, 2: xxiv–xxx, "Cuentas," and "Tarifa," *BRAH* 77 (1920): 434–37, no. 20; López Dapena, *Cuentas*, 157–76, 408–18; García Fitz, "Defensa," 278–79, 306.

48. Gaibrois, "Tarifa," *BRAH* 74 (1919): 522, and 76 (1920): 422–23, no. 3.

49. *CSIV*, 86, ch. 9; *CLC*, 1:125; Gaibrois, *Sancho IV*, 2:169, n. 1, and 171–72, 175, n. 1,

and 1:xxix, lxxx, xci, and "Tarifa," *BRAH* 76 (1920): 422–23, no. 3; López Dapena, *Cuentas*, 130–56, 418–32.

50. Gaibrois, *Sancho IV*, 1:xxxix–xl, lxxx–lxxxv; García Fitz, "Defensa," 278–81, 306–8.

51. García Fitz, "Defensa," 281–83, 307–8.

52. Gaibrois, *Sancho IV*, 1:171, 173–75, and 3:ccxcvi–ccxcvii, no. 441; Pereda Llerena, *Burgos (1254–1293)*, 353–55, no. 283.

53. Gaibrois, *Sancho IV*, 2:xxiv "Cuentas," and "Tarifa," *BRAH* 74 (1919): 522–23; López Dapena, *Cuentas*. 407; Nieto Soria, *Sancho IV*, 110–20.

54. Masià i de Ros, *Jaume II*, 17, and *Relación*, 1:42; Giménez Soler, *Corona*, 30 n. 2; Dufourcq, *L'Espagne*, 223.

55. *CSIV*, 86, ch. 9; Gaibrois, *Sancho IV*, 2:174–77, and "Tarifa," *BRAH* 76 (1920): 421–22, no. 2.

56. Ballesteros, *Sevilla*, cclxviii, no. 245; *CSIV*, 86, ch. 9; Giménez Soler, *Corona*, 28; Gaibrois, *Sancho IV*, 2:194 n. 1.

57. Ibn Khaldūn, *Histoire*, 4:131–32.

58. Gaibrois, *Sancho IV*, "Cuentas," 1:xxxvi, lxxxii, lxxxiii, and "Tarifa," *BRAH* 74 (1919): 525; López Dapena, *Cuentas*, 449.

59. Gaibrois, *Sancho IV*, 2:177; Jacopo d'Oria, *Annales Ianuenses*, 146–47.

60. *CSIV*, 86, ch. 9; Ibn Abī Zarʿ, *Rawd al-Qirtās*, 2:696–97; Ibn Khaldūn, *Histoire*, 4:132; Arié, *L'Espagne*, 77–78, citing Ibn al-Khatīb, *Aʿmāl*, 291; Torres Delgado, *Granada*, 207–9; García Fitz, "Acontecimientos," 54–61.

61. Jacopo d'Oria, *Annales Ianuenses*, 146; *CSIV*, 86, ch. 9; *CDIE*, 1:676; Jofre de Loaysa, *Crónica*, 138, ch. 222.52; Ibn Abī Zarʿ, *Rawd al-Qirtās*, 2:697; Ibn Khaldūn, *Histoire*, 4:132.

62. Gaibrois, *Sancho IV*, 2:181–82, and "Tarifa," *BRAH* 74 (1919): 526–28; Manzano Rodríguez, *Intervención*, 141–44.

63. *CSIV*, 86, ch. 9.

64. Sancho IV, *Castigos e documentos para bien vivir ordenados por el rey don Sancho IV*, ed. Agapito Rey (Bloomington: Indiana University Press, 1952), 33 (prologue), 75 (ch. 10), 190 (ch. 40), and 127–32 (ch. 21), esp. 132.

65. *CSIV*, 86, ch. 9; Gaibrois, *Sancho IV*, 2:182–83, 195, and "Tarifa," *BRAH* 74 (1919): 419; Torres Delgado, *Granada*, 207–8; García Fitz, "Conquista de Tarifa," 119–23.

66. Masiá de Ros, *Relación*, 2:9–10, no. 3/14, and *Jaume II*, 20–21; Gaibrois, *Sancho IV*, 2:186–87, and 3:ccxciii, no. 436; Giménez Soler, *Corona*, 28 n. 1; Dufourcq, *L'Espagne*, 222–23, citing ACA Reg. 252, fol. 44–46.

67. Gaibrois, *Sancho IV*, 1:ciii; Ibn Khaldūn, *Histoire*, 4:131–34; Ibn Abī Zarʿ, *Rawd al-Qirtās*, 2:696–97.

68. Gaibrois, *Sancho IV*, 2:192–94, and "Tarifa," *BRAH* 76 (1920): 430–31, no. 19; López Dapena, *Cuentas*, 342–43; Goñi Gaztambide, *Historia*, 204–5.

69. Gaibrois, "Tarifa," *BRAH* 75 (1919): 349–55; Manzano Rodríguez, *Intervención*, 139–46; Arié, *L'Espagne*, 78; Torres Delgado, *Granada*, 208–9; Nieto Soria, *Sancho IV*, 120–22.

70. *CSIV*, 87, ch. 9; Gaibrois, *Sancho IV*, 2:199–202; Nieto Soria, *Sancho IV*, 122–23; Masiá de Ros, *Relación*, 1:44–46.

71. Masià i de Ros, *Jaume II*, 17–20; Gimenez Soler, *Corona*, 29–30; Dufourcq, *L'Espagne*, 224; Zurita, *Anales*, 2:443–45.

72. Nieto Cumplido, *Regionalismo*, 155, no. 20; *CLC*, 1:106–17, 118; Gaibrois, "Tarifa," *BRAH* 76 (1920): 422–23, no. 3.

73. Gaibrois, "Tarifa," *BRAH* 76 (1920): 423, no. 4; Ibn Abī Zarʿ *Rawd al-Qirṭās*, 2:698; Ibn Khaldūn, *Histoire*, 4:132–33; Manzano Rodríguez, *Intervención*, 147–48; Harvey, *Islamic Spain*, 160–61.

74. Ibn Abī Zarʿ *Rawd al-Qirṭās*, 2:700–703; Ibn Khaldūn, *Histoire*, 4:133–34; Gaibrois, "Tarifa," *BRAH* 76 (1920): 430–33, no. 19; Manzano Rodríguez, *Intervención*, 148–49; Torres Delgado, *Granada*, 210 n. 71.

75. Gaibrois, *Sancho IV*, 2:229, 251, and "Tarifa," *BRAH* 76 (1920): 423, no. 5; Dufourcq, *L'Espagne*, 226–27, citing ACA Reg. 98, fol 170v; Giménez Soler, *Corona*, 33; Lopez, *Genova*, 173–74.

76. Masià i de Ros, *Jaume II*, 27–28; Giménez Soler, *Corona*, 33; Gaibrois, *Sancho IV*, 2:293–94.

77. *CSIV*, 88, ch. 10; Dufourcq, *L'Espagne*, 227–28, citing ACA Reg. 252, fol. 77, and Reg. 99, fol. 2 v; Gaibrois, *Sancho IV*, 2:229, 275–77, 290–91, 3:cclxxi–cclxxii, no. 544, and "Tarifa," *BRAH* 76 (1920): 55–56, 68–70, 103, 423–25, nos. 6, 7–18.

78. Antonio Muñoz Torrado, *La Iglesia de Sevilla en el siglo XIII: Estudio histórico* (Seville: Imprenta de Izquierdo, 1914), 145; Nieto Soria, *Sancho IV*, 125.

79. José Alemany, "Milicias cristianas al servicio de los sultanes musulmanes del Almagreb," in *Homenaje a D. Francisco Codera en su jubilación del profesorado: Estudios de erudición oriental*, ed. Eduardo Saavedra (Zaragoza: Mariano Escar, 1904), 133–69, esp. 144–46; Pedro Barrantes Maldonado, *Ilustraciones de la Casa de Niebla*, *MHE* 9 (1857): 134–35; Dufourcq, *L'Espagne*, 216.

80. *CSIV*, 87, ch. 10; Gaibrois, *Sancho IV*, 2:230, 251, and "Tarifa," *BRAH* 76 (1920): 53–57, 65–66; López Dapena, *Cuentas*, 668.

81. López Dapena, *Cuentas*, 200–201, 290, 635–65; Gaibrois, "Tarifa," *BRAH* 76 (1920): 134–38, 444–48, no. 30, and *Sancho IV*, 3:cccxcv–cd, no. 583; García Fitz, "Defensa," 284–302, 308–20.

82. Gaibrois, *Sancho IV*, 2:260–61, 280–84, and 1:xliii, and "Tarifa," *BRAH* 76 (1920): 123–33; López Dapena, *Cuentas*, 192–214, 436–37.

83. López Dapena, *Cuentas*, 115–20, 460–61, 474–76; Gaibrois, *Sancho IV*, 2:258, and 3:cdiv–cdvii, no. 592.

84. López Dapena, *Cuentas*, 130–77; Gaibrois, *Sancho IV*, 3:ccclxxviii–ccclxxxi, cccxc–cccxci, nos. 556–58, 561, 575, and "Tarifa," *BRAH* 76 (1920): 438–41, nos. 21–25.

85. Gaibrois, *Sancho IV*, 2:294–97, and 3:ccclx–ccclxv, ccclxvi–ccclxxiii, ccclxxxiv, ccclxxxi–ccclxxxii, ccclxxxvi–ccclxxxviii, nos. 526–28, 533–37, 540, 545, and "Tarifa," *BRAH* 76 (1920): 430–39, nos. 19–20; López Dapena, *Cuentas*, 342–67.

86. Gaibrois, *Sancho IV*, 3:ccclx–ccclxi, ccclxiv–ccclxvi, ccclxx–ccclxxi, nos. 524–25, 529, 531–32, 539, 541; López Dapena, *Cuentas*, 349–50.

87. López Dapena, *Cuentas*, 355–60; Gaibrois, *Sancho IV*, 3:ccclxxiv, ccclxxxi–ccclxxxii,

ccclxxxvi–ccclxxxviii, cccxciii, nos. 548, 562, 570–71, 578; García Fitz, "Defensa," 284–305, 308–9.

88. *CSIV*, 88, ch. 10; Ibn Abī Zarʿ, *Rawd al-Qirṭās*, 2:702–3; Ibn Khaldūn, *Histoire*, 4:134.

89. *CSIV*, 88, ch. 10; Ibn Abī Zarʿ, *Rawd al-Qirṭās*, 2:702–3; Ibn Khaldūn, *Histoire*, 4:134; Gaibrois, "Tarifa," *BRAH* 76 (1920): 63–65.

90. *CSIV*, 88–89, ch. 11; Jofre de Loaysa, *Crónica*, 142, ch. 224.54.

91. *MFIV*, 2:145–47, no. 102; Manuel Gonzalez Jiménez, "Guzmán el Bueno y su tiempo," in *Les Espagnes médiévales: Aspects économiques et sociaux: Mélanges offerts à Jean Gautier Dalché, Annales de la Faculté des Lettres et Sciences humaines de Nice* 46 (1983): 237–46; Isabel Mille Jiménez, "Guzmán el Bueno en la historia y en la literatura," *Revue Hispanique* 78 (1930): 311–409. Alfred Morel-Fatio, "La lettre du roi Sanche IV à Alonso Pérez de Guzmán sur la défense de Tarifa (2 janvier 1295)," in *Études sur l'Espagne* 3rd ser. (Paris: E. Bouillon, 1904), 1–23, proved that a congratulatory letter from Sancho IV published by Barrantes Maldonado, *Ilustraciones*, 169, is false.

92. Gaibrois, "Tarifa," *BRAH* 74 (1919): 418–19, and 76 (1920): 145–47.

93. Masià i de Ros, *Jaume II*, 21–27; Gaibrois, "Tarifa" *BRAH* 76 (1920): 442–43, nos. 26–29; Dufourcq, *L'Espagne*, 230–33.

94. Ibn Abī Zarʿ, *Rawd al-Qirṭās*, 2:702–3; *CSIV*, 89, ch. 11; Manzano Rodríguez, *Intervención*, 157; Gaibrois, *Sancho IV*, 2:326–29; García Fitz, "Conquista de Tarifa," 121–25.

95. López Dapena, *Cuentas*, 660–65; Gaibrois, "Tarifa," *BRAH* 76 (1920): 152–60; 77 (1920): 212–15, no. 31; García Fitz, "Defensa," 295–97.

96. Of the 900,000 *maravedíes* levied on the Jews for galleys from Seville, Juan Mathe had received 212,000, leaving a balance of 688,000. A new galley was built for 10,000 *maravedíes* and four were purchased from the Genoese for 33,000. Thus in order to reach the 1,401,000 needed to maintain the fleet until 1 April, 1,189,000 was required.

97. The transcription by Gaibrois, "Tarifa," *BRAH* 77 (1920): 215, no. 30, is *entena*; López Dapena, *Cuentas*, 664 read *escenas*, which makes no sense. I must thank Francisco García Fitz for help in interpreting some of these terms.

98. López Dapena, *Cuentas*, 660–65.

99. Gaibrois, *Sancho IV*, 2:376, and 3:cdviii–cdix, no. 594. Juan Mathe died on 9 August 1299. Fernán Pérez Maimón was last recorded as *almirante* on 28 June 1300; *MFIV*, 2:218.

100. F. Javier Pereda Llerena, *Documentación de la Catedral de Burgos (1294–1316)* (Burgos: Garrido Garrido, 1984), 13–14, no. 304; Gaibrois, *Sancho IV*, 2:361 n. 1; Goñi Gaztambide, *Historia*, 204–5.

101. Eliseo Vidal Beltrán, "Privilegios y franquicias de Tarifa," *Hispania* 17 (1957): 3–78, esp.16–18, no. 1; Ladero Quesada and González Jiménez, "Gibraltar," 232–33, no. 9.

102. *CSIV*, 70, ch. 1, erroneously dated the grant to Zaccaria at the beginning of the reign. González Jiménez, "De al-Qanatir," 45, 48–51, nos. 1–3; López Dapena, *Cuentas*, 660.

103. Gaibrois, *Sancho IV*, 3:ccclxxxiii–ccclxxxvi, ccclxxxix, cccxc–cccxciv, cdi–cdii, nos. 564, 568–69, 572–74, 576, 579, 585–86. See also letters to Dinis, ibid., 3:ccclxxxiv-ccclxxxv, nos. 566–67.

104. Gaibrois, *Sancho IV*, 2:362–63, and 3:cccxciv, no. 580; Masià i de Ros, *Jaume II*, 26–27.

105. Gaibrois, *Sancho IV*, 2:364–69, and 3:cccliv–ccclv, cdvii–cdviii, nos. 512–13, 593; Dufourcq, *L'Espagne*, 234–36, 344.

106. Juan Manuel, "Tractado que fizo don Juan Manuel sobre las armas que fueron dadas a su padre el Infante don Manuel, et por que el et sus descendientes pudiesen facer caballeros non lo siendo, et de como paso la fabla que con el rey don Sancho ovo ante que finase," in Pascual de Gayangos, ed., *Escritores en prosa anteriores al siglo XV*, BAE 51:257–64, esp. 263.

107. *CSIV*, 89–90, ch. 12–13; Jofre de Loaysa, *Crónica*, 146, ch. 224.57.

CHAPTER 6. CRUSADES OF GIBRALTAR, ALMERÍA, AND ALGECIRAS

1. The *Crónica de Fernando IV* (*CFIV*) was edited by Cayetano Rosell, *BAE* 66:91–170, and by Antonio Benavides, *Memorias de Fernando IV de Castilla*, 2 vols. (Madrid: José Rodríguez, 1869) (*MFIV*), 1:1–242. Benavides also published nearly 600 royal charters. I cite Rosell's edition of *CFIV*.

2. César González Mínguez, *Fernando IV de Castilla (1295–1312): La guerra civil y el predominio de la nobleza* (Valladolid: Universidad de Valladolid, 1976), and *Fernando IV, 1295–1312* (Palencia: Diputación Provincial and Editorial La Olmeda, 1995), and "Fernando IV (1295–1312): Perfíl de un reinado," *ETF* 17 (2004): 223–44. I cite the first of these studies.

3. María Josefa Sanz Fuentes, "Cartas de hermandad concejíl en Andalucía: El caso de Écija," *HID* 5 (1978): 413–18, no. 1; Agustín Múñoz y Gómez, "Concejos de Córdoba, Sevilla y Jerez de la Frontera: Carta inédita de su hermandad en 1296," *BRAH* 36 (1900): 306–16; Nieto Cumplido, *Regionalismo*, 169–76, 183–91, nos. 23, 25.

4. Luis Suárez Fernández, "Evolución histórica de las hermandades castellanas," *Cuadernos de Historia de España* 16 (1951): 52–55, no. 4; Nieto Cumplido, *Regionalismo*, 177–83, no. 24; Carmen Argente del Castillo Ocaña, "Las hermandades medievales en el reino de Jaén," *Andalucía medieval: Actas del I Congreso de Historia de Andalucía, diciembre de 1976*, 2 vols. (Córdoba: Monte de Piedad y Caja de Ahorros, 1978), 2:21–32.

5. *CODOM*, 3:110–16, no. 112; *MFIV*, 2:46–51, no. 29.

6. *CFIV*, 93–97, 100–103, ch. 1–2; Jofre de Loaysa, *Crónica*, 150–73, ch. 225.59–69; *MFIV*, 2: 2–3, 53, 59, 61–63, 68–71, 86–87, nos. 2, 33, 39, 41–43, 48–50, 69–70; Zurita, *Anales*, 2:493–505; Masiá de Ros, *Relación*, 1:53–66.

7. Ibn Khaldūn, *Histoire*, 4:138; *CFIV*, 101, ch. 1; Al-Makkarī, *History*, 2:346; Arié, *L'Espagne*, 79–81; Torres Delgado, *Granada*, 212–13; Harvey, *Islamic Spain*, 162–63.

8. Masià i de Ros, *Jaume II*, 33–40, 188–89, and *Relación*, 1:66–67; *MFIV*, 2:74–75, 98–99, nos. 53–54, 69; Alarcón y Santón and García de Linares, *Documentos árabes*, 1–3, no. 1; Giménez Soler, *Corona*, 37–41, 46; Dufourcq, *L'Espagne*, 233–36, 348–49.

9. Masià i de Ros, *Jaume II*, 47–48, 189–90, and *Relación*, 1:67–80; *MFIV*, 2:115–16, 124, nos. 81, 89. See also *MFIV*, 2:161–67, nos. 116–18.

10. Zurita, *Anales*, 2:514–16; Masià i de Ros, *Jaume II*, 40; *MFIV*, 2:99, no. 70; González Mínguez, *Fernando IV*, 61–62; Harvey, *Islamic Spain*, 162–63.

11. *CFIV*, 103, 106, ch. 2; Barrantes Maldonado, *Ilustraciones*, 186–88; Diego Ortíz de Zúñiga, *Anales eclesiásticos y seculares de la muy noble y muy leal ciudad de Sevilla*, 5 vols. (Madrid: Imprenta Real, 1795–96; reprint with new introd., Seville: Guadalquivir, 1988), 4:157; Arié, *L'Espagne*, 82; Torres Delgado, *Granada*, 213–14.

12. *CFIV*, 107–8, ch. 2; González Mínguez, *Fernando IV*, 64–65.

13. Nieto Cumplido, *Regionalismo*, 191–99, no. 26.

14. *MFIV*, 2:145–46, 580–82, nos. 102, 392; Ladero Quesada and González Jiménez, "Gibraltar," 233–35, nos. 10–11, 13.

15. *CFIV*, 111, 115, ch. 4–5; Ortíz de Zúñiga, *Anales*, 4:161–62; González Mínguez, *Fernando IV*, 85–86.

16. Masià i de Ros, *Jaume II*, 41–42; Giménez Soler, *Corona*, 52 nn. 1–2.

17. Andrés Giménez Soler, *El sitio de Almería de 1309* (Barcelona: Casa Provincial de Caridad, 1904), 78–79, and *Corona*, 53 n. 1, 55.

18. Nieto Cumplido, *Regionalismo*, 199–201, no. 27.

19. Masià i de Ros, *Jaume II*, 42–43; Giménez Soler, *Corona*, 57 n. 1, 58 n. 1, 60 n. 1; Al-Makkarī, *History*, 2:346; Melchor M. Antuña, "Conquista de Quesada y Alcaudete," *Religión y Cultura* 20 (1932): 61–70, 386–95; Arié, *L'Espagne*, 82–83; Torres Delgado, *Granada*, 213.

20. Masià i de Ros, *Jaume II*, 49–52, 93–103, 107–14; Giménez Soler, *Corona*, 53 n. 2; *MFIV*, 2:203–6, nos. 149–50; Arié, *L'Espagne*, 82.

21. Masià i de Ros, *Jaume II*, 117–23, and *Relación*, 2:46, 50–52, no. 31/100; Giménez Soler, *Corona*, 61 n. 2, 68–70, and *Juan Manuel*, 248–49, no. 32; *MFIV*, 2:229–31, 252–54, nos. 169, 181; Zurita, *Anales*, 2:604–5; Dufourcq, *L'Espagne*, 352 n. 3; González Mínguez, *Fernando IV*, 105–6.

22. Masià i de Ros, *Jaume II*, 123–27, 131–33, 137–44, 195–202, and *Relación*, 1:87–88, 2:58–59, 60–61, nos. 37/109, 39/114; Giménez Soler, *Corona*, 71–73 nn. 1–2, 76–81; Alarcón y Santón and García de Linares, *Documentos árabes*, 4–6, 7–10, no. 3.

23. Giménez Soler, *Corona*, 75 nn. 1–2, 83 n. 1, and *Juan Manuel*, 253–54, no. 37; Masià i de Ros, *Jaume II*, 43–44, 55–56, and *Relación*, 1:96–97, 2:60–61; Ángel Canellas López, "Aragón y la empresa del Estrecho en el siglo XIV: Nuevos documentos del Archivo Municipal de Zaragoza," *EEMCA* 2 (1946): 15; Arié, *L'Espagne*, 83; Dufourcq, *L'Espagne*, 352–53; Torres Delgado, *Granada*, 212; Vidal Castro, "Historia," 102–3; González Mínguez, *Fernando IV*, 117–27.

24. A. Marcos Pous, "Los dos matrimonios de Sancho IV de Castilla," *Cuadernos de trabajo de la Escuela Española de Historia y Arqueología en Roma* 8 (1956): 106–8, no. 11; Masiá de Ros, *Relación*, 1:92–93; Giménez Soler, *Corona*, 74 n. 1.

25. *MFIV*, 2:232–34, 267–69, nos. 170, 190; Pereda Llarena, *Burgos (1294–1316)*, 130–33, no. 367.

26. Al-Makkarī, *History*, 2:346; Lafuente Alcántara, *Inscripciones*, 209–11.

27. Masià i de Ros, *Jaume II*, 57–63; Harvey, *Islamic Spain*, 165–70.

28. Ibn Khaldūn, *Histoire*, 4:157–58; Ibn Abī Zarʿ, *Rawd al-Qirtās*, 2:707; Al-Makkarī, *History*, 2:346–47; Arié, *L'Espagne*, 84–85; Torres Delgado, *Granada*, 225–26; Vidal Castro, "Historia," 115.

29. *CLC*, 1:161–68; *MFIV*, 2:344–46, no. 229; *CFIV*, 123–25, ch. 10; Jofre de Loaysa, *Crónica*, 195, ch. 227.87; González Mínguez, *Fernando IV*, 130–42.

30. *MFIV*, 2:315–16, no. 213; Masiá de Ros, *Relación*, 1:94.

31. *CFIV*, 128–29, ch. 10–11; Giménez Soler, *Juan Manuel*, 262–64, 273–74, nos. 46, 57; *MFIV*, 2:383–84, no. 250.

32. Masià i de Ros, *Jaume II*, 58, 62, and *Relación*, 1:97–140, 2:61–63, nos. 40/115, 41/118.

33. Giménez Soler, *Corona*, 88–91; Masià i de Ros, *Jaume II*, 145–46 and 67–72; Dufourcq, *L'Espagne*, 355–61.

34. *MFIV*, 2:351–53, 359–60, nos. 234, 240; González Mínguez, *Fernando IV*, 149–64.

35. *MFIV*, 2:353–54, 515, nos. 235, 348; Juan Torres Fontes, *Documentos de Fernando IV, CODOM* 5 (Murcia: Academia Alfonso X el Sabio, 1980), 31–33, no. 25; Goñi Gaztambide, *Historia*, 263–64.

36. *CFIV*, 131–33, ch. 11; Jofre de Loaysa, *Crónica*, 195–96, ch. 227.87–89; Giménez Soler, *Juan Manuel*, 286–87, no. 74; Masiá de Ros, *Relación*, 2:64–65, no. 43/123; Arié, *L'Espagne*, 85; Torres Delgado, *Granada*, 225–27; González Mínguez, *Fernando IV*, 164–66.

37. Masià i de Ros, *Jaume II*, 77–85, 87–89; Dufourcq, *L'Espagne*, 379, citing ACA Reg. 334, fol. 174v, 175, and Cartas árabes, caja 2, nos. 84, 97; Alarcón y Santón and García de Linares, *Documentos árabes*, 160–62, 184–85, nos. 79, 84 bis; Giménez Soler, *Juan Manuel*, 284–87, 291, nos. 71–77, 82, and *Almería*, 23.

38. *MFIV*, 2:413–29, nos. 279–89, and 2:412, 432–34, 445–46, 449–61, 464–67, 473–76, 487–88, 498, nos. 277, 291–93, 299, 301–16, 318–20, 324–25, 327, 333, 337; Masiá de Ros, *Relación*, 2:110–20, no. 70/219; Jofre de Loaysa, *Crónica*, 198–216, ch. 227.90–92, ch. 228.93–100; Giménez Soler, *Corona*, 96–99, 111–12; González Mínguez, *Fernando IV*, 173–201; Dufourcq, *L'Espagne*, 377–78.

39. Giménez Soler, *Almería*, 85–86, and *Corona*, 112.

40. Alarcón y Santón and García de Linares, *Documentos árabes*, 157–60, no. 78; Giménez Soler, *Corona*, 112, and *Almería*, 26–27, 85–86; Canellas López, "Aragón," 46–52; Charles Dufourcq, "Nouveaux documents sur la politique africaine de la Couronne d'Aragon," *Analecta Sacra Tarraconensia* 26 (1953): 319–20, no. 68.

41. Dufourcq, *L'Espagne*, 380–81, citing ACA Reg. 334, fol. 175; Arié, *L'Espagne*, 86–87.

42. Giménez Soler, *Corona*, 116 n. 1, 117 n. 1, and *Almería*, 85; Masià i de Ros, *Jaume II*, 283–84; Dufourcq, *L'Espagne*, 383–84, citing ACA Cartes reials diplomàtiques, Jaime II, caja 14, no. 2766, and ACA Reg. 236, fol. 239; Al-Makkarī, *History*, 2:347.

43. Ibn Khaldūn, *Histoire*, 4:161, 173–74, 176–79; Ibn Abī Zarʿ, *Rawd al-Qirtās*, 2:707–9; Arié, *L'Espagne*, 87; Manzano, *Intervención*, 160–62, 173–76; Mosquera Merino, *Señoría de Ceuta*, 306–17; Charles Dufourcq, "La question de Ceuta au XIIIe siècle," *Hespéris* 42 (1955): 67–127.

44. Ángel Canellas López. "Datos para la historia de los reinos peninsulares en el

primer tercio del siglo XIV: IV Génesis del tratado de Alcalá de Henares," *BRAH* 145 (1959): 256–59, 279–80, no. 16; Giménez Soler, *Almería*, 28–29, 87–88.

45. Manzano Rodríguez, *Intervención*, 321–69; Arié, *L'Espagne*, ch. 4; Torres Delgado, "Ejército," 202–7.

46. Ibn Abī Zarʿ, *Rawd al-Qirṭās*, 2:709–15; Ibn Khaldūn, *Histoire*, 4:167–69, 180–83; *Al-Hulal*, 203; González Mínguez, *Fernando IV*, 279–80; Dufourcq, *L'Espagne*, 384–85; Arié, *L'Espagne*, 86–88; Harvey, *Islamic Spain*, 165–70; Vidal Castro, "Historia," 115–16.

47. Giménez Soler, *Corona*, 122 n. 1, and *Almería*, 33–35, 89, 90–92, 100–102; Masià de Ros, *Jaume II*, 403–4.

48. Masià i de Ros, *Jaume II*, 281, 291–316, and *Relación*, 1:150–55, 2:218–19, no. 112 bis/318; Dufourcq, *L'Espagne*, 386, citing ACA Reg. 3335, fol. 330, and ACA CRD Jaime II, caja 17, no. 3383; Zurita, *Anales*, 2:687.

49. *MFIV*, 2:621–26, nos. 416–19; Masià i de Ros, *Jaume II*, 317–18, 406, and *Relación*, 1:155–59, 2:230–32, no. 119/338; Giménez Soler, *Corona*, 121 n. 1.

50. *CFIV*, 161–62, ch. 16; Zurita, *Anales*, 2:702–3; *CGPIII*, 167, ch. 38; Canellas López, "Datos," 249–55, and "Aragón," 17–18; González Mínguez, *Fernando IV*, 280–83; Dufourcq, *L'Espagne*, 389–90; Manzano Rodríguez, *Intervención*, 177–78.

51. Muntaner, *Crònica*, 7:6, ch. 246.

52. *CFIV*, 162, ch. 16; Giménez Soler, *Almería*, 94–98, no. 10, and *Corona*, 137–38, and *Juan Manuel*, 364–66, nos. 192–95; Masià i de Ros, *Jaume II*, 386; González Mínguez, *Fernando IV*, 283–85.

53. Masià i de Ros, *Jaume II*, 321–24, and *Relación*, 1:159–60; Giménez Soler, *Juan Manuel*, 366, no. 195.

54. Fita, *Actas*, 155–56, no. 1.

55. Finke, *Acta Aragonensia*, 2:764–67, 878–79, nos. 556–57, and 3:xxvii–xxviii, 3:193–97, no. 90; *Regestum Clementis Papae V*, 8 vols. (Rome: Typographia Vaticana, 1884–92), nos. 224, 233; Giménez Soler, *Corona*, 127–30; Goñi Gaztambide, *Historia*, 266–67.

56. Giménez Soler, *Corona*, 131 n. 2, 133, n. 1; Masiá de Ros, *Relación*, 2:236–39, no. 123/345; Finke, *Acta Aragonensia*, 3:200–202, no. 92; Goñi Gaztambide, *Historia*, 269–70.

57. Dufourcq, *L'Espagne*, 390, citing ACA Reg. 335, fols. 258–59; Zurita, *Anales*, 2:709.

58. *MFIV*, 2:644, 650–51, nos. 436, 439–40; Masià i de Ros, *Jaume II*, 325–26; *Regestum Clementis Papae V*, 3:96–100, nos. 3989–90; Giménez Soler, *Corona*, 134–36.

59. *Regestum Clementis Papae V*, 3:117–23, nos. 4046–51; *MFIV*, 2:657–59, no. 443; Masiá de Ros, *Relación*, 2:233–34, no. 121/342.

60. Finke, *Acta Aragonensia*, 2:880–82, no. 559.

61. Johannes Vincke, *Documenta selecta mutuas civitatis Arago-Cathalaunicae et Ecclesiae relationes illustrantia* (Barcelona: Bibliotheca Balmes, 1936), 93–94, no. 148; Finke, *Acta Aragnensia*, 3:202–3, no. 93; Goñi Gaztambide, *Historia*, 271.

62. Masià i de Ros, *Jaume II*, 326–29; *Regestum Clementis Papae V*, nos. 4519–21, 4524; Goñi Gaztambide, *Historia*, 272.

63. Finke, *Acta Aragonensia*, 2:771, no. 482; Goñi Gaztambide, *Historia*, 272.

64. Masià i de Ros, *Jaume II*, 329–34; *Regestum Clementis Papae V*, nos. 5090, 5092, 5094.

65. *MFIV*, 2:791–93, no. 486; Finke, *Acta Aragonensia*, 3:207–11, no. 97, and 2:773, 778–79, 888–89, nos. 483, 486, 566; Goñi Gaztambide, *Historia*, 273.

66. *Regestum Clementis Papae V*, nos. 5091, 5093, 5095; Masiá de Ros, *Relación*, 2:241–42, no. 125/360; Goñi Gaztambide, *Historia*, 274; José Manuel Calderón Ortega and Francisco Javier Díaz González, "Los almirantes del 'siglo de oro' de la marina castellana medieval," *ELEM* 24 (2001): 311–64, esp. 312–15.

67. Éphrem Longpré, "Le *Liber de acquisitione Terrae Sanctae* du bienheureux Ramon Llull," *Criterion* 3 (1927): 265–78; *Epistola Raymundi ad Regem Aragoniae* in Finke, *Acta Aragonensia* 2:879, no. 557; Pamela Drost Beattie, "'Pro exaltatione sanctae fidei catholicae': Mission and Crusade in the Writings of Ramon Llull," in Larry J. Simon, ed., *Iberia and the Mediterranean World of the Middle Ages: Studies in Honor of Robert I. Burns, S.J.*, 2 vols. (Leiden: Brill, 1995), 1: 113–29; Goñi Gaztambide, *Historia*, 252–62.

68. Masià i de Ros, *Jaume II*, 410–11, 424–27, 430–33; *MFIV*, 2:659–64, nos. 444–48; Capmany, *Tratados*, 517; Ibn Marzūq, *El Musnad*, 104.

69. Vicente Salavert y Roca, *Cerdeña y la expansión mediterránea de la Corona de Aragón (1297–1314)*, 2 vols. (Madrid: CSIC, 1956), 2:413–14, nos. 332, 347; Masià i de Ros, *Jaume II*, 291, 341–42; Giménez Soler, *Corona*, 140–41, and *Almería*, 99–100, 141; Dufourcq, *L'Espagne*, 393; Torres Delgado, *Granada*, 239–40.

70. Arié, *L'Espagne*, 88–89, citing ACA Reg. 238, fol. 47v; Giménez Soler, *Juan Manuel*, 363–64, no. 192, and *Almería*, 92–94; Pedro Díaz Cassou, *Serie de los obispos de Cartagena, sus hechos y su tiempo* (Madrid: Fortanet, 1895), 27; *MFIV*, 2:670–71, 785–86, nos. 456–57, 538.

71. Ibn Khaldūn, *Histoire*, 4:184; Al-Makkarī, *History*, 2:347–48, quoting Ibn al-Khatīb; *CAXI*, 205, ch. 53; *GCAXI*, 1:403, ch. 68; Giménez Soler, *Almería*, 92–94, 99–100, and *Corona*, 143–45; Dufourcq, *L'Espagne*, 393–94; Harvey, *Islamic Spain*, 171–80.

72. Masià i de Ros, *Jaume II*, 350–51; Rica Amrán-Tedghi, "El papel de Ceuta en la política exterior de Jaime II de Aragón," *Anales de la Universidad de Alicante: Historia Medieval* 11 (1996–97): 465–478, esp. 470–75.

73. Ibn Abī Zarʿ, *Rawd al-Qirṭās*, 2:715–19; Manzano, *Intervención*, 167–79; Andrés Gimenez Soler, "Expedición de Jaime II a la ciudad de Almería," *Boletín de la Real Academia de Buenas Letras de Barcelona* 2 (1903–4): 302–3; Torres Delgado, *Granada*, 227–30.

74. Alarcón y Santón and García de Linares, *Documentos árabes*, 164–65, no. 81; *MFIV*, 2:659–64, 669, nos. 444–48, 453; Vidal Castro, "Historia," 118–19.

75. Dufourcq, *L'Espagne*, 394–99, citing Madrid, Archivo de la Real Academia de la Historia, Colección Salazar, A-2, fols. 50–52, and ACA Reg. 335, fols. 291v–292r; Zurita, *Anales*, 2:715. Mosquera Merino, *Señoría de Ceuta*, 317–51.

76. Ibn Abī Zarʿ, *Rawd al-Qirṭās*, 2:717; Ibn Khaldūn, *Histoire*, 4:183–84, 205; Mosquera Merino, *Señoría de Ceuta*, 353–60.

77. Masià i de Ros, *Jaume II*, 369–71, and *Relación*, 1:160–62; *MFIV*, 2:691–92, no. 476.

78. Carmen María Marugán Vallvé, "El sitio de Almería de 1309: El desarrollo de la Campaña militar," in *Almería entre culturas (siglos XIII–XVI): Actas del Coloquio, Almería,*

19, 20 y 21 de abril de 1990, 2 vols. (Almería: Instituto de Estudios Almerienses, 1990), 185, no. 2; Zurita, *Anales*, 2:715; Dufourcq, *L'Espagne*, 400–401.

79. *CFIV*, 163, ch. 17; Giménez Soler, *Juan Manuel*, 366, no. 196.

80. Rui de Pina, *Crónica de D. Dinis* (Porto: Livraria Civilização, 1945), 235–37, ch. 12; Manuel García Fernández, "Las relaciones internacionales de Alfonso IV de Portugal y Alfonso XI de Castilla en Andalucía: La participación portuguesa en la Gran Batalla del Estrecho, 1325–1350," *RFLH* 3 (1986): 201–16, esp. 203.

81. Giménez Soler, *Corona*, 160 nn. 2–3; Masiá de Ros, *Relación*, 2:242–44, no. 126/361.

82. *CFIV*, 163, ch. 17; Gonzalo de la Finojosa, "Continuación," 106:46–47, ch. 248; *CDIE*, 1:677; Dufourcq, *L'Espagne*, 401 n. 7, citing Francisco Bofarull y Sans, *Memorias de la Real Academia de Buenas Letras* 7 (1901): 74–75; Harvey, *Islamic Spain*, 172–73.

83. *MFIV*, 2:708–10, no. 495; Ladero Quesada and González Jiménez, "Gibraltar," 237–41, nos. 14–16.

84. Ibn Khaldūn, *Histoire*, 4:204–5; Giménez Soler, *Corona*, 161 n. 1.

85. *MFIV*, 2:696, no. 483; González Mínguez, *Fernando IV*, 293–94.

86. Ibn Khaldūn, *Histoire*, 4:183–14; Ibn Abī Zarʿ, *Rawd al-Qirtās*, 2:717–18.

87. Alarcón y Santón and Garcia de Linares, *Documentos árabes*, 165–69, no. 82; *MFIV*, 2:694, no. 479; Giménez Soler, *Corona*, 159 n. 1; Dufourcq, *L'Espagne*, 401–2.

88. Masià i de Ros, *Jaume II*, 371–72, 374–76, and *Relación*, 1:162–65; Giménez Soler, *Juan Manuel*, 367–69, no. 197; Dufourcq, *L'Espagne*, 403–4.

89. *CFIV*, 163–64, ch. 17; Masiá de Ros, *Jaume II*, 373, and *Relación*, 2:244–47, no. 126 bis/363; Giménez Soler, *Juan Manuel*, 368–71, nos. 197–200, and *Almería*, 60 n.1; Zurita, *Anales*, 2:716–17.

90. *MFIV*, 2:760–63, no. 525; Giménez Soler, *Juan Manuel*, 373, no. 203, and *Corona*, 175 n. 1; Hilda Grassotti, "Un empréstito para la conquista de Sevilla: Problemas que suscita," in *Miscelánea de estudios sobre instituciones castellano-leonesas* (Bilbao: Editorial Nájera, 1978), 272, citing Madrid, Biblioteca Nacional, MS 4357, no. 103; González Mínguez, *Fernando IV*, 289–90.

91. Giménez Soler, *Juan Manuel*, 368–70, nos. 197, 198; *CFIV*, 162–64, ch. 17.

92. Giménez Soler, *Almería*, and "Expedición de Jaime II," 290–335; Cynthia L. Chamberlin, "'Not All Martyrs or Saints': The Aragonese-Castilian Crusade Against Granada, 1309–1310," *Comitatus* 23 (1992): 17–45; I. S. Allouche, "La relation du siège d'Almería en 709 (1309–1310) d'après de nouveaux manuscrits de la Durrat al-Hiǧāl," *Hespéris* 16 (1933): 122–38.

93. Marugán Vallvé, "Sitio de Almería," 2:172–73, citing documents from ACA Reg. 308, 344. María Desamparados Martínez San Pedro, "Jaime II y la Cruzada de Almería," *Anales de la Universidad de Alicante: Historia Medieval* 11 (1996): 579–86.

94. Zurita, *Anales*, 2:713–14; Muntaner, *Crònica*, 7:6, ch. 245–46; *CFIV*, 163, ch. 17; Masiá de Ros, *Relación*, 2:234–36, 240–41, nos. 121/342, 122.343, 123/345, 124/347.

95. Ahmad ibn al-Qādī, *Durrat al Hijāl*, in René Basset, "Le siège d'Almería en 709," *Journal Asiatique* 10th ser. 10 (1907): 275–303; Claudio Sánchez Albornoz, *La España musulmana según los autores islamitas y cristianos medievales*, 7th ed., 2 vols. (Madrid:

Espasa-Calpe, 1986), 2:386–92; Harvey, *Islamic Spain*, 174–75; Évariste Lévi-Provençal, "Un Zağal hispanique sur l'expédition aragonaise de 1309 contre Almería," *Al-Andalus* 6 (1941): 377–99, esp. 398–99.

96. *CGPIII*, 168, ch. 38; *The Chronicle of San Juan de la Peña: A Fourteenth-Century Official History of the Crown of Aragón*, tr. Lynn H. Nelson (Philadelphia: University of Pennsylvania Press, 1991), 96, ch. 38 (*CSJP*); Ramon Muntaner, *Crònica*, 7:7, ch. 246; Marugán Vallvé, "Sitio de Almería," 184, no. 1; Ibn al-Qāḍī, *Durrat al Hijāl*, in Basset, "Siège d'Almería," 293; Giménez Soler, *Almería*, 57–59.

97. Finke, *Acta Aragonensia*, 2:884, no. 561, 3:206, no. 96; Salavert y Roca, *Cerdeña*, 2:526–27; Zurita, *Anales*, 2:718–20.

98. Ibn al-Qāḍī, *Durrat al-Hijāl*, in Basset "Siège d'Almeria," 293–97, 301; Ibn Khaldūn, *Histoire*, 204–5; Al-Makkarī, *History*, 2:348; Harvey, *Islamic Spain*, 175–76.

99. Marugán Vallvé, "Sitio de Almería," 185–86, no. 2; Zurita, *Anales*, 2:727–29; Harvey, *Islamic Spain*, 175–76.

100. Masià i de Ros, *Jaume II*, 339–40; Giménez Soler, *Corona*, 163–64 n. 1, and *Almería*, 61–63; Manzano Rodríguez, *Intervención*, 345–46.

101. *CFIV*, 163–64, ch. 17; González Mínguez, *Fernando IV*, 296.

102. *MFIV*, 2:707–8, nos. 492–94; Masià i de Ros, *Jaume II*, 391–92, 473; Giménez Soler, *Corona*, 165 n. 1, and *Almería*, 64; Dufourcq, *L'Espagne*, 404.

103. Ibn al-Qāḍī, *Durrat al Hijāl*, in Basset "Siège d'Almeria," 302–3.

104. Giménez Soler, *Corona*, 162–66; 164 n. 1, and *Juan Manuel*, 172, no. 201; Masià i de Ros, *Jaume II*, 377–84, 452–53.

105. *CFIV* 164, ch. 17; *MFIV*, 2:719–23, 773–76, nos. 502–3, 532–33.

106. Giménez Soler, *Corona*, 166 n. 1, 175 n. 2; Masià i de Ros, *Jaume II*, 386–89.

107. Giménez Soler, *Corona*, 167–70; Masiá de Ros, *Relación*, 1:167–68, 2:250–51, no. 129/374; *MFIV*, 2:760–63, no. 525; Arié, *L'Espagne*, 89–93; Torres Delgado, *Granada*, 233–38.

108. *MFIV*, 2:756, no. 521; Giménez Soler, *Corona*, 176 nn. 1–2, 177–79 n. 1, 182 n. 1; Masià i de Ros, *Jaume II*, 392–93, 443.

109. *CGPIII*, 168, ch. 38; *CSJP*, 96–97, ch. 38; Muntaner, *Crònica*, 7:6–10, ch. 245–47.

110. Masiá de Ros, *Relación*, 2:244–50, 256–57, 258–60, nos. 126 bis/363, 127/368, 132/380, 133/385, 135/386.

111. *CFIV*, 168–69, ch. 19; *MFIV*, 2:736–37, 789–91, 793–99, 800–805, 811, 822–23, nos. 510, 541–44, 546, 550, 560; González Mínguez, *Fernando IV*, 303–16.

112. Ibn Abī Zar', *Rawd al-Qirṭās*, 2:718–19; Ibn Khaldūn, *Histoire*, 4:188; *CAXI*, 314–15, ch. 224–25; Zurita, *Anales*, 2:741–42; Alemany, "Milicias," 145, 147, 149; Dufourcq, *L'Espagne*, 457–58, citing ACA Reg. 336, fol. 29v; Benavides, *MFIV*, 1:227, n. 1; Manzano Rodríguez, *Intervención*, 187–92.

113. Ibn Abī Zar', *Rawd al-Qirṭās*, 2:724; Ibn Khaldūn, *Histoire*, 4:216; Giménez Soler, *Corona*, 183 n. 3.

114. *CAXI*, 206, ch. 54; *GCAXI*, 1:406, ch. 69; Al-Makkarī, *History*, 2:348–49; Giménez Soler, *Corona*, 183 n. 2, 184–85 n. 2; Arié, *L'Espagne*, 92–93; Torres Delgado, *Granada*, 245.

115. *CFIV*, 169, ch. 19–20; Giménez Soler, *Corona*, 184 nn. 1– 2; *MFIV*, 2:365–67, 820, 861–63, nos. 243, 558, 582–83; González Mínguez, *Fernando IV*, 314–24.

116. *MFIV*, 2:712, no. 497; Giménez Soler, *Corona*, 172 n. 1, 173–74 n. 1, and *Almería*, 64–72, 106–13; Masià i de Ros, *Jaume II*, 335–36, 387–88; Zurita, *Anales*, 2:736.

117. Benavides , *MFIV*, 1:225 n. 1, and *MFIV*, 2:725–26, 743–45, nos. 505, 515; González Mínguez, *Fernando IV*, 299.

118. Manuel Milián Boix, "El fondo 'Instrumenta Miscellanea' del Archivo Vaticano: Documentos referentes a España (853–1782)," *Anthologica Annua* 15 (1967): 531; Zurita, *Anales*, 2:736; González Mínguez, *Fernando IV*, 299.

119. *Regestum Clementis Papae V*, nos. 5492, 5485, 6939, 6941, cited by Peter Linehan, "The Church, the Economy and the *Reconquista* in Early Fourteenth-Century Castile," *Revista Española de Teología* 43 (1983): 275–302, reprinted in his *Past and Present in Medieval Spain* (Aldershot: Variorum/Ashgate, 1992), XI:275–302.

120. Fita, *Actas*, 156, no. 2.

121. *Regestum Clementis Papae V*, nos. 8459–64; Goñi Gaztambide, *Hstoria*, 282.

122. Giménez Soler, *Corona*, 185 n. 3.

123. *CFIV*, 169–70, ch. 20; Finke, *Acta Aragonensia*, 3:230, no. 108; Torres Delgado, *Granada*, 245–46; Masiá de Ros, *Relación*, 1:175–88.

124. *CAXI*, 173, ch. 1; *GCAXI*, 1:275, ch. 1; Gonzalo de la Finojosa, "Continuación," 106:47, ch. 248.

125. *Regestum Clementis Papae V*, no. 9727, cited by Linehan, "The Church," 283.

126. Finke, *Acta Aragonensia*, 2:781–83, nos. 488–89; Vicente Salavert y Roca, "La isla de Cerdeña y la política internacional de Jaime II de Aragón," *Hispania* 10 (1950): 265; Goñi Gaztambide, *Historia*, 282.

127. Giménez Soler, *Corona*, 183.

CHAPTER 7. EARLY CRUSADES OF ALFONSO XI'S REIGN

1. *Crónica de Alfonso XI (CAXI)*; *Gran crónica de Alfonso XI (GCAXI)*, ed. Diego Catalán; Rodrigo Yáñez, *Poema de Alfonso XI*, ed. Tomás Antonio Sánchez, in *Poetas castellanos anteriores al siglo XV (PAXI 1864)*; and ed. Yo Ten Cate.

2. See Nicolas Agrait, "Monarchy and Military Practice During the Reign of Alfonso XI of Castile (1312–1350)" (Ph.D. dissertation, Fordham University, 2003), and "The Reconquest During the Reign of Alfonso XI (1312–1350)," in Donald J. Kagay and Theresa Vann, eds., *On the Social Origins of Medieval Institutions: Essays in Honor of Joseph F. O'Callaghan* (Leiden: Brill, 1998), 149–66, and "The Experience of War in Fourteenth-Century Spain: Alfonso XI and the Capture of Algeciras (1342–1344)," in L. J. Andrew Villalon and Donald J. Kagay, eds., *Crusaders, Condottieri, and Cannon: Medieval Warfare in Societies Around the Mediterranean* (Leiden: Brill, 2003), 213–38; José Sánchez-Arcilla Bernal, *Alfonso XI, 1312–1350* (Palencia: La Olmeda, 1995).

3. *CAXI*, 173–77, ch. 1–6; *GCAXI*, 1:276–91, ch. 1–7; *CDIE*, 1:677; Giménez Soler,

Juan Manuel, 409–10, 413–20, 432–33, 435–36, 451–55, 457, nos. 244, 249–55, 258, 276, 278, 303, 307; Masiá de Ros, *Relación*, 1:189–97; Fita, *Actas*, 149–51.

4. Nieto Cumplido, *Regionalismo*. 205–12, no. 29; Sanz Fuentes, "Cartas de hermandad concejíl," 419–24; Argente del Castillo Ocaña, "Hermandades medievales," 21–32; Manuel García Fernández, "La Hermandad General de Andalucía durante la minoría de Alfonso XI de Castilla," *HID* 12 (1985): 351–75, and "Las hermandades municipales andaluzas en tiempos de Alfonso XI," *AEM* 19 (1989): 329–43, and "Las relaciones castellano-mariniés en Andalucía en tiempos de Alfonso XI: La participación norteafricana en la guerra por el control del Estrecho, 1312–1350," in García Arenal and Viguera, *Relaciones*, 249–71, esp. 254.

5. Ibn Khaldūn, *Histoire*, 4:216.

6. Giménez Soler, *Juan Manuel*, 431–32, 435, nos. 272–73, 277; Manuel García Fernández, "Regesto documental andaluz de Alfonso XI (1312–1350)," *HID* 15 (1990): 3, no. 2.

7. Masià i de Ros, *Jaume II*, 446–47; Giménez Soler, *Corona*, 186 n. 1; Manuel García Fernández, "Jaime II y la minoría de Alfonso XI (1312–1325): Sus relaciones con la sociedad política castellana," *HID* 18 (1991): 143–81, and "Don Dionis de Portugal y la minoría de Alfonso XI de Castilla (1312–1325)," *RFLH* 9 (1992): 25–51.

8. Masià i de Ros, *Jaume II*, 293, 487–88; García Fernández, "Regesto," 5, nos. 10–11; Giménez Soler, *Juan Manuel*, 437, 441–42, 449–50, nos. 281, 287, 301; Lafuente y Alcántara, *Inscripciones*, 31–32, 213–16; Al-Makkarī, *History*, 2:349–50; Arié, *L'Espagne*, 93; Torres Delgado, *Granada*, 246–47.

9. Giménez Soler, *Corona*, 187 n. 1, 188 nn. 1–2, 189 n. 1, 196 n. 1, and *Juan Manuel*, 460–61, no. 315; Masià i de Ros, *Jaume II*, 474–77, 479–81, 485–86; Harvey, *Islamic Spain*, 178–87.

10. Giménez Soler, *Corona*, 190 n. 1, 191 n. 1, 192 n. 1, 195–96 n. 1, and *Juan Manuel*, 447, 463–64, nos. 297, 320; Masià i de Ros, *Jaume II*, 457, 488–89; *CAXI*, 177–78, 179, ch. 6, 8; *GCAXI*, 1:289–90, 295, ch. 7, 9; Vigil, *Oviedo*, 169, no. 104.

11. Ubieto Arteta, *Cuéllar*, 156–58, no. 71.

12. *CAXI* 180, 206, ch. 8, 55; *GCAXI*, 1:296–98, 407, ch. 10–11, 70; García Fernández, "Regesto," 8–9, nos. 27a–28a, 29–30; Giménez Soler, *Juan Manuel*, 469–71, nos. 329, 332–33, and *Corona*, 198–99 n. 1, 199 nn. 1–2, 200–202, 203 n. 1; Masià i de Ros, *Jaume II*, 458–59, 463–64, 490, 493–94, 499–501, 504.

13. Fita, *Actas*, 151–54, no. 2; Linehan, "The Church," 283–84; *CAXI*, 178, ch. 6; *GCAXI*, 1:290, ch. 7.

14. *CDACA*, 40:49–53; Finke, *Acta Aragonensia*, 2:850–51, no. 531.

15. Reg. Vat. 64, ep. 1902, and Reg. Av. 5, fol. 117v, cited by Goñi Gaztambide, *Historia*, 283; Guillaume Mollat, *Lettres communes: Jean XXII, analysées d'aprés les registres dits d'Avignon et du Vatican*, 17 vols. (Paris: A. Fontemoing, 1904–47), no. 2338.

16. Finke, *Acta Aragonensia*, 3:L, extract from ACA Reg. 251, fol. 118; Goñi Gaztambide, *Historia*, 286–87.

17. Finke, *Acta Aragonensia*, 2:789–90, nos. 492–93; 3:318–19, no. 151; Masiá de Ros, *Relación*, 1:197–98; Zurita, *Anales*, 3:95; *PAXI (1864)*, stanzas 1–18.

18. Reg. Av. 5, fol. 357a, Reg. Vat. 65, ep. 2125a, and Reg. Vat. 63, epp. 1001–2, cited by Goñi Gaztambide, *Historia*, 284; Mollat, *Lettres*, nos. 2924–25.

19. Reg. Av. 5, fol. 219a, and Reg. Vat. 63, ep. 155, cited by Goñi Gaztambide, *Historia*, 285; Mollat, *Lettres*, no. 2921.

20. Reg. Av. 5, fol. 357b, Reg. Vat. 65, ep. 2125c, and Reg. Vat. 63, ep. 1003, cited by Goñi Gaztambide, *Historia*, 285; Mollat, *Lettres*, no. 2926.

21. Reg. Av. 5, fol. 356b, and fol. 250b, Reg. Vat. 65, epp. 2123–24, Reg. Vat. 63, ep. 1000, cited by Goñi Gaztambide, *Historia*, 285; Emil Friedberg, *Corpus Iuris Canonici*, 2 vols. (Leipzig: Tauchnitz, 1879–81), 2:1214; Mollat, *Lettres*, no. 2922.

22. Al-Makkarī, *History*, 2:350–51.

23. Finke, *Acta Aragonensia*, 2:790, no. 494; Reg. Av. 8, fol. 343a, Reg. Vat. 67, ep. 477, ACA Bulas pontificias, leg. 29, no. 24, cited by Goñi Gaztambide, *Historia*, 286.

24. Giménez Soler, *Corona*, 193–94 n. 1, 209 n. 3, 210 n. 1; Masià i de Ros, *Jaume II*, 457–63.

25. *CAXI*, 206, ch. 75; *GCAXI*, 1:407, ch. 70.

26. ACA Bulas pontificias, leg. 28, no. 6, Reg. Vat. 110, fol. 102, ep. 325, Reg. Vat. 109, fol. 37, ep. 152, cited by Goñi Gaztambide, *Historia*, 286.

27. Ibn ʿAbī Zarʿ, *Rawd al-Qirtās*, 2:727; Ibn Khaldūn, *Histoire*, 4:199–200; Manzano Rodriguez, *Intervención*, 196–201; Dufourcq, *L'Espagne*, 467.

28. *CAXI*, 180–82, ch. 10–11; *GCAXI*, 1:300–305, ch. 13–15; Giménez Soler, *Juan Manuel*, 471, no. 335; García Fernández, "Regesto," 12, no. 44; Francisco de Asís Veas Arteseros, *Documentos de Alfonso XI*, CODOM 6 (Murcia: Academia Alfonso X el Sabio, 1997), 18, no. 19.

29. Giménez Soler, *Juan Manuel*, 471–73, nos. 336, 338–39; *CAXI*, 182, ch. 12; *GCAXI*, 1:306–7, ch. 16.

30. Reg. Av. 9, fol. 464b–466b, 483a, and Reg. Vat. 68, epp. 1547, 1688–89, 1694–95, cited by Goñi Gaztambide, *Historia*, 285–86; Mollat, *Lettres*, nos. 7864, 8020–22, 8026–27.

31. Finke, *Acta Aragonensia*, 3:345–52, nos. 164–65; Giménez Soler, *Corona*, 206–7 n.1, 209 n. 1; Reg. Vat. 337, fol. 359, cited by Goñi Gaztambide, *Historia*, 287–88.

32. Giménez Soler, *Juan Manuel*, 474–75, no. 341; Masià i de Ros, *Jaume II*, 465–68.

33. Ibn Khaldūn, *Histoire*, 4:205–6; Manzano Rodríguez, *Intervención*, 199, 212.

34. *GCAXI*, 1:310–12, ch. 18–20; *PAXI (1864)*, stanzas 1–18; García Fernández, "Regesto," 13, nos. 47–48.

35. Giménez Soler, *Juan Manuel*, 475–76, no. 343, and *Corona*, 211 nn. 1–2; Masià i de Ros, *Jaume II*, 507–8.

36. *CAXI*, 183, ch. 13; *GCAXI*, 1:313–15, ch. 20, and 465–67, ch. 11, of the critical version of *CAXI*; *PAXI (1864)*, stanzas 19–27; Al-Makkarī, *History*, 2:350, also An-Nuwayrī, cited by Gayangos, in Al-Makkarī, *History*, 535 n. 23.

37. *PAXI (1864)*, stanzas 28–39; *CAXI*, 195, 200, ch. 33, 43; *GCAXI*, 1:362–63, 382, ch. 44, 55; Gonzalo de la Finojosa, "Continuación," 106:47, ch. 249; Agrait, "Experience of War," 217 n. 18.

38. *CAXI*, 183–84, ch. 14; *GCAXI*, 1:316–18, ch. 21; *PAXI (1864)*, stanzas 40–48; *CDIE*, 1:677; *Chronicon de Cardeña*, *ES* 23:376–77; Juan Manuel, *El libro de los estados*, ed. Ian R. Macpherson and Robert Brian Tate (Madrid: Clásicos Castalia, 1991), bk. 1, ch. 77.

39. *CAXI*, 184, ch. 14; *GCAXI*, 1:318–19, ch. 21; *PAXI (1864)*, stanzas 49–52.

40. Ibn Khaldūn, *Histoire*, 2:206; Al-Makkarī, *History*, 2:350–52; Arié, *L'Espagne*, 96–97; Andrés Giménez Soler, "La expedición a Granada de los infantes don Juan y don Pedro en 1319," *RABM* 11 (1904): 353–60, and 12 (1905): 24–36; Zurita, *Anales*, 3:129–30.

41. Reg. Vat. 70, ep. 24, cited by Goñi Gaztambide, *Historia*, 291–92; Mollat, *Lettres*, no. 12046.

42. *CAXI*, 184, ch. 14; *GCAXI*, 1:319, ch. 21, n. 71; García Fernández, "Hermandad General," 354–55; Nieto Cumplido, *Regionalismo*, 213–26, nos. 30–33; Argente del Castillo Ocaña, "Hermandades," 26 n. 19, 32.

43. Ortega y Cotes, *Bullarium*, 177–79; Fidel Fita, "El concilio nacional de Palencia en 1321," *BRAH* 52 (1908): 47–48, no. 9; Giménez Soler, *Corona*, 217 n. 1, and *Juan Manuel*, 478–79, nos. 347–49.

44. García Fernández, "Hermandad General," 363–64, 370–73, no. 1.

45. Giménez Soler, *Juan Manuel*, 488–89, no. 355, and *Corona*, 212 n.2. Masià i de Ros, *Jaume II*, 508–12.

46. Nieto Cumplido, *Regionalismo*, 227–29, no. 35; García Fernández, "Regesto," 16–17, nos. 60–62, 64, and "Hermandad General," 374–75, no. 2.

47. *CAXI*, 184–91, ch. 14–26; *GCAXI*, 1:323–44, 350, ch. 22–33, 37, and 471–77, ch. 34–36, of the critical version of *CAXI*; *PAXI (1864)*, 479, stanzas 75–78; *CLC*, 1:337–72; *MFIV*, 1:680–86, no. 33; *CDIE*, 1:677; Goñi Gaztambide, *Historia*, 289; Mollat, *Lettres*, no. 14136; Masiá de Ros, *Relación*, 1:198–207.

48. Mollat, *Lettres*, nos. 14284–87; Goñi Gaztambide, *Historia*, 291; Adeline Rucquoi, "El cardenal legado Guillaume Peyre de Godin," *Revista Española del Derecho Canónico* 47 (1990): 493–516.

49. Rui de Pina, *Crónica de D. Dinis*, 303–5, ch. 26; *MH*, 1:133–40; García Fernández, "Relaciones internacionales," 203–4, and "Don Dionis de Portugal," 37–38.

50. Masià i de Ros, *Jaume II*, 512–13; Giménez Soler, *Corona*, 214 n. 1, 215 n. 2, 220 n. 1, and *Juan Manuel*, 70, 490, no. 358; Finke, *Acta Aragonensia*, 3:386–87, no. 175; Goñi Gaztambide, *Historia*, 289; García Fernández, "Regesto," 16, nos. 60–61.

51. Masià i de Ros, *Jaume II*, 517–26, 531–40; Giménez Soler, *Corona*, 216 n. 1, 218 n. 1, 219 n.1, 221–24, 225 n. 2, 226 n. 2, 228 n.1, 229–32, and *Juan Manuel*, 496–97, 500, 503, nos. 367, 370, 372, 379; Alarcón y Santón and García de Linares, *Documentos árabes*, 31–36, 55–58, nos. 13–15, 27.

52. *CAXI*, 200, 206–7, ch. 43, 55; *GCAXI*, 1:382, 407–9, ch. 55, 70; Al-Makkarī, *History*, 2:352–53; Gimenez Soler, *Corona*, 225, n. 1, 226, n. 1; Lafuente Alcántara, *Inscripciones*, 215–19; Ibn Khaldūn, *Histoire*, 4:237; Arié, *L'Espagne*, 98; Torres Delgado, *Granada*, 262–63; Harvey, *Islamic Spain*, 187–89.

53. *CAXI*, 197–203, ch. 37–49; *GCAXI*, 1:373–85, 393–95, ch. 50–57, 62; *PAXI (1864)*, stanzas 196–246; *CDIE*, 1:678; Gonzalo de la Finojosa, "Continuación," 106:48, ch. 249; *CLC*, 1:372–400; Giménez Soler, *Juan Manuel*, 532, no. 420; Masiá de Ros, *Relación*, 1:207–10; García Fernández, "Regesto," 24, no. 96.

54. *CLC*, 1:393, art. 10; García Fernández, "Hermandad General," 19, and "Algunas

consideraciones sobre los objetivos politicos de la Hermandad General de Andalucía," *Medievalismo* 2 (1992): 61–65, esp. 64–65.

55. *CAXI*, 196–97, ch. 36; *GCAXI*, 1:366–68, ch. 47–48; Giménez Soler, *Juan Manuel*, 514, 516, nos. 395, 399; Calderón Ortega and Díaz González, "Los almirantes del 'siglo de oro,'" 315–26.

56. Reg. Vat. 133, fol. 225v, ep. 1325, cited by Goñi Gaztambide, *Historia*, 297.

57. *CAXI*, 207, ch. 56; *GCAXI*, 1:410, ch. 71; O'Callaghan, *Reconquest*, 191–92; Harvey, *Islamic Spain*, 187–89.

58. *CDIE*, 1:678; *CAXI*, 202–205, ch. 46; *GCAXI*, 1:386–91, ch. 58–60; *PAXI (1864)*, stanzas 188–95; Gonzalo de la Finojosa, "Continuación," 106:48, ch. 249; Torres Delgado, *Granada*, 269–70.

59. Giménez Soler, *Juan Manuel*, 532, no. 419; Reg. Vat. 114, ep. 541–42, cited by Goñi Gaztambide, *Historia*, 298.

60. Ibn Khaldūn, *Histoire*, 4:216; Giménez Soler, *Corona*, 233, nn. 1–2; Arié, *L'Espagne*, 98–100; Torres Delgado, *Granada*, 265–72; Harvey, *Islamic Spain*, 187.

61. *CAXI*, 203–4, ch. 498; *GCAXI*, 1:397–98, ch. 64; *PAXI (1864)*, stanzas 247–65, 283–84.

62. Giménez Soler, *Juan Manuel*, 516, no. 397.

63. Reg. Vat. 113, fol. 225, ep. 1324, cited by Goñi Gaztambide, *Historia*, 296.

64. Goñi Gaztambide, *Historia*, 296, 644–45, no. 3.

65. Isabel Montes Romero-Camacho, "La documentación de Alfonso XI conservada en el Archivo de la Catedral de Sevilla," *ELEM* 3 (1982): 138, 140, nos. 8, 14; Ortíz de Zúñiga, *Anales*, 2:56–58, 87; García Fernández, "Regesto," 19, no. 75; Ballesteros, *Sevilla*, ccciv.

66. Finke, *Acta Aragonensia*, 2:837, no. 518, and "Nachträge und Ergänzungen zu den Acta Aragonensia (I-III)," *Spanische Forschungen der Görresgesellschaft: Gesammelte Aufsätze zu Kulturgeschichte Spaniens* I Reihe, 4 (1933): 355–56, reprinted in *Acta Aragonensia*, 3:706–7.

67. Reg. Vat. 114, epp. 747, 749, cited by Goñi Gaztambide, *Historia*, 297–98, and 293.

68. Manuel Rojas Gabriel, "Guerra de asedio y expugnación castral en la frontera con Granada: El reinado de Alfonso XI de Castilla como paradigma (1325–1350)," *RFLH* ser. 2, 15 (1998): 875–900.

69. Giménez Soler, *Corona*, 238 n. 2; Veas Arteseros, *Alfonso XI*, 87–88, no. 74.

70. *CAXI*, 206–7, ch. 57–58; *GCAXI*, 1:399–400, 411–12, ch. 55, 72; *PAXI (1864)*, stanzas 286–88; Gonzalo de la Finojosa, "Continuación," 106:48, ch. 249; *CDIE*, 1:678; Giménez Soler, *Juan Manuel*, 545–46, 549, nos. 440–41, 446; Veas Arteseros, *Alfonso X*, 100–101, no. 93.

71. Romualdo Escalona, *Historia del Real Monasterio de Sahagún* (Madrid, 1782; reprint, León: Ediciones Leonesas, 1982), 652–53, no. 293; Manuel Rojas Gabriel, *Olvera en la Baja Edad Media (siglos XIV–XV)* (Cádiz: Diputación Provincial, 1988), 157–59.

72. *PAXI (1864)*, stanzas 289–90; García Fernández, "Regesto," 29, no. 119; O'Callaghan, *Reconquest*, 206–8.

73. *CAXI*, 209, ch. 59; *GCAXI*, 1:414, ch. 74; Gonzalo de la Finojosa, "Continuación," 106:48, ch. 249; Cesáreo Fernández Duro, *La marina de Castilla desde su orígen y pugna con la de Inglaterra hasta la refundición en la Armada Española* (Madrid: El Progreso Editorial, 1894), 77; Antonio de Capmany y de Montpalau, *Memorias históricas sobre la marina, comercio y artes de la antigua Ciudad de Barcelona*, 4 vols. in 3 (Madrid: A. de Sancha, 1779–92), 3:14–28.

74. Ibn Khaldūn, *Histoire*, 4:216; Manzano Rodríguez, *Intervención*, 200–201.

75. *CDIE*, 1:678–79; Gonzalo de la Finojosa, "Continuación," 106:49, ch. 249; García Fernández, "Relaciones internacionales," 205.

76. António Caetano de Sousa, *Provas da História genealogica da casa real portuguesa*, 6 vols. in 12, ed. Manuel Lopes Almeida and César Pegado (Coimbra: Atlantida, 1946–52), 1:355–77, no. 27.

77. Veas Arteseros, *Alfonso XI*, 89–98, nos. 77–91; Giménez Soler, *Juan Manuel*, 533, 537–40, 543, nos. 421, 428, 430, 432, 435; Fernando Arias Guillén, "Los discursos de la guerra en la *Gran Crónica de Alfonso XI*," *Miscelánea Medieval Murciana* 31 (2007): 9–21, esp. 11–12.

78. Giménez Soler, *Juan Manuel*, 551–59, no. 450, 452; Veas Arteseros, *Alfonso XI*, 103–5, nos. 96–106; *CAXI*, 209–10, ch. 70; *GCAXI*, 1:417–18, ch. 75; *PAXI (1864)*, stanzas 294–99.

79. Demetrio Mansilla, *La documentación española del Archivo del Castel S. Angelo (395–1498)* (Rome: Iglesia Nacional Española, 1958), 66, no. 125.

80. *CAXI*, 213–14, ch. 76; *GCAXI*, 1:438–39, ch. 88; Reg. Vat. 114, fol. 226v–228, cited by Goñi Gaztambide, *Historia*, 299; Giménez Soler, *Juan Manuel*, 569–70, no. 465.

81. Raynaldus, *Annales*, a. 1328, nos. 76–78; Reg. Vat. 87, ep. 2477, Reg. Av. 30, fol. 631, 633v, and Archivio Sant'Angelo, Armario II, caja 2, no. 12, cited by Goñi Gaztambide, *Historia*, 299.

82. Mansilla, *Castel S. Angelo*, 66–67, no. 126; Mollat, *Lettres*, nos. 41566–68; Reg. Vat. 87, epp. 2476, 2478, and Reg. Avin. 30, fol. 623v, 633, 636b, cited by Goñi Gaztambide, *Historia*, 299–300.

83. Mansilla, *Castel S. Angelo*, 67, no. 127.

84. Giménez Soler *Juan Manuel*, 534, 550, 560–64, 567–69, nos. 423, 448, 454, 456, 458, 462, 464, and *Corona*, 237 n. 2; Zurita, *Anales*, 3:294–96; Francisco de Moxó y de Montoliu, "La relación epistolar entre Alfonso XI y Alfonso IV en el Archivo de la Corona de Aragón," *ELEM* 3 (1982): 173–95; Masiá de Ros, *Relación*, 1:211–14; María Martínez Martínez and Manuel Sánchez Martínez, "El reino de Murcia en la alianza castellano-aragonesa contra el sultanato nazarí (1329)," *RFLH* ser. 2, 15 (1998): 1135–68.

85. Veas Arteseros, *Alfonso XI*, 122–26, no. 119, and 144–51, nos. 126–30; Giménez Soler, *Corona*, 235 n. 1, 236, n. 1; Masiá de Ros, *Relación*, 2:319–23, nos.174/12, 176/17; Moxó y de Montoliu, "Relación," 178, nos. 13, 15; *CAXI*, 218–21, ch. 74–75, 78; *GCAXI*, 455–57, 462–63, ch. 95–96, 99; *CDIE*, 1:679; Gonzalo de la Finojosa, "Continuación," 106:50, ch. 249; Zurita, *Anales*, 3:312–14, 321–24; Juan Torres Fontes, "El tratado de Tarazona y la campaña aragonesa en el reino de Granada (1328-1330)," *ROEL* 7–8 (1986–87): 3–19; Manuel

Sánchez Martínez, "Guerra, avituallamiento del ejército y carestías en la Corona de Aragón: La provisión del cereal para la expedición granadina de Alfonso el Benigno (1329–1333)," *HID* 20 (1993): 523–45.

86. Manuel Sánchez Martínez, "La contribución valenciana a la cruzada granadina de Alfonso IV de Aragón (1327–1335)," *Primer Congreso de Historia del País Valenciano celebrado en Valencia del 14 al 18 de abril de 1971*, 4 vols. (Valencia: Universidad de Valencia, 1973–81), 2:579–98.

87. Giménez Soler, *Corona*, 239 n. 2, and *Juan Manuel*, 576, no. 477.

88. ACA Reg. 562, fols. 93, 101, cited by Finke, "Nachträge," in *Acta Aragonensia*, 3:728; Giménez Soler, *Corona*, 243 n. 3, 244 n. 1; Masiá de Ros, *Relación*, 2:320–21, no. 175/16; Moxó y de Montoliu, "Relación," 179–80, nos. 26–28; Zurita, *Anales*, 3:325; Sánchez Martínez, "Guerra," 546–48, no. 1.

89. Ángels Masià i de Ros, "Aportaciones al estudio de los 'Pastorellos' en la Corona de Aragón," in *Homenaje a Millás Vallicrosa*, 2 vols. (Barcelona: CSIC, 1954–56), 2:9–30.

90. Finke, "Nachträge," in *Acta Aragonensia* 3:722–33.

91. Reg. Vat. 113, ep. 1676, and Reg. 646, no. 4, cited by Goñi Gaztambide, *Historia*, 298.

92. Joaquim Miret i Sans, "Negociacions diplomatiques d'Alfons III de Catalunya-Aragó ab el rey de França per la croada contra Granada," *Anuari de l'Institut d'Estudis Catalans* 2 (1908–9): 265–336, esp. 318–20, nos. 7–8; idem, "Ramón de Melany, embajador de Alfonso IV en la corte de Francia," *Boletín de la Real Academia de Buenas Letras de Barcelona* 2 (1903–4): 199–202.

93. Finke, *Acta Aragonensia*, 3:544–45, 547, and "Nachträge," 490–96, no. 41; Giménez Soler, *Corona*, 238–39 nn. 1–3, 242 n. 2, and *Juan Manuel*, 577, no. 479.

94. Marianne Mahn-Lot, "Philippe d'Évreux, roi de Navarre, et un projet de croisade contre le royaume de Grenade (1329–1331)," *Bulletin Hispanique* 46 (1944): 227–33; Reg. Vat. 115, epp. 1992–94, Reg. Vat. 94, ep. 916, cited by Goñi Gaztambide, *Historia*, 302; Mollat, *Lettres*, no. 48660.

95. Giménez Soler, *Corona*, 243 nn. 1–2; Finke, *Acta Aragonensia*, 3:545, no. 256, and "Nachträge," 725–26.

96. Reg. Vat. 94, ep. 945, and Reg. Avin. 270, fol. 334a, cited by Goñi Gaztambide, *Historia*, 302–3; Mollat, *Lettres*, no. 48478.

97. Reg. Vat. 116, ep. 240, cited by Goñi Gaztambide, *Historia*, 303; Finke, *Acta Aragonensia*, 3:548, no. 256; Francisco Miquel Rosell, *Regesta de letras pontificias en el Archivo de la Corona de Aragón, Sección de Cancillería real (Pergaminos)* (Madrid: CSIC, 1948), no. 544.

98. Reg. Vat. 115, ep. 2062, cited by Goñi Gaztambide, *Historia*, 303; Giménez Soler, *Corona*, 243 n. 2; Moxó y de Montoliu, "Relación," 181, no. 34.

99. Rui de Pina, *Chronica de el rey Dom Afonso o Quarto* (*CAIV*), 68–74, ch. 24–25.

100. *MH*, 1:162–65, no. 76; Finke, "Nachträge," in *Acta Aragonensia*, 3:728–31, no. 41; Giménez Soler, *Corona*, 244–45 nn. 1–2; Moxó y de Montoliu, "Relación," 180, nos. 32–33; Luis Vicente Díaz Martín, "Las fluctuaciones en las relaciones castellano-portuguesas durante el reinado de Alfonso IV," *RFLH* ser. 2 15 (1998): 1231–54, esp. 1236; García Fernández, "Relaciones internacionales," 206.

101. *CAXI*, 222–25, 229, ch. 80, 82–84, 94; *GCAXI*, 1:467–69, 472–73, 476–77, 494, ch. 100–101, 103–5, 115; *PAXI (1864)*, stanza 347; Gonzalo de la Finojosa, "Continuación," 106:50, ch. 249; *CDIE*, 1:679; Rui de Pina, *CAIV*, 15, ch. 4; *CLC*, 1:401–37; Giménez Soler, *Juan Manuel*, 575–76, 580, 582, nos. 475–76, 484, 487, and *Corona*, 247 n. 2; *CDAXI*, 287–89, nos. 158–59; García Fernández, "Regesto," 38, nos. 160–61; Veas Arteseros, *Alfonso XI*, 175, no. 155.

102. Jean Froissart, *Chroniques*, ed. Siméon Luce, Gaston Raynaud, and Léon Minot, 13 vols. (Paris: Mme Ve Renouard, 1869), 1:41–42, bk. 1, ch. 7, and *The Chronicles of England, France and Spain by Sir John Froissart* (London: J. M. Dent, 1906), 15–17.

103. John Barbour, *The Bruce, or The Book of the Most Excellent and Noble Prince, Robert de Broyss, King of Scots*, ed. Walter W. Skeat, 2 vols. (Edinburgh: William Blackwood, 1894), 2:184–92, bk. 20, vv. 210–510; José Enrique López de Coca Castañer, "Cruzados escoceses en la frontera de Granada (1330)," *AEM* 18 (1988): 245–61.

104. Angus MacKay, "Andalucía y la guerra del fin del mundo," in Emilio Cabrera, ed., *Andalucía entre Oriente y Occidente (1236–1492): Actas del V Coloquio Internacional de Historia Medieval de Andalucía* (Córdoba: Diputación Provincial, 1986), 329–42, esp. 329–30.

105. *CAXI*, 225, ch. 85; *GCAXI*, 1:479, ch. 106; *MH*, 1:176; García Fernández, "Relaciones internacionales," 206–7; Miguel Ángel Ladero Quesada, "Portugueses en la frontera de Granada," *ELEM* 23 (2000): 67–100, esp. 71–72.

106. *CAXI*, 226–27, ch. 86–88; *GCAXI*, 1:481–84, ch. 107–9; *PAXI (1864)*, vv. 350–58; Gonzalo de la Finojosa, "Continuación," 106:51, ch. 249; Veas Arteseros, *Alfonso XI*, 175–76, no. 156; Giménez Soler, *Juan Manuel*, 582, 584, nos. 487, 489, and *Corona*, 247 n. 1; Vidal Beltrán, "Tarifa," 21, no. 3; Torres Delgado, *Granada*, 274–75.

107. Consuelo Gutiérrez del Arroyo, *Privilegios reales de la Orden de Santiago en la Edad Media: Catálogo de la Serie existente en el Archivo Histórico Nacional* (Madrid: Junta técnica de Archivos, Bibliotecas y Museos, 1946), 295, nos. 702–3; Giménez Soler, *Corona*, 245 n.3; Moxó y de Montoliu, "Relación," 182, no. 46; García Fernández, "Regesto," 38, no. 164; Veas Arteseros, *Alfonso XI*, 177–81, nos. 158–59.

108. Giménez Soler, *Corona*, 240–41 n. 1, 245, 246 n. 1, 247 n. 1, 247–48 n. 2, and *Juan Manuel*, 578–81, 583–88, nos. 481–86, 488, 490–95; Moxó y de Montoliu, "Relación," 179, 181, 182, nos. 21, 36, 38, 42; Veas Arteseros, *Alfonso XI*, 157, 160–61, 175–76, nos. 137, 140, 142, 156–57; Masiá de Ros, *Relación*, 2:325–26, no. 177/18; *CAXI*, 227, ch. 89; *GCAXI*, 1:486, ch. 110; Zurita, *Anales*, 3:326–27, 329, 334.

109. Giménez Soler, *Corona*, 248–49 n. 1; Moxó y de Montoliu, "Relación," 183, 184, nos. 48, 53–54; Masiá de Ros, *Relación*, 2:330–32, nos. 178/29, 179/30, 180/31, and 1:218–19.

110. *CAXI*, 227, ch. 91; *GCAXI*, 1:489, ch. 112; Veas Arteseros, *Alfonso XI*, 186–92, nos. 166–68; Giménez Soler, *Corona*, 249–50 n. 2, 251 n. 1, and *Juan Manuel*, 589–90, nos. 498–99; Gonzalo de la Finojosa, "Continuación," 106:51, ch. 249; Zurita, *Anales*, 3:335; Nicolas Agrait, "Castilian Military Reform Under the Reign of Alfonso XI (1312–50)," *Journal of Medieval Military History* 3 (2005): 88–126, esp. 114.

111. Masiá de Ros, *Relación*, 1:220–21, 2:326–30, 334–35, nos. 178/29, no. 181/40; Moxó y de Montoliu, "Relación," 182, 184, 188, 191, nos. 47, 54, 58–61, 90, 106; Miret i Sans,

"Negociacions," 324–26, no. 12; Giménez Soler, *Corona*, 251 n. 1, 252 nn. 1–3, 254 n. 1, and *Juan Manuel*, 596–97, 601–2, nos. 506–7, 512; Zurita, *Anales*, 3:347–49, 362–63.

112. *CAXI*, 228–30, ch. 93, 95; *GCAXI*, 1:493, 496–97, ch. 114, 116; Baer, *Jews*, 1:325–26; Sánchez Albornoz, *España*, 2:221.

113. Reg. Vat. 116, ep. 300, cited by Goñi Gaztambide, *Historia*, 297; Joseph F. O'Callaghan, "Las definiciones medievales de la Orden de Montesa, 1326–1468," *Miscelánea de Textos Medievales* 1 (1972): 212–51, reprinted in *Spanish Military Order of Calatrava*, ch. 10.

114. *CAXI*, 231–32, ch. 97; *GCAXI*, 1:501, ch. 118; *PAXI (1864)*, stanzas 1558, 1674; Alfonso Ceballos-Escalera y Gila, *La orden y divisa de la Banda real de Castilla* (Madrid: Ediciones Iberoamericanas, 1993).

115. *CAXI*, 233–36, ch. 99–101; *GCAXI*, 1:506–14, ch. 120–22; *PAXI (1864)*, stanzas 388–414; Claudio Sánchez Albornoz, "Un ceremonial inédito de la coronación de los reyes de Castilla," in his *Estudios sobre las Instituciones medievales españolas* (México, D.F.: Universidad Nacional Autónoma de México, 1965), 739–63; Peter Linehan, "The Mechanics of Monarchy: Knighting Castile's King, 1332," *History Today* 43 (1993): 26–32, and "Ideología y liturgia en el reinado de Alfonso XI de Castilla," in Adeline Rucquoi, ed., *Génesis medieval del Estado moderno: Castilla y Navarra (1250–1370)* (Valladolid: Ambito, 1987), 229–43; María del Pilar Ramos Vicent, *Reafirmación del poder monárquico en Castilla: La coronación de Alfonso XI* (Madrid: Universidad Autónoma de Madrid, 1983).

CHAPTER 8. LOSS OF GIBRALTAR AND THE CRUSADE OF SALADO

1. For Marinid history, see *CAXI*, 310–16, ch. 214–39, and *GCAXI*, 2:201–36, ch. 214–38; see also Ibn Marzūq, *El Musnad*.

2. Ibn Khaldūn, *Histoire*, 4:217; Ibn al-Khatīb, *Historia*, 101; *CAXI*, 232–33, 314–15, ch. 98, 232–33; *GCAXI*, 1:504–5, ch. 119; Moxó y de Montoliu, "Relación," 189, nos. 93, 95.

3. Ibn Khaldūn, *Histoire*, 4:217; *CAXI*, 238–40, 242–45, ch. 103, 105–6, 108–10; *GCAXI*, 2:11, 16–18, 24–31, ch. 124, 126–27, 129–31; *PAXI (1864)*, stanzas 362, 415–27, 423–25; Rui de Pina, *CAIV*, 22–23, ch. 5; Al-Qalqašandi, *Subh al-aʿšā*, 8:92, cited by Manzano Rodríguez, *Intervención*, 221–23; Giménez Soler, *Juan Manuel*, 598–601, nos. 510–11.

4. *CAXI*, 241–48, ch. 107, 109, 111–14; *GCAXI*, 2:22–23, 32–40, ch. 128, 132–35; *PAXI (1864)*, stanzas 426–32; Ibn Khaldūn, *Histoire*, 4:217–19; Ibn Marzūq, *El Musnad*, 323; *Chronicon Conimbricense*, *ES* 23:345; García Fernández, "Regesto," 49, no. 221; Giménez Soler, *Juan Manuel*, 602–3, no. 513; Manuel López Fernández, "El itinerario del ejército castellano para desercar Gibraltar en 1333," *ETF* ser. 3, 18 (2005): 185–207, and "Los caminos y cañadas de Tarifa en los itinerarios del rey Alfonso XI de Castilla," *Aljaranda* 53 (2004): 5–10, and "Los itinerarios de Alfonso XI desde Sevilla al Campo de Gibraltar en sus campañas del Estrecho," *HID* 33 (2007): 309–27.

5. *CAXI*, 248–49, ch. 115; *GCAXI*, 2:41, 233, ch. 136, 237; Zurita, *Anales*, 3:364–66; Arié, *L'Espagne*, 101; Torres Delgado, *Granada*, 282; Manzano Rodríguez, *Intervención*, 224–26.

6. *CAXI*, 249–50, ch. 116; *GCAXI*, 2:43–46, ch. 137; *PAXI (1864)*, stanzas 433–59.

7. Manuel López Fernández, "Sobre la ubicacíon del real y del trazado de la cava que mandó hacer Alfonso XI en el istmo frente a Gibraltar en 1333," *ETF* ser. 3, 16 (2003): 151–68.

8. Masiá de Ros, *Relación*, 2:335–39, nos. 182/43, 183/44, 184/45, 185/47, 186/49, and 1:221–23; Giménez Soler, *Corona*, 255 n. 1, and *Juan Manuel*, 603–4, no. 514; Moxó y de Montoliu, "Relación," 190–91, nos. 100–106.

9. Rui de Pina, *CAIV*, 22–23, ch. 5; García Fernández, "Relaciones internacionales," 207.

10. *CAXI*, 250–53, ch. 117–20; *GCAXI*, 2:47–55, ch. 138–41.

11. Ibn Khaldūn, *Histoire*, 4:218; *CAXI*, 255–56, ch. 121–23; *GCAXI*, 2:58–63, ch. 143–44; Masiá de Ros, *Relación*, 1:223–25; Manzano Rodríguez, *Intervención*, 227.

12. *CAXI*, 256–58, ch. 124–26; *GCAXI*, 2:64–69, ch. 145–47; *PAXI (1864)*, stanzas 460–65; Rui de Pina, *CAIV*, 24–25, ch. 5; Ibn Khaldūn, *Histoire*, 4:218–19; Veas Arteseros, *Alfonso XI*, 284, no. 247; Giménez Soler, *Corona*, 255–56 n. 3, and *Juan Manuel*, 604, no. 515; Manzano Rodríguez, *Intervención*, 229–30; López Fernández, "El itinerario," 207.

13. García Fernández, "Regesto," 51, 53, nos. 227a, 229, 240.

14. *CAXI*, 258, ch. 126–27; *GCAXI*, 2:69–72, ch. 147–49; *PAXI (1864)*, stanzas 465–66; Ibn Khaldūn, *Histoire*, 4:237–38; Al-Makkarī, *History*, 2:355; Zurita, *Anales*, 3:376–77; Manzano Rodríguez, *Intervención*, 230, 351–58; Torres Delgado, *Granada*, 288–89; Harvey, *Islamic Spain*, 190–205.

15. Alarcón y Santón and García de Linares, *Documentos árabes*, 61–63, 66–70, nos. 30, 32–32 bis; Giménez Soler, *Corona*, 255–56 n.3, and 256 n. 2; Veas Arteseros, *Alfonso XI*, 293.

16. *CAXI*, 259–60, 315, ch. 129, 234; *GCAXI*, 2:78–79, ch. 151; *PAXI (1864)*, stanzas 470–82; Masiá de Ros, *Relación*, 2:340–41, 343–44 nos. 186/49, 188/53; Veas Arteseros, *Alfonso XI*, 304, no. 263; Giménez Soler, *Corona*, 257–58; García Fernández, "Relaciones castellano-mariníes," 258–60; Torres Delgado, *Granada*, 290–91.

17. Giménez Soler, *Juan Manuel*, 609–14, nos. 521–22, 524–27, and *Corona*, 257 n. 1, 257–59, 259–60 n. 1, 261 nn. 1–2; Alarcón y Santón and García de Linares, *Documentos árabes*, 87–92; Moxó y de Montoliu, "Relación," 191, nos. 109, 111; Masiá de Ros, *Relación*, 2:341, nos. 186/49, 188/53, 189/60; *CCPIV*, 69–92, ch. 2; Arié, *L'Espagne*, 101–2.

18. Giménez Soler, *Juan Manuel*, 605–8, nos. 517–19; *CCPIV*, 86–88, ch. 2; Zurita, *Anales*, 3:376–78, 414–22.

19. *CAXI*, 260–64, 267–69, 272–83, 286–92, 294–95, ch. 131–37, 140, 152, 154–63, 165–72, 175, 177–85, 188–90; *GCAXI*, 2:81–94, 99–100, 124–95, 249–53, 258, ch. 153–59, 162, 176–97, 200–202, 210, 248–51, 254; *PAXI (1864)*, stanzas 489–92, 622–75; Pedro López de Ayala, *Crónica de Juan I*, *BAE* 68:95, Año 7, ch. 5.

20. *CAXI*, 258–59, 266, 292–93, ch. 128, 141, 186; *GCAXI*, 2:75–76, 101–2, ch. 150, 163; *PAXI (1864)*, stanza 472; *CLC*, 1:443–46; Agrait, "Military Reform," 99–107.

21. *CAXI*, 268, 315, ch. 144, 235; *GCAXI*, 2:108–9, 223, ch. 166, 230; Manzano Rodríguez, *Intervención*, 237–39; Moxó y de Montoliu, "Relación," 192–93, nos. 118, 120, 124.

22. Ibn Khaldūn, *Histoire*, 4:229; Ibn Marzūq, *El Musnad*, 325–27, ch. 38; *GCAXI*, 2:238–46, ch. 239–46; *CAXI*, 315–16, ch. 237; *PAXI (1864)*, stanzas 676–87.

23. García Fernández, "Relaciones internacionales," 208–9; J. M. Vidal, *Benoit XII (1334–1342): Lettres closes et patentes interessant les pays autres que la France*, 2 vols. (Paris: Fontemoing and Boccard, 1913–50), nos. 1364–69, 1618–22, 1846, 2300–1, 2469; *MH*, 1:123–24, no. 81; Goñi Gaztambide, *Historia*, 317–18; Georges Daumet, *Étude sur l'alliance de la France et de la Castille au XIVe et au XVe siècles* (Paris: E. Bouillon, 1898), 130, no. 2.

24. *CDACA*, 7:87–98, nos. 5–7; Giménez Soler, *Corona*, 263, 264 n. 1, 265 nn. 1–2, and *Juan Manuel*, 634–36, nos. 558–59; Zurita, *Anales*, 3.448–57, 467–72; Francesc Sevillano i Colom, "Crisi hispano-musulmana: Un decenni crucial en la reconquista (1330–1340)," *Estudis d'Historia Medieval* 3 (1970): 55–74.

25. *CDACA*, 7:78–84, 98–101, nos. 2, 8–9; Giménez Soler, *Juan Manuel*, 636, no. 560; *CAXI*, 294–95, ch. 190–91, 194; *GCAXI*, 2:253, 256, ch. 250, 253; *CCPIV*, 94–95, ch. 2; J. A. Robson, "The Catalan Fleet and Moorish Sea-Power (1337–1344)," *English Historical Review* 74 (1959): 386–408.

26. Giménez Soler, *Corona*, 266–67 n. 4, 267–68 n. 1; *CDACA*, 7:84–87, nos. 3–4.

27. Vidal, *Benoit XII: Lettres closes*, nos. 752, 10957; Goñi Gaztambide, *Historia*, 318.

28. Raynaldus, *Annales*, a. 1339; J. M. Vidal, *Benoit XII (1334–1342): Lettres communes analysées d'après les registres dit d'Avignon et du Vatican*, 3 vols. (Paris: Fontemoing, 1902–11), no. 8043; Goñi Gaztambide, *Historia*, 316.

29. Georges Daumet, "Une semonce du pape Benoît à Pierre IV d'Aragon, pour ses relations fréquentes et intimes avec les musulmans," *Bulletin Hispanique* 7 (1905): 305–7; Goñi Gaztambide, *Historia*, 319–20.

30. Baer, *Jews*, 1:354–60, citing *Shebeth Yehuda*; *CAXI*, 288, ch. 178; *GCAXI*, 180, ch. 204.

31. Giovanni Villani (d. 1348), *Cronica*, ed. Ignazio Moutier, 8 vols. (Florence: Magheri, 1823), 6:196; *CAXI*, 296–300, ch. 195–99; *GCAXI*, 2:260–69, ch. 255–59; *PAXI (1864)*, stanzas 609–837; *CLC*, 1:456–76; Veas Arteseros, *Alfonso XI*, 427–30, nos. 375–79; *CDAXI*, 460–62, no. 271.

32. *CAXI*, 300–302, ch. 199–200; *GCAXI*, 2:269–87, ch. 260–65; *PAXI (1864)*, stanzas 852–85; Ibn Khaldūn, *Histoire*, 4:229–30; Ibn Marzūq, *El Musnad*, 124, 187, 327, ch. 6, 15, 38; *CSPRP*, 2:301–7; Rui de Pina, *CAIV*, 131–36, ch. 50; Gonzalo de la Finojosa, "Continuación," 106:54–55, ch. 249; Pedro López de Ayala, *Crónica de Pedro I*, *BAE* 66:402, Año 1, ch. 1; Manzano Rodríguez, *Intervención*, 243–49; Ambrosio Huici Miranda, *Las grandes batallas de la reconquista durante las invasiones africanas (almorávides, almohades, y benimerines)* (Madrid: CSIC, 1956), 336–38.

33. Alfonso XI, *Libro de la Montería*, 2 vols., ed. José Gutiérrez de la Vega (Madrid: M. Tello, 1877), 2:385, bk. 3, ch. 29.

34. *CAXI*, 302–5, ch. 201–5; *GCAXI*, 2:291–300, ch. 267–71; *PAXI (1864)*, stanzas 837–51; Vidal, *Benoit XII: Lettres closes*, no. 2631.

35. *CAXI*, 305–6, ch. 206; *GCAXI*, 2:301–2, ch. 272.

36. *GCAXI*, 2:287–88, ch. 265; *PAXI (1864)*, stanza 910.

37. *GCAXI*, 2:288–90, ch. 266; *PAXI (1864)*, stanzas 886–914, 915–43 (the sultan's letter).

38. Adam Murimuth, *Continuatio chronicarum*, ed. Edward M. Thompson, Rolls Series (London: Eyre and Spottiswoode, 1889), appendix, 263, gives the French text and a modern English translation.

39. Manzano Rodríguez, *Intervención*, 223 n. 604, citing Abū l-Hasan's letter to the sultan, in al-Qalqašandī, *Subh al-aʿšā*, 8:92.

40. *CDACA*, 7:100–101, 107–8, nos. 10, 12; Giménez Soler, *Corona*, 272 nn. 2, 4; *CAXI*, 303, 306 ch. 202, 207; *GCAXI*, 2:294, 308–9, ch. 268, 276.

41. *CAXI*, 306–8, ch. 208–9; *GCAXI*, 2:310–19, ch. 277–81; Ibn Khaldūn, *Histoire*, 4:230–31; *PAXI (1864)*, stanzas 944–90, esp. 909; *CSPRP*, 1:311; Rui de Pina, *CAIV*, 138–41, ch. 51; Gonzalo de la Finojosa, "Continuación," 106:56, ch. 249; Villani, *Cronica*, 6:210; Manzano Rodríguez, *Intervención*, 250, 253; Huici, *Batallas*, 338–39; Robson, "Catalan Fleet," 399–400; Manuel López Fernández, "Del desastre de Getares a la Victoria del Salado: La crítica situación de la zona del Estrecho en 1340," *ETF* ser. 3, 20 (2007): 135–62, esp. 135–49.

42. *CDACA*, 7:108–15, nos. 14–16, 18; Giménez Soler, *Corona*, 268 n. 1, and *Juan Manuel*, 636, no. 561; Ahmad al-Nāsirī al-Salāwī, "Kitāb al-Istiqsā, Tome Quatrième. Les Mérinides," tr. Ismael Hamet, *Archives Marocaines* 33 (1934): 218; Canellas López, "Aragón," 31; García Fernández, "Regesto," 73, no. 327.

43. Vidal, *Benoit XII: Lettres closes*, no. 2803; Goñi Gaztambide, *Historia*, 320.

44. *CAXI*, 308–9, ch. 210–11, 213; *GCAXI*, 2:320–23, 326, ch. 282–83, 285; *PAXI (1864)*, stanzas 1011–37; *CSPRP*, 2:314; Rui de Pina, *CAIV*, 123–24, 127–29, ch. 51; García Fernández, "Relaciones internacionales," 210; Díaz Martín, "Fluctuaciones," 1248–49; Ladero Quesada, "Portugueses," 72–73.

45. *CDACA*, 7:115–29, nos. 19–21, 23, 25; Giménez Soler, *Corona*, 268–69 nn. 1–2, and *Juan Manuel*, 637, no. 563; *CAXI*, 309, ch. 212; *GCAXI*, 2:324–25, ch. 284; *CCPIV*, 103, ch. 2.

46. *CAXI*, 309, ch. 212; *GCAXI*, 2:324–25, ch. 284; Georgius Stella and Ioannes Stella, *Annales genuenses*, ed. Giovanni Petti Balbi (Bologna: Zanichelli, 1975), 134; Vidal, *Benoit XII: Lettres closes*, nos. 2573–74, 2801; Goñi Gaztambide, *Historia*, 320–32; Robson, "Catalan Fleet," 400; López Fernández, "Desastre de Getares," 150–54.

47. Rogelio Pérez Bustamante, "Benedicto XII y la cruzada del Salado," in *Homenaje a Fray Justo Pérez de Urbel*, 2 vols. (Silos: Abadía de Silos, 1976–77): 1:177–203, esp. 196–203; Reg. Vat. 128, ep. 14–15, and Reg. Avin. 54, fol. 58, 64v, cited by Goñi Gaztambide, *Historia*, 323; Raynaldus, *Annales*, 16:120–21, a. 1340, nos. 40–43; Vidal, *Benoit XII: Lettres communes*, nos. 8103–4; *PAXI (1864)*, stanzas 1006–7.

48. Reg. Vat. 128, ep. 16–17 and Reg. Avin. 54, fol. 63v, 65, cited by Goñi Gaztambide, *Historia*, 323; Vidal, *Benoit XII: Lettres communes*, nos. 8104–6; Mansilla, *Castel S. Angelo*, 72–73, nos. 138–139; *CAXI*, 318, ch. 242; *GCAXI*, 2:342, ch. 293.

49. Vidal, *Benoit XII: Lettres closes*, nos. 8355, 2792; Mansilla, *Castel S. Angelo*, 73, no. 140; Goñi Gaztambide, *Historia*, 324.

50. *CAXI*, 318, ch. 242; *GCAXI*, 2:343, ch. 293.

51. Vidal, *Benoit XII: Lettres closes*, nos. 2862–67; Goñi Gaztambide, *Historia*, 326.

52. *CDACA*, 7:129–41, nos. 26–28; Canellas, "Aragón," 57–59; Giménez Soler, *Corona*, 269–70; Zurita, *Anales*, 3:448–50; Goñi Gaztambide, *Historia*, 322–23.

53. Nicolae Iorga, *Notes et extraits pour servir à l'histoire des croisades au XVe siècle* 4th ser., 3 vols. (Bucharest: Academia Romana, 1915–16), 3–5; Francesco A. Ugolini, "Avvenimenti, figure e costumi di Spagna in una cronaca italiana del Trecento," in *Italia e Spagna: Saggi sui rapporti storici, filosofici, artistici fra le due civiltà* (Florence: LeMonnier, 1941), 91–122, esp. 104–5.

54. Ibn Khaldūn, *Histoire*, 4:232; *GCAXI*, 2:329–33, ch. 286–88; *CAXI*, 316, ch. 239; *PAXI (1864)*, stanzas 991–1002; *CSPRP*, 2:315, ch. 55; Manzano Rodríguez, *Intervención*, 256; Huici, *Batallas*, 342.

55. *CAXI*, 316–18, ch. 240–42; *GCAXI*, 2:334–48, 353–61, ch. 289–95, 297–300; *PAXI (1864)*, stanzas 1003–10; *CSPRP*, 2:316–17; Rui de Pina, *CAIV*, 145–46, ch. 53; Ibn Khaldūn, *Histoire*, 4:232; Huici, *Batallas*, 342–46; Manzano Rodríguez, *Intervención*, 256–59.

56. *PAXI (1864)*, 1116–95; *CAXI*, 318–20, ch. 243–44; *GCAXI*, 2:349–52, 362–67, ch. 296, 301–4; *CSPRP*, 2:323, 335; Rui de Pina, *CAIV*, 148–55, ch. 55–56.

57. *CAXI*, 320, ch. 245; *GCAXI*, 2:369–78, ch. 305–9; *PAXI (1864)*, stanzas 1080–1115; Rui de Pina, *CAIV*, 146–47, ch. 54; Huici, *Batallas*, 349–50; Manzano Rodríguez, *Intervención*, 259; Manuel López Fernández, "La actuación de las flotas de Castilla y de Aragón durante el cerco meriní a Tarifa en el año 1340," *Aljaranda* 64 (2007): 3–10.

58. José Filipe Mendeiros, "O Santo Lenho da Sé de Évora," *A Cidade de Évora* 10, nos. 33–34 (Julho–Dezembro 1953): 259–98.

59. *CAXI*, 321–23, ch. 246–48; *GCAXI*, 2:379–85, ch. 310–12; *PAXI (1864)*, stanzas 1196–1266; *CSPRP*, 2:330–31; Rui de Pina, *CAIV*, 155–59, ch. 57; Ladero Quesada, "Portugueses," 73.

60. *GCAXI*, 391–406, ch. 314–21; *CAXI*, 323, ch. 248; *PAXI (1864)*, stanzas 1270–1301, 1339–1408; *CSPRP*, 2:333, 336; Rui de Pina, *CAIV*, 160–61, ch. 57; García Fernández, "Regesto," 74, no. 331.

61. *GCAXI*, 2:386–90, 406–10, ch. 313–14, 321–23; *CAXI*, 323–24, ch. 248–50; *PAXI (1864)*, stanzas 1409–49; Huici, *Batallas*, 346–54; García Fernández, "Regesto," 75, no. 332; López Fernández, "Los caminos y cañadas," 5–10; Wenceslao Segura González, "La batalla del Salado según Gil de Albornoz," *Aljaranda* 58 (2005): 9–15.

62. *GCAXI*, 2:418–21, ch. 326–27; *CAXI*, 324–25, ch. 250–51; *PAXI (1864)*, stanzas 1302–38, 1450–96; Ibn Khaldūn, *Histoire*, 4:232–33.

63. *GCAXI*, 2:419–21, ch. 326–27; *PAXI (1864)*, stanzas 1497–1512; Diego Catalán Menéndez Pidal, "La oración de Alfonso XI en Salado: El poema, la crónica inédita y la historia," *BRAH* 131 (1952): 247–66; Juan Beneyto Pérez, *El cardenal Albornoz: Canciller de Castilla y caudillo de Italia* (Madrid: Espasa-Calpe, 1950), 150–52, and *El cardenal Albornoz: Hombre de la iglesia y de estado en Castilla y en Italia* (Madrid: Fundación Universitaria Española, 1986), 96–100.

64. *Chronique de Jean le Bel*, ed. Jules Viard and Eugène Déprez, 2 vols. (Paris: Renouard, 1904–5), 1:216, ch. 40.

65. *GCAXI*, 2:420–21, ch. 327; *CAXI*, 325, ch. 251. See the archbishop's letter of 30 October 1340 in Ugolini, "Avvenimenti," 121–22.

66. *PAXI (1864)*, stanzas 1513–37.

67. Rui de Pina, *CAIV*, 166–69, ch. 59; Huici, *Batallas*, 381–87; Bernardo Vasconcelos e Sousa, "O sangue, a cruz e a coroa: A memória do Salado em Portugal," *Penélope: Fazer e Desfazer Historia* 2 (1989): 28–48.

68. The date of the battle, as commemorated by Alfonso XI in his charters, was Monday, 30 October. Although *CAXI* and *GCAXI* dated it Monday, 28 October, that was a Saturday. *PAXI (1864)*, stanzas 1802–3, dated it on the eve of All Saints' Day, 31 October. According to Ibn al-Khatīb, the date was 7 jumada I in the year 741, i.e., Sunday, 29 October. Luis Seco de Lucena, "La fecha de la batalla del Salado," *Al-Andalus* 19 (1954): 228–31; Huici, *Batallas*, 362–64.

69. *GCAXI*, 2:422–25, ch. 328–29; *CAXI*, 325–26, ch. 251; *PAXI (1864)*, stanzas 1538–1652; Gonzalo de la Finojosa, "Continuación," 106:56–61, ch. 249.

70. *GCAXI*, 2:426–29, ch. 330; *CAXI*, 325–26, ch. 251.

71. *GCAXI*, 2:429–30, ch. 330; *CAXI*, 326–27, ch. 251; *PAXI (1864)*, stanzas 1653–91; *CSPRP*, 2:342.

72. Mūsā, emir of Tlemcen, "El Collar de Perlas," tr. Mariano Gaspar Remiro in Huici, *Batallas*, 379–80.

73. *GCAXI*, 2:430–31, ch. 330; *CAXI*, 327, ch. 251; *PAXI (1864)*, stanzas 1645, 1690–1790; *CSPRP*, 2:340–43; Rui de Pina, *CAIV*, 170–71, ch. 59; Ibn Khaldūn, *Histoire*, 4:232–34; Huici, *Batallas*, 359–60; *Chronique de Jean le Bel*, 1:213–18, ch. 40; Villani, *Cronica*, 6:224; Mariano Pérez Castro, "Estudios históricos-militares: La batalla del Salado," *Revista de España* 25 (1872): 552–65; Robert Ricard, "La relation portugaise de la bataille du Salado (1340)," *Hespéris* 43 (1956): 7–27; López Fernández, "Desastre de Getares," 154–62; Agrait, "Experience of War," 218–21, and "Reconquest," 155–56.

74. *GCAXI*, 2:433–34, ch. 330; *CAXI*, 327, ch. 251; *PAXI (1864)*, stanzas 1791–1811; Ibn Khaldūn, *Histoire*, 4:233–34: Al-Makkarī, *History*, 2:355–56; Ibn Marzūq, *El Musnad*, 188, ch. 15; Huici, *Batallas*, 356–62, 380–81; Manzano Rodríguez, *Intervención*, 262–66.

75. *GCAXI*, 2:434–36, ch. 330; *CAXI*, 327–28, ch. 251; *PAXI (1864)*, stanzas 1843–90; Giménez Soler, *Corona*, 271; *CCPIV*, 103, ch. 2.

76. *PAXI (1864)*, stanzas 1812–42. See "Profecías de Merlin" in "El Baladro del Sabio Merlin," in Adolfo Bonilla y San Martín, ed., *Libros de Caballerías: Primera Parte* (Madrid: Bailly/Bailliére, 1907), 19–22.

77. *GCAXI*, 2:436, ch. 330; *CAXI*, 328, ch. 251; Huici, *Batallas*, 364–67; García Fernández, "Regesto," 75, no. 331.

78. *GCAXI*, 2:438, ch. 331. O'Callaghan, *Cantigas*, ch. 9.

79. *CAXI*, 329–30, ch. 253; *GCAXI*, 2:443, ch. 333.

80. Ibn Marzūq, *El Musnad*, 381, ch. 52.

81. *CAXI*, 329–30, ch. 253; *GCAXI*, 2:442–43, ch. 333; *PAXI (1864)*, stanzas 1791–99; *CSPRP*, 2:349; Rui de Pina, *CAIV*, 178–79, ch. 59; *CDACA*, 7:149, no. 34; Ladero Quesada, "Portugueses," 73–74.

82. Gonzalo Argote de Molina, *Nobleza del Andaluzia* (Hildesheim: Olms, 1975), 183, bk. 2, ch. 82; García Fernández, "Regesto," 75, nos. 333–35.

83. Rodrigo Amador de los Ríos, "La Bandera del Salado," *BRAH* 21 (1892): 464–71, and *Trofeos militares de la Reconquista: Estudio acerca de las enseñas musulmanas del Real Monasterio de las Huelgas (Burgos) y de la Catedral de Toledo* (Madrid: Fortanet, 1893), 119–74; Wenceslao Segura González, "Los pendones de la batalla del Salado," *Aljaranda* 66 (2007): 9–16; Huici, *Batallas*, 366 n. 3.

84. Beneyto Pérez, *Albornoz: Canciller*, 331–32, and *Albornoz: Hombre*, 291–93; Ugolini, "Avvenimenti," 119–22; Goñi Gaztambide, *Historia*, 329; Segura González, "La batalla del Salado según Gil de Albornoz," 9–15; Agrait, "Experience of War," 221–23.

85. Juan Manuel Sierra López, *El Misal Toledano de 1499* (Toledo: Instituto Teológico San Ildefonso, 2004), 338–39.

86. Manuel Dualde Serrano, *Solidaridad espiritual de Valencia con las victorias cristianas del Salado y de Algeciras* (Valencia: CSIC, 1950), 76–77.

87. Vasconcelos e Sousa, "O sangue," 32, citing Solange Corbin, "Fêtes portugaises: Commemoration de la victoire chrétienne de 1340 (Rio-Salado)," *Bulletin Hispanique* 49 (1947): 212, 216.

88. *CAXI*, 330–31, ch. 254; *GCAXI*, 2:445–46, ch. 334; *CSPRP*, 2:338; Rui de Pina, *CAIV*, 178, ch. 59.

89. *CAXI*, 330–31, ch. 254; *GCAXI*, 2:446–47, ch. 334; *PAXI (1864)*, stanzas 1891–1928; Goñi Gaztambide, *Historia*, 331–32; Léopold Duhamel, *Une ambassade à la cour pontificale: Épisode de l'histoire des palais des papes* (Avignon: Sequin, 1883); Guillaume Mollat, *The Popes at Avignon, 1305–1378* (New York: Harper Torchbooks, 1965), 315.

90. Vidal, *Benoit XII: Lettres closes*, no. 2976; Raynaldus, *Annales*, a. 1340, nos. 52–54; Goñi Gaztambide, *Historia*, 330.

91. Raynaldus, *Annales*, a. 1341, no. 2; Vidal, *Benoit XII: Lettres closes*, no. 3078; *MH*, 1:199–201, no. 87; Goñi Gaztambide, *Historia*, 332.

92. *CDACA*, 7:142–47, nos. 28, 30–32, and 7:138–41, no. 27; Giménez Soler, *Corona*, 270 n. 2.

93. *CAXI*, 328–29, ch. 252; *GCAXI*, 2:439–41, ch. 331; *PAXI (1864)*, stanza 1723.

94. García Fernández, "Relaciones castellano-mariníes," 265.

95. Huici, *Batallas*, 367–71.

96. *CAXI*, 180–81, ch. 10; Huici, *Batallas*, 377–79.

CHAPTER 9. CRUSADE OF ALGECIRAS AND GIBRALTAR

1. *CAXI*, 331, ch. 255; *GCAXI*, 2:448–49, ch. 335. From here on *GCAXI* repeats, without alteration, *CAXI*, until the beginning of the siege of Algeciras in 1344.

2. Baer, *Jews*, 1:447 n. 43a.

3. *GCAXI*, 2:449, ch. 335; Giménez Soler, *Juan Manuel*, 638, no. 565; Peter Linehan, "The Beginnings of Santa María de Guadalupe and the Direction of Fourteenth-Century Castile," *Journal of Ecclesiastical History* 36 (1985): 284–304; reprinted in his *Past and Present in Medieval Spain*, chap. 12.

4. *MH*, 1:178–94, 199–201, nos. 84–87; García Fernández, "Relaciones internacionales," 212–13.

5. Raynaldus, *Annales*, a. 1341, no. 4–9.

6. *CAXI*, 331–35, ch. 256–58; *CSPRP*, 2:350, ch. 63; *PAXI (1864)*, stanzas 1947–2006; Gonzalo de la Finojosa, "Continuación," 106:61, ch. 249; Ibn Khaldūn, *Histoire*, 4:234; González Crespo, *CDAXI*, 478–79, no. 285; García Fernández, "Regesto," 75–79, nos. 336–37, 347, 350, 354; Manzano Rodríguez, *Intervención*, 267–68.

7. Raynaldus, *Annales*, a. 1341, no. 7; Vidal, *Benoit XII: Lettres closes*, no. 3200; Goñi Gaztambide, *Historia*, 332.

8. *CAXI*, 333, 335, ch. 257, 259; *CDACA* 7:147–48, 150–57, nos. 33, 35, 37–40.

9. *CAXI*, 335, ch. 259.

10. *PAXI (1864)*, stanzas 2059–65; O'Callaghan, *Reconquest*, 1–21.

11. *CAXI*, 335–38, ch. 259–63; Salvador de Moxó, *La alcabala: Sobre sus orígenes, concepto y naturaleza* (Madrid: CSIC, 1963); O'Callaghan, *Cortes*, 37, 38, 144–45; Agrait, "Experience of War," 223–24.

12. *CAXI*, 338, ch. 263; *PAXI (1864)*, stanzas 2064–71; Rui de Pina, *CAIV*, 180–81, ch. 60.

13. Agrait, "Experience of War," 227.

14. *CDACA*, 7:157–59, no. 41; Giménez Soler, *Corona*, 273.

15. Montes Romero-Camacho, "Alfonso XI," 148, nos. 44–45; García Fernández, "Regesto,"80–81," nos. 356–60; Ladero Quesada and González Jiménez, "Gibraltar," 242–43, no. 18.

16. *CAXI*, 339–42, ch. 264–67; *PAXI (1864)*, stanzas 2072–2124; Ibn Khaldūn, *Histoire*, 2:235; Masiá de Ros, *Relación*, 1:238–39.

17. *CAXI*, 342–43, ch. 267.

18. *PAXI (1864)*, stanzas 2026–33, 2039, 2044–58, 2138–42; *CAXI*, 343, ch. 268–69; García Fernández, "Regesto," 81, no. 363.

19. Giménez Soler, *Corona*, 273–74; Agrait, "Experience of War," 226–32.

20. *CAXI*, 344–46, ch. 270–72; *PAXI (1864)*, stanzas 2010–22, 2130–34; Manzano Rodríguez, *Intervención*, 271–79.

21. Ortíz de Zúñiga, *Anales*, 2:109–10; García Fernández, "Regesto," 82, no. 368.

22. *CAXI*, 344, 359, ch. 270, 289.

23. Paul E. Chevedden, "The Artillery of King James I the Conqueror," in Paul E. Chevedden, Donald J. Kagay, and Paul Padilla, eds., *Iberia and the Mediterranean World of the Middle Ages: Essays in Honor of Robert I. Burns, S.J.* (Leiden: Brill, 1996), 47–94, and "The Hybrid Trebuchet: The Halfway Step to the Counterweight Trebuchet," in Kagay and Vann, *Social Origins*, 179–222; and Paul E. Chevedden, Zvi Shiller, and Donald J. Kagay, "The Traction Trebuchet: A Triumph of Four Civilizations," *Viator* 31 (2000): 433–86.

24. *CAXI*, 347–60, ch. 273–91; *PAXI (1864)* stanzas 2143–93; Agrait, "Experience of War," 226–38.

25. *CAXI*, 364–65, ch. 299; *PAXI (1864)*, stanzas 2287–94; Giménez Soler, *Juan Manuel*, 641, no. 570; García Fernández, "Regesto," 82, nos. 364, 367.

26. *PAXI (1864)*, stanzas 2294–2306, esp. 2302.

27. *CAXI*, 347, 350, ch. 273, 276.

28. *CAXI*, 345–46, 350, ch. 272, 276; Ladero Quesada, "Portugueses," 74.

29. *CAXI*, 357–58, ch. 287; *CDACA*, 7:160–69, nos. 42–46; Giménez Soler, *Corona*, 274–75.

30. *CAXI*, 350, 353, ch. 276, 280

31. *CAXI*, 352–55, ch. 280–81, 284.

32. *CAXI*, 357, 360–61, ch. 286, 291–92, 294.

33. *CAXI*, 344, 356, 358, ch. 270, 285, 288; *Chronique de Jean le Bel*, 1:219, ch. 40.

34. Daumet, *Étude*, 1–5, 125–31, nos. 1, 3.

35. *CAXI*, 360, 362, 369–71, ch. 292, 295, 306–7, 309; *PAXI (1864)*, stanzas 2274–81; Rymer, *Foedera*, 2.4:167; Christopher Tyerman, *England and the Crusades, 1095–1588* (Chicago: University of Chicago, 1988), 277–78.

36. *Chaucer's Canterbury Tales*, ed. Alfred W. Pollard, 2 vols. (London: Macmillan, 1907), 1:3–4; MacKay, "Andalucía," 329.

37. *CAXI*, 361, 363–64, ch. 294, 295, 297; *PAXI (1864)*, stanzas 2238–43.

38. *PAXI (1864)*, stanzas 2281–86; *CAXI*, 361, 368–69, ch. 294, 304.

39. *CAXI*, 370–71, ch. 308–9.

40. *CAXI*, 363–64, 367, 377, ch. 297, 298, 302, 319; Baer, *Jews*, 1:359–60.

41. Raynaldus, *Annales*, a. 1343, no. 37; Goñi Gaztambide, *Historia*, 333.

42. Georges Daumet, "Jean de Rye au siège d'Algeciras," *Bulletin Hispanique* 12 (1910): 265–74.

43. *PAXI (1864)*, stanza 2290.

44. *CAXI*, 354, 360, ch. 282, 291; Luciano Serrano, *Cartulario del Infantado de Covarrubias* (Valladolid: Cuesta, 1907), 195, no. 164; Justiniano Rodríguez Fernández, *Las juderías de la provincia deLeón* (León: Centro de Estudios e Investigación San Isidoro, 1976), 212–15; Florencio Marcos Rodríguez, *Catálogo del Archivo catedralicio de Salamanca (siglos XII–XV)* (Salamanca: Universidad Pontificia de Salamanca, 1962), 109, nos. 565, 567.

45. Mansilla, *Castel S. Angelo*, 76–77, nos. 146–48; Luciano Serrano, "Alfonso XI y el papa Clemente VI durante el cerco de Algeciras," in *Cuadernos de Trabajos de la Escuela Española de Arqueología e Historia en Roma* 3 (Madrid: Junta para Ampliación de Estudios e Investigaciones Científicas, 1915), 11–14, 17, 26–27, no. 3, 27–33; Agrait, "Military Reform," 123; Peter Spufford, *Handbook of Medieval Exchange* (London: Royal Historical Society, 1986), 158.

46. Raynaldus, *Annales*, a. 1343, no. 36; Serrano, "Alfonso XI," 33, no. 7; Goñi Gaztambide, *Historia*, 332–33; Agrait, "Military Reform," 120.

47. *CAXI*, 367–68, ch. 303; *PAXI (1864)*, stanzas 2194–2212, 2230–33; Archivo de la Catedral de Toledo, v. 12.0.1.10.

48. *CAXI*, 361–63, ch. 293, 296; *PAXI (1864)*, stanzas 2365–2413.

49. *CAXI*, 365–66, 375, ch. 300, 315.

50. *CAXI*, 366–74, 377–78, 301–13, 319, ch. 321; *PAXI (1864)*, stanzas 2347–56; *CSPRP*, 2:353, ch. 63; Ibn Marzūq, *El Musnad*, 327, ch. 38; Manzano Rodríguez, *Intervención*, 277.

51. *CAXI*, 378–79, ch. 322–23.
52. *CAXI*, 379–80, ch. 324; Ibn Khaldūn, *Histoire*, 2:235–36.
53. Ibn Marzūq, *El Musnad*, 327, ch. 38.
54. *CAXI*, 380–81, ch. 325; *PAXI (1864)*, stanzas 2310–14; *CDACA*, 7:170–71, no. 47.
55. *CAXI*, 381–83, ch. 326–28.
56. *CAXI*, 383–85, ch. 329–31; *PAXI (1864)*, stanzas 2414–45.
57. *CDACA*, 7:171–75, nos. 48–50; Manzano Rodríguez, *Intervención*, 279.
58. *CAXI*, 385–88 ch. 332–35.
59. *CAXI*, 388–89, ch. 336; *PAXI (1864)*, stanzas 2445–49; Giménez Soler, *Corona*, 275 n. 5; Masiá de Ros, *Relación*, 2:363, no. 195/34; García Fernández, "Relaciones castellano-mariníes," 266–67.
60. *CDACA*, 7:176–77, 188, nos. 51, 54; Giménez Soler, *Juan Manuel*, 642–43, no. 574; Veas Arteseros, *Alfonso XI*, 460, no. 405; Giménez Soler, *Corona*, 277.
61. *CAXI*, 389, ch. 336; Giménez Soler, *Juan Manuel*, 642, nos. 572–73, and *Corona*, 276 n. 1; Masiá de Ros, *Relación*, 2:363–64, no. 195/34.
62. *CAXI*, 389–90, ch. 336–37; *PAXI (1864)*, stanzas 2450–56. Rodrigo Yáñez's *Poema* ends here. *Chronicon Conimbricense*, *ES* 23:345; Beneyto, *El Cardenal Albornoz*, 106–7.
63. Ibn Khaldūn, *Histoire*, 2:236; Ibn Marzūq, *El Musnad*, 163–64, ch. 12; Agrait, "Reconquest," 157–61, and "Experience of War" 226–32.
64. Gonzalo de la Finojosa, "Continuación," 106:68, ch. 249.
65. Jaime de Villanueva, *Viage literario a las iglesias de España*, 22 vols. (Madrid: Imprenta Real: 1803–52), 9:236.
66. *CDACA*, 7:180–81, no. 52.
67. Raynaldus, *Annales*, a. 1344, nos. 50, 52; Mansilla, "Cádiz y Algeciras," 269, no. 8.
68. Rymer, *Foedera*, 2.4:163–65; Daumet, *Étude*, 9.
69. *CDACA*, 7:186–89, no. 54; Giménez Soler, *Corona*, 277 n. 1, 279–80 n. 1, 281–84.
70. *CAXI*, 389–90, ch. 336. At this point the *Royal Chronicle* ends. Three chapters recording the siege of Gibraltar and the king's death in 1350 were added as an appendix. Gonzalo de la Finojosa, "Continuación," 106:61–68, ch. 249; María del Carmen de León-Sotelo Casado and Esther González Crespo, "Notas para el itinerario de Alfonso XI en el período de 1344 a 1350," *ELEM* 5 (1986): 575–89, esp. 576–77; García Fernández, "Regesto," 86, nos. 382–84.
71. García Fernández, "Regesto," 87–88, nos. 389, 391; Fernández Duro, *Marina*, 471.
72. Antonio Torremocha Silva, *El Ordenamiento de Algeciras (1345): Datos sobre la conquista, repoblación, y organización de la ciudad en el siglo XIV* (Algeciras: Roca, 1983), 91–95.
73. Mansilla, "Cádiz y Algeciras," 265–68, nos. 5–7.
74. Antonio Torremocha Silva and Ángel J. Sáez Rodríguez, "Algeciras Medieval," in Mario Ocaña, ed., *Historia de Algeciras*, 2 vols. (Cádiz: Diputación de Cádiz, 2001), 1:201.
75. *CAXI*, 389, ch. 336.
76. *CAXI*, 389, ch. 336; Montes Romero-Camacho, "Alfonso XI," 150–51, nos. 54–55; Agrait, "Military Reform," 123.

77. Archivo Municipal de Sevilla, carpeta 2, no. 46; Rafael Ramírez de Arellano, *Historia de Córdoba desde su fundación hasta la muerte de Isabel la Católica*, 4 vols. (Ciudad Real: Hospicio Provincial, 1915–19), 4:106.

78. *CLC*, 1:477–83 (Alcalá, art. 3, 5), 483–92 (Burgos, art. 3), 627–37 (León, art. 19, 24); González Crespo, *CDAXI*, 502–3, no. 301; León Sotelo Casado and González Crespo, "Notas," 579–80; O'Callaghan, *Cortes*, 38, 44, 145–46.

79. *CLC*, 1:492–593 (*Ordenamiento de Alcalá*), 593–626 (*Cuaderno* of Alcalá); Ángel Luis Molina Molina, *Documentos de Pedro I*, *CODOM* 7 (Murcia: Academia Alfonso X el Sabio, 1978), 23–28, no. 19.

80. Daumet, *Étude*, 9–16, 132–51, 156–57, nos. 4–18, 22–24.

81. Rymer, *Foedera*, 2.4:180–81, 186, 194, and 3.1:25–26, 39; Daumet, *Étude*, 16–18, 152–54, nos. 19–21.

82. Rymer, *Foedera*, 2.4:267; Fernández Duro, *Marina*, 417–18, no. 16.

83. Real Academia de la Historia, Colección Salazar, M 114, no. 4, cited by Fernández Duro, *Marina*, 472; Pérez Embid, *Almirantazgo*, 34.

84. Álvaro Pelayo [Álvaro Pais], *Speculum regum*, ed. and tr. Miguel Pinto de Meneses as *Espelho dos reis*, 2 vols. (Lisbon: Instituto de Alta Cultura, 1955), 1:4.

85. Álvaro Pelayo, *Speculum regum*, 1:6, 8; O'Callaghan, *Reconquest*, 14–17.

86. Álvaro Pelayo, *Speculum regum*, 1:10

87. Álvaro Pelayo, *Speculum regum*, 1:12.

88. Álvaro Pelayo, *Speculum regum*, 1:16, 22.

89. Florentino Pérez Embid, *Los descubrimientos en el Atlántico y la rivalidad castellano-portuguesa hasta el Tratado de Tordesillas* (Seville: Escuela de Estudios Hispano-Americanos, 1948), 73–74.

90. *MH*, 1:207–14, no. 89; Charles Coquelines et al., eds., *Bullarum, privilegiorum et diplomata romanorum pontificum amplissima collectio*, 37 vols. in 50 (Rome: Hieronymus Mainardus, 1733–1857), 3.2:296–98; José Zunzunegui, "Los orígenes de las misiones en las Canarias," *Revista Española de Teología* 1 (1941): 361–408, esp. 385, no. 1.

91. Eugène Déprez, Jean Glenisson, and Michel Mollat, eds., *Lettres closes, patentes et curiales du pape Clément VI (1342–1352) se rapportant a la France*, 4 vols. (Paris: Fontemoing, 1901–61), 2:310–12, 333–35, nos. 1314–15, 1348–49; *MH*, 1:214–16, nos. 90–91; Zunzunegui, "Canarias," 386–93, nos. 2–11.

92. *MH*, 1:228–29, nos. 95–96; Zunzunegui, "Canarias," 393–94, nos. 12–13; Vitorino de Magalhães Godinho, *Documentos sobre a Espansão portuguesa*, 3 vols. (Lisbon: Gleba/Cosmos, 1943–56), 1:29–31; Goñi Gaztambide, *Historia*, 334–35.

93. *MH*, 1:217–28, nos. 92–94; García Fernández, "Relaciones internacionales," 214.

94. *MH*, 1:201–6, no. 88; Pérez Embid, *Descubrimientos*, 69–72.

95. *MH*, 1:230–34, no. 97; Déprez, Glenisson, and Mollat, *Clément VI*, 2:313–15, no. 1317; Zunzunegui, "Canarias," 394, no. 15.

96. Antonio Rumeu de Armas, *España en el Africa atlántica*, 2 vols. (Madrid: Instituto de Estudios Africanos, 1956–57), 2:1–2, no. 1; Déprez, Glenisson, and Mollat, *Clément VI*, 2:312–13, no. 1316; *MH*, 1:234–35, no. 98; Raynaldus, *Annales*, a. 1344, no. 50.

97. *MH*, 1:237, no. 100; *CCPIV*, 241, ch. 4; Zurita, *Anales*, 4:10–11, 20–21; Joseph F. O'Callaghan, "Castile, Portugal, and the Canary Islands: Claims and Counterclaims, 1344–1479," *Viator* 24 (1993): 287–309.

98. *CAXI*, 390, ch. 338; Ibn Marzūq, *El Musnad*, 322–23, ch. 38; Collins, *Arab Conquest*, 30–31.

99. Ibn Battūta, *Voyages d'Ibn Battutah*, ed. and tr. C. Defrémery and B. R. Sanguinetti, 2nd ed., 4 vols. (Paris: Imprimerie Nationale, 1873–79), 4:353–55.

100. Masiá de Ros, *Relación*, 2:364–66, no. 196/35; Zurita, *Anales*, 4:32–35.

101. Ibn Khaldūn, *Histoire*, 4:246–71; Manzano Rodríguez, *Intervención*, 293–95.

102. *CAXI*, 390, ch. 338; Manzano Rodríguez, *Intervención*, 299–300.

103. Gaspar Remiro, *Correspondencia*, 143–57, 164–83; Manzano Rodríguez, *Intervención*, 296.

104. Veas Arteseros, *Alfonso XI*, 488, 490, 496, nos. 426, 428, 434.

105. León Sotelo-Casado and González Crespo, "Notas," 587–88; Veas Arteseros, *Alfonso XI*, 492–513, nos. 430–44.

106. Giménez Soler, *Corona*, 289–91; Zurita, *Anales*, 4:176–78; Masiá de Ros, *Relación*, 2:367, no. 197/37.

107. Rui de Pina, *CAIV*, 192–93, ch. 63; García Fernández, "Relaciones internacionales," 214.

108. Raynaldus, *Annales*, a. 1344, n. 50, a. 1346, n. 61; José Rius Serra, "Los rótulos de la Universidad de Valladolid," *Analecta Sacra Tarraconensia* 16 (1943): 92; Goñi Gaztambide, *Historia*, 333–34; Ramírez de Arellano, *Córdoba*, 4:106–7.

109. Veas Arteseros, *Alfonso XI*, 501 no. 437.

110. González Crespo, *CDAXI*, 595–97, no. 339.

111. Molina Molina, *Documentos de Pedro I*, 3–4, no. 4.

112. Veas Arteseros, *Alfonso XI*, 498, 502–7, 510–13, nos. 436, 438–41, 443–44; José A. Martín Fuertes and César Álvarez Álvarez, eds., *Archivo histórico municipal de León: Catálogo de los documentos* (León: Ayuntamiento de León, 1982), 75, no. 131.

113. Veas Arteseros, *Alfonso XI*, 509, no. 442; León-Sotelo Casado and González Crespo, "Notas," 588; García Fernández, "Regesto," 106, no. 474; Agrait, "Military Reform," 123–24.

114. José López Agurleta, *Bullarium equestris ordinis S. Iacobi de Spatha* (Madrid: Juan de Ariztia, 1719), 324; Gutiérrez del Arroyo, *Privilegios*, 311, no. 752.

115. Alarcón y Santón and García de Linares, *Documentos árabes*, 196–201, no. 99; Manzano Rodríguez, *Intervención*, 297 n. 862; Agrait, "Experience of War," 233–35.

116. Ángel Vaca Lorenzo, "La peste negra en Castilla: La primera et grande pestilencia que es llamada mortandad grande," *Fundación* 4 (2001–2): 19–50, and "La peste negra en Castilla: Aportación al estudio de algunas de sus consecuencias económicas y sociales," *Studia Historica: Historia Medieval* 2 (1984): 89–107, and "La peste negra en Castilla (Nuevos testimonios)," *Studia Historica: Historia Medieval* 8 (1990): 159–73.

117. Veas Arteseros, *Alfonso XI*, 488, no. 425; Arié, *L'Espagne* 396–98, 435–36.

118. Molina Molina, *Documentos de Pedro I*, 1–2, nos. 1–2; Luis Díaz Martín, *Itinerario de Pedro I de Castilla: Estudio y Regesta* (Valladolid: Universidad de Valladolid, 1975), 269, no. 435.

119. *CAXI*, 390–92, ch. 338–39. Pedro López de Ayala, in his *Crónica de Pedro I*, BAE 66:401–6, Año Primero, ch. 1–5, repeated the last chapters of *CAXI*. Gonzalo de la Finojosa, "Continuación," 106:69, ch. 249; Clara Estow, *Pedro the Cruel of Castile, 1350–1369* (Leiden: Brill, 1995), 1–13.

120. Ibn Khaldūn, *Histoire*, 4:291; Al-Makkarī, *History*, 2:356–57; Lafuente Alcántara, *Inscripciones*, 222–31; Arié, *L'Espagne* 104–5.

121. *CAXI*, 391, ch. 338.

122. Ibn al-Khatīb, in Miguel Casiri, *Bibliotheca arabico-hispana escurialensis*, 2 vols. (Madrid: Antonio Pérez de Soto, 1760–70), 2:303, cited by Giménez Soler, *Corona*, 263.

CHAPTER 10. WAGING THE CRUSADE OF GIBRALTAR

1. *Espéculo: Texto jurídico atribuído al Rey de Castilla Don Alfonso el Sabio*, ed. Robert A. MacDonald (Madison, Wis.: Hispanic Seminary, 1990); *Las Siete Partidas del Rey Don Alfonso el Sabio*, ed. Real Academia de la Historia, 3 vols. (Madrid: Imprenta Real, 1801); *Las Siete Partidas*, tr. Samuel P. Scott, ed. Robert I. Burns, S.J., 5 vols. (Philadelphia: University of Pennsylvania Press, 2001).

2. See also Alfonso X, *Fuero real*, ed. Gonzalo Martínez Díez, José Manuel Ruiz Asencio, and C. Hernández Alonso (Ávila: Fundación Claudio Albornoz, 1988), 1,2; 3,13; 4,19; Joseph F. O'Callaghan, "War (and Peace) in the Law Codes of Alfonso X," in Villalon and Kagay, *Crusaders*, 3–18; Francisco Luis Pascual Sarría, "Las obligaciones militares establecidas en los ordenamientos de las Cortes castellano-leonesas durante los siglos XIII y XIV," *Revista de Estudios histórico-jurídicos* 25 (2003): 147–85.

3. Juan Gil de Zamora, *Liber de preconiis Hispaniae*, 347–76; Flavius Vegetius Renatus, *Vegetius: Epitome of Military Science*, tr. N.P. Milner (Liverpool: Liverpool University Press, 1993).

4. Sancho IV, *Castigos e documentos*, 172–73, ch. 46.

5. Juan Manuel, *El libro de los estados*; *Libro de los doze sabios o tractado de la nobleza y lealtad*, ed. John K. Walsh (Madrid: Anejos de la Boletin de la Real Academia Española, 1975).

6. José María Gárate Córdoba, "El pensamiento militar en el Código de las Siete Partidas," *Revista de Historia Militar* 13 (1963): 7–60, esp. 19–21; Ana Belén Sánchez Prieto, *Guerra y guerreros en España según las fuentes canónicas de la Edad Media* (Madrid: E.M.E., 1990).

7. *CSM*, 2:281, no. 360; *DAAX*, 253–54, no. 231; O'Callaghan, *Alfonso X and the Cantigas*, 86–90, 93–95, 194–96.

8. José Antonio Maravall, "Del regimen feudal al regimen corporativo en el pensamiento de Alfonso X," *BRAH* 157 (1965): 213–68, esp. 249.

9. Hilda Grassotti, "El deber y el derecho de hacer guerra y paz en León y Castilla," in *Estudios medievales españolas* (Madrid: Fundación Universitaria Española, 1981), 43–132; *El fuero viejo*, ed. Ignacio Jordán de Asso y del Río and Miguel de Manuel y Rodríguez (Madrid: Joaquín Ibarra, 1771), 1.1.1.

10. *Poema de Fernán González*, ed. Alonso Zamora Vicente (Madrid: Espasa-Calpe, 1946), vv. 66, 75; Gárate Córdoba, "Pensamiento," 46–52.

11. García Fernández, "Regesto," 38, no. 160.

12. Eloy Benito Ruano, *Hermandades en Asturias durante la Edad Media* (Oviedo: La Cruz, 1972), 57–58, no. 1; Escudero, "Súplica," 58–59; O'Callaghan, *Learned King*, 243–44.

13. *CJI*, 7:42–44, ch. 382; Rui de Pina, *CAIV*, 155–59, ch. 57.

14. Francisco García Fitz, "La composición de los ejércitos medievales," in José Ignacio de la Iglesia Duarte, ed., *La guerra en la Edad Media: XVII semana de estudios medievales* (Logroño: Instituto de Estudios Riojanos, 2007), 85–146.

15. *CAX (GJ)*, 180–81, ch. 63; *CAX*, 50–51, ch. 63; Gárate Córdoba, "Pensamiento," 23–24.

16. Gaibrois, *Sancho IV*, 1:58–60, and 3:l–li, no. 79.

17. *CAX (GJ)*, 208, ch. 74; *CAX*, 58, ch. 74; Carlos de Ayala Martínez, *Las órdenes militares hispánicas en la Edad Media (siglos XII–XV)* (Madrid: Marcial Pons, 2007), 405–610; Philippe Josserand, *Église et pouvoir dans la Péninsule Ibérique: Les ordres militaires dans le royaume de Castille (1252–1369)* (Madrid: Casa de Velázquez 2004), 233–99.

18. Regina Sanz de la Maza Lasoli, *La Orden de Santiago en la corona de Aragón* (Zaragoza: Instituto Fernando el Católico, 1980), 1:335, no. 142.

19. Agrait, "Monarchy and Military Practice," 43; O'Callaghan, *Reconquest*, 143–46.

20. Juan Manuel, *Libro del caballero et del escudero*, *BAE* 51:234–56; Gárate Córdoba, "Pensamiento," 12–19.

21. *Fuero real*, 4,19,4–5; *Fuero viejo*, 1,3,1.

22. *CAXI*, 266, ch. 141; *GCAXI*, 2:101–2, ch. 163.

23. *CLC*, 1:443–46; *CAXI*, 292–93, ch. 186; Agrait, "Military Reform," 102–7; Álvaro Soler del Campo, *La evolución del armamento medieval en el reino castellano-leonés y al-Andalus (siglos XII–XIV)* (Madrid: Ministerio del Ejército, 1993); Ada Bruhn de Hoffmeyer, *Arms and Armour in Spain: A Short Survey*, 2 vols. (Madrid: CSIC, 1972–82); Gárate Córdoba, "Pensamiento," 17–19

24. James A. Powers, *A Society Organized for War: The Iberian Municipal Militias in the Central Middle Ages, 1000–1284* (Berkeley: University of California Press, 1988), 112–35.

25. Antonio Ballesteros, "Las Cortes de 1252," *Anales de la junta para ampliación de estudios e investigaciones científicas* 3 (1911): 141–42; James F. Powers, "Two Warrior-Kings and Their Municipal Militias: The Townsman-Soldier in Law and Life," in Burns, *Worlds*, 95–125.

26. González Díez, *Burgos*, 93–96, 106–11, nos. 26, 32; *MHE*, 1:89–100, 224–28, nos. 43–44, 102; Rafael Ureña y Smenjaud, ed., *Fuero de Cuenca* (Madrid: Academia de la Historia, 1935), 861–62; José Benavides Checa, ed., *El fuero de Plasencia* (Rome: Lobesi, 1896), 170; O'Callaghan, *Learned King*, 92–94.

27. *CAX (GJ)*, 26, ch. 9; *CAX*, 109, ch. 9, p. 109; *Crónica de la población de Ávila*, ed. Amparo Hernández Segura (Valencia: Anubar, 1966), 49; Iglesia Ferreiros, "Privilegio general"; Juan Martín Carramolino, *Historia de Ávila, su provincia y obispado*, 3 vols. (Madrid: Librería Española, 1872), 2:491; Ubieto Arteta, *Cuéllar*, 60–66, no. 21; Timoteo Domingo Palacio, *Documentos del Archivo general de la Villa de Madrid*, 6 vols. (Madrid: Imprenta Municipal, 1888–1943), 1:96–102; Juan Agapito y Revilla, *Los privilegios de Valladolid* (Valladolid: Sociedad Castellana de Excursiones, 1906), 54, 78; Evelyn Procter, *Curia and Cortes in León and Castile, 1072–1295* (Cambridge: Cambridge University Press, 1980), 211–12, 250–59, no. 7.

28. Ureña y Smenjaud, *Cuenca*, 867–68; Pedro Fernández del Pulgar, *Historia secular y eclesiástica de Palencia*, 4 vols. (Madrid: F. Nieto, 1679–80), 3:330–32; Antonio Floriano, *Documentación histórica del Archivo municipal de Cáceres (1229–1471)* (Cáceres: Diputación Provincial, 1987), 21, no. 9.0; *DAAX*, 369–70, 429–30, 497–98, nos. 342, 404, 471; Ballesteros, *Alfonso X*, 791–93.

29. Teófilo Ruiz, *Sociedad y poder real en Castilla* (Barcelona: Ariel, 1981), 145–98, and *Crisis and Continuity: Land and Town in Late Medieval Castile* (Philadelphia: University of Pennsylvania, 1994), 175–286.

30. *MHE*, 1:315, no. 140; Rodrigues Lapa, *Cantigas d'escarnho*, 3, 6, 11–12, 27–28, 37–39, 44–45, 48–49, nos. 2, 6, 9, 16, 21, 24, 26; O'Callaghan, *Alfonso X and the Cantigas*, 107–9.

31. *CLC* 1:450–53, 548–51; Agrait, "Monarchy and Military Practice," 34–42, 74–77.

32. *CLC*, 1:617–19; Agrait, "Military Reform," 99–101.

33. Manuel González Jiménez, "La caballería popular en Andalucía (siglos XIII al XV)," *AEM* 15 (1985): 315–29, esp. 321; José Manuel Pérez Prendes, "El origen de los caballeros de cuantía y los cuantiosos de Jaén en el siglo XV," *Revista Española de Derecho Militar* 9 (1968): 31–86; Agrait, "Monarchy and Military Practice," 42–45, 81–85.

34. John E. Keller and Richard P. Kinkade, *Iconography in Medieval Spanish Literature* (Lexington: University Press of Kentucky, 1984), plate 15; John E. Keller and Annette Grant Cash, *Daily Life Depicted in the Cantigas de Santa Maria* (Lexington: University Press of Kentucky, 1998), 16–18, 52, plate 60, 68; García Cuadrado, *Cantigas*, 264–307.

35. Agrait, "Monarchy and Military Practice," 61–71.

36. Agrait, "Monarchy and Military Practice," 79–81, and "Military Reform," 107–8.

37. Ibn Abī Zarʿ, *Rawd al-Qirtas*, 2:660; *CSIV*, 70–71, 73, ch. 2, 3.

38. Giménez Soler, *Corona*, 241 n. 3.

39. *GCAXI*, 2:406–10, ch. 321–23; *CAXI*, 323–24, ch. 248–50; Huici, *Batallas*, 346–48, 367–71.

40. *CAXI*, 269, ch. 343.

41. Giménez Soler, *Corona*, 241 n. 3; on the Nasrid army see Arié, *L'Espagne*, 238–48.

42. García Cuadrado, *Cantigas*, 308–14; O'Callaghan, *Alfonso X and the Cantigas*, illustration 11.

43. Amador de los Ríos, "Bandera del Salado," 464–71.

44. Gárate Córdoba, "Pensamiento," 21–23.

45. Gárate Córdoba, "Pensamiento," 26–35; Inés Carrasco, *Los cargos de la hueste real en tiempos de Alfonso X: Estudio onomasiológico* (Granada: Universidad de Granada, 1992).
46. Arié, *L'Espagne*, 257–65.
47. *CAXI*, 206, ch. 55; *GCAXI*, 407–8, ch. 70; Arié, *L'Espagne*, 261.
48. Hilda Grassotti, "Sobre la retenencia de castillos en la Castilla medieval," in *Estudios medievales españoles*, 261–81.
49. *CSIV*, 88–89, ch. 11.
50. Ibn Abī Zarʿ, *Rawd al-Qirtas*, 2:598–602; *CAX (GJ)*, 178–80, 208, ch. 62, 74; *CAX*, 49–50, 58, ch. 62, 74; *CAXI*, 183–84, ch. 14; *GCAXI*, 1:316–18, ch. 21; John Barbour, *The Bruce*, 2: 184–92, bk. 20, vv. 210–510.
51. Luis García de Valdeavellano, *Curso de historia de las instituciones españolas de los orígines al final de la edad media* (Madrid: Revista de Occidente, 1968), 628.
52. The *Espéculo* (4,12,17) included a form letter of appointment for various officials including an admiral; Pérez Embid, *Almirantazgo*, 25–27.
53. *CSIV*, 70, 86, ch. 1, 8; *CAXI*, 309, ch. 212; *GCAXI*, 2:324–25, ch. 284.
54. García Cuadrado, *Cantigas*, 339–50.
55. Ibn Khaldūn, *Histoire*, 4:230–31; *CAXI*, 306–8, 339–42, ch. 208–9, 264–67; *GCAXI*, 2:310–19, ch. 277–81.
56. Aquilino Iglesia Ferreirós, *Historia de la traición: La traición regia en León y Castilla* (Santiago de Compostela: Universidad de Compostela, 1971); Gárate Córdoba, "Pensamiento," 31–32, 46–52.
57. Veas Arteseros, *Alfonso XI*, 456, no. 403.
58. O'Callaghan, *Reconquest*, 146–47; Powers, *Society*, 162–87; Hilda Grassotti, "Para la historia del botín y de las parias en Castilla y León," in her *Miscelánea*, 135–221; Gárate Córdoba, "Pensamiento," 39–41, 59–60; Pedro Andrés Porras Arboledas, "Dos casos de erechamiento de cabalgadas (Murcia, 1334–1392)," *Estudos em homenagem ao Professor Doutor José Marques* (Porto: Universidade de Porto, 2009), 261–69.
59. Agrait, "Military Reform," 113.
60. Ayala Martínez, *Órdenes*, 604–12; Gárate Córdoba, "Pensamiento," 24–25, 41–42, 44–46; Powers, *Society*, 136–61, 188–206; James W. Brodman, *Charity and Welfare: Hospitals and the Poor in Medieval Catalonia* (Philadelphia: University of Pennsylvania Press, 1998).
61. Arié, *L'Espagne*, 264.
62. O'Callaghan, *Cantigas*, 92–93, and *Reconquest*, 147–49; Pedro Marín, *Miraculos romanzados*; Gil de Zamora, *De preconiis Hispaniae*, 151; Manuel González Jiménez, "Esclavos andaluces en el reino de Granada," in *Actas del III Coloquio de Historia Medieval Andaluza: La Sociedad Medieval Andaluza: Grupos no privilegiados* (Jaén: Diputación Provincial, 1984), 327–38; Cossío, "Cautivos de moros en el siglo XIII."
63. James W. Brodman, *Ransoming Captives in Crusader Spain: The Order of Merced on the Christian-Islamic Frontier* (Philadelphia: University of Pennsylvania Press, 1986), and "Municipal Ransoming Law on the Medieval Spanish Frontier," *Speculum* 60 (1985): 318–30; Ayala Martínez, *Órdenes*, 606–10.

64. *CAX (GJ)*, 40–43, ch. 15; *CAX*, 11, ch. 15; *CSIV*, 84–85, ch. 7–8; *CFIV*, 131–33, ch. 11; Giménez Soler, *Corona*, 167–70.

65. *CAXI*, 227, 259–60, 315, ch. 91, 129, 234; *GCAXI*, 1:489, ch. 112, 2:78–79, ch. 151; Alarcón y Santón and García de Linares, *Documentos árabes*, 61–63, no. 30.

66. *CDACA*, 7:176–77, no. 51; Giménez Soler, *Juan Manuel*, 642–43, no. 574.

67. López Dapena, *Cuentas*.

68. López Dapena, *Cuentas*, 660–65; Gaibrois, "Tarifa," *BRAH* 76 (1920): 152–60, and 77 (1920): 212–15, no. 31.

69. Miguel Ángel Ladero Quesada, *Fiscalidad*, 33–40, 75–105, 121–39, 155–74, and "Las transformaciones de la fiscalidad regia castellano-leonesa en la segunda mitad del siglo XIII (1252–1312)," in *Historia de la Hacienda española (Épocas antigua y medieval)* (Madrid: Instituto de Estudios Fiscales, 1982), 321–406, and "Fiscalidad regia y génesis del Estado en la Corona de Castilla (1252–1504)," *ETF* 3 (1991): 95–135; O'Callaghan, *Cortes*, 143–44; Procter, *Curia*, 195–99.

70. Rodríguez Díez, *Astorga*, 715–20; *CAX (GJ)*, 49–53, 214–19, ch. 18, 75; *CAX*, 13, 59–60, ch. 18, 75; Vigil, *Oviedo*, 75, no. 41; *CSIV*, 86, ch. 8–9; *CLC*, 1:125; *CFIV*, 162, 169, ch. 16, 19–20; *CAXI*, 182, 222–23, ch. 12, 80; *GCAXI*, 1:306–7, 467–69, ch. 16, 100–101.

71. Gaibrois, *Sancho IV*, 2:xxiv–xxx, "Cuentas," and "Tarifa," *BRAH* 77 (1920): 434–37, no. 20; López Dapena, *Cuentas*, 157–76, 408–18; García Fitz, "Defensa," 278–79, 306.

72. Gaibrois, "Tarifa," *BRAH* 74 (1919): 522, and 76 (1920): 422–23, no. 3.

73. Gonzalo Martínez Díaz, ed., *Libro Becerro de las Behetrías*, 3 vols. (León: Centro de Estudios e Investigaciones, 1981), 2:180–81, 108.

74. Ladero Quesada, *Fiscalidad*, 41–52; Agrait, "Military Reform," 110–12; O'Callaghan, *Cortes*, 189–91.

75. *PCG*, 2:745, ch. 1069; *CAX (GJ)*, 5–7, ch. 1; *CAX*, 4, ch. 1.

76. Ladero Quesada, *Fiscalidad*, 47–50, and "Transformaciones," 362; Agrait, "Military Reform," 114; Grassotti, "Para la historia."

77. Procter, *Curia*, 54–57, 82–85, 186–95; O'Callaghan, *Cortes*, 130–51; Ladero Quesada, *Fiscalidad*, 54–70, 175–79.

78. Joseph F. O'Callaghan, "The Beginnings of the Cortes of León-Castile," *American Historical Review* 74 (1969): 1503–37, reprinted in *Alfonso X, the Cortes, and Government in Medieval Spain* (London: Ashgate, 1997), chap. 9.

79. *CAX (GJ)*, 117, ch. 41; *CAX*, 30–31, ch. 40; *MHE* 2:79–80, no. 209; *CFIV*, 96, 169, ch. 1, 20; *CAXI*, 182, 199, 222–24, 273, 354, ch. 12, 40, 80, 82, 155, 282; *GCAXI*, 1:307, 378, 468, ch. 16, 52, 101, and 2:126, ch. 177; *CLC*, 1:99–106.

80. *CAX (GJ)*, 49, 67, 76–92, 132–35, 193–95, 216–20, ch. 18, 21, 23–25, 47, 68–69, 75; *CAX*, 13, 17, 21–22, 35, 53–54, 59–60, ch. 18, 21, 23–25, 47, 68–69, 75; *CLC*, 1:85–86; *MHE*, 1:305, 308–24, 339–41, nos. 137, 140, 153; González Díez, *Burgos*, 125, 127, 129–30, nos. 40, 42, 44; Vigil, *Oviedo*, 75, no. 41.

81. *CSIV*, 86–89, ch. 8–11; *CLC*, 1:99–106, 125; *CFIV*, 93, ch. 1.

82. *CFIV*, 107, 111, 115, 117, 119, 123–25, 133, 139–40 144, 146, 151, 160, 162, 169, ch. 2, 4–5, 7–8 10–11, 13–16, 20.

83. *CAXI*, 179–82, 187–93, 195, 199, 222–24, 273–74, 287, 298, 330–31, ch. 8–10, 12, 19–27, 29, 31, 40, 80, 154–55, 177, 196, 253–55; *GCAXI* 1:295, 327–46, 353, 359, 378, ch. 9, 24–34, 40, 42, 52, and 2:125–27, 443–49, 467–78, 471–73, ch. 34, 101, 103, 176–77, 332–35; Agrait, "Military Reform," 115–18.

84. Ladero Quesada, "Transformaciones," 332–33.

85. *CAXI*, 259, 335–38, ch. 128, 259–63; *GCAXI*, 2:75–76, ch. 150; Moxó, *La alcabala*; Ladero Quesada, *Fiscalidad*, 175–91; Agrait, "Military Reform," 118–19.

86. O'Callaghan, *Cortes*, 132–33; Procter, *Curia*, 201–2; Ladero Quesada, *Fiscalidad*, 191–207.

87. Berger, *Registres d'Innocent IV*, 1:377, no. 2538; Goñi Gaztambide, *Historia*, 184.

88. Ballesteros, "Cortes de 1252," 114–43, art. 44; O'Callaghan, *Learned King*, 53–54.

89. Jordan, *Clément IV*, 350–52, nos. 890, 896; Domínguez Sánchez, *Gregorio X*, 368–69, no. 214; Gay, *Nicolas III*, 338–40, 342–44, nos. 739–41, 743.

90. *MFIV*, 2:232–34, no. 170; *Regestum Clementis Papae V*, no. 9727.

91. *MFIV*, 2:657–59, no. 443; Finke, *Acta Aragonensia*, 2:764–67; *Regestum Clementis Papae V*, 117–23, nos. 4046–51.

92. Reg. Vat. 68, ep. 1694, cited by Goñi Gaztambide, *Historia*, 285; Mollat, *Lettres*, no. 2921; *CAXI*, 181, ch. 11; *GCAXI*, 302, ch. 14.

93. Finke, *Acta Aragonensia*, 2:790, no. 494.

94. Mansilla, *Castel S. Angelo*, 66–67, nos. 126–27; Reg. Vat. 87, ep. 2477, cited by Goñi Gaztambide, *Historia*, 299–300.

95. *MH*, 1:162–65, no. 76.

96. Vidal, *Benoit XII: Lettres communes*, nos. 8043, 8103–4; Goñi Gaztambide, *Historia*, 316, 323.

97. Serrano, "Alfonso XI," 33, no. 7; Veas Arteseros, *Alfonso XI*, 502, no. 435; Goñi Gaztambide, *Historia*, 332–33; Agrait, "Military Reform," 121–22.

98. O'Callaghan, *Cortes*, 133; Ladero Quesada, *Fiscalidad*, 217–22.

99. "Empréstito pedido por D. Fernando III el Santo a los conceios de Galicia para atender a los gastos de la guerra con los árabes el año 1248 dos meses antes de la toma de Sevilla," *Boletín de la Comisión de Monumentos de Orense* 3 (1909): 385–87; Grassotti, "Un empréstito," 261–65.

100. *MHE*, 1:69, no. 33; Agapíto y Revilla, *Los privilegios de Valladolid*, 48–49, no. 29-XI; Sánchez Ruano, *Salamanca*, xx, 166.

101. Vigil, *Oviedo*, 46, no. 22; *CAX (GJ)*, 130–31, 200–202, ch. 45, 72; *CAX*, 34–35, 55–56, ch. 45, 72; Procter, *Curia*, 201.

102. *MFIV*, 2:760–63, no. 525; López Dapena, *Cuentas*, 284; Giménez Soler, *Juan Manuel*, 373, no. 203; Rui de Pina, *Crónica de D. Dinis*, 235–37, ch 12.

103. *CAXI*, 245, 259, 323, 368, ch. 111, 128, 248, 304; *GCAXI*, 2:32, 76, 385, ch. 132, 150, 312.

104. Mansilla, *Castel S. Angelo*, 76–77, nos. 147–48; Serrano, "Alfonso XI," 13–14, 27–33, nos. 4–7; *CAXI*, 368, ch. 303; *PAXI (1864)*, stanzas 2209, 2230–33; Agrait, "Military Reform," 122–23.

105. Torres Fontes, *Fernando IV*, 31–33, no. 25.
106. *CLC*, 1:58, art. 17; *CAX (GJ)*, 7, ch. 1; *CAX*, 4, ch. 1.
107. Giménez Soler, *Juan Manuel*, 367–69, no. 197; *El libro de los castigos o consejos* or *Libro infinido*, BAE 51:264–75, esp. 269, ch. 6; *CAXI*, 241–42, ch. 107; *GCAXI*, 2:22–23, ch. 128; Agrait, "Military Reform," 106.
108. Agrait, "Military Reform," 105–6, tables 1 and 2.
109. *CSIV*, 87, ch. 10; Gaibrois, *Sancho IV*, 1:61, cliv, 2:230, 251, and "Tarifa," *BRAH* 76 (1920): 53–57, 65–66; López Dapena, *Cuentas*, 668.
110. *CAX*, ch. 69; *CSIV*, 70, 86, ch. 1–2, 8.
111. López Dapena, *Cuentas*, 660–65; Gaibrois, "Tarifa," *BRAH* 76 (1920): 152–60; 77 (1920): 212–15, no. 31.
112. *GCAXI*, 2:324–25, ch. 284; Agrait, "Military Reform," 109, n. 99; Ladero Quesada, *Fiscalidad*, 335–36.
113. López Dapena, *Cuentas*, 288–91, 766–68.
114. *CFIV*, 159–60, ch. 15–16.
115. *CAXI*, 180–81, ch. 10; *GCAXI*, 1:300–301, ch. 13; O'Callaghan, *Cortes*, 147–48; Agrait, "Military Reform," 118; Hilda Grassotti, "Los apremios fiscales de Alfonso XI," in Manuel Peláez, ed., *Historia económica y de las instituciones financieras en Europa* (Málaga: Universidad de Málaga, 1990), 3435–62.
116. Giménez Soler, *Corona*, 241 n. 3.
117. O'Callaghan, *Reconquest*, 17–22.
118. *PAXI (1864)*, stanzas 2238–43; O'Callaghan, *Reconquest*, 184.
119. Quintana Prieto, *Inocencio IV*, 2:711, no. 833; Rodríguez de Lama, *Alejandro IV*, 74–77, 83–84, nos. 53, 62; Villar García, *Segovia*, 280–81, 284, nos. 169, 171.
120. *DAAX*, 313–16, no. 286; Colmenares, *Segovia*, 1:264; Mingüella, *Sigüenza*, 1:599–601, no. 225; Domínguez Sánchez, *Clemente IV*, 111–15, 118–19, 127–31, 260–63, nos. 4–5, 10, 20, 140.
121. Domínguez Sánchez, *Gregorio X*, 343–45, no. 195; Raynaldus, *Annales*, a. 1276, no. 20 fragment; Goñi Gaztambide, *Historia*, 202.
122. Muñoz Torrado, *Iglesia de Sevilla*, 145; Nieto Soria, *Sancho IV*, 125.
123. *MFIV*, 2:353–54, 515, nos. 235, 348; Torres Fontes, *Fernando IV*, 31–33, no. 25; Goñi Gaztambide, *Historia*, 263–64.
124. *MFIV*, 2:644, 650–51, 657–59, nos. 436, 439–40, 443; Masià i de Ros, *Jaume II*, 325–26; *Regestum Clementis Papae V*, 3:96–100, 117–23, nos. 3989–90, 4046–51; 8459–64; Goñi Gaztambide, *Historia*, 282.
125. Reg. Vat. 65, ep. 2125a, and Reg. Vat. 63, epp. 1001–2, and Reg. Vat. 68, epp. 1547, 1688–89, 1694–95, cited by Goñi Gaztambide, *Historia*, 284–86; Mollat, *Lettres*, nos. 2924–25, 7864, 8020–22, 8026–27.
126. Mansilla, *Castel S. Angelo*, 66–67, no. 126; Mollat, *Lettres*, nos. 41566–68; Reg. Vat. 87, cpp. 2476, 2478, and Reg. Avin. 30, fol. 623v, 633, 636b, cited by Goñi Gaztambide, *Historia*, 299–300.
127. Reg. Vat. 128, ep. 14–15, cited by Goñi Gaztambide, *Historia*, 323; Raynaldus,

Annales, 16:120–21, a. 1340, nos. 40–43; Vidal, *Benoit XII: Lettres communes*, nos. 8103–4; *MH*, 1:178–94, 199–201, nos. 84–87.

128. Reg. Vat. 128, nos. 14–17, cited by Goñi Gazambide, *Historia*, 332–33; Vidal *Benoit XII: Lettres communes*, nos. 8103–6; Raynaldus, *Annales*, a. 1343, no. 36; Serrano, "Alfonso XI," 33, no. 7.

129. Brundage, *Canon Law and the Crusader*.

130. Linehan, "Preaching the Crusades," 129–54; Rodríguez de Lama, *Alejandro IV*, 124–25, no. 117; *MFIV*, 2:353–54, nos. 235; Torres Fontes, *Fernando IV*, 31–33, no. 25; Goñi Gaztambide, *Historia*, 323.

131. Al-Qabtawrī, *Rasā'il*, 113–21, cited by Mosquera Merino, *Señoría de Ceuta*, 191–93.

132. Matthew Paris, *Chronica majora*, 5:170; Quintana Prieto, *Inocencio IV*, 2:837–38, no. 955; Finke, *Acta Aragonensia*, 2:880–82, no. 559.

133. Al-Makkarī, *History*, 2:350–51; Giménez Soler, *Juan Manuel*, 583–84, no. 488; Iorga, *Notes et extraits*, 3–5; O'Callaghan, *Reconquest*, 180–85.

134. O'Callaghan, *Alfonso X and the Cantigas*, 172–91, esp. 186–91.

135. *CSIV*, 85, ch. 8; O'Callaghan, *Alfonso X and the Cantigas*, 38.

136. *CAXI*, 233–34, ch. 99; *GCAXI*, 1:506–508, ch. 120.

137. *CSM*, 2:310–11, no. 374; O'Callaghan, *Alfonso X and the Cantigas*, 152–53.

138. Linehan, *Spanish Church*, 242; Gaibrois, *Sancho IV*, 3:cclxxxii, no. 420.

139. Gaibrois, *Sancho IV*, 1:lxxxii, "Cuentas," and "Tarifa," *BRAH* 74 (1919): 525; López Dapena, *Cuentas*, 449.

140. Giménez Soler, *Juan Manuel*, 368–70, nos. 197–98; *CFIV*, 162–64, ch. 17.

141. *Regestum Clementis Papae V*, nos. 5091, 5093, 5095; Goñi Gaztambide, *Historia*, 274.

142. Vidal, *Benoit XII: Lettres closes*, nos. 2862–67; Goñi Gaztambide, *Historia*, 326.

143. O'Callaghan, *Reconquest*, 191–92; *CAXI*, 318, ch. 242; *GCAXI*, 2:343, ch. 293; Zurita, *Anales*, 2:713–14.

144. Rui de Pina, *CAIV*, 166–71, ch. 59; Mendeiros, "O Santo Lenho."

145. Ibn Marzūq, *El Musnad*, 381, ch. 52.

146. Gárate Córdoba, "Pensamiento," 35–38.

147. *GCAXI*, 2:418–21, ch. 326–27; *CAXI*, 325, ch. 251; *PAXI (1864)*, stanzas 1497–1512; Rui de Pina, *CAIV*, 166–69, ch. 59.

148. O'Callaghan, *Reconquest*, ch. 8.

149. Ibn Abī Zar', *Rawd al-Qirtas*, 2:598–600, 609–12.

150. *GCAXI*, 2:422–25, ch. 328–29; *CAXI*, 325–26, ch. 251; *PAXI (1864)*, stanzas 1538–1652.

151. *PAXI (1864)*, stanzas 28–39, 188–95, 681–96, 852–85, 2143–93; *CAXI*, 302, ch. 200; *GCAXI*, 1:388–89, 2:51, 2:261, 2:280, ch. 59, 139, 255, 263; O'Callaghan, *Reconquest*, 193–99.

152. Gárate Córdoba, "Pensamiento," 12–13, 43; Ariel Guiance, "Morir por la patria, morir por la fe: La ideología de la muerte en la *Historia de rebus Hispaniae*," *Cuadernos de Historia de España* 73 (1991): 75–106, esp. 91–100.

153. *Poema de Fernán González*, ll. 549–62; *PCG*, 2:404–5, ch. 700; Ibn Khaldūn, *Histoire*, 4:103.
154. *CAXI*, 202–5, ch. 46; *GCAXI*, 1:386–91, ch. 58–60; *PAXI (1864)*, stanzas 188–95.
155. *GCAXI*, 2:438, ch. 331; Linehan, "Beginnings."
156. *CJI*, 8:34, ch. 445; *CSIV*, 86, ch. 9; *PAXI (1864)*, stanzas 289–90; García Fernández, "Regesto," 29, no. 119; O'Callaghan, *Reconquest*, 206–8.
157. Mansilla, "Cádiz y Algeciras," 265–68, nos. 5–7; Domínguez Sánchez, *Clemente IV*, 245–47, no. 128; *CAXI*, 389–90, ch. 336–37; *PAXI (1864)*, stanzas 2450–56.

CHAPTER 11. THE AFTERMATH: THE STRAIT OF GIBRALTAR TO 1492

1. *PCG*, 2:772–73, ch. 1132.
2. O'Callaghan, *Reconquest*, 1–21.
3. Gaibrois, *Sancho IV*, 3:ccl–lvii, no. 384; *MHE*, 3:453; Álvaro Pelayo, *Speculum regum*, 1:12; O'Callaghan, "Castile, Portugal, and the Canary Islands."
4. O'Callaghan, *Reconquest*, 7–17, and "The Mudejars of Castile and Portugal in the Twelfth and Thirteenth Centuries," in James M. Powell, *Muslims Under Latin Rule, 1100–1300* (Princeton, N.J.: Princeton University Press, 1990), 11–56.
5. Richard Fletcher, *The Quest for El Cid* (New York: Knopf, 1990).
6. Alemany, "Milicias," esp. 144–46.
7. *CAX (GJ)*, 92–116, ch. 27–40; *CAX*, 23–31, ch. 27–40; *CSIV*, 88–89, ch. 11.
8. Manzano Rodríguez, *Intervención*, 298–99.
9. Manzano Rodríguez, *Intervención*, 293–305.
10. Manzano Rodríguez, *Intervención*, 321–71, esp. 366–69; Arié, *L'Espagne*, 106–21.
11. Ibn Khaldūn, *Histoire*, 4:405–11; Arié, *L'Espagne*, 119; Manzano Rodríguez, *Intervención*, 304; Harvey, *Islamic Spain*, 206–19.
12. I. I. Macdonald, *Don Fernando de Antequera* (Oxford: Dolphin, 1948), ch. 5.
13. Arié, *L'Espagne*, 121–45; Ladero Quesada, *Granada*, 94–118; Harvey, *Islamic Spain*, 220–74.
14. Goñi Gaztambide, *Historia*, 380–94, 671–76, no. 15.
15. Goñi Gaztambide, *Historia*, 392–93.
16. Arié, *L'Espagne*, 147–78; Ladero Quesada, *Granada*, 119–63, and *Castilla y la conquista del Reino de Granada* (Granada: Diputación Provincial, 1987); Harvey, *Islamic Spain*, 275–323; Felipe Fernández-Armesto, *Ferdinand and Isabella* (New York: Dorset, 1977), 89–105.
17. Bailey W. Diffie and George Winius, *Foundations of the Portuguese Empire, 1415–1580* (Minneapolis: University of Minnesota Press, 1977), esp. ch. 4–9.
18. José Martins da Silva Marques, *Descobrimentos Portugueses: Documentos para a sua história*, 2 vols. (Lisbon: Instituto para a Alta Cultura, 1944), 1:291–320, no. 281; O'Callaghan, "Castile," 300–303.

19. Rodrigo Sánchez de Arévalo, *Vergel de los principes*, BAE 116:312.
20. Diego de Valera, *Epistola* 24, BAE 116:31.
21. Goñi Gaztambide, *Historia*, 465–76; Erika Rummel, *Jiménez de Cisneros: On the Threshold of Spain's Golden Age* (Tempe: Arizona Center for Medieval and Renaissance Studies, 1999), 29–52.

Bibliography

NARRATIVE SOURCES: CHRISTIAN

Adam Murimuth. *Continuatio Chronicarum.* Ed. Edward M. Thompson. Rolls Series. London: Eyre and Spottiswoode, 1889.
Anales Toledanos III. ES 23: 411–24.
Annales Ianuenses. Monumenta Germaniae Historica. Scriptores. 18:11–356.
Bernat Desclot. *Crònica.* Ed. M. Coll i Alentorn. 5 vols. Barcelona: Barcino, 1949–51.
Chronicle of Alfonso X. Tr. Shelby Thacker and José Escobar. Lexington: University Press of Kentucky, 2002.
Chronicle of Pere III of Catalonia (Pedro IV of Aragon). Tr. Mary Hillgarth. 2 vols. Toronto: Pontifical Institute of Mediaeval Studies, 1980.
The Chronicle of San Juan de la Peña: A Fourteenth-Century Official History of the Crown of Aragón. Tr. Lynn H. Nelson. Philadelphia: University of Pennsylvania Press, 1991.
Chronicon de Cardeña. ES 23:371–81.
Chronicon Conimbricense. ES 23:326–56.
Chronicon Marchiae Tarvisinae et Lombardiae (aa. 1207–1270). Ed. L. A. Botteghi. Città di Castello: S. Lapi, 1916.
Chronique catalane de Pierre IV d'Aragon III de Catalogne. Ed. Amédée Pagès. Toulouse: E. Privat, 1941.
Chronique de Jean le Bel. 2 vols. Ed. Jules Viard and Eugène Déprez. Paris: Renouard, 1904–5.
Cossío, José María. "Cautivos de moros en el siglo XIII: El texto de Pero Marín." *Al-Andalus* 7 (1942): 49–112.
Crónica de Alfonso X. BAE 66:1–66.
Crónica de Alfonso X según el Ms. II/2777 de la Biblioteca del Palacio Real (Madrid). Ed. Manuel González Jiménez. Murcia: Real Academia Alfonso X el Sabio, 1998.
Crónica de Alfonso XI. BAE 66:173–392.
Crónica de Fernando IV. BAE 66:93–170. Also in Antonio Benavides, ed., *Memorias de Fernando IV de Castilla.* 2 vols. Madrid: José Rodríguez, 1869. 1:1–242.
Crònica de Jaume I. Ed. J. M. Casacuberta and E. Bagüe. 9 vols. Barcelona: Barcino, 1926–62.

Crónica de Sancho IV. BAE 66 : 69–90.
Crónica de la población de Ávila. Ed. Amparo Hernández Segura. Valencia: Anubar, 1966.
Crónica dos sete primeiros reis de Portugal. Ed. Carlos da Silva Tarouca. 2 vols. Lisbon: Academia Portuguesa da Historia, 1952.
Crónicas anónimas de Sahagún. Ed. Antonio Ubieto Arteta. Zaragoza: Anubar, 1987.
Crónicas de los reyes de Castilla desde don Alfonso el Sabio hasta los católicos don Fernando y doña Isabel. Ed. Cayetano Rosell. 3 vols. BAE 66, 68, 70. 1875. Reprint Madrid: Real Academia Española, 1953.
"Fragmento del itinerario del Hermano Mauricio y del señor Andrés Nicolas, año 1273." In José García Mercadal, *Viajes de extranjeros por España desde los tiempos más remotos hasta fines del siglo XVI.* Madrid: Sociedad General Española de Librería, 1952. 223–24.
Georgius et Ioannes Stella. *Annales Genuenses.* Ed. Giovanni Petti Balbi. Bologna: Zanichelli, 1975.
Giovanni Villani. *Cronica.* Ed. Ignazio Moutier. 8 vols. Florence: Magheri, 1823.
González Jiménez, Manuel. "Unos anales del reinado de Alfonso X." *BRAH* 192 (1995):461–91.
Gonzalo de la Finojosa. "Continuación de la Crónica del Arzobispo Don Rodrigo Jiménez de Rada." Ed. Marqués de Fuensanta in Martín Fernández de Navarrete et al., eds., *Colección de documentos inéditos para la historia de España.* 112 vols. Madrid: Calera and others, 1841–95. Vols. 105–6.
La Gran Conquista de Ultramar: Biblioteca Nacional MS 1187. Ed. Louis Cooper. Madison, Wis.: Hispanic Seminary, 1989.
Gran crónica de Alfonso XI. Ed. Diego Catalán. 2 vols. Madrid: Gredos, 1977.
Jacopo d'Oria. *Annales Ianuenses.* Ed. Cesare Imperiale. *Fonti per la Storia d'Italia* 5 (1929).
Jean Froissart. *Chroniques.* Ed. Siméon Luce, Gaston Raynaud, and Léon Minot. 13 vols. Paris: Mme Ve Renouard, 1869.
———. *The Chronicles of England, France and Spain by Sir John Froissart.* London: J.M. Dent, 1906.
Jofre de Loaysa. *Crónica de los reyes de Castilla Fernando III, Alfonso X, Sancho IV, y Fernando IV (1248–1305).* Ed. Antonio García Martínez. Murcia: Diputación de Murcia, 1961.
John Barbour. *The Bruce or the Book of the Most Excellent and Noble Prince, Robert de Broyss, King of Scots.* Ed Walter W. Skeat. 2 vols. Edinburgh: William Blackwood, 1894.
Juan Manuel. *Chronicon Domini Joannis Emmanuelis.* In *MFIV,* 1:675–80.
Matthew Paris. *Chronica Majora.* Ed. H. R. Luard. 7 vols. Rolls Series. London: Longman, 1872–83.
Pedro López de Ayala. *Crónica de Pedro I.* BAE 66:393–614.
Pedro Marín. *Los miraculos romanzados de como sacó Santo Domingo de Silos los cautivos de la catividad.* Ed. Sebastián de Vergara. Madrid: Francisco del Hierro, 1736.
Poema de Fernán González. Ed. Alonso Zamora Vicente. Madrid: Espasa-Calpe, 1946.
Primera crónica general de España. Ed. Ramón Menéndez Pidal. 2 vols. Madrid: Gredos, 1955.

Ramon Muntaner. *Crònica.* Ed. Enric Bagüe. 2nd ed. 9 vols. Barcelona: Barcino, 1927–52.
Raynaldus, Odoricus. *Annales ecclesiastici ab anno MCXCVIII ubi desinit Cardinalis Baronius.* Ed. J. D. Mansi. 15 vols. Lucca: Leonardo Venturini, 1738–47.
Rodrigo Yáñez. *Poema de Alfonso XI.* Ed. Tomás Antonio Sánchez. In *Poetas castellanos anteriores al siglo XV.* Madrid: M. Rivadeneyra, 1864. 477–551.
———. *Poema de Alfonso XI.* Ed. Yo Ten Cate. Madrid: CSIC, 1956.
Rui de Pina. *Chronica de el rey Dom Afonso o Quarto.* Lisbon: Paulo Craesbeeck, 1653. Reprint Lisbon: Biblion, 1936.
———. *Crónica de D. Dinis.* Porto: Livraria Civilização, 1945.
Sturla Thordarson. *Hakonar saga Hakonarsonar.* In C. R. Unger, ed., *Codex Frisianus: En Samlung af norske Konge-Sagaer.* Christiania: P. T. Mallings, 1871. 387–583.

NARRATIVE SOURCES: MUSLIM

Al-Dhakhīra al-Saniyya fī ta'rikh al-dawla al-marīniyya. Ed. Mohammed Ben Cheneb. Algiers: Bastide, 1920.
Al-Dhakhīra al-Saniyya fī ta'rikh al-dawla al-marīniyya. Ed. A. Benmansour. Rabat: Dar al-Mankhur, 1972.
Al-Himyarī. *Kitāb al-Rawd al-mi'tar.* Tr. María Pilar Maestro González. Valencia: Gráficas Bautista, 1963.
Al-Hulal al-Mawsiyya: Crónica árabe de las dinastías almorávide, almohade y benimerín. Tr. Ambrosio Huici Miranda. *Colección de crónicas árabes de la Reconquista* 1. Tetuán: Editora Marroquí, 1952.
Al-Makkarī, Ahmad ibn Mohammed. *History of the Mohammedan Dynasties in Spain, Extracted from the Nafhu t-tib min ghosni-l-Andalusi-r-rattab wa tarikh Lisanu-d-Din ibni-l-Khattīb.* Tr. Pascual de Gayangos. 2 vols. London: Oriental Translation Fund, 1840–43. Reprint New York: Johnson, 1964.
Ibn Abī Zar'. *Rawd al-Qirtās.* Tr. Ambrosio Huici. 2 vols. Valencia: Anubar, 1964.
Ibn Battūta. *Voyages d'Ibn Battutah.* Ed. and tr. C. Defrémery and B. R. Sanguinetti. 2nd ed. 4 vols. Paris: Imprimerie Nationale, 1873–79.
Ibn 'Idhārī. *Al-Bayān al-Mugrib fī Ijtisār ajbār Muluk al-Andalus wa al-Magrib.* Tr. Ambrosio Huici. 2 vols. Tetuán: Editora Marroquí, 1954.
Ibn Khaldūn. *Histoire des Berbères et des dynasties musulmanes de l'Afrique septentrionale.* Tr. Baron de Slane. 4 vols. Paris: Imprimerie du Gouvernement, 1852–56.
Ibn al-Khatīb. *Al-Ihāta fī akhbār Garnāta.* Ed. Muhammad 'Abd Allāh 'Inān. 4 vols. Cairo: Maktabat al-Khānjī, 1973–77.
———. *Al-Lamha al-badriyya fī l-dawla al-nasriyya.* Ed. Ahmad 'Āsī and Muhibb al-dīn al-Khatīb. Beirut: Dār al-Afāq al-Jadīdah, 1978.
———. *Historia de los reyes de la Alhambra: El resplandor de la luna llena (Al-Lamha al-badriyya).* Ed Emilio Molina López, tr. José María Casciaro Ramírez. Granada: Universidad de Granada, 1998.

Ibn al-Qāḍi, Ahmad. *Durrat al Hijāl.* In René Basset, "Le siège d'Almería en 709," *Journal Asiatique* 10th ser. 10 (1907): 275–303.
Ibn Marzūq. *El Musnad: Hechos memorables de Abū l-Hasan, sultán de los Benimerines.* Ed. and tr. María Jesús Viguera. Madrid: Instituto Hispano-Arabe de Cultura, 1977.
Lévi-Provençal, Évariste. "Un zaǧal hispanique sur l'expédition aragonaise de 1309 contre Almería." *Al-Andalus* 1 (1941): 377–99.

LITERARY SOURCES

Alfonso XI. *Libro de la Montería.* 2 vols. Ed. José Gutiérrez de la Vega. Madrid: M. Tello, 1877.
Alvar, Carlos. *La poesia trovadoresca en España y Portugal.* Barcelona: Planeta, 1977.
Álvaro Pelayo [Álvaro Pais]. *Speculum regum.* Ed. and tr. Miguel Pinto de Meneses as *Espelho dos reis.* 2 vols. Lisbon: Instituto de Alta Cultura, 1955.
"El Baladro del Sabio Merlin." In Adolfo Bonilla y San Martín, ed., *Libros de Caballerías: Primera Parte.* Madrid: Bailly/Bailliére, 1907. 1–162.
Cantigas de Santa Maria. Ed. Walter Mettmann. 4 vols. Coimbra: Universidad de Coimbra, 1959–74. Reprint, 2 vols. Vigo: Edicions Xerais de Galicia, 1981.
Chaucer, Geoffrey. *Chaucer's Canterbury Tales.* Ed. Alfred W. Pollard. 2 vols. London: Macmillan, 1907.
Diego de Valera. *Epistolas. BAE* 116:3–51.
Fita, Fidel. "Biografías de San Fernando y de Alfonso el Sabio por Gil de Zamora." *BRAH* 5 (1885): 308–28.
Juan Gil de Zamora. *Liber de preconiis civitatis Numantine.* In Fidel Fita, "Dos libros (inéditos) de Gil de Zamora." *BRAH* 5 (1884): 131–200.
———. *Liber de preconiis Hispaniae.* Ed. Manuel de Castro y Castro. Madrid: Universidad de Madrid, 1955.
Juan Manuel. *El libro de los estados.* Ed. Ian R. Macpherson and Robert Brian Tate. Madrid: Clásicos Castalia, 1991.
———. *El libro de los castigos o consejos* o *Libro infinido, BAE* 51:264–75
———. *Libro del caballero et del escudero. BAE* 51:234–56.
———. "Tractado que fizo don Juan Manuel sobre las armas que fueron dadas a su padre el Infante don Manuel, et por que el et sus descendientes pudiesen facer caballeros non lo siendo, et de como paso la fabla que con el rey don Sancho ovo ante que finase." In Pascual de Gayangos, ed., *Escritores en prosa anteriores al siglo XV. BAE* 51:257–64.
Libro de los doze sabios o tractado de la nobleza y lealtad. Ed. John K. Walsh. Madrid: Anejos de la Boletin de la Real Academia Española, 1975.
Montoya Martínez, Jesús. *Cancionero de Santa María de el El Puerto.* El Puerto de Santa María: Ayuntamiento, 2006.
Rodrigo Sánchez de Arévalo. *Vergel de los principes. BAE* 116:311–41.

Rodrígues Lapa, Manuel. *Cantigas d'escarnho e de mal dezir dos cancioneiros medievais galego-portugueses.* 2nd ed. Coimbra: Galaixa, 1970.
Sancho IV. *Castigos e documentos para bien vivir ordenados por el rey don Sancho IV.* Ed. Agapito Rey. Bloomington: Indiana University Press, 1952.
Vegetius Renatus, Flavius. *Vegetius: Epitome of Military Science.* Tr. N. P. Milner. Liverpool: Liverpool University Press, 1993.

DOCUMENTARY SOURCES

Agapito y Revilla, Juan. *Los privilegios de Valladolid.* Valladolid: Sociedad Castellana de Excursiones, 1906.
Alarcón y Santón, Maximiliano, and Ramón García de Linares. *Los documentos árabes diplomáticos del Archivo de la Corona de Aragón.* Madrid: E. Maestre, 1940.
Alfonso X. *Espéculo: Texto jurídico atribuído al Rey de Castilla Don Alfonso el Sabio.* Ed. Robert A. MacDonald. Madison, Wis.: Hispanic Seminary, 1990.
———. *Fuero real.* Ed. Gonzalo Martínez Díez, José Manuel Ruiz Asencio, and C. Hernández Alonso. Ávila: Fundación Claudio Albornoz, 1988.
———. *Setenario.* Ed. Kenneth Vanderford. Buenos Aires, 1945. Reprint Barcelona: Crítica, 1984.
———. *Las Siete Partidas.* Tr. Samuel P. Scott, ed. Robert I. Burns, S.J. 5 vols. Philadelphia: University of Pennsylvania Press, 2001.
———. *Las Siete Partidas del Rey Don Alfonso el Sabio.* Ed. Real Academia de la Historia. 3 vols. Madrid: Imprenta Real, 1801.
Argente del Castillo Ocaña, Carmen. "Las hermandades medievales en el reino de Jaén." In *Andalucía medieval: Actas del I Congreso de Historia de Andalucía, diciembre de 1976.* 2 vols. Córdoba: Monte de Piedad y Caja de Ahorros, 1978. 2:21–32.
Ayala Martínez, Carlos de. *Libro de privilegios de la Orden de San Juan de Jerusalén en Castilla y León (siglos XII–XV).* Madrid: Editorial Complutense, 1995.
Ballesteros, Antonio. "Las Cortes de 1252." *Anales de la junta para ampliación de estudios e investigaciones científicas* 3 (1911): 114–43.
Barrios García, Ángel, Alberto Martín Expósito, and Gregorio del Ser Quijano. *Documentación medieval del Archivo municipal de Alba de Tormes.* Salamanca: Universidad de Salamanca, 1982.
Barrios García, Ángel, José María Monsalvo Antón, and Gregorio del Ser Quijano. *Documentación medieval del Archivo municipal de Ciudad Rodrigo.* Salamanca: Diputación Provincial de Salamanca, 1988.
Benavides, Antonio. *Memorias de Fernando IV de Castilla.* 2 vols. Madrid: José Rodríguez, 1869.
Benavides Checa, José, ed. *El fuero de Plasencia.* Rome: Lobesi, 1896.
Berger, Élie. *Les registres d'Innocent IV.* 4 vols. Bibliothèque des Écoles Françaises d'Athènes et de Rome ser. 2, no. 1. Paris: Thorin, 1884–1921.

Bourel de la Roncière, Charles, et al. *Les registres d'Alexandre IV (1254–1261)*. 3 vols. Bibliothèque des Écoles Françaises d'Athènes et de Rome ser. 2, no. 15. Paris: Fontemoing, 1902–59.

Canivez, J. M. *Statuta capitulorum generalium Ordinis Cisterciensis*. 8 vols. Louvain: Revue d'Histoire ecclésiastique, 1933–41.

Capmany y de Montpalau, Antonio. *Antiguos tratados de paces y alianzas entre algunos reyes de Aragón y diferentes principes infieles de Asia y Africa desde el siglo XIII hasta el XV*. Madrid: Imprenta Real, 1786.

Colección de documentos inéditos del Archivo de la Corona de Aragón. Ed. Prosper Bofarull et al. 41 vols. Barcelona: Imprenta del Archivo, 1847–1910.

Coquelines, Charles, et al., eds. *Bullarum, privilegiorum et diplomata romanorum pontificum amplissima collectio*. 37 vols. in 50. Rome: Hieronymus Mainardus, 1733–1857.

Cortes de los antiguos reinos de León y Castilla. 5 vols. Madrid: Real Academia de la Historia, 1861–1903.

Daumet, Georges. "Les testaments d'Alphonse X le Savant, roi de Castille." *Bibliothèque de l'École des Chartes* 67 (1906): 70–99.

Del Estal, Juan Manuel. *Documentos inéditos de Alfonso X el Sabio y del Infante, su hijo, Don Sancho*. Alicante: Juan Manuel del Estal, 1984.

Déprez, Eugène, Jean Glenisson, and Michel Mollat, eds. *Lettres closes, patentes et curiales du pape Clement VI (1342–1352) se rapportant a la France*. 4 vols. Paris: A. Fontemoing, 1901–61.

Díaz Martín, Luis. *Itinerario de Pedro I de Castilla: Estudio y Regesta*. Valladolid: Universidad de Valladolid, 1975.

"Documentos de la época de D. Alfonso el Sabio." *MHE* 1:1–344; 2:1–135.

"Documentos de la época de D. Sancho el Bravo." *MHE* 3:421–68.

Domínguez Sánchez, Santiago. *Documentos de Clemente IV (1265–1268) referentes a España*. León: Universidad de León, 1996.

———. *Documentos de Gregorio X (1272–1276) referentes a España*. León: Universidad de León, 1997.

———. *Documentos de Nicolás III (1277–1280) referentes a España*. León: Universidad de León, 1999.

Dufourcq, Charles. "Nouveaux documents sur la politique africaine de la Couronne d'Aragon." *Analecta Sacra Tarraconensia* 26 (1953): 291–322.

"Empréstito pedido por D. Fernando III el Santo a los conceios de Galicia para atender a los gastos de la guerra con los árabes el año 1248 dos meses antes de la toma de Sevilla." *Boletín de la Comisión de Monumentos de Orense* 3 (1909): 385–87.

Escudero, J. M. "Súplica hecha al Papa Juan XXI para que absolviese al rey de Castilla, D. Alfonso X, del juramento de no acuñar otra moneda que los dineros prietos." *RABM* 2 (1872): 58–59.

Fernández, Luis. "Colección diplomática del monasterio de San Pelayo de Cerrato." *Hispania Sacra* 26 (1973): 281–324.

Fernández Gómez, Marcos, Pilar Ostos Salcedo, and María Luisa Pardo Rodríguez, eds. *El libro de privilegios de la ciudad de Sevilla.* Seville: Ayuntamiento de Sevilla, 1993.

Finke, Heinrich. *Acta Aragonensia: Quellen zur deutschen, italienischen, französischen, spanischen, zur Kirchen- und Kulturgeschichte aus der diplomatischen Korrespondenz Jaymes II (1291–1327).* 3 vols. Berlin, 1908–22. Reprint Aalen: Scientia Verlag, 1966.

———. "Nachträge und Ergänzungen zu den Acta Aragonensia (I–III)." *Spanische Forschungen der Görresgesellschaft: Gesammelte Aufsätze zu Kulturgeschichte Spaniens* 1 Reihe, 4 (1933): 355–536. Reprint, Finke, *Acta Aragonensia,* 3.

Fita, Fidel. *Actas inéditas de Siete Concilios españoles celebrados desde el año 1282 hasta el de 1314.* Madrid: F. Maroto, 1882.

———. "El concilio nacional de Palencia en 1321." *BRAH* 52 (1908): 17–48.

García Fernández, Manuel. "Regesto documental andaluz de Alfonso XI (1312–1350)." *HID* 15 (1990): 1–125.

Floriano, Antonio. *Documentación histórica del Archivo municipal de Cáceres (1229–1471).* Cáceres: Diputación Provincial, 1987.

Fricaud, Émile. "1283 (682 H): Des émissaires du Sultan Qalāwūn dans la Castille d'Alphonse X et de son fils Sanche IV." *TextArab* 40 (July–August 1996): 8–9.

Friedberg, Emil. *Corpus Iuris Canonici.* 2 vols. Leipzig: Tauchnitz, 1879–81.

El fuero Viejo. Ed. Ignacio Jordán de Asso y del Río and Miguel de Manuel y Rodríguez. Madrid: Joaquín Ibarra, 1771.

Gaspar Remiro, Mariano, ed. *Correspondencia diplomática entre Granada y Fez (siglo XIV): Extractos del "Raihana Alcuttab" de Lisaneddin Abenal-jatif el andalosi.* Granada: El Defensor, 1916.

Gay, Jules. *Les registres de Nicolas III (1277–1280): Recueil des bulles de ce pape.* Bibliothèque des Écoles Françaises d'Athènes et de Rome ser. 2, no. 14. Paris: Fontemoing, 1898–1938.

González, Julio. *Repartimiento de Sevilla.* 2 vols. Madrid: CSIC, 1951. Reprint Seville: Ayuntamiento de Sevilla, 1998.

González Crespo, Esther. *Colección documental de Alfonso XI: Diplomas reales conservados en el Archivo Histórico Nacional, Sección de Clero, Pergaminos.* Madrid: Universidad Complutense, 1985.

———. "Inventario de documentos de Alfonso XI relativos al reino de Murcia." *ELEM* 17 (1994): 235–59.

González Díez, Emiliano. *Colección diplomática del Concejo de Burgos (884–1369).* Burgos: Ayuntamiento de Burgos, 1984.

González Jiménez, Manuel. *Diplomatario andaluz de Alfonso X.* Seville: El Monte, Caja de Huelva y Sevilla, 1991.

———. "Repartimiento de Carmona: Estudio y edición." *HID* 8 (1981): 59–84.

González Jiménez, Manuel, and Antonio González Gómez. *El libro del repartimiento de Jerez de la Frontera: Estudio y edición.* Cádiz: Instituto de Estudios Gaditanos, Diputación Provincial, 1980.

Guiraud, Jean. *Les registres de Grégoire X (1271–1276): Recueil des bulles de ce pape.* Bibliothèque des Écoles Françaises d'Athènes et de Rome ser. 2, no. 12. Paris: Fontemoing, 1892–1906.

———. *Les registres d'Urbain IV (1261–1264): Recueil des bulles de ce pape.* 4 vols. Bibliothèque des Écoles Françaises d'Athènes et de Rome ser. 2, no. 13. Paris: Fontemoing, 1892–1958.

Gutiérrez del Arroyo, Consuelo. *Privilegios reales de la Orden de Santiago en la Edad Media: Catálogo de la Serie existente en el Archivo Histórico Nacional.* Madrid: Junta técnica de Archivos, Bibliotecas y Museos, 1946.

Hernández Díaz, José, Antonio Sancho Corbacho, and Francisco Collantes de Terán, eds. *Colección diplomática de Carmona.* Seville: Editorial de la Gavida, 1941.

Huici Miranda, Ambrosio, and María Desamparados Cabanes Pecourt. *Documentos de Jaime I de Aragón.* 5 vols. thus far. Valencia: Anubar, 1976–88.

Iglesia Ferreirós, Aquilino. "El privilegio general concedido a las Extremaduras en 1264 por Alfonso X: Edición del ejemplar enviado a Peñafiel el 15 de abril de 1264." *AHDE* 53 (1983): 456–521.

Jordan, Edouard. *Les registres de Clément IV (1265–1268): Recueil des bulles de ce pape.* 2 vols. Bibliothèque des Écoles Françaises d'Athènes et de Rome ser. 2, no. 11. Paris: Thorin, 1893–1945.

Langlois, Ernest. *Les registres de Nicolas IV (1288–1292): Recueil des bulles de ce pape.* Bibliothèque des Écoles Françaises d'Athènes et de Rome ser. 2, no. 5. Paris: Thorin, 1886–93.

López Agurleta, José. *Bullarium equestris ordinis S. Iacobi de Spatha.* Madrid: Juan de Ariztia, 1719.

López Dapena, Asunción. *Cuentas y gastos (1292–1294) del Rey D. Sancho IV el Bravo (1284–1295).* Córdoba: Monte de Piedad y Caja de Ahorros, 1984.

López Ferreiro, Antonio. *Fueros municipales de Santiago y de su tierra.* Santiago de Compostela, 1895. Reprint Madrid: Castilla, 1975.

Magalhães Godinho, Vitorino de. *Documentos sobre a Espansão portuguesa.* 3 vols. Lisbon: Gleba/Cosmos, 1943–56.

Mansilla, Demetrio. *La documentación española del Archivo del Castel S. Angelo (395–1498).* Rome: Iglesia Nacional Española, 1958.

———. *La documentación pontificia de Honorio III (1216–1227).* Rome: Instituto Español de Historia Ecclesiástica, 1965.

Marcos Rodríguez, Florencio. *Catálogo del Archivo catedralicio de Salamanca (siglos XII–XV).* Salamanca: Universidad Pontificia de Salamanca, 1962.

Martín Fuertes, José A., and César Álvarez Álvarez, eds. *Archivo histórico municipal de León: Catálogo de los documentos.* León: Ayuntamiento de León, 1982.

Martínez Díaz, Gonzalo, ed. *Libro Becerro de las Behetrías.* 3 vols. León: Centro de Estudios e Investigaciones, 1981.

Mas Latrie, Louis de. *Traités de paix et de commerce et documents divers concernant les rélations des chrétiens avec les arabes de l'Afrique septentrionale a moyen âge.* 2 vols. Paris, 1866. Reprint Philadelphia: Burt Franklin, 1963.

Masià i de Ros, Ángels. *Jaume II: Aragó, Granada i Marroc*. Barcelona: CSIC, 1989.
Masiá de Ros, Ángeles. *Relación castellano-aragonesa desde Jaime II a Pedro el Ceremonioso*. 2 vols. Barcelona: CSIC, 1994.
Milián Boix, Manuel. "El fondo 'Instrumenta Miscellanea' del Archivo Vaticano: Documentos referentes a España (853–1782)." *Anthologica Annua* 15 (1967): 489–1014.
Molina Molina, Ángel Luis. *Documentos de Pedro I. CODOM 7*. Murcia: Academia Alfonso X el Sabio, 1978.
Mollat, Guillaume. *Lettres communes: Jean XXII, analysées d'après les registres dits d'Avignon et du Vatican*. 17 vols. Paris: A. Fontemoing, 1904–47.
Montes Romero-Camacho, Isabel. "La documentación de Alfonso XI conservada en el Archivo de la Catedral de Sevilla." *ELEM* 3 (1982): 135–56.
Monumenta Henricina. 15 vols. Coimbra: Comissação executivo das comemorações do V centenário da morte do Infante D. Henrique, 1960–74.
Moxó y de Montoliu, Francisco de. "La relación epistolar entre Alfonso XI y Alfonso IV en el Archivo de la Corona de Aragon." *ELEM* 3 (1982): 173–95.
Muñoz Torrado, Antonio. *La Iglesia de Sevilla en el siglo XIII: Estudio histórico*. Seville: Imprenta de Izquierdo, 1914.
Múñoz y Gómez, Agustín. "Concejos de Córdoba, Sevilla y Jerez de la Frontera: Carta inédita de su hermandad en 1296." *BRAH* 36 (1900): 306–16.
Olivier-Martin, F. *Les registres de Martin IV (1281–1285): Recueil des bulles de ce pape*. Bibliothèque des Écoles Françaises d'Athènes et de Rome ser. 2, no. 16. Paris: Fontemoing, 1901–35.
Ortega y Cotes, Ignacio José, et al. *Bullarium Ordinis Militiae de Calatrava*. Madrid: A. Marín, 1761.
Palacio, Timoteo Domingo. *Documentos del Archivo general de la Villa de Madrid*. 6 vols. Madrid: Imprenta Municipal, 1888–1943.
Pereda Llarena, F. Javier. *Documentación de la Catedral de Burgos (1254–1293)*. Burgos: Garrido Garrido, 1984.
———. *Documentación de la Catedral de Burgos (1294–1316)*. Burgos: Garrido Garrido, 1984.
Quintana Prieto, Augusto. *La documentación pontificia de Inocencio IV (1243–1254)*. 2 vols. Rome: Instituto Español de Historia Ecclesiástica, 1987.
Regestum Clementis Papae V. 8 vols. Rome: Typographia Vaticana, 1884–92.
Rius Serra, José. "Los rótulos de la Universidad de Valladolid," *Analecta Sacra Tarraconensia* 16 (1943): 87–134.
Rodríguez de Lama, Ildefonso. *La documentación pontificia de Alejandro IV (1254–1261)*. Rome: Instituto Español de Historia Ecclesiástica, 1981.
Rosell, Francisco Miquel. *Regesta de letras pontificias en el Archivo de la Corona de Aragón, Sección de Cancillería real (Pergaminos)*. Madrid: CSIC, 1948.
Rymer, Thomas. *Foedera, conventiones, litterae et cuiuscunque acta publica inter reges Angliae et alios quosvis imperatores, reges, pontifices, principes*. 3rd ed. 10 vols. The Hague: Joannes Neaulme, 1739–45.

Sacy, Silvestre de. "Mémoire sur une correspondance de l'empereur de Maroc Yakoub, fils d'Abd-alhakk, avec Philippe-le-Hardi, conservée dans les Archives du Royaume." *Histoire et Mémoires de l'Institut Royal de France, Académie des Inscriptions et Belles Lettres* 9 (1831): 478–506.

Sánchez Ruano, Julián. *Fuero de Salamanca.* Salamanca: Sebastián Cerezo, 1870.

Sanz Fuentes, María Josefa. "Cartas de hermandad concejíl en Andalucía: El caso de Écija." *HID* 5 (1978): 403–29.

———. "Repartimiento de Écija." *HID* 3 (1976): 535–51.

Serrano, Luciano. *Cartulario del Infantado de Covarrubias.* Valladolid: Cuesta, 1907.

Sousa, António Caetano de. *Provas da História genealogica da casa real portuguesa.* 6 vols. in 12. Ed. Manuel Lopes Almeida and César Pegado. Coimbra: Atlantida, 1946–52.

Torres Fontes, Juan, ed. *Colección de documentos para la historia del reino de Murcia.* 22 vols. thus far. Murcia: Academia Alfonso X el Sabio, 1963–.

———. *Documentos de Alfonso X el Sabio. CODOM* 1. Murcia: Academia Alfonso X el Sabio, 1963.

———. *Documentos de Fernando IV. CODOM* 5. Murcia: Academia Alfonso X el Sabio, 1980.

———. *Documentos del siglo XIII. CODOM* 2. Murcia: Academia Alfonso X el Sabio, 1969.

———. "El estatuto concejil murciano en la época de Alfonso X el Sabio." In *Documentos del siglo XIII. CODOM* 2. Murcia: Academia Alfonso X el Sabio, 1969. xxiii–lxxvi.

———. *Fueros y privilegios de Alfonso X el Sabio al reino de Murcia. CODOM* 3. Murcia: Academia Alfonso X el Sabio, 1973.

———. *Repartimiento de Lorca.* Murcia: Academia Alfonso X el Sabio, 1977.

———.*Repartimiento de Murcia.* Murcia: Academia Alfonso X el Sabio, 1960.

———. *Repartimiento de Orihuela.* Murcia: Academia Alfonso X el Sabio, 1988.

Ubieto Arteta, Antonio. *Colección diplomática de Cuéllar.* Segovia: Diputación Provincial, 1961.

Ureña y Smenjaud, Rafael, ed. *Fuero de Cuenca.* Madrid: Academia de la Historia, 1935.

Veas Arteseros, Francisco de Asís. *Documentos de Alfonso XI. CODOM* 6. Murcia: Academia Alfonso X el Sabio, 1997.

Vidal, J. M. *Benoit XII (1334–1342): Lettres closes et patentes interessant les pays autres que la France.* 2 vols. Paris: A. Fontemoing and E. Boccard, 1913–50.

———. *Benoit XII (1334–1342): Lettres communes analysées d'après les registres dit d'Avignon et du Vatican.* 3 vols. Paris: A. Fontemoing, 1902–11.

Vidal Beltrán, Eliseo. "Privilegios y franquicias de Tarifa." *Hispania* 17 (1957): 3–78.

Vigil, Ciriaco Miguel. *Colección histórico-diplomática del ayuntamiento de Oviedo.* Oviedo: Pardo-Gusano, 1889.

Villar García, Luis Miguel. *Documentación medieval de la catedral de Segovia (1115–1300).* Salamanca: Universidad de Salamanca, 1990.

Vincke, Johannes. *Documenta selecta mutuas civitatis Arago-Cathalaunicae et Ecclesiae relationes illustrantia.* Barcelona: Bibliotheca Balmes, 1936.

MODERN WORKS

Agrait, Nicolas. "Castilian Military Reform Under the Reign of Alfonso XI (1312–1350)." *Journal of Medieval Military History* 3 (2005): 88–126.
———. "The Experience of War in Fourteenth-Century Spain: Alfonso XI and the Capture of Algeciras (1342–1344)." In Villalon and Kagay, eds., *Crusaders*. 213–38.
———."Monarchy and Military Practice During the Reign of Alfonso XI of Castile (1312–1350)." Ph.D. dissertation, Fordham University, New York, 2003.
———. "The Reconquest During the Reign of Alfonso XI (1312–1350)." In Kagay and Vann, eds., *Social Origins*. 149–66.
Alemany, José. "Milicias cristianas al servicio de los sultanes musulmanes del Almagreb." In *Homenaje a D. Francisco Codera en su jubilación del profesorado: Estudios de erudición oriental.* Ed. Eduardo Saavedra. Zaragoza: Mariano Escar, 1904. 133–69.
Allouche, I. S. "La relation du siège d'Almerie en 709 (1309–1310) d'après de nouveaux manuscrits de la Durrat al-Higal." *Hespéris* 16 (1933): 122–38.
Almazán, Vicente. "El viaje de la princesa Cristina a Valladolid (1257–1258) según la Saga islandesa del rey Hakon." *Archivos Leoneses* 73 (1983): 101–10.
Al-Nāsirī al-Salāwī, Ahmad. *Kitāb al-Istiqsā*. Tome quatrième, *Les Mérinides*. Tr. Ismael Hamet. *Archives Marocaines* 33 (1934): 1–621.
Amador de los Ríos, Rodrigo. "La Bandera del Salado." *BRAH* 21 (1892): 464–71.
———. *Trofeos militares de la Reconquista: Estudio acerca de las enseñas musulmanas del Real Monasterio de las Huelgas (Burgos) y de la Catedral de Toledo.* Madrid: Fortanet, 1893.
Amrán-Tedghi, Rica. "El papel de Ceuta en la política exterior de Jaime II de Aragón." *Anales de la Universidad de Alicante: Historia Medieval* 11 (1996–97): 465–78.
Antón Solé, Pablo. "La iglesia gaditana en el siglo XIII." In *Cádiz en el siglo XIII: Actas de las "Jornadas Conmemorativas del VII Centenario de la muerte de Alfonso X el Sabio."* Cádiz: Universidad de Cádiz, 1983. 37–48.
Antuña, Melchor M. "Conquista de Quesada y Alcaudete." *Religión y Cultura* (1932): 61–70, 386–95.
Argote de Molina, Gonzalo. *Nobleza del Andaluzia*. Hildesheim: Olms, 1975.
Arias Guillén, Fernando. "Los discursos de la guerra en la *Gran Crónica de Alfonso XI*." *Miscelánea Medieval Murciana* 31 (2007): 9–21.
Arié, Rachel. *L'Espagne musulmane au temps des Nasrides (1232–1492)*. Paris: Boccard, 1973.
———. "Les rélations diplomatiques et culturelles entre musulmans d'Espagne et musulmans d'Orient au temps des Nasrides." *Mélanges de la Casa de Velázquez* 1 (1965): 87–107.
Arribas Palau, Mariano. "Los Benimerines en los pactos concordados entre Aragón y Granada." In *Actas del Primer Congreso de Estudios Árabes e Islámicos, Córdoba 1962*. Madrid: Comité Permanente del Congreso de Estudios Árabes e Islámicos, 1964. 179–88.
Ayala Martínez, Carlos de. "Alfonso X, Beaucaire y el fin de la pretensión imperial." *Hispania* 47 (1987): 5–31.

———.*Directrices fundamentales de la política penínsular de Alfonso X: Relaciones castellano-aragonesas de 1252 a 1263*. Madrid: Universidad Autónoma de Madrid, 1986.

———."La monarquía y las órdenes militares durante el reinado de Alfonso X." *Hispania* 178 (1991): 409–65.

———. *Las órdenes militares hispánicas en la Edad Media (siglos XII–XV)*. Madrid: Marcial Pons, 2007.

———. "Paces castellano-aragonesas de Campillo-Agreda (1281)." *ELEM* 5.2 (1986): 151–68.

Baer, Yitzhak. *A History of the Jews in Christian Spain*. 2 vols. Philadelphia: Jewish Publication Society, 1966.

Ballesteros y Beretta, Antonio. *Alfonso X el Sabio*. 1963. Reprint Barcelona: El Albir, 1984.

———. *El itinerario de Alfonso el Sabio*. Madrid: Tipografía de Archivos, 1935.

———. "Itinerario de Alfonso el Sabio." *BRAH* 104 (1934): 49–88, 455–516; 105 (1934): 123–80; 106 (1935): 83–150; 107 (1935): 21–76, 381–418; 108 (1936): 15–42; 109 (1936): 377–460.

———.*La Reconquista de Murcia por el Infante D. Alfonso de Castilla*. Murcia: Noues, 1959.

———. *Sevilla en el siglo XIII*. Seville: Juan Pérez Torres, 1913.

———. "La toma de Salé en tiempos de Alfonso X el Sabio." *Al-Andalus* 8 (1943): 89–128.

Barrantes Maldonado, Pedro. *Ilustraciones de la Casa de Niebla*. MHE 9 (1857): 1–534.

Beattie, Pamela Drost. "'Pro exaltatione sanctae fidei catholicae': Mission and Crusade in the Writings of Ramon Llull." In Larry J. Simon, ed., *Iberia and the Mediterranean World of the Middle Ages: Studies in Honor of Robert I. Burns, S.J.* 2 vols. Leiden: Brill, 1995. 1:113–29.

Bejarano Rubio, Amparo. "La frontera del reino de Murcia en la política castellano-aragonesa del siglo XIII." In Miguel Rodríguez et al., *Alfonso X el Sabio*. 199–212.

Beneyto Pérez, Juan. *El cardenal Albornoz: Canciller de Castilla y Caudillo de Italia*. Madrid: Espasa-Calpe, 1950.

———.*El cardenal Albornoz: Hombre de iglesia y de estado en Castilla y en Italia*. Madrid: Fundación Universitaria Española, 1986.

Benito Ruano, Eloy. *Hermandades en Asturias durante la Edad Media*. Oviedo: La Cruz, 1972.

Berger, Élie. *Saint Louis et Innocent IV: Étude sur les rapports de la France et du Saint-Siège*. Paris: Thorin & Fils, 1893.

Borrero Fernández, Mercedes. "La frontera de Sevilla con el reino de Granada en tiempos de Alfonso X." In Segura Graíño, ed., *Relaciones*. 13–21.

Brodman, James W. *Charity and Welfare: Hospitals and the Poor in Medieval Catalonia*. Philadelphia: University of Pennsylvania Press, 1998.

———. *Ransoming Captives in Crusader Spain: The Order of Merced on the Christian-Islamic Frontier*. Philadelphia: University of Pennsylvania Press, 1986.

———. "Municipal Ransoming Law on the Medieval Spanish Frontier." *Speculum* 60 (1985): 318–30.

Bruhn de Hoffmeyer, Ada. *Arms and Armour in Spain: A Short Survey*. 2 vols. Madrid: CSIC, 1972–82.

Brundage, James A. *Medieval Canon Law and the Crusader.* Madison: University of Wisconsin Press, 1969.

Burns, Robert I., S.J. *Muslims, Christians and Jews in the Crusader Kingdom of Valencia: Societies in Symbiosis.* Cambridge: Cambridge University Press, 1984.

———. "Warrior Neighbors: Alfonso el Sabio and Crusader Valencia, an Archival Case Study in His International Relations." *Viator* 21 (1990): 147–202.

———, ed. *The Worlds of Alfonso the Learned and James the Conqueror: Intellect and Force in the Middle Ages.* Princeton, N.J.: Princeton University Press, 1985.

Cádiz en el siglo XIII: Actas de las "Jornadas Conmemorativas del VII Centenario de la muerte de Alfonso X el Sabio." Cádiz: Universidad de Cádiz, 1983.

Caldcrón Ortega, José Manuel, and Francisco Javier Díaz González. "Los almirantes del 'siglo de oro' de la marina castellana medieval." *ELEM* 24 (2001): 311–64.

———. "Los almirantes y la política naval de los reyes de Castilla en el siglo XIII." *Anuario de la Facultad de Derecho de Alcalá de Henares* 8 (1998–99): 103–25.

Canellas López, Ángel. "Aragón y la empresa del Estrecho en el siglo XIV: Nuevos documentos del Archivo Municipal de Zaragoza." *EEMCA* 2 (1946): 7–73.

———. "Datos para la historia de los reinos peninsulares en el primer tercio del siglo XIV: IV Génesis del tratado de Alcalá de Henares." *BRAH* 145 (1959): 231–86.

Capmany y de Montpalau, Antonio de. *Memorias históricas sobre la marina, comercio y artes de la antigua Ciudad de Barcelona.* 4 vols. in 3. Madrid: A. de Sancha, 1779–92.

Carramolino, Juan Martín. *Historia de Ávila, su provincia y obispado.* 3 vols. Madrid: Librería Española, 1872.

Carrasco, Inés. *Los cargos de la hueste real en tiempos de Alfonso X: Estudio onomasiológico.* Granada: Universidad de Granada, 1992.

Catalán Menéndez Pidal, Diego. *Un cronista anónimo del siglo XIV (La Gran Crónica de Alfonso XI: Hallazgo, estilo, reconstrucción).* La Laguna, Canarias: Universidad de la Laguna, 1955.

———. *La Estoria de España de Alfonso X: Creación y evolución.* Madrid: Universidad Autónoma de Madrid, 1992.

———. "La historiografía en verso y en prosa de Alfonso XI a la luz de nuevos textos." *BRAH* 154 (1964): 79–126; *BRAH* 156 (1966): 55–87; and *AEM* 2 (1965): 257–98.

———. "La oración de Alfonso XI en el Salado: El poema, la crónica inédita y la historia." *BRAH* 131 (1952): 247–66.

———. *Poema de Alfonso XI: Fuentes, dialecto, estilo.* Madrid: Gredos, 1953.

———. *La tradición manuscripta en la Crónica de Alfonso XI.* Madrid: Gredos, 1974.

Ceballos-Escalera y Gila, Alfonso. *La orden y divisa de la Banda real de Castilla.* Madrid: Ediciones Iberoamericanas, 1993.

Cereijo Martínez, Concepción. "La política marina de Alfonso X: La toma de Salé en la Crónica de Alfonso X y en las Fuentes musulmanas." *Revista de Historia Naval* 25 (2007): 37–57.

Chamberlin, Cynthia L. "'The King Sent Them Very Little Relief': The Castilian Siege of Algeciras, 1278–1279." In Villalon and Kagay, eds., *Crusaders.* 193–212.

———. "'Not All Martyrs or Saints': The Aragonese-Castilian Crusade Against Granada, 1309–1310." *Comitatus* 23 (1992): 17–45.

Chevedden, Paul E. "The Artillery of King James I the Conqueror." In Paul E. Chevedden, Donald J. Kagay, and Paul Padilla, eds., *Iberia and the Mediterranean World of the Middle Ages: Essays in Honor of Robert I. Burns, S.J.* Leiden: Brill, 1996. 47–94.

———. "The Hybrid Trebuchet: The Halfway Step to the Counterweight Trebuchet." In Kagay and Vann, *Social Origins*, 179–222.

Chevedden, Paul E., Zvi Shiller, and Donald J. Kagay. "The Traction Trebuchet: A Triumph of Four Civilizations." *Viator* 31 (2000): 433–86.

Collins, Roger. *The Arab Conquest of Spain, 710–797*. Oxford: Blackwell, 1989.

———. *Visigothic Spain, 491–711*. Oxford: Blackwell, 2004.

Colmenares, Diego. *Historia de la insigne Ciudad de Segovia*. New ed. 3 vols. Segovia: Academia de Historia y Arte de San Quirce, 1969–75.

Cómez Ramos, Rafael. *Las empresas artísticas de Alfonso X*. Seville: Diputación Provincial de Sevilla, 1979.

———. "Notas sobre las atarazanas de Sevilla." *Archivo Hispalense* 254 (2000): 165–77.

Daumet, Georges. *Étude sur l'alliance de la France et de la Castille au XIVe et au XVe siècles*. Paris: E. Bouillon, 1898.

———. "Jean de Rye au siège d'Algeciras." *Bulletin Hispanique* 12 (1910): 265–74.

———. *Mémoire sur les relations de la France et de la Castille de 1255 à 1320*. Paris: A. Fontemoing, 1913.

———. "Une semonce du pape Benoît XII à Pierre IV d'Aragon, pour ses relations trop fréquentes et intimes avec les musulmans." *Bulletin Hispanique* 7 (1905): 305–7.

Del Estal, Juan Manuel. *Alicante, de villa a ciudad (1252–1490)*. Alicante: Juan Manuel del Estal, 1990.

———. "Problemática en torno a la conquista y repoblación de las ciudades musulmanes de Orihuela y Alicante por Alfonso X el Sabio." In *La ciudad hispánica durante los siglos XIII al XVI*. 2 vols. Madrid: Universidad Complutense, 1985. 2: 798–810.

Diago Hernando, Máximo. "La monarquía castellana y los Staufer: Contactos políticos y diplomáticos en los siglos XII y XIII." *ETF* 8 (1995): 51–83.

Díaz Cassou, Pedro. *Serie de los obispos de Cartagena, sus hechos y su tiempo*. Madrid: Fortanet, 1895.

Díaz Martín, Luis Vicente. "Las fluctuaciones en las relaciones castellano-portuguesas durante el reinado de Alfonso IV." *RFLH* ser. 2, 15 (1998): 1231–54.

Diffie, Bailey W., and George Winius. *Foundations of the Portuguese Empire, 1415–1580*. Minneapolis: University of Minnesota Press, 1977.

Dualde Serrano, Manuel. *Solidaridad espiritual de Valencia con las victorias cristianas del Salado y de Algeciras*. Valencia: CSIC, 1950.

Dufourcq, Charles-Emmanuel. *L'Espagne catalane et le Maghrib aux XIIIe et XIVe siècles*. Paris: Presses Universitaires de France, 1966.

———. "La question de Ceuta au XIIIe siècle." *Hespéris* 42 (1955): 67–127.

———. "Un projet castillane du XIIIe siècle: La croisade d'Afrique." *Revue d'histoire et du civilisation du Magreb* 1 (1966): 26–51.

Duhamel, Léopold. *Une ambassade à la cour pontificale: Épisode de l'histoire des palais des papes.* Avignon: Seguin, 1883.

Escalona, Romualdo. *Historia del Real Monasterio de Sahagún.* Madrid, 1782. Reprint León: Ediciones Leonesas, 1982.

Estow, Clara. *Pedro the Cruel of Castile, 1350–1369.* Leiden: Brill, 1995.

Fernández-Armesto, Felipe. *Ferdinand and Isabella.* New York: Dorset, 1977.

Fernández del Pulgar, Pedro. *Historia secular y eclesiástica de Palencia.* 4 vols. Madrid: F. Nieto, 1679–80.

Fernández Duro, Cesáreo. *La marina de Castilla desde su orígen y pugna con la de Inglaterra hasta la refundición en la Armada Española.* Madrid: El Progreso Editorial, 1894.

Fletcher, Richard. *Moorish Spain.* Berkeley: University of California Press, 1992.

———. *The Quest for El Cid.* New York: Knopf, 1990.

Gaibrois de Ballesteros, Mercedes. *Historia del reinado de Sancho IV.* 3 vols. Madrid: RABM, 1922–28.

———. *María de Molina, tres veces reina.* 1936. Reprint Madrid: Espasa-Calpe, 1967.

———. "Tarifa y la política de Sancho IV de Castilla." *BRAH* 74 (1919): 418–36, 521–29; 75 (1919): 349–55; 76 (1920): 53–77, 123–60, 420–48; 77 (1920): 192–215. Reprint *Tarifa y la política de Sancho IV.* Madrid: Real Academia de la Historia, 1920.

Gárate Córdoba, José María. "El pensamiento militar en el Código de las Siete Partidas." *Revista de Historia Militar* 13 (1963): 7–60.

García Arenal, Mercedes, and María J. Viguera, eds. *Las relaciones de la Península ibérica con el Magreb (siglos XIII–XIV).* Madrid: CSIC, 1988.

García Cuadrado, Amparo. *Las Cantigas: El Códice de Florencia.* Murcia: Universidad de Murcia, 1993.

García de Valdeavellano, Luis. *Curso de historia de las instituciones españolas de los orígenes al final de la edad media.* Madrid: Revista de Occidente, 1968.

García Fernández, Manuel. "Algunas consideraciones sobre los objetivos politicos de la Hermandad General de Andalucía." *Medievalismo* 2 (1992): 61–65.

———. "Don Dionis de Portugal y la minoría de Alfonso XI de Castilla (1312–1325)." *RFLH* 9 (1992): 25–51.

———. "La defensa de la frontera de Granada en el reinado de Alfonso XI de Castilla, 1312–1350." In Segura Graíño, *Relaciones.* 37–54.

———. "Fortificaciones fronterizas andaluzas en tiempos de Alfonso XI de Castilla (1312–1350)." *Castillos de España* 95 (1988): 51–58.

———. "La frontera de Granada a mediados del siglo XIV." *Revista de Estudios Andaluces* 9 (1987): 69–86.

———. "La Hermandad General de Andalucía durante la minoría de Alfonso XI de Castilla, 1312–1325." *HID* 12 (1985): 311–70.

———. "Las hermandades municipales andaluzas en tiempos de Alfonso XI." *AEM* 19 (1989): 329–43.

———. "Jaime II y la minoría de Alfonso XI (1312–1325): Sus relaciones con la sociedad política castellana." *HID* 18 (1991): 143–81.
———. "La política internacional de Portugal y Castilla en el umbral de la Baja Edad Media: Nuevas reflexiones sobre los viejos sistemas de alianzas dinásticas peninsulares (1279–1357)." *Revista de Ciencias Históricas* 14 (1999): 61–80.
———. *El reino de Sevilla en tiempos de Alfonso XI (1312–1350)*. Seville: Diputación Provincial, 1989.
———. "Las relaciones castellano-mariníes en Andalucía en tiempo de Alfonso XI: La participación norteafricana en la guerra por el control del Estrecho, 1312–1350." In García Arenal and Viguera, eds. *Relaciones*. 249–73.
———. "Las relaciones internacionales de Alfonso IV de Portugal y Alfonso XI de Castilla en Andalucía: La participación portuguesa en la Gran Batalla del Estrecho, 1325–1350." *RFLH* 3 (1986): 201–16.
García Fitz, Francisco. "Los acontecimientos político-militares de la frontera en el último cuarto del siglo XIII." *Revista de Historia Militar* 32 (1988): 9–71.
———. "Alfonso X, el reino de Granada y los Banū Ašqīlūla: Estrategias políticas de disolución durante la segunda mitad del siglo XIII." *AEM* 27 (1997): 216–37.
———. "Alfonso X y sus relaciones con el Emirato granadino: Política y guerra." *Alcanate* 4 (2004–5): 35–77.
———. *Castilla y León frente al Islam: Estratégias de espansión y tácticas militares (siglos XI–XIII)*. Seville: Universidad de Sevilla, 1998.
———. "La composición de los ejércitos medievales." In José Ignacio de la Iglesia Duarte, eds., *La guerra en la Edad Media: XVII semana de estudios medievales*. Logroño: Instituto de Estudios Riojanos, 2007. 85–146.
———. "La conquista de Tarifa en la estrategia de expansión castellano-leonesa del siglo XIII." In Manuel González Jiménez, ed. *Tarifa en la Edad Media*. Tarifa: Ayuntamiento de Tarifa, 2005. 103–25.
———. "La defensa de la frontera del bajo Guadalquivir ante las invasiones benimerines del siglo XIII." In García Arenal and Viguera, *Relaciones*. 275–323.
———. "La frontera castellano-granadina a fines del siglo XIII." In Segura Graíño, *Relaciones*. 23–35.
———. "¿Hubo estrategía en la edad media? A propósito de las relaciones castellano-musulmanas durante la segunda mitad del siglo XIII." *RFLH* ser. 2, 15 (1998): 837–54.
———. "¿Una España musulmana, sometida y tributaria? La España que no fue." *HID* 31 (2004): 227–48.
García Sanjuan, Alejandro. "La conquista de Niebla por Alfonso X." *HID* 27 (2000): 89–112.
———. "Mercenarios cristianos al servicio de los musulmanes en el norte de África durante el siglo XIII." In Manuel González Jiménez and Isabel Montes Romero-Camacho, eds., *La Península ibérica entre el Mediterráneo y el Atlántico, siglos XIII–XV*. Cádiz: Diputación de Cádiz, 2006. 436–47.
Gaspar Remiro, A. "Relaciones de la Corona de Aragón con los estados musulmanes de

Occidente." *Revista del Centro de Estudios históricos de Granada y su reino* 13 (1923): 125–292.
Gelsinger, Bruce. "A Thirteenth-Century Norwegian-Castilian Alliance." *Medievalia et Humanistica*, n.s., 10 (1981): 55–80.
Gibert, Rafael. "Almirante en la historia del derecho." *Revista de la Facultad de Derecho de la Universidad Complutense de Madrid* 18 (1976): 137–51.
Giménez Soler, Andrés. *La Corona de Aragón y Granada: Historia de las relaciones entre ambos reinos*. Barcelona: Casa Provincial de Caridad, 1908.
———. *Don Juan Manuel: Biografía y estudio crítico*. Zaragoza: F. Martínez, 1932.
———. "La expedición a Granada de los infantes don Juan y don Pedro en 1319." *RABM* 11 (1904): 353–60; 12 (1905): 24–36.
———. "Expedición de Jaime II a la ciudad de Almería," *Boletín de la Real Academia de Buenas Letras* 2 (1903–4): 290–335.
———. *El sitio de Almería de 1309*. Barcelona: Casa Provincial de Caridad, 1904.
Gonzaga de Azevedo, Luis. *História de Portugal*. 6 vols. Lisbon: Biblion, 1940–44.
González, Cristina. *La tercera crónica de Alfonso X: "La gran conquista de Ultramar."* London: Tamesis, 1992.
———. "El último sueño de Alfonso X: La gran conquista de Ultramar." *Exemplaria Hispánica* 1 (1991–92): 97–117.
González, Julio. "Origen de la marina real de Castilla." *RABM* 54 (1948): 229–53.
———. *Reinado y diplomas de Fernando III*. 3 vols. Córdoba: Monte de Piedad y Caja de Ahorros, 1986.
González Arévalo, Raúl. "La costa del reino de Granada en la documentación náutica italiana (siglos XIV–XVI)." *ELEM* 31 (2008): 7–36.
González Jiménez, Manuel. "Alcala de Guadaira en el siglo XIII: Conquista y repoblación." *Anales de la Universidad de Alicante* 6 (1987): 135–58.
———. *Alfonso X el Sabio*. Barcelona: Ariel, 2004.
———. *Alfonso X el Sabio, 1252–1284*. Palencia: Diputación Provincial, 1993.
———. "La caballería popular en Andalucía (siglos XIII al XV)." *AEM* 15 (1985): 315–29.
———. "Cortes de Sevilla de 1261." *HID* 25 (1998): 295–311.
———. "De al-Qanatir al Gran Puerto de Santa María." In *El Puerto de Santa María entre los siglos XIII y XVI: Estudios en homenaje a Hipólito Sancho de Sopranis en el centenario de su nacimiento*. El Puerto de Santa María: Ayuntamiento de El Puerto de Santa María, 1995. 37–52.
———. "Esclavos andaluces en el reino de Granada." In *Actas del III Coloquio de Historia Medieval Andaluza: La Sociedad Medieval Andaluza: Grupos no privilegiados*. Jaén: Diputación Provincial, 1984. 327–38
———. *Fernando III el Santo: El rey que marcó el destino de España*. Seville: Fundación José Manuel Lara, 2006.
———. "Genoveses en Sevilla (siglos XIII–XV)." In *Serta gratulatoria in honorem Juan Regulo*. La Laguna: Universidad de La Laguna, 1988. 421–31.
———. "Guzmán el Bueno y su tiempo." In *Les Espagnes médiévales: Aspects économiques*

et sociaux: Mélanges offerts à Jean Gautier Dalché. Annales de la Faculté des Lettres et Sciences Humaines de Nice 46 (1983): 237–46.

———. "La obra repobladora de Alfonso X en las tierras de Cádiz." In *Cádiz en el siglo XIII: Actas de las "Jornadas Conmemorativas del VII Centenario de la muerte de Alfonso X el Sabio."* Cádiz: Universidad de Cádiz, 1983. 7–20.

———. "Osuna en el siglo XIII." In Manuel García Fernández and Juan José Iglesias Rodríguez, eds. *Osuna entre los tiempos medievales y modernos (siglos XIII–XVIII)*. Seville: Universidad de Sevilla, 1995. 27–38.

———. "Poblacion y repartimiento de Écija." In *Homenaje al Profesor Juan Torres Fontes*. 2 vols. Murcia: Universidad de Murcia, 1987. 1:691–711.

———. "El Puerto de Santa María en tiempos de Alfonso X el Sabio." In Manuel González, Alfonso Jiménez, Jesús Montoya, and José Luis Tejada, eds., *Nuestros orígenes históricos como el Puerto de Santa María*. El Puerto de Santa María: Ayuntamiento de El Puerto de Santa María, 1989. 11–31.

———. "Relaciones de las órdenes militares castellanas con la Corona (siglos XIII–XIV)." *HID* 18 (1991): 209–22.

———. "Las relaciones entre Portugal y Castilla durante el siglo XIII." *RFLH*, ser. 2, 15 (1998): 1–24.

———. *La repoblación de la zona de Sevilla durante el siglo XIV: Estudio y documentación.* Seville: Universidad de Sevilla, 1975.

———, ed. *Sevilla 1248: Congreso Internacional Conmemorativo del 750 Aniversario de la Conquista de la Ciudad de Sevilla por Fernando III, Rey de Castilla y León.* Madrid: Fundación Ramón Areces, 2000.

González Jiménez, Manuel, Mercedes Borrero Fernández, and Isabel Montes Romero-Camacho. *Sevilla en tiempos de Alfonso X el Sabio*. Seville: Ayuntamiento de Sevilla, 1987.

González Mínguez, César. *Fernando IV de Castilla (1295–1312): La guerra civil y el predominio de la nobleza*. Valladolid: Universidad de Valladolid, 1976.

———. *Fernando IV, 1295–1312*. Palencia: Diputación Provincial and Editorial La Olmeda, 1995.

———. "Fernando IV (1295–1312): Perfíl de un reinado." *ETF* 17 (2004): 223–44.

Goñi Gaztambide, José. *Historia de la bula de la cruzada en España*. Vitoria: Editorial del Seminario, 1955.

Goodman, Anthony. "Alfonso X and the English Crown." In Miguel Rodríguez et al., *Alfonso X el Sabio*. 39–54.

———. "England and Iberia in the Middle Ages." In Michael Jones and Malcolm Vale, eds. *England and Her Neighbours, 1066–1453: Essays in Honour of Pierre Chaplais*. London: Hambledon, 1988.

Grassotti, Hilda. "Los apremios fiscales de Alfonso XI." In Manuel Peláez, ed., *Historia económica y de las instituciones financieras en Europa*. Málaga: Universidad de Málaga, 1990. 3435–62.

———. "El deber y el derecho de hacer guerra y paz en León y Castilla." In *Estudios medievales españolas*. Madrid: Fundación Universitaria Española, 1981. 43–132.

———. *Estudios medievales españolas*. Madrid: Fundación Universitaria Española, 1981.
———. *Miscelánea de estudios sobre instituticiones castellano-leonesas*. Bilbao: Editorial Nájera, 1978.
———. "Para la historia del botín y de las parias en Castilla y León." In *Miscelánea de estudios sobre instituticiones castellano-leonesas*. Bilbao: Editorial Nájera, 1978. 135–221.
———. "Sobre la retenencia de castillos en la Castilla medieval." In *Estudios medievales españolas*. Madrid: Fundación Universitaria Española, 1981. 261–81.
———. "Un empréstito para la conquista de Sevilla: Problemas que suscita." In *Miscelánea de estudios sobre instituciones castellano-leonesas*. Bilbao: Editorial Nájera, 1978. 225–73.
Guiance, Ariel. "Morir por la patria, morir por la fe: La ideología de la muerte en la *Historia de rebus Hispaniae*." *Cuadernos de Historia de España* 73 (1991): 75–106.
Guichard, Pierre. *Un señor musulman en la España cristiana: El ra'is de Crevillente (1243–1318)*. Alicante: Instituto de Estudios Alicantinos, 1976.
Harvey, L. P. *Islamic Spain, 1250 to 1500*. Chicago: University of Chicago Press, 1990.
Herculano, Aleixandre. *História de Portugal desde o começo da monarquia até o fim do reinado de D. Afonso III*. 9th ed. 8 vols. Lisbon: Livraria Bertrand, n.d.
Hernández, Francisco J. "Relaciones de Alfonso X con Inglaterra y Francia." *Alcanate* 4 (2004–5): 167–242.
Hernández Vegas, Mateo. *Ciudad Rodrigo: La catedral y la ciudad*. 2 vols. Salamanca: Imprenta Comercial Salmantina, 1935.
Huici Miranda, Ambrosio. *Las grandes batallas de la reconquista durante las invasiones africanas (almorávides, almohades, y benimerines)*. Madrid: CSIC, 1956.
———. "La toma de Sale por la esquadra de Alfonso X." *Hespéris* 39 (1952): 41–52.
Iglesia Ferreirós, Aquilino. *Historia de la traición: La traición regia en León y Castilla*. Santiago de Compostela: Universidad de Compostela, 1971.
Iorga, Nicolae. *Notes et extraits pour servir à l'histoire des croisades au XVe siècle*. 4th ser. 3 vols. Bucharest: Academia Romana, 1915–16.
Josserand, Philippe. *Église et pouvoir dans la Péninsule Ibérique: Les ordres militaires dans le royaume de Castille (1252–1369)*. Madrid: Casa de Velázquez 2004.
Kagay, Donald J., and Theresa Vann, eds. *On the Social Origins of Medieval Institutions: Essays in Honor of Joseph F. O'Callaghan*. Leiden: Brill, 1998.
Keller, John E., and Annette Grant Cash. *Daily Life Depicted in the Cantigas de Santa Maria*. Lexington: University Press of Kentucky, 1998.
Keller, John E., and Richard P. Kinkade. *Iconography in Medieval Spanish Literature*. Lexington: University Press of Kentucky, 1984.
Kennedy, Hugh. *Muslim Spain and Portugal: A Political History of Al-Andalus*. London: Longman, 1996.
Kinkade, Richard P. "Alfonso X, *Cantiga* 235, and the Events of 1269–1278." *Speculum* 67 (1992): 284–323.
Ladero Quesada, Miguel Angel. *Castilla y la conquista del Reino de Granada*. Granada: Diputación Provincial, 1987.

———. *Fiscalidad y poder real en Castilla (1252–1369)*. Madrid: Editorial Complutense, 1993.
———. "Fiscalidad regia y génesis del Estado en la Corona de Castilla (1252–1504)." *ETF* 3 (1991): 95–135.
———. *Granada: Historia de un país islámico (1232–1571)*. Madrid: Gredos, 1969.
———. "Portugueses en la frontera de Granada." *ELEM* 23 (2000): 67–100.
———. "Las transformaciones de la fiscalidad regia castellano-leonesa en la segunda mitad del siglo XIII (1252–1312)." In *Historia de la Hacienda española (Épocas antigua y medieval)*. Madrid: Instituto de Estudios Fiscales, 1982. 321–406.
Ladero Quesada, Miguel Angel, and Manuel González Jiménez. "La poblacion en la frontera de Gibraltar y el repartimiento de Vejer (siglos XIII y XIV)." *HID* 4 (1977): 199–204.
Lafuente y Alcántara, Emilio. *Inscripciones árabes de Granada*. Madrid: Imprenta Nacional, 1859.
Latham, J. Derek. *The Rise of the Azafids of Ceuta*. Tel Aviv: Tel Aviv University, 1972.
León-Sotelo Casado, María del Carmen de, and Esther González Crespo. "Notas para el itinerario de Alfonso XI en el período de 1344 a 1350." *ELEM* 5 (1986): 575–89.
Linehan, Peter. "The Beginnings of Santa María de Guadalupe and the Direction of Fourteenth-Century Castile." *Journal of Ecclesiastical History* 36 (1985): 284–304. Reprinted in his *Past and Present in Medieval Spain*, chap. 12.
———. "The Church, the Economy and the *Reconquista* in Early Fourteenth-Century Castile." *Revista Española de Teleología* 43 (1983): 275–302. Reprinted in his *Past and Present in Medieval Spain*, ch. 11.
———. "El cuatro de mayo de 1282." *Alcanate* 4 (2004–5): 147–66.
———."Ideología y liturgia en el reinado de Alfonso XI de Castilla." In Adeline Rucquoi, ed., *Génesis medieval del Estado moderno: Castilla y Navarra (1250–1370)*. Valladolid: Ambito, 1987. 229–43.
———. "The Mechanics of Monarchy: Knighting Castile's King, 1332." *History Today* 43 (1993): 26–32.
———. *Past and Present in Medieval Spain*. Aldershot: Variorum/Ashgate, 1992.
———. "*Quaedam de quibus dubitans*: On Preaching the Crusades in Alfonso X's Castile." *HID* 27 (2000): 129–54.
———. *The Spanish Church and the Papacy in the Thirteenth Century*. Cambridge: Cambridge University Press, 1971.
Longpré, Éphrem. "Le *Liber de acquisitione Terrae Sanctae* du bienheureux Ramon Llull." *Criterion* 3 (1927): 265–78
Loperráez, Juan. *Descripción histórica del Obispado de Osma*. 3 vols. Madrid: Imprenta Real, 1788.
López, Atanasio. "Cruzada contra los saracenos en el reino de Castilla predicada por los franciscanos de la Provincia de Santiago." *Archivo Ibero-Americano* 9 (1918): 322–27.
———. *Memoria histórica de los obispos de Marruecos desde el siglo XIII*. Madrid: n.p., 1920.
Lopez, Roberto. *Genova marinara nel duecento: Benedetto Zaccaria, ammiraglio e mercante*. Milan: Giuseppe Principato, 1933.

López de Coca Castañer, José Enrique. "Cruzados escoceses en la frontera de Granada (1330)." *AEM* 18 (1988): 245–61.
López Fernández, Manuel. "La actuación de las flotas de Castilla y de Aragón durante el cerco meriní a Tarifa en el año 1340." *Aljaranda* 64 (2007): 3–10.
———. "Los caminos y cañadas de Tarifa en los itinerarios del rey Alfonso XI de Castilla." *Aljaranda* 53 (2004): 5–10.
———. "Del desastre de Getares a la Victoria del Salado: La crítica situación de la zona del Estrecho en 1340." *ETF* ser. 3, 20 (2007): 135–62.
———. "El itinerario del ejército castellano para desercar Gibraltar en 1333." *ETF* ser. 3, 18 (2005): 185–207.
———. "Los itinerarios de Alfonso XI desde Sevilla al Campo de Gibraltar en sus campañas del Estrecho." *HID* 33 (2007): 309–27.
———. "Sobre la ubicacíon del real y del trazado de la cava que mandó hacer Alfonso XI en el istmo frente a Gibraltar en 1333." *ETF* ser. 3, 16 (2003): 151–68.
Macdonald, I. I. *Don Fernando de Antequera*. Oxford: Dolphin, 1948.
MacKay, Angus. "Andalucía y la guerra del fin del mundo." In Emilio Cabrera, ed., *Andalucía entre Oriente y Occidente (1236–1492): Actas del V Coloquio Internacional de Historia Medieval de Andalucía*. Córdoba: Diputación Provincial, 1988. 329–42.
Mahn-Lot, Marianne. "Philippe d'Évreux, roi de Navarre, et un projet de croisade contre le royaume de Grenade (1329–1331)." *Bulletin Hispanique* 46 (1944): 227–33.
Mansilla, Demetrio. "Creación de los obispados de Cádiz y Algeciras." *Hispania Sacra* 10 (1957): 243–71.
———. *Iglesia castellano-leonesa y curia romana en los tiempos del rey San Fernando*. Madrid: CSIC, 1945.
Manzano Rodríguez, Miguel Ángel. *La intervención de los Benimerines en la Península Ibérica*. Madrid: CSIC, 1992.
Maravall, José Antonio. "Del regimen feudal al regimen corporativo en el pensamiento de Alfonso X." *BRAH* 157 (1965): 213–68.
Marcos Pous, A. "Los dos matrimonios de Sancho IV de Castilla." *Cuadernos de trabajo de la Escuela Española de Historia y Arqueología en Roma* 8 (1956): 7–108.
Marín Buenadicha, María Inmaculada. "Una contradicción historiográfica: El suceso de Salé." In Miguel Rodríguez et al., *Alfonso X el Sabio*. 225–36.
Martínez, H. Salvador. *Alfonso X el Sabio: Una biografía*. Madrid: Polifemo, 2003.
Martínez Martínez, María, and Manuel Sánchez Martínez. "El reino de Murcia en la alianza castellano-aragonesa contra el sultanato nazarí (1329)." *RFLH* ser. 2, 15 (1998): 1135–68.
Martínez Montávez, Pedro. "Relaciones de Alfonso X de Castilla con el sultán mameluco Baybars y sus sucesores." *Al-Andalus* 27 (1962): 343–76.
Martínez San Pedro, María Desamparados. "Jaime II y la Cruzada de Almería." *Anales de la Universidad de Alicante: Historia Medieval* 11 (1996): 579–86.
Martínez Valverde, Carlos. "La campaña de Algeciras y la conquista de esta plaza." *Revista de Historia Militar* 25 (1981): 7–41.

Martins da Silva Marques, José. *Descobrimentos Portugueses: Documentos para a sua história.* 2 vols. Lisbon: Instituto para a Alta Cultura, 1944.

Marugán Vallvé, Carmen María. "El sitio de Almería de 1309: El desarrollo de la campaña militar." In *Almería entre culturas (siglos XIII–XVI): Actas del Coloquio, Almería, 19, 20 y 21 de abril de 1990.* 2 vols. Almería: Instituto de Estudios Almerienses, 1990. 171–86.

Masià i de Ros, Àngels. "Aportaciones al estudio de los 'Pastorellos' en la Corona de Aragón." In *Homenaje a Millás Vallicrosa.* 2 vols. Barcelona: CSIC, 1954–56. 2:9–30.

Mendeiros, José Filipe. "O Santo Lenho da Sé de Évora." *A Cidade de Évora* 10, nos. 33–34 (Julho–Dexembro 1953): 259–98.

Menéndez Pidal, Juan. *Noticias acerca de la Orden militar de Santa María de España instituída por Alfonso X.* Madrid: RABM, 1907.

Miguel Rodríguez, Juan Carlos de, Angela Múñoz Fernández, and Cristina Segura Graiño, eds. *Alfonso X el Sabio: Vida, obra y época: Actas del Congreso internacional de estudios medievales conmemorativos del VII Centenario de la muerte de Alfonso el Sabio.* Madrid: Sociedad Española de Estudios Medievales, 1989.

Mille Jiménez, Isabel. "Guzmán el Bueno en la historia y en la literatura." *Revue Hispanique* 78 (1930): 311–409.

Mingüella, Toribio. *Historia de la diócesis de Sigüenza.* 3 vols. Madrid: RABM, 1900–1913.

Miret i Sans, Joaquim. "Negociacions diplomatiques d'Alfons III de Catalunya-Aragó ab el rey de França per la croada contra Granada." *Anuari de l'Institut d'Estudis Catalans* 2 (1908–9): 265–336.

———. "Ramón de Melany, embajador de Alfonso IV en la corte de Francia." *Boletín de la Real Academia de Buenas Letras de Barcelona* 2 (1903–4): 199–202.

Mitre Fernández, Emilio. "De la toma de Algeciras a la campaña de Antequera." *Hispania* 32 (1972): 71–122.

Mollat, Guillaume. *The Popes at Avignon, 1305–1378.* New York: Harper Torchbooks, 1965.

Montoya Martínez, Jesús. "Las Cantigas de Santa Maria, fuente para la historia gaditana." In *Cádiz en el siglo XIII: Actas de las "Jornadas Conmemorativas del VII Centenario de la muerte de Alfonso X el Sabio."* Cádiz: Universidad de Cádiz, 1983. 173–91.

———. "El Castillo de Chincoya." *Boletín de Estudios Gienenses* 101 (1980):17–25.

———. "Historia de Andalucía en las Cantigas de Santa María." In *Andalucía medieval: Actas del I Congreso de Historia de Andalucía, diciembre de 1976.* 2 vols. Córdoba: Monte de Piedad y Caja de Ahorros, 1978. 1:259–69.

Morel-Fatio, Alfred. "La lettre du roi Sanche IV à Alonso Pérez de Guzmán sur la défense de Tarifa (2 janvier 1295)." *Études sur l'Espagne* 3rd ser. Paris: E. Bouillon, 1904. 1–23.

Mosquera Merino, María del Carmen. *La señoría de Ceuta en el siglo XIII: Historia política y económica.* Ceuta: Instituto de Estudios Ceutíes, 1994.

Moxó, Salvador de. *La alcabala: Sobre sus orígenes, concepto y naturaleza.* Madrid: CSIC, 1963.

Munch, P. A., Tomás Antonio Sánchez, Pascual de Gayangos, Antonio Ballesteros Beretta, and Juan Pérez de Guzmán y Gallo. "La princesa Cristina de Noruega y el infante don Felipe, hermano de don Alfonso el Sabio." *BRAH* 74 (1919): 45–61.

Nieto Cumplido, Manuel. *Orígenes del regionalismo andaluz, 1235–1325.* Córdoba: Monte de Piedad y Caja de Ahorros de Córdoba, 1979.
Nieto Soria, José Manuel. *Sancho IV, 1284–1295.* Palencia: Diputación Provincial, Editorial La Olmeda, 1994.
O'Callaghan, Joseph F. *Alfonso X and the Cantigas de Santa Maria: A Poetic Biography.* Leiden: Brill, 1998.
———. *Alfonso X, the Cortes, and Government in Medieval Spain.* London: Ashgate, 1997.
———. "The Beginnings of the Cortes of León-Castile." *American Historical Review* 74 (1969): 1503–37. Reprinted in *Alfonso X, the Cortes, and Government in Medieval Spain.* Chap. 9.
———. "Castile, Portugal, and the Canary Islands: Claims and Counterclaims, 1344–1479." *Viator* 24 (1993): 287–309.
———. "The Cortes and Royal Taxation During the Reign of Alfonso X." *Traditio* 27 (1971): 379–98. Reprinted in *Alfonso X, the Cortes, and Government in Medieval Spain.* Chap. 4.
———. *The Cortes of Castile-León, 1188–1350.* Philadelphia: University of Pennsylvania Press, 1989.
———. *A History of Medieval Spain.* Ithaca, N.Y.: Cornell University Press, 1975.
———. "Las definiciones medievales de la Orden de Montesa, 1326–1468." *Miscelánea de Textos Medievales* 1 (1972): 213–51. Reprinted in *The Spanish Military Order of Calatrava and its Affiliates.* Chap. 10.
———. *The Learned King: The Reign of Alfonso X of Castile.* Philadelphia: University of Pennsylvania Press, 1993.
———. "The Mudéjars of Castile and Portugal in the Twelfth and Thirteenth Centuries." In James M. Powell, ed. *Muslims Under Latin Rule, 1100–1300.* Princeton, N.J.: Princeton University Press, 1990. 11–56.
———. "Origin and Development of Archival Record-Keeping in the Crown of Castile-León." In Lawrence J. McCrank, ed., *Discovery in the Archives of Spain and Portugal: Quincentenary Essays, 1492–1992.* New York: Haworth, 1993. 3–18.
———. "Paths to Ruin: The Economic and Financial Policies of Alfonso the Learned." In Burns. *Worlds.* 41–67.
———. *Reconquest and Crusade in Medieval Spain.* Philadelphia: University of Pennsylvania Press, 2003.
———. *El rey sabio: El reinado de Alfonso X de Castilla.* Spanish tr. Manuel González Jiménez. Seville: Universidad de Sevilla, 1996.
———. *The Spanish Military Order of Calatrava and Its Affiliates.* London: Variorum, 1975.
———. "War (and Peace) in the Law Codes of Alfonso X." In Villalon and Kagay, eds. *Crusaders.* 3–18.
Ortíz de Zúñiga, Diego. *Anales eclesiásticos y seculares de la muy noble y muy leal ciudad de Sevilla.* 5 vols. Madrid: Imprenta Real, 1795–96. Reprint with new intro., Seville: Guadalquivir, 1988.
Pascual Sarría, Francisco Luis. "Las obligaciones militares establecidas en los ordenamientos

de las Cortes castellano-leonesas durante los siglos XIII y XIV." *Revista de Estudios histórico-jurídicos* 25 (2003): 147–85.

Pérez Bustamante, Rogelio. "Benedicto XII y la cruzada del Salado." In *Homenaje a Fray Justo Pérez de Urbel*. 2 vols. Silos: Abadía de Silos, 1976–77. 1: 177–203.

———. *El gobierno y la administración de los reinos de la Corona de Castilla (1230–1474)*. 2 vols. Madrid: Universidad Autónoma, 1976.

Pérez Castro, Mariano. "Estudios históricos-militares: La batalla del Salado." *Revista de España* 25 (1872): 552–65.

Pérez Embid, Florentino. *El almirantazgo de Castilla hasta las capitulaciones de Santa Fe*. Seville: Universidad de Sevilla, 1944.

———. *Los descubrimientos en el Atlántico y la rivalidad castellano-portuguesa hasta el Tratado de Tordesillas*. Seville: Escuela de Estudios Hispano-Americanos, 1948.

———. *La frontera entre los reinos de Sevilla y Portugal*. Sevilla: Ayuntamiento de Sevilla, 1975.

———. "La marina real castellana en el siglo XIII." *AEM* 6 (1969): 158–65.

Pérez Prendes, José Manuel. "El origen de los caballeros de cuantía y los cuantiosos de Jaén en el siglo XV." *Revista Española de Derecho Militar* 9 (1968): 31–86.

Pérez Villamil, Juan. "Orígen e instituto de la Orden militar de Santa María de España." *BRAH* 74 (1919): 243–71.

Porras Arboledas, Pedro Andrés. "Dos casos de erechamiento de cabalgadas (Murcia, 1334–1392)." *Estudos em homenagem ao Professor Doutor José Marques*. Porto: Universidade de Porto, 2009. 261–69.

Powers, James F. *A Society Organized for War: The Iberian Municipal Militias in the Central Middle Ages, 1000–1284*. Berkeley: University of California Press, 1988.

———. "Two Warrior-Kings and Their Municipal Militias: The Townsman-Soldier in Law and Life." In Burns, *Worlds*, 95–125.

Procter, Evelyn. *Curia and Cortes in León and Castile, 1072–1295*. Cambridge: Cambridge University Press, 1980.

Pryor, John H. *Geography, Technology and War: Studies in the Maritime History of the Mediterranean, 649–1571*. Cambridge: Cambridge University Press, 1988.

Purcell, Maureen. *Papal Crusading Policy, 1244–1291*. Leiden: Brill, 1975.

Ramírez de Arellano, Rafael. *Historia de Córdoba desde su fundación hasta la muerte de Isabel la Católica*. 4 vols. Ciudad Real: Hospicio Provincial, 1915–19.

Ramos Vicent, María del Pilar. *Reafirmación del poder monárquico en Castilla: La coronación de Alfonso XI*. Madrid: Universidad Autónoma de Madrid, 1983.

Reilly, Bernard F. *The Contest of Christian and Muslim Spain, 1031–1157*. London: Blackwell, 1992.

———. *The Kingdom of León-Castilla Under King Alfonso VI, 1065–1109*. Princeton, N.J.: Princeton University Press, 1988.

Ricard, Robert. "La relation portugaise de la bataille du Salado (1340)." *Hespéris* 43 (1956): 7–27.

Robson, J. A. "The Catalan Fleet and Moorish Sea-Power (1337–1344)." *English Historical Review* 74 (1959): 386–408.

Rodgers, Paula K. "Alfonso X Writes to His Son: Reflections on the *Crónica de Alfonso X*." *Exemplaria Hispanica* 1 (1991–92): 60–79.

Rodríguez de la Peña, Manuel Alejandro. "La cruzada como discurso político en la cronística alfonsí."*Alcanate* 2 (2000–2001): 23–41.

Rodríguez Díez, Matías. *Historia de la ciudad de Astorga.* 2nd ed. Astorga: Porfirio López, 1909.

Rodríguez Fernández, Justiniano. *Las juderías de la provincia de León.* León: Centro de Estudios e Investigación San Isidoro, 1976.

Rodríguez García, José Manuel. "Fernando III y sus campañas en el contexto Cruzado Europeo, 1217–1252." *Archivo Hispalense* 234–36 (1994): 205–17.

———. "Henry III, Alfonso X of Castile and the Crusading Plans of the Thirteenth Century (1245–1274)." In Björn Weiler and Ifor Rowlands, eds., *England and Europe in the Reign of Henry III (1216–1272).* Aldershot: Ashgate, 2002. 99–120.

———. "La marina alfonsí al asalto de Africa, 1240–1280: Consideraciones estratégicas e historia." *Revista de Historia Naval* 85 (2004): 27–55.

Rojas Gabriel, Manuel. "Guerra de asedio y expugnación castral en la frontera con Granada: El reinado de Alfonso XI de Castilla como paradigma (1325–1350)." *RFLH* ser. 2, 15 (1998): 875–900.

———. *Olvera en la Baja Edad Media (siglos XIV–XV).* Cádiz: Diputación Provincial, 1988.

Roldán Castro, Fátima. "Ibn Mahfuz en Niebla (siglo VII/XIII)." *Anaquel de Estudios Árabes* 4 (1993): 161–78.

Rubiera Mata de Epalza, María Jesús. "Los Banū Escallola, la dinastía granadina que no fue." *Andalucía Islámica* 2–3 (1981–82): 85–94.

Rucquoi, Adeline. "El cardenal legado Guillaume Peyre de Godin." *Revista Española del Derecho Canónico* 47 (1990): 493–516.

Ruiz, Teófilo. *Crisis and Continuity: Land and Town in Late Medieval Castile.* Philadelphia: University of Pennsylvania, 1994.

———. *Sociedad y poder real en Castilla.* Barcelona: Ariel, 1981.

Rumeu de Armas, Antonio. *España en el Africa atlántica.* 2 vols. Madrid: Instituto de Estudios Africanos, 1956–57.

Rummel, Erika. *Jiménez de Cisneros: On the Threshold of Spain's Golden Age.* Tempe: Arizona Center for Medieval and Renaissance Studies, 1999.

Salavert y Roca, Vicente. *Cerdeña y la expansion mediterránea de la Corona de Aragón (1297–1314).* 2 vols. Madrid: CSIC, 1956.

———. "La isla de Cerdeña y la política internacional de Jaime II de Aragón." *Hispania* 10 (1950): 211–65.

Samargo, Juan de. "Obispado de Ceuta." *Transfretana: Revista del Instituto de Estudios Ceutíes* 6 (1994): 129–35.

Sánchez Albornoz, Claudio. *La España musulmana según los autores islamitas y cristianos medievales.* 7th ed. 2 vols. Madrid: Espasa-Calpe, 1986.

———. "Un ceremonial inédito de la coronación de los reyes de Castilla." In *Estudios sobre las Instituciones medievales españolas.* México, D.F.: Universidad Nacional Autónoma de México, 1965. 739–63.

Sánchez-Arcilla Bernal, José. *Alfonso XI, 1312–1350*. Palencia: La Olmeda, 1995.
Sánchez de Mora, Antonio. "Nuño González de Lara: 'El más poderoso omne que sennor ouiese et más honrado de Espanna.'" *HID* 31 (2004): 631–44.
Sánchez Herrero, José. "El episcopología medieval gaditano, siglos XIII al XV." *ELEM* 1 (1980): 443–65.
Sánchez Martínez, Manuel. "La contribución valenciana a la cruzada granadina de Alfonso IV de Aragón (1327–1335)." In *Primer Congreso de Historia del País Valenciano celebrado en Valencia del 14 al 18 de abril de 1971*. 4 vols. Valencia: Universidad de Valencia, 1973–81. 2: 579–98.
———. "Guerra, avituallamiento del ejército y carestías en la Corona de Aragón: La provisión del cereal para la expedición granadina de Alfonso el Benigno (1329–1333)." *HID* 20 (1993): 523–45.
Sánchez Prieto, Ana Belén. *Guerra y guerreros en España según las fuentes canónicas de la Edad Media*. Madrid: E.M.E., 1990.
Sánchez Saus, Rafael. "Cádiz en la época medieval." In Francisco Javier Lomas Salmonte, Rafael Sánchez Saus, Manuel Bustos, Alberto Ramos Santana, and José Luis Millán Chivite, *Historia de Cádiz*. Cádiz: Sílex, 2005. 147–281.
Sancho de Sopranis, Hipólyto. *Historia de Jerez de la Frontera*. 3 vols. Jerez: Jerez Industrial, 1964–65.
———. "La incorporación de Cádiz a la Corona de Castilla bajo Alfonso X." *Hispania* 9 (1949): 355–86.
———. "La repoblación y repartimiento de Cádiz por Alfonso X." *Hispania* 15 (1955): 490–503.
Sanz de la Maza Lasoli, Regina. *La Orden de Santiago en la corona de Aragón*. Zaragoza: Instituto Fernando el Católico, 1980.
Scheffer-Boichorst, Paul. "Kleinere Forschungen zur Geschichte Alfons X von Castilien." *Mitteilungen des Instituts für Österreichische Geschichtsforschung* 9 (1888): 226–48.
Seco de Lucena, Luis. "Embajadores granadinos en El Cairo." *Miscelánea de Estudios árabes y hebraicos* 4 (1955): 5–30.
———. "La fecha de la batalla del Salado." *Al-Andalus* 19 (1954): 228–31.
Segura González, Wenceslao. "La batalla del Salado según Gil de Albornoz." *Aljaranda* 58 (2005): 9–15.
———. "Los pendones de la batalla del Salado." *Aljaranda* 66 (2007): 9–16.
Segura Graíño, Cristina, ed. *Relaciones exteriores del reino de Granada: IV Coloquio de Historia Medieval Andaluza*. Almería: Instituto de Estudios Almerienses, 1988.
Serrano, Luciano. "Alfonso XI y el papa Clemente VI durante el cerco de Algeciras." In *Cuadernos de Trabajos de la Escuela Española de Arqueología e Historia en Roma* 3. Madrid: Junta para Ampliación de Estudios e Investigaciones Científicas 1915. 1–35.
Sevillano i Colom, Francesc. "Crisi hispano-musulmana: Un decenni crucial en la reconquista (1330–1340)." *Estudis d'Historia Medieval* 3 (1970): 55–74.
Sierra López, Juan Manuel. *El Misal Toledano de 1499*. Toledo: Instituto Teológico San Ildefonso, 2004.

Socarras, Cayetano J. *Alfonso X of Castile: A Study on Imperialistic Frustration.* Barcelona: Ediciones Hispam, 1976.

Soler del Campo, Álvaro. *La evolución del armamento medieval en el reino castellano-leonés y al-Andalus (siglos XII–XIV).* Madrid: Ministerio del Ejército, 1993.

Spufford, Peter. *Handbook of Medieval Exchange.* London: Royal Historical Society, 1986.

Suárez Fernández, Luis. "Evolución histórica de las hermandades castellanas." *Cuadernos de Historia de España* 16 (1951): 6–78.

Torremocha Silva, Antonio. *Algeciras entre la Cristiandad y el Islam: Estudio sobre el cerco y la conquista de Algeciras por el rey Alfonso XI de Castilla.* Algeciras: Instituto de Estudios Campogibraltareños, 1994.

———. *El Ordenamiento de Algeciras (1345): Datos sobre la conquista, repoblación, y organización de la ciudad en el siglo XIV.* Algeciras: Roca, 1983.

Torremocha Silva, Antonio, and Ángel J. Sáez Rodríguez. "Algeciras Medieval." In Mario Ocaña, ed., *Historia de Algeciras.* 3 vols. Cádiz: Diputación de Cádiz, 2001. Vol. 1.

Torres Balbás, Leopoldo. "Atarazanas hispano-musulmanas." *Al-Andalus* 11 (1946): 179–209.

———. "La mezquita de al-Qanatir y el santuario de Alfonso el Sabio en el Puerto de Santa Maria." *Al-Andalus* 8 (1942): 417–37.

Torres Delgado, Cristóbal. *El antiguo reino nazarí de Granada (1232–1340).* Granada: Anel, 1974.

———. "El ejército y las fortificaciones del reino nazarí de Granada." *Gladius*, special vol. (1988): 197–217.

Torres Fontes, Juan. "La cautividad en la frontera gaditana (1275–1285)." In *Cádiz en el siglo XIII: Actas de las "Jornadas Conmemorativas del VII Centenario de la muerte de Alfonso X el Sabio."* Cádiz: Universidad de Cádiz, 1983. 75–92.

———. "Jaime I y Alfonso X: Dos criterios de repoblación." In *Actas del VII Congreso de Historia de la Corona de Aragón.* Barcelona: Fidel Rodríguez Ferrán, 1962. 329–40.

———. "Los mudéjares murcianos en la Edad Media." In *Actas del III Simposio Internacional de Mudejarismo.* Teruel: Instituto de Estudios Turolenses, 1986. 55–66.

———. "El obispado de Cartagena en el siglo XIII." *Hispania* 13 (1953): 340–401, 515–80.

———. "La Orden de Santa María de España." *AEM* 11 (1981): 794–821.

———. "La Orden de Santa María de España." *Miscelánea Medieval Murciana* 3 (1977): 75–118.

———. "La Orden de Santa María de España y el Maestre de Cartagena." *Murcia Murgetana* 10 (1952): 95–102.

———. "La Orden de Santa María de España y el Monasterio de Santa María la Real de Murcia." *Alcanate* 2 (2000–2001): 83–96.

———. *La reconquista de Murcia en 1266 por Jaime I de Aragón.* Murcia: CSIC, 1967.

———. "El tratado de Tarazona y la campaña aragonesa en el reino de Granada (1328–1330)." *Roel* 7–8 (1986–87): 3–19.

Tyerman, Christopher. *England and the Crusades, 1095–1588.* Chicago: University of Chicago Press, 1988.

Ugolini, Francesco A. "Avvenimenti, figure e costumi di Spagna in una cronaca italiana del Trecento." In *Italia e Spagna: Saggi sui rapporti storici, filosofici, artistici fra le due civiltà*. Florence: LeMonnier, 1941. 91–122.

Vaca Lorenzo, Ángel. "La peste negra en Castilla: Aportación al estudio de algunas de sus consecuencias económicas y sociales." *Studia Historica: Historia Medieval* 2 (1984): 89–107.

———. "La peste negra en Castilla: La primera et grande pestilencia que es llamada mortandad grande." *Fundación* 4 (2001–2): 19–50.

———. "La peste negra en Castilla (Nuevos testimonios)." *Studia Historica: Historia Medieval* 8 (1990): 159–73.

Vasconcelos e Sousa, Bernardo. "O sangue, a cruz e a coroa: A memória do Salado em Portugal." *Penélope: Fazer e Desfazer Historia* 2 (1989): 28–48.

Veas Arteseros, Francisco de Asís, and María del Carmen Veas Arteseros. "Alférez y Mayordomo Real en el siglo XIII." *Miscelánea Medieval Murciana* 13 (1986): 29–48.

Vidal Castro, Francisco. "Historia política." In María Jesús Vigueira Molins, ed., *El reino nazarí de Granada (1232–1492)*. In *Historia de España fundada por Ramón Menéndez Pidal*. Madrid: Espasa-Calpe, 2000. 3: 47–208.

Viguera, María Jesús. "La intervención de los Benimerines en al-Andalus." In García Arenal and Viguera, eds., *Relaciones*. 237–48.

———. "Religión y política de los Benimerines." *Ilu* (1995): 285–88.

Villalon, L. J. Andrew, and Donald J. Kagay, eds. *Crusaders, Condottieri, and Cannon: Medieval Warfare in Societies Around the Mediterranean*. Leiden: Brill, 2003.

Villanueva, Jaime de. *Viage literario a las iglesias de España*. 22 vols. Madrid: Imprenta Real: 1803–52.

Zunzuñegui, José. "Los orígenes de las misiones en las Canarias." *Revista Española de Teología* 1 (1941): 361–408.

Zurita, Jerónimo. *Anales de la Corona de Aragón*. Ed. Ángel Canellas López. 9 vols. Zaragoza: CSIC, 1970–85.

Index

'Abd al-Ḥaqq, Marīnid envoy, 91, 92, 93, 253
'Abd al-Rahmān b. Abū l-Hasan, Marīnid emir's son, 183, 198
'Abd al-Wāhid b. Abū Yūsuf, Marīnid emir's son, 57
Abraham el Barchilón, tax collector, 90
Abū 'Inān Fāris, Marīnid emir, 213, 214, 216, 262
Abū Hafs 'Umar al-Murtadā, Almohad caliph, 24, 27
Abū Hātim al-'Azafī, lord of Ceuta, 78, 86, 110
Abū Ishāq Ibrāhīm, governor of Guadix, 65
Abū l'Abbās Ahmad, Marīnid emir, 263
Abū l-Hasan 'Alī, Marīnid emir, 10, 161–63, 165–68, 170–72, 174–77, 182–85, 188, 190–92, 197, 198, 203, 204, 206–8, 213–16, 228, 251, 252, 262
Abū Muhammad b. Ashqīlūlā, governor of Murcia, 37, 65, 68
Abū l-Qāsīm al-'Azafī, lord of Ceuta, 24
Abū l-Rabī' Sulaymān, Marīnid emir, 121, 122
Abū Mālik 'Abd al-Wāhid b. Abū l-Hasan 'Alī, Marīnid emir's son, 162
Abū Sa'īd Faraj b. Ismā'īl, *arráez* of Málaga, 134
Abū Sa'īd 'Uthmān b. Abū Yūsuf, Marīnid emir, 134, 137, 141, 143, 154, 185
Abū Tābit 'Āmir, Marīnid emir, 121
Abū 'Umar Tāshufīn b. Abū l-Hasan, Marīnid emir's son, 183
Abū Ya'qūb Yūsuf, Marīnid emir, 93, 95, 121, 261
Abū Yūsuf Ya'qūb b. 'Abd al-Haqq, Marīnid emir, 18, 25, 27, 34, 35, 38, 56, 57, 61–70, 72–76, 78, 82–94, 103, 111, 134, 252, 257, 260
Abū Zayd, king of Valencia, 45
acémilas, 89, 96, 105, 239

adelantado de la mar, 22, 26
adelantado mayor de la frontera, 62, 89, 115, 149
adelantado mayor de Murcia, 148, 149
Afonso III, king of Portugal, 9, 30, 38, 49, 225
Afonso IV, king of Portugal, 9, 152, 156, 163, 164, 167, 170, 173–77, 179, 182–84, 186–89, 191, 192, 196, 197, 212, 214, 220, 225, 244, 249, 252, 254, 262
Africa, 3, 4, 7, 9, 13–18, 21, 22, 25, 29, 39, 40, 45, 55, 66, 67, 71, 97, 110, 111, 150, 171, 175, 183, 210–13, 238, 257, 259, 263–65
Agreda, 22
Aguilar de la Frontera, 6, 32
Al-Andalus, 3, 4, 9, 86, 134, 204, 209
Al-Azraq, Mudéjar lord, 66
Alberite River, 169
Alboaquez (al-Wātiq), king of Murcia, 37, 50, 52
Alcácer Seguir, 65, 69, 72, 83, 90, 96, 97, 121
Alcalá de Benzaide (Alcalá la Real), 41, 44, 56, 79, 169, 190–91, 217, 226; treaty, 49–50, 54, 57, 59, 61, 238, 239
Alcalá de Guadaira, 90
Alcalá de Henares, 70, 75; assembly, 209; Cortes, 209; treaty, 122–23
Alcalá de los Gazules, 6, 61, 78, 90, 94, 117, 169
Alcalá del Río, 72, 97
Alcanatir. See El Puerto de Santa María
Alcántara, master of, 130, 144, 165, 168, 169, 172, 245; Order of, 78, 94, 170, 222
Alcaraz, 46
Alcaudete, 6, 116, 118, 120, 122, 135, 136, 144, 147
Alcolea del Río, 73
Alexander IV, pope, 16, 19, 21, 37, 248
Alexander VI, pope, 264
Alexandria, 20, 71

366 Index

Alfonso III, king of Aragón, 95, 96
Alfonso IV, king of Aragón, 154, 155, 156, 159, 160, 164, 166, 225, 226, 238
Alfonso VI, king of León-Castile, 4, 170
Alfonso VIII, king of Castile, 187
Alfonso X, king of Castile, 7, 8, 9, 10, 11–87, 89, 90, 112, 119, 120, 124, 160, 184, 204, 219, 223, 224, 233, 238, 239, 240, 243–47, 250, 254, 256, 259, 260
Alfonso XI, king of Castile, 8, 10, 136, 137–217, 220–24, 226, 231, 238–40, 242, 243–45, 247, 251, 252, 254, 256, 257, 261–65
Alfonso, bishop of Coria, 222
Alfonso de Cartagena, bishop of Burgos, 264
Alfonso de la Cerda, 80, 81, 84, 88, 96, 97, 113, 114, 118–20
Alfonso Fernández el niño, son of Alfonso X, 62, 76
Alfonso Jofre Tenorio, admiral, 152, 162, 165, 172, 233
Alfonso Méndez de Guzmán. master of Santiago, 169
Alfonso Ortíz Calderón, prior of the Hospital, 175, 202
Alfonso Pérez de Guzmán, *el bueno*, 104, 107, 108, 110, 114–16, 128, 129, 231, 245, 246, 258, 259, 261, 264
Algarbe (Algarve), 30, 31, 38
Algeciras, 4, 5, 7, 8, 28, 31–32, 34, 36, 51, 57, 60, 65, 66, 68–70, 72–78, 80, 83, 85–87, 90, 92, 94–96, 98–100, 103, 108–37, 141, 149, 152, 161–63, 167, 169, 171–75, 183, 189–217, 225, 226, 231, 235, 238–47, 262, 263, 265; *Ordenamiento*, 208
Algeria, 97, 213, 257
Alhama, 113
Alhamar, 139
Alhambra, 138, 145, 149
Alicante, 5, 18, 46, 52, 53, 56, 113, 120, 148, 213
Alicún, battle, 139
Al-Makkarī, historian, 9, 140, 145, 183, 250
Almería, 3, 5, 62, 112, 118, 122, 125, 127, 129, 130, 133, 135, 136, 140, 152, 154, 216, 231, 251, 261; crusade, 131–32
almirante de la mar, 14, 22, 89, 110, 152
almirante de Sevilla, 90
Almodóvar del Río, 65
Almohads, 3, 7, 24, 25, 28, 29, 65, 94, 95, 239, 256
almojarifazgo, 160, 215
almojarife mayor, 80, 160

Almoravids, 3, 28, 65, 94, 239, 256
Almúñecar, 5, 127, 134
Álvar Díaz de Asturias, magnate, 57, 58
Álvar Pérez de Guzmán, magnate, 177
Álvaro Pelayo, bishop of Silves, 210, 212, 257, 264
Andalucía, 10, 20, 33, 36, 38, 39, 41, 44, 50–53, 55, 58, 59, 62, 74, 89, 98, 102, 137, 139, 146, 149, 153, 158, 187, 192, 193, 195, 206, 211, 223, 224, 226, 256, 260
Andreu, bishop of Valencia, 45
Andújar, 41, 73, 82, 112, 116
Annales Ianuenses, 89, 100, 101
Annibale de Ceccano, bishop of Frascati, 185
Anonymous of Sahagún, 12
Antequera, 48, 149, 150, 152, 159, 169, 216, 253, 263, 264
Aragón, Cortes, 45; Crown of, 5, 10, 78, 114, 124, 125, 148, 154; kingdom, 10, 16, 22, 62, 63, 66, 74, 90, 95,-98, 102, 103, 105, 109, 112–18, 120, 122–25, 127, 129, 130, 133, 134, 138, 139, 146, 148, 154–56, 159–61, 165, 167, 168, 173, 174, 187, 198, 207, 208, 212, 215, 225, 234, 239, 244, 248, 257, 260, 261, 264
Archidona, 48, 73, 169
Arcila, 121
Arcos de la Frontera, 6, 12, 31, 37, 38, 51, 90, 170
arcos de saetas de estribera, arcos de saetas de dos pies, 109
Ardales, 149, 150
Arjona, 73, 82, 112, 114, 146
Arnald de Vilanova, physician, 131
Astorga, bishop, 130; bishopric, 105
Asturias, 7, 99, 177
Atlantic Ocean, 4, 6, 12, 23–25, 30, 54, 121, 177, 213, 235, 256
Avignon, 62, 185, 199
Ávila, 61, assembly, 191, 243; bishop, 173, 215
Avis, Order of, 176
Ayamonte, 152
'Azafids of Ceuta, 121

Babylon, sultan of, 123, 170–71
Badajoz, kingdom of, 87
Baena, 6, 48; truce of, 146–48
Baetica, 210, 211
Baeza, 41, 65, 73, 82, 86, 112, 146; *pendón*, 150, 251
Banda, Order of La, 160–61
Banū Ashqīlulā, 35, 44, 48–50, 54–63, 65, 70, 72, 74, 79, 95, 260

Banū Marin. *See* Marinids
Barbour, John, archdeacon of Aberdeen, 157
Barcelona, 24, 139, 192, 216; bishop, 47; Corts, 45
Bartolomé, bishop of Cádiz and Algeciras, 209
Baybars, Mamlūk sultan, 20, 71
Bayonne, 71, 78
Baza, 148, 226
Beatrice of Swabia, wife of Fernando III, 16, 58
Beaucaire, 62, 63, 66
Bedmar, 6, 113, 115, 118–20, 122, 133, 138
Bélmez de la Moraleda, 41, 141
Benamejí, 6, 73, 164, 190, 197
Benaxixar, 139
Benedetto Zaccaria, Genoese admiral, 89, 96, 100, 104, 110, 234, 247
Benedict XII, pope, 168, 170, 172–74, 185, 186, 189–91, 198, 244, 249, 251
Benet, archbishop of Tarragona, 45
Benimerines. See Marinids
Berbers, 9
Bernat Rocaberti, viscount of Cabrera, 198, 200, 214
Bernat de Sarrià, Catalan envoy, 116, 117
Biscay, Bay of, 14, 51, 52, 54, 100, 103, 157, 195, 199
Blanche, wife of Fernando de la Cerda, 74
Blanche of Castile, mother of Louis IX, 8
Bonavena or Bonavía, Micer, Genoese mariner, 110
Boniface VIII, pope, 118, 119, 123, 244
Braga, archbishop, 189
Buñol, 56
Burgos, 48, 61, 74, 75, 88, 163, 166, 245; assembly, 85, 90, 191, 209, 223, 224, 240, 259; Cortes, 55, 57, 70, 72, 119, 238, 240–42, 247; diocese, 99, 239; Ordinance, 209, 223, 224, 246

Cabra, 6, 163
Cádiz, 6 21–23, 28, 29, 31, 34, 38, 51, 52, 94, 173, 175, 259, 260; bishop, 40, 193, 209; bishopric, 48, 105, 254; Gulf, 6, 31, 38, 259
Cairo, 71, 83
Calahorra, 46; bishopric, 99, 239
Calatayud, 98, 135
Calatrava, master of, 53, 60, 101, 113, 127, 144, 146, 246; Order of, 12, 37, 38, 53, 56, 66, 69, 75, 78, 79, 116, 124, 149, 222

Calatrava la nueva, 37, 39
Caliphate of Córdoba, 3
Cambil, 139
Campillo, treaty, 120, 121
Campillo de Arenas, 85
Canary Islands, 210–13, 257, 264
Cañete de las Torres, 73
Cañete la Real, 158
Cantabrian ports 21, 91, 94, 234, 239
cantigas d'escarnho, 48, 224
Cantigas de Santa Maria, 9, 13, 23, 99, 184, 225, 227, 228, 231, 234, 237, 250
Cantillana, 73
Carcabuey, 190
Carlo Pessagno (Peçanho), Portuguese admiral, 192, 196
Carmona, 90, 91, 193
Carrión, assembly, 141, 242, 247
Cartagena, 5, 18, 52,-54, 77, 105, 113, 172, 175, 213; bishop, 47, 127, 147, 159
Castellar de la Frontera, 141, 206
Castile, 1, 4, 6–8, 10, 12, 13, 15–18, 24–28, 30, 32, 35, 37, 40, 44–46, 50, 52–55, 57, 62, 63, 67, 69, 70, 71, 74–76, 78, 80, 82–84, 90, 93–98, 100, 102–4, 108–14, 116–24, 127, 129, 130, 132, 133, 136–38, 142, 144, 145, 148, 150, 152, 153, 155, 156, 159, 160, 162, 164, 165, 167, 169, 170, 172, 173, 175, 178, 179, 182–89, 191, 195–98, 204, 206, 207, 209, 210, 215, 218, 223, 225, 231, 233, 234, 238, 240, 244, 248, 249, 252, 253, 256–59, 261–65
Castro del Río, 163
Castrourdiales, 94
Catalonia, 14, 61, 62, 108
Cazorla, 6, 41
Celestine V, pope, 104, 110
Ceuta, 4, 23–29, 31–34, 36, 50, 63, 65, 72, 76, 86, 92, 95, 103, 110, 121, 122, 126, 127, 129, 130, 133, 136, 141, 143, 148, 172, 183, 192, 199, 239, 250, 264, 265
Charles of Anjou, king of Naples, 14
Charles of Valois, son of Philip III, 84
Christ, Order of, 156, 158
Cisneros, Francisco Jiménez de, cardinal, 265
Ciudad Real, 79
Ciudad Rodrigo, 44
Clement IV, pope, 37, 39–41, 45, 47, 49, 50, 51, 67, 71, 110, 244, 248
Clement V, pope, 123–25, 126, 131, 135, 136, 139, 140, 143, 151, 160, 244, 248, 251

Clement VI, pope, 201, 202, 208, 209, 211, 212, 215, 244, 245, 249, 254
Comares, 95
Compostela. *See* Santiago de Compostela
Constanza, wife of Fernando IV, 97, 130, 245
Córdoba, 3, 5, 6, 32, 41, 44, 51, 65–69, 73, 78, 79, 81–83, 85, 86, 89, 94, 103, 112, 114,-16, 137, 139, 140, 141, 143–46, 149, 150, 153, 157, 163, 164, 184, 193, 197, 209, 216, 220, 240, 243, 256; bishop, 119, 222; treaty 120, 122, 238
Coria del Río, 66
Corsica, 117, 124, 148
Cortes: Alcalá de Henares, 209; Cuéllar, 115, 241; Haro, 238, 241; Palencia, 256; Segovia, 241; Seville, 29, 238, 241; Toledo, 11, 15, 16, 18, 20, 25, 88, 250; Valladolid, 21, 89, 102, 115, 135, 141, 147, 238, 240, 241, 242, 246; Zaragoza, 45
cosas vedadas, 207
Cote, 94
Crevillente, 46
Cuéllar, Cortes, 115, 241
Cuenca, bishop, 36, 37, 147, 173; bishopric, 119

decima, 40, 41, 45, 47, 49, 66, 74, 78, 123–26, 135, 136, 139–43, 146–48, 151, 153–56, 168, 173, 174, 188, 189, 202, 209, 212, 215, 243–44, 249
Derby, Henry, earl of, 199, 210, 241
Diego López de Haro, lord of Vizcaya, 57, 83, 130
Diego Sánchez de Funes, nobleman, 41
Dinis, king of Portugal, 9, 78, 82, 97, 100, 107, 113, 114, 118, 119, 128, 135, 147, 174, 245
Douglas, Sir James, 157, 158, 225, 232
Dufourcq, Charles, 18, 63, 117

Écija, 32, 34, 39, 49, 62, 90, 91, 112, 160, 193, 197, 198; battle, 67–70, 83, 232, 252, 260
Edward I, king of England, 71, 78, 82
Edward III, king of England, 155, 198, 199, 208
Egidio Boccanegra, admiral, 173, 190, 192, 193, 197, 199, 204, 208, 210, 234
Egypt, 7, 18, 19, 20, 21, 71, 126, 171
El Puerto de Santa María, 6, 22–23, 25, 26, 27, 29, 30, 31, 32, 34, 51, 54, 81, 90, 91, 94, 110, 184, 250, 254, 259, 260
Elche, 46, 52, 53, 120

Elda, 46
empréstito, 245
Enrique II, king of Castile, 263
Enrique, Infante, son of Fernando III, 12, 16, 22, 35, 50, 111, 112, 114, 116, 119, 261
Enrique, illegitimate son of Alfonso XI, 177
Escalona, 152
Espéculo, 218, 219, 220, 236, 253
Esteban Bernáldez, naval captain, 100
Estepa, 6, 49, 78, 197
Estepona, 5, 101, 129, 141, 193, 198, 203, 214
Estoria de Espanna, 253
Évora, 176
Extremadura, 32, 52, 70, 99, 109, 141, 206, 223, 240; Ordinance, 224

Fadrique, Infante, son of Fernando III, 35, 50, 72, 83
Fadrique, Infante, illegitimate son of Alfonso XI, 177
Felipe, Infante, brother of Alfonso X, 17, 57, 58, 258
Felipe, Infante, son of Sancho IV, 130, 141, 146, 147, 149
Ferdinand and Isabella, 1, 264, 265
Fernán Pérez Maimón, chancellor of the privy seal, 92, 108, 110, 247
Fernán Ruiz de Asturias, magnate, 57
Fernán Sánchez de Valladolid, chancellor, historian, 8, 252
Fernando III, king of Castile, 6–8, 11, 12, 13, 24, 118, 144, 219, 237, 239, 243, 245, 250, 253, 256, 257, 259
Fernando IV, king of Castile, 8, 9, 10, 111, 112–36, 138, 147, 213, 216, 218, 238, 239, 240, 241, 244, 245, 246, 248, 249, 250, 261, 265
Fernando, marquess of Tortosa, 198
Fernando de Antequera, 264
Fernando de la Cerda, Infante, son of Alfonso X, 55, 60, 62, 65, 70, 211, 260
Fez, 94, 96, 107, 127, 129, 162, 165, 166, 213
fonsadera, 31, 32, 48, 49, 89, 90, 96, 99, 105, 202, 215, 239, 241
France, 155, 174
Fuente de la Peña, 93
Fuero real, 244

Gaibrois, Mercedes, 10, 101, 103, 107, 108
Galera, 149
galera, ship duty, 239

Index   369

Galicia, 99, 241
García Fitz, Francisco, 99
García, archbishop of Seville, 101, 254
Gascony, 15, 16, 71
Gaston de Béarn, count of Foix, 199, 200, 225
Gaucín, 129
Genoa, 24, 32, 39, 96, 97, 173, 190, 204, 207, 212, 234
Germany, 155, 174, 198
Getares, 192, 193
Gibraleón, 30
Gibraltar, 162, 262–63, 265; conquest, 128–29; loss, 162–63; ports, 4–5; siege, 163–65, 213–15; strait, 1–4
Gil de Albornoz, archbishop of Toledo, 168, 174, 178, 182, 183, 189, 193, 202, 221, 222, 252
Gil Gómez de Roa, magnate 57
Giménez Soler, Andrés, 10, 136, 183
Godefroy, count of Los, 198
Goñi Gaztambide, José, 21, 174
González, Julio, 14
González Jiménez, Manuel, 10, 21
Gonzalo, archbishop of Toledo, 98
Gonzalo de la Finojosa, bishop of Burgos, 9
Gonzalo Ibáñez de Aguilar, nobleman, 82
Gonzalo Martínez de Oviedo, master of Alcántara, 168, 169, 172
Gonzalo Ruiz Girón, master of Santiago, 79
Granada, 1, 3, 5–7, 9–11, 13, 15, 20, 23–25, 28, 29, 31–38, 44, 48–50, 55–63, 65, 66, 68, 70, 72, 73–76, 78, 81, 82, 85, 86, 89, 92, 93, 95–98, 100–103, 105, 108, 110–24, 127, 129, 130, 132, 133–41, 143–52, 154, 156, 159, 160–63, 165–67, 169, 170, 176, 177, 182–84, 188, 190, 197, 198, 203, 204–9, 214, 216, 217, 226, 237–39, 258, 260–64
Gregory X, pope, 53, 62, 63, 66, 67, 69, 71, 74, 244, 248
Guadalajara, 102
Guadalete River, 23, 29, 31, 51, 93, 177
Guadalhorce River, battle, 149–50, 161, 251, 254
Guadalquivir River, 5, 6, 12, 13, 50, 65, 73, 115, 193, 256, 260
Guadalupe, shrine of the Virgin Mary, 189, 254
Guadamecí River, 182, 192
Guadarranque River, 163, 205
Guadiana River, 5
Guadiaro River, 103, 198, 203

Guadix, 35, 58, 60, 65, 95, 118, 138, 139, 147, 149, 226
Guadateba River, 157, 158
Guardamar, 113
Guillaume Peyre de Godin, cardinal, 147
Gutierre Gómez, archbishop of Toledo

Haakon, king of Norway, 17, 31
Hafsid dynasty, 19, 22, 35
Hagar, slave girl, 39
Haro, Cortes, 238, 241
Henry III, king of England, 7, 14, 15, 16, 19, 31
hermandad, 41, 82, 112, 113, 115, 116; of Asturias, 220; of Burgos, 242; of Carrión, 242;
of León and Galicia, 241
Hermandad General de Andalucía, 137, 139, 146–49
Holy Land, 1, 6–8, 11, 15, 16, 17, 19–22, 39–41, 44, 53, 62, 66, 67, 71, 74, 75, 80, 87, 97, 98, 120, 123, 125, 126, 139–43, 148, 151, 154, 156–58, 174, 202, 218, 219, 244, 248, 249, 250, 257, 265
Holy Roman Empire, 11, 21, 59
*Holy Sepulchre, 157; Order of the, 40, 105
hospitals, 151, 236
Hospital, Order of the, 41, 75, 124, 159, 160, 175, 176, 191, 202, 251
Huelva, 30, 52
Huércal, 159
Huéscar, 6, 149, 231

Ibn Abī Zarʿ, chronicler, 9, 65–68, 72, 74–76, 83, 86, 92– 94, 96, 102, 103, 107, 108
Ibn al-Ahmar, king of Granada, 6, 13, 15, 20, 23–25, 28, 29, 31–38, 44, 48, 49, 50, 55–59, 61, 65, 237–39, 260
Ibn Ashqīlūlā, governor of Málaga, 48
Ibn Baṭṭūṭa, traveler, 213
Ibn Hūd, ʿAbd Allāh, king of Murcia, 6, 12, 52; *arráez* of Crevillente, 46
Ibn ʿIdhārī, historian, 9, 26,-29, 34, 50
Ibn Khaldūn, historian, 3, 4, 9, 65, 69, 79, 83, 86, 91, 96, 100–103, 129, 145, 165, 166, 169, 182
Ibn al-Khatīb, historian, 9, 182, 217, 231
Ibn Mahfūt, king of Niebla, 6, 12, 30, 34
Ibn Marzūq, historian, 10, 163, 169, 204, 213
Ibrāhīm ibn ʿUthmān, 151
Indalecio, St., 131, 251
Infantes de la Cerda, 70, 74, 117

Iñigo López de Orozco, *capitan mayor de los trabucos y engeños*, 195
Innocent IV, pope, 7, 14, 15, 25, 37, 104, 243, 248
Innocent V, pope, 71, 74, 248
Innocent VIII, pope, 264
Isabel, wife of Jaime II, 97, 110
Isidore of Seville, St., 150, 251, 253
Ismāʿīl I, Abū l-Walīd, king of Granada, 134, 138–41, 143–48, 149, 262
Italica, 72
Italy, 12, 14, 17, 111, 174
Iznalloz, battle, 113
Iznatoraf, 41

Jacopo Colonna, cardinal, 125
Jaén, 5, 6, 25, 31, 32, 41, 56, 65, 66, 69, 73, 79, 82, 86, 91, 94, 112, 114, 116, 118, 119, 136, 138, 139, 146, 147, 149, 193, 237, 256; bishop 153, 222; kingdom, 41, 80, 81, 203
Jaime I, king of Aragón, 21–22, 24, 31, 35, 38, 44–50, 52, 53, 55, 56, 61–63, 66, 69, 71, 220, 225, 254, 260
Jaime II, king of Aragón, 96–98, 100–104, 108, 110, 112–43, 145–48, 150, 151, 154, 155, 225, 238–40, 249–51, 257, 261
Jaime, Infante, son of Alfonso X, 87
Jaspert, viscount of Castellnou, 126–30
Jean de Rye, 201
Jerez de la Frontera, 6, 12, 13, 23, 27, 29–31, 34, 35–39, 44, 50–52, 65, 69, 71, 73, 90–94, 97, 103, 112, 128, 133, 163, 169, 170, 175–77, 192, 193, 201, 231, 239, 241, 250, 254, 259–61
Jerusalem, 17, 72, 154, 158, 186, 248
Jews, 39, 80, 94, 104, 109, 168, 244
Jimena de la Frontera, 6, 129, 141, 214
João, son of Afonso IV of Portugal, 163
Jofre de Loaysa, historian, 8, 91, 92, 120
Jofre Gilabert de Cruilles, Catalan admiral, 167, 171
John XXII, pope, 139–41, 146, 147, 149,-51, 153–56, 160, 174, 244, 249
John, count of Luxembourg, 155
Juan II, king of Castile, 263
Juan, Infante, son of Alfonso X, 81, 91–93, 107, 111, 113–16, 118, 122, 123, 133–35, 137, 141, 143–46, 246, 259, 261, 262
Juan *el tuerto*, son of Infante Juan, 147, 149, 242
Juan Alfonso de Guzmán, duke of Medina Sidonia, 264

Juan Alfonso de Haro, magnate, 166
Juan García de Villamayor, admiral, 22, 26, 233
Juan Gil de Zamora, Fray, 7, 218
Juan González, master of Calatrava, 53, 60,
Juan Manuel, 111, 130, 133–35, 141, 146–55, 157, 159, 161–64, 166, 177, 180, 207, 213, 218, 219, 221, 227, 228, 229, 232, 237, 242, 246, 250, 251, 253, 254, 261. See also *Libro de los estados*
Juan Martínez de Leyva, envoy to Avignon, 185
Juan Mathe de Luna, *camarero mayor*, 89, 104, 108, 110, 247
Juan Núñez de Lara, magnate, 57, 58, 111, 180, 246
Juan Osórez, master of Santiago, 119–20
Juan Sánchez de Bedmar, nobleman, 113, 115
Julian, count, 101, 213

Kinkade, Richard, 61
Kristin of Norway, 17, 18

La Coruña, 54, 94
La Higueruela, battle, 264
La Peña del Ciervo, 177, 180
Ladero Quesada, Miguel Ángel, 242
Larache, 55
Laredo, 239
Las Cuevas del Becerro, 158
Las Huelgas de Burgos, 145, 161
Las Navas de Tolosa, 61, 155, 187, 217, 256
Lebrija, 12, 37, 38, 51, 169
León, assembly, 191, 209, 240–43; bishopric, 99; kingdom, 4, 7, 15, 16, 40, 52, 69, 102, 109, 130, 141, 173, 186, 210, 223
Leonor, daughter of Alfonso Pérez de Guzmán, 110
Leonor de Guzmán, mistress of Alfonso XI, 167, 252
Libro de los castigos, 101, 218, 221, 227, 231
Libro de los estados, 218, 219, 221, 227–29, 231–33, 237, 251, 253, 254
Libro de los doze sabios, 219, 221, 223, 225, 228, 229
Linehan, Peter, 41
Lisbon, 28, 107, 177, 184, 196, 212
Locubín, 122, 169, 190
Lombardy, 63, 80
Lope de Mendoza, magnate, 57
Lope Fernández de Aín, bishop of Morocco, 16

Index 371

Lope Díaz de Haro, lord of Vizcaya, 57, 58, 69, 92, 93
Lorca, 37, 47, 52, 113, 132, 159, 203, 206, 214
Louis IX, king of France, 7, 8, 17, 19
Lubrín, 127
Lucena, 6
Luis de la Cerda, 110, 211, 212
Luque, 6

Madrid, 240; assembly, 169; Cortes, 123, 156, 238, 240, 242; treaty, 167
Maghrib, 100
Málaga, 3, 5, 35, 36, 48, 55, 58, 60, 65, 68, 74, 75, 78, 85, 86, 94, 95, 101, 118, 122, 134, 136, 152, 190, 198, 216, 265
Mallorca, 139, 173, 187, 196, 197, 208
Manuel, Infante, brother of Alfonso X, 45, 46, 66, 82
Manuel Pessagno (Peçanho), Portuguese admiral, 147, 173, 175, 177
Manzano Rodríguez, Miguel Ángel, 35, 74, 105, 108
Marbella, 5, 48, 79, 141, 152, 183, 214, 262, 263
Marchena, 90; near Almería, 129, 132
María de Molina, 88, 100, 102, 110–12, 115–17, 130, 137, 138, 146, 147, 241, 242, 250, 261
Marinids (Banū Marīn, Benimerines), 10, 11, 18, 19, 24, 25, 27–29, 33–36, 38, 48, 51, 54–56, 59, 60–94, 96–98, 102–4, 107, 110, 111, 114, 116, 118, 121, 124, 127, 129, 133, 137, 141, 152, 156, 157, 161, 162, 169, 170, 172, 173, 187, 191, 193, 197, 199, 203–5, 208, 210, 212, 213, 216, 218, 220, 222, 226, 231, 235, 240, 245, 250, 252, 257, 259–65
Marrakech, 3, 25, 65, 83
Marseille, 16, 17, 24
Martin IV, pope, 81, 82, 84, 87, 88
Martos, 6, 73, 116, 149; battle, 67, 69, 232, 248, 260
Marzamosa (Qasr Masmuda), naval battle, 96
Mateu Mercer (Mercader), Catalan admiral, 196, 197
Matrera, 12, 37, 38, 190
Matthew Paris, historian, 7, 8
Mauritania, 3, 4, 7, 211, 257
Mazalquivir, 265
Medina del Campo, assembly of bishops, 99, 138, 241; Cortes, 119, 141, 238, 241, 242
Medina Sidonia, 12, 31, 35, 37, 38, 51, 78, 90, 94, 115, 117, 169, 170, 264

Mediterranean Sea, 1, 3–5, 9, 216, 256, 257
Melilla, 265
Moclín, battle, 79, 80, 190, 222, 232, 260
Molinaseca, 113
moneda blanca, 133
moneda forera, 70, 88, 90, 95, 135, 141, 201, 209, 215, 240–43, 245
Monteagudo, treaty, 97, 257
Montesa, Order of, 161
Montiel, 86
Morocco, 1, 3, 6, 7, 9–11, 16, 17, 19, 20, 22, 24–26, 28, 30–33, 51, 57, 58, 61, 63, 65, 69, 70, 74–76, 80, 84, 86, 88–91, 94, 96–98, 100–103, 107, 108, 110, 113, 116, 122, 123, 126–29, 133, 134, 136, 147, 160, 162, 165, 173–75, 183, 188, 189, 191, 193, 195, 198, 201–4, 206, 208, 211, 213, 217, 219, 226, 228, 233, 238, 248, 256–61, 264–65
Morón de la Frontera, 6, 12, 73, 78, 94, 170
mudéjars, 11, 12, 32, 34–59, 66, 71, 110, 148, 220, 224, 254, 260
Muhammad I, king of Granada. *See* Ibn al-Ahmar
Muhammad II, king of Granada, 49, 58, 60,-63, 65, 66, 68, 70, 72–76, 78, 81, 82, 85, 86, 89, 92, 93, 95,-98, 100–103, 105, 108, 110, 111, 113–18, 136, 238, 239, 260, 261
Muhammad III, king of Granada, 118–21, 123, 127, 134, 136, 238, 261
Muhammad IV, king of Granada, 137, 148–51, 152, 154, 159, 160–63, 165, 206, 238, 262
Muhammad V, king of Granada, 209, 263
Muhammad b. Ismāʿīl, governor of Algeciras, 149
Muhammad, prophet, 13, 68, 85, 125, 141, 153, 172, 175, 176, 180, 185, 207, 211, 219, 251–53, 258
Mula, 113
Mulawiya River, 97, 257
Murcia, 5, 46, 47, 132, 206, 207, 214–16, 220, 243; bishop, 250; king 12, 13, 34, 239; kingdom, 5–7, 22, 33, 36–39, 44, 48, 49, 50, 52–53, 55, 58, 66, 87, 89, 96, 103, 113, 114, 116–18, 120, 135, 138, 139, 148, 149, 154, 159, 167, 189, 203, 208, 220, 254, 260
Mūsā II, emir of Tlemcen, 182

Napoleone Orsini, cardinal, 140
Nasr (Abū l-Juyūsh Nasr), king of Granada, 127, 129, 132, 133, 134, 136, 137, 138, 139, 147, 238, 261, 262

Nasrid dynasty, 6, 29, 32, 34, 35, 41, 55, 56, 59, 61, 62, 63, 68, 79, 82, 94, 95, 96, 102, 114, 117, 118, 119, 121, 122, 129, 132, 133, 138, 139, 145, 149, 152, 157, 161, 162, 165, 177, 190, 203, 204, 206, 208, 217, 237, 239, 259, 260, 261, 262, 263

Navarre, kingdom, 15, 16, 66, 155, 168, 173, 174, 187, 199, 200, 201, 225

Nicholas III, pope, 54, 74, 75, 78, 244

Nicholas IV, pope, 98, 104

Nicola de Prato, cardinal bishop of Ostia, 131

Niebla, kingdom of, 5, 6, 7, 12, 13, 29, 30–31, 34, 91, 193, 239, 259, 260

Norway, 16, 17, 18

Nuño González de Lara, magnate, 12, 29, 36, 37, 48, 55, 57, 58, 62, 66, 67, 68, 69, 70, 83, 87, 231, 232, 260; Nuño, son, 55

Olmedo, assembly, 138

Olvera, 6, 152, 153, 157, 159, 161, 254

Oran, 18, 19, 265

Orce, 149

Orihuela, 46, 52, 120

Ortegícar, 158

Osuna, 6, 39, 78

Oviedo, 21, 31, 245

Palencia, assembly, 241; bishopric, 99, 239; Cortes, 256

Palma del Río, 65, 137, 146, 193, 197

Palmones River, 4, 163, 193; battle, 205–206, 208

parias, tribute, 6, 239

Pedro III, king of Aragón, 71, 74, 78, 82, 84, 85, 88, 89, 90, 93

Pedro IV, king of Aragón, 166, 167, 168, 172, 173, 174, 177, 186, 190, 192, 195, 196, 197, 206, 207, 208, 212, 213, 214, 215; *Chronicle of*, 9

Pedro I, king of Castile, 216, 263,

Pedro, Infante, son of Alfonso X, 71, 76, 77, 78, 81, 82

Pedro, Infante, brother of Fernando IV, 122, 133, 134, 135, 136, 137, 138, 139, 140, 141, 142, 143, 144, 145, 149, 151, 161, 232, 242, 249, 250, 253, 262

Pedro Gómez de Barroso, bishop of Cartagena, 159

Pedro López de Ayala, *adelantado mayor de Murcia*, 226, 247; historian, 169

Pedro Lorenzo, archdeacon of Cádiz, 23

Pedro Marín, 237

Pedro Martínez de Fe, admiral, 26, 75, 77, 90, 233, 246,

Pedro Núñez de Guzmán, master of Santa María and Santiago, 54, 79

Pelayo Pérez Correa, master of Santiago, 13, 44

Peñafiel, 152

Peñaflor, 146

Pere de Moncada, admiral, 177, 183, 187, 190, 192, 193, 196

Philip III, king of France, 70, 80, 82, 83, 84, 85, 90

Philip IV, king of France, 96

Philip VI, king of France, 155, 156, 160, 168, 189, 198, 199, 202, 210, 244, 245

Philip of Évreux, king of Navarre, 155, 199, 200, 225

Pisa, 16–17, 24, 39

Poema de Fernán González, 236, 253

Porcuna, 73

Portugal, 5, 28, 30, 38, 40, 49, 78, 82, 97, 98, 100, 103, 107, 113–15, 118, 119, 128, 135, 147, 152, 155, 156, 161–63, 167, 170, 173–75, 179, 182, 184–86, 189, 193, 195, 197, 212, 216, 220, 225, 233, 234, 245, 249, 251, 252, 262, 265; *Chronicle of the First Seven Kings of Portugal*, 9

Priego, 85, 169, 190

Pruna, 6, 152

Puerto del Muradal, El, 86

Qalawūn, sultan of Egypt, 83

Qayrawān, 213, 215

Quesada, 6, 41, 113, 114, 118, 120, 122, 133, 136, 138, 144

Rabat, 25, 26

Raimundo Danza di Vintimiglia, 32

Ramón Bonifaz of Burgos, mariner, 14

Ramon Llull, 126, 265

Ramon Muntaner, historian, 122, 133

Remondo, archbishop of Seville; bishop of Segovia, 21

Requena, 55, 61

Richard de Labret of d'Albret, viscount of Tartas, 161

Richard of Cornwall, 17, 56

Ridwān, *hājib*, 237

Robert Bruce, king of Scotland, 157, 225

Rodrigo, archbishop of Santiago, 100

Rodrigo, Visigothic king, 101, 115, 179, 180, 213, 252, 256
Rodrigo Díaz de Vivar, el Cid, 150, 258
Rodrigo Jiménez de Rada, archbishop of Toledo, historian, 9, 187
Rodrigo Pérez Ponce, master of Calatrava, 101, 113, 246
Rodrigo Sánchez de Arévalo, 264
Rodrigo Yáñez, poet, 8, 150, 170, 172, 174, 183, 191, 196, 199, 201, 248
Roger Bernard, viscount of Castelbon, 199, 200
Ronda, 65, 72, 78, 79, 83, 85, 94, 103, 113, 118, 129, 134, 141, 152, 157, 159, 169, 197, 198, 214, 226, 262, 263
Rota, 38, 73, 90, 94
Roy García de Santander, mariner, 22
Roy López de Mendoza, admiral, 14, 22, 233
Rudolf of Habsburg, emperor, 63
Rufin, Micer, Genoese soldier, 104
Rute, 6, 138, 149

Salado, crusade, 162–88, 197, 203, 208, 210, 212, 217, 220, 222, 226, 228, 233, 236, 239, 242, 244, 245, 248, 249, 250–52, 254, 262
Salamanca, 44, 49
Salé, 24–29, 31, 32, 34, 75, 237, 259
Salisbury, William Montague, earl of, 199, 225
Samuel ibn Wakar, physician, 160
San Juan de la Peña, abbey, 131
San Millán de la Cogolla, 253
Sancho II, archbishop of Toledo, 49, 58 67, 69, 70, 221, 232, 248, 260
Sancho IV, king of Castile, 8, 9, 10, 88–111, 113, 115, 119, 120, 124, 218, 220, 222, 226, 231, 238, 239, 241, 242, 244–47, 250, 254, 257, 260, 261, 265; Infante, 54, 57, 69, 70, 74, 75, 79, 82, 85, 89, 240, 260. See also *Libro de los castigos*
Sancho Martínez de Jódar, nobleman, 41
Sancho Pérez de Jódar, nobleman, 82
Sancho Sánchez de Jódar, nobleman, 82
Sanlúcar de Barrameda, 6, 38, 73, 90, 91, 115
Santa María de España, Order of, 53–54, 78, 79
Santiago (St. James), 134, 150, 177; war cry 144, 150, 164, 169, 182, 195, 198, 252, 253
Santiago, master of, 13, 25, 44, 54, 116, 144, 149, 165, 169, 177, 180, 190, 222, 232, 248; Order of, 40, 48, 49, 66, 75, 78, 79, 86, 94, 119–20, 124, 158, 197, 206, 215, 222, 260

Santiago de Compostela, 172; archbishop, 100, 105, 130, 151; archdiocese, 15, 49; pilgrimage, 91, 96, 161, 250; provincial council, 98, 250
Santiesteban del Puerto, 86, 146
Santo Domingo de Silos, 237
Santo Lenho, relic of the Holy Cross, 176, 179, 251
Sarah, wife of Abraham, 39
Sardinia, 117, 124, 127, 135, 148, 159, 174
Segovia, assembly, 21; bishop, 21, 36, 37; bishopric, 99, 239, Cortes, 241
Segura, river, 46, 120; sierra de, 169
servicio, 49, 55, 72, 75, 90, 95, 99, 103, 105, 119, 123, 135, 138, 139, 141, 191, 215, 240–43
Setenario, 7
Seuilly, Henry, lord of, 155
Seville, 1, 3, 5–7, 11–15, 17, 20, 21, 24, 27, 30–32, 35, 36, 38, 39, 44, 49, 51–53, 55, 62, 63, 66, 67, 69, 71–76, 78, 80–83, 89–92, 94–96, 99–101, 105, 109, 110, 114–16, 128, 130, 137, 151, 152, 156, 157, 159, 160, 163, 164, 166, 167, 169, 173, 175, 176, 184, 189, 190, 192, 193, 195, 197, 199, 200, 210, 216, 223, 224, 226, 234, 240, 243–45, 249–51, 253, 256; archbishop, 39, 71, 101, 104, 116, 129, 137, 139, 140, 144, 146, 153, 209, 222, 249, 254; archbishopric, 23; kingdom, 87, 89, 147, 259, 260; Cortes, 29, 238, 241
Sicily, 14, 16, 17, 82, 84, 113
Siete Partidas, 36, 218, 219, 220, 222, 225, 227–29, 233–37, 251, 253
Siles, 169
Siliebar, 12
Silves, bishop of, 210
Simón, bishop of Sigüenza, 36, 37
Simón Boccanegra, doge of Genoa, 173, 204
Simón Pérez de Bedmar, nobleman, 113
Simón Ruiz de los Cameros, magnate, 57, 72, 83
sisa, 105, 241
soldadas, 57, 104, 222, 246
Syria, 20, 126

Tagunt, Taount, 18, 19
Tagus River, 53
Talavera la Reina, 86
Tangier, 4, 18, 27, 28, 55, 63, 65, 76–78, 92, 103, 107, 113, 121, 129, 264
Tarazona, treaty of, 154, 160

Tarifa, 4, 6, 7, 31, 32, 34, 36, 51, 60, 65, 69, 70, 72, 88–111, 113–18, 120, 128, 129, 145, 146, 167, 172, 174–77, 179, 180, 183, 187, 188, 192, 226, 231, 238, 239, 241, 242, 246–48, 250, 254, 258–62, 264, 265
Tarik ibn Ziyad, 4, 213
Tarragona, archbishop, 45, 47; province, 208
Teba, 149, 150, 157–59, 161, 225, 231, 232
Temple, Order of the, 124, 160
Tempul, 133
Tenetu, Thenecii, 19
tercias reales, 15, 41, 49, 75, 78, 118, 123, 135, 136, 139–41, 143, 146, 151, 153, 156, 168, 173, 174, 188, 192, 202, 210, 215, 243–44, 249
Tetuán, 265
Theobald of Blazón, French noble, 155
Tingitana, 3, 264
Tíscar, 6, 144
Tlemcen, 18, 19, 56, 61, 65, 76, 78, 93– 95, 98, 101, 104, 113, 119, 121, 134, 137, 148, 162, 163, 165, 166, 182, 184, 259
Toledo, 18, 51, 53, 86, 111, 140, 152, 163, 167, 170, 176, 184, 240, 245; archbishop, 49, 58, 67, 69, 70, 98, 122, 124, 140, 141, 146, 147, 168, 174, 178, 193, 221, 232, 248, 250, 252, 260; archbishopric, 119, 135, 242; archdeacon, 8; church of Santa Leocadia, 49; Cortes, 11, 15, 16, 18, 20, 25, 88, 250; kingdom, 141
Torre Alháquime, 152
Tres Crónicas, 8
Tripoli, 97
Tunis, 12, 19, 22, 31, 35, 36, 50, 182, 188, 213, 214, 257
Tunisia, 97, 213

Úbeda, 41, 65, 73, 82, 86, 112, 113, 115, 116, 118, 138, 143, 146, 147, 177
Urban IV, pope, 51
'Uthmān, emir of Tlemcen, 95, 104
'Uthmān b. Muhammad b. 'Abd al-Haqq, Marinid prince, 253
'Uthmān ibn Abī l-'Ulā, military commander, 121, 129, 132, 139, 143, 144, 149, 157, 158, 165

Valencia, 45, 71, 131, 175, 185, 192, 216; bishop, 45, 47, 122, 125; Corts, 154; kingdom, 46, 66, 110, 116, 117, 138, 139, 146, 148, 167, 174, 213; Muslim king, 25, 258
Valencia de Alcántara, 169
Valladolid, 8, 17, 18, 44, 105, 128, 163, 223, 244, 245, 252; assembly, 82, 240; Cortes, 21, 89, 102, 115, 135, 141, 147, 238, 240–42, 246; council, 98
Vasco Pérez de Meira, *alcaide* of Gibraltar, 163
Vejer de la Frontera, 6, 12, 38, 51, 52, 56, 59, 65, 90, 94, 97, 98, 115, 117, 245
Vélez, 226
Vera, 226
Vienne, Council, 139
Vilches, 86
Villar García, Luis, 19
Villarreal, 38, 65, 79, 80, 137
Villasirga, shrine of the Virgin Mary, 250
Violante, wife of Alfonso X, 35, 37, 44, 58, 61, 62, 74, 75, 80, 82
Virgin Mary, 9, 13, 19, 23, 38, 41, 47, 52, 53, 62, 63, 66, 73, 80, 81, 189, 221, 228, 250, 251, 254
Visigoths, 3, 7, 13, 179, 191, 210, 211, 257
Vizcaya, 57, 69

William, count of Hainaut, 155
William, count of Jülich, 155

Yagmurāsan b. Zayyān, emir of Tlemcen, 61, 76, 78
Yūsuf I, Abū l-Hajjaj, king of Granada, 165–67, 169, 170, 176, 177, 182–84, 188, 190, 197, 198, 203–8, 214, 217, 226, 238, 262
Yūsuf of Écija, *almojarife mayor*, 160

Zag de la Maleha, tax farmer, 80
Zahara, 6, 83, 214
Zambra, 6
Zamora, 218; assembly, 191, 240, 243; Cortes, 241; Ordinance, 286 n. 74
Zaragoza: Cortes, 45; Muslim kings, 258; treaty, 117

Acknowledgments

After completing my book *Reconquest and Crusade in Medieval Spain*, I realized the importance of extending my work beyond the middle of the thirteenth century. By then the peninsular reconquest had reduced Islamic Spain to the kingdom of Granada, a vassal state of Castile. In the following century the kings of Castile and Granada and the sultans of Morocco struggled to control the Strait of Gibraltar. My intention is to study that conflict from the reign of Alfonso X in the second half of the thirteenth century through that of his namesake, Alfonso XI, in the first half of the fourteenth. In two earlier books on Alfonso X, I touched on some of the themes in this study. I debated whether to go over the same ground, but I decided that a proper understanding of the battle for the Strait required that I do so. In the process I have reviewed the documentation previously employed and more recent publications, especially those of my good friend Manuel González Jiménez of the Universidad de Sevilla.

Among the scholars who kindly assisted me by providing copies of articles, translations, or commentaries are: Manuel García Fernández, Universidad de Sevilla; Miguel Ángel Manzano Rodríguez, Universidad de Salamanca; Francisco García Fitz, Universidad de Extremadura; José Manuel Rodríguez García, Universidad Autónoma de Madrid; Alejandro García Sanjuan, Universidad de Huelva; Nicolás Agrait, Long Island University; Paul Chevedden, University of California, Los Angeles; Donald Kagay, Albany State University; John Clark, Fordham University; James Todesca, Armstrong Atlantic State University; Theresa Earenfight, Seattle University; Theresa Vann, Hill Museum and Manuscript Library, Collegeville, Minnesota; and Ahmed Salama, Marlboro College. I must also remember my good friend and collaborator Robert I. Burns, S.J., of the University of California, Los Angeles, who died in 2008. For more than forty years he led a small band of American scholars interested in the history of medieval Spain. Happily, through his dedication and example, their number has increased!

I am grateful to the Biblioteca de El Escorial, the Patrimonio Nacional de España, and Edilán, S.A., for permission to use illustrations from the *Cantigas de Santa Maria*. I must also thank Daniela Ialeggio O'Callaghan and Gordon Thompson for creating the maps. Antonio Torremocha Silva graciously permitted an adaptation of his map of medieval Algeciras and Wenceslao Segura González of his map of the battle of Salado.

Throughout this book I use the term Moor, though in modern parlance it is sometimes seen as offensive. Derived from *maurus*, a resident of ancient Mauritania, or Morocco, medieval writers consistently employed the vernacular *moro* to refer to Muslims. Also following medieval practice, I use the word "Spain" to refer to the entire Iberian Peninsula.

I have attempted to be consistent in using Castilian, Portuguese, or Catalan forms when speaking of people and places in those kingdoms. For Arabic transliteration I have generally followed the guidelines of the *International Journal of Middle East Studies*. Unless otherwise indicated, all translations used in this book are my own.

I dedicate this book to my masters in the study of medieval history. From Cyril E. Smith of Marquette University I learned the fundamental techniques of historical research. James S. Donnelly Sr. and Jeremiah F. O'Sullivan of Fordham University introduced me to institutional and monastic history. Gerhart B. Ladner, also of Fordham, opened my eyes and mind to the importance of ideas and artistic symbols as manifestations of the medieval worldview. In paying homage to all of my masters, now deceased, I wish to affirm my gratitude to them for educating me and guiding my steps on the road to scholarship. May they, indeed, rest in peace!